10/05

PERIKLEAN ATHENS AND ITS LEGACY

Problems and Perspectives

EDITED BY JUDITH M. BARRINGER
AND JEFFREY M. HURWIT

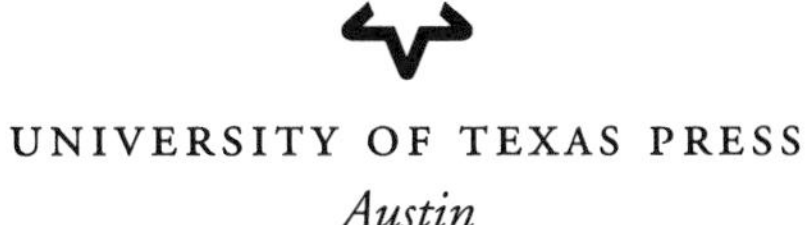

UNIVERSITY OF TEXAS PRESS
Austin

Printed in the United States of America

First edition, 2005

♾ The paper used in this book meets the minimum requirements of ANSI/NISO Z39.48-1992 (R1997) (Permanence of Paper).

LIBRARY OF CONGRESS CATALOGING-IN-PUBLICATION DATA

Periklean Athens and its legacy : problems and perspectives / edited by Judith M. Barringer and Jeffrey M. Hurwit.— 1st ed.
p. cm.
"In honor of J. J. Pollitt."
Includes bibliographical references and index.
ISBN 0-292-70622-7 (hardcover : alk. paper)
1. Art Greek—Greece—Athens. 2. Art Greek—Influence. 3. Art, Classical—Greece—Athens. 4. Art—Greece. I. Barringer, Judith M., 1959–. II. Hurwit, Jeffrey M., 1949– III. Pollitt, J. J. (Jerome Jordan), 1934–
N5650.P47 2005
709′.38′5—dc22
2004021789

IN HONOR OF J. J. POLLITT

This book has been made possible through the generosity of

The Yale University Art Gallery
The Department of Classics, Yale University
The Department of the History of Art, Yale University
The Office of the Provost, Yale University

CONTENTS

NOTE ON ABBREVIATIONS XI

JEROME JORDAN POLLITT: A BIBLIOGRAPHY XIII

INTRODUCTION XV

ACKNOWLEDGMENTS XXI

1. Perikles as General 1
Donald Kagan

THE ART OF CLASSICAL AND PERIKLEAN ATHENS

2. Bail Oinochoai 13
John H. Oakley

3. A Farewell with Arms: Departing Warriors on Athenian Vases 23
Susan B. Matheson

4. The Girl in the *Pithos:* Hesiod's *Elpis* 37
Jenifer Neils

5. The Judgment of Helen in Athenian Art 47
H. A. Shapiro

6. Composition and Content on Classical Murals and Vases 63
John Boardman

7. The Painting Program in the Stoa Poikile 73
Mark D. Stansbury-O'Donnell

8. Feminizing the Barbarian and Barbarizing the Feminine: Amazons, Trojans, and Persians in the Stoa Poikile 89
David Castriota

9. Notes on the Subject of the Ilissos Temple Frieze 103
Randall L. B. McNeill

10. "Periklean" Cult Images and Their Media 111
Brunilde Sismondo Ridgway

11. Athena at Pallene and in the Agora of Athens 119
Evelyn B. Harrison

THE PERIKLEAN AKROPOLIS

12. The Parthenon and the Temple of Zeus at Olympia 135
Jeffrey M. Hurwit

13. The Parthenon Frieze and Perikles' Cavalry of a Thousand 147
Ian Jenkins

14. Alkamenes' Prokne and Itys in Context 163
Judith M. Barringer

15. Interpretations of Two Athenian Friezes: The Temple on the Ilissos and the Temple of Athena Nike 177
Olga Palagia

THE LEGACY OF PERIKLEAN ATHENS

16. Alpheos to the Orontes: An Unusual Echo of the Pheidian Zeus at the Syrian Port of Seleukia Pieria 195
Cornelius C. Vermeule III

17. Kosmetai, the Second Sophistic, and Portraiture in the Second Century 201
Eve D'Ambra

18. A Rhetorical Perikles 217
W. Martin Bloomer

19. On Some Motives Supposed Present in Self-Portraits of Pheidias and Others 233
Creighton Gilbert

20. Early Photography and the Reception of Classical Antiquity: The Case of the Temple of Athena Nike 237
Peter J. Holliday

THE LEGACY OF JEROME J. POLLITT

21. Greek Art and Culture since *Art and Experience in Classical Greece* 255
Elizabeth A. Meyer and J. E. Lendon

WORKS CITED 277

ABOUT THE CONTRIBUTORS 297

INDEX 301

NOTE ON ABBREVIATIONS

Modern journal and book abbreviations and references to ancient texts generally follow the guidelines of the *American Journal of Archaeology* 104 (2000): 10–24. Exceptions to this format are the abbreviations for *Para* for J. D. Beazley, *Paralipomena* (Oxford 1971) and *Addenda*[2] for T. H. Carpenter, *Beazley Addenda*[2] (Oxford 1989).

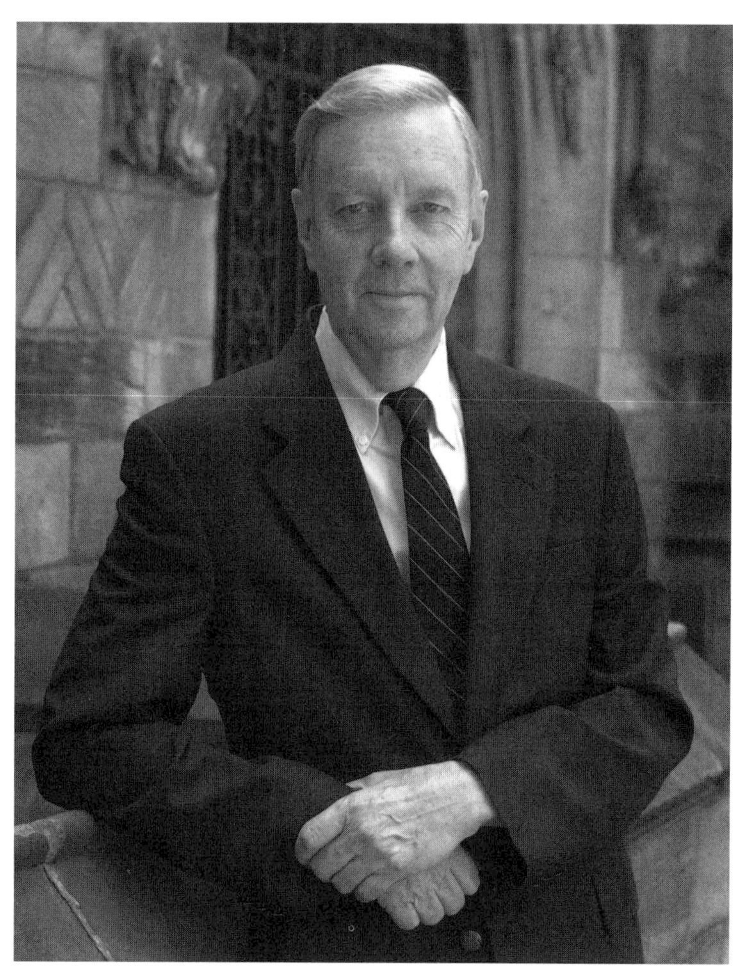

J. J. Pollitt
Michael Marsland / Yale University

JEROME JORDAN POLLITT:

A BIBLIOGRAPHY

BOOKS

The Art of Ancient Greece: Sources and Documents (Prentice-Hall 1965; rev. Cambridge University Press 1990).

The Art of Rome c. 753 B.C.–A.D. 337: Sources and Documents (Prentice-Hall 1966; reprint, Cambridge University Press 1983).

Art and Experience in Classical Greece (Cambridge University Press 1972).

The Ancient View of Greek Art: Criticism, History, Terminology (Yale University Press 1974).

Greek Vases at Yale, coedited with Susan Matheson (Yale University Art Gallery 1975).

Art in the Hellenistic Age (Cambridge University Press 1986).

Personal Styles in Greek Sculpture, coedited with Olga Palagia (Cambridge University Press 1996).

ESSAYS AND ARTICLES

"Fragment of a Sacred Calendar and Other Inscriptions from the Attic Deme of Teithras," *Hesperia* 30 (1961) 293–298.

"Professional Art Criticism in Ancient Greece," *Gazette des Beaux-Arts* 64 (1964) 317–330.

"The Egyptian Gods in Attica: Some Epigraphical Evidence," *Hesperia* 34 (1965) 125–130.

"The Explosion of Santorini (Thera) and Its Place in the Aegean Bronze Age," in *Problems in Ancient History,* edited by Donald Kagan, 2nd edition, (1975) 135–145.

"The Ethos of Polygnotos and Aristeides," in *Essays in Archaeology and the Humanities,* In Memoriam Otto J. Brendel (1976) 49–54.

"The Impact of Greek Art on Rome," *TAPA* 108 (1978) 155–174.

"Kernoi from the Athenian Agora," *Hesperia* 48 (1979) 205–233.

"Early Classical Greek Art in a Platonic Universe," in *Greek Art: Archaic into Classical,* edited by C. Boulter (Cincinnati 1985) 96–111.

"Pots, Politics, and Personifications," *YaleBull* (Spring 1987) 8–15.

"Greek Sculpture and Gems," and "Greek Painting and Mosaic," in *Civilization of the Ancient Mediterranean,* edited by M. Grant and R. Kitzinger (New York 1988) 1701–1725, 1749–1770.

"Art: Archaic to Classical," in *The Cambridge Ancient History* 5, 3rd edition (Cambridge 1992) 171–183.

"Art, Politics, and Thought in Classical Greece," in *The Greek Miracle: Classical Sculpture from the Dawn of Democracy,* edited by D. Buitron-Oliver (Washington, D.C., 1993) 31–44.

"What Is Hellenistic about Hellenistic Art? A Response," in *Hellenistic Art and Culture,* edited by Peter Green (Berkeley 1993) 90–110.

"Rome, the Republic and the Early Empire," in *The Oxford History of Classical Art,* edited by J. Boardman (Oxford 1993) 217–295.

"Art: Classical to Hellenistic," in *The Cambridge Ancient History* 6, 3rd edition (Cambridge 1994) 647–660.

"The Canon of Polykleitos and Other Canons," in *Polykleitos, the Doryphoros, and Tradition,* edited by W. G. Moon (Madison 1995) 19–25.

"The Uses of Classical Myth," *Fenway Court* (Journal of the Isabella Stewart Gardner Museum, 1995) 11–26.

"Masters and Masterworks in the Study of Classical Sculpture," in *Personal Styles in Greek Sculpture,* edited by O. Palagia and J. J. Pollitt (Cambridge 1996) 1–15.

"Art, ancient attitudes to," *Oxford Classical Dictionary,* 3rd edition (Oxford 1996) 178–179.

"The Meaning of the Parthenon Frieze," in *The Interpretation of Architectural Sculpture in Greece and Rome,* edited by D. Buitron-Oliver (Studies in the History of Art 49, Washington, D.C., 1997) 51–63.

"New Perspectives on the Art of Pergamon," (review article) *AJA* 103 (1999) 337–339.

"Patriotism and the West Pediment of the Parthenon," in *Periplous: Papers on Classical Art and Archaeology Presented to Sir John Boardman,* edited by G. R. Tsetskhladze, A. J. N. W. Prag, and A. M. Snodgrass (London 2000) 220–227.

"The Phantom of a Rhodian School," *From Pergamon to Sperlonga,* edited by N. De Grummond and B. Ridgway (Berkeley 2000) 92–110.

"Περί Χρωμάτων: The Role of Color in Ancient Greek Art and Architecture 700–31 B.C." In Περί Χρωμάτων: *What Ancient Greek Painters Thought about Colors,* edited by M. A. Tiverios and D. S. Tsiafakis (Thessaloniki 2002) 1–8.

"Epigonos," *Künstlerlexikon der Attika* I, edited by R. Vollkommer (Munich 2001) 206–208.

"Euthykrates," *Künstlerlexikon der Attika* I, edited by R. Vollkommer (Munich 2001) 239–240.

"Thrasymedes," *Künstlerlexikon der Attika,* edited by R. Vollkommer, forthcoming.

INTRODUCTION

Jerome Jordan Pollitt earned his B.A. from Yale College in 1957 and his Ph.D. from Columbia University in 1963 under the direction of Otto Brendel. He returned to Yale to begin his teaching career and spent the next thirty-six years instructing undergraduate and graduate students in Classical and Hellenistic Greek art and archaeology.

Rising through the ranks at Yale, he was promoted to full professor in 1973 and held his first endowed chair, the John M. Schiff Professorship of Classical Archaeology and History of Art, from 1990 to 1995. In 1995 he was named Sterling Professor of Classical Archaeology and the History of Art, another illustrious chair that he held until his retirement from teaching in 1998, when he was granted emeritus status. It is a mark both of the esteem in which he was held by his colleagues and of his own dedication to his university that during his career at Yale he held numerous leadership posts, including Chair of Classics, Chair of History of Art, and Dean of the Graduate School of Arts and Sciences.

Jerry Pollitt's many books and articles reflect a remarkably broad range of interests and expertise and exemplify an uncommon interdisciplinary and humanistic approach to the field. For four decades he has been perhaps the most outstanding representative of an increasingly rare breed: the art historian/archaeologist who is completely conversant with Greek, Latin, and the ancient written sources. Indeed, his published dissertation, "The Ancient View of Greek Art," offers a compendium of, and commentary upon, the ancient texts on ancient art, the closest thing we have to an art history written by the Greeks and Romans themselves.

With his interest in what the Greeks thought and wrote about their own art, Pollitt pioneered and anticipated interest in the viewer's experience of art, a subject that has recently begun to occupy archaeologists and historians of ancient art more and more. Other publications include collections of translated sources on Greek art and Roman art, which are not only useful to the specialist but are also especially illuminating for the student and layman. Furthermore, these works also reflect another extraordinary aspect of his work and interests: his training and publications in both Greek and Roman art. Such ambidexterity is rare.

Perhaps his most dramatic contributions to the field(s) of Classical Archaeology and Ancient Art History are his books, *Art and Experience in Classical Greece* (1972) and *Art in the Hellenistic Age* (1986). The first marked a watershed moment in the history of the field by elegantly and succinctly introducing and applying the concept of cultural context to the study of Classical Greek art (ca. 480–323 B.C.). The second extended this method to the notoriously complex and unwieldy Hellenistic period (ca. 323–31 B.C.), with dazzling results. Both of these publications are "classics" in the field and are regularly assigned as textbooks in classrooms. Perhaps more important, they also make excellent reading for specialist and nonspecialist alike, offering thoughtful and elegant examinations of two of the richest and most productive periods of human history.

His joint appointment in Classics and History of Art at Yale University testifies to his versatility and breadth, as do his numerous professional duties and honors, which straddle the increasingly (or has it always been?) blurry divide between Classical Archaeology and Ancient Art History. He was Editor-in-Chief of the *American Journal of Archaeology* from 1973 to 1977, served on the advisory boards of both the *Art Bulletin* (1984–1998) and the *American Journal of Archaeology* (1986–1992), and was Chairman of the Publications Committee of the American School of Classical Studies from 1982 to 1985. His honorary lectureships as Howland Lecturer at the National Gallery of Art in Washington, D.C., in 1980; Thompson Lecturer for the Archaeological Institute of America in 1991; Hilldale Lecturer at the University of Wisconsin in 1993; and Townsend Lecturer at Cornell University in 1995 also attest to this range.

His honors at Yale include the William Clyde De-Vane Medal from the Yale Chapter of Phi Beta Kappa for distinguished scholarship and undergraduate teaching in 1984 and the prestigious Wilbur Lucius Cross Medal awarded by the Alumni Association of the Yale Graduate School for scholarship, teaching, and academic administration. Moreover, his extraordinary contributions to the profession have been internationally recognized by his election as Honorary Member of The Society for the Promotion of Hellenic Studies in London in 1997 and as Mitglieder of the Deutsches Archäologisches Institut in Berlin in 1998, two of the highest honors that any classicist can receive.

Philologist and archaeologist, Hellenist and Romanist, archaeologist and art historian, academic and now novelist, Jerry Pollitt has offered the very best of critical inquiry and sound scholarship to the profession for some forty years. His undergraduate and graduate courses at Yale on various topics of Classical and Hellenistic Greek art are justifiably legendary. His lectures vividly combined humor, clarity, and above all, erudition worn lightly and stylishly. His graduate seminars were engaging explorations of fairly broad categories, such as Greek vase painting, reflective of his broad range and depth of knowledge. One of the most successful undergraduate lecture courses at Yale was "Periklean Athens," the brainchild of Jerry Pollitt, Don Kagan, and the late John Herington—archaeologist, historian, and philologist, three colleagues, three friends. The course's interdisciplinary scope and integrated approach embodied the cultural context method that Pollitt embraced in his scholarship and enabled this trio to share their knowledge of, and enthusiasm for, this period of cultural achievement with several generations of undergraduates and their fortunate graduate teaching assistants. To all of his courses he brought dedication, wit, knowledge, and *humanitas.*

The collection of essays offered here by students and colleagues of Jerry Pollitt is devoted to the topic of Periklean Athens, defined quite broadly beginning with its formative stages at the close of the Persian Wars, which is, in fact, where the Yale course began, through its proper period from Perikles' ascendancy in Athens to his death in 429. The essays in the volume go on to consider the impact of Perikles and Periklean Athens on the Romans and the reception of Periklean Athens and its cultural achievements in later periods.

Appropriately, Donald Kagan begins this collection with a consideration of Perikles' military strategy and his performance as *strategos.* Perikles has been defended and criticized by both ancient and modern writers for his performance as general, and Kagan offers a review and reassessment of Perikles' strategy before and during the Peloponnesian War, concluding that its linear quality and Perikles' lack of perspicacity about warfare ultimately harmed the Athenian cause.

John Oakley, Susan Matheson, Jenifer Neils, and Alan Shapiro offer explorations of various topics in vase painting. John Oakley takes up the topic of funerary customs in Early Classical Athens and their manifestation in painted form on an Athenian bail oinochoe, which is unique in providing us with the sole visual depiction from the ancient Greek world of the deposition of a corpse in a coffin. Oakley argues that bail oinochoai, predecessors of Classical white-ground lekythoi, should be recognized as another class of funerary vessel. Susan Matheson sheds light on Early Classical and Classical Athenian vase paintings of warriors' departures. Reading such scenes together with literature and related depictions in their historical context, Matheson explains them as revelatory of the role of the ephebe in the *polis* and links them to the concept of Periklean *ethos.* The rare depiction of Elpis (Hope) in Pandora's jar is the subject of Jenifer Neils' paper, which looks at the only previously identified depiction of this subject, dating to the mid fifth century B.C., and then identifies two more examples. The myth of Pandora was clearly of importance to Periklean Athens—it decorated the base of the Athena Parthenos statue housed in the Parthenon—and Neils concludes her essay with a consideration of the myth's significance. Women and the trouble they cause as reflected in Greek myth also form the topic of Alan Shapiro's essay as he examines depictions of Helen in Attic vase painting, sculpture, and literature from ca. 490 to 420 B.C. As Shapiro demonstrates, vase painters provide surprisingly sympathetic portrayals of Helen, and his sensitive readings reveal keen psychological insight on the part of Classical vase painters.

The Stoa Poikile in the Athenian Agora is the subject of three contributors to this volume: John Boardman, Mark Stansbury-O'Donnell, and David Castriota, who each consider different aspects of the famed mural paintings that once adorned the Stoa's walls. Boardman begins with the relationship between painted vases and Polygnotos' mural paintings at Delphi, then moves to the Stoa Poikile paintings, with special emphasis on the Marathon scene as described by Pausanias. By means of extant vases, Boardman addresses certain elements of the Marathon painting's composition and character. Stansbury-O'Donnell turns his attention to the arrangement of the paintings based on Pausanias' account and the recent excavations at the Stoa and also speculates about later modifications to the original organization. Stansbury-O'Donnell then broadens his view to consider the role of the paintings in the career and chronology of the painter Polygnotos and suggests that Polygnotos' political views may have shaped his creative production. In his essay on the Stoa Poikile, David Castriota focuses on the subjects of the paintings: the battle of Marathon, the Amazonomachy, the Ilioupersis, and the purported battle of Oinoe. He draws on literary evidence to propose that the paintings formed a coherent thematic program designed to underscore similarities between Persians, Amazons, and defeated Trojans and to glorify Greek achievements.

With the contributions of Randall McNeill, Brunilde S. Ridgway, and Evelyn B. Harrison, the collection moves to the realm of sculpture, both architectural and freestanding. McNeill takes up the old riddle of the interpretation of the Ilissos temple frieze, which he accepts as dating to the 430s. His careful examination and new observation of details lead him to endorse the view first put forward in the nineteenth century that the frieze depicts scenes from the Ilioupersis, a theme that he views as particularly well suited to the frieze's political and historical context. Brunilde Ridgway and Evelyn Harrison both consider cult statues in Periklean Athens. After refining the definition of "cult image," Ridgway questions the appropriateness of particular media to various cult statues. Bringing in material from other regions to elucidate the Athenian material, she surveys the evidence for marble, chryselephantine, and bronze, highlighting their use and suitability for particular circumstances. Harrison takes up a specific case—the report of Pausanias about cult statues he saw in the temple of Ares in the Athenian Agora—and offers several new proposals regarding the temple's cult statues. This temple, which was constructed at Pallene in the second half of the fifth century and then moved to the Athenian Agora during the Augustan period, was, according to Harrison, originally dedicated to Athena and embellished with a bronze statue of the goddess by Lokros of Paros, reflected in the Athena Giustiniani type. When the temple was moved, a statue of Ares by Alkamenes, familiar to us from the Ares Borghese type, was taken from the Areopagos and paired with the Athena in the temple newly dedicated to Ares.

This traversal through the Athenian Agora leads us to the Athenian Akropolis, where Jeffrey Hurwit explores the Parthenon's architectural and sculptural relation to its immediate chronological predecessor, the Temple of Zeus at Olympia (470–456 B.C.). Tracing a kind of *agon* between the two buildings in the second half of the fifth century, Hurwit suggests that the Parthenon can be in part considered an artistic and intellectual response to its Olympian predecessor and that the Zeus temple in critical ways responded to the Parthenon in turn. Ian Jenkins reexamines the prominent horsemen on the Parthenon frieze against the background of Perikles' cavalry reform, which resulted in an increase in their numbers. Regarding the disposition of the sculpted horsemen in conjunction with this historical event, Jenkins provides new insights into the design of the frieze and argues that although the frieze surely alludes to the recent new organization of the cavalry, it does so subtly. Judith Barringer explores one of the sculptural dedications on the Athenian Akropolis, the group of Prokne and her son Itys of ca. 430–410, in its physical landscape. Viewed in a visual context replete with allusions to the early history of Athens, the Prokne and Itys dedication was designed, Barringer argues, to inspire and perhaps console contemporary Athenians as they experienced the tragic losses of the Peloponnesian War. In an essay concerning two related architectural sculptures, Olga Palagia revisits the Ilissos frieze, discussed by Randall McNeill above, together with the friezes, particularly the east frieze, of the temple of Athena Nike on the Akropolis. Singling out details and offering fresh observations and identifications, Palagia posits iconographical interpretations for the two friezes: like McNeill, she thinks that some of the Ilissos frieze concerns the Ilioupersis but argues that Odysseus' visit to Hades is also included on the slabs, and further suggests that the temple was dedicated to Artemis Agrotera. Palagia sees the birth of Athena on the east frieze of the Athena Nike temple and concludes with a brief consideration of how these related frieze cycles, together with the Parthenon frieze, offered variety in physical disposition and narrative program during the second half of the fifth century.

The following five essays demonstrate the long shadow and profound influence of Periklean Athens in the Roman and post-Classical periods. Cornelius Vermeule presents an echo of Pheidias' Olympian Zeus, famed in antiquity, in a seated marble statue of Zeus of the first or second centuries A.D. from the Roman provincial city of Seleukia Pieria. Eve D'Ambra examines the vexing issue of the role of Greek ideology and cultural trappings in Roman self-definition in her essay on portraits of second-century A.D. Athenian *kosmetai.* Arguing against conventional notions of "Greek" and "Roman," D'Ambra instead suggests more nuanced readings that acknowledge the cosmopolitanism and complexities of Athenians working and living under Roman rule. Portraiture is also the subject of Creighton Gilbert's contribution, which considers the phenomenon of self-portraiture in the Renaissance. Looking for possible motivations for Renaissance self-portraits, Gilbert reviews an earlier case, the purported self-portrait of Pheidias on the shield of the Athena Parthenos statue reported by Cicero. Martin Bloomer also takes up the issue of portraiture, but in his case, the portrait is a written, not a visual one. Bloomer examines Plutarch's biography of Perikles to reveal a carefully constructed rhetorical account designed to counter critics of Perikles and shape the reception of this historical figure by a skeptical audience. Peter Holliday brings us back to the Athenian Akropolis as he discusses the reception of Classical Antiquity by nineteenth-century photographers and archaeologists. Using the Temple of Athena Nike as a focal point, Holliday explores how the past was put to use for later, more modern concerns.

Finally, Elizabeth Meyer and J. E. Lendon consider another legacy of Periklean Athens: J. J. Pollitt's *Art and Experience in Classical Greece.* Their provocative essay measures the response to Pollitt's ground-breaking book of 1972 and traces the course of scholarship in Classical Archaeology since then, much of which implicitly takes aspects of Pollitt's innovative approach as starting points. Meyer and Lendon's evaluations assess how well various theories explain why a particular phenomenon occurs in the visual arts at a particular moment and why art changes over time. While Pollitt's legacy may be detected in more recent scholarly trends, especially in the debate over the meaning of "culture," the authors conclude that Pollitt's cultural contextual approach, represented by his reading of Periklean Athens, continues to stand as a necessary and exemplary model of scholarship.

The contributors to this volume are just some of many beneficiaries of Jerome Pollitt's teaching, scholarship, and generosity. Many others have not been able to participate but nonetheless extend their warmest wishes to our honorand. Among these are Susan Alcock, Adolph Borbein, Gail Hoffman, Faith Hentschel, Christine Kondoleon, Amy C. Smith, and Marion True. None have benefited more from Jerry's teaching, guidance, and friendship than the two editors of this volume, which we offer and dedicate to him with profound gratitude.

JUDITH M. BARRINGER
Edinburgh

JEFFREY M. HURWIT
Eugene, Oregon

ACKNOWLEDGMENTS

The editors wish to thank each other and the contributors for their efforts and goodwill. We also wish to express our gratitude to Jim Burr, of the University of Texas Press, for his consideration, guidance, and patience; Carolyn Cates Wylie, who oversaw the editorial process; and Nancy Moore, for her careful and conscientious copyediting. The editors also wish to express our profound thanks to Jock Reynolds at the Yale University Art Gallery, John Matthews in the Classics Department of Yale University, Ned Cooke in the Department of the History of Art at Yale University, and Emily Bakemeier and the Office of the Provost, Yale University, for their great interest in this project and for their generosity. The publication of this volume was possible only with their financial support.

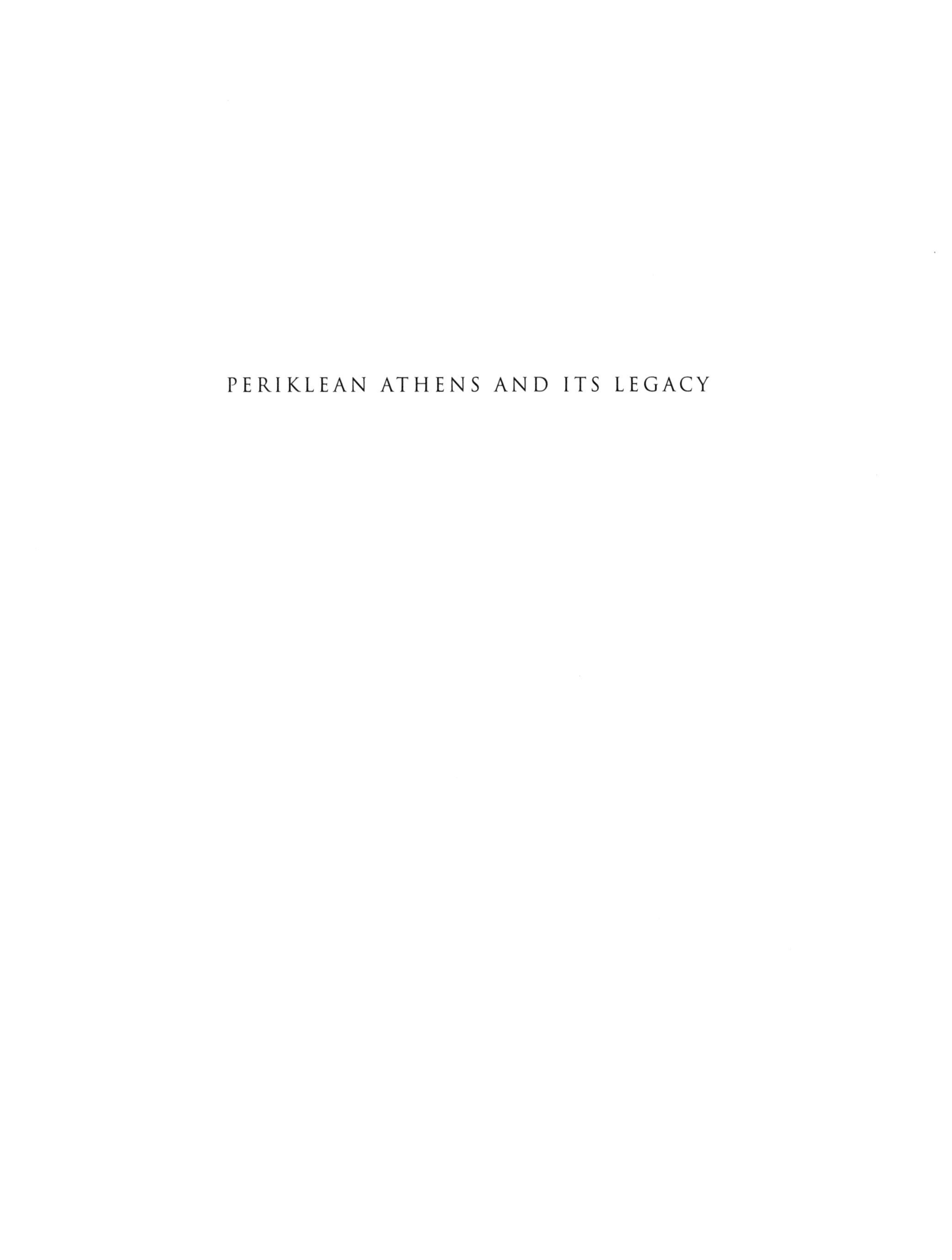

PERIKLEAN ATHENS AND ITS LEGACY

I

PERIKLES AS GENERAL

DONALD KAGAN

It is a great privilege to participate in honoring my colleague of more than three decades, Jerry Pollitt. As teacher, scholar, university citizen, and colleague, he has been a model and an inspiration. His intelligence, high standards, common sense, and good humor have brought him outstanding success in all his undertakings and the admiration of the many who have benefited from them. I have been among them and have had the great good fortune to collaborate with him as a teacher and as an administrator, as well as a departmental colleague. He has taught me much about the Greeks, about scholarship, and about what a college and a university ought to be. I offer him thanks for all these gifts and congratulations for all his achievements. The following essay develops ideas he has heard before in lectures I have given in the course on Periklean Athens we helped invent and taught together for years. Our work there has been one of the great experiences in my professional life.

Near the end of his biography of Perikles, Plutarch describes the great Athenian leader on his deathbed. The best men of Athens and his personal friends gathered in his room were discussing the greatness of his virtues and the power he held. Thinking he was asleep, "they added up his achievements and the number of his trophies, for as general he had set up nine commemorating a victory on behalf of the city."[1]

There is no good reason to doubt the story, and it is a useful reminder to the modern reader. We are inclined to think of Perikles primarily as a great political leader, a brilliant orator, a patron of the arts and sciences, the man whose work in the peaceful arts shaped the "Golden Age of Athens." We must not forget, however, that the office to which the people elected him for some thirty years, from which he carried on these activities was that of *strategos,* general, and that to the Athenians, its incumbents' foremost responsibility was to lead armies and navies into battle.

From his own until modern times, Perikles' talents as a general have been criticized and defended. In 431, the first year of the Peloponnesian War, when his strategy called for the Athenians to huddle behind the walls of their city while the invading Peloponnesian army ravaged their lands in Attika:

> The city was angry with Perikles. . . . They abused him because, as their general, he did not lead them out into battle, and they held him responsible for all they were suffering.[2]

In the next year, after another invasion and destruction of their crops and farms and after a terrible plague had struck them, crowded behind the city walls by his strategy, "they blamed Perikles for persuading them to go to war and held him responsible for their misfortunes."[3] At a lower level, the poet Hermippos presented a comedy in the spring of 430 that gives us an idea of what must have been a common charge against the reluctant general: cowardice. He addresses Perikles as follows:

> King of the Satyrs, why won't you ever lift a spear but instead only use dreadful words to wage the war, assuming the character of the cowardly Teles? But if a little knife is sharpened on a whetstone you roar as though bitten by the fierce Kleon.[4]

The title of this essay is a translation of the most vehement modern attack, *Perikles als Feldheer* by Dr. Julius von Pflugk-Harttung.[5] A veteran of the Franco-Prussian war and an appreciative student of what he took to be the lessons taught by Clausewitz, he believed he had "acquired some useful knowledge of the science of war"[6] that led him vigorously and entirely to condemn Perikles' generalship. In Perikles' conduct of the Peloponnesian War, he says, we see "expeditions without inner unity, without the possibility of greater results."

> To avoid danger Perikles regularly gave away important advantages. . . . Over all we find the effort to lose no battle but nowhere to win one. As much as Perikles' personal courage operated in battle and in the assembly, so little did he have of that courage proper to a general, which boldly risks the life of thousands at the decisive moment; as such he belongs to those, one may say a philosophical group, which brings everything as neatly as possible into the system and plan, instead of acting openly and vigorously. It is a fact that Perikles, the chief advocate of the anti-Spartan policy, never offered a single battle against the Spartans.[7]

At the higher level of strategy the critique is no less severe: "Perikles was a good Minister of War who made far-sighted preparations, but as general he did not know how to make good use of the existing situation." He was

> a great *Bürgermeister,* in the true sense of the word; there the rich many-sidedness of his nature came into play, his superiority to corruption, everything petty and paltry . . . yet he lacked the prophet's vision and the certain luck of the born statesman, above all, the recklessness which is often needed to lead what has begun to the goal. . . . As a leader of foreign policy he was not comparable to a Themistocles, as a general not even approximately to a Cimon.[8]

Perikles, however, has been fortunate in his defenders. In antiquity his performance was justified and praised by Thukydides, a contemporary, a general himself and the historian of the period whose interpretations have dominated opinion ever since he wrote. For all the objectivity of his style, he tells the story very much from Perikles' viewpoint. When, for instance, he describes the revolt against the Athenian leader in the second year of the war and the Athenians' unsuccessful effort to make peace, this is how he describes the aftermath:

> Being totally at a loss as to what to do, they attacked Perikles. And when he saw that they were exasperated and doing everything as he had anticipated, he called an assembly (since he was still general). He wanted to put confidence into them and, leading them away from their anger, to restore their calm and their courage.[9]

He reports three of Perikles' speeches at length, without reporting those of his opponents, with the result that the reader is made to see the situation through Perikles' eyes. Finally, he makes his own judgment perfectly clear, coming down firmly and powerfully on the side of Perikles and against his critics:

> As long as he led the state in peacetime he kept to a moderate policy and kept it safe, and it was under his leadership that Athens reached her greatest heights; and when the war came it appears that he also judged its power correctly.
>
> Perikles lived for two years and six months after the war began, and after his death his foresight about the war was acknowledged still more. For he had said that if the Athenians stayed on the defensive, maintained their navy and did not try to expand their empire in wartime, thereby endangering the state, they would win out. But they acted opposite to his advice in every way . . . and when their efforts failed they harmed the state's conduct of the war.[10]

In spite of his successors' departure from his strategy and the disasters that resulted, in spite of the entry of the Persian Empire into the enemy ranks, the Athenians held out for ten years after the disastrous Sicilian expedition and twenty-seven years in all. "So more than abundant were Perikles' reasons for his own prediction that Athens would have won in a war against the Peloponnesians alone."[11]

Plutarch accepted Thukydides' judgment and added further defense against the charges of cowardice and lack of enterprise. To Plutarch the actions that provoked such accusations instead revealed prudence, moderation, and a desire to protect the safety of Athenian soldiers. In 454 Perikles led a seaborne expedition into the Corinthian Gulf. Thukydides merely reports that he defeated the Sikyonians in battle and ravaged the territory and besieged the important city of Oeniadae, though he failed to take it, and sailed home. Obviously answering later criticism, Plutarch concludes his account of these events by saying that Perikles returned to Athens "having showed himself to be formidable to the enemy but a safe and effective commander to his fellow-citizens. For no misfortunes struck the men on the expedition."[12] In 437 he sailed into the Black Sea on a mission of imperial consolidation that amounted to little more than "showing the flag" to the local barbarians, an action too insignificant to be noticed by Thukydides. Plutarch, however, does not miss the chance to meet the criticism directed against his hero. On this campaign Perikles "displayed the magnitude of his forces and the fearlessness and confident courage with which they sailed wherever they liked and placed the entire sea under their power."[13]

In 446, when Boiotia was in rebellion, the bold and ambitious general Tolmides convinced the assembly to send him at the head of an army to put down the uprising. Plutarch reports that Perikles "tried to restrain and persuade him in the assembly, making his famous remark that if he would not listen to Perikles, he would not go wrong in waiting for time, the wisest counselor." Tolmides went, nevertheless, and the result was a disaster. The Athenians suffered many casualties, Tolmides was killed, and Boiotia was lost. Plutarch's comment is that this incident "brought great fame and goodwill [to Perikles] as a man of prudence and patriotism."[14]

Later in the same year, rebellion broke out in Euboia, and Megara revolted, opening the road for a Peloponnesian invasion of Attika. Perikles led an Athenian army out to meet the invading army, but instead of fighting a battle, he convinced the Spartans to withdraw and then to negotiate a peace. In retrospect, no doubt, his critics accused him of missing a chance for victory in the field. Thukydides reports the Peloponnesian withdrawal without comment or explanation, but Plutarch uses this action to respond in almost poetic language to later charges that accompanied the Peloponnesian invasion in 431, reporting that his enemies "threatened and denounced him, and choruses sang mocking songs to his shame and insulted his generalship for its cowardice and for abandoning everything to the enemy."[15]

The Peloponnesians, he tells us, expected the Athenians to fight out of anger and pride, "but to Perikles it appeared terrible to fight a battle against 60,000 Peloponnesians and Boiotian hoplites (for that was the number of those who made the first invasion) and to stake the city itself on the outcome."[16] He reports Perikles' calming language to the excited Athenians in 431, "saying that trees though cut and lopped, grew quickly, but if men were destroyed it was not easy to get them again." Here he turned the charges of cowardice and lack of enterprise on their heads and did so more fully in a passage that sums up his view of Perikles' generalship:

> In his generalships he was especially famous for his caution. He never willingly undertook a battle that involved great risk or uncertainty, nor did he envy or emulate those who took great risks, won brilliant success, and were admired as great generals. He always said to his fellow-citizens that as far as it was in his power they would live forever and be immortals.[17]

Of the many modern scholars who have been persuaded by this view, none has argued more forcefully in favor of Perikles' generalship than Hans Delbrück, perhaps the most renowned military historian of his day and still a respected figure in that field. Annoyed by the critiques lately leveled at Perikles' generalship by such distinguished German historians as Karl Julius Beloch and M. W. Duncker, as well as by Pflugk-Harttung's vigorous assault, he wrote a thorough defense in 1890 under the title *Die Strategie des Perikles, erlaütert durch die Strategie Friedrichs des Grossen* (The Generalship of Perikles Explained through the Generalship of Frederick the Great).[18] His main effort is to justify Perikles' conduct of the Peloponnesian War that began in 431, the subject of the greatest criticism leveled at the Athenian general.

Perikles' strategy did not aim at defeating the Spartans in battle but was meant to convince them that war against Athens was futile. His strategic goals, therefore, were entirely defensive. The Athenians were to reject battle on land, abandon their fields and homes in the country to Spartan devastation, and retreat behind their walls. Meanwhile, their navy would launch a series of commando raids on the coast of the Peloponnesos. This strategy would continue until the frustrated enemy was prepared to make peace. The naval raids and landings were not meant to do serious harm but to annoy the enemy and to suggest how much damage the Athenians could do if they chose. The strategy was not to exhaust the Peloponnesians physically or materially but psychologically.

No such strategy had ever been attempted in Greek history, for no state before the coming of the Athenian imperial democracy ever had the means to try it. To do so was not easy, for this unprecedented strategy ran directly against the grain of Greek tradition. Willingness to fight and bravery and steadfastness in battle became the essential characteristics of the free man and the citizen. Perikles' strategy of passivity, therefore, ran counter to the teachings of the Greek tradition.

Most Athenians, however, were farmers whose lands and homes were outside the walls. The Periklean strategy required them to look on idly while their houses, crops, vines, and olive trees were damaged or destroyed. In the face of these facts, as well as of the power of tradition and its cultural values, it is hard to understand, even in retrospect, how Perikles could convince the Athenians to adopt his strategy.

Delbrück, keenly aware of Athens' numerical inferiority on land, was convinced of the soundness of Perikles' approach:

> The structure of the Peloponnesian War . . . obliges us to give him a position not simply among the great statesmen, but also among the great military leaders of world history. It is not his war plan as such that bestows this right on him (for the fame of the commander is gained not by word but by deed), but rather the gigantic power of decision that accompanied it, not to halt with a half-measure, but to plunge in whole-heartedly and give up completely what had to be sacrificed, the entire Attic countryside, and in addition the strength of personal authority that was able to make such a decision understandable to a democratic national assembly and to gain their approval. The execution of this decision is a strategic deed that can be compared favorably with any victory.[19]

Delbrück tries to bolster his case by comparing Perikles with Frederick the Great, king of Prussia in the eighteenth century. During the Seven Years' War, Frederick applied what Delbrück calls a "strategy of exhaustion" instead of the "strategy of annihilation" in which one army seeks out the other to bring it to decisive battle with the goal of destroying its nation's ability to resist. Such a strategy is sometimes adopted by, or forced upon, the weaker side in a conflict because no other choice promises success. In the twentieth century, the North Vietnamese Communists used it with success against the United States. Superior firepower brought the Americans victory in set battles but was not so effective in dealing with various forms of guerrilla warfare. The Communists, therefore, avoided battles for the most part. Continuing warfare over years without a decisive result fed division and discontent in the United States and ultimately exhausted the American will to fight.

In the Second Punic War, Rome repeatedly suffered crushing defeats in battle at the hands of Hannibal. The Romans, therefore, chose the tactics of Quintus Fabius Maximus, avoiding battle, harassing the enemy with guerrilla warfare, until they grew stronger, and Hannibal, far from home and cut off from it by sea, grew weaker and was compelled to withdraw.

Perikles' was unlike these strategies in many ways. Unlike the Vietnamese Communists and the Romans, he never attempted a set battle on land. The Vietnamese wore down Americans' resolve by inflicting casualties on their forces. The Romans avoided battle only so long as they had to. Their ultimate aim was to defeat the enemy in standard battles, which, finally, they did, in Italy, Spain, and Africa. Delbrück's comparison with Frederick's strategy is no less faulty. The Prussian monarch was driven to it by combat losses in set battles fought over two years and by the absence of an alternative. He needed to avoid battle to survive. Only good fortune, not calculated war plans, could save him. He succeeded as much by good fortune as by strategy. Britain came to his aid with financial assistance, and the death of the Russian empress broke up the coalition of his enemies, allowing him to escape from the war unbeaten.

The situation confronting Perikles was entirely different. No helpful ally stood in the wings, and no fortunate accident divided his opponents. Since he avoided all fighting on land against the Spartans, he inflicted no casualties, as the Vietnamese and Romans did. They, and Frederick, moreover, aimed at fighting and winning battles when the odds were more favorable. The core of Perikles' plan, however, was to avoid all land battles, to show that the Peloponnesians could do Athens no serious harm and so exhaust them psychologically, to make them see reason and understand that their efforts were futile and could not bring victory. The plan did not work. The element of chance, the unexpected and incalculable, intervened *against* Perikles and Athens in the form of the terrible plague that ultimately killed a third of the population. All this encouraged the Peloponnesians, who refused to be discouraged and continued to fight. When Perikles died, the Athenian treasury was running dry, his plan lay in ruins, and there was no prospect for victory. Only when his successors turned to a more aggressive strategy did the Athenians level the playing field and achieve a position that allowed them to hold out for twenty-seven years and almost brought victory.

It is not surprising, then, that Perikles' strategy in the Peloponnesian War has brought criticism that raises questions about his capacity as a military leader, even from sober and friendly scholars. Georg Busolt regarded the strategy as "fundamentally right" but still thought that it was "somewhat one-sided and doctrinaire, and in its execution it was lacking in energetic procedure and in the spirit of enterprise."[20] Hermann Bengtson defends the plan against its critics but concedes "that the carrying out of the offensive part of the plan appears to modern viewers as not very energetic and resolute."[21] They are influenced, no doubt, by the knowledge that Perikles' successors took some actions that did not risk significant land battles or numerous casualties yet produced important successes. In the spring of 425 the brilliant and daring general Demosthenes conceived and executed a plan to seize and fortify the promontory of Pylos at the southwestern tip of the Peloponnesos. From there the Athenians could launch raids at will and encourage the escape or rebellion of the helots, Sparta's enslaved population. His success panicked the Spartans, who allowed several hundred of their troops to be trapped and captured on the island of Sphakteria, just opposite Pylos. They immediately proposed a peace, which the Athenians refused.

Later in the same spring the Athenians seized and garrisoned the island of Kythera, just off the southeastern tip of the Peloponnesos. Immediately, they began to launch raids against the mainland. Thukydides reports that the Spartans suffered a kind of nervous collapse:

> The Spartans . . . sent garrisons here and there throughout the country, deciding the number of

> hoplites by what seemed necessary at each place. In other respects they were very much on guard for fear that there would be a revolution against the established order . . . , and from every direction a war rose up around them which was swift and defied precaution. . . . In military affairs they now became more timid than ever before, since they were involved in a naval contest, outside their normal conception of preparation for war, and in this unaccustomed area they fought against the Athenians, to whom the omission of an enterprise was always a loss in respect to what they had expected to achieve. At the same time, the misfortunes that had struck them in such numbers unexpectedly and in such a short time caused great terror, and they were afraid that another calamity might again strike them sometime like the one on the island [Sphakteria]. For this reason they were less daring in going into battle, and they thought that whatever they undertook would turn out badly because they had no self-confidence as a result of having little previous experience with misfortune.[22]

In the light of results such as these it is natural to ask why did the enterprises that produced them need to wait until the fifth year of the war? Why did Perikles not use them at once? His failure to do so is the most weighty of the charges brought against him, and Delbrück uses much effort and ingenuity to defend him. He is forced to concede, however, that a more aggressive offensive effort would have been helpful. He believes that the attack Perikles led against Epidauros in 430 was meant to take and hold that city. "If any such conquest had succeeded, any success in Acarnania, any campaign of devastation, however intensive, any fortification of a coastal spot in Messenia would disappear in comparison." Taking Epidauros would have threatened the neighboring states near the coast as well. It might bring peace at once or, at least, cool the ardor for war among Sparta's allies. Why, then, did Perikles wait and then do so little? "We do not know" is Delbrück's answer.[23]

The failure by so learned, clever, and determined a scholar, and by his many other defenders, to explain their hero's behavior in this way is a powerful sign that they have taken the wrong path. Perikles did not mean to use any serious offensive measures to wear down the enemy's *ability* to fight. His goal was psychological and intellectual: to convince the Spartans and their allies that victory was impossible, that the Athenians could easily sustain the only damage the enemy could inflict, the ravishment of Attika, and to show the allies that the Athenians could do them considerable harm if they chose. Athens' carefully calculated limited offensive efforts were meant to deliver a message without inciting the enemy, just as the carefully calculated limited attacks by U.S. forces in Vietnam aimed at putting pressure on the enemy without causing their Chinese supporters to intervene. The strategy called for delicate action and judgment. The offensive part of the plan was deliberately to do little harm, for actions that were too aggressive might anger the enemy and harden their determination. The goal was to depress the enemy's spirit by showing that there was no way for them to win, to destroy their *will* to fight. Then they could be expected to make a negotiated peace that would return to the status quo ante bellum, only made more secure by the demonstration that it could not be overthrown by force, which was Perikles' aim in the war.

That strategy failed, as had Perikles' diplomatic maneuvers in the period leading to war from 433 to 431. When civil war in Epidamnos, a remote town on the fringes of the Greek world, threatened to bring a great war between the Peloponnesian League and the Athenian Empire, Perikles pursued a policy of restrained, limited intervention meant to deter Corinth, Sparta's important ally, without driving the Spartans and all their Peloponnesian allies into a war against Athens. That effort also failed and resulted in the terrible war Perikles had wanted to avoid.

Do these great strategic failures fully make the case for his critics? Were they the result of cowardice or lack of enterprise and resolution? A fair examination of his performance suggests otherwise. The charge of personal cowardice is absurd: even Pflugk-Harttung concedes that his "personal courage operated in battle and in the assembly."[24] No Athenian who led armies and navies in many battles, repeatedly setting up trophies of victory, could have escaped condemnation had he shown any sign of cowardice, nor could he have been reelected general year after year.

Nor did he fail to demonstrate boldness and enterprise. In 446 the very survival of Athens and its empire was threatened. The most menacing rebellions broke out close to home, first at Euboia, then at Megara. Perikles swiftly took an army to put down the first and just as swiftly withdrew on news of the second, which opened the door to a Peloponnesian invasion of Attika. He arrived in time to persuade the Spartans to withdraw and returned at once to Euboia to suppress the rebellions there.[25] Again, when the island of Samos launched a dangerous rebellion in 440, Perikles took personal charge, acting promptly and decisively, taking the Samian rebels by surprise, ultimately forcing them to surrender by means of a naval blockade.

To be sure, these expeditions were against lesser opponents, not the Spartans, and they were not serious land battles but were on the Athenians' preferred element, the sea. They show, however, that Perikles' frequent caution did not derive only from a temperamental tendency or a character flaw but from thought and calculation. The main reason he avoided land battles against the Spartans and their Peloponnesian allies is because he was certain to lose: the numbers were decisively against him.

Yet it is fair to say that he was more careful than bolder generals. No *polis* was prodigal with its citizens in battle, and it behooved a general, especially in a democratic state, to keep the casualty lists as low as possible. We must remember that Athenian *strategoi*, generals, were not only military leaders but also politicians who needed to be elected to their posts. No doubt, Perikles sincerely took pride in the prudence and economy of his leadership, but it could not have hurt his political popularity when he boasted to the Athenians that "as far as it was in his power they would live forever and be immortals."[26] Such considerations help explain his cautious performance; nevertheless, there is no evidence to suggest that he was one of those rare military geniuses who belong in the ranks of the Hannibals, the Caesars, the Alexanders, the Pattons, who understand the limits of rational calculation in war and the need to seize opportunity boldly when it offers. Perikles was a "soldier's general," an Omar Bradley rather than a George Patton, or perhaps a Bernard Montgomery, who seeks battle only when the odds are heavily in his favor. He lacked the flare and the boldness of a Kimon, the daring and ruthlessness that seeks victory at any cost.

Another element has been suggested to explain the Periklean strategy. Says one critic:

> Pericles, himself, was rather an Admiral than a General. . . . The Athenian Admiralty it was which framed the strategy at the outset of the war. Not Perikles the Bürgermeister but Perikles the Admiral invented the "strategy of exhaustion," a strategy which came near to ruining Athens in a couple of years and could never have won her the victory.[27]

There is some merit in this analysis. The Athenians under Perikles had built a grand strategy that was based on naval power that might seem to suit a maritime empire whose homeland was an island, such as Great Britain's, or a power that dominates a continent and is separated from other great powers by two great oceans, like the United States. Athens' geographical situation was not so fortunate, for the city was attached to the mainland, offering targets of coercion not available to the enemies of the great Anglo-Saxon countries.

Perikles tried to cancel that disadvantage by building the long walls connecting the city to its fortified harbor, turning the city into an island. It was an extraordinary strategy, far ahead of its time in its reliance on human reason and technology and its rejection of traditional ways of fighting that cost lives and gave the enemy an advantage. At the same time, he abandoned all ideas of further expansion and devised a policy aimed at preserving peace and the status quo that perfectly suited Athenian interests. Such a policy depended for success on an extraordinary amount of rationality on everyone's part. The Athenians must be content with what they had and abandon hopes for extension of their power. There were always Athenians who objected to that. But while he lived, Perikles had the wisdom and the political strength to restrain and control them.

What he could not control were the other states. Unexpected changes and shifts in power are the normal condition of international history. Herodotos underscored the inevitable and unforeseeable shifts in the power of states:

> I shall go forward with my history describing equally the greater and lesser cities. For the cities that were formerly great, have most of them become insignificant;

> and such as are at present powerful, were weak in the olden time.[28]

Paul Kennedy writes in the same vein about our own world that

> wealth and power, or economic strength and military strength, are always relative, and since all societies are subject to the inexorable tendency to change, then the international balances can *never* be still, and it is a folly of statesmanship to assume that they ever could be.[29]

These changes have always taken place because international relations are guided only partially and spasmodically by rational calculation of material advantage. Always at work, as well, are greed, ambition, jealousy, resentment, anger, hatred and Thukydides' triad of fear, honor, and interest. In the world as it has been, therefore, a state satisfied with its situation and wishing to preserve peace cannot rely on a reasoned response to its reasoned policies but must anticipate challenges that seem unreasonable. The Spartans and their allies ought to have recognized that they had no realistic strategy to promise victory over Perikles' reliance on defense and refusal to fight a major land battle, but resentment and anger at Athenian power and the fear that it might ultimately undermine their own alliance and security led them to fight. As is usual in human history, they were more influenced by the memory of the Athenians' failure to fight a traditional battle and negotiate a peace in 446 than by the recognition that the new technology, in the form of the long walls, made it unnecessary for Athens to risk such a battle in the future. To deter a war in such circumstances required some offensive threat to the Peloponnesians, whose menace was great and impossible to underestimate, that would make the fear of immediate consequences of war stronger than all the emotions leading to war.

Perikles, however, had come to think of Athens as an invulnerable island since its acquisition of a fleet, a vast treasury to support it, and defensible walls. For such a state to adopt a defensive strategy is natural. It had developed a unique and enviable way of fighting that used these advantages and avoided much of the danger and unpleasantness of ordinary warfare. It allowed the Athenians to concentrate their forces quickly and attack island and coastal enemies before they were prepared; it permitted them to strike others without danger to their own city and population. Success in this style of warfare made it seem the only one necessary, and defeats with great losses on land made the Athenians reluctant to take risks by fighting on land.

Offensive action should be taken as a last resort, only when it was unavoidable. Perikles carried this approach to its logical conclusion by refusing to use a land army even in defense of the homeland, much less launching offensive efforts that might do the enemy serious harm. The enemy's passionate refusal to see reason made "the Athenian way of warfare" inadequate, and Perikles' strategy was a form of wishful thinking that failed.

For a state like Athens in 431, satisfied with its situation and capable of keeping the enemy at bay, the temptation to avoid the risks of offensive action is great, but it contains dangers. It tends to create a rigid way of thinking that leads men to apply a previously successful strategy or one supported by a general theory to a situation in which it is not appropriate, but it may have other disadvantages as well. Its capacity to deter potential enemies from provoking a war is severely limited. Deterrence by standing behind a strong defensive position and thereby depriving the enemy of the prospect of victory assumes a high degree of rationality and a strong imagination on his part. When the Spartans invaded Attika in 431, they must have thought they were risking little. Even if the Athenians refused to fight, even if they persisted in that refusal for a long time, both of which seemed unlikely and unnatural, the Spartans would risk little more than time and effort. In any case, their own lands and city would be safe. Had the Athenians possessed the capacity to strike where they were vulnerable, and had that capacity been obvious to all, Perikles' strategy of deterrence might have been effective.

Once the war came, there was no way to win without abandoning the Athenian way of war and the Periklean strategy. As Perikles lay dying in the fall of 429, his strategy was a failure. After three campaigning seasons, the Peloponnesians showed no sign of exhaustion. On the contrary, they had just lately refused an offer of peace and fought on with the determination to destroy Athenian power forever. The Athenians, on the other hand, had seen their lands and homes ravaged repeatedly, their crops and trees burned and destroyed. They also suffered from the plague, which was killing great numbers of them and destroying their moral fiber. In the anecdote at the beginning of this essay, Plutarch tells of Perikles' response to the praise of his military prowess. He expressed astonishment that they should be praising what was the result of good fortune as much as his own talents and what many others had accomplished. Instead, he said, they should be praising the finest and most important of his claims to greatness: "that no Athenian now alive has put on mourning clothes because of me."[30] That assertion, the last words of Perikles reported to us, must have astounded his audience, as they would have surprised any other Athenian. Even his friends would have had to admit that his policy had contributed at least something to the coming of the war and that his strategy had something to do with the intensity of the destruction caused by the plague. His final words show how deeply he felt the wounds caused by the widespread accusations hurled against him and his stubborn refusal to admit he had been wrong. He had applied his great intelligence to his city's needs, and reason told him that he was not responsible for the results, which he must have believed to be temporary. If his fellow-citizens would have the wisdom and courage to hold to his strategy, they would win out. So he believed, and so did his great contemporary Thukydides.

More than two millennia later Clausewitz saw war through very different eyes. "War," he said,

> is more than a true chameleon that slightly shapes its characteristics to the given case. As a total phenomenon its dominant tendencies always make war a paradoxical trinity—composed of primordial violence, hatred, and enmity, which are to be regarded as a blind natural force, of the play of chance and probability within which the creative spirit is free to roam; and its elements of subordination, as an instrument of policy, which makes it subject to reason alone. . . .
>
> These three tendencies are like three different codes of law, deep-rooted in their subject and yet variable in their relationship to one another. A theory that ignores any one of them or seeks to fix an arbitrary relationship between them would conflict with reality to such an extent that for this reason alone it would be totally useless.[31]

Like most generals in history and unlike its few military geniuses, Perikles saw war as essentially a linear phenomenon, "subject to reason alone," and understood too little its other aspects. For that he and his people paid a great price.

NOTES

1. Plut. *Per.* 38.3.
2. Thuk. 2.21.3.
3. Thuk. 2.59.2.
4. *Fates,* cited by Plut. *Per.* 33.7.
5. Pflugk-Harttung 1884.
6. Pflugk-Harttung 1884, vi.
7. Pflugk-Harttung 1884, vi: "About the collection of nine trophies for P (Plut. *Per.* 38) it has long been necessary to meditate and to count avoidance of defeats as successes."
8. Pflugk-Harttung 1884, 110–123.
9. 2.59.3.
10. 2.15.6.
11. 2.65.
12. *Per.* 19.4.
13. *Per.* 20.1.
14. *Per.* 18.2–3.
15. *Per.* 33.6.
16. *Per.* 33.3. All modern scholars agree that the true number was probably half that figure or less.
17. *Per.* 18.1.
18. His conclusions and some of his arguments are restated in Delbrück 1920.
19. Renfroe 1990, 137.
20. Busolt 1904, 901.
21. Bengtson 1965, 221, n.5.
22. Thuk. 4.55.
23. Delbrück 1890, 121.
24. Pflugk-Harttung 1884.
25. Thuk. 1.114.
26. *Per.* 18.1.
27. B. W. Henderson 1927, 67–68.
28. Hdt. 1.5.
29. Kennedy 1987, 536.
30. *Per.* 38.4.
31. Clausewitz 1984, 1.1.28, 89.

THE ART OF CLASSICAL AND PERIKLEAN ATHENS

2

BAIL OINOCHOAI

JOHN H. OAKLEY

Fifth-century Athens witnessed a striking series of changes in funerary customs. Not long after the start of the century, large-scale sculpted stone monuments stopped decorating private graves, a change usually attributed to the so-called *post aliquanto* funerary decree mentioned by Cicero (*Leg.* 2.25–26) limiting the size, cost, and manner of decorating the graves. At the same time, the number of children's graves increased dramatically, and burials were no longer allowed in the city.[1] A decade or two later, Athenian men who had fallen on behalf of the city started to be interred in the *Demosion Sema,* a public burial ground. Each year their interment was marked by a public ceremony, the highlight of which was a funerary oration (*epitaphios logos*) extolling the virtues of the dead and the city of Athens, given by a noteworthy individual chosen by the city. The speech of Perikles, as reported by the historian Thukydides (2.35–46), is the earliest such oration presented in full. It offers the most clearly articulated expression of Periklean ideals preserved from antiquity, as our honoree notes in his well-known book, *Art and Experience in Classical Greece.*[2] Historians now believe that the Demosion Sema and the epitaphios logos were first established around 470 B.C., customs that continued during the Periklean period.[3]

The archaeological record also indicates other changes around 470 B.C. that remained in effect in Periklean Athens and are probably connected with the institution of the Demosion Sema and the epitaphios logos. The earliest preserved casualty list, giving the names by deme of those who died fighting for Athens in a given year, dates to 465/64 B.C., and white-ground lekythoi with polychrome painting and primarily funerary scenes started around 470 B.C.; these vases became a staple grave offering in Periklean Athens.[4] They, however, were not the first special type of Athenian funerary vase with iconography devoted primarily to funerary ritual. Several special varieties of black-figure ware were the forerunners of the white lekythoi, including black-figure loutrophoroi, funerary plaques, eggs, and phormiskoi.[5] In this paper I will focus on another type of black-figure antecedent, one that has

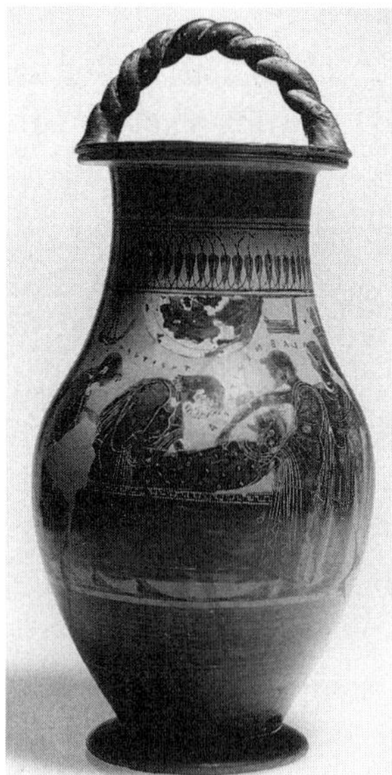
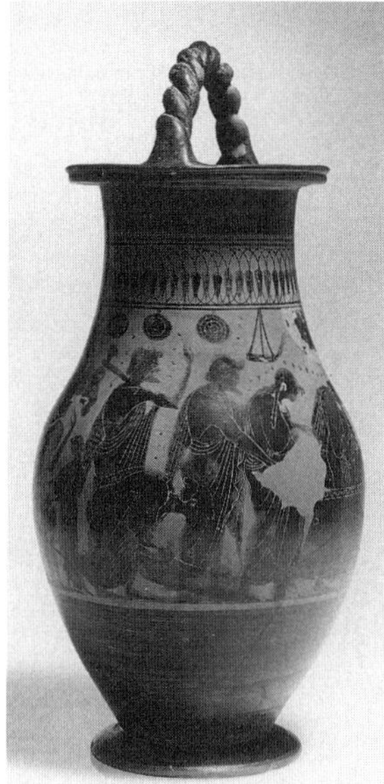
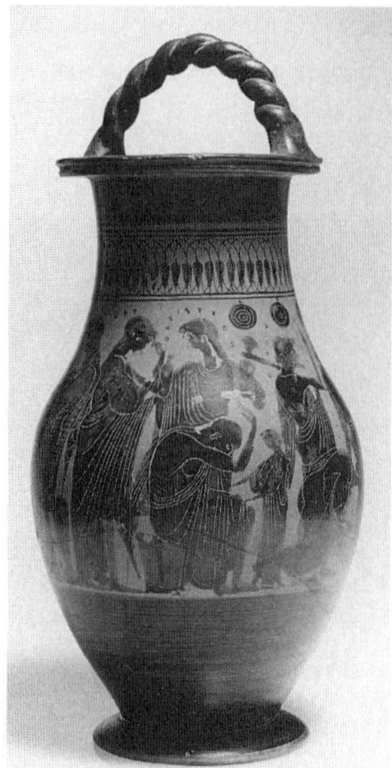
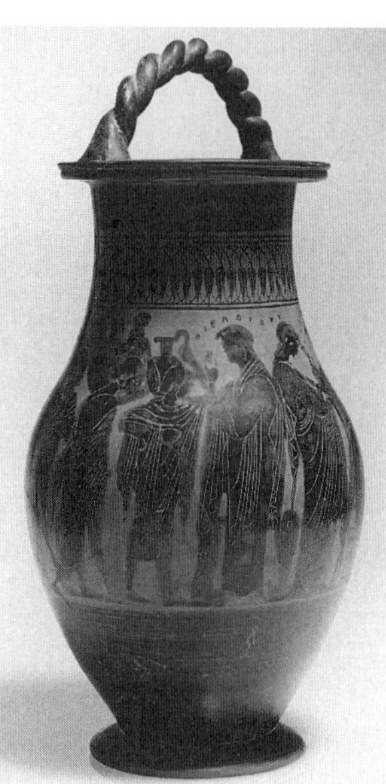

FIGURES 2.1–4. *Attic black-figure bail oinochoe, Sappho Painter (ca. 500–480 B.C.). Bowdoin College Museum of Art, Brunswick, Maine, 1984.023. Museum Purchase with Funds from the Adela Wood Smith Trust in Memory of Harry de Forest Smith 1891. Photos courtesy of the Museum.*

never received proper attention as a funerary vase, nor has its form been treated fully: the bail oinochoe (a jug with upwardly arched handle).

The finest bail oinochoe known is in the Bowdoin College Museum of Art (Appendix No. 1: Figs. 2.1–4). Although photographs of the vase have been published, no thorough publication of it exists, nor is there a complete and accurate description. For these reasons, and because it is the only known depiction in Greek vase painting of a corpse being placed into the coffin, I describe and analyze the picture first.

The decorated frieze that runs continuously around the vessel's body employs three groups of figures. The most important group is centered on the main side (Fig. 2.1), where two women and a bearded man lower the corpse of another bearded man into a coffin having the form of a wooden chest with legs. A battlement pattern between horizontal lines decorates the top of the casket, and the two small circles on the body below it are elements commonly found on other chests.[6] Similarly shaped chests in a variety of materials had been used in Greece as coffins since the Bronze Age. The corpse is completely enveloped in a shroud (ἔνδυμα) decorated with small circles, except for the head, which bears a red wreath. Both women bend over; the first has her arms wrapped around the lower body of the corpse, and the second probably did also, but the section showing her lower arms and the bottom of the corpse is lost. They wear *chiton* and mantle, as do all the women on this vase, and their hair is cut short and tattered from mourning, the first's more so than the second's. The man's left hand rests under the corpse's shoulder; his right grasps the top of the upper body. Like the other males in the picture, he wears a mantle.

Above the figures are two inscriptions, one of which appears to make sense. It starts slightly behind the head of the standing man on the right and is written retrograde and can be read as: λαβ<έ> με λιτ(ώ)τα<τα>—"hold me very gently," a statement very appropriate for handling a corpse.[7] All the other inscriptions spread throughout the scene are nonsense, with the possible exception of part of two on the back of the vase, one beginning with οὔτις ("nobody"), the other with οἴ ἐγώ ("poor me").[8] They illustrate a preference for certain letters: ι, λ, μ, ο, σ, and τ. These, except for λ, are the ones used to spell the most common lamentation cries in Athenian tragedy (ὀτοτοῖ, οἴμοι, and αἰαῖ), suggesting that the nonsense inscriptions are meant to imitate the sounds of these laments. Another woman with short hair, perhaps the dead man's mother or wife, reaches toward the corpse from behind the standing man.

The lower half of a shield hangs above the dead man, perhaps his own. Much of the white slip covering it has chipped away. Directly to the right of the shield a lamp with lit wick is shown in profile upon an L-shaped shelf. Another lamp with a blazing, upturned end is suspended by three strings on the other side of the shield.[9] These burning lamps indicate that the action takes place inside at night, probably in the men's room, the *andron.*

Behind the two women stands a bearded man who extends both hands out towards the corpse (Fig. 2.2); his left arm runs behind the second woman, the hand appearing near her breast. Another stands behind him wearing a red headband and giving the valediction with his raised right hand. This gesture is often made by males in scenes of the *prothesis,* and it is mentioned by the fifth-century tragedians, such as Aischylos (*Cho.* 8–9).[10] The same man also carries an axe over his left shoulder, indicating that he is the carpenter who has made the coffin; he is probably there to put on the lid, once the corpse is in place. Next to him a woman bends over, picking up a basket with four lekythoi. This is the earliest known representation of the funerary basket. They are commonly shown on white-ground lekythoi in scenes of either a visit to the tomb or the preparations for the visit.[11] The woman, in any case, makes ready for the funerary procession to the grave, the *ekphora.*

Above the three figures hang three disc-shaped objects decorated with concentric circles; the one closest to the coffin also has rows of short lines radiating out from the three outer circles. It is uncertain what they represent. Joan Mertens suggests to me that they could be phialai hung on the wall and shown from the underside, the small central circle in the middle of each delineating the omphalos. At the top of each, however, is a small round mark. Is this a part of a hook or pin upon which the object hangs, or is it actually part of the object, in which case they are not phialai? Sabine Weber suggests that they are lamps. Another possibility is that they may be composed of a material used to purify the air of bad smells.[12]

The second group (Fig. 2.3), consisting of four figures, comes next. An old man sits in the center on a block seat, head bent over in mourning, as indicated by his raised right arm. Only traces of his white hair remain. This is a pose used elsewhere for grieving or agitated figures, such as the seer in depictions of the Departure of Amphiaraos or Priam, when he is about to be slain at Troy.[13] A young girl stands before the seated man, reaching towards his lap, apparently consoling him. They probably represent the dead man's father and daughter. The woman standing behind him holds up an alabastron in her left hand, while raising the right to her face. She appears to be wiping away tears of grief, for a similar pose is found on a white-ground lekythos by the Inscription Painter in Athens.[14] Representations of crying are rare in Greek art. Further supporting this interpretation is the woman shown behind the man, who attempts to comfort the crying woman by placing her right hand on the other's left shoulder. Parts of a *diphros* (backless stool) can be seen near them; a block stool overlaps one of the chair's legs, but the leg is unexpectedly visible to the viewer, because the gloss for it is darker than that for the stool.

The final group (Fig. 2.4) consists of two short men carrying vessels on their shoulders, who move towards a woman with straggly hair facing them and standing by a diphros. She gestures with both arms to the men. The first man is bearded and holds the back handle of a hydria with his left hand; the vase sits on his back and shoulder. The second supports a hemispherical container with articulated rim on his left shoulder with his right hand. A rectangular object, along with two more rectangular-like objects having nearly rounded tops, uneven contours, and interior details, protrude from the vessel. The latter two give the appearance of wrung cloth. The closest parallels in form for this vessel are a hemispherical basket, a type normally shown in connection with food, often hanging in the background of banqueting scenes,[15] and a coarse ware tub, such as those found in the excavations of the Athenian Agora.[16] This suggests that the basket/pot might contain food, and, therefore, the two outer objects might be butchered meat. If so, we might understand this group as preparing for the *perideipnon* (περίδειπνον), the funerary feast, which will take place later that day after the deceased is buried.[17] The andron, the probable location of this scene, was the largest room in the house, where dining normally took place.

More likely, however, the group shows part of the preparations for the *prosphagma* (πρόσφαγμα), a sacrifice made either at home before the ekphora or after it at the grave.[18] When the sacrifice took place is debated. If they are going to the grave, the liquid in the hydria, as Sabine Weber suggests, may have been used for the *aponimma* (ἀπόνιμμα), when a pit was dug to the west of the grave after burial, and water was poured into it, followed by a prayer.[19] The woman bending over to pick up the funerary basket, who was noted earlier, is a step behind them in getting ready.

Another less likely possibility is that the vessels allude to an earlier action, the preparation of the corpse for burial. Water was used to bathe the corpse, which was then wrapped in an ἔνδυμα. Might the outer objects in the basket/pot actually be crumpled clothing or, as Sabine Weber suggests, sponges? Even less likely is that the vessels are in some way connected with the water placed outside the door of the deceased's house, so that visitors could purify themselves upon leaving. The container for this water is referred to in the literary sources as an ὄστρακον, πηγαῖον, and ἀρδάνιον.[20]

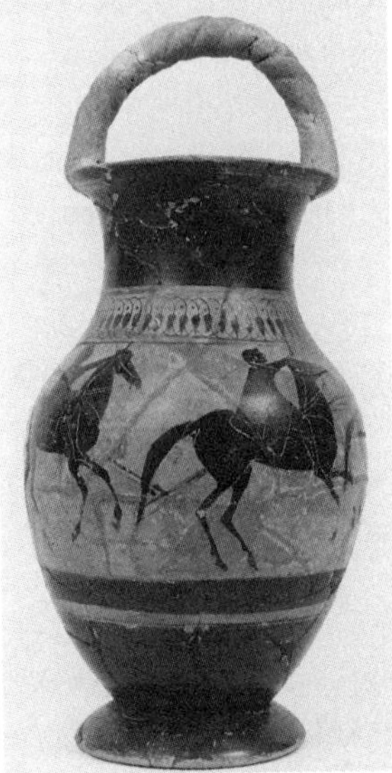

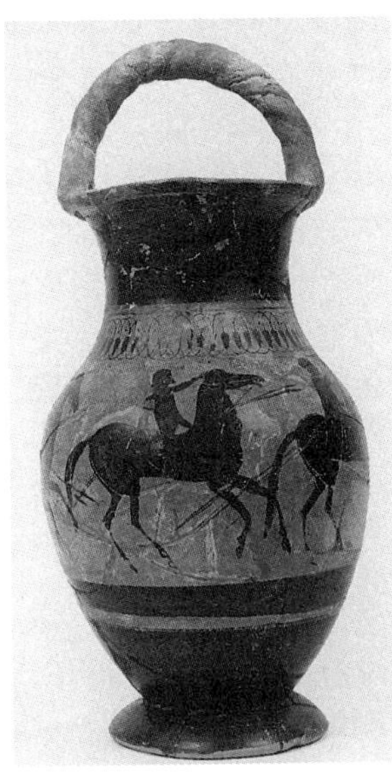

FIGURES 2.5–6. *Attic black-figure bail oinochoe. Quebec, Laval University Museum D 12. Photos courtesy of the Museum.*

The frieze on the Bowdoin bail oinochoe supplies one of the most remarkable pictures of funerary rites from ancient Greece. The range of actions and the emotions shown are exceptional: from the solemn act of placing the corpse gently into the coffin at night, to the grieving mourners being consoled by their relatives, to the preparation for the funeral feast or sacrifice. Also noteworthy are the depictions of specific objects such as the funerary basket with lekythoi, the coffin, the lamps, and the hanging discs (phialai?).

The artist who decorated this vase, the Sappho Painter (ca. 500–480 B.C.), was primarily a painter of late black-figure lekythoi, many of them white ground, who had a side interest in funerary vases.[21] Several other remarkable depictions of Attic funerary rites are by his hand. These include the earliest Attic picture of a visit to the tomb and the only known scene with the deposition of the coffin into a grave, both on a loutrophoros in Athens, as well as the prothesis on a funerary plaque in the Louvre, where inscriptions give the familial relationship of many of the participants, as well as their laments. Still another loutrophoros by him in Bonn shows horsemen at the tomb.[22] The Sappho Painter liked to place inscriptions on his vases, but many of them are nonsense, or sometimes, as on the bail oinochoe, one or more make sense among others that do not.[23]

All seven known figured bail oinochoai date to the first quarter of the fifth century.[24] I list them in addition to the Attic black-gloss ones in the Appendix at the end. Four (Nos. 1–4), including the one at Bowdoin, have the body of an olpe with a splaying foot and twisted, upwardly arched (bail) handle connected to either side of the rim. The handles on two are missing (Nos. 3–4); that on the vase at Bowdoin (No. 1; Figs. 2.1–4) is black, that on the example in Quebec (No. 2; Figs. 2.5–6) reserved. The rim of the Bowdoin bail oinochoe is flat on top and in two degrees; two others that preserve their rims (Nos. 2–3) have ones that flair outwards. Four (Nos. 1–4) have a frieze of hanging lotus buds above their pictures; the one in Quebec has a reserved band as well below the image. All four (Nos. 1–4) appear to come from different workshops.

The body on an unpublished example in Athens (No. 5) does not have the shape of an olpe but comes closest to Beazley's form Vb. A concave upper part is used for the neck and shoulder and is set above a rounded lower body. The figured scene is placed high on the shoulder, and there is no pattern-band above. The bail handle is twisted and in reserve. The two remaining figured ones (Nos. 6–7; Figs. 2.7–8) both have bodies of form Vb, the upper part being clearly set off from the lower, and both are probably from the same workshop. Their tripartite handles are black; only traces of the handle on No. 7 (Fig. 2.8) remain. The rims are flat on top and offset from the neck, and each has a splaying, disc foot. Above the picture on one

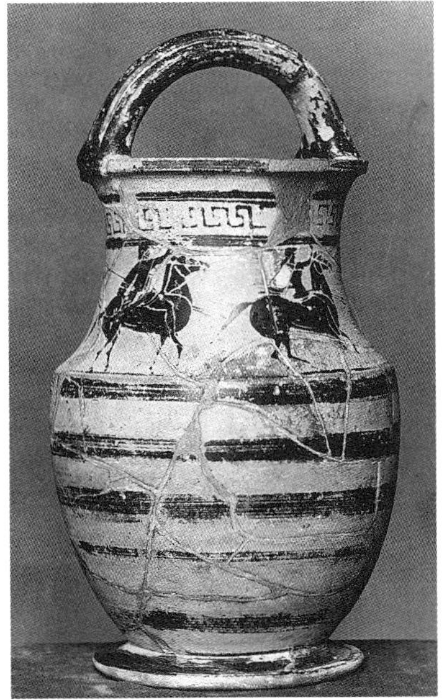

FIGURE 2.7. *Attic black-figure bail oinochoe. Dresden, Staatliche Kunstsammlungen ZV 2955. Photo courtesy of the Museum.*

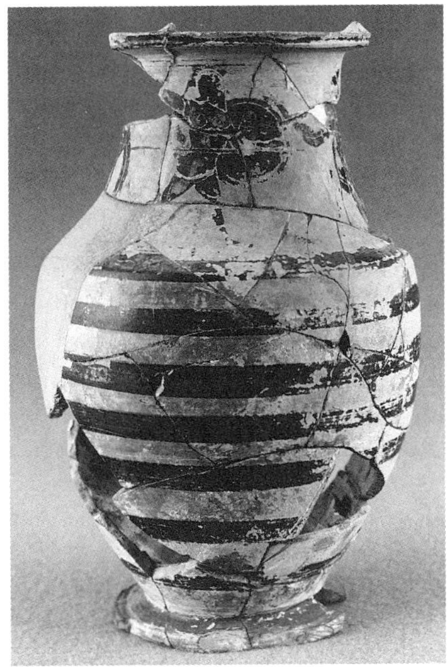

FIGURE 2.8. *Attic black-figure bail oinochoe. Dresden, Staatliche Kunstsammlungen ZV 2956. Photo courtesy of the Museum.*

(No. 6; Fig. 2.7) is a key pattern; black stripes decorate the bodies of both, a scheme found on a number of other nearly contemporary vases.[25] Thus, there are two variants of bail oinochoai, one having the body of an olpe, the other of form Vb.

The same two variants are found in Attic black gloss. An unpublished example in Athens (No. 8) has the first form, the central plait of its otherwise reserved handle painted red. Seven others take the second form (Nos. 9–15; Fig. 2.9), four with twisted handle (Nos. 9, 11, 14, and 15), three with a plain black one (Nos. 10, 12, and 13). They all date to the fifth or fourth century: at least one to the first half of the fifth century (No. 15), one to the third quarter (No. 11), another to the last quarter (No. 10), and one to the second quarter of the fourth century (No. 14).

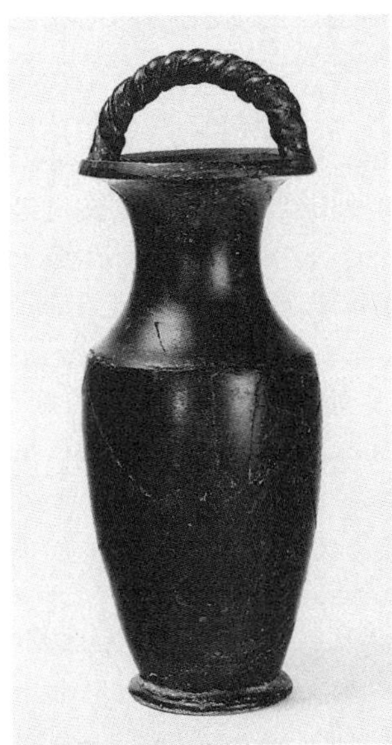

FIGURE 2.9. *Attic black-gloss bail oinochoe. Athens, N. P. Goulandris Foundation–Museum of Cycladic Art, inv. no. 490. Photo courtesy of the Museum.*

All the black-gloss and the figured bail oinochoai with known provenance come from Athens, Attika, or nearby Aigina, and those with a known or suspected context derive either from a grave or an offering pit connected with graves. This indicates that they are Attic funerary vessels that were used as grave gifts and in ritual connected with burial, functions that are also implied by the scenes on a majority of the figured ones, as the Bowdoin piece helps to illustrate. Three others (Nos. 2, 5, and 6) depict a cavalcade going around the vessel. The riders on two (Nos. 2 and 6) wear Thracian cloaks (*zeirai*), hold spears, and stretch an arm out in the gesture of valediction. Similar riders are found on other funerary vases, including black-figure and red-figure loutrophoroi, black-figure amphoriskoi, and black-figure phormiskoi.[26] The riders are probably best thought of as taking part in the ekphora, not in a contemporary, real-life ekphora, rather one that is symbolic of earlier aristocratic funerals, so as to indicate the worthiness of the deceased. The third (No. 5) shows naked riders going toward a tripod, which suggests funeral games.

The scenes on the remaining three vases are not necessarily funerary, but the pictures are not inappropriate for funerary vessels. One in Dresden of the second form shows a warrior fighting a Skythian archer (No. 7; Fig. 2.8). Another type of funerary vessel that started to be made around the time of this vase is the battle-loutrophoros, whose battle scenes sometimes pit Amazons against Greeks. Skythians, like Amazons, are foreigners, and so the basic equation of foreigner versus Greek is common to both scenes.[27] The two remaining bail oinochoai show processions. The image on one once in Berlin (No. 3) has six pairs of figures, each comprised of a woman with a diphros atop her head and a boy holding a *lagobolon* over his shoulder, onto which is tied a dead fox and a dead hare. A fragment of another in Frankfurt (No. 4; Fig. 2.10) preserves both the top of a man carrying a vessel on his shoulder, almost certainly a hydria of the same form as shown carried by the short man on the Bowdoin bail oinochoe, and most of the upper half of a woman carrying a basket on her head. They may be part of a funerary procession, although nothing definitively indicates this.

Twisted handles and plain bail handles are known already in Attic pottery from the Late Bronze Age,[28] and from that time on there is a long and nearly continuous tradition in Attika of oinochoai with twisted handles, many of which were used as funerary vessels.[29] Bail handles are also found on other black-figure vases, including miniature baskets and siphons.[30] Normally the handle on an oinochoe runs vertically between the mouth and body, its primary function to facilitate easy and controlled pouring, although the vase is also often carried by it—not always successfully, when full, because liquid can spill out. Bail handles, however, are used primarily on oinochoai for carrying and sometimes for hanging.

Literary sources cite a variety of liquids that were used in Athenian funerary rites for libations, including honey, milk, wine, oil, and water.[31] Of these, water is the logical choice as the preferred liquid for bail oinochoai, since the others are more valuable liquids, which are better suited for a vessel designed primarily for careful, controlled pouring. Additionally, Sparkes and Talcott suggest that bail oinochoai were derived from the *kados,* a much larger common coarse-ware or metal vessel for drawing well-water in the sixth and fifth centuries B.C.[32] Water, as we have already noted, played a role in various parts of the funerary ritual.[33] One could posit a connection between any of these roles and these vessels, or cleverly suggest new ones, but any such suggestion would be pure speculation.

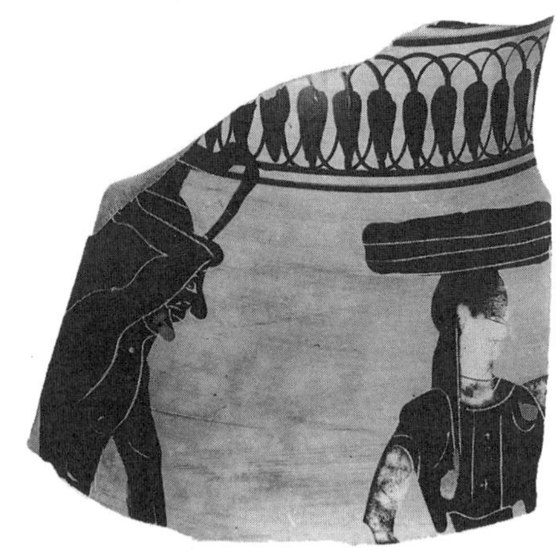

FIGURE 2.10. *Fragment of an Attic black-figure bail oinochoe. Frankfurt, Städtische Galerie Liebieghaus IN 524. Photo courtesy of the Museum.*

In the case of the Bowdoin bail oinochoe, we see reflected the beginnings of an interest in new types of funerary subjects at the start of the fifth century, as the painters moved away from the traditional picture of the prothesis to depicting other parts of the funerary ritual. The Sappho Painter was a leader in this regard. The deposition of the corpse into the coffin, however, was apparently not a subject that found favor with the clientele of the Kerameikos, for, again, this is the only example we have of it. This should not be a surprise, because it is one of the most emotional moments in a funeral, the last time one actually sees the deceased, and an act one would not want to remember. Instead, other scenes, such as the visit to the grave, as shown on the Sappho Painter's loutrophoros in Athens,[34] and the preparations for a visit to the grave, as inferred from the woman with a funerary basket on the Bowdoin bail oinochoe, become the preferred ones on the white-ground lekythos.[35] Thus, the images on the late black-figure predecessors to the Periklean white-ground lekythoi, such as the bail oinochoe, are harbingers of things to come, and the bail oinochoe can now be recognized as a special class of Attic funerary vase that takes its place beside the black-figure loutrophoros, funerary plaque, egg, and phormiskos as the immediate antecedents to the Classical Athenian white lekythos.

APPENDIX

The following abbreviations are used:

Db. = Diameter of Base

Dm. = Diameter of Mouth

Ht. = Height

All measurements are in centimeters.

BLACK FIGURE

1. Brunswick, Maine, Bowdoin College Museum of Art 1984.023

Ht. 37.3, Ht. without handle 30.4–7, Dm. 13.9, Db. 11.4–5.

A dead man placed into his coffin; mourners; procession.

Paralipomena 247 (Sappho Painter); *Addenda*² 126–127; *GBA* 1394 (March 1985), *La Chronique* 27; Kurtz 1975, 133, n. 7; Boardman 1974, fig. 266; Kurtz and Boardman 1971, pls. 37–38; *CAH* Plates to Volume 4, 168, no. 218a–c; *AJA* 95 (1991) 635, fig. 4; Immerwahr 1998, vol. 2, no. 2854; Laxander 2000, pl. 68:1–4; Huber 2001, 107–108, no. 108; *AntK* 45 (2002) pl. 3:1–2; Jubier-Galinier, forthcoming, fig. 5: Neils and Oakley 2003, 166 and 297–298, cat. no. 112.

Figs. 2.1–4

2. Quebec, Laval University D 12 (now on loan to Montreal, Musée des Beaux-Arts)

From Greece.

Ht. 27.3–5, Ht. with handle 35.2, Dm. 13.2, Db. 11.4–5, Max. D. 17.1.

Cavalcade.

Oakley 2003, 36–37, fig. 3.2 and 103, cat. no. 12.

Figs. 2.5–6

3. Once Berlin, Staatliche Museen, Antikensammlung VI 3330 (destroyed)

From Athens.

Ht. without handle 25.7.

Procession of youths and women.

AA (1895) 36; *Monatshefte* 11 (1918) pl. 11, fig. 6.

4. Frankfurt, Liebieghaus IN 524, fr.

Probably from Athens.

Ht. 3.7, W. 4.1.

Procession.

CVA Frankfurt 2 Germany 30 pl. 58:2; Flashar 2003, 197–198, no. 243.

Fig. 2.10

5. Athens, National Museum 12950

From Vari.

Ht. 25.9, Ht. without handle 19.9, Dm. 10.9, Db. 10.1.

Cavalcade.

6. Dresden, Staatliche Kunstsammlungen ZV 2955

From Aigina.

Ht. 32.0, Ht. without handle 25.0, Db. 13.5.

Cavalcade.

AA (1925), cols. 104, 108–109, no. 18; col. 109, fig. 11.

Fig. 2.7

7. Dresden, Staatliche Kunstsammlungen ZV 2956

From Aigina.

Ht. without handle 26.2, Db. 11.1.

Hoplite fighting a Skythian archer.

AA (1925) cols. 109–110, no. 19.

Fig. 2.8

BLACK GLOSS

8. Athens, National Museum 18021

Ht. 32.1, Ht. without handle 25.9, Db. 10.76.

Sparkes and Talcott 1971, 203, n. 13, no. 2; Clark 1992, 181, n. 49.

9. Athens, N. P. Goulandris Foundation, Museum of Cycladic Art 490

Ht. 29.8, Ht. without handle 24.8, Dm. 11, Db. 7.8.

Marangou 1985, 111, no. 157.

Fig. 2.9

10. Athens, Kerameikos hS 51

From Athens, Kerameikos Grave hS 51.

Ht. 20.2, Ht. without handle 16.4, Dm. 7.2–8, Db. 7.2 (restored).

AM 81 (1966) 51, no. 102 and Beil. 41:2.

11. Athens, Kerameikos Inv. 1553

From Athens, Kerameikos Grave S 21.

Ht. 30.6, Ht. without handle 26.4.

Sparkes and Talcott 1971, 203, n. 13, no. 3; Kunze-Götte et al. 1999, pl. 57:1, 4.

12. Athens, Kerameikos HS 28/29

From Athens, Kerameikos Grave HS 28/29.

Ht. 20.7, Ht. without handle 16.8, Dm. 8.6–9.0, Db. 6.5–6.

Sparkes and Talcott 1971, 203, n. 13, no. 4.

13. Athens, Kerameikos HS 56

From Athens, Kerameikos Grave HS 56.

Ht. 19.3, Ht. without handle 16.5, Dm. 8.4–5, Db. 6.4–5.

Sparkes and Talcott 1971, 203, n. 13, no. 5.

14. Athens, Kerameikos

From Athens, Kerameikos, Opferstelle Eck 43.

Ht. 25.9, Dm. 10.8.

Kovacsovics 1990, 57 and pl. 43:54.1.

15. Athens, Third Ephoria

From Athens, grave at Konstantinoupoleos St. between Salaminas and Plataion Strs.

ADelt 22 (1967) *Chronika* 1, 97 and pl. 90:e.

NOTES

I would like to thank the following for their help in preparing this article: G. Adler, P. C. Bol, D. von Bothmer, Y. Brandt, A. J. Clark, G. Deschênes-Wagner, A. Ferris, M. Kelly, L. J. Latman, J. R. Mertens, A. Nielsen, D. Plantzos, O. Palagia, J. Stroszeck, and Sabine Weber. After submission of this paper, Sabine Weber presented a poster about this type of vase at the *Internationales Vasen-Symposium* in Kiel, September 24–28, 2001. I profited from a good discussion with her about these vases, and she brought Nos. 14 and 15 in the Appendix to my attention. She also kindly sent me copies of the pertinent pages in her dissertation. I also greatly profited from my exchange with C. Jubier-Galinier who also sent me copies of her work.

1. Houby-Nielsen 1995, 145–150.

2. Pollitt 1972, 68.

3. See most recently: Frangeskou 1999, 315, n. 2, with additional bibliography; and also Clairmont 1983, 7–17; Garland 1985, 89–93; Pritchett 1985, 106–124; Loraux 1986, 13–76. Stupperich (1977, 238) prefers a Kleisthenic date.

4. *IG* I^2 928: Clairmont 1983, 127–130 and pls. 15–16, for the casualty list; for the start of the white-ground lekythos, see Oakley 2001.

5. For black-figure plaques, see most recently Mommsen 1997 and see her list of black-figure loutrophoroi with funerary scenes, pp. 66–71. For phormiskoi and eggs, see most recently Kefalidou 2001 and Hatzivassilou 2001, and also Sparkes and Talcott 1971, 181, with earlier bibliography.

6. See Brümmer 1985, esp. 59–68, for the use of chests as burial containers.

7. Weber 2000, 439, suggests the reading λαβ<έ> εὖ ἰ(τ for θ)ύ τά, which would read, "hold it good and straight."

8. Jubier-Galinier, forthcoming.

9. A similar lamp is depicted on the reverse of a stamnos by Smikros: Brussels, Musées Royeaux d'Art et d'Histoire A 717: *ARV*[2] 20:1 and 1619; *Paralipomena* 322; *Addenda*[2] 154; Neer 2002, 88, figs. 41–42.

10. Other references include Eur. *Al.* 768 and *Supp.* 772. See most recently Mommsen 1997, 20; Hame 1999, 55. See also Reiner 1938, 35–49; Neumann 1965, 85–89.

11. Kurtz and Boardman 1971, 149; Kurtz 1988, 149. For

the baskets, see also Fairbanks 1914, 213–233; Kurtz 1975, passim; Reilly 1989, 417–418; Kurtz 1990, 108; Hame 1999, 84. For baskets in general, see Amyx 1958, 164–175; Lissarrague 1995.

12. See Hame 1999, 29–31, for this problem.

13. E.g., Once Berlin, Staatliche Museen F 1655: *CorVP* 571–572, no. 66; FR 3, pl. 121 and New York, Metropolitan Museum of Art 06.1021.99: *ARV*[2] 220,4; *LIMC* 7, pl. 406, Priamos 94. See also the mourner (Hekuba?) on the side of the new sarcophagus from Gümüşçay with the sacrifice of Polyxena: *Studia Troica* 6 (1996) 258, fig. 11.

14. Athens, National Museum 1958: *ARV*[2] 748,2 and 1668; *Paralipomena* 413; *Addenda*[2] 284; Kurtz 1975, pl. 19:3.

15. Amyx 1958, 268–271, pl. 51:a.

16. Sparkes and Talcott 1971, 366, nos. 1847–1848, pl. 88.

17. Hame 1999, 96–101.

18. Most recently, Hame 1999, 513–555.

19. Weber 2000, 313.

20. Hame 1999, 36–37.

21. *ABL* 94–130, 225–229; *ABV* 507–508, 702; *Paralipomena* 246–247; *Addenda*[2] 126–127; Boardman 1974, 148–149; Kurtz 1975, 79–81, 118–120, 133, 149–150; Frel 1983, 35; Jubier 1999.

22. Athens, National Museum 450: *ABL* 229,59; *CVA* Athens 1 Greece 1 pls. 8:1–2, 9:3. Paris, Louvre MNB 905: *ABL* 229,58; Denoyelle 1994, 112–113, no. 51. Bonn, Akademisches Kunstmuseum 1002a: *AA* (1935) 448–449, no. 23, 457–458, fig. 34; Mommsen 1997, 69, no. 46.

23. *ABL* 96–97; Jubier-Galinier, forthcoming.

24. The first to collect and discuss these is Clark 1992, 142–143, 180–185.

25. Clark 1992, 184–185.

26. Mommsen 1997, 21–22. She now believes that the Thracians did take part in some contemporary ekphorai: "Donne e cavalieri traci nel culto funebre in Attica," a paper presented at the conference *Il Greco, Il Barbaro e la Ceramica Attica* held in Catania, Sicily, May 14, 2001. The papers from this congress are to be published.

27. For battle loutrophoroi, see especially Beazley 1932; van den Driessche 1973; Stupperich 1977, 155–162; Clairmont 1983, 74–85. Two new ones with an Amazonomachy are Athens, N. P. Goulandris Foundation, Museum of Cycladic Art A 15369 (on loan): *Athens: The City beneath the City* (Athens 2000), 369–370, no. 410; and Athens, National Museum 13032A: *ADelt* 49 (1994) *Chronika* 1, pl. 5:d.

28. Mountjoy 1999, 567, 569 no. 325, 528–529 nos. 145 and 147, 521–522 nos. 110–111, 589–590 no. 438. For bail handles, see Weber 2000, 25–36.

29. E.g., Late Helladic III: Mountjoy 1999, 589–590, nos. 436–437. Geometric: Athens, Kerameikos 300; Coldstream 1968, pl. 5:a. Seventh Century: Kübler 1970, pls. 27, 62. Some black-figure oinochoai were clearly made as funerary vessels, such as Athens, Kerameikos 40: *ABV* 19,2; Kübler 1970, pls. 93, 95–96.

30. E.g., Siphon: Oxford, University of Mississippi 77.3.74; Shapiro 1981, 138–139; *CVA* Robinson 3 USA 7 pl. 3:1. Baskets: *ABV* 658, 121–124. For other shapes with basket handles, see Sparkes and Talcott 1971, 203, n. 14.

31. Graf 1981; Garland 1985, 113–115; Hame 1999, 83–85.

32. Sparkes and Talcott 1971, 203.

33. See also Kurtz and Boardman 1971, 149–150.

34. Athens, National Museum 450: above, n. 22.

35. Oakley (forthcoming).

3

A FAREWELL WITH ARMS

DEPARTING WARRIORS ON ATHENIAN VASES

SUSAN B. MATHESON

Both place and time were changed, and I dwelt nearer to those eras of history that had most attracted me.

HENRY DAVID THOREAU, *Walden*

Art and Experience in Classical Greece was my first introduction to J. J. Pollitt's work, long before I was introduced to the author himself. Since that first encounter, which opened for me a new way of looking at Greek art, the humanist philosophy of *Art and Experience* has been an inspiration and its clarity a model. Its author has been a consistent and gratefully received influence on my work but an even more profound influence on my life.

DEPARTURE OF WARRIOR SCENES

Images of warriors taking leave of their families on the eve of battle can be heart-wrenching and inspiring to the sympathetic viewer today, and there is subtle but compelling evidence on red-figure vases from Periklean Athens that the same held true in fifth-century Greece. Scenes of departing warriors on Athenian vases portray universal human emotions such as sadness, distress, love, and pride through gesture and expression, while social ideals such as honor, civic duty, and family devotion are evoked through composition, setting, and dress. The notable popularity of departure scenes in Classical Athenian vase painting can be seen to reflect contemporary civic and personal values, as well as the historical fact of military service and frequent warfare during this period. The content of departure scenes enriches the understanding of aspects of Athenian life in this period that we otherwise derive from literary sources, some of which are significantly later, and from monumental art, notably the sculptures of the Parthenon. In some cases, the vases offer information not available from any other contemporary source. This paper will focus on departure scenes on vases beginning with those by the Early Classical Altamura and Niobid Painters and continuing through the end of the fifth century.[1]

Scenes of departing warriors first appear on black-figure vases, where departing epic heroes and mortal Athenians alike are carried to war in chariots.[2] Archaic red-figure vase painters occasionally follow this model.[3] In a related subject, the *extispicy* (examination of the entrails) that often preceded a departure is shown in black figure and early red figure.[4] Athenian hoplites taking leave of their families also appear in black-figure compositions that are closely related to the more common scenes of warriors arming: a hoplite arms or departs surrounded by members of his family.[5] Both show the hoplite in the company of a small group; the presence of a libation in the departure scenes is the primary difference between arming and departure. Early red-figure departure scenes, which are infrequent, develop from these family scenes.[6] Classical departures, which comprise the vast majority of such scenes in red-figure vase painting, in turn grow out of the Late Archaic departures, but they are considerably more varied in significant details.

Several key elements form the foundation on which the departure scenes of the Classical period are built. An armed warrior, generally in the center of the composition, is the focus. He is sometimes bearded, more often not. He wears and bears basic hoplite gear: at a minimum a helmet (often Corinthian), a round shield, and a spear.[7] He may also have a sword in a scabbard, wear body armor (various types of corselets and cuirasses), and have greaves. A woman will be present, preparing for a libation, and an older man will also be there. The libation is a determining narrative element in Classical departure scenes and the key to distinguishing these scenes from those of arming. On the surface, the scenes appear quite consistent, almost formulaic. Yet within a relatively set framework there is sufficient variation to differentiate several important events related to the military service that anchored the life of every Athenian man.

Two critical points in an Athenian male's life are relevant to his military service and to the scenes examined here.[8] At age 18, as most scholars reconstruct the chronology, a young man officially became an adult, a citizen, and an *ephebe*. He served as an ephebe for two years, undergoing military training that was supported by the state and as a member of the *peripoloi*, that is, the home guard, who acted as the guards of the frontier.[9] At the age of twenty, he became a hoplite, and he remained so from age 20 through age 29 (inclusive, at both Athens and Sparta), with the potential for being called up for active service until the age of 60. Not all Athenian males became hoplites, however. Some joined the cavalry instead; they, too, are illustrated on vases.[10]

These stages of life are reflected in what I see as two types of departure scenes: (1) the departure of a hoplite who is actually leaving for battle or extended military campaign and (2) the departure of ephebes for some stage of their two-year training and military service guarding the Athenian frontiers and the associated presentation of the arms of a hoplite at the dedication of the ephebe.[11]

Here, I will treat these two types of scenes but make no pretense of being comprehensive; rather my goal is, through the selective examination of Classical vases, to suggest the complexity and ambiguity of these departure scenes and propose an interpretation that links them as closely to the training of ephebes as to actual warfare. Unquestionably there is inconsistency in the details of the departure scenes, introducing ambiguity that Richard Neer, writing about earlier vases, proposes is intentional.[12] Whether deliberate or not, this ambiguity allows the vases to yield multiple complementary interpretations. What follows should thus be understood as one approach to a single part of a large and complex subject. Future research might explore the relation of arming and departure scenes, departures of warriors compared to those of civilians on Athenian white-ground lekythoi and grave stelai, and the use of mythological and epic names in departures and daily-life scenes of all sorts.

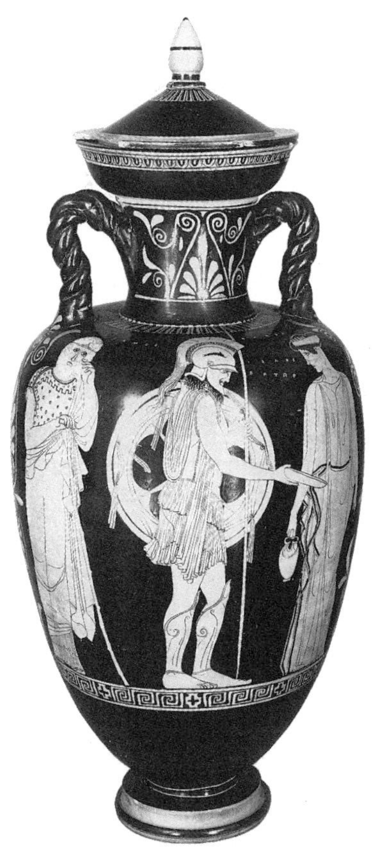

FIGURE 3.1. *Attic red-figure neck amphora by the Hector Painter, side A: Departure of Hektor. Vatican City, Museo Gregoriano Etrusco 16570. Photo courtesy of the Museum.*

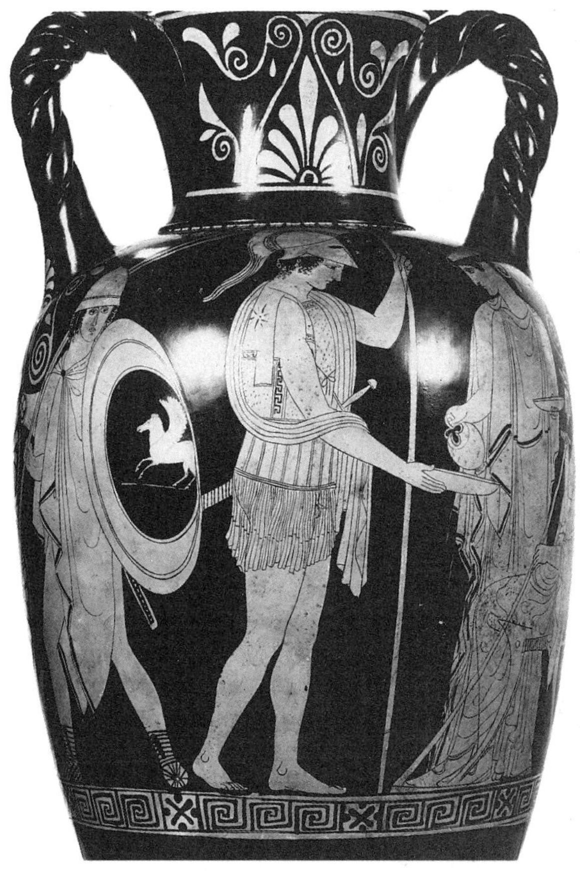

FIGURE 3.2. *Attic red-figure neck amphora by the Hector Painter, side A: Departure of a warrior. Brussels, Royal Library of Belgium, Coin Cabinet, Lucien de Hirsch coll. nr. 15. Photo courtesy of the Museum.*

DEPARTING WARRIORS

Scenes of warriors departing for battle feature a warrior who is generally bearded and in full hoplite armor (helmet, round shield, spear or spears, sword, corselet or cuirass, and greaves; Fig. 3.1).[13] There is considerable variety in the armor, suggesting that, with the exception of the shield and spear, hoplites provided their own equipment.[14] Shield devices, where visible, are varied, although the lion seems to be the most frequent. Helmets vary from the common Corinthian and Attic to Thracian and the occasional Chalkidian. Body armor can be an individually fitted muscle cuirass, or, more frequently, a composite corselet or cuirass of scales, leather, or quilted fabric. The armor is worn over a short chiton. Not all the departing hoplites are bearded (Fig. 3.2). This is consistent with the occurrence of bearded and beardless hoplites together in arming scenes.[15] Nor are all the departing bearded hoplites fully armed. Some do not wear their body armor or greaves, although virtually all wear their helmets and have shield and spear in hand.

The hoplite takes leave of members of his family, generally a woman, likely his mother, and a bearded man, sometimes balding or white haired. This distinguished elder should be his father. He is generally seated or leaning on a staff. Sometimes the hoplite and the bearded, older man clasp hands. Much has been written about this gesture, especially as it appears on grave reliefs, but none of it is truly conclusive with regard to scenes such as this on vases.[16] By itself, the handclasp can be a gesture of farewell or of greeting.[17] In these scenes, however, it is combined not with gestures of greeting, such as raised hands, but with gestures of sadness and mourning, such as a head held in the hand or drapery held out in distress. The combination of gestures leaves us in no doubt that these scenes show departures, not arrivals.

The primary role of the woman in these scenes is to prepare or assist in the libation. In most of these libations, the warrior holds a phiale, while the woman standing next to him holds an oinochoe, sometimes in the act of pouring. Less frequently, the woman holds both vessels, while the warrior does something else, perhaps clasping hands with his father or keeping both hands on his weapons.

In the most thinly peopled versions of the scene, where only an older man (presumably the father) and a woman are present with the hoplite, the woman is most likely the mother. Her importance in this context is confirmed by at least two independent sources. First, in departure scenes on other vases where the figures are given names from epic poetry, the woman in the departures (and in the closely related arming scenes) is given the name of the hero's mother; second, the mothers of the fallen soldiers in the Peloponnesian War are singled out for special sympathy by Perikles in the Funeral Oration (Thuk. 2.44.3).

Where there are two women present, the second should, in my view, be read as the warrior's wife, or, if she is wearing the hairstyle of an unmarried woman, as his sister or fiancée, although these distinctions cannot be said to be absolute. There do seem to be cases where the woman nearest the warrior is likely to be his wife, but she generally does not participate in the libation. Occasionally someone hands the hoplite his helmet as part of the departure. As in the arming scenes, this is generally the hoplite's mother, but on occasion several family members and more than the helmet are involved. Such a combination of arming and departure is readily understandable as a reflection of real life, but it softens the border between arming and departures as vase-painting subjects.

Elements suggesting a setting for the scene are occasionally introduced. A column is the most common. Sometimes there is an altar. A column in conjunction with an altar suggests a sanctuary, or, more likely, the domestic altar in the courtyard of a house. A seat (either a *klismos* or a stool), when used by the old bearded male relative and shown by itself or in conjunction with a column, would indicate a domestic setting. Occasionally there is a door, generally signifying a house. A palm tree alone or in conjunction with an altar would indicate an outdoor sanctuary, as Christiane Sourvinou-Inwood has shown.[18] An exceptional two-sided hydria in the Vatican Museums, on which a single scene of a warrior departing extends across both sides of the vase, shows an outdoor location by placing the altar near a closed door and column and the seated older man next to a palm tree.[19] The setting is confirmed by introducing a woman seated on a rock near a small tree, a vignette placed over the hydria's handle. Outdoor sanctuary settings are quite rare, indicating that most of the departures take place in a domestic context. The predominance of domestic settings among the surviving vases further suggests that departures in which no setting is indicated should also be read as domestic.

The departing hoplite is sometimes accompanied by a servant or a comrade in arms.[20] This figure generally wears a short *chiton* or *chlamys* and a *pilos* helmet or *petasos*, and he often carries a spear (Fig. 3.3). Where the companion carries the hoplite's armor, he is probably a servant, but where both the hoplite and the companion are armed, the companion is more likely to be a comrade. The warrior's dog may also accompany him. Occasionally there is a horse: transportation to the Front.

Epic names are sometimes given to all the participants. The name vase of the Hector Painter (Fig. 3.1), in the Vatican Museums, for example, bears inscriptions naming each of the figures.[21] Hektor is shown as a mature hoplite (albeit a Trojan in Greek dress) going off to a real war. Hekuba, his mother, gives him wine for an offering. His father, Priam, appears to know his son's fate. Such inscribed vases help to determine the identification of the woman in similar three-figure scenes without inscriptions as the mother of the warrior. Other named warriors include Neoptolemos, Skeparnos, and Lykaon; Hektor is the most frequent.

Such epic scenes are descendants of early red-figure arming scenes with heroic casts, such as the amphora by Euthymides in Munich with Hektor arming, Hek-

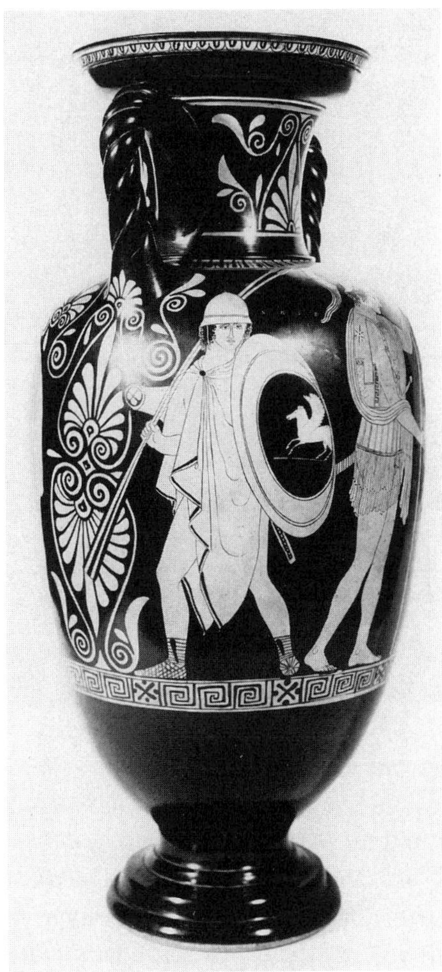

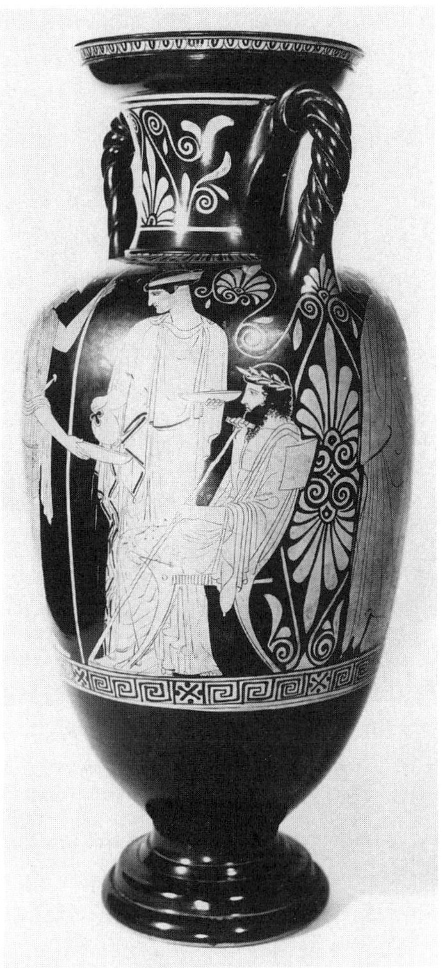

FIGURES 3.3:A–B. *Attic red-figure neck amphora by the Hector Painter, side A: Departure of a warrior. Brussels, Royal Library of Belgium, Coin Cabinet, Lucien de Hirsch coll. nr. 15. Photos courtesy of the Museum.*

uba assisting, and Priam looking on,[22] and black-figure departure scenes in which the departing warrior, conveyed in a chariot, and his family are named to indicate the departure of Hektor. Most black-figure departure scenes are chariot departures, and it has been suggested that the presence of the chariot, which was not in use in sixth-century Athens when these vases were made but was known to have been used in the distant (epic) past, elevates all these departures to the heroic level, even when the figures are not named.[23]

The simultaneous departure of two or more warriors occurs on several vases, among them a volute krater in Boston by the Niobid Painter that, although uninscribed, has been interpreted as a scene from epic poetry.[24] In the crowded scene on the vase, a beardless warrior dressed in armor is about to receive his helmet from a young woman who touches his hand gently in farewell, while other women cluster about the couple. One bears a phiale; another, a wreath; and a third, a fine textile sash. Another woman stands before a door. An older man is seated in a chair, near a column. A shield and sword hang from the rafters. Under the handle of the vase another warrior takes leave, flanked by two bearded men, both wearing wreaths, one with white hair and beard. Erika Simon has identified the young warrior with long curly hair as Achilles, and she interprets the scene as the hero leaving the daughters of Lykomedes.[25] The woman touching Achilles' hand would then be Deidameia, Achilles' secret bride, and the moment of leaving virtually the same as the moment of their marriage. This convincing interpretation would make the Boston krater another example of

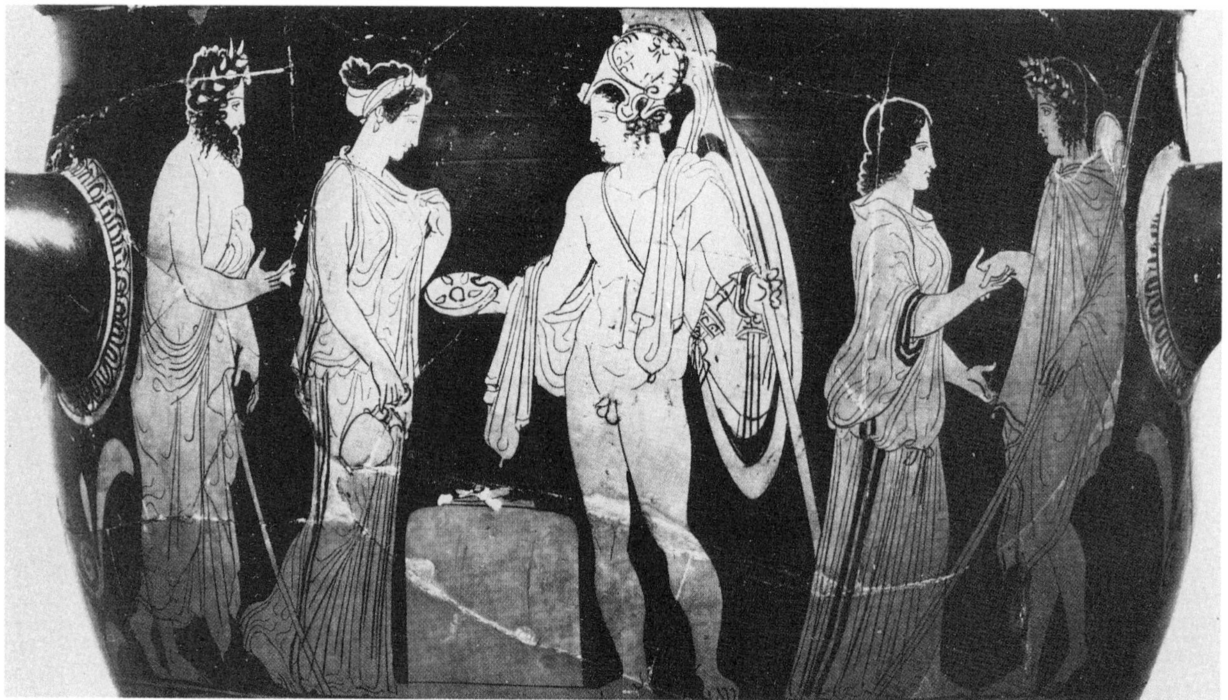

FIGURE 3.4. *Attic red-figure bell krater by the Dinos Painter, side A: Departure of Pandion and Oineus. Syracuse, Museo Archeologico Nazionale 30747. Photo after* LIMC, *by permission.*

a heroic departure, as well as one of the few departure scenes to go beyond simple leave-taking or libation.

A second dual departure appears on a bell krater by the Dinos Painter in Syracuse (Fig. 3.4).[26] In this scene, a nude warrior, wearing a chlamys over one shoulder, a decorated Corinthian helmet, and a scabbard with sword and bearing a shield and spear, holds a phiale over an altar as he makes an offering. This helmeted warrior is inscribed Pandion, a mythical Athenian king, son of Erichthonios, and one of the ten Athenian eponymous heroes, for whom nudity would be appropriately called heroic.[27] A woman, unnamed, stands on the opposite side of the altar from him, holding an oinochoe and grasping her peplos at the shoulder in a sign of distress. To the right is a second couple consisting of another young man (Oineus, also an eponymous hero), wearing a chlamys and petasos and holding two spears, who clasps hands with a young woman (Choiros) dressed in a sleeved chiton. At the far left, a bearded man (Akamas, yet another eponymous hero) stands leaning on a staff and gesturing towards the two couples before him. Akamas and Oineus wear wreaths, indicating the ceremonial nature of the scene.

The situation in which these three Athenian heroes find themselves seems not to refer to a specific mythical episode, and the scene is better understood as another instance of transforming a common departure into something heroic. As Uta Kron has written about this vase, "The three Attic *Phylenheroen* take leave of their loved ones as the Athenians of the time of the Peloponnesian War must so often have done."[28]

Evelyn Harrison argues for a close connection between Pandion and departing warriors.[29] She cites a second representation of the hero as a departing warrior, this time light armed, on an oinochoe by the Eretria Painter in Palermo.[30] In this scene, Pandion prepares to pour a libation, a key element in departure scenes. Harrison combines the Dinos Painter's representation of Pandion with the nearly contemporary first reference to the statue of Pandion in the Athenian Agora in ancient literature (Aristophanes' *Peace,* first performed in 421 B.C.) to support her suggestion that this statue of the hero might have shown him as a "young soldier preparing for an expedition."[31] As that passage declares,

> Tis tomorrow that the soldiers leave the town; one poor wretch has brought no victuals, for he knew not he must go 'till he on Pandion's statue spied the list and found twas so, reading there his name inserted.[32]

Harrison suggests further, citing scholiasts on Aristophanes, that the statue of Pandion in the Agora might have been the place where lists of soldiers being called up for specific expeditions were posted. Whether this, or Harrison's alternative proposal that the poet cited Pandion because "the image of his statue was appropriate,"[33] is the case, the contemporary association of Pandion and warrior's departures provides critical support for an interpretation of Pandion's nudity as heroic. The civic nature of this heroism is clearly indicated by the use of an eponymous hero's name in this departure, adding a new dimension to the epic heroism of earlier scenes such as the departure on the Hector Painter's name vase.

Harrison's suggestions about the relation between the images of Akamas and Oineus, the two other eponymous heroes on the Dinos Painter's krater, and their statues in the Agora are beyond the scope of this paper, except insofar as they would confirm that the vase paintings are more closely associated with contemporary public art and civic values than with the mythical or epic past.[34]

Nude warriors such as Pandion bearing hoplite gear represent a small proportion of the total number of departure scenes. Although lacking the body armor that they would need in real battle, they may still be read as departing warriors.[35] Other elements in the scene, including the participants and their gestures (especially the woman's mourning gesture), the libation, and the frequent indications of setting are consistent with departures in which the hoplite is clothed and fully armed. Most of the examples with a nude warrior known to me include inscriptions naming the warrior and the other figures in the scene. The majority of these names come from Trojan epic. The Dinos Painter's krater naming the warrior Pandion is a possible exception, although he is associated on the vase with Akamas, who is known at Troy. On the Lykaon Painter's amphora in New York (Fig. 3.5), for example, the nude and beardless warrior is named Neoptolemos, although the father figure is named Anthiochos, not Achilles.[36]

It is tempting to suggest that the nudity itself has epic or heroic implications. Nudity is traditionally the garb of gods and heroes, and Athenian men who sacrifice their lives in the service of their *polis* are characterized as heroes and their tombs as shrines by Perikles in the Funeral Oration (Thuk. 2.43.2–3). Depicting a departing Athenian soldier in the nudity of heroes and with the name of an epic hero obviously, then, characterizes that warrior as a hero. The scenes with named participants may thus be read simultaneously as episodes from epic or myth and as scenes of heroized mortals. One might think of them as inspirational: visual calls to heroism.

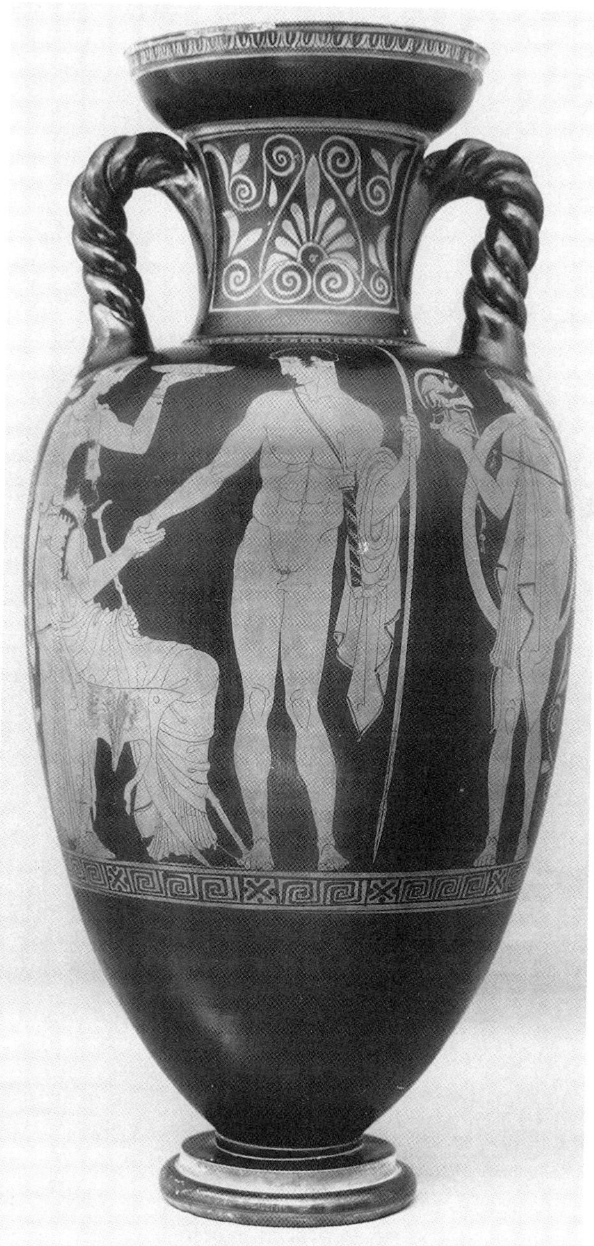

FIGURE 3.5. *Attic red-figure neck amphora by the Lykaon Painter, side A: Departure of Neoptolemos. New York, The Metropolitan Museum of Art, Rogers Fund, 1906 (06.1021.116). Photo courtesy of the Museum.*

DEPARTING EPHEBES

The primary distinction between scenes of an ephebe departing—for training, service in the home guard, or a ceremony—and a hoplite departing for battle is that the ephebe neither is bearded nor wears armor. The ephebe is shown as a beardless young man, dressed in a short chiton and often wearing or carrying a chlamys. A stamnos by Polygnotos in Capua is typical (Fig. 3.6).[37] Occasionally he wears the chalmys alone. He may wear his helmet and hold his shield and spear. Sometimes he wears a petasos, which has suggested a link between hunting and warfare to some scholars, although the petasos may simply indicate travel.[38] As with other departure scenes, the young warrior stands in the midst of his family, and a libation is under way. The supporting figures are the fundamental family members seen in the hoplite departures, namely, the ephebe's father and mother, and occasionally his sister or brother. Settings are generally domestic or absent. As with hoplite departures, I would consider the scenes lacking architectural or landscape elements to be domestic as well.

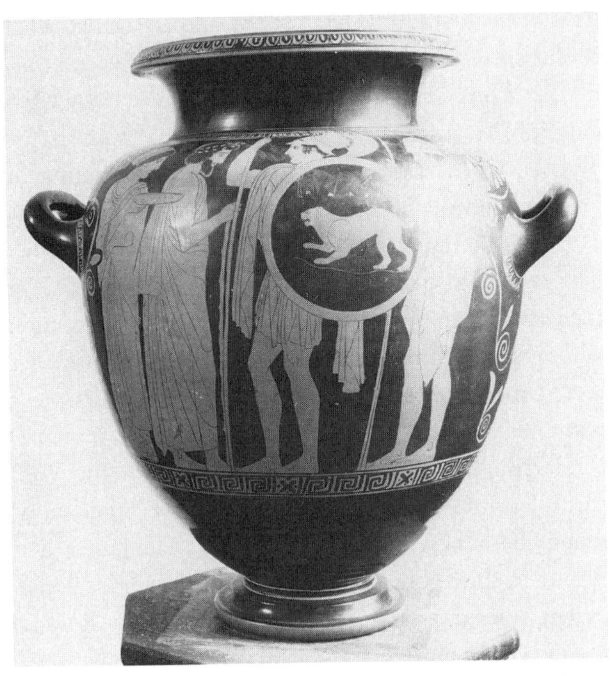

FIGURE 3.6. *Attic red-figure stamnos by Polygnotos, side A: Departure of an ephebe. Capua, Museo Campano 7530. Photo by Hutzel, Inst. Neg. Nr. 64.2239, courtesy of the Deutsches Archäologisches Institut, Rome.*

It is possible to read these scenes as marking the departure of the ephebe for a ceremony that will initiate him into adulthood as a hoplite or a member of the cavalry.[39] The position of the woman as the ephebe's mother is prominent, symbolizing her role as the provider of sons for the service of Athens, and echoing Perikles' words in the Funeral Oration in which he exhorts Athenian women to bear sons to replace the soldiers who had fallen in the first campaigns of the Peloponnesian War (Thuk. 2.44.3).

Complementary evidence for such ceremonies in the fifth century comes from scenes marking the investiture of young men into the cavalry, an alternative to hoplite service at the conclusion of the ephebic term. A pelike by the Dinos Painter in the Bowdoin College collection shows a light-armed youth entering the family on horseback.[40] Barefoot and dressed in a chlamys, he wears a wreath, a sign that he has been engaged in a ritual. He approaches his mother, who holds libation vessels, and his father, who sits in front of a column. A young woman with long hair, probably his unmarried sister, stands at the far right.

Nike sometimes appears in these scenes, either with or instead of the ephebe's mother, as on an amphora by the Peleus Painter in Ferrara (Fig. 3.7).[41] Occasionally, Nike holds the oinochoe for the libation.[42] Somewhat surprisingly, the goddess of victory does not appear in scenes of the fully armed hoplite departing for war, where the emotion of the departure and thus the human dimension of the event are emphasized. Given the frequency of war in Classical Greece, Ronald Ridley rightly states—"From the Persian wars to the battle of Chaironeia, Athens was at war two years out of three, and had not a decade of continuous peace"[43]—scenes of hoplites departing for an actual battle or campaign could have commemorated any one of several departures at any time during a decade or more of hoplite service.

The departure of an ephebe at the start of his service in the peripoloi, by contrast, happened only once. In a sense, it was thus a more ritualized event and as such might readily have suggested the need for divine protection and stimulated the wish to have Nike present at the departure. Nike thus serves as the protector of Athens' new citizen-soldiers as they depart on their first official tour of duty, her presence the equivalent of Athena's in scenes of a hoplite arming before battle

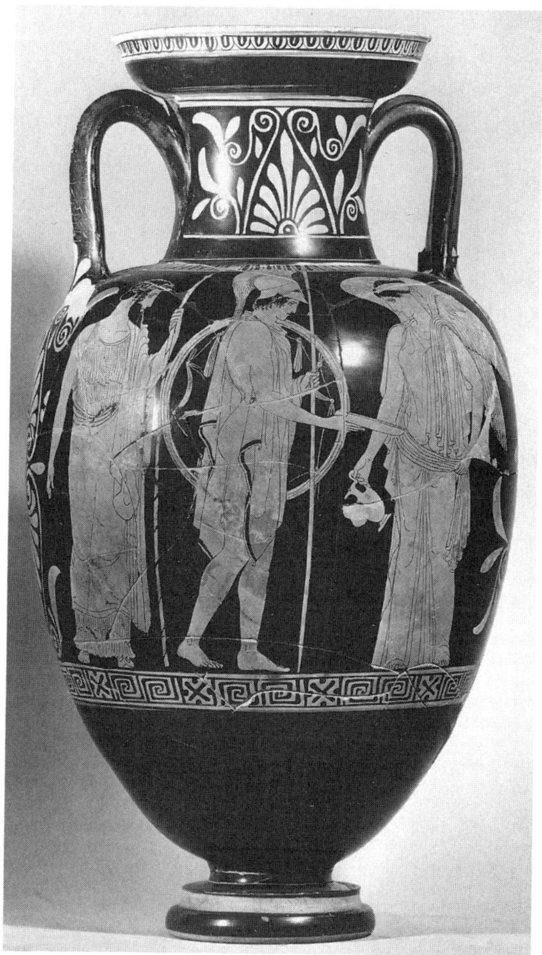

FIGURE 3.7. *Attic red-figure neck amphora by the Peleus Painter, side A: Departure of an ephebe. Ferrara, Museo Archeologico Nazionale di Spina 2894. Photo: Hirmer Verlag, München, neg. no. 571.0097.*

or setting off to war.[44] Nike is closely associated with Athena, whether held in the hand of the Athena Parthenos or crowning Athena in the Gigantomachy of the Parthenon's east metopes. When Nike is present, there is generally only one other participant besides the ephebe—either a man or a woman, apparently the mother or father—and the settings are either neutral or with a column or an altar and palm tree to suggest a sanctuary. This is evidence for the shift in these scenes away from the domestic focus of the hoplite departure scenes.

Another possible interpretation for the presence of Nike in some of these scenes, especially those with sanctuary settings, would classify them not as departures but as scenes related to military games and contests.[45] Ridley proposes the existence of ongoing military training for hoplites throughout the duration of their service, arguing further that the growth of gymnasia derived from the need for hoplites to keep in shape.[46] Ridley cites images on Greek vases as evidence for such military training, including scenes such as that on a red-figure kylix in London in which hoplites run in precise order while raising their spears as if to throw them.[47] Further, he believes that scenes of the *hoplitodromos* and the *pyrrhic* dance (competitive events in which a foot race [*hoplitodromos*] and a dance were executed while wearing armor) on vases are primary evidence for competitions involving military skills, competitions designed to encourage maintenance and improvement of the skills needed in phalanx battle.[48] The name vase of the Lykaon Painter in London and its replica in the Vatican show Nike making an offering to a nude bearded warrior.[49]

Competitors in the hoplitodromos and the pyrrhic dance are shown nude on vases, and they are generally bearded, as are the Lykaon Painter's nude warriors; perhaps nudity in this case, as combined with the presence of Nike, relates the scene to athletic competition. The epic names borne by the Lykaon Painter's warriors would add a heroic dimension to the victory. One might then suggest that the presence of Nike, the goddess of victory in competition even more than in warfare, indicates that the Peleus Painter's amphora in Ferrara (Fig. 3.7) shows a victorious contestant in such a military competition. The beardless young man on this vase, dressed only in a chlamys, his helmet resting back on his head, his spear and shield in hand, extends a phiale to Nike, who holds an oinochoe. The bearded male figure at left holds a staff wrapped in a diagonal band and wears a wreath. Neither of these attributes is common for the older men in departure scenes, but they are typical attributes of officials at competitions. Arguing against this interpretation, however, is the beardless youthfulness of the armed "victor" in contrast to the bearded state of contestants on hoplitodromos and pyrrhic vases. It would be preferable, perhaps, to consider the older man as a military trainer for the ephebe who is present at the young man's dedication ceremony or an official presiding at the event. Nike's role here would then be the equivalent of that in the ephebic departure scenes.

Fourth-century evidence for the *ephebeia*[50] indicates that at the end of the first year of their two-year training and service, ephebes were invested with shield and spear by the state. No literary source confirms that this was true in the fifth century, but scenes on fifth-century vases suggest that it was. There is certainly evidence for the ritual character of the bestowal of arms: on a bell krater in the manner of the Niobid Painter in Chicago, the ephebe is virtually enthroned as he receives his arms.[51] Members of his family bring ritual items such as a sash and a sprig of greenery, in addition to the shield. On a pelike by the Kleophon Painter in Boston, the ephebe wears a patterned garment that has much in common with the ceremonial tunic called the *ependytes,* further underscoring the ritual nature of the bestowal of arms.[52]

There is also evidence for the connection of Athena, embodying the polis, with this ritual: on an amphora by the Niobid Painter in St. Petersburg, for example, a hoplite receives his helmet from Athena.[53] The shield that she will give him rests at her feet. Related is a stamnos by the Altamura Painter in Paris, on which an ephebe, dressed in a short patterned chiton (again like an ependytes) and wearing a *tainia* bound around his head, extends his greaves toward Athena.[54] Behind him an older man holds his sword. The young man approaches Athena bending slightly in a deferential pose as he receives his armor or dedicates it and himself to the goddess.

The presence of Athena in these scenes symbolizes the civic nature of Athenian military service in the fifth century. The oath taken by the ephebes, in the fourth-century text as we have it in a late fourth-century inscription from Acharnai, confirms the idea that all who take it are citizen soldiers:

> I will not disgrace these sacred arms, and I will not desert the comrade beside me wherever I shall be stationed in a battle line. I will defend our sacred and public institutions and I will not hand over to the descendants the fatherland smaller, but greater and better, so far as I am able, by myself or with the help of all. I will obey those who for the time being exercise sway reasonably and the established laws and those which they will establish reasonably in the future, if anyone seek to destroy them, I will not admit it so far as I am able, by myself or with the help of all. I will honor the sacred traditional institutions.
>
> Witnesses are the gods Aglauros, Hestia, Enyo, Enyalios, Ares and Athena Areia, Zeus, Thallo, Auxo, Hegemone, Herakles, and the boundaries of the fatherland, wheat, barley, vines, olive-trees, fig-trees.[55]

In this oath, obeying the laws and honoring the sacred and public institutions are as important as standing by one's comrades in arms. Defense is to be exercised for the preservation of these laws and institutions as much as it is for the preservation of the boundaries of the state. The obligation to do so is sacred.

The final departure of a warrior takes place at the tomb. In a fragmentary loutrophoros by the Kleophon Painter in Athens, warriors and an old man mourn a departed comrade.[56] On a few white-ground lekythoi, warriors appear in scenes at the tomb, where an old man mourns or a woman brings a funerary offering.[57] The scene is comparable to those in which the man appears in traveling garb; the warrior is distinguished from the other men solely by his arms.

Warriors also appear in scenes where a farewell is being exchanged with a woman. Two such scenes occur on white-ground lekythoi by the Achilles Painter, in Athens and London.[58] On the Athens vase, the warrior offers his helmet to a woman who is presumably his wife, as a token of remembrance. On the London lekythos, the woman has risen from her seat to receive the helmet, which she now holds. The vessels hanging on the wall suggest a domestic interior as the setting for the farewell. The farewell is thus symbolic, the more so since the warrior's arms were generally buried with him.

Such apparently intimate scenes raise the issue of emotion in all the departure images. On the Achilles Painter's lekythoi, emotion is expressed sometimes through traditional gestures but more frequently by the intensity of the gaze that bridges the space between the living and the dead. The same intensity of gaze reveals emotion on the bell krater by the Dinos Painter in Syracuse (Fig. 3.4), where both women look into the eyes of their men. A downward glance, as that of the central woman on the stamnoi by the Kleophon Painter in Munich (Fig. 3.8) and St. Petersburg,[59] conveys sad-

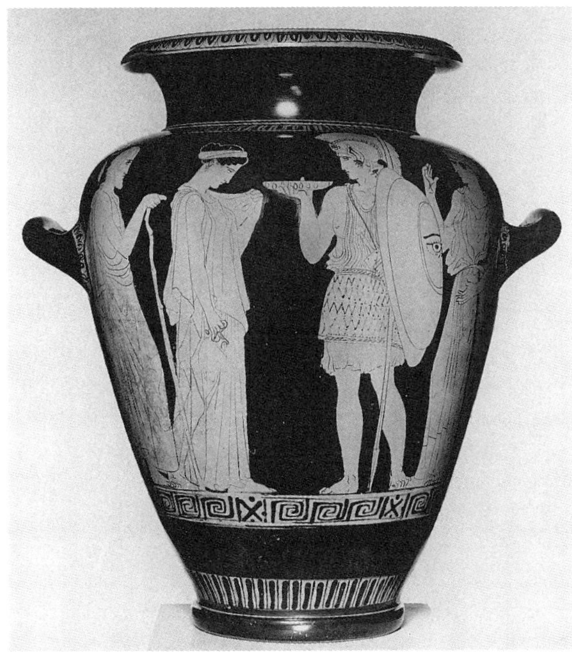

FIGURE 3.8. *Attic red-figure stamnos by the Kleophon Painter, side A: Departure of a warrior. Staatliche Antikensammlungen und Glyptothek München, inv. no. 2415. Photo courtesy of the Museum.*

ness, as does the wrinkled brow of Priam at Hektor's departure in the Hector Painter's name vase (Fig. 3.1). Emotion is also expressed through gesture, as in that of the warrior's wife on the Kleophon Painter's stamnoi or the Dinos Painter's krater, or those of the Kleophon Painter's mourning warriors on the Athens loutrophoros, or that of the Hector Painter's Priam.

In all Classical departure scenes there is a focus on the individual. This confirms Ridley's characterization of the Athenian army as a "citizen militia,"[60] and it emphasizes the warrior's role both within his family and as an Athenian citizen. Scenes of warriors departing thus convey two ideas that were fundamental to Athenian life. The first is the emphasis on the family. The warrior's coming of age and departure are seen in the context of his parents and wife far more often than in the company of his comrades in arms. The realities of war must have been vividly in the minds of Athenians throughout the fifth century, and the grief and fear at departure of warrior sons and husbands were undoubtedly equally real. The knowledge of these realities brought foreboding to the dedication of a young man as a hoplite, and it must have contributed to the somber tenor of all the arming and departure scenes. The need to invoke divine protection for their sons must have inspired the frequent addition of Nike to the family circle in these scenes.

The second is the emphasis on the hoplite's civic role. The ephebic oath is fundamentally a civic oath. The virtues extolled by Perikles in the Funeral Oration are civic virtues. The dedication of a son to the service of Athens fulfilled the mother's civic duty in the same way that the father's civic duty was fulfilled by his previous service as a hoplite. For the hoplite himself, the twelve years that he dedicated to the service of Athens was a period of his life during which he especially needed divine protection. It is fitting and proper that he should embark on each stage of his life with sober reflection and an offering to the gods.

It was a Spartan mother who exhorted her departing warrior son to return "with his shield or on it." Nike, Athena, and the identification of hoplites with heroes on Athenian vases were meant to serve as the same inspiration. An Athenian mother would undoubtedly have exhorted her son to the same heroic behavior. But it was the Athenians who emphasized the effect of war on the individual in the context of the family, and Athenian vase painters who portrayed these concerns in art. The departing warrior left with the love of his family, the inspiration of gods and heroes, and the knowledge that he served Athens as part of a company of citizen-soldiers. The emphasis on these ideas is what distinguishes scenes of departing warriors on vases of the Classical period from those that came before. These vases, designed for use by individuals, are as much about Athenian civic values in the Classical period as is the Parthenon itself.

NOTES

My sincere thanks are offered to Judy Barringer and Jeff Hurwit for the grand gesture of this volume, their dedication in seeing it through, and their kindness in inviting me to be a part of it.

1. See Pemberton 1977, 64–65; Lissarrague 1989, 44–45. I first explored this subject in Matheson 1995, 269–276, and hope to develop it further in the near future.

2. Typical are vases by the Antimenes Painter and the Priam Painter; see Wrede 1916.

3. E.g., London, British Museum E16, a cup by Oltos with Ajax leaving home; *ARV*[2] 61, 75.

4. They have been discussed recently by Lissarrague 1989, 48–50.

5. E.g., those on two sides of an amphora by the Amasis Painter in New York, The Metropolitan Museum of Art, 56.171.10; *ABV* 150, 3; *Paralipomena* 62, 3; Von Bothmer 1985, 86–89.

6. E.g., an amphora by the Kleophrades Painter in Munich, Antikensammlungen 2305; *ARV*[2] 182, 4.

7. Defined as basic hoplite equipment by Snodgrass 1967, 49–63.

8. The following is drawn from Pélékides 1962; Barringer 2001, 47–53.

9. Whether the ephebeia existed in the fifth century, and if so, the extent to which it resembled the ephebeia described in the *Athenaia Politeia* of the fourth in which Aischines served (2.11, as noted by Ridley 1979, 532–533), are debated and beyond the scope of this paper. Barringer 2001, 47–53, provides an excellent, cautionary review of the debate. I am convinced by the arguments offered by Ridley in favor of a fifth-century ephebeia that included military training, the gift of shield and spear by the state, and frontier service, and follow that position here. See also Siewert 1977, who provides some fifth-century allusions to the ephebic oath. Snodgrass 1967, 59, cites Arist. [*Ath. Pol.*] 41.4 as evidence for a state-bestowed shield and spear.

10. Cf. Ridley 1979, 511.

11. Vernant 1974, 37–38, suggests that they show the departure of ephebes for the ceremony that will elevate them to hoplite status. See also Bažant 1987, 36. A related event described in the ancient sources is the annual presentation of eighteen-year-old Athenian war orphans to the public at the start of the Dionysia; see Strauss 1993, 2, citing Thukydides, Lysias, Plato, and Aristotle.

12. Neer 2002.

13. Snodgrass 1967, 58–59.

14. Ridley 1979, 520, notes the relation between the variety and the concept of non-standard-issue privately supplied armor, but he does not draw the conclusion that the vases show variety to reflect this reality. As Ridley points out, the need to supply their own armor meant that there was a property qualification for hoplite service, even when, as in the fourth century if not before, the hoplite's shield and spear were provided by the state.

15. E.g., Brygos Painter cup in the Vatican, Museo Gregoriano Etrusco; *ARV*[2] 373, 48.

16. E.g., McNiven 1982.

17. See McNiven 1982, 37–38, who suggests that these scenes could all be arrivals.

18. Sourvinou-Inwood 1985.

19. Vatican, Museo Gregoriano Etrusco 17882; *ARV*[2] 614, 11; Prange 1989, 221–222, GN76, pls. 18–19.

20. Ridley 1979, 510, notes that slaves were used extensively in non-combatant roles, especially for carrying armor and baggage.

21. Vatican, Museo Gregoriano Etrusco 16570; *ARV*[2] 1036, 1; Matheson 1995, 401, no. 1, pl. 77.

22. Munich, Antikensammlungen 2307; *ARV*[2] 26, 1; Lissarrague 1989, fig. 63.

23. Wrede 1927, 354–358.

24. Museum of Fine Arts, 33.56; *ARV*[2] 600, 12.

25. Simon 1963, 57–59.

26. Syracuse, Museo Archeologico Regionale 30747; *ARV*[2] 1153, 17; *LIMC* 1, s.v. Akamas et Demophon, 440, no. 25, pl. 340 [U. Kron]; *LIMC* 7, 163, no. 10, s.v. Pandion [A. Nercessian]; Matheson 1995, 147–149, 384, D18, pl. 132.

27. On Pandion, see A. Nercessian in *LIMC* 7, s.v. Pandion.

28. U. Kron in *LIMC* 1, s.v. Akamas et Demophon, 445 (translation mine).

29. Kron 1976, 264, P8, pl. 13:2; Harrison 1979b, 72–75.

30. *ARV*[2] 1249; Lezzi-Hafter 1971, pls. 30:2, 4; 32.

31. Harrison 1979b, 75.

32. Ar. *Pax* 1181–1184, tr. B. B. Rogers, Loeb edition, Cambridge 1950, 109.

33. Harrison 1979b, 75.

34. Akamas: Harrison 1979b, 75–76; Oineus: 77–78.

35. For a possible association of nude warriors with athletic competitions, see below.

36. Metropolitan Museum of Art 06.1021.116; *ARV*[2] 1944, 1; Matheson 1995, 431, L1, pl. 64.

37. Capua, Museo Campano 7530; *ARV*[2] 1028, 5; Matheson 1995, 15, 346 P4, pl. 7.

38. Lissarrague 1989, 46; Barringer 2001, 47–53.

39. This has also been suggested by Vernant 1974, 37–38. See also Bažant 1987, 36.

40. Brunswick, Maine, Bowdoin College Museum of Art 1895.2; *ARV*[2] 1155, 41; Matheson 1995, 390, D46, pl. 174.

41. Ferrara, Museo Nazionale Archeologico di Spina 2894; *ARV*[2] 1039, 11; Matheson 1995, pl. 87.

42. Niobid Painter krater, Ferrara, Museo Archeologico Nazionale di Spina T740; *ARV*[2] 599, 6; Lissarrague 1989, fig. 66.

43. Ridley 1979, 509.

44. Arming before battle: amphora by the Antimenes Painter, Rome, Capitoline Museum 88; *ABV* 270, 66; Lissarrague 1989, 47, fig. 64. Athena accompanying a warrior: amphora, Group of Würzburg 199, Würzburg, Martin von

Wagner Museum I.199; *ABV* 287, 5; Lissarrague 1989, 46, fig. 65.

45. Lissarrague (1989, 39–44) also links the youthful warrior to athletics and hunting.

46. Ridley 1979, 535–546.

47. London, British Museum E322, cited by Ridley 1979, 535.

48. Ridley (1979, 535) suggests that British Museum E322, in fact, shows a hoplitodromos. On vases showing the pyrrhic dance, see Poursat 1968.

49. British Museum E379: *ARV*[2] 1045, 3; Matheson 1995, 431, L3, pl. 66; Vatican, Museo Gregoriano Etrusco 16574; *ARV*[2] 1045, 4; Matheson 1995, 431, L4, pl. 67. Nike carries a *kerykeion,* which might identify her as Iris were she not named as NIKH by inscription on the London pelike; perhaps the kerykeion, as the attribute of Hermes, should be linked to travel.

50. *Ath. Pol.* 42, as noted by Ridley 1979, 519.

51. Art Institute 1922.2197: *ARV*[2] 610, 21; Prange 1989, 212, GN35.

52. Museum of Fine Arts 03.793; *ARV*[2] 1145, 37.

53. St. Petersburg, State Hermitage Museum 2227; *ARV*[2] 604, 52; Prange 1989, 195, N68.

54. Paris, Musée du Louvre C 10832; *ARV*[2] 593, 48; Prange 1989, 69, A62, pl. 15.

55. On the ephebic oath, see Siewert 1977. This translation is by J. Plescia, amended by Siewert 1977, 103. Scholars have noted features of the oath itself that point to a fifth-century ephebeia. Siewert quotes and discusses references or allusions to the oath in fifth-century texts, Perikles' speeches as presented by Thukydides among them. See also Barringer 2001, 47–53.

56. National Archaeological Museum 1700 (CC1477); *ARV*[2] 1146, 50.

57. Old man mourning: Achilles Painter, Berlin Staatliche Museen 1983.1, Oakley 1997, no. 273, pl. 141. Woman with offering: Achilles Painter, Athens, National Archaeological Museum 12745; Oakley 1997, no. 251, pl. 131.

58. London, British Museum D51: *ARV*[2] 1000, 201; Oakley 1997, no. 276, pl. 143:A–B. Athens, National Archaeological Museum 1818; *ARV*[2] 998, 161; Oakley 1997, no. 218, pl. 114.

59. St. Petersburg, State Hermitage Museum Ë1148: *ARV*[2] 1143,3: Matheson 1995, 406, K3, pl. 122.

60. Ridley 1979, 509.

4

THE GIRL IN THE *Pithos*

HESIOD'S *Elpis*

JENIFER NEILS

Writing a century ago in the *Journal of Hellenic Studies,* the British classicist Jane Ellen Harrison corrected a widespread misconception regarding the myth of Pandora. She wrote: "No myth is more familiar than that of Pandora, none perhaps has been so completely misunderstood. Pandora is the first woman, the beautiful mischief: she opens the forbidden box, out comes every evil that flesh is heir to; hope only remains. The box of Pandora is proverbial, and that is the more remarkable as she never had a box at all."[1] What she opened was—in the word used by Hesiod and all other writers up to the twelfth century after Christ—a *pithos.* The story of this pithos and its contents is first told in Hesiod's *Works and Days,* 90–99:

> Since before this time the races of men had been living on earth
> free from all evils, free from laborious work, and free from
> all wearing sicknesses that bring their fates down on men
> [for men grow old suddenly in the midst of misfortune];
> but the woman, with her hands lifting away the lid from the great jar [pithos],
> scattered its contents, and her design was sad troubles for mankind.
> Hope [*Elpis*] was the only spirit that stayed there in the unbreakable
> closure of the jar, under its rim, and could not fly forth
> abroad, for the lid of the great jar closed down first and contained her;
> this was by the will of cloud-gathering Zeus of the aegis.
>
> TRANS. LATTIMORE 1959

It is surprising that this graphic image of a female personification trapped under the rim of a large jar was not seized upon by ancient Greek artists, if only for its humor. The entry on Elpis in the *Lexicon Iconographicum Mythologiae Classicae,* however, lists only one possible image.[2] In this paper I will reexamine this sole visual representation of Pandora's pithos containing Elpis, discuss the controversial meaning of

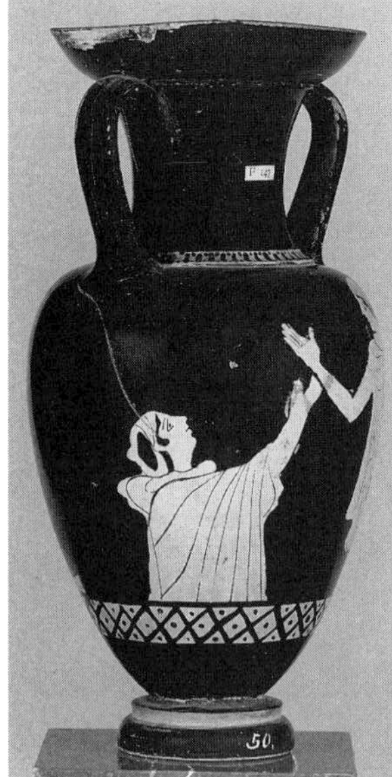

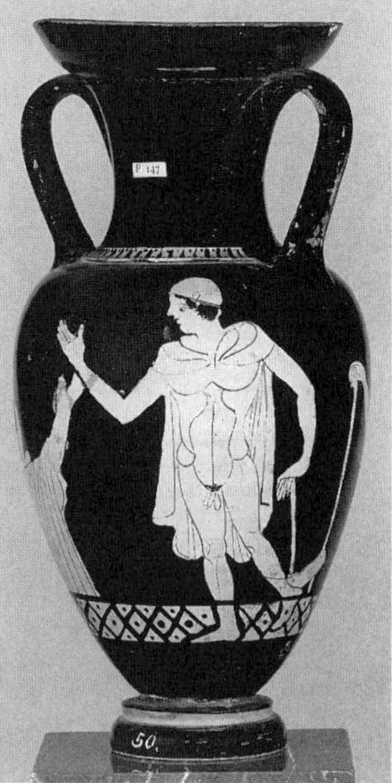

FIGURES 4.1–2. *Campanian red-figure neck amphora attributed to the Owl Pillar Group, ca. 450–425 B.C. Obverse: Pandora and Hephaistos (?). London, British Museum F 147. Photo courtesy of the Trustees of the British Museum, © Copyright The British Museum.*

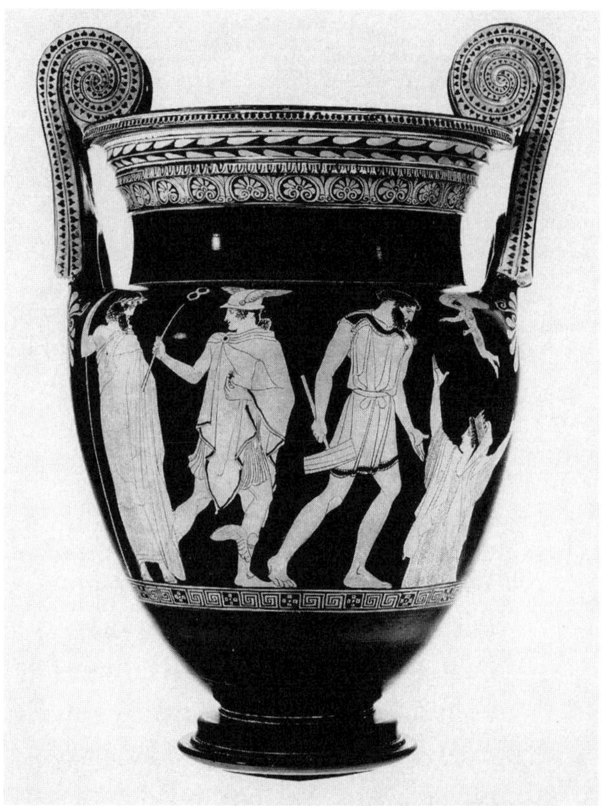

FIGURE 4.3. *Attic red-figure volute krater attributed to the Workshop of Polygnotos, ca. 450 B.C. Zeus, Hermes, Epimetheus, Pandora, and Eros. Oxford, Ashmolean Museum G275. Photo courtesy Ashmolean Museum, Oxford.*

its contents, and attempt to add two additional representations to this limited repertoire.

First, the only extant illustration of Elpis is a South Italian neck amphora from the Basilicata, now in the British Museum (Figs. 4.1–2, 4.6–8).[3] An inaccurate line drawing of its figures, made when it was still in the Vivenzio collection in Naples, was published as early as 1900.[4] In 1943 Beazley attributed the vase to his Owl Pillar Group, a workshop located in Campania that seems to have been operative from around the mid fifth century B.C.[5] According to Beazley, the approximately sixty decorated vases in this group "imitate, in a semi-barbarous style, Attic originals from the second and third quarters of the fifth century." He went on to say, "I do not pretend to understand all the subjects."[6]

The subject of the obverse (Figs. 4.1–2) seems clear enough: the *anodos* of a draped woman in the presence of a male figure wearing a workman's cap and *chlamys* and leaning on a mallet-like tool. On the basis of the inscribed Attic volute krater from the Workshop of Polygnotos in Oxford (Fig. 4.3),[7] the pair is usually identified as Pandora and Epimetheus, her future husband. Ge, Aphrodite, and Persephone also rise from the ground but usually not with the assistance of a man (as opposed to a satyr) with a hammer, and so Pandora is the most likely label for the woman.[8] The male's stance, dress, and age, however, are unlike those of Epimetheus on the Polygnotan krater. Rather, his pose recalls that of a sculptor resting after his labors, as on the Foundry Painter's name-vase (Fig. 4.4).[9] His cap is that of a smith, as also seen on the same vase just to the left (as well as on the opposite side). In dress and age (i.e., beardless) the young man on Figure 4.2 is closer to the one labeled Hephaistos on the white-ground cup in London (Fig. 4.5) that represents a later moment in the myth of Pandora (there called "Anesidora"), namely, her decking out by Athena and Hephaistos, as described by Hesiod (*Op.* 70–72).[10] While both Epimetheus and Hephaistos carry the hammer as an attribute, the pilos-like cap is closely associated with the smith god.[11]

Ancient texts also support this identification. In both the *Theogony* (571–572) and the *Works and Days*

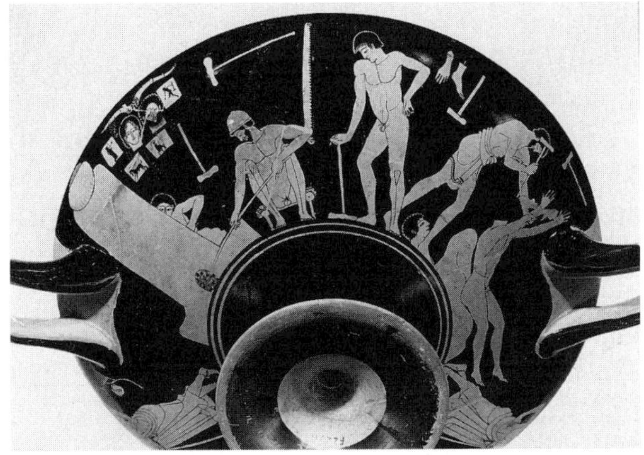

FIGURE 4.4. *Attic red-figure kylix attributed to the Foundry Painter, ca. 470 B.C. Bronze-casting workshop. Berlin, Staatliche Museen, Antikensammlung F 2294. Photo by Ingrid Geske, courtesy of the Staatliche Museen zu Berlin–Preussischer Kulturbesitz Antikensammlung.*

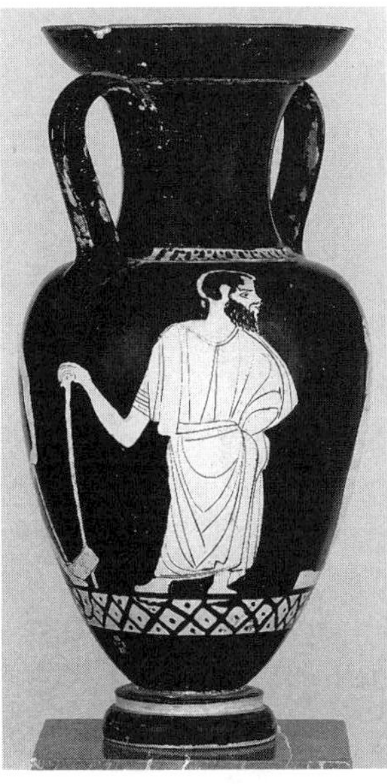

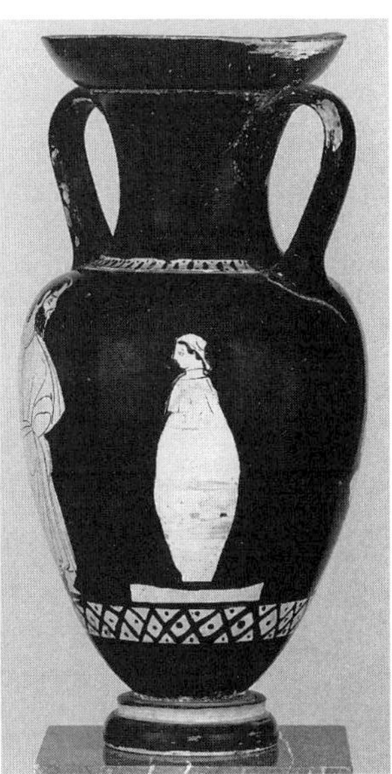

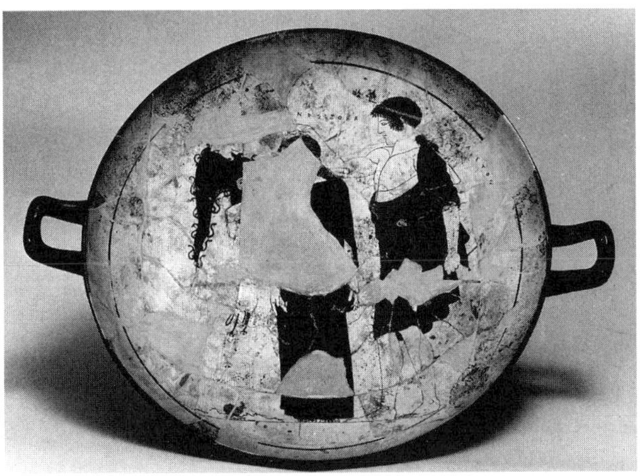

FIGURE 4.5. *Attic white-ground kylix by the Tarquinia Painter, ca. 460 B.C. Athena, Anesidora, and Hephaistos. London, British Museum D 4. Photo courtesy of the Trustees of the British Museum, © Copyright The British Museum.*

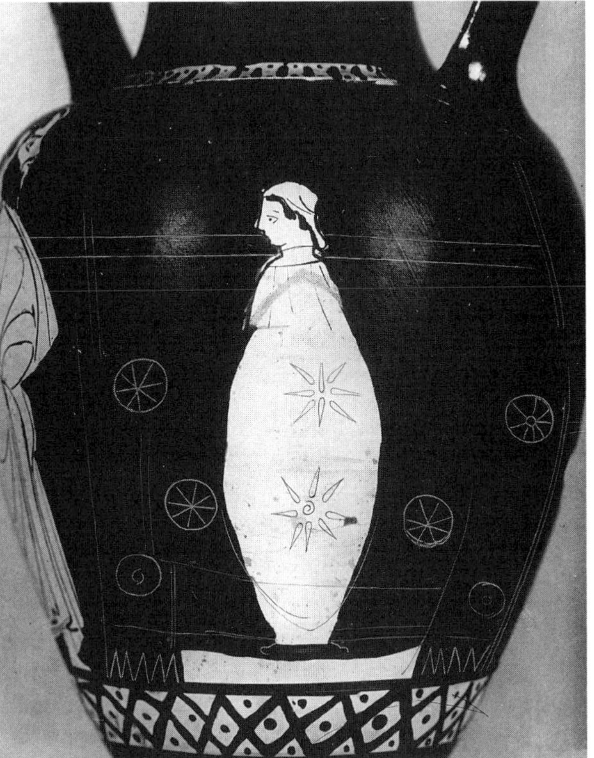

FIGURES 4.6–8. *Campanian red-figure neck amphora attributed to the Owl Pillar Group, ca. 450–425 B.C. Reverse: Zeus (?) and Elpis. London, British Museum F 147. Photo courtesy of the Trustees of the British Museum, © Copyright The British Museum.*

(60–63), Zeus specifically orders Hephaistos to create Pandora from earth and water. Thus, in spite of some doubts recently expressed by John Boardman in an article on Pandora in the West,[12] we should certainly see here Pandora with her maker Hephaistos. She is shown emerging from the ground not because she is a chthonic or earth goddess, as Jane Harrison argued, but because she is made of earth.

The other side of this vase in London (Figs. 4.6–8) is more problematic, but I think easily explained if one adheres to the Hesiodic account. A bearded man with a staff, dressed in what appears to be a *himation* over a sleeved *chiton,* is looking toward a tall, ovoid jar out of which emerges a small head covered by a head cloth, and so is presumably female. The jar is naturally taken to be the pithos given by Zeus to Pandora because of her appearance on the other side. Later we will discuss the identity of the woman in the jar, but first, who is the man? He has been identified as Hephaistos by many, and Prometheus by a few.[13] Hephaistos, as we have tried to prove, probably appears in the adjacent scene on the vase; moreover, in any event, in the myth as recorded by ancient authors, he has nothing to do with the pithos. Prometheus, the original culprit who stole fire from the gods and warned his brother Epimetheus not to receive any gift from Zeus, namely, Pandora, is also not involved with the pithos. Nor does the man's staff on the vase resemble a fennel stalk, his instrument for stealing fire. Again the dress and age of the man suggest an older, possibly divine figure. Hermes serves as a messenger in this myth, as well as on the Oxford vase (Fig. 4.3), but he is a youthful god and otherwise attired. In the passage dealing with the pithos (*Op.* 94–105), the only male mentioned is Zeus. In fact, in his pose, dress, and beard, the male on the Campanian neck amphora closely resembles Zeus on the Oxford krater.

If this male spectator is Zeus, then the girl in the pithos is surely Elpis. It is by the order of Zeus that Elpis remains in the jar, and the evils and diseases that emerge from the pithos are there by the will of Zeus, according to Hesiod. In the *Iliad* (24.527–528) Zeus has two jars (*pithoi*), one containing good and the other, evil. It must be the latter that he sent to earth to punish mankind for the transgressions of Prometheus, and Pandora, the "beautiful evil," serves as his agent for the opening of the jar. So the Campanian vase juxtaposes two analogous scenes: female evil contemplated by male divinity.

Together they constitute the two main phases of the account as told in the *Works and Days:* at the beginning of the tale Pandora is produced by Hephaistos, and at the end of the episode the pithos filled with evil is closed by the will of Zeus. The Campanian vase painter, surely influenced by a more sophisticated Attic model, used an artistic device known as antithetic responsion to relate these two episodes.[14] In both instances the female evil is concealed in a deceptive exterior, either an alluring virgin or an innocent-looking (but curiosity-arousing) jar. The male fabricators of these "crafty snares" are standing before their creations—both of which will bring unending woe to mankind, according to Hesiod's account.

Having reinterpreted this admittedly peculiar vase, let us turn now to the problematic Elpis who has opened a virtual Pandora's box of scholarly speculation.[15] Few commentators seem to agree as to the quality—good, bad, or neutral—of this Elpis or as to why she remains in the jar, for the benefit or to the detriment of mankind. There are four possible scenarios:[16] (1) The first is the most positive reading, and in my opinion the most un-Hesiodic, namely, that Elpis is positive, that is, Hope, and is stored in the jar for mankind.[17] (2) The second is that Elpis is good but is being kept from mankind as an additional punishment. (3) The third possibility is that Elpis is the last of the evils in the jar, that is, false hope, is reserved *for* man or (4) *from* which man is being spared.

Logic would opt for the fourth scenario for the following reasons.[18] Because the jar contains evil, Elpis cannot be positive in this context. In fact, later in the same poem, Hesiod actually qualifies Elpis as "empty" (l. 498) and "not good" (l. 500). Elpis serves to take away man's industriousness, rendering him lazy and prone to evil. Housed in a jar of evils, Elpis then must be negative, but why does Zeus command it to remain within? Since the other evils have escaped to do damage among mankind, false hope must have been retained at the last minute so that man could not become lazy. In this new, harsher world order in which man must labor for his living (*bios*), good hope for the future is a necessity, whereas false hope would be a formula for extinction. Hence, to preserve man, Zeus, at the last minute, imprisons Elpis. Other interpreters have claimed that Elpis is ambiguous, potentially either good or bad depending on the circumstances, somewhat like the personifications Eris (strife vs. competition) or Aidos (shame vs. modesty).[19] Perhaps the visual imagery can support our reading of Hesiod's Elpis as an evil entrapped in the pithos.

The jar has been construed either as a storage pithos, hence, a sort of pantry, or as a bronze vessel, in which case it is a strongbox or prison. In Greek art, clay storage pithoi are usually set into the ground, like the one into which king Eurystheus takes refuge when Herakles returns with the live Erymanthian boar.[20] While such jars are normally used for the storage of agricultural produce, they can also contain potentially harmful substances, as the wine that inebriates the Centaurs in the Herakles and Pholos episode.

Many scholars wish to see a close analogy between Pandora herself, made from clay, and the clay pithos that dispenses evils, and they have even identified the girl in the jar as Pandora.[21] They ignore, however, Hesiod's description of Pandora's pithos as *arrektoisi* or unbreakable. This adjective, which is usually applied to objects of metal, such as gold fetters and hobbles in Homer (*Il.* 13.37, 15.20), would strongly imply that the jar is made of metal rather than earthenware, which is obviously capable of being broken.

A closer analogy from Homer (*Il.* 5.385–391) is the unbreakable bronze jar into which the god Ares is locked up by Otos and Ephialtes.[22] Diodorus Siculus (4.12.1–2) states that when Herakles returned with the live Erymanthian boar Eurystheus hid himself in a *bronze* pithos. That storage jars could be made of metal is also indicated by Herodotos' (1.51) mention of four silver pithoi dedicated at Delphi by King Kroisos. If Pandora's unbreakable pithos is metal, then it is probably meant to be a prison or stronghold to lock things within, rather than a storage vessel.

The evidence of the London amphora supports this reading. There are two iconographic peculiarities of this pithos as depicted on the Campanian neck amphora that merit discussion. One is the extensive use of preliminary sketch lines, incised before the application of the slip but not used in the final decoration (Fig. 4.8). These consist of a foot in two degrees for the pithos, two eight-pointed stars on its surface, and six rosettes scattered in the field around it. As we have already noted, clay pithoi are usually set into the ground and so do not need a foot. Hence, this is a possible indication on the part of the artist of a non-earthenware jar.

As for the other seemingly decorative motifs, such designs are not normally found in fifth-century vase-painting, and so one can only speculate about their purpose. Two similar stars appear in the background of the tondo of the Brygos Painter's cup in Berlin that shows the moon goddess Selene driving her chariot through the night sky.[23] One finds similarly formed gold spangles on the drapery of Fayum portrait figures.[24] It would thus seem that the Campanian vase painter is attempting to indicate a gleaming, that is, metallic, surface. The incised rosettes outside the jar might be abstract symbols of the evils emitted by its opening. They seem to float in the vicinity of the jar like the *keres* released from the sunken pithos by Hermes on a white-ground lekythos in Jena.[25]

The rectilinear structure surrounding the pithos is less easily explained.[26] It may have been inspired by the bronze fence surrounding Tartaros mentioned by Hesiod in the *Theogony* (726–727). Some scholars believe that Hesiod conceived of Tartaros as a kind of pot, since it seems to have a neck around which Night is poured three times.[27] Such a description of a large vessel surrounded by a fence may have been the initial inspiration for the vase painter, who then changed his mind and omitted this elaborate setting in favor of a simpler composition.

The other oddity is the form of the pithos, in particular its segmented collar-like shoulder decoration. This is not a feature common to clay vessels of any shape. The closest artistic parallel I can find for the lappeted collar is a Mesopotamian gold vase from the royal tombs of Ur.[28] It is admittedly far removed geographically and chronologically from our vase, but it does demonstrate the use of such collars on metal vessels. Taken altogether, the indication of a gleaming surface, the foot, and the elaborate collar support the reading of Hesiod's unbreakable pithos as a metal vessel.

In spite of all the complex literature on the subject, the simplest explanation seems the best. Elpis, because she resides in a jar containing evils, must herself be negative, that is, false expectation, rather than hope. The pithos in which she is imprisoned is metallic. Although Pandora closes the lid, it is the will of Zeus that false hope not be let loose in the world where it would serve to deprive men of incentive to action. The moral lesson for Perses, Hesiod's lackadaisical brother, is that the gods have indirectly given mortals hope by sparing them from false expectation.

We turn now to the other possible representations of Elpis. The first is a small (11.6 cm in height) ovoid vase with an aryballos mouth set atop a female head (Figs. 4.9–12).[29] The Museum of Fine Arts in Boston acquired it in 1901 via the dealer Edward Perry Warren, who bought it in Paris, with a probable provenance of Thebes. While at first one might call it simply a head

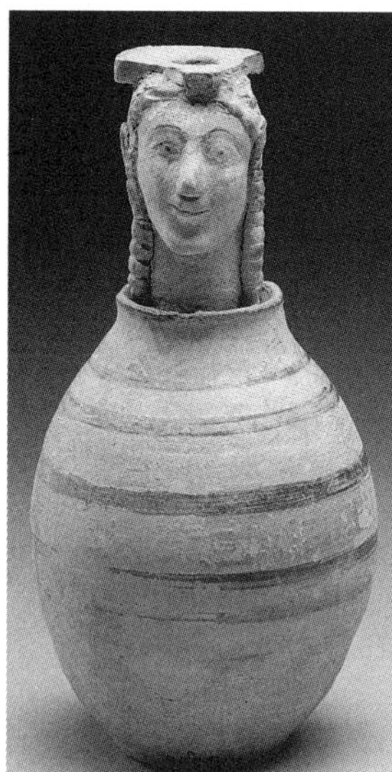
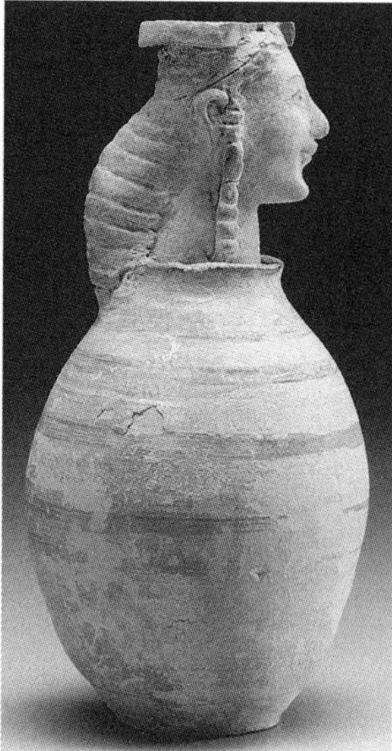
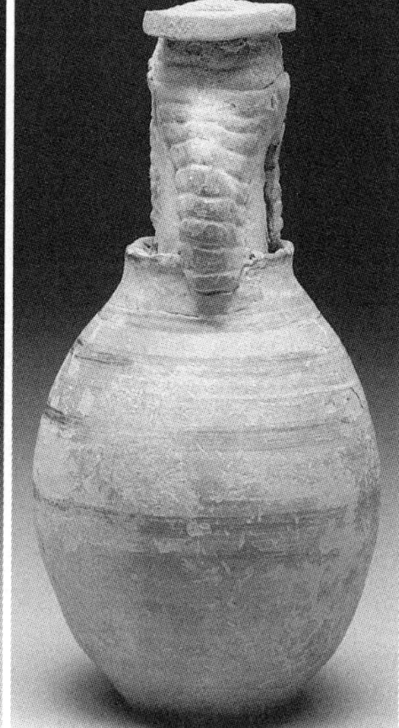
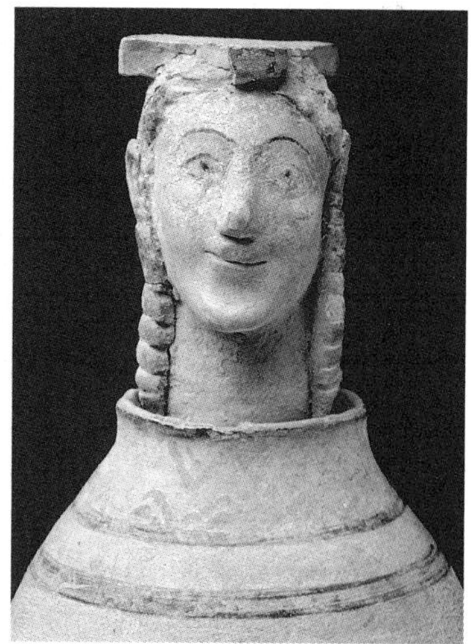

FIGURES 4.9–12. *Boiotian plastic aryballos, ca. 625–600* B.C. *Boston, Museum of Fine Arts 01.8056. Henry Lillie Pierce Fund. Photo © 2003 Museum of Fine Arts, Boston.*

aryballos, like proto-Corinthian perfume vases with plastic female heads, upon closer inspection one can see that the head and neck are not actually part of the vase but are emerging from within its simple rim. This feature is particularly evident in the treatment of the locks of hair framing the face: they are attached to the neck and descend *inside* the rim. The ovoid shape of the vessel closely resembles the painted pithos on the Campanian neck amphora, and both have their lower bodies slipped. There is decoration at the rim of the vase consisting of a band of reversing chevrons. The Boston female in the jar lacks a head scarf but has a fillet around her head (incised at the sides) and a thick shank of hair at the back, which was used by the coroplast to anchor the head to the jar's rim.

In addition to the curious fact of the head emerging from the jar, there are two other intriguing features of this small vase. The aryballos mouth is large and sits directly atop the woman's head, in contrast to other female-head perfume flasks, on which the mouth is smaller and is connected to the head via a narrow neck.[30] In fact, the mouth is large enough in diameter to form the lid of the vessel. The other interesting feature is the woman's enigmatic expression, consisting of a crooked smile or smirk (Fig. 4.12).

The provenience of this vase is telling: it is said to be from Thebes. The dull reddish fabric of the vase supports such a find spot, although there is no exact Boiotian parallel for this vase.[31] Closest in style and format are the Boiotian pyxides on which female heads often serve as knobs for the lids.[32] Their heads, however, do not emerge from within the containers. It is not completely far-fetched that the description of Elpis in the *Works and Days* inspired this unique ceramic creation. With a stylistic date of ca. 625–600 B.C., the Boston vase is not far removed in time from the Theban poet Hesiod (ca. 700 B.C.).

If the Boston vase is a second representation of Elpis in the pithos, what does it add to our understanding of this particular personification? As a perfume flask, the Boston aryballos contained a substance that was known for its seductive qualities and its association with Aphrodite. In the *Works and Days* (70–71) the goddess bestows on Pandora both *charis* (grace) and *pothos* (sexual longing) to attract men. Thus, Pandora, like the substance in a perfume bottle, is a "crafty snare" for men that leads to their downfall. Just as Aphrodite's gifts veil the shameless and deceitful Pandora, so perfume masks the debilitating effects of women's lust: both are ruses and so traps for men. As such, this vase may represent a bit of humor on the part of the Boiotian potter.[33]

Another possible representation of Elpis is from fifth-century Athens and was once part of a high-relief marble frieze, fragments of which have been excavated over the years in the Agora.[34] Evelyn Harrison identified the disparate and fragmentary figures as deities taking part in the birth of Pandora, the same theme that decorated the base of the Athena Parthenos. She labels a youthful male head Hephaistos and a bearded one, Prometheus (although might he be Zeus?). Harrison identifies an archaizing female head as Pandora, while another (Fig. 4.13) she describes as having a "strange" or slightly wicked expression. It is considerably larger than the other heads of the frieze, and its flat top indicates that it once reached to the very top of the relief slab. Given the height and size of the figure, Harrison concludes that "she can hardly have been standing erect as a full figure."[35] She, therefore, identifies this enigmatic figure as Eris, who, according to Homer (*Il.* 4.442–443), is small at first but then grows so quickly that her head touches the sky while she still walks upon the ground.

An alternative might be Elpis, who, if posed within a large pithos, could reach to the top of the frieze, with the upper molding serving as the lid of the jar. What Harrison calls "the discrepancy between the two sides of the face" is analogous to the lopsided grin of the girl on the Boston aryballos. Facial expressions are extremely rare in Greek art, but a smirk seems a particularly apt way to characterize an otherwise attribute-less personification of false hope. Also, Elpis is perhaps more pertinent to the Pandora myth than is the personification Eris, who appears in a much earlier section of Hesiod's *Works and Days* (11–26). The original location of this relief is unknown, but Harrison speculates that it may once have adorned an altar of Athena on the Akropolis.[36]

Due to the fragmentary nature of this relief, it is unclear whether Pandora was shown as a half-length figure rising out of the ground (as on the Oxford krater, Fig. 4.3, and British Museum neck amphora, Fig. 4.1) or already fully formed as on the Parthenos base, the Anesidora cup (Fig. 4.5) and other Attic vase paintings.[37] The seemingly autochthonos birth of Pandora is not in the Hesiodic text and so appears to be an invention of the Athenians.[38] The myth of autochthony was, of course, one near and dear to their hearts: "We are a race not gathered out of foreign lands, but born from this soil" (Eur. *Erechtheus*).[39] This concept, which was so essential to the Athenians' self-image, realized its fullest expression in the myth of the birth of Erichthonios. The artistic representations of his birth from Ge, impregnated by Hephaistos, show the earth goddess as a half-length figure rising from the ground, offering the newborn to its surrogate mother Athena.[40] These, which predate the representations of Pandora, could well have influenced the vase paintings of her anodos.

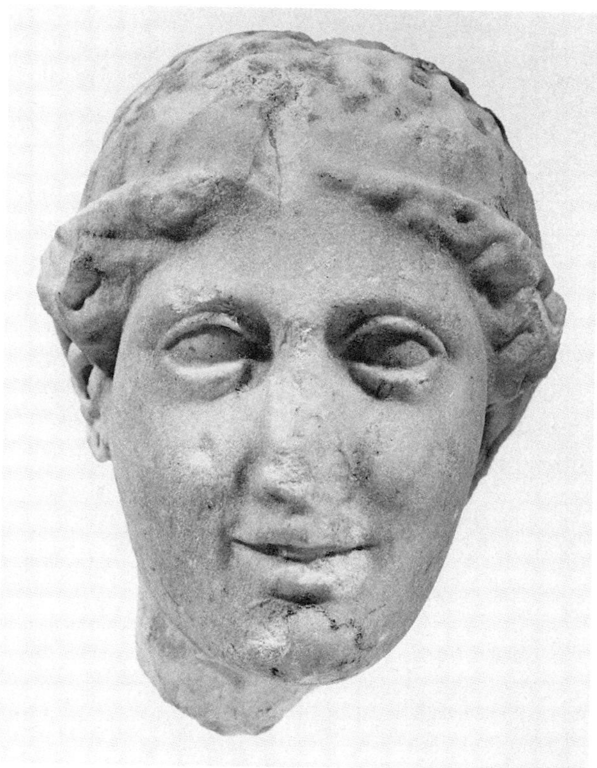

FIGURE 4.13. *Marble female head from a high-relief frieze, ca. 425 B.C. Athens, Agora inv. S 2331. Photo courtesy of the American School of Classical Studies at Athens, Agora Excavations.*

These myths have close parallels that may have contributed to their related iconography. Both Pandora and Erichthonios are children, so to speak, of the god Hephaistos. Athena plays a crucial role in both: dressing Pandora in finely wrought garments (*Theog.* 573–575) and accepting Erichthonios into a richly woven receiving blanket. Both myths involve a closed container (basket, pithos), the unauthorized opening of which causes dire consequences (suicide of the daughters of Kekrops, evils escaping). The parallelism and importance to the Athenians of these two births are manifested in their appearance on the bases of two of the most important cult statues in the city: the birth of Erichthonios on the base of the statue group of Hephaistos and Athena in their joint temple,[41] and the birth of Pandora on the base of the Athena Parthenos in the Parthenon.[42] Another feature that links these mythological births is the presence of Zeus, who is often added as an observer of the birth of the future Attic king, in spite of his playing no role in the myth.[43] These deities, Athena, Zeus, and Hephaistos, are the principal deities of the *polis* and, as such, occupy pride of place in the Parthenon's sculptural program, in the east pediment and in the center of its Ionic frieze.

The myth of Pandora is clearly one that was appropriated by the Athenians and used for purposes very different from those of Hesiod. In Athens the myth accentuates the roles of Athena and Hephaistos in the creation of the first woman, as shown on the Anesidora cup (Fig. 4.5) and the base of the Athena Parthenos. Pandora's secondary role as the dispenser of evils would seem to have been suppressed, but as we have tried to demonstrate, it is not missing altogether. The presence of the pithos with Elpis trapped inside can be seen as a subtle allusion to the nature of Pandora/woman and the power of Zeus. In this sense, Elpis plays a key role, for she demonstrates that in spite of the evils brought to the world by the race of women, in the end Zeus spared mankind one crucial *kakon* that could lead to his destruction: false hope.

NOTES

Unlike Pandora and her jar, Jerry Pollitt's far-ranging curiosity about the classical world has opened avenues of research and scattered pearls of wisdom for which all of us who work in this complex area are immensely grateful.

A version of this paper was delivered at the conference "Personification in the Greek World" organized by Emma Stafford, School of Classics, University of Leeds, and Judith Herrin, Centre for Hellenic Studies, King's College London, held September 11–13, 2000, at the Institute of Classical Studies, University of London. I am grateful to the audience, and in particular Lloyd Llewellyn-Jones, for their comments. I also thank Dyfri Williams and Lucilla Burn for enabling me to examine the Campanian neck amphora in the British Museum, and John Hermann at the Museum of Fine Arts, Boston, for permission to study the Boiotian aryballos.

1. J. E. Harrison 1900, 99. The misconception that Pandora opened a box resulted from a textual corruption; *pyxis* was substituted for *pithos* in the early sixteenth century. On the later pictorial history of Pandora's "box," see Panofsky and Panofsky 1962.

2. Elpis is not included in Shapiro 1993. On personification in general, see Stafford 2000.

3. British Museum F 147. See *LIMC* 3, s.v. Elpis, no. 13 [F. W. Hamdorf] (with earlier bibliography); Trendall 1967, 667, no. 3.

4. The drawing, made by Costanzo Angelini in 1798, was published in Patroni 1900, pl. 29. It was later reproduced in A. B. Cook 1940, 350, fig. 233; and J. E. Harrison 1955 (1922), 280, fig. 70. Harrison (1955, 282) interpreted the two scenes as the *anodos* of Kore and the making of Pandora by Hephaistos. Cook (1940, 350–352) identified the two scenes as Greek cult (evocation of Ge) and Egyptian cult (consultation of the Isis jar) respectively. This drawing was apparently unknown to H. B. Walters, who listed the vase in his British Museum catalogue (1896, 71).

5. Owl Pillar Group: Beazley 1943; Trendall 1967, appendix I, 667–673; Hadzisteliou-Price 1974; Trendall 1983, 309–310. Beazley (1928, 77) earlier described the group as "a class of vases, chiefly neck-amphorae, made by barbarians, probably somewhere in Campania, in the latter part of the fifth century. . . . He prefers drawing large figures in the Greek manner, and his figurework is marvelously crude."

6. Beazley 1943, 66.

7. Oxford, Ashmolean Museum G275; *ARV*[2] 601, 23. See Reeder 1995, 284–286, no. 81 (with earlier bibliography).

8. See Bérard 1974.

9. Berlin, Antikensammlung F2294. *ARV*[2] 400, 1. See Neils 2000.

10. London, British Museum D4 (1885.1-28-1); *ARV*[2] 869, 55. See Reeder 1995, 279–281, no. 79.

11. As pointed out by Brommer 1978, 24.

12. Boardman 2000a, 52: "surely not a Hephaistos who has just made Pandora."

13. For a list of these identifications, see *LIMC* 7, s.v. Pandora no. 5 [M. Oppermann].

14. The close relationship of Hephaistos and Zeus with Pandora may also be seen on a Tyrrhenian neck amphora by the Kyllenios Painter in Leipzig (T3323; *ABV* 96, 6), on which Hephaistos leads a woman, probably Pandora, on a mule-drawn cart to an enthroned Zeus with other deities present. See *CVA* Leipzig 2, pls. 6.1, 7.1–4; Paul 1995, 8–9 and 56, no. 3. For problems concerning the identification of this scene, see Brommer 1978, 27. In *Theog.* 585–589, Hephaistos leads his creation Pandora into the company of men and gods who are awed by it.

15. On Elpis in general, see Waltz 1910; Gow 1914; Séchan 1929; Trancsényi-Waldapfel 1955; Lendle 1957; Fink 1958, 65–71; Neitzel 1976; Pucci 1977, 104–105; Ogden 1998; Lauriola 2000.

16. These are based on the commentary of Verdenius 1985, 66–71.

17. This theory is espoused by Beall 1989.

18. West (1978, 169–170) admits that the text seems illogical but argues that logic is not relevant to Hesiod's meaning.

19. Elpis as ambiguous: Noica 1984; J.-P. Vernant 1989; Zeitlin 1995a, 53.

20. A vase in the Owl Pillar Group in fact depicts a man's head (Eurystheus?) emerging from a pithos with a tall rim set into the ground: Marseilles, Borley Collection 2869. See Hadzisteliou-Price 1974, pl. 47:a. This terracotta pithos is very different in shape and placement from the one on the amphora in the British Museum.

21. So J. E. Harrison 1955 (1922), 282: "The short deformed man would be Hephaistos, and Pandora, half woman half vase, may be conceived as issuing from her once famous *pithos.*" She was misled by the drawing, which shows a crown in front of the base on which the pithos rests; these are simply zigzag lines, which also appear behind the base. Cf. also Sissa 1990, 155: "The two [woman and jar] are so closely associated that a Campanian-style amphora preserved in London depicts a Pandora standing not alongside a jar but in the form of a jar, observed with satisfaction by a club-footed artisan." See also her n. 40 on p. 228, and Maaskant-Kleibrink 1989, 9–10. For further discussion of the vase/female body analogy, see G. Hoffmann 1985; DuBois 1988, 45–49; Zeitlin 1995a, 53. Zeitlin (1995b, 59–60) summarizes her argument: "The image of Pandora's jar . . . is a substitute for, and analogy to, the woman's womb, according to which Elpis is the child (or the hope of a child) and Pandora's acts of removing and replacing the lid of the jar represent the breaching of her virginity and the subsequent closure that is necessary for pregnancy to occur." I fail to see how Pandora can be responsible for her own loss of virginity and subsequent pregnancy, especially as the Greeks believed that the male alone was responsible for conception.

22. For the nature of the jar and other instances of the adjective *arrektos,* see Walcot 1961.

23. Berlin, Antikensammlung 2293; *ARV*^{2} 370, 10.

24. Such stars appear on the mantle of a woman in a Fayum portrait in the Cleveland Museum of Art (1971.137). See Berman and Bohac 1999, 506–507, no. 400. They are said to indicate the gleam of spangles sewn onto the garment.

25. Jena, Friedrich-Schiller-Universität 338. *ARV*^{2} 760, 41, near the Tymbos Painter. See J. E. Harrison 1955 (1922), 43, fig. 7. Cf. also the white-ground lekythos with winged figures hovering over a pithos, found in the Kerameikos (see *AM* 81, 1966, 31, no. 51.1, pl. 21:1).

26. Boardman (2000a, 52) suggested that "the painter had in mind some sort of cosmic setting for his subject which he was unable to realise when it came to the painting."

27. Walcot 1966, 61; Penglase 1994, 209–211.

28. Philadelphia University Museum, Philadelphia B16692. See Zettler and Horne 1998, 70–72, no. 15. An Egyptian Dynasty 18 stone vessel with a faience collar on a travertine stand is another example of an ostrich egg-shaped jar with a protruding, decorative rim; see Brunner-Traut and Brunner 1981, 126, pl. 2.

29. Boston, Museum of Fine Arts 01.8056. See Fairbanks 1928, 184, no. 539, pl. 51.

30. See Higgins 1959, pls. 4–9 (Rhodian female busts). Two other unusual aryballoi with female heads are (1) J. Paul Getty Museum 91.AE.26, a seventh-century Cretan aryballos with Daidalic head formerly in the Erlenmeyer Collection (see Sotheby's London 9 July 1990, lot 21), and (2) Geneva HR 31, a sixth-century cockle-shell aryballos with Archaic head of Aphrodite (?) from Selinos (see *Geneva* 38, 1990, 84, fig. 3:c).

31. In fact, there are few Boiotian plastic vases extant. Cf. Higgins (1959, 45): "It is unlikely that there was in Boiotia a strong independent tradition for the manufacture of plastic vases."

32. E.g., Boston, Museum of Fine Arts 98.898. See Fairbanks 1928, pl. 50, no. 542.

33. For Pandora as a ruse, see Faraone 1992, 101–102.

34. See E. B. Harrison 1986.

35. E. B. Harrison 1986, 116.

36. In Neils 2001, 216, I speculate that the relief might be that hypothesized by Manolis Korres for the east porch of the Parthenon. Like the other sculptures of the east façade, it would tie in iconographically with the Athena Parthenos inside the cella.

37. Namely, the kalyx krater attributed to the Niobid Painter in London (British Museum E467; *ARV*^{2} 601, 23) and the fragmentary rhyton by Sotades from Paphos (*ARV*^{2} 764, 6; Lubsen-Admiraal and Hoffmann, 1995).

38. See Penglase (1994, 200–209), however, who finds parallels for her anodos in Mesopotamian creation myths.

39. On Athenian autochthony, see Rosivach 1987; Loraux 2000.

40. Birth of Erichthonios: Shapiro 1998; *LIMC* 4, s.v. Erechtheus, 923–951 [U. Kron]; Neils 1983. To these may be added a fragmentary red-figure krater, ca. 400–380 B.C., in Paros (inv. 3255) published by Kaufman-Samara 1999, which preserves the three daughters of Kekrops, with Erichthonios on one of their laps, and Athena.

41. Hephaisteion base: E. B. Harrison 1977; Delivorrias 1997.

42. For the Parthenos base, see most recently Hurwit 1995.

43. Another instance of the cross-fertilization between the iconography of these two scenes is the presence of Epimetheus on the kalyx krater attributed to the Nikias Painter in Richmond, which depicts the birth of Erichthonios. See Oakley 1987.

5

THE JUDGMENT OF HELEN IN ATHENIAN ART

H. A. SHAPIRO

Near the end of Book 3 of Homer's *Iliad,* Helen and Paris find themselves together in their bedchamber in the palace of Priam, brought together there by the goddess Aphrodite. Paris professes his ardor, now stronger than ever:

> Come, then, rather let us go to bed and turn to love-making. Never before as now has passion enmeshed my senses, not when I took you the first time from Lakedaimon the lovely and caught you up and carried you away in seafaring vessels, and lay with you in the bed of love on the island of Kranae, not even then, as now, did I love you and sweet desire seize me.[1]

Helen makes no reply, but the poet continues, with his usual matter-of-fact tone, "So speaking, he led the way to the bed; and his wife went with him" (3.447).

This amiable conclusion to the scene would be less surprising if Helen had not greeted Paris only moments before with these bitter words:

> So you came back from fighting. Oh, how I wish you had died there beaten down by the stronger man, who was once my husband. (3.428–429)

Yet no sooner has she poured forth this withering scorn upon her second, Trojan husband than, melting at the sight of his extraordinary good looks, she abruptly changes her tone, briefly worries that he might get hurt if he reenters the battle, and then follows him silently to bed just as, ten years before, she had followed him to Troy. This may be the first recorded instance of Fatal Attraction.[2]

Like all their fellow Greeks, sculptors and vase painters were fascinated, and confounded, by this story of a respectable married woman who left her husband, her child, and her native country to follow—and marry—a handsome foreigner she barely knew. At no time and place was the discussion of Helen's guilt or innocence more intense than in Athens in the age of Perikles and the subsequent years of the

Peloponnesian War. J. J. Pollitt has probably done more than any scholar to explore the ways in which Greek visual artists of the Classical period contributed to the ongoing moral and ethical discussions that engaged contemporary philosophers and poets.[3] The purpose of this paper is to consider how painters and sculptors of the fifth century participated in the absorbing conversation on the nature of Helen.

HELEN AND PARIS: FROM GEOMETRIC TO HIGH CLASSICAL

Perhaps the grandest expression of Helen's story in Athenian art is the great red-figure skyphos in the Museum of Fine Arts, Boston, which is the masterpiece of the painter Makron and his potter Hieron, made about 490 B.C. (Figs. 5.1–2).[4] The two scenes form a sequence, separated by ten years: Paris leading Helen away from Sparta on one side (Fig. 5.1), Menelaos recovering his wayward wife during the night that Troy fell, on the other (Fig. 5.2). I leave aside here the recent proposal of Martin Robertson, that the scene on Side B takes place not at the Fall of Troy but many years earlier, even before the war started, when Menelaos came on an embassy to reclaim his wife.[5] Robertson was inspired by the observation that Priam, who sits beneath one handle, looks surprisingly youthful, not white-haired or -bearded as we might expect. The difficulties with this bold and eccentric suggestion have been well discussed by Guy Hedreen.[6]

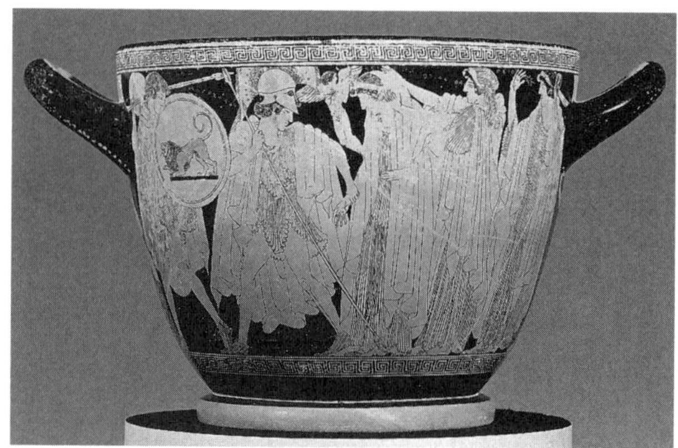

FIGURE 5.1. *Attic red-figure skyphos by Makron. Paris leading Helen from Sparta. Boston, Museum of Fine Arts 13.186. Francis Bartlett Donation of 1912. Photo © 2003 Museum of Fine Arts, Boston.*

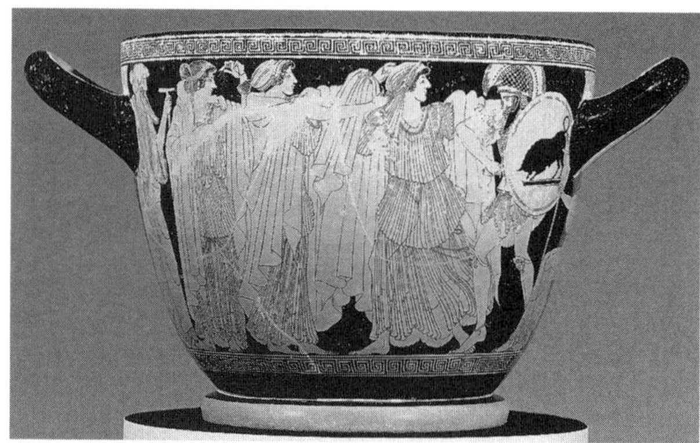

FIGURE 5.2. *Side B of the skyphos in Fig. 5.1. Recovery of Helen by Menelaos. Photo © 2003 Museum of Fine Arts, Boston.*

Apart from Helen herself, one figure recurs in both scenes on the skyphos: Aphrodite. First, Aphrodite encourages Helen along, playing, as Sir John Beazley observed, the role we would expect of the mother of the bride;[7] then, on the other side, she shields Helen from the wrath of her murderous husband. This is very much the Homeric Aphrodite, managing and manipulating the mortal actors, especially Helen, like a master puppeteer. If she is the mother of the bride, then Peitho (Persuasion) is the bridesmaid, as she attends upon the goddess.[8] The abducted Helen looks completely passive, almost inert, neither resisting nor a willing accomplice. Her bridal veil already anticipates the wedding that awaits her in Troy. Under the other handle stands a boy, possibly her son (Homer gives her only a daughter, as we shall see, but another tradition speaks of a son as well).[9] This particular episode, Helen's departure from Sparta, is never described in Homer (the passage in *Il.* 3 quoted above is the fullest reminiscence of it), but I think this is just how the poet would have imagined it. Though separated by more than two centuries, Homer and Makron have much the same conception of Helen as the innocent and helpless pawn of Aphrodite.

That this should be so is far from obvious, since in the intervening years another tradition had grown up, one hostile to Helen, blaming her and holding her personally responsible for all the suffering occasioned by the war at Troy. We find this view first in the poet

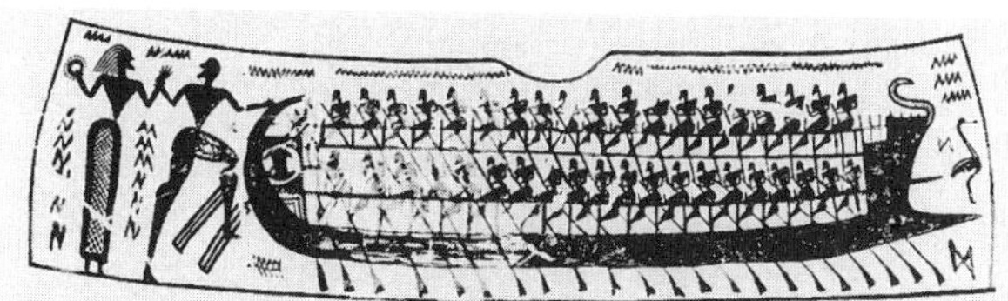

FIGURE 5.3. *Late Geometric bowl from Thebes. Helen and Paris boarding the ship for Troy (?). London, British Museum 1899.2–19.1. After K. Schefold,* Frühgriechische Sagenbilder *(Munich 1964), pl. 5:c.*

Alkaios of Mytilene, about 600 B.C.,[10] and it may have been echoed soon after by the western Greek poet Stesichoros, who was famously struck blind by Helen for his insolence.[11] This negative portrayal reaches a fever pitch with Aischylos, an Athenian and a near contemporary of Makron, in the choruses of the *Agamemnon:*

> Helen? In a manner befitting her name, destroyer of ships, destroyer of men, destroyer of cities [ἑλένας, ἕλανδρος, ἑλέπτολις, an untranslatable series of puns], from the delicate curtains of her bedchamber she sailed. . . . (687–691, trans. R. Lattimore)

Just as all Greek poetry stands in some relation to its predecessors, so too all vase paintings are part of a visual tradition. The low survival rate of Athenian vases means that there is a constant danger that our iconographical picture may be badly skewed. On present evidence, however, it seems that, while Makron's picture of Helen and Menelaos on Side B of the Boston skyphos stands in a long and rich tradition in Athens from the black-figure period,[12] his scene of Paris and Helen leaving Sparta is virtually unique. A remote ancestor may be the well-known Late Geometric bowl in the British Museum (Fig. 5.3), around 700, which I believe, along with some scholars, shows Paris and Helen embarking on the ship that will take them to Troy.[13]

But Helen and Paris are never shown together—in any context—on extant Attic black-figure vases. A Corinthian painter shows their wedding in Troy, visualized as an elaborate chariot procession.[14] The Greeks apparently had no difficulty with the idea that, although she clearly had no time to divorce Menelaos, Helen married Paris immediately upon their arrival in Troy. (We recall that Homer refers to Helen as Paris's wife, ἄκοιτις, at *Il.* 3.447.) The painter of a so-called

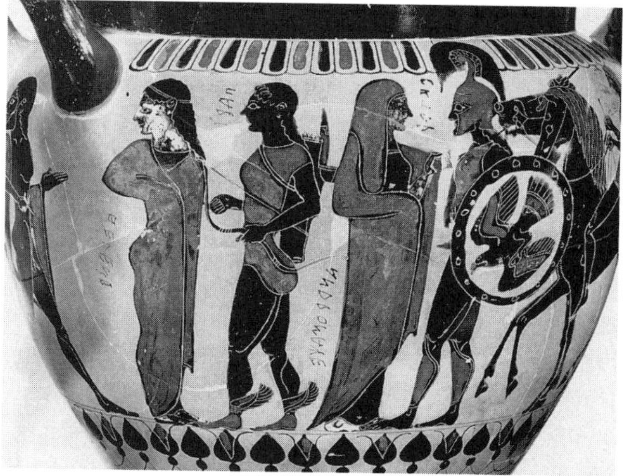

FIGURE 5.4. *Chalkidian black-figure krater. Helen and Paris with Andromache and Hektor. Würzburg, Martin-von-Wagner Museum der Universität L 160. Photo: Museum, courtesy of I. Wehgartner.*

Chalkidian krater (Fig. 5.4), probably a Greek resident in South Italy in the middle of the sixth century, gives us what may be the only reflection in the visual arts of the Archaic tradition hostile to Helen.[15] She and Paris are rather pointedly juxtaposed with Hektor and Andromache, those paragons of marital fidelity. Not only that, but Helen turns away from Paris as if in disgust, calling to mind her rebuke of him quoted above.

But, the Geometric krater aside, the scene of Helen and Paris's departure from Sparta enters the visual repertoire only with Makron. Moreover, the only instance in Archaic red figure other than the Boston skyphos is also by Makron, on his cup in Berlin.[16] Though the scene is superficially similar to the Boston version, there are interesting changes in the cast of characters. Aineias, Paris' Trojan companion (who is also on the Boston skyphos), turns to meet the remonstration of an agitated woman labeled Timandra, one of Helen's sisters (we shall hear more of her presently), and the two bearded men watching from the far side are her stepfather, King Tyndareos, and his brother Ikarios (the latter familiar from Hom. *Od.* as Penelope's father). The other side of this cup shows one of the most imaginative versions we have of the Judgment of Paris, featuring an Aphrodite surrounded by a band of fluttering Erotes. The two scenes, then, form a meaningful temporal and narrative sequence, as on the Boston skyphos, with the focus now more on Paris than on Helen.

Unless the fragmentary state of our evidence is once again playing tricks on us, it is very striking that Makron's two masterful scenes of Helen and Paris had no influence on contemporary or later painters. This particular moment, Paris leading Helen out of Sparta on foot, is never again depicted in Attic red figure. In fact, for the next two generations, it is not easy to find *any* vases that bring these two characters together. A white-ground pyxis in Basel of about 460 gives a unique depiction of the couple's arrival in Troy (Figs. 5.5–6).[17] King Priam is less than pleased by his son's acquisition of a trophy wife. The *Kypria* told of how Paris' departure for Sparta was accompanied by dire warnings from the seer Helenos and his sister, the prophetess Kassandra,[18] and we may suppose that his return to Troy with Helen was similarly ill-omened. The extraordinary sense of foreboding in Priam's face and the hand raised in despair may be likened to the famous Old Seer on the contemporary East Pediment of the Temple of Zeus at Olympia.[19]

A few fragments are all that remain of what was once a splendid white-ground krater of the same period, now in the Cincinnati Art Museum.[20] Parts of four figures survive: Helen, looking pensive and probably seated; Aphrodite, releasing a small Eros from her hand; and a standing youth in traveler's attire. The scene almost certainly represented the first meeting of Helen and Paris, with Aphrodite providing the essential catalyst in Eros. The youth, who stands near the handle, is probably not Paris himself but a subsidiary figure, such as Aineias.

There is, unfortunately, no complete vase close enough in subject to help us visualize what this krater might have looked like. In some important ways it anticipates a much-discussed little vase some thirty years later in date (Figs. 5.7–11).[21] This delicate perfume vessel, a pointed amphoriskos, the name-vase of the Heimarmene Painter, substitutes for the realism of Late Archaic art a mixture of fantasy and allegory that is but one of the modes favored by High Classical vase painting.[22] Helen, veiled and sunk in thought, a finger raised pensively to her lip, sits in the lap of Aphrodite, who places a reassuring arm around her shoulder (Figs. 5.7–8). Persuasion (Peitho) stands quietly by. But here Aphrodite's tender, motherly concern makes us briefly lose sight of the fact that it is not a blushing bride she comforts but a married woman on the brink of committing adultery. The ancient viewer may have lost sight of this as well, for exactly this visual formula is later adapted for scenes of the shy, hesitant bride receiving encouragement on her wedding day, all the way

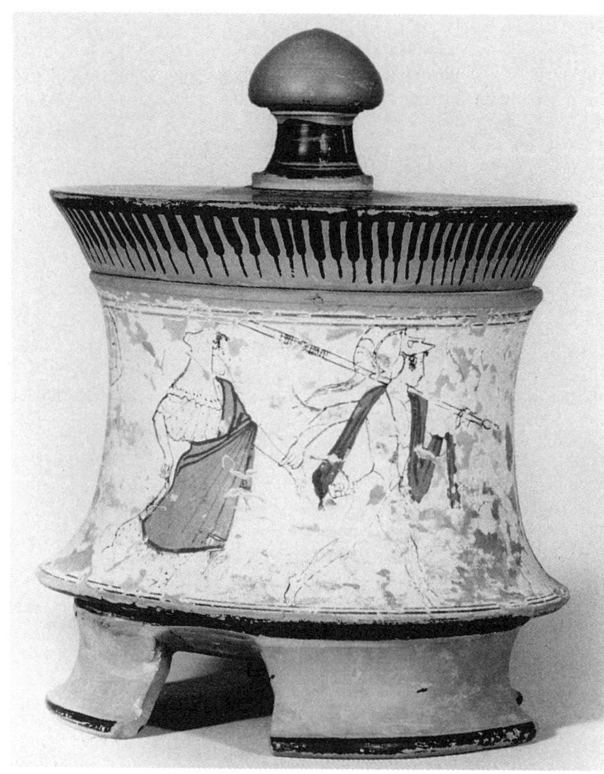

FIGURE 5.5. *Attic white-ground pyxis. Arrival of Helen and Paris in Troy. Antikenmuseum Basel und Sammlung Ludwig Kä 431, once on loan from the Käppeli Collection. Photo: Claire Niggli.*

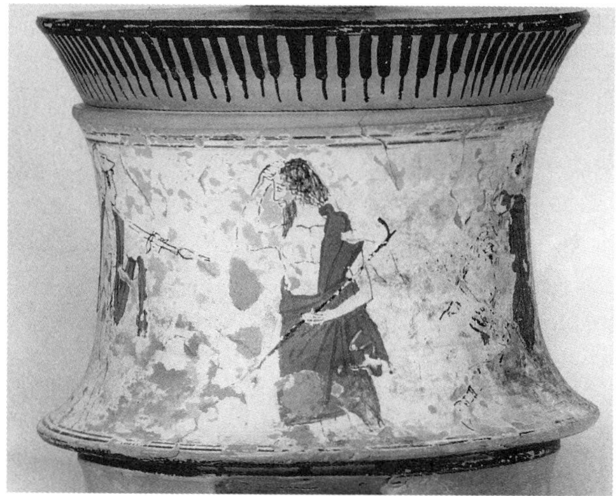

FIGURE 5.6. *Detail of the pyxis in Fig. 5.5. Priam receiving Paris and Helen. Antikenmuseum Basel und Sammlung Ludwig Kä 431, once on loan from the Käppeli Collection. Photo: Claire Niggli.*

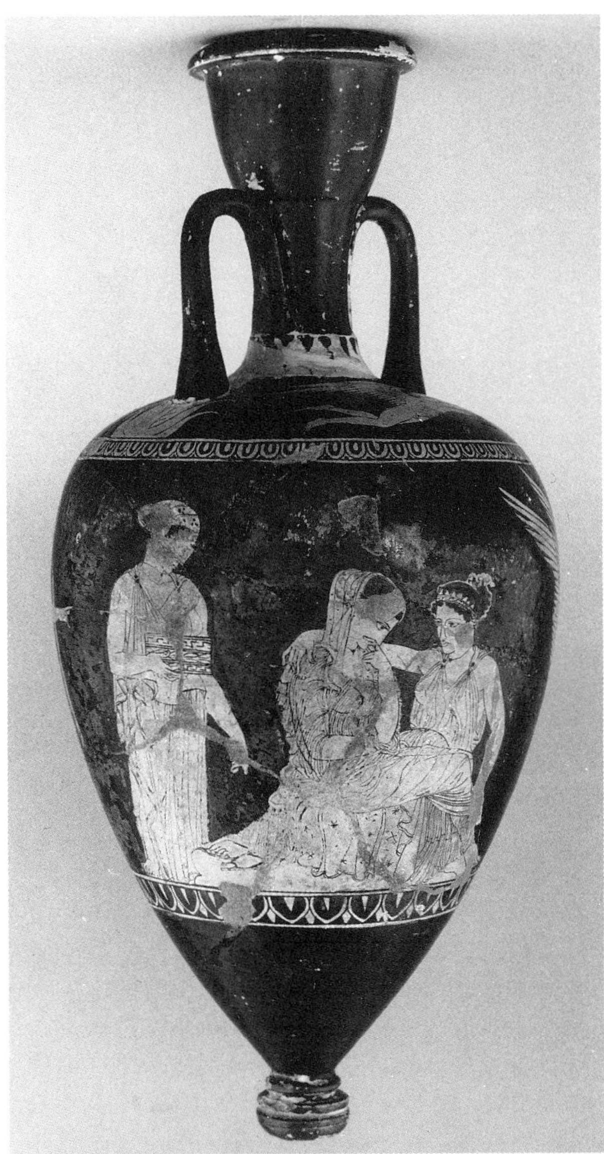

FIGURE 5.7. *Attic red-figure pointed amphoriskos. Meeting of Paris and Helen. Antikensammlung, Staatliche Museen zu Berlin–Preussischer Kulturbesitz 30036. Photo: J. Tietz-Glagow.*

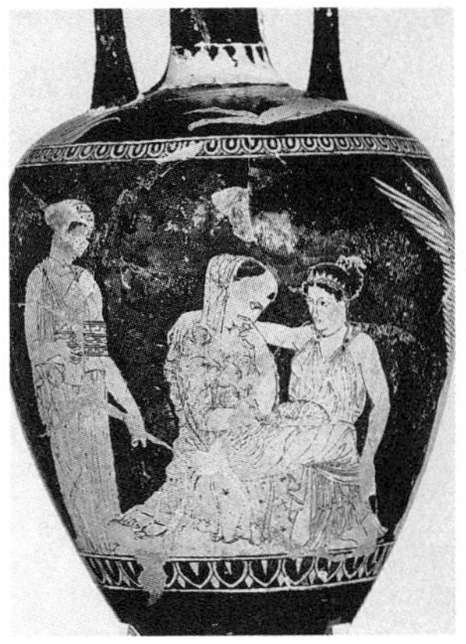

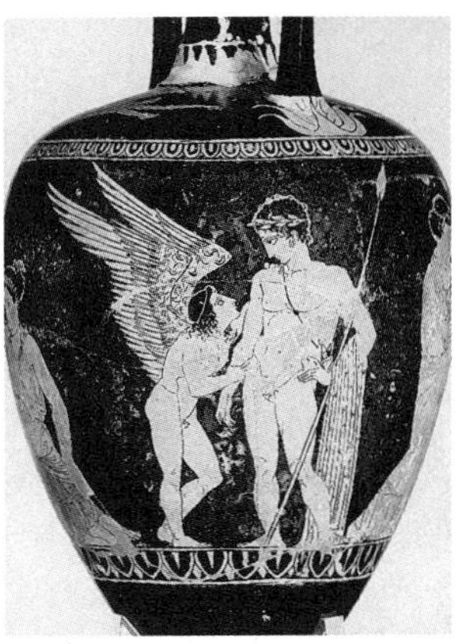

FIGURE 5.8 (LEFT). *Detail of the amphoriskos in Fig. 5.7. Helen in the lap of Aphrodite. Antikensammlung, Staatliche Museen zu Berlin–Preussischer Kulturbesitz 30036. Photo: I. Luckert.*

FIGURE 5.9 (RIGHT). *Detail of the amphoriskos in Fig. 5.7. Paris and Himeros. Antikensammlung, Staatliche Museen zu Berlin–Preussischer Kulturbesitz 30036. Photo: I. Luckert.*

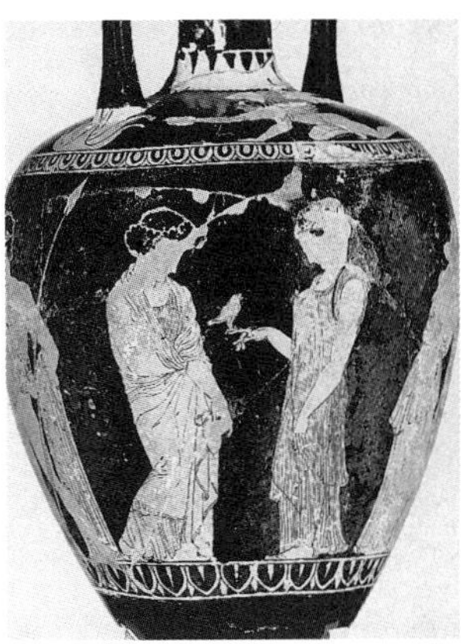

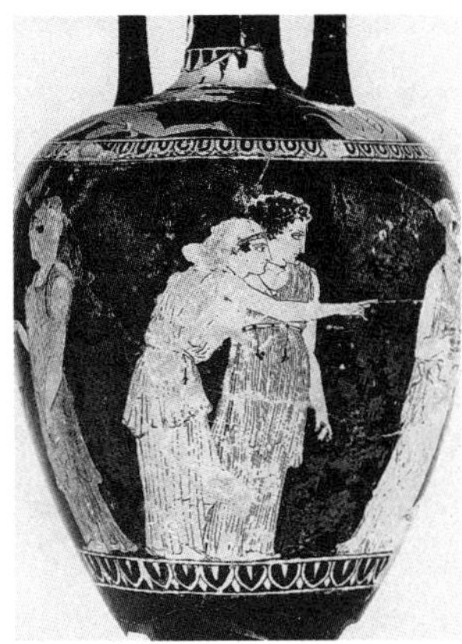

FIGURE 5.10 (LEFT). *Detail of the amphoriskos in Fig. 5.7. Heimarmene and unnamed woman. Antikensammlung, Staatliche Museen zu Berlin–Preussischer Kulturbesitz 30036. Photo: I. Luckert.*

FIGURE 5.11 (RIGHT). *Detail of the amphoriskos in Fig. 5.7. Nemesis and Tyche. Antikensammlung, Staatliche Museen zu Berlin–Preussischer Kulturbesitz 30036. Photo: I. Luckert.*

down to the great Roman painting known as the Aldobrandini Wedding.[23]

Paris, meanwhile, stands apart, not yet making eye contact with his prize (Fig. 5.9). His improbable nudity is clearly meant to emphasize his extraordinary beauty, which, as he reminds Hektor at *Iliad* 3.64–66, is a gift from Aphrodite and not to be despised. The Eros-like creature tugging at his arm is in fact labeled Himeros ("desire": the very word Paris himself used to describe the desire that seizes hold of him: με γλυκὺς ἵμερος αἱρεῖ, *Il.* 3.446). With his penetrating gaze, Himeros infuses an irresistible desire for Helen into the young prince.[24]

The scene is framed by four more women, all allegorical figures, who set it within a broader, one might say cosmic framework. Nemesis, who points an accusing finger (Fig. 5.11), is the retribution that will follow from this fateful encounter; her companion, Tyche, the chance that has brought the lovers together; Hei-

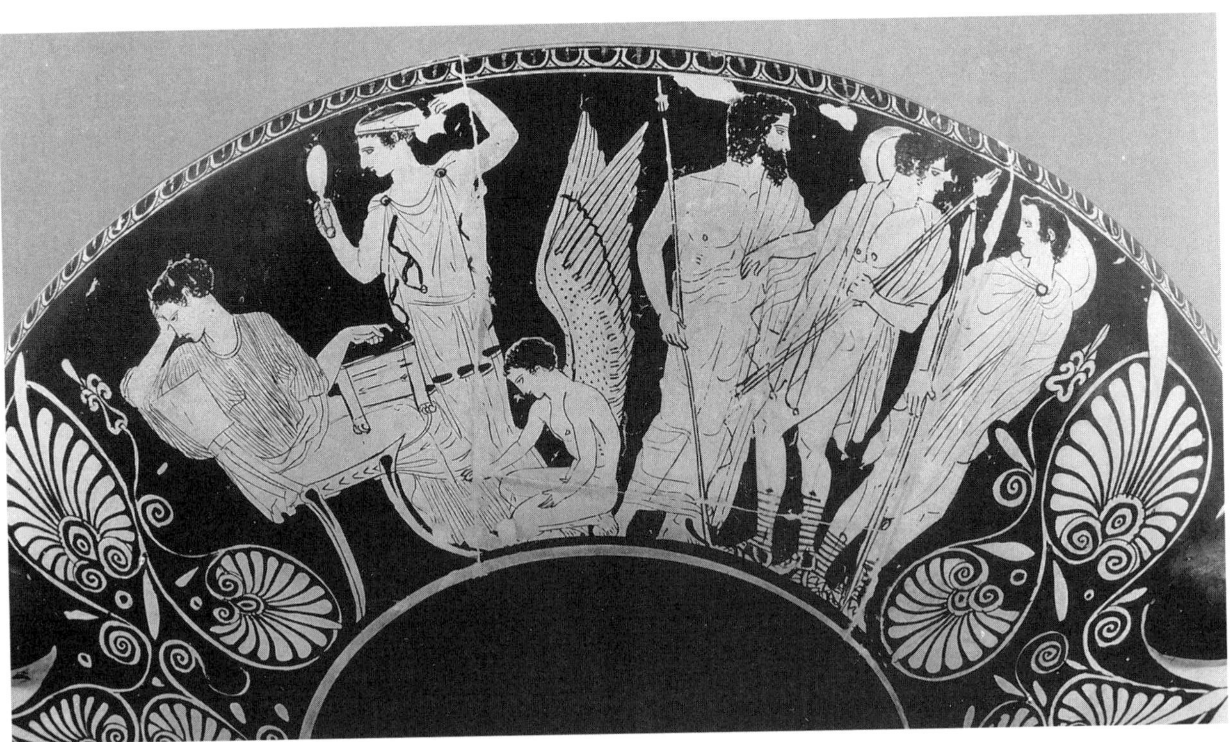

FIGURE 5.12. *Attic red-figure cup. Menelaos introducing Paris to Helen. Antikensammlung, Staatliche Museen zu Berlin–Preussischer Kulturbesitz F 2536. Photo: J. Tietz-Glagow.*

marmene, contemplating a bird held by her companion (Fig. 5.10), is literally that which has been ordained by Fate and the gods. The fourth inscription is unfortunately lost. Such sophisticated allegory is unlikely to be the invention of a vase painter, an impression reinforced by marble reliefs of the Roman period that obviously quote the same pictorial source from which our amphoriskos derives.[25] Perhaps it was a wall painting from the School of Polygnotos or a panel painting of the kind that hung in the Pinakotheke in the Propylaia at the entrance to the Athenian Akropolis.[26]

The painter is clearly sympathetic to Helen's predicament, while also at pains to point out, in the personifications, the disastrous and unintended consequences of her actions.

The literary sophistication of the scene and its sense of dark foreboding had long seemed unique in the Classical iconography of Helen's story. The latter can now, however, be matched on the recently published Kerameikos hydria (to be discussed in detail below), while the former now finds an interesting parallel on a vase a half-century later in date.[27] The scene belongs to a substantial group within the latest Attic red figure (ca. 400–350) depicting the first encounter of Helen and Paris in a well-populated idyllic landscape (cf. Figs. 5.24–26).[28] The surprising discovery by Elke Böhr and Tonio Hölscher of previously unnoticed inscriptions adds an entirely new dimension. In particular, the elegant woman seated at the far left, holding out a wreath in the direction of the standing Paris, is labeled Habrosyne ("softness, luxury, decadence").[29] The politically charged word *habrosyne* had, since the Archaic period, been emblematic of a kind of "orientalism" (to borrow Edward Said's term), the Greek view of the Eastern "other" as luxury-loving, decadent, and hence morally and ethically inferior.[30] On the Berlin vase (and many other vases of its period), the habrosyne of the Eastern barbarian Paris is expressed visually in the exceptionally ornate, Persianizing costume.[31]

Yet allegory and fantasy are only one strand in High Classical art. Another is the deflation of divine and heroic themes into a world of bourgeois domesticity, such as we often see happening in the plays of Euripides. A cup in Berlin (Fig. 5.12), painted in the decade 440–430, marks, I think, a unique attempt to understand the mind of Helen on that fateful day when Paris appeared, unexpectedly, in Sparta.[32] The scene must be set inside the palace of Menelaos, for Helen sits on a backed chair, a *klismos,* of the type favored by fifth-century Athenian matrons. She has been caught by surprise at her toilette. Eros busies himself at her feet, tying on a sandal, while an attendant holds Helen's mirror and takes the opportunity to admire herself. Helen, meanwhile, was evidently about to take something from the jewelry box on her lap, but suddenly three men have intruded on her privacy. Her husband Menelaos greets the two young Trojan princes, Paris and Aineias, just arrived (they wear the typical traveling gear of *chlamys, petasos,* and boots), and ushers them in to meet his wife. Clearly Helen has seen Paris before he has noticed her, and she quickly turns away, distraught, clutching her forehead. The whole scene has such an astonishingly modern feel about it that we have the feeling we could easily supply the dialogue:

> Menelaos: Honey, look who's here! All the way from Troy.
>
> Helen (aside): Please God, don't let him see me with my hair like this!

What has actually thrown Helen into such distress is, of course, her first glimpse of Paris's devastating good looks. The *topos* is familiar elsewhere in Greek myth, perhaps best captured in verse by Apollonios' description of Medea's erotic distress after she has first glimpsed the handsome Jason (*Argon.* 3.451–471).

We cannot know if our painter was inspired by a scene from a now-lost tragedy that he had seen on the stage of the Theater of Dionysos. But I think such an assumption would be unnecessary. His subtle understanding of Helen's conflicted emotional state is akin to Homer's, when he pictures Helen's anguished self-flagellation at the recollection of her shameful behavior:

> I wish bitter death had been what I wanted, when I came hither following your son [she speaks these verses to Priam], forsaking my chamber, my kinsmen, my grown child, and the loveliness of girls my own age. (3.173–175)

Consistently, the vase painters portray Helen in a humane and sympathetic light, as Homer had done, and ignore or suppress the hostile tradition.

HELEN AS AN ATTIC HEROINE

To return briefly to the Heimarmene Painter's amphoriskos: the figure of Nemesis would also have reminded the Athenian viewer of another association, the epic tradition that made Helen the daughter of Zeus by the goddess Nemesis.[33] According to this version, it was at Rhamnous, on the east coast of Attika, that Zeus, in the form of an eagle, coupled with Nemesis. The egg that resulted from this union was then brought to Leda and Tyndareos in Sparta, where Helen was hatched. A series of red-figure vases starting about 430 records the moment before Helen emerged from the egg, with Leda looking on in amazement (Figs. 5.13–14).[34] Also present are usually Tyndareos as well as Helen's twin brothers, the Dioskouroi, Kastor and Polydeukes (Fig. 5.13).[35] The story was known not only in Athens: one of the most remarkable versions is on a huge muglike vessel that is said to be of Lakonian fabric.[36] Here, unlike in the Attic versions, Helen has started to break out of her shell, anticipating a scene that will turn into a kind of burlesque on the fourth-century vases of South Italy.[37]

The sudden appearance of the story ca. 430, primarily on Athenian vases, must, I think, be linked to cult activities in Attika. In these same years, a temple was going up to Nemesis at Rhamnous, possibly designed by the same master architect as the Hephaisteion above the Agora and other temples in Athens and Attika.[38] The cult statue of Nemesis was the masterpiece of Agorakritos, and fragments of it still survive,[39] along with a number of relief figures from the elaborately carved base (Fig. 5.15).[40] Thanks to Pausanias (1.33.8), we know the subject of the base: Helen being introduced to her real mother, Nemesis, by her stepmother Leda. Other members of Helen's family filled out the scene.[41] In other words, the Nemesis worshipped at Rhamnous was best known to the Athenians

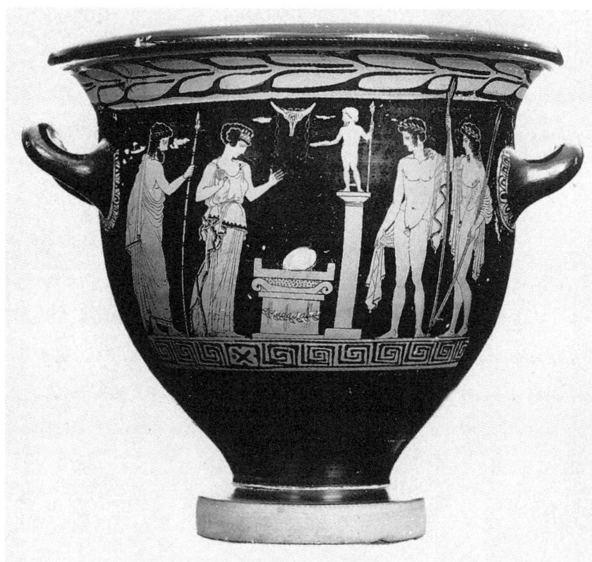

FIGURE 5.13. *Attic red-figure bell-krater. Birth of Helen. Akademisches Kunstmuseum der Universität Bonn, inv. 78. Photo: W. Klein, courtesy of W. Geominy.*

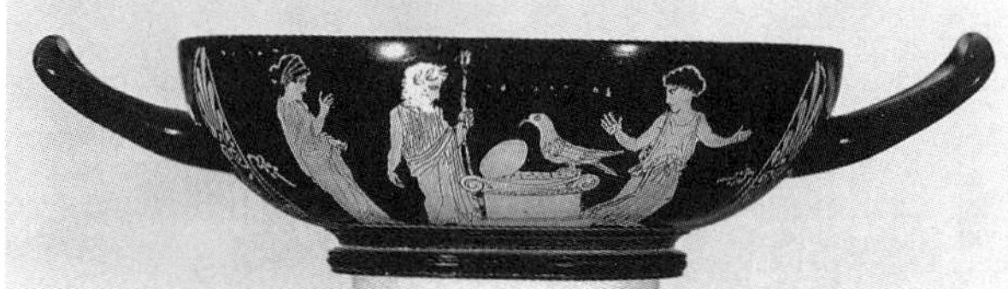

FIGURE 5.14. *Attic red-figure cup by the Xenotimos Painter. Birth of Helen. Boston, Museum of Fine Arts 99.539. Henry Lillie Pierce Fund. Photo © 2003 Museum of Fine Arts, Boston.*

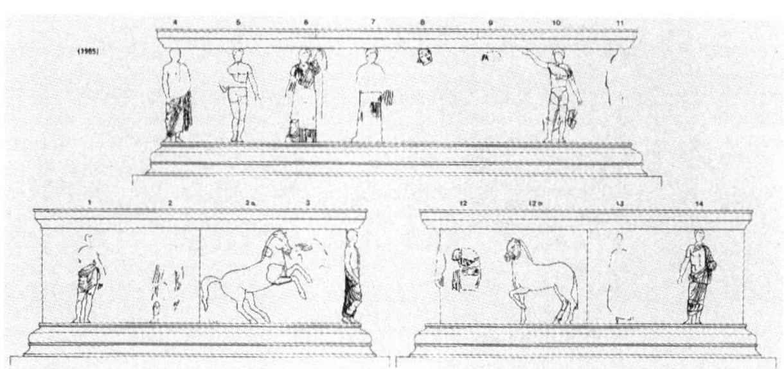

FIGURE 5.15. *Base of the cult statue of Nemesis at Rhamnous. Reconstruction drawing. After Petrakos 1986, 106, fig. 8.*

as the mother of Helen, who was thus co-opted as an Athenian heroine. A sacrificial calendar of the fourth century attests the worship of Helen at another site in Attika, Thorikos,[42] and a late lexicographer tells us that an island off the coast of Attika (otherwise called Makronisos) was named for Helen because she rested there on the way home from Troy (Paus. 1.35.2).

This Athenian claim to the Spartan Helen would have had a particular resonance on the eve of the Peloponnesian War. In 431 the comic poet Kratinos staged his play *Nemesis,* a satire on the outbreak of the war, in which Helen was evidently portrayed as Sparta's revenge on Athens (her *nemesis*), and Perikles travestied as Zeus, author of the war.[43]

The purpose of this brief excursus has been to show that by the later fifth century, Helen not only was the literary heroine of epic verse but also had been integrated into Athenian religion as a heroine of cult. The vase painters are well aware of both aspects.

HELEN IN THE LATE FIFTH CENTURY: HEROINE OR WHORE?

The last two decades of the fifth century witnessed an unusually intense scrutiny and reevaluation of Helen in several media, particularly in Athens. Gorgias of Leontini in Sicily, who had first dazzled the Athenians with his rhetorical pyrotechnics on a diplomatic mission in 427, wrote an *Encomium of Helen,* in which he set out to rehabilitate her reputation.[44] Harking back to the Iliadic tradition, he portrays Helen as the victim of Eros (though he does not mention Aphrodite), as well as of Tyche (chance), Ananke (necessity), and Peitho (persuasion), who are all post-Homeric creations but, as we have seen on the vases, traditional components of the myth.[45] Euripides, meanwhile, put Helen on the stage twice in the space of a few years. In the *Trojan Women* of 416, she comes face to face with Menelaos at the end of the war (in the scene referred to above) and, with a canny eloquence worthy of Gorgias, pleads her case for mercy, placing the blame on Aphrodite (948–950).

Yet only a few years later, in 412, Euripides suddenly reversed himself by staging a play—the *Helen*—in which he accepted the Stesichorean tradition that the real Helen never went to Troy but only her *eidolon,* or phantom, while she was stranded in Egypt.[46] (That story, by the way, so important in the literary tradition,

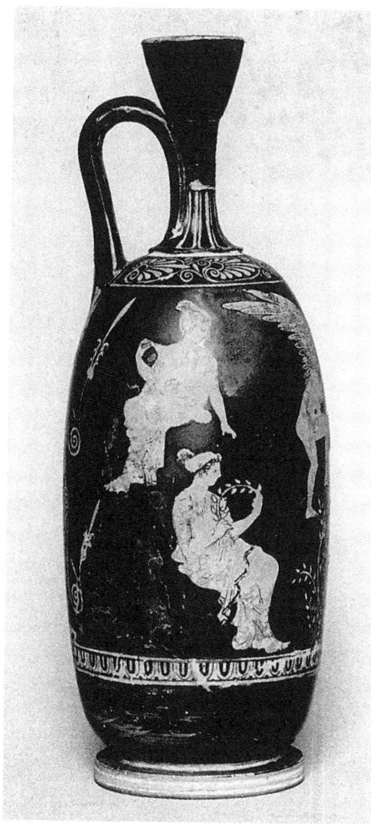

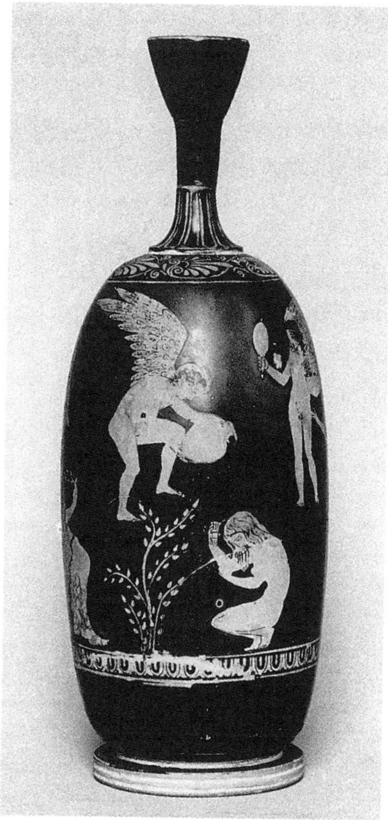

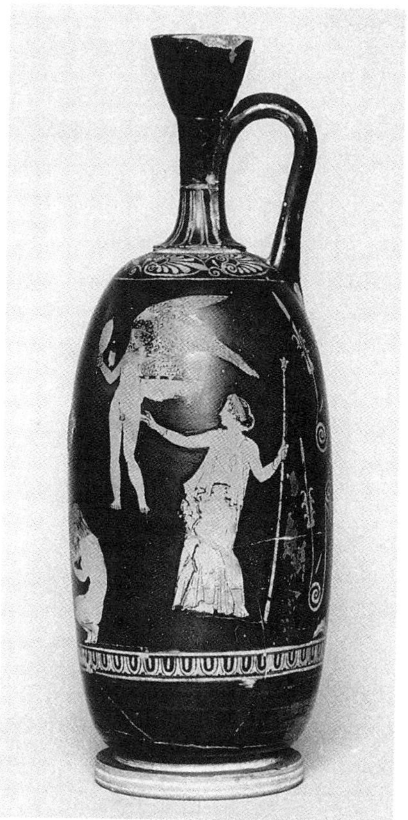

FIGURE 5.16 (LEFT). *Attic red-figure acorn lekythos. Eukleia. Formerly London, Embiricos Collection. Photo courtesy of A. Lezzi-Hafter.*

FIGURE 5.17 (CENTER). *Another view of lekythos in Fig. 5.16. Helen bathing. Photo courtesy of A. Lezzi-Hafter.*

FIGURE 5.18 (RIGHT). *Another view of lekythos in Fig. 5.16. Aphrodite. Photo courtesy of A. Lezzi-Hafter.*

did not interest the painters at all, perhaps because it would, by definition, be impossible for them to distinguish the real from the false Helen.)

How, then, did the visual arts respond to this plethora of different and conflicting Helens? How did the painters contribute to the ongoing discussion on the nature of Helen? It is surely no coincidence that the iconography of Helen on red-figure vases of the last quarter of the fifth century is richer and more complex than in any other period of Greek art.

About 410 B.C. Zeuxis, the celebrated fresco painter and native of Herakleia in Sicily, stunned the art world when he unveiled his portrait of Helen in Kroton.[47] He had received permission from the city fathers to study five of the fairest virgins of the city, in the nude, and composed his Helen from the best elements of each, claiming that "he did not believe it possible to find in one body all the things he looked for in beauty, since nature has not refined to perfection any single object in all its parts" (Cic. *Inv. rhet.* 2.1.1). Aside from her nudity, we are not told by our ancient sources just how Zeuxis depicted his Helen, but Robert Sutton has recently made a convincing case that she was shown bathing.[48] In other words, she would have been a forerunner of the earliest monumental statue of a nude Aphrodite, the mid-fourth-century Knidia of Praxiteles, who has just disrobed for her bath.[49]

If Sutton is right, then we may have a precious reflection of the great painting by Zeuxis on an exquisite little perfume vessel from the Workshop of the Meidias Painter (Figs. 5.16–18).[50] Helen (her name is inscribed) crouches beside a leafy tree as Eros pours water for her bath from a hydria (Fig. 5.17). A second Eros-like figure above is labeled Pothos, or Longing. He is often paired with Himeros, whom we met on the Berlin amphoriskos, on vases of this period.[51] Aphrodite, holding her divine scepter, observes from the right (Fig. 5.18). Particularly interesting is the woman seated at the left, who appears to be plaiting a wreath for Helen (Frontispiece, Fig. 5.16). She is labeled Eukleia (Good Repute), a personification who appears not infrequently in the retinue of Aphrodite on vases from the Meidian workshop.[52] But here I believe she carries a special significance. Gorgias had written that Helen should be absolved of the *duskleia* (ill repute) into which she had fallen (*Hel.* 6), and Euripides, in the *Helen,* has the chorus pray to the Dioskouroi to bring their sister back, to remove the *duskleia* of her marriage to a barbarian (lines 1500–1507). On our lekythos, Helen's *duskleia* has been replaced by its opposite, Eukleia.[53]

How is it that Helen has regained her good reputation, paradoxically, now that she is, for the first time, shown in the nude? Most Greek male viewers, after all, would have subscribed to the notion that a woman removes her modesty (*aidos*) along with her clothing (e.g., Hdt. 1.8.3). The answer may lie in her bath. Pausanias (2.2.3) records a spot called "the Bath of Helen," a salt stream opposite Kenchreai, near Corinth, and another source mentions a "Spring of Helen" where she bathed on the island of Chios (Steph. Byz. s.v. Helene).[54] There are indications that the motif of bathing was not simply an activity drawn from daily life but carried a ritual significance. Hera, for example, bathed every year in a spring called Kanathos, near Nauplia, to regain her virginity (Paus. 2.38.2). Bathing represents the washing away of impurity; Helen's bath restores her virginity and, with it, her reputation.

As we have seen, the vase painters almost invariably present Helen as the favorite of Aphrodite, who acts as a combination of mother, big sister, and manager. The goddess' concern for her protégé is always benevolent. There is no hint of their strained relationship in the *Iliad,* where, at one point, Helen defiantly refuses Aphrodite's command to join Paris, and the full wrath of the goddess is briefly brought down on her (3.411–414). But the painters did, I believe, understand Aphrodite's vengeful nature, too. They knew the story, first recorded in a fragment of Stesichoros,[55] that Tyndareos had once omitted to sacrifice to Aphrodite, and to punish him she made his daughters διγάμους τε καὶ τριγάμους καὶ λιπεσάνορας ("twice-married and thrice-married and husband-deserters"). "Thrice-married" is clearly a reference to Helen, who, after the death of Paris, married Deiphobos, another Trojan prince, her third husband.[56] Hesiod, in his *Catalogue of Women,* specifies two other unfaithful sisters of Helen: Klytaimnestra, who left Agamemnon for Aigisthos, and Timandra, who left her husband Echemon.[57] Timandra's name—"she who honors her husband"—must have sounded in this context rather ironic.

This story seems to be one of several that lie behind the remarkable gathering of women on a fragmentary hydria that is one of the masterpieces of the Meidias Painter (Figs. 5.19–23).[58] The vase was once an offering at a woman's grave in the Athenian Kerameikos. The German excavators have dated it in the decade 430 to 420,[59] which seems to me perhaps a little too early.

Nine women are spread around the shoulder of the hydria (Fig. 5.23), most of them casually disposed in pairs, as is typical for the painter and his associates.[60] Angelika Schöne's careful scrutiny of the damaged surface brought to light more traces of the inscribed names only a few years ago, although the fragments themselves started to turn up as stray finds in the Kerameikos excavations as early as 1915.[61]

The focal point of the group is clearly the seated figure of Helen, holding a small Eros in her lap (Figs. 5.19–20). She bends her head and seems to listen intently to Eros' words. Eros substitutes here for Aphrodite (as in Gorgias), who is not present in the scene. His outstretched arm gestures toward Hermione, the daughter Helen will leave behind when she goes to Troy (Fig. 5.20). Phylonoe leans on Helen's shoulder but appears lost in her own thoughts (Fig. 5.19). To the left of them is the more animated pair of Klytaimnestra conversing with Phoibe (Fig. 5.19), and behind Klytaimnestra is a nurse (her name cannot quite be made out) holding the baby Orestes (Fig. 5.21). To Helen's right is the pair of Hermione (only the top of her head and bottom of her hem preserved) and Hilaira (Fig. 5.20). Finally, at the far right, a seated figure, Timandra, is paired with a woman whose name has not survived (Fig. 5.22).

Several of these women are known from earlier Athenian vases (and of course from the poets and mythographers), though never in a gathering quite like this

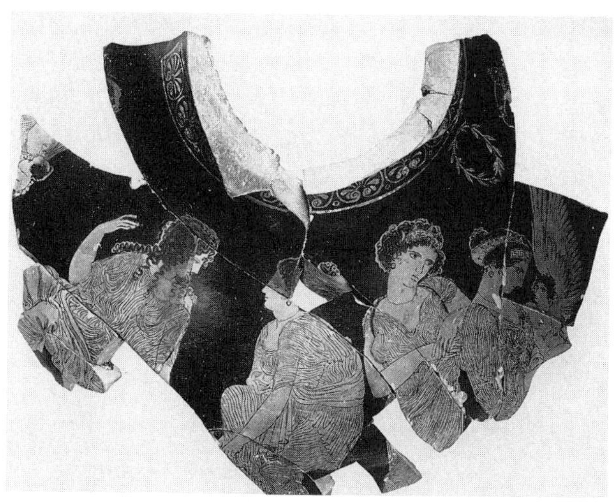

FIGURE 5.19. *Detail of Attic red-figure hydria by the Meidias Painter. Klytaimnestra, Phoibe, Phylonoe, and Helen with Eros. Athens, Kerameikos 2712. Photo: Deutsches Archäologisches Institut, Athens, neg. nr. KER 6254.*

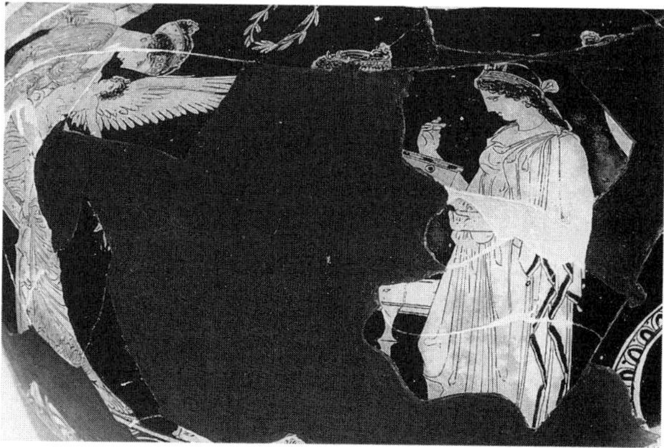

FIGURE 5.20. *Detail of hydria in Fig. 5.19. Helen with Eros, Hermione, and Hilaira. Photo: Deutsches Archäologisches Institut, Athens, E. F. Gehnen, neg. nr. KER 15166.*

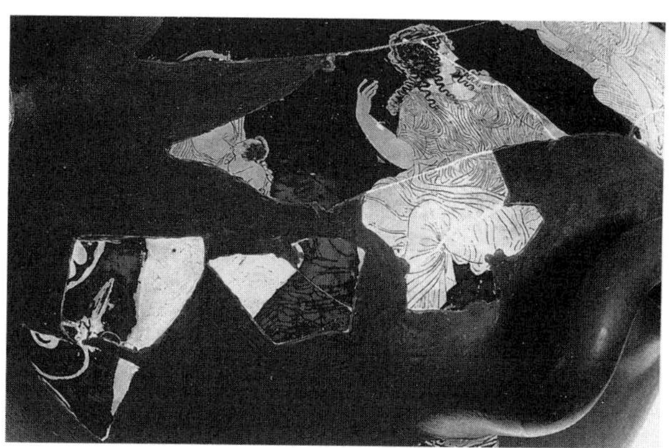

FIGURE 5.21. *Detail of the hydria in Fig. 5.19. Nurse suckling Orestes, Klytaimnestra. Photo: Deutsches Archäologisches Institut, Athens, E. F. Gehnen, neg. nr. KER 15169.*

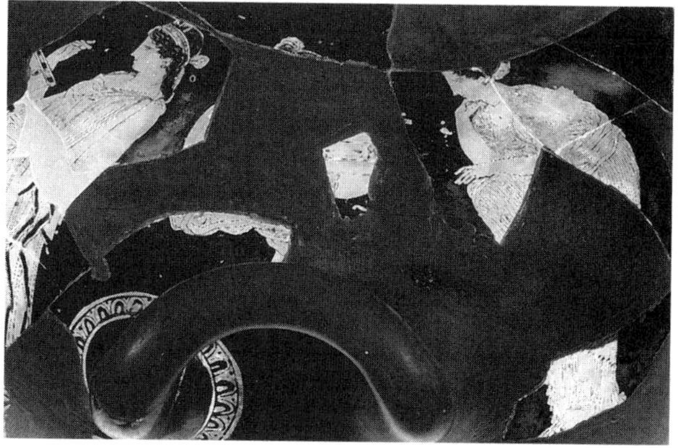

FIGURE 5.22. *Detail of the hydria in Fig. 5.19. Hilaira, Timandra, and unidentified woman. Photo: Deutsches Archäologisches Institut, Athens, E. F. Gehnen, neg. nr. KER 15167.*

one. Timandra, the third unfaithful sister, had witnessed Helen's departure with Paris on Makron's cup in Berlin[62] and also appears inscribed on a cup by the Codrus Painter closer in date to our hydria.[63] Phoibe appears as a sister of Helen and the Dioskouroi as early as an Attic black-figure hydria of the mid sixth century.[64] She reappears on a magnificent red-figure stamnos in Athens, showing Helen being carried off by Theseus (her first affair, long before Menelaos or Paris),[65] and in Euripides' *Iphigenia at Aulis,* produced in 405, Phoibe is said to be a daughter of Leda and Tyndareos (lines 50–51).

Hilaira is one of the Daughters of Leukippos, which makes her a cousin of Helen, and she appears labeled on the most famous version of the Dioskouroi abducting the Leukippidai, the Meidias Painter's name vase in London.[66] It is not clear whether the painter intended to include both Leukippidai on the Kerameikos hydria; if so, the other could be the woman at the extreme right who has lost her label (Fig. 5.22).[67] Helen was closely associated in cult with her cousins—and sisters-in-law, once they married the Dioskouroi—the Leukippidai: the egg from which she was born could still be seen in their sanctuary in Sparta in Pausanias' time (3.16.1).

Phylonoe, who leans so familiarly on Helen, is again one of her sisters (that makes five altogether in this one

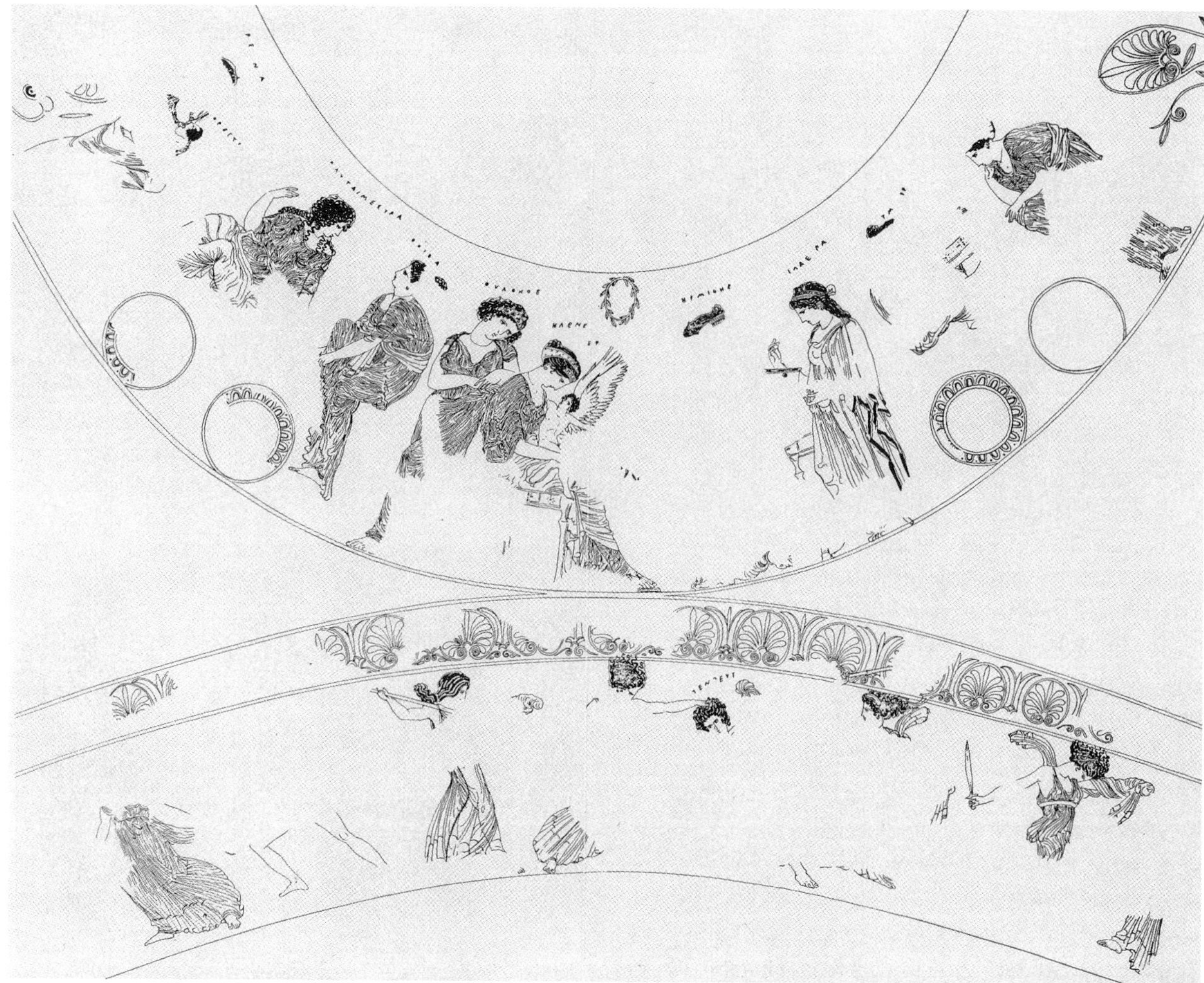

FIGURE 5.23. *Rollout drawing of the hydria in Fig. 5.19. Helen and her Sisters. After* AM *105 (1990) Beilage 7.*

scene) and, like Helen, she was worshipped in Lakonia.[68] The Xenotimos Painter, a contemporary of the early Meidias Painter, portrayed Phylonoe as part of the family gathering that witnesses Helen's birth from the egg, on his cup in Boston.[69] Exceptionally, those who surround the egg here include not only Leda and Tyndareos but Klytaimnestra, labeled by inscription (Fig. 5.14). The kinship of Helen and Klytaimnestra (never apparent in the visual arts before this period) was also on the Meidias Painter's mind when he painted the Kerameikos hydria, which includes Klytaimnestra and her baby Orestes (Fig. 5.21).

I have adduced a long list of comparanda to emphasize the point that, no matter how many literary sources we may discover for the figures on a given vase, it is essential to establish the iconographical tradition in which the painter was working. While most of the Meidias Painter's figures here do belong to an Attic visual tradition, two elements seem to be original with him. This is the only inscribed representation of Hermione on an Athenian vase,[70] and the depiction of Orestes as an infant is also unique.[71] That both Hermione and Orestes appear in the same scene is surely not by accident.

If the story of the punishment of Tyndareos and the infidelity of his daughters hangs like a dark cloud over this picture, then the presence of Helen's and Klytaimnestra's offspring adds an ominous note that carries over into the next generation. Just as Klytaimnestra fobbed the little Orestes off on a distant friend as her affair with Aigisthos was heating up (Aisch. *Ag.* 877–881), so Helen left behind the child Hermione

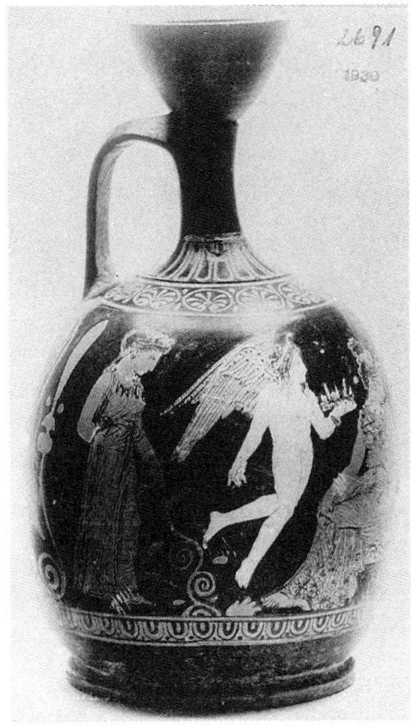
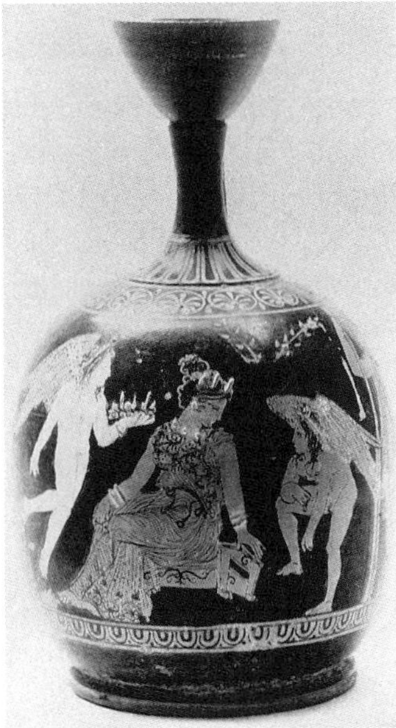
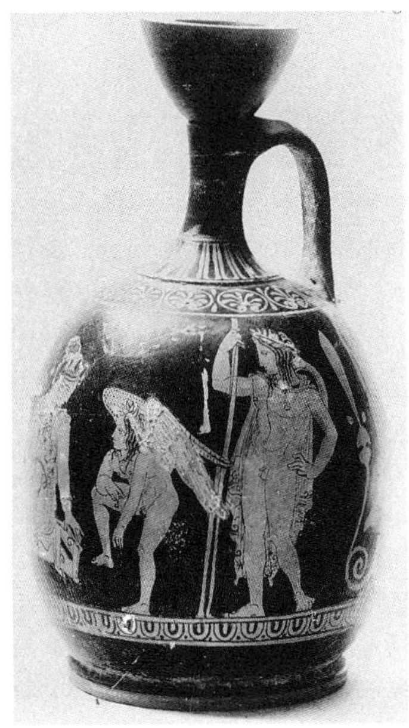

FIGURE 5.24. *Attic red-figure squat lekythos. Meeting of Helen and Paris. Berlin, Antikenmuseum inv. 4906. Photo: Deutsches Archäologisches Institut, Rome, neg. nr. 51-68.*

FIGURE 5.25. *Another view of the squat lekythos in Fig. 5.24. Photo: Deutsches Archäologisches Institut, Rome, neg. nr. 51-65.*

FIGURE 5.26. *Another view of the squat lekythos in Fig. 5.24. Photo: Deutsches Archäologisches Institut, Rome, neg. nr. 51-80.*

when she followed Paris, and Menelaos entrusted the girl, ironically, to Klytaimnestra. This much we are told by the ever-gloomy Elektra in Euripides' *Orestes* (lines 63–65, 1184), produced in 408, who explicitly links the two disastrous mothers:

> Poor Tyndareos. What daughters he fathered! Helen and my mother, Klytaimnestra! And both disgraced in the eyes of Hellas. (lines 249–250)

Both were not only *lipesanores* (husband-deserters), as Stesichoros called them, but deserters of their children as well. Yet fate had stranger things in store for these two abandoned children, for in the dénouement of Euripides' melodrama, Orestes, in a mad frenzy, first threatens to run Hermione through with his sword, then ends up marrying her on the instructions of Apollo (lines 1573–1624). That Euripides did not invent this bizarre story is suggested by the scene on an amphora of about 430 now in Kassel.[72] Orestes menaces Hermione, who has taken refuge at an altar, while Apollo calmly surveys the scene and looks ahead to its happy, if peculiar, resolution.

The Meidias Painter must have known this too, but his scene is pervaded by a quiet melancholy that portends no happy endings. Indeed, his choice of theme for the frieze decorating the body of the vase brings little joy either: the frenzied maenads of Thebes dismembering their young king Pentheus (Fig. 5.23). The two parts of the vase seem to be linked by their preoccupation with women out of control, women subverting the natural order of men.[73]

But what of Helen herself? As we have observed, the vase painters are consistently sympathetic to her and, for a brief period from about 440 to 420, even explore her psychological turmoil and emotional conflict with a remarkable degree of empathy and understanding. By the last years of the century, however, scenes of Helen and Paris, though more numerous than ever, have been reduced to a bland formula with neither tension nor sexual charge. They are merely a happy and handsome couple, often meeting in an idyllic landscape (Figs. 5.24–26).[74] A number of these vases are of very modest quality, and a fairly high percentage were found in Attika.[75] This suggests that, as a popular grave offering for women, the story was gradually stripped of its psychological complexity, the two protagonists seen only as exemplars of beauty, good fortune, and romance.[76] Indeed, what could be more romantic than the illicit lovers, locked in a steamy embrace, on a tall-boy lekythos (a companion in shape and style to the Bathing Helen vase, Figs. 5.16–18), in the J. Paul Getty Museum?[77] But the passion here is exceptional. Paris' exotic appeal is now often enhanced by clothing him in Phrygian garb—elaborately patterned cloak and felt cap—perhaps inspired by the stage.[78]

One exception to the usual bland scene is an unusual object, a ceramic egg (*oön*), again from a tomb in Athens, but now in the Metropolitan Museum of Art.[79] It is the earliest known example of Paris carrying off Helen in a chariot, a motif familiar enough from other myths of marriage-by-abduction, such as the Dioskouroi and the Daughters of Leukippos seen earlier.[80] Aphrodite watches with grim satisfaction as her plan is realized. Helen is once again the helpless, passive victim, as on Makron's skyphos; only the galloping chariot reflects a romanticized vision perhaps best paralleled by the story of Pelops and Hippodameia.[81] The egg, though not normally part of the ceramic repertoire, does have well-established funerary connotations.[82] One wonders if it did not also seem particularly appropriate for Helen, given the circumstances of her birth.

In his *Encomium of Helen,* Gorgias admires the ability of the painter to combine form and color into a work of art that delights the eye. For us, the viewer, he says, the experience of viewing is a νόσος ἡδεῖα, a "sweet disease" (18). Zeuxis' painting of Helen at her bath must have had just such an effect on its original viewers. In the formalized medium of red-figure vase painting, the play of color is much reduced compared to the subtle palette that must have been available to wall painters like Zeuxis. But, as we contemplate the lovely Helen on the finest red-figure vases, we may appreciate the almost hypnotic power of a simple form combined with the most subtle and delicate brushwork that characterizes the best work in this medium. It too causes its own νόσος ἡδεῖα, and I hope the honorand of this volume may long be infected.

NOTES

I would like to thank the editors of this volume for the invitation to join in honoring a scholar who, though never my teacher, has long been an inspiration for all my work on the interconnections of Greek literature and art. This paper was first presented as a Leventritt Lecture at Harvard in 1997, at the invitation of Aaron J. Paul.

1. *Il.* 3.441–446 (tr. R. Lattimore).

2. For a subtle analysis of this episode, see Lendle 1968.

3. In such papers as Pollitt 1976 and Pollitt 1985.

4. Boston, Museum of Fine Arts 13.186; *ARV*^{2} 458, 1; Kunisch 1997, pls. 98–99.

5. Robertson 1995.

6. Hedreen 1996, 176–177; Hedreen 2001, 54–57. On yet another version of the Recovery of Helen by Makron, a white-bearded Priam sits on an altar, calmly observing as Helen flees her irate husband: cup, Princeton, University Art Museum y1990-20a–b + y1990-54; Kunisch 1997, 129, pl. 45.

7. Beazley in CB 1963, vol. 3, 35.

8. On Peitho, see Shapiro 1993, 186–207.

9. Sources in CB 1963, vol. 3, 34.

10. *PMG* fr. 42.

11. On the Archaic literary tradition on Helen, see the excellent summary by Kannicht 1969, 21–48, and, on Stesichoros and Helen, Bassi 1993.

12. See Ghali-Kahil 1955, 71–113.

13. London, British Museum 1899.2-19.1; for a recent discussion, summarizing other views, see Snodgrass 1998, 33–35.

14. New York, Metropolitan Museum of Art 27.116; Amyx 1988, 196, no. 5, pl. 79. A contemporary Attic vase, a lebes gamikos by Sophilos, also depicts Helen's wedding: Izmir, Archaeological Museum inv. 3332; *ABV* 40, 2; Bakir 1982, 69, pls. 39–45. The groom is here not named, and Sutton (1997–1998, 28) says his identity is uncertain. But since Helen's brothers the Dioskouroi are also in attendance, this must be Helen's marriage to Menelaos in Sparta.

15. Würzburg, Martin von Wagner Museum L160; Simon 1981, 63–64, pl. XIX.

16. Berlin, Antikensammlung 2291; *ARV*^{2} 459, 4; Kunisch 1997, pls. 94–95 and p. 129 for a comparison of this cup and the Boston skyphos.

17. Basel, Antikensammlung und Sammlung Ludwig Kä 431; *CVA* Basel 3 Schweiz 7 pl. 56.

18. Davies, *EGF* 31, l.12–16.

19. Well discussed by Pollitt 1972, 29, 34, fig. 12.

20. Inv. 1962.386–388; *ARV*^{2} 634, 5; Ghali-Kahil 1955, pl. 10.

21. Berlin, Antikensammlung 30036; *ARV*^{2} 1173, 1. I have discussed this vase at some length already, in Shapiro 1986,

11–14, and Shapiro 1993, 194–195.

22. On the important role of personifications on Classical red-figure vases, see the comments of Pollitt 1987.

23. Simon 1986, 220–221, pls. 32–33.

24. For Himeros in vase painting, see Shapiro 1993, 111–122; *LIMC* 5, s.v. Himeros, 425–427 [A. Hermary].

25. Froning 1981, 66.

26. Paus. 1.22.6; Travlos *Athens,* 482, 491, fig. 618.

27. Hydria by the Jena Painter, Berlin, Antikensammlung V.I.3768; *ARV*[2] 1516, 81; Ghali-Kahil 1955, pl. 15:3–4; Böhr 2000; *CVA* Berlin 9 Deutschland 74, pls. 40–42.

28. For parallels, see below and Ghali-Kahil 1955, pls. 12, 14, 20.

29. The inscription was originally read and published as Aphrosyne ("thoughtlessness"; Böhr 2000) but was subsequently recognized as Habrosyne: *CVA* Berlin 9 Deutschland 74, 66.

30. For a full study of the semantics of habrosyne, see Kurke 1992.

31. On the identification of Trojans and Persians in fifth-century Athens, see Erskine 2001; M. C. Miller 1997.

32. Berlin, Antikensammlung F 2536; *ARV*[2] 1287, 1; Ghali-Kahil 1955, pl. 9; cf. the recent discussion in Sutton 1997–1998, 31, who observes that, despite Helen's conflicted state at the moment, Eros' action, lacing up her sandals to depart, points clearly to the eventual outcome.

33. For the somewhat contradictory sources on the parentage and birth of Helen, see *LIMC* 4, s.v. Helene 498 [L. Kahil]. See also the recent discussion of Mayer (1996, 9–11) on the "dysfunctional family" of Helen and Nemesis in the epic genealogy.

34. *LIMC* 4, s.v. Helene, nos. 1–13 [L. Kahil]; *LIMC* 6, s.v. Leda, nos. 28–32 [L. Kahil]. On the iconography, see Bottini 1988.

35. Bell krater: Bonn, Akademisches Kunstmuseum inv. 78; *ARV*[2] 1171, 4; *LIMC* 3, s.v. Dioskouroi, no. 185 [A. Hermary]. The statue of a bearded god on a column suggests that the setting is a Lakonian sanctuary of Zeus, who is symbolically present at the birth of his daughter.

36. Athens, National Museum 19947; *LIMC* 4, 503, s.v. Helene, no. 4 [L. Kahil]; Karouzou 1985.

37. *LIMC* 4, s.v. Helene, nos. 5–9 [L. Kahil].

38. Miles 1989. For a recent interpretation of the political context, see Knittlmayer 1999.

39. Despinis 1971.

40. Kallipolitis 1978; Petrakos 1981. The reconstruction reproduced here (Fig. 5.15) is that of Petrakos 1986, 106, fig. 8.

41. See Lapatin 1992 and, most recently, Palagia (2000, 62–68), who suggests that the occasion is the wedding of Helen's daughter Hermione to Neoptolemos, son of Achilles, at Sparta.

42. Daux 1984, 149; Lyons 1997, 47.

43. Kratinos fr. 115 (Kassel-Austin); Schwarze 1971, 33; Mayer 1996, 11–12. I have briefly discussed this play, and the scenes of Helen's birth, in Shapiro 1999, 105–106.

44. MacDowell 1982. Cf. Braun (1982), who argues that the *Encomium* is a rhetorical showpiece, not meant to be taken seriously, and, for a different view, Porter 1993.

45. Only Ananke is not attested on vases before the fourth century: *LIMC* 1, s.v. Ananke, 757–758 [E. Simon].

46. Kannicht 1969; Austin 1994, ch. 6. Hdt. 2.112–120 also records this version, and it probably originated with Stesichoros: see Kannicht 1969, 25. For an alternative view, that this story was already known to Hesiod, see Nagy 1990, 419–423.

47. Pollitt 1990a, 149–151.

48. Sutton 1997–1998, 41.

49. See Havelock 1995.

50. *ARV*[2] 1690; 1705; current whereabouts unknown; sold at auction in 1993: Christie's (London) 28.4.1993, no. 30. I have discussed the vase briefly in Shapiro 1993, 77–78; see also Sutton 1997–1998, 41.

51. E.g., the hydria by the Meidias Painter with Himeros and Pothos drawing the chariot of Aphrodite: Florence, Museo Archeologico Etrusco 81947; *ARV*[2] 1312, 2; Simon 1981, pl. 218.

52. Hampe 1955; Shapiro 1993, 70–78; *LIMC* 4, s.v. Eukleia, 48–51 [A. Kossatz-Deissmann].

53. On Helen's escape from duskleia (through cult), see Foley 1992, 132, 145–146.

54. On these and other cults and cult places of Helen, see Clader 1976, 69–71; Larson 1995, 69–70, 80–81, and passim. For Helen's cults in Attika, see Kearns 1989, 158.

55. Stesichoros fr. 46 *PMG* = 223 Campbell.

56. *LIMC* 3, s.v. Deiphobos, 363 [L. Kahil].

57. Hes. *Cat.* fr. 176; see West 1988.

58. Athens, Kerameikos Museum 2712; *ARV*[2] 1313, 6; Burn 1987, 69–70, pls. 44–45; Schöne 1990.

59. Knigge 1975, 134; Schöne 1990, 164, n. 9.

60. Cf., e.g., the Meidian hydriai illustrated in L. Burn 1987, pls. 22–23, 27–29.

61. For the history of the vase's discovery, see Schöne 1990, 163–164.

62. Above, n. 16.

63. Rome, Museo Gregoriano Etrusco Vaticano, Astarita 125–127; *ARV*[2] 1269, 6; Beazley 1960.

64. Basel, Antikensammlung und Sammlung Ludwig (no inv. no.); *LIMC* 3, s.v. Dioskouroi, no. 180 [A. Hermary].

65. Athens, National Museum 18063; *ARV*[2] 1028, 13; Matheson 1995, 348, 68, pl. 53. On Helen and Theseus, see most recently Shapiro 2000a.

66. London, British Museum E224; *ARV*[2] 1313, 5; L. Burn 1987, pls. 3–5.

67. In some sources (e.g., Paus. 2.27.5) the second Leukippid is named Phoibe, not to be confused with our Phoibe, sister of Helen. The name Phoibe is inscribed in a scene of

the Rape of the Leukippidai on a black-figure Chalkidian fragment (*LIMC* 3, s.v. Dioskouroi, no. 194 [A. Hermary]) but does not occur in Attic scenes of the subject.

68. Wide 1893, 350; *LIMC* 7, s.v. Phylonoe I, 408 [L. Kahil].

69. Boston 99.539; *ARV*^{2} 1142, 1; CB 1963, vol. 3, pl. 99. On scenes of the Birth of Helen, see above, p. 53 and n. 34.

70. *LIMC* 5, s.v. Hermione, 388–389 [L. Kahil]. Palagia (2000, 67) has argued convincingly that Hermione occupied an important position on the Nemesis base, beside her mother Helen.

71. At least unique in this context; elsewhere, the baby Orestes figures in another myth, that of Telephos: see *LIMC* 7, s.v. Telephos, 866–868 [M. Strauss].

72. Kassel, Staatliche Kunstsammlungen T43; *ARV*^{2} 1206, 1; *LIMC* 5, s.v. Hermione, no. 3 [L. Kahil].

73. Schöne (1990, 176–177) rightly sees a link between the two scenes in that both depict a god's curse (Aphrodite's above, Dionysos' below). She goes on, however, to see a political allusion as well in the juxtaposition of the two stories: Sparta and Thebes were both Athens' archenemies in the early years of the Peloponnesian War, both shown here under a curse.

74. Squat lekythos: Berlin, Berlin Antikensammlung inv. 4906; *ARV*^{2} 1336, 4; *LIMC* 4, s.v. Helene, no. 88 [L. Kahil]. For other examples, see Ghali-Kahil 1955.

75. E.g., the lekythos illustrated here (above, n. 74); also *LIMC* 4, s.v. Helene, nos. 89, probably 91, no. 92, and no. 120 [L. Kahil].

76. On the increasing assimilation of Helen and Paris to prototypes of the ideal bride and groom, see Sutton 1997–1998.

77. Malibu 91.AE.9; Sutton 1997–1998, 37, fig. 16, and see Sutton's discussion of the scene, pointing out how it "blurs the boundaries between myth and contemporary life," making it impossible to be certain that the lovers (who are not labeled) are really Helen and Paris.

78. E.g., the pelike Harvard, Arthur M. Sackler Museum 1925.30.46; *ARV*^{2} 1341, bottom, 1; Ghali-Kahil 1955, pl. 25. Cf. the discussion of Paris in Eastern dress on the Berlin hydria, above, n. 29.

79. New York 1971.258.3; *ARV*^{2} 1256, 1; Ghali-Kahil 1955, pl. 5.

80. Above, n. 66.

81. E.g., on the well-known red-figure amphora Arezzo, Museo Nazionale Archeologico 1460; *ARV*^{2} 1157, 25; Simon 1981, pls. 224–225.

82. Nilsson 1902; Bettini 1988.

6

COMPOSITION AND CONTENT ON CLASSICAL MURALS AND VASES

JOHN BOARDMAN

It is a commonplace of our studies to hold that vase scenes with figures set on different levels in the field (up/down, as I shall call them) are influenced by or may even copy mural compositions of the Early Classical period, notably those that we associate with the name of Polygnotos and that we know from Pausanias' description of his work at Delphi. We are led to judge that these were typical of his work, and of the work of his contemporary, Mikon of Athens, and seem to be justified in this by the vase scenes that, especially from the mid century on, display the composition.

There are, however, different types of multilevel vase scenes, and we need to ask ourselves whether these all derive from murals, and if so whose, or whether some are the vase painter's own answer, however prompted, to newly perceived problems of narrative display, which may depend as much on the constraints of his craft as on the example of other media. There also remain problems of interpretation for the wall paintings themselves. Our honorand has addressed these problems of Classical paintings and vases more than once;[1] I can offer little new to his observations and those of other scholars, but it is a field in which the balance of probabilities can always be adjusted and answers proposed and in which close observation of the primary evidence can still, as ever, yield important results.

Reconstructions of Polygnotos' Delphi paintings have long been a scholarly exercise. The latest, by Mark Stansbury-O'Donnell in two articles in the *AJA,* must be those that best reflect the text,[2] but this is not a subject on which the last word will ever be spoken.[3] Pausanias can be obscure, and whole books can be, and have been, written about his use of a single preposition. But the resultant reconstruction drawings still look a little odd. The field is not as well filled as we expect from Greek artists, or as Carl Robert's old drawings presented it, nor is it easy to posit windows or doors or fixed furniture in the Lesche at Delphi to fill the gaps. Different media often observe different iconographic conventions, so reconstructing Polygnotos after Athenian vase scenes is not easy and perhaps wrong.

Although the figures in his Delphi *Ilioupersis* were named, many are virtually unknown to us from other sources, and the inscriptions may have been retouched by Pausanias' day. He even thought the painter could have made up some of them (10.25.2), and they would have been interpreted by him in the terms of the second century A.D., not the fifth B.C. In the Troy picture, we might prefer to take what Pausanias describes as the Lesser Ajax at an altar, with a pre-rape group of Kassandra beside him, for him taking refuge from angry Greeks, rather than taking an oath. Could the painter really have avoided showing the deaths of Priam and Polyxena, rather than having one a corpse and the other a captive; where is Hekabe; where are Aineias and Anchises? Were all the names original, and did Pausanias omit some parts of the painting by design or accident? After all, he forgot to mention one of the metopes in the Temple of Zeus at Olympia, and the paintings were far more confusing. But we can be sure of the overall compositions, and almost sure about how they filled the walls of the Knidian Lesche, with roughly half-life-sized figures.

Polygnotos was a Thasian, Ionian, and perhaps the more disposed therefore to create frieze compositions in the Ionic manner. Major painting on wall or panel had a longer pedigree in Asia Minor than it did on the Greek mainland, as we may now judge from the palace and tomb paintings of Gordion and Lykia. Although these give no hint of other than frieze compositions, they come from a new political unit, the Persian empire, where major displays of narrative had been the up/down friezes cut in low relief, and painted, on Mesopotamian palace walls. This was not a genre that the Persian homeland encouraged, but it may have flourished more modestly in the western empire, to affect Polygnotan painting. When he was a young man in Thasos, the island was much involved in Persian affairs and even arts.[4] Earlier homeland Greek compositions of this type are unknown, and attempts to reconstruct them from vase scenes are surely misguided, even when the suggestion is made that a very youthful Polygnotos worked in Athens before the Persian sack.[5] Nor can the occasional placing of one figure above another, determined by the field and apparent on vases from the Geometric period on, be in any way relevant.[6]

The up/down mural compositions at Delphi seem to have been mainly static, with action confined to very small groups and with no interaction between groups and figures other than, it may be, by glance or gesture. The pictures seem to ask to be enjoyed piecemeal, and although a ship or a wall might seem to provide a focus, it is not the focus we would look for in a Classical composition in preference to some heroic action or figure. This is what we find on the vases, where even a static scene has focal figures, while registers of fighting figures are very closely knit, even though they can often be resolved into formulaic groups.

The Niobid Painter's name-vase in Paris is our first with the new composition; it has one static scene (Fig. 6.1), with one focal figure (to this I shall return, below), and an action scene (the killing of the Niobids) with a clear narrative focus. The scenes are up/down and have the cut-off figures in a landscape setting that seem a hallmark of the murals. But this vase is exceptional even among the painter's known works. The scheme is unique for him too, so far as we know, and it is only after some years that we meet again these up/down compositions on vases, and then for close-knit fighting scenes such as Amazonomachies.

By contrast, the Niobid Painter's Amazonomachies, and those of his immediate following, employ a quite different but equally novel compositional scheme, which soon gets used for other subjects: the variable ground line with a frieze still basically one-figure high. These carry suggestions of different ground lines in a comparatively narrow band, enabling some variation of level between figures in single action groups and far more overlapping of figures than red-figure artists had found suitable to their technique, where figures too easily dissolve into each other. There are cut-off figures, too, but the overlapping looks more like an alternative to the Polygnotan scheme than a vase painter's adaptation of it.[7] The style better suited vase painters skilled enough to design large-figure scenes, yet it seems unlikely to have been their invention. For all we know, it was the scheme of other murals, such as the Amazonomachies by Mikon in Athens. It remained popular for vases into the fourth century and is the one favored for the incised bronze cistae of Praeneste, inspired by Classical Greek compositions, and on some stone votive reliefs. It may have had a somewhat different source of

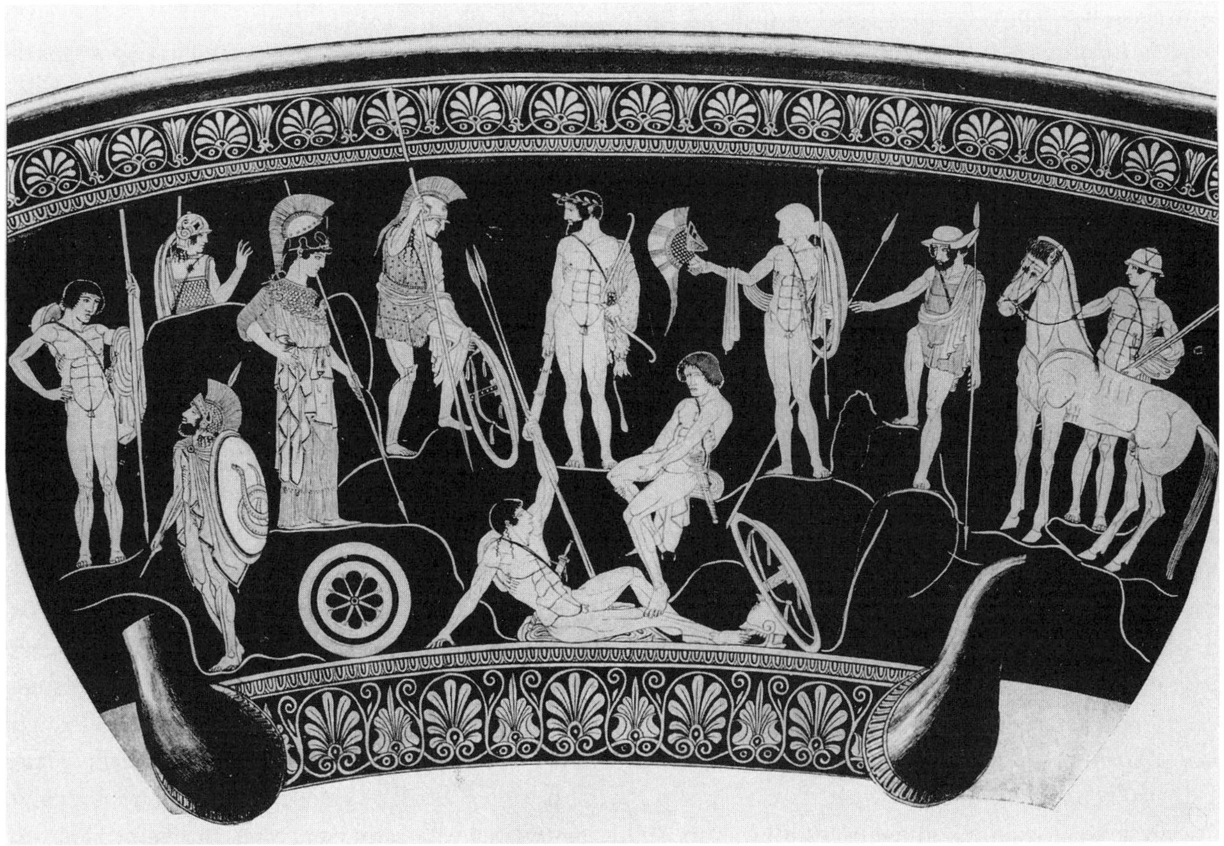

FIGURE 6.1. *Volute krater by the Niobid Painter. Paris, Louvre G 341, from Orvieto. Drawing after* FR, *pl. 108.*

inspiration from that for the up/down scenes, possibly still mural, and certainly monumental.

Our sources fail us in reconstructing other murals (I come to Mikon's *Marathon* painting below). Pliny (*HN* 35.138) describes a painting by Polygnotos' brother Aristophon as *numerosa tabula,* presumably like his brother's. A prime problem in determining inspiration from mural painting for vase scenes is the apparent unwillingness of the vase painter to do more than copy a general scheme of composition and probably themes. This is clearly true where sculpture was the model. Even unusual individual figures, like the Hektor clasping his knee in the *Nekyia* at Delphi (Paus. 10.31.5), are in fact anticipated on vases (for Odysseus at the Mission to Achilles). The lack of close correlation in figures and groups between treatments of the same theme by different or even the same artists demonstrates this clearly enough, and where we know a major multilevel composition that might well have inspired vase scenes—the Parthenos shield—the absence of any copies of the most distinctive figures and groups, or even juxtaposition of the more commonplace ones, shows how little the painter was concerned with simple copying. A survey of the recorded titles of fifth-century paintings produces very few obvious correlations with the choice of scenes for vases. There is communication between the media in style and composition, not subject.

John Barron suggested that a physical trait on some figures in vase scenes might well be taken to have been closely inspired by their treatment on murals. It is the boldly articulated superficial muscle pattern of the upper abdomen, which is shown as triple pairs above the navel, not the usual double pairs of the period; thus for the Herakles and others in Figure 6.1.[8] But this does not appear for the same figures in scenes otherwise related in subject or style. It may indeed have been a feature of the larger mural figures, but it is not "deformity" or "erroneous," and in no way does it hark back to Archaic modes, for all that in some respects Polygnotos was a sub-Archaic artist. The sextuple division above the navel is in fact more lifelike than the quadruple—what in the modern gymnasium is referred to as a "six-pack." It is a sign of the closer anatomical rendering that, on most vases, was becoming less conspicuous as the style of drawing became looser but was being more scrupulously observed in sculpture.

One possible example of a mural copied on vases occurs towards the end of the fifth century. It involves the Suessula Painter's Gigantomachy amphora in Paris. Von Salis showed that "free replicas, differently arranged, of figures" on the vase (Beazley's words in *ARV*² 1345) appear on fragments of two other vases, of different shapes and, probably, by different painters.[9] That the figures are rearranged shows that no simple copying is involved, but we have something close to evidence for a "model" here. The style suggests that the model did not belong to the period of Polygnotos, yet if it was a mural (no Gigantomachy of the late fifth century is recorded), then it was Polygnotan in form. All other evidence suggests that the Polygnotan scheme was short-lived for murals, though not for vases, and so perhaps the model here was another vase.

Few styles in painting in the later fifth century and the fourth brought new techniques and interests—not wall covering but panel pictures, probably with fewer figures and relying on new skills with line, shade, color, and chiaroscuro. To judge from the Macedonian paintings and copies in Italy, the preferred compositions had more in common with the variable-ground lines of the fifth century than with the Polygnotan up/down. This is probably why Polygnotos was remembered rather than copied in later centuries and why only one of his paintings is recorded as having been taken to Rome: that of a warrior who may have been climbing either up or down—perhaps a fragment or excerpt from a multilevel mural (Pliny *HN* 35.59).

The scheme has a mixed history on vases. Well into the fourth century we can still find fine examples of focused up/down pictures of Polygnotan type on several vases. Otherwise, it is used to compose both static and action pictures, and court scenes around a Dionysos or Herakles. The more populous multifigure scenes are resolved into registers without dividing lines, recalling the fifth-century kalyx kraters with two separate registers, but generally of dissimilar subjects. This recurs in the reliefs at Trysa and on the Nereid Monument. Without dividing lines, it is the scheme of the Attic Pronomos vase and that generally adopted for the large Apulian kraters. With the just possible exception of the Suessula Painter Gigantomachy, there is nothing to suggest that such compositions, up/down or register, are other than the deliberate and outmoded choice of the painters themselves, who found in them a satisfactory means of expressing narrative groups on shapes that lent themselves more to squarish compositions than to friezes, which might be more subtly composed on one or more ground lines.

I turn now from this general consideration of major compositions on wall or vase to the particular problems of the painting of the battle of Marathon in the Stoa Poikile in Athens. There are very few direct sources for this, and Pausanias is far less informative about paintings in Athens than he is at Delphi. There is even confusion about the painter, though the consensus seems to have been for the Athenian Mikon, with Panainos, brother or nephew of Pheidias, as second choice. The latter is not a contender; his career seems mainly later, with his brother. The choice of Marathon for a painting fits well with early years when the connection with Kimon and the desire to glorify his father Miltiades was still strong; thus, in the period immediately after the construction of the Stoa, itself sponsored by the Kimonian supporter, Peisianax.[10]

Pausanias saw four major paintings in the Stoa: a battle of Oinoe, an Amazonomachy, a sack of Troy, and the battle of Marathon. The best modern account of the evidence for the last is by Eve Harrison in the *AJA* for 1972, where due account is taken of the records of the battle, from Herodotos to the sophist Polemon, which might be thought influenced by the painting.[11] We cannot, of course, be sure about these sources, and it is unlikely that Polemon, composing imaginary honorific speeches on Kynegeiros and Kallimachos, generals who fell at Marathon, would have felt constrained to mention only those actions and figures that appeared in the painting.

The other paintings deserve a brief comment. We cannot judge the *Amazonomachy* by Mikon, which might have followed any of the schemes discussed, with few or many figures, at many levels or perhaps with a variable ground line. Nor can we judge the *Sack of Troy* by Polygnotos. We may not simply assume that it was like the one at Delphi. Pausanias picks out only the Greek leaders conferring over the misdeeds of the Lesser Ajax and an assembly of captured Trojan women, two subjects out of many at Delphi. It seems to have belonged to a whole program of paintings for the Stoa and of course has its Kimonian and Persian War associations too. Polygnotos was said to have shown Laodike, daughter of Priam, with the features of Elpinike, Kimon's sister (Plut. *Kim.* 4). Whether Polygnotos intended this or not, the fact that the connection was made by someone, presumably at an early date, is significant. There can be no question of true portraiture, but since Laodike was said by Homer to have been the most beautiful of the Trojan women, he may well have singled her out and given her distinctive features—color of hair, for example—that permitted comparison. Polygnotos himself was said to have had an affair with Elpinike; so, indeed, was her brother Kimon. Among the Trojan women, Laodike was exactly the right figure to choose, however, since she was associated in myth with Theseus' sons, and the Kimon/Theseus association is well documented. She was said to have had a child by Akamas when he came with the mission to ask for the return of Helen; the child was Munitos/Munichos, eponym of Mounychia, the Attic harbor; and after Troy, his mother was said to have accompanied Akamas home.[12]

The painting of the battle of Oinoe presents the real problem. It is mentioned only by Pausanias, who does not name its painter—points of some significance. He took it to represent an engagement between the Athenians and the Spartans at Argive Oinoe, an encounter that he mentioned also in describing the Argive dedication commemorating it at Delphi (10.10.3). The date of the battle has occasioned no little discussion, even its historicity, to which I shall add nothing.[13] That such an event should be dignified by a painting in the Stoa has rightly been greeted with some surprise, since it seems hardly to qualify for such distinction. A solution proposed by the late David Francis, with Michael Vickers, seems to me in essence though not in detail to provide a possible answer.[14] A similar solution had recommended itself to me for quite different reasons, though from the same clue, and with quite different results for our understanding of the paintings in the Stoa. There are some grave objections, and the Francis/Vickers theory rather adds to them, but it is worth consideration, and along the way it enables us to develop a somewhat different view from the traditional one of the Marathon painting.

In brief, the proposal is that the Oinoe of the battle seen by Pausanias was not the Argive Oinoe but the Oinoe near Marathon, and that this was, in fact, another Marathon painting in the Stoa, related in some way to the one more fully described. Francis and Vickers thought it was a full-scale complement to it, balancing the whole scheme, with the allegorical paintings of *Troy* and the *Amazonomachy* dividing the two *Marathon* paintings. I shall return to *Oinoe* but wish first to consider *Marathon* as described by Pausanias and as elucidated by Harrison in 1972.

Pausanias says little enough: it is described as a painting of the men who fought at Marathon:

> The Boiotians from Plataia and men from Attika are coming to grips with the barbarians: the contest is evenly balanced. But in the heart of the battle the barbarians are in flight, pushing each other into the marsh, and the painting ends with the Phoenician ships, and with Greeks slaughtering barbarians as they jump into them. The hero Marathon, from whom the plain is named, is there, with Theseus like one rising out of the earth, and Athena and Herakles. . . . In the picture of the fighting you can most clearly make out the generals Kallimachos, who was chosen to be commander-in-chief, and Miltiades, and the hero Echetlos. (1.16.1)

The description is confusing, with no clear indication of who was where, and it may very well be that what Pausanias saw was not itself in very good order. I have a strong suspicion that by his day, six hundred years after the execution of the painting, it was in extreme disrepair. He commented on the illegibility of some of the paintings in the Pinakotheke in the Propylaia, and we are told that Polygnotos' painting at Thespiae had to be touched up a century later by Pausias (Plin. *HN* 35.123). Fortunately, prominent figures in the painting are mentioned by several other sources, listed and quoted by Harrison. From Synesius' description of its removal by a proconsul in the fourth century A.D., it is clear that the painting was on boards, *sanidas,* and there must have been reason and opportunity enough for deterioration over the centuries.[15] The state of the paintings at Delphi was clearly much healthier—either thanks to the technique of painting or to the way they had been kept in better repair and perhaps restored by a temple administration with an eye to the tourist—than the Athenian paintings were, cared for by a civic administration.

Harrison makes a convincing case for a tripartite composition in the painting, with three focal figures: Miltiades urging on his men, a figure dwelt on by other sources; the general Kallimachos staggering on upright though already shot through by enemy missiles, another figure who had played on the imagination of ancient viewers; and the third, the evocative figure of Kynegeiros, clinging to a Persian ship and having his hand severed. She places all these in a single frame, but if we try to reconstruct details, serious difficulties emerge. Although the action might in some way seem to center on each of the focal figures, it would basically have been composed in a frieze, two figures high or less on the analogy of Delphi, with victorious Athenians advancing from the left, and defeated Persians, fighting, fleeing, or scrambling onto ships at the right.

The transitions between three such essentially disparate scenes are difficult to imagine, especially since in the first, at least, the Persians were facing left. Moreover, we are taken in a single picture from the opening of hostilities on one side of the plain at Marathon to their close at the other side. This is a far more dramatic change in time and location for a single composition viewed as a whole than any we know in Greek art. The Parthenon frieze, which could not be viewed as a whole, appears to offer a far more restricted range in time and place, and the sequence can be understood as a logical one without shifts and turns around different foci. It seems to me more likely that the painting as described was divided into three separate but closely juxtaposed panels, each with a central figure, an Athenian general. Two died on the battlefield; the third, Miltiades, survived but not for long, and he died before the painting was made. Each panel had its own character as a battle scene: the equally balanced fight with Miltiades urging on the Athenians and allies; the Persian flight with the living-dead Kallimachos; the rout at the ships and Kynegeiros' desperate bravery.[16]

But should this have been all? Might there not have been another, the real first panel, with the marshaling of hosts, meeting with the Plataians, and perhaps the first blows exchanged? This is surely where a composition such as that described by Pausanias as of the battle of Oinoe would fit very well indeed. He was himself puzzled by its content: "This is not a drawing of the full event, the rage of battle, or particular deeds of daring, but the first moments of a battle as the armies come to grips" (1.15.1). We would then have a full sequence of the battle in four tableaux, from marshaling to the final discomfiture of the enemy. Oinoe must have appeared as eponymous nymph of the village that lay on one of the approaches to the plain from the north, on the route of the Plataians hurrying to the battlefield. She was perhaps not an insignificant figure and surely named. Her brothers found a place on the base of the statue of Nemesis at Rhamnous (Paus. 1.33.8), itself a memorial to the defeat of the Persians.

To accept this solution we have to assume that the Oinoe panel had been badly damaged and probably removed from its proper place at the start of the main sequence. This would explain Pausanias' difficulty in describing its content, its lack of a named painter, and why no one else mentions it as a separate entity, since it was not one, until damage required its removal. It must have been removed by Polemon's time, only a few years before Pausanias' visit; thus, the sophist describing the *Marathon* sequence would have had no reason to specify details from it.[17] Pausanias describes the Oinoe panel as "first" in the stoa. Perhaps it had been removed to a side wall. His sequence is otherwise *Amazonomachy—Sack of Troy—Marathon;* but possibly all panels had been rearranged.

The Francis/Vickers solution leaves the panel separate, with the Spartan "enemy" being really the friendly Plataians approaching Marathon from the route past Oinoe, to join the assembled Athenian army, though Pausanias says the Athenians were already coming to blows with the enemy. They suggest as a centerpiece, a council of war with Miltiades presiding, which is hardly a theme for a major painting to match the main *Marathon* battle picture. On my theory, whatever opponents were shown were mistaken for hostile Greeks (Spartans) by Pausanias, or they were indeed the friendly Plataians and fighting had not, in fact, yet broken out. The meeting of two forces could have been managed with them in parallel groups, but perhaps, if on a separate panel, better facing each other. The state of the panel may not have allowed of any accurate description, and Pausanias (or his source), having decided that this was a battle, naturally identified hostility. As for the focus for the *Oinoe* panel, it might have been one or more of the Athenian generals, possibly welcoming the Plataians whose role in the battle was always acknowledged by Athens. Demosthenes also makes clear that Plataian assistance was made explicit in the painting, by their "Boiotian helmets" (*Neaer.* 94).[18]

Oinoe must have been labeled; otherwise, she would not have been identifiable. We are told that the figure of Miltiades was not labeled, at his request. He survived; were other Greeks who did not survive labeled? Possibly not; there would have been no difficulty identifying the main figures: Miltiades the belligerent, dying Kallimachos, handless Kynegeiros. Superhuman figures, however, might well have been labeled: Oinoe, the hero Marathon, perhaps Echetlos, though he might be recognized from the plowshare he wielded. Mikon the Athenian, whose painting this was, need not have observed Polygnotan conventions about labeling or even possibly composition. At Delphi all Polygnotos' figures were labeled, but it is not surprising that a painter would have felt it necessary to be reticent about mortals still alive or recently dead, whatever status they may have been accorded by their fellow-citizens after their heroic achievements on the battlefield of Marathon.

What of the other, divine figures? Pausanias names Theseus "like one rising out of the earth" (not actually rising from the earth, then), Athena, and Herakles. In his colorful account of the battle, not the painting, Polemon names also Pan, Hera, Demeter, and Kore, but we need not accommodate all or any of them. Robert reconstructed the painting with a line of deities in the upper register, following the later practice in up/down vase compositions, especially the Apulian. Harrison saw the difficulties but also assembled the deities at the top of her picture. Her sketch has, of course, to be very considerably extended laterally to make any sense and would then present the same problems that Robert had, unless the gods were floating in independent groups; they could hardly have been engaged in the battle itself beside the Athenians, whatever stories there may have been about apparitions on the battlefield. If the proportions of the Stoa walls and the figures in the painting were at all like those for the Lesche at Delphi, there would have been no room for a divine register over the battle scenes.

There was a long tradition in Greek art for showing deities in a separate field from the action in which they are concerned, from the east frieze of the Siphnian Treasury at Delphi, through the Hephaisteion east frieze where they are isolated on their rocky islands, to the Parthenon north metopes, west end, and indeed the frieze where they are also insulated from the mortal by their stature and the heroes. So, for the Marathon painting, should we consider the possibility of a separate panel for divine and certain heroic figures, adjacent to the fighting, and more probably at the end, to judge from Pausanias, than in the middle? If so, we have a very good model for such a panel in the Niobid Painter's name-vase (Fig. 6.1), with Athena, Herakles, and a possible Theseus in an emergent pose. He rose from a chasm, and one of the physical features of Oinoe was the chasm, *charadra,* nearby.

Eve Harrison again comes to our aid in her discussion of the vase scene in the *Art Bulletin* of 1972.[19] She reverts to an earlier explanation for it as the assembly of heroes before Marathon, argues it skillfully and, to my mind, in the main convincingly. The suggestion was proposed first by Hauser and repeated by other scholars with various degrees of adherence, most recently by Martine Denoyelle, with other observations to which I return below.[20] The scene even includes the intimation of Spartan interest, though too late for the battle, with the probable Dioskouroi in their *piloi* appearing in the wings. We have Athena, Herakles centrally, and a Theseus below him in what is certainly not an emergent pose but that evokes one, and is combined with the figure seated above him making what seems like a "helping hand."[21] The other figures are surely the Athenian tribal heroes (the snake blazon is prominent) who were also to be celebrated in Pheidias' bronze group commemorating Marathon and erected at Delphi.

There is, however, also an unmistakable weariness in the figures, surely resting after a fight, not before it—stooping, reclining, seated, the "helping hand"

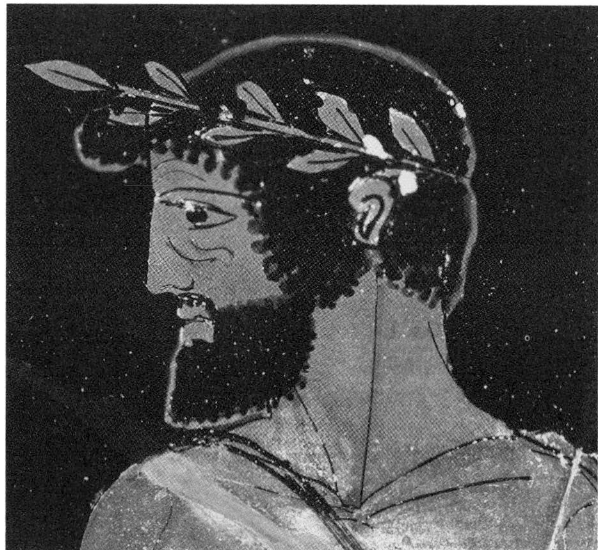

FIGURE 6.2. *Photograph detail of the head of Herakles on Fig. 6.1. Photo courtesy Département des Antiquités grecques, étrusques et romaines, Musée du Louvre, Paris.*

with deeply furrowed brow. Herakles too has remarkable features not perceptible in most illustrations, with a furrowed brow, deep folds under the eyes, even gritted teeth—all this only clearly visible in enlargement (Fig. 6.2); Mikon was famed for his life studies.[22] The Spartan Dioskouroi, who are arriving in time only to view the field, seem to suggest the aftermath of victory, not a period of preparation. Harrison thought the original of the vase scene might have been in the Theseion in Athens. I would suggest another home, in the Stoa Poikile, as the final panel of the Marathon battle sequence, with the vase scene perhaps more than just vaguely recalling its composition and content.[23]

The scene itself deserves a closer look. It is, with the Niobids on the other side, the earliest surviving example of the new compositional technique on a vase, followed at some distance by others, as I have remarked. So it may not yet be generalizing, as they are, what had become a common scheme for such scenes, but be more directly inspired—what will perhaps prove to be a unique occurrence. Moreover, it may reveal a very early stage in addressing the problem of laying out and executing such compositions on vases.

Cleaning the vase for the new Greek vase displays in the Louvre has revealed much more, well described by Martine Denoyelle. After the figures had been laid out and probably painted in all detail, the background

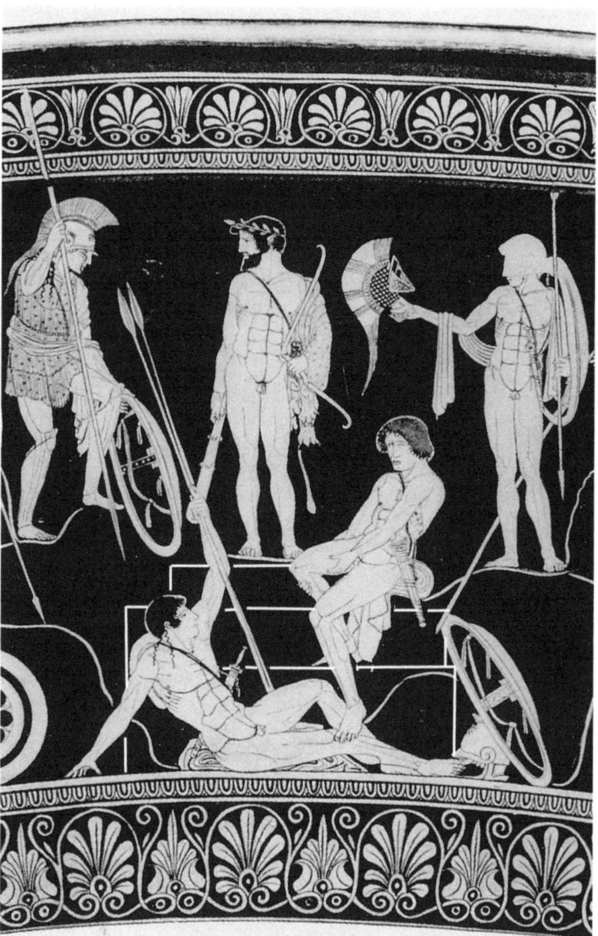

FIGURE 6.3. *Detail of Fig. 6.1, adding the intended but abandoned base for Herakles.*

was filled in; this was the usual mode, it seems. On the background, ground lines for the figures (a novelty for red figure) on both sides of the vase were sketched in fine relief line. The lines were then painted in white, some of them quite disregarding the relief guide lines.[24] But, apart from the ground lines for figures, there were also light relief lines, forming a stepped base on which Herakles stands, and these were not painted over at all (Fig. 6.3 shows them painted on in white) but remained unobserved for two and a half millennia!

So we have in these lines a scheme that in the end, the painter decided to abandon. It had been in his mind to show Herakles on a base, like a statue or victor, but he decided in preference to make all the figures "real." Herakles was at any rate the focus, with his divine patron, the city goddess, to one side, two figures away. His role at Marathon was generally acknowledged; it was in a Herakles sanctuary that the Athenian army was drawn up before the battle, and in another, at Kynosarges in Athens, that the victorious army assembled after a forced march as the Persian fleet arrived off Phaleron.[25] This is a period in which the hero was still the goddess' prime support, with a status that even the "new" Theseus was never quite to attain.[26] If we ask why the painter did not simply in the first place draw an outlined reserved base, such as appear on other red-figure vases, we might answer that he was influenced by its appearance on the wall painting, where it would have been drawn in outline.

Herakles is presented as both the weary victor and the presiding power. The painter decided to favor an image presenting the former, rather than a figure on a base (surely a statue base, as Denoyelle rightly argues), which would have been a less real presence beside his comrades in arms. Yet he is also statuesque for all the painterly and realistic presentation of his pose and features. This is the live counterpart of the Herakles statue with lionskin and bow in the left hand, the club held on the ground with the right, which was devised in the second quarter of the fifth century and which we know in various copyist versions: the Cherchel and the Boston/Oxford statuettes, often associated with Myron and at any rate a near contemporary of the Niobid Painter's vase.[27] Was its original a Marathon memorial or part of one? Whatever the inspiration of the Herakles—a statue, a painting, or the imagination of a gifted vase painter—his head (Fig. 6.2) is a poignant and powerful study of a mortal hero ravaged and distressed by battle.

NOTES

1. Pollitt 1972, 44–45; Pollitt 1976; Pollitt 1992a, 317–320.

2. Stansbury-O'Donnell 1989, 1990.

3. Cousin 2000 is the latest essay of reconstruction and explanation.

4. Cf. Boardman 2000b, 249.

5. Boardman 1984a on one such attempt.

6. Some sort of precursor in Protocorinthian: Payne 1931, 95, n. 1 (= *JHS* 71 [1951] pl. 29:a).

7. Some examples: Boardman 1989a, figs. 12, 13; notably in the work of the Painters of the Woolly Satyrs, and of the Berlin Hydria.

8. Barron 1972.

9. As Boardman 1989a, 168, figs. 329, 330.

10. For the Kimonian monuments and iconography of Athens, see Castriota 1992, ch. 2.

11. Harrison 1972b.

12. I note there is an Amazon Laodoke behind Theseus on the Aison Amazonomachy (Naples, Museo Archeologico Nazionale RC 239; *ARV*² 1174, 6; Simon and Hirmer 1976, pl. 220, upper left).

13. On this recently, see Francis and Vickers 1985a; Schreiner 1988; Develin 1993 (dates about 390 B.C.); Pritchett 1994, ch. 1 (painting = battle of Orneai).

14. Francis and Vickers 1985b. For a full account of the Oinoe problem and the arrangement of the Stoa paintings, see Stansbury-O'Donnell in this volume.

15. I see no reason to doubt Synesius, who had no cause to invent the record, but some scholars (e.g., Pritchett 1994) think the paintings were on the marble walls.

16. The three-panel scheme is well argued in Mazzaro 1978.

17. Cf. Pausanias' problem with one of the Mikon paintings in the Theseion, the product of time and the painter's obscurity: 1.17.2.

18. *Pilos* helmets would identify either Boiotians or Spartans for the likes of Pausanias. Boiotian pilos helmets might indeed resemble Median helmets like that dedicated at Olympia, but Greek art does not show Persian warriors with such helmets.

19. Harrison 1972a.

20. Denoyelle 1997. I am most grateful to her for comment on the vase.

21. The pair then recalls Theseus and Peirithoos in the Underworld, which is where some, notably Barron 1972, place the whole scene, followed by Robertson 1992, 181–182; but for this, and for other suggestions (the Seven against Thebes), too much else is awry, although the Underworld association, as Theseus' immediately precedent home before the battle, is relevant.

22. E. B. Harrison 1972a, 392–394, remarks on the anxious attitudes and features. The furrowed brow appears also on the Dioskouros at the left, being quizzed by the Athenian hero with the snake-blazoned shield. Recall the blind Epizelos in the *Marathon* painting; and Pausanias' description of the family of Antenor painted by Polygnotos at Delphi: "All their faces express the result of calamity" (10.27.4); or the awful Eurynomos baring his teeth (10.28.4). On whether this has anything to do with the Polygnotan *ethos*, see Pollitt 1976. Herakles' expression on the vase is as that of wounded warriors in vase painting, rather than the rather supercilious smile of Riace Warrior A.

23. Unfortunately, the Stoa Poikile itself cannot help us,

although the building so identified has been judged fitted for attached panels. Indeed, the very identity of the excavated Classical stoai of the Agora remains a matter for debate: cf. Robertson 1999 on the Basileios and the Herms.

24. This use of relief lines as guides for ground lines in such compositions seems not to have been followed on later vases but is unique.

25. Hammond 1988, 510–513.

26. The promotion of Theseus in the new Athenian democracy did not, could not, involve positive demotion of Herakles, Athena's first and continuing champion.

27. *LIMC* 4, s.v. Herakles, 751 [O. Palagia]. Some have thought the original to be the work of Onatas, dedicated by the Thasians at Olympia; ibid., p. 788, no. 1266. Or could it have been at Kynosarges?

7

THE PAINTING PROGRAM IN THE STOA POIKILE

MARK D. STANSBURY-O'DONNELL

The fame of the Stoa Poikile is due in part to the group of philosophers who taught there, and became known as the Stoics, and to the suite of paintings found on wooden panels on its walls. Representing the battle of Marathon, the battle of the Amazons and Athenians, and the assembly of the Greek leaders following the sack of Troy, these works as well as some others are frequently mentioned in surviving literary sources.[1] While these testimonials give us a sense of the familiarity of the paintings to the citizens of Athens, they do not provide us with sufficient information to reconstruct the individual paintings in detail, nor do they by themselves provide an unambiguous description of their arrangement and scale within the building.[2]

This situation has led to a variety of proposals reconstructing the original painting program, with quite different results in its overall meaning. The discovery and identification of the Stoa's remains two decades ago, however, has provided an opportunity to reexamine the literary testimony and to suggest a solution to the problem based on a convergence of several lines of evidence. Following a discussion of the arrangement of the paintings in the Stoa and a description of the original painting program and its later modification, I finally would like to offer a few speculations about the career and work of Polygnotos.

THE ARRANGEMENT OF THE PAINTINGS WITHIN THE STOA POIKILE

We can begin to consider the elements of the original painting program of the Stoa Poikile by considering the dimensions and features of the building itself. The Stoa, as revealed by the excavations, was 42.37 m long and 11.51 m deep, with a long colonnade facing south toward the Agora and enclosed rear and side walls (Figs. 7.1, 7.4).[3] Doric columns faced the Agora (Figs. 7.2–3), while Ionic columns supported

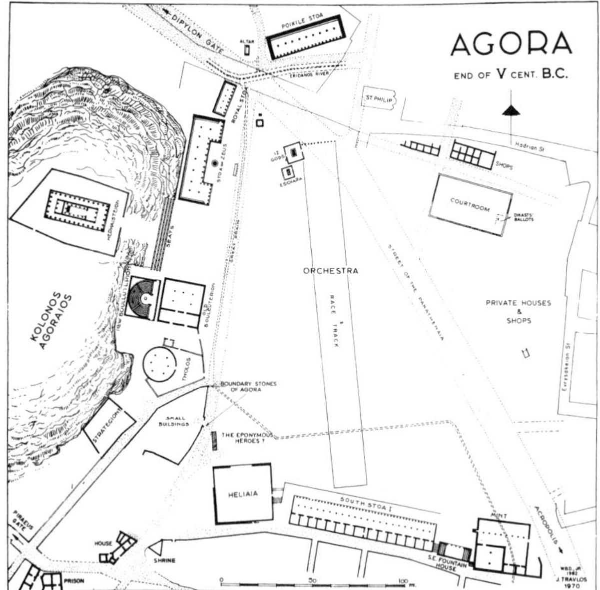

FIGURE 7.1. *Restored plan of the Agora, ca. 400 B.C. Travlos and Dinsmoor, after T. L. Shear 1984, fig. 2. Courtesy American School of Classical Studies at Athens.*

the interior superstructure, a combination of orders that was to reappear shortly in the Periklean buildings on the Akropolis.[4] It is likely that there were nine columns in the center, marking off ten double bays, each about 4 m wide and 10 m deep. The interior height of the Stoa, based on the restored elevation and section, was over 4.5 m.

Leaving aside for the moment the question of the specific date of the structure, it is generally agreed that the Stoa is part of the Kimonian building program in Athens. One distinctive feature of Kimonian patronage appears to have been the use of large-scale paintings on the interiors of buildings.[5] For example, the Theseion, an earlier Kimonian building, featured large interior paintings by at least one of the painters mentioned as working at the Stoa: Mikon. The Anakeion, the sanctuary of the Dioskouroi, also featured paintings by Mikon and by Polygnotos. Given these circumstances, we can presume that at least some painting was intended for the Stoa from the beginning. The placement of a bench across the back (north side) of the Stoa's interior indicates that the back wall was the primary location of the paintings, although no blocks above the foundations have been found in situ to verify whether additional works were also affixed to the side walls.[6] Based on the later testimony of Bishop Synesios, it is probable that these were wooden panel paintings that were removed finally from the Stoa sometime around 400 A.D.[7] As John Boardman discusses in his essay in this volume, this medium means that the paintings could be relocated and that Pausanias' text indicates only where the panels were when he saw them. It is entirely possible that the paintings were rearranged in antiquity. For the purposes of this discussion, however, I will assume that Pausanias saw all the four paintings in their original placement.

The problem in defining and understanding the original painting program begins to appear when one examines the most detailed account of them in the guidebook of Pausanias (1.15.1–3) and attempts to correlate it with the excavated remains. After describing the Hephaisteion and other structures on the northwest side of the Agora, Pausanias reenters the Agora proper and describes the Stoa Poikile (Fig. 7.1). Given his position, it is likely that he entered the building ("the stoa, which is called poikile from its paintings") at the west end of the colonnade. He then goes on to tell us that[8]

> this stoa contains first a scene with the Athenians drawn up against the Lakedaimonians at Oinoë in the territory of Argos. The painting does not show the highpoint of the struggle, nor has the action reached the point where there is already a display of valorous deeds, but rather the battle is just beginning and they are still in the process of coming to grips with one another. On the middle wall the Athenians and Theseus are shown fighting the Amazons. . . . After the Amazons come the Greeks who have taken Troy and also the kings who have gathered together on account of the outrageous act of Aias against Kassandra. The painting includes Aias himself and also Kassandra and other captive women. The final part of the painting represents those who fought at Marathon.

From Pausanias' text it is clear that there are four separate paintings, which he describes in succession as he moves through the building, going most likely from left to right.[9] Placement of the paintings within the building, however, is more difficult. Reconstructions of the paintings' arrangement in the Stoa have included placing all four paintings on the back wall, moving from left to right, placing *Oinoe* and *Marathon* in a symmetrical and pendant relationship with each other.[10]

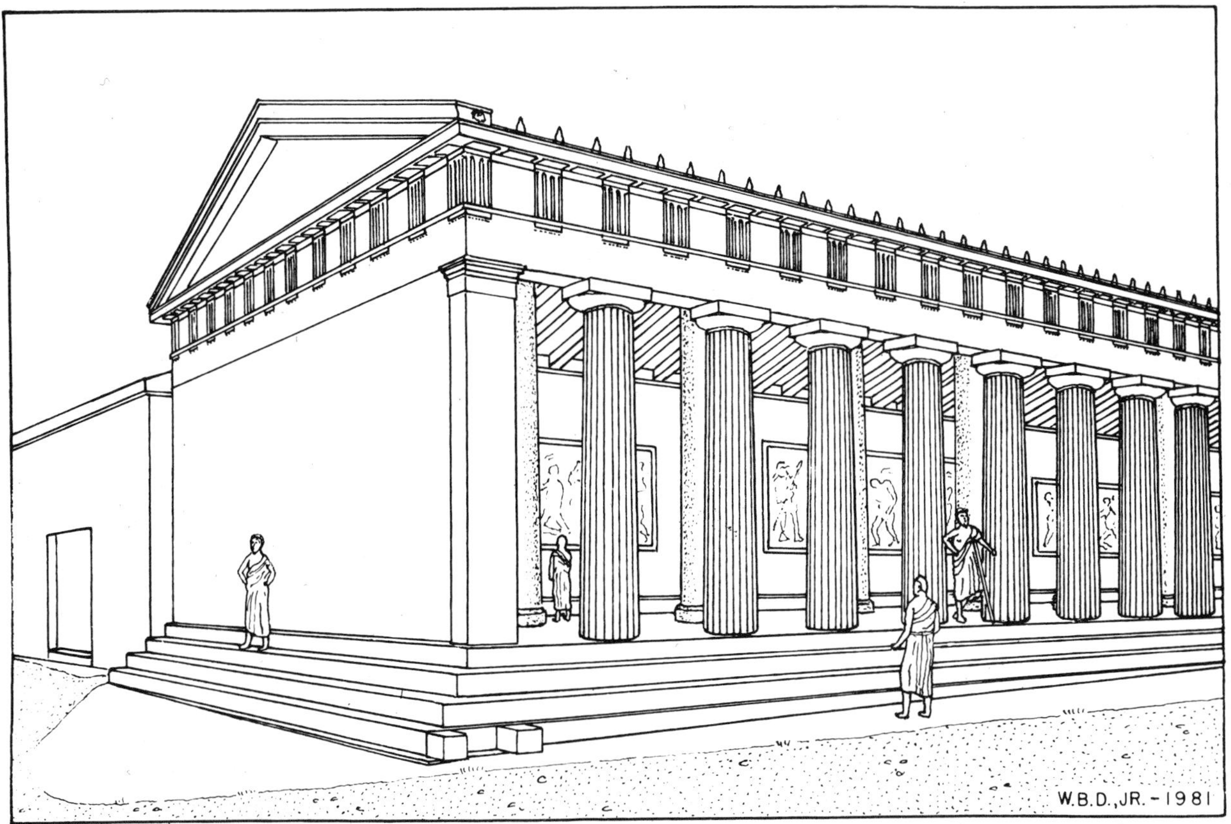

FIGURE 7.2. *Perspective rendering of the Stoa Poikile. Travlos and Dinsmoor, after T. L. Shear 1984, fig. 8. Courtesy American School of Classical Studies at Athens.*

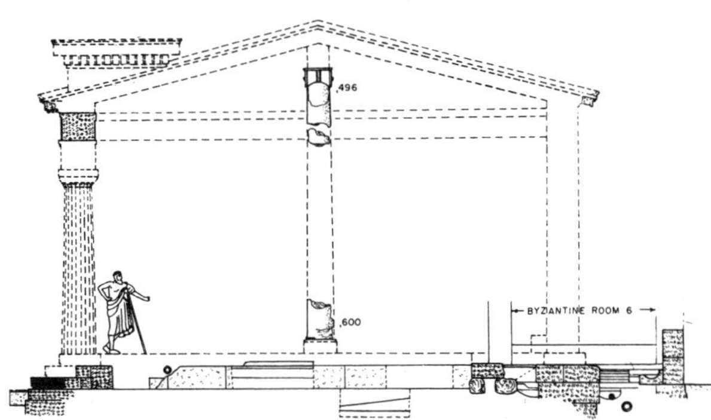

FIGURE 7.3. *Section with restorations of the Stoa Poikile. Travlos and Dinsmoor, after T. L. Shear 1984, fig. 7. Courtesy American School of Classical Studies at Athens.*

Alternatively, the first of the paintings, *Oinoe,* has been placed on the short, western side wall, with the other three paintings along the back wall of the Stoa. A final possibility is to place *Oinoe* and *Marathon* on the end walls, while the others were in the center.

The central issue regarding the arrangement of the paintings concerns the *Battle of Oinoe:* whether or not one believes that Pausanias is correct in his naming of the painting's subject and that the painting's subject fits with the themes of the other paintings.[11] Those who view it as a later addition generally point to the anti-Spartan character of the painting as being inconsistent with Kimonian policies and patronage. Others reinterpret Pausanias' identification of the subject, usually with the idea that the painting is part of the original program and that he has misunderstood the subject matter. Still others accept Pausanias' interpretation but see it as an effort by Kimon and his followers to show their patriotism following his expulsion and the change of Athenian policy toward Sparta.

We will return to these points later, but it suffices to say that a solution based exclusively on the strength or weakness of Pausanias' testimony is not likely since it hinges upon one's belief in his credibility as well as the relative brevity of his description. A consideration of the scale and size of the Stoa paintings in light of the excavations of the building, however, does bring another source of evidence to bear upon the problem,

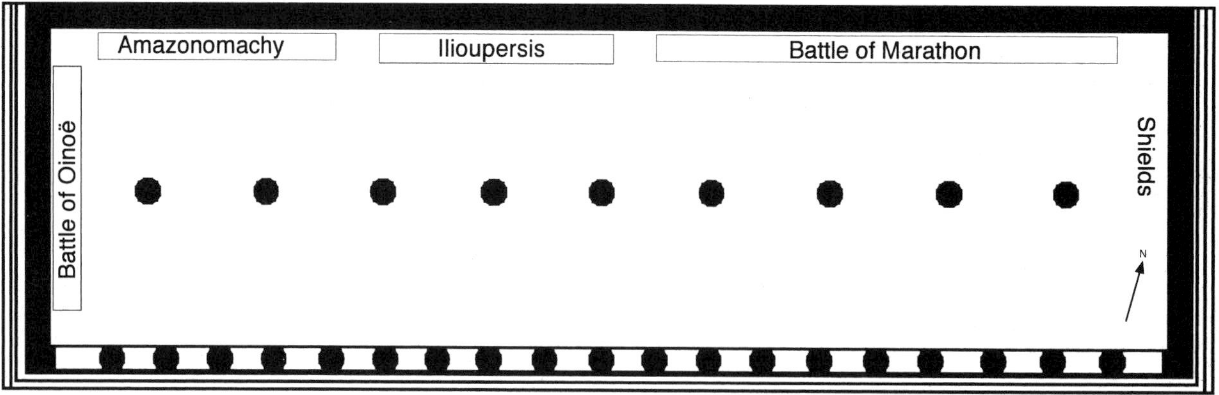

FIGURE 7.4. *Plan of the Stoa Poikile with proposed arrangement of paintings, by M. D. Stansbury-O'Donnell, adapted from Fig. 7.1.*

as do efforts to reconstruct the individual paintings in the Stoa and a second painting of the *Ilioupersis* by Polygnotos in the Lesche of the Knidians at Delphi. A solution based collectively on these sources may provide a way out of the impasse.

To begin, we can assume that Pausanias described both the order of paintings and their compositions in the same direction as he viewed them. While Pausanias does not specifically say on which wall the first painting is, he does state immediately after his description of *Oinoe* that "in the middle of the walls," or on the central wall (ἐν δὲ τῷ μέσῳ τῶν τοίχων, 1.15.2), is the second painting, the *Amazonomachy.* Pausanias' reference to the center or middle (i.e., back) wall at this point would mark a change of direction or reorientation not unlike his description of the pediment of the Temple of Zeus at Olympia, where he uses the figure of Zeus in the middle of the pediment as a point of reference when beginning his description and when returning to it to change direction and describe the other side of the pediment: "An image of Zeus is placed in the center of the pediment, and to the right of Zeus is Oinomaos. . . . To the left of Zeus are Pelops and Hippodameia."[12] Pausanias similarly indicates a change in direction as well as subject in describing the paintings in the *Theseion* at Athens:[13]

> There are paintings here of the Athenians fighting the Amazons. . . . Also painted in the sanctuary of Theseus is the battle of the Lapiths and Centaurs. . . . The painting on the third wall is not very clear to those who have not heard what they tell about it, in part because of its age and in part because Mikon did not depict the whole story.

In the Stoa, he similarly signals a change in location within the building, accompanied by a new painting and a change in subject matter.[14]

Pausanias describes the third painting, the *Ilioupersis,* as simply next to the *Amazonomachy* (ἐπὶ δὲ ταῖς Ἀμαζόσιν, 1.15.2). Later on, in first mentioning *Marathon,* Pausanias states that it is "at the end of the painting" (τελευταῖον δὲ τῆς γραφῆς, 1.15.2). The use of the singular here is consistent with the way in which he refers to the overall painting program at Delphi, but there is no indication of a change in location from the *Amazonomachy* and *Ilioupersis.* Since he associated the *Amazonomachy* specifically with the central wall, and places the *Ilioupersis* and then *Marathon* as next in order, the implication is that *Marathon* is the end of a series of paintings on the middle or back wall that began with the *Amazonomachy.*[15] This being the case, there would be no painting on the right end wall of the Stoa, at least at the time of Pausanias, while the *Battle of Oinoe* would be on the left end wall apart from the other paintings (Fig. 7.4).

A consideration of the size of the individual paintings and their placement within the Stoa lends support to this arrangement. While we have no concrete information on scale and size of the Stoa paintings, Pausanias' brief description of the *Ilioupersis* by Polygnotos is very similar to the central portion of a large painting on the same theme that the artist did at Delphi. The relevant section of the Delphi painting, showing the Greek leaders, Aias, Kassandra, and captives, occupied the east wall of the Lesche, which was about 7.8 m wide.[16] The Lesche reconstruction allows a scale of about 1 m for an individual figure, and a total height of about 3 m above the dado for the painting itself. These dimensions and scale would also work for the Stoa Poikile. Panel paintings about 2.5–3.0 m high would fit with the size of the Stoa, whose back, interior wall was about 4.5 m high. In addition, each bay of the Stoa was about 4 m long, allowing a painting like the Delphi *Ilioupersis* to fit comfortably across two bays of the Stoa. If the paintings were part of the original building program, then it is likely that the size of the paintings fit with the structural articulation of the building. Fitting the *Ilioupersis* across two bays of the Stoa would provide a painting containing about twenty to thirty figures. Such a scale would also work for the *Amazonomachy,* which might have included even more figures depending on the amount of overlapping in the composition. The proportions of such a painting would be about 1:2.5 or 1:3.

To judge from Pausanias' more detailed description of it as well as other testimony, it is not likely that the *Battle of Marathon* was the same size as the other pictures, if its figural scale was even close to that of the other paintings. The *Battle of Marathon* had three distinct portions, one where the battle was just beginning, another where it was fully engaged, and another where the Persians have fled to their ships. The number of figures and objects in this painting is much greater than is suggested for the *Ilioupersis* or *Amazonomachy,* and it is probable, given the scale of the tripartite compositions of Polygnotos in the Lesche at Delphi, that *Marathon* extended easily to twice the width of the *Ilioupersis* and *Amazonomachy* individually. If so, the painting would have been about 16 m long and about 1:6 in proportion, fitting across the equivalent of four bays of the Stoa. Schematic reconstructions of the painting to date have tended to be about 1:2 or 1:3 in proportion, but these diagrams did not attempt to determine the extent of the number and massing of figures.[17] With all the features such as hoplite ranks and single combats reflected in surviving monuments and other elements such as ships, the width of the painting would necessarily be greater than the previous two paintings along the wall.

Considering, therefore, the dimensions and bay size of the Stoa and the possible scale of its paintings, particularly the larger size of the *Marathon* painting, I would place the three paintings on the back wall (*Amazonomachy, Ilioupersis, Marathon*), filling the equivalent of eight of the ten bays of the building (Fig. 7.4). If there were a break equal to one bay (4 m) between the paintings, or if the paintings were set back from the corner about the width of one-half bay (2 m), with the same distance between the paintings themselves, the total spacing would equal 8 m or two full bays, making the length of the painted surface (32 m) and the spacing (8 m) cover the full ten bays of the Stoa (Fig. 7.4).

Of these two potential schemes for spacing, I prefer the latter in that it places the center of the end paintings midway between the interior columns and thus provides an unobstructed view of the midpoint of the paintings when standing directly in front of them inside the Stoa, although this is not a major consideration, given the open quality of the building and the multiple vantage points. A distance of 2 m between the paintings would also provide room for small paintings or other objects to be added at later times, which may account for the placement of other works or trophies that sources mention in the Stoa, such as a portrait of Sophokles or the painting of the *Suppliant Herakleidai.*[18] This arrangement of the paintings would have left Pausanias at the northeast corner of the building when he finished his description of *Marathon.* The Spartan shields that he describes as the last of the major objects in the Stoa could then have fit at the right end of the Stoa, at the opposite end of the building from the painting of the *Battle of Oinoe.*

If *Marathon* were twice as large as the other two paintings, it could well be that two artists collaborated on it. Indeed, the literary testimony mentions both Mikon and Panainos as painters of *Marathon.*[19] Since Mikon is consistently mentioned as the painter of the *Amazonomachy,* it is conceivable that a young Panainos worked with Mikon on the painting of *Marathon,* perhaps as an assistant. Given Mikon's reputation for large-scale action painting, it is entirely possible that Panainos concentrated on the more prominent figural portrayals, such as Miltiades in the *Battle of Marathon,* as Pliny (35.57) states. That Panainos later gained renown working with his brother Pheidias ensured that, unlike other assistants through time, he would not be forgotten at the Stoa.

THE *Battle of Oinoe* AND THE MODIFICATION OF THE STOA'S ORIGINAL PROGRAM

Based on this analysis, I would propose that the original painting program of the Stoa Poikile consisted of three paintings along the back wall of the building: the *Amazonomachy,* the *Ilioupersis,* and the *Battle of Marathon* (Fig. 7.4). The two smaller paintings had mythological subjects that represented Greek triumphs over Asiatic foreigners. The larger painting showed a historical triumph over a similar foe, but at the distance of a generation, it was a subject that should be seen as mythohistorical. The scale of *Marathon* gave it a visual equivalence to the other two paintings, establishing in the minds of viewers a perfect parallel between the actions of their remote ancestors and their more recent forebears. Thus the actual battle of Marathon is promoted as equal to the mythological past and a proper foundation for the current actions of Athens. The choice of subjects also reflects symbolically on the Persian victories of Kimon and his father Miltiades. The latter was triumphant at Marathon and portrayed in the painting, while his son pursued further battles against the Persians in the 470s and 460s.[20] According to this logic, the *Ilioupersis* may have commemorated the sack of Eion in 477/6 and the *Amazonomachy,* the defeat of Dolopes at Skyros in 476/5. Thus the exploits of father and son stand in roughly equal importance for the prominence of Athens in the 460s.

Before considering further implications of this reconstruction of the painting program, we need to account for the *Battle of Oinoe* and where it fits into the history of the Stoa Poikile. This painting poses complications for a number of reasons, beginning with Pausanias as the only testimony for such a battle. By itself, this would raise questions about the reliability of his identification of the subject of the painting as Argive Oinoe, except that he also mentions the battle a second time and in a different context in describing the Argive dedication at Delphi from the spoils of the same battle (10.10.3–5). This would imply that Argos and Athens were allies in the battle, which leads some to place the battle, if it occurred, during the first phase of the war (461–452) in which the two states were allied against the Spartans, and Athens was ruled by the opponents of Kimon. This timing would therefore follow Kimon's exile from Athens in 461, so that the placement of the painting in the Stoa could be seen either as a repudiation of Kimon's more pro-Spartan policies or as Kimon's profession of Athenian loyalty during exile.[21]

That the *Oinoe* painting dates from the 450s, however, raises several problems. As many scholars have noted, it would be unprecedented to depict a contemporary battle immediately after the fact. Even the battle of Marathon waited well over twenty years and the death of some of the key participants before it became acceptable as a subject, and the special significance of that battle would argue against an even quicker transition from recent events to mythohistory for the battle of Oinoe.

Some scholars would get around this difficulty of the painting's subject and its consequences for dating by reinterpreting Pausanias' mysterious battle. Jeffery, for example, proposes that the *Oinoe* picture is actually the Athenian expedition led by Theseus to recover the Argive heroes killed before Thebes, and indeed Pausanias mentions elsewhere that the Athenians marched by Oinoe on their way to Thebes.[22] In some versions of the story, a truce was negotiated before the battle became fully engaged, and this might fit the general moment described by Pausanias for the *Oinoe* painting. This action was also, as Jeffery points out, one of the five glories of Athens described by Herodotos (9.26–28), the others being Marathon, Troy, the Amazonomachy, and the Suppliant Herakleidai. As mentioned earlier, there is also testimony about the presence of a painting on the last subject also in the Stoa Poikile, thus making *Oinoe/Rescue of the Argive Heroes* an integral part of the overall program for the Stoa in Jeffery's proposal.

The problem with this interpretation is that the Athenians should be confronting Thebans, and not Spartans, in the painting of *Oinoe.* Further, the Athenians only passed through Oinoe but did not face the Thebans there. The overall program of the five glories also faces difficulties in that the testimony for the *Suppliant Herakleidai* is meager compared to that for the other three main paintings. The testimony, from the scholia to Aristophanes' *Ploutos,* identifies the painter as Pamphilos and states that it was in "the stoa of the

Athenians."[23] Pamphilos, as Wycherley points out, was active in the fourth century, and it is not certain that the painting was in the Stoa Poikile and not another stoa. Such a painting may well have existed in Athens, but the later dating would at least imply that it was not part of the original program, even if it were in the Stoa Poikile. Perhaps the scholiast's placement of the painting of the *Herakleidai* in a stoa is the result of confusion with the visually similar representation of the *Ilioupersis* at the Stoa Poikile.[24] Even if it were in the Stoa Poikile and the testimony were reliable, the painting would then date to the fourth century B.C. and would be gone by Pausanias' time. On the whole, there do not seem to be sufficient grounds for developing either *Oinoe* or the *Suppliant Herakleidai* as part of the original program of the Stoa Poikile, representing the five glories of Athens.

Francis and Vickers made a second attempt to reinterpret the *Battle of Oinoe* and to place it into the context of the original painting program. They proposed that Pausanias switched Argive Oinoe for Marathonian Oinoe and that the picture actually represents the arrival of the Plataians the night before the battle of Marathon.[25] With this emendation, they would make all four paintings part of the original program along the back wall of the Stoa, with the two paintings concerning the battle of Marathon at the ends and the mythological paintings in the center. This creates a symmetry and balance visually as well as thematically, using four roughly equal paintings. The proposal also removes the difficulty caused by the anti-Spartan character of Argive *Oinoe* in a Kimonian building program.[26] In a Kimonian building project, a painting that depicted Athenians and Spartans about to do battle would be unlikely, as would a depiction of a contemporary event that never, like Marathon, assumed heroic proportions in the succeeding generation.

The difficulties with the theory of Marathonian Oinoe, however, are several. First, Pausanias seems to place *Oinoe* on a different wall than the other paintings, a position that a consideration of the dimensions and articulation of the Stoa and the scale of the three other paintings confirms. Second, it would be highly unusual in monumental painting to have two discrete paintings from the same story. If the paintings did constitute a cyclical narrative (and the painting of *Marathon* itself is already quite sophisticated in its coordination of space and time and the viewer's position), then the paintings would have been more sensibly connected by being placed next to each other to form a series, like multiscene narratives on metopes.[27] Such a placement (*Marathonian Oinoe/Marathon//Amazonomachy/Ilioupersis*) would still maintain the principles of balance and symmetry but would develop the narrative more clearly. As it is, Pausanias himself did not see any connection between *Oinoe* and *Marathon.* If there were a connection, then the separation of the paintings was such an impediment to the viewer (Pausanias) that it was completely ineffective or misleading. This suggests that the two paintings were not intended to be connected directly as a cyclical narrative.

Third, Pausanias identifies the soldiers in *Oinoe* as Lakedaimonians and Athenians and states that they are coming into confrontation with one another. Whether this identification was the result of an inscription or a visual index such as their armor is unknown, but Pausanias expresses no doubt about the identity of the participants. Further, the action that Pausanias describes leaves little room for considering the image as showing a meeting of allies rather than foes. Ultimately, the subject matter does not cause Pausanias any trouble, and so one must assume his explanation, even if it is his own without the aid of an inscription or guide, conforms to what he saw. Presumably Plataians would have been wearing Boiotian armor, as pseudo-Demosthenes indicates in his reference to the *Battle of Marathon:* "And even now the painting in the Poikile Stoa displays memorials of their valor. They are depicted coming to your aid promptly, each with such speed as he can—they are the men with the Boeotian hats."[28] Pausanias also mentions the Plataians rushing to battle in his description of *Marathon:* "The final part of the painting represents those who fought at Marathon. The Boeotians who inhabit Plataea and the Attic force are coming to grips with the barbarians. In this section the struggle is an equal match."[29] If the figures in the *Oinoe* painting had been wearing Boiotian armor, it would seem likely that Pausanias would comment on the contradiction with his identification of the figures as Spartans.

Despite these difficulties, I agree with Francis and Vickers that it is most likely that the original program of the Stoa was designed with balance and symmetry. Placing *Oinoe* on a side wall destroys this symmetry and suggests that it was not part of the original painting program. Clearly, however, it was a large-scale painting, and its placement in the Stoa must have been a significant public decision; certainly it seemed to Pausanias to fit with the overall painting program of the building.[30] The same principles of balance and symmetry in the original program should, therefore, apply to *Oinoe.* Rather than simply discarding the painting if it were not part of the original program, one must find a context in which it would be added to the Stoa and in which it would be balanced by other new programmatic elements.

J. G. Taylor has recently dealt with these problems and the tension between accepting and emending Pausanias.[31] He points out that the label "Oinoe" did not bother Pausanias, but there is a problem in connecting it with the battle at Argive Oinoe that Pausanias mentions in his description of the Argive monument to the battle at Delphi. If this battle were part of the Argive-Athenian alliance against Sparta during the first war, why then are the Argive forces missing from the painting of *Oinoe*? The Plataian allies are included in *Marathon,* and so it is reasonable to expect that the Argive allies would have been included in *Oinoe.* Taylor's suggestion is that neither the painting nor its label, if any, specified which Oinoe is represented in the picture and that Pausanias, being already familiar with the major monument for the battle of that name with the same Spartan foes at Delphi, has himself supplied the modifier "Argive" to guide his reader. If so, then it is possible that the painting does represent a battle of Oinoe between Spartans and Athenians but not necessarily at Argive Oinoe. Taylor proposed that the painting represented the battle at Oinoe on the Boiotian/Attic border in 431 at the beginning of the Archidamian War. The painting would have been done in conjunction with the installation of the shields from the Athenian victories during the Archidamian War at Sphakteria and Skione. This would put the date of the painting between 425 and 421, the dates of those two battles, and 411, when Oinoe was lost.[32]

The reconstruction of the Stoa's program proposed here would support Taylor's argument in that the painting of *Oinoe* on the west wall of the Stoa would stand as a pendant to the shield trophies from the battles on the eastern side and would show the initial encounter of the Archidamian War against the tangible results of its conclusion. This arrangement would maintain the overall symmetry of the Stoa's art program but would add a new layer, placed on the end walls, in front of the original program showing the mythological battles with Trojans and Amazons and the mythohistorical battles with the Persians. This addition to the program would continue to show Athens' superiority, now over a Hellenic foe, and justification for her policies during the Peloponnesian War as a continuation of the earlier struggles and triumphs of myth and mythohistory.

The victory at Sphakteria actually marked a change in military strategy for Athens, one that cemented the position of Kleon as a leader of Athens.[33] By placing the trophies from that victory opposite the initial successful defense of Athens under Perikles during the first year of the war, the new program would help to portray Kleon's decisions as consistent with the goals of Perikles, who might well have altered Athens' strategy as the war dragged on in the early 420s, had he lived. Since the initial battle at Oinoe was not so much a defeat of the Spartans as a successful defense against them, the less dramatic character of the painting described by Pausanias would fit generally the historical circumstances of the battle.

Taylor's hypothesis has much to recommend it and requires the least amount of reinterpretation of Pausanias and other sources about the Stoa and its construction. Within the context of the Stoa's organization, it also provides a thematic connection between the painting of *Oinoe* and the shields and links their placement in the Stoa as part of a coordinated change to that building's program. There is still the problem of representing such a recent historical battle, but as Stähler and Krumeich point out, the relative rarity of historical painting in the fifth century means that there is no consistent "rule" about it.[34] Indeed, linking the painting to the victory at Sphakteria would provide the momentum that might have been necessary to stimulate commissioning such a work as *Oinoe,* which would have been about a decade in the past by the time it was commemorated. A recent paper by Peter Schultz would see another contemporary example of the use of a historical subject, Demosthenes' victory over the Ambrakiots in 426, on the frieze of the Temple of Athena Nike.[35]

Arguing also for a later dating for the *Oinoe* painting, in the late 420s or early 410s, is that the painter of the work is not recorded in any literary testimony.[36] There is ample testimony for the attribution of the three other paintings to Mikon, Polygnotos, and Panainos, but there exists no trace of an artist for the painting of *Oinoe*. How the information for the work of the three named artists was initially preserved, whether in the Stoa itself or elsewhere, is not known, but if *Oinoe* were part of the original program, it would be reasonable to expect that the information about its painter would have survived along with the other attributions. That only Pausanias of all our sources even records the painting, and only as part of a systematic description of the whole Stoa, would suggest that the *Oinoe* painting came to hold a minor and relatively unimportant place in the imagination of Athenian viewers and was not equivalent to the other three paintings. Placement on a side wall would contribute physically and visually to this relatively minor status, as would Athens' ultimate loss of Oinoe and the Peloponnesian War, making the painting and shields somewhat hollow as a boast.

THE STOA POIKILE AND THE CAREER OF POLYGNOTOS

Placing the *Battle of Oinoe* as part of a later programmatic change to the Stoa brings us back to the question of the date of the Stoa and its original program, a question that also bears on speculation about the chronology of the career of Polygnotos. The construction of the structure, according to the dating of pottery sherds found in the excavation, falls in the decade between 470 and 460, a period that is consistent with the style of the architectural carving.[37] Literary sources confirm this dating by telling us that Peisianax, brother-in-law to Kimon, paid for the construction of the Stoa and that the building was also known as the Peisianakteos in a number of sources.[38] Since Kimon was exiled from Athens in 462/1, it is likely that the building was finished or mostly finished by that time, given the close association of its funder Peisianax with Kimon. Undoubtedly, the building was part of the Kimonian propaganda program, as were the earlier Theseion with its paintings and other structures, and was possibly paid for with proceeds from the Persian campaigns.[39] Given the pattern of Kimonian decoration of buildings, the three paintings within the building would be part of the original building program and its functions. This would make the date of the paintings fall into the later 460s.[40]

The dating is important for speculating on the career of Polygnotos, and particularly the paintings that he did in the Lesche at Delphi. The artist represented the *Ilioupersis* as part of both programs, and by all accounts, the two paintings were very similar in their composition, mood, and subjects. It would be logical to assume that the paintings were close to one another in date, but whether Delphi or the Stoa version came first is uncertain from the available evidence. Robert Kebric would date the Delphi paintings to the early 460s, no later than 468 or 467, on two grounds.[41] First, the *Ilioupersis* was identified by an epigram attributed to Simonides. The poet is traditionally said to have died in 468, and so the epigram would be one of the last works of his career. Kebric also states that the Knidians built the Lesche with proceeds from the victory over the Persians at Eurymedon. Kebric and some others would place the battle in 469, so that the Knidians could have begun work on the Lesche in the following year and have commissioned the epigram before Simonides died.

More recently, Ernst Badian has argued persuasively and in great detail that the battle of Eurymedon fits best into the year 466.[42] If so, this would be too late for an epigram by Simonides, at least with the traditional dates of the poet.[43] In a discussion of the epigram, Page proposes that Simonides was not the author of the epigram and that it may have been composed by Polygnotos himself.[44] Given the doubts about the dating of Eurymedon and the authorship of Simonides, it seems that there is not a compelling reason to date the Lesche paintings before 465. It is also probable that funds for the Stoa came from the same general source as the Lesche, and that the period of the later 460s would be one that favored undertaking a number of building projects.[45]

Given Polygnotos' close associations with Kimon, it would make more sense that the painter was employed first in Athens on the Stoa during Kimon's ascendancy. It is possible that both the Lesche and the Stoa were completed before Kimon was expelled in 461, but it is equally possible that Polygnotos left Athens when his patron did and sought projects elsewhere. If so, the Lesche would follow the Stoa paintings, perhaps in 460 or shortly thereafter. We do know that Polygnotos later returned to his home in Thasos by the early 440s, and so there seems to be no substantial reason to associate the painter directly with Athens during the decade of the 450s.[46] During this time, he may well have worked outside Athens, perhaps at the sanctuary of Athena at Plataia. This building, constructed with funds from the spoils of the victory at Marathon in 490, had a statue of Athena made by Pheidias as well as a painting of Odysseus and the Suitors by Polygnotos in its pronaos.[47]

There is no conclusive proof about the sequence of the Stoa and the Lesche paintings, but I would like to speculate about the consequences for the career and development of Polygnotos by placing the Lesche paintings after the Stoa, around 460 or shortly thereafter. It should be noted first that work on the Stoa may already have been under way when the Athenians turned their attention to Thasos in 465. That island, following the victory at Eurymedon, had quarreled with Athens over the control of trade and mining. Kimon defeated the Thasian navy and besieged the island, which surrendered in the third year of the campaign, probably in 463.[48] While being granted Athenian citizenship and, notably, doing the painting in the Stoa for no fee, Polygnotos does not seem to have abandoned his connections with his homeland and held office there later in the 440s.

Just what Polygnotos' sentiments were about the subjugation of Thasos are unknown, and it is not likely that he would have jeopardized his position in Athens simply to protest an accomplished fact. Given his close associations with Kimon, including rumored affairs with his sister Elpinike, there was undoubtedly a mixture of feelings on the matter. Once Kimon was expelled from Athens, however, there would be less conflict for Polygnotos, and leaving for Delphi to execute a commission could well have been a graceful exit for him from a less than favorable political climate.

What is of great interest in thinking about politics and art is to consider the Delphi paintings in the context of the post-Eurymedon period and how an artist such as Polygnotos might have reflected upon the situation in his art. As Kebric, Castriota, and others have pointed out, there are references to Athens in the Lesche paintings and likely in the Stoa *Ilioupersis* as well.[49] For example, in the Lesche *Ilioupersis,* Polygnotos included the figure of Theseus' son Demophon, who was awaiting the decision about his grandmother Aithra's freedom. Theseus' other son Akamas is shown in the center section of the painting among the Greek leaders witnessing the oath of Aias. It is likely that the Stoa *Ilioupersis* also featured Akamas and Demophon among the Greek leaders, but the only figures who are specifically named in any of our sources are Aias, Kassandra, and Laodike.[50] In the Delphi *Nekyia,* Polygnotos also painted Theseus and Peirithoös sitting on chairs. As reconstructed from Pausanias' descriptions, Theseus and Demophon are located toward the corners of the north wall of the Lesche, about equidistant from the center of the wall (Fig. 7.5).[51] This placement in a pendant relationship surely links them in the minds of viewers and brings forth three generations of Athens' leading family. Kebric would see their inclusion at Delphi as fundamental to the pro-Athenian leanings of the Lesche's painting program.[52]

Given the relatively minor role of Athenians in the Trojan war, the prominent inclusion of the sons of Theseus in artistic representations of Troy is usually seen as promoting the mythical importance of Athens as a parallel to its contemporary role in Greek events. Certainly the inclusion in the Lesche *Ilioupersis* of Theseus' other son, Akamas, among the Greek leaders judging Aias places Athens and its heroes among the elite of Greek cities.[53] If Akamas and Demophon were also included in the Stoa *Ilioupersis,* the intent would be clear and straightforward. As Castriota proposes, we would have a scene of the Greek leaders dealing with

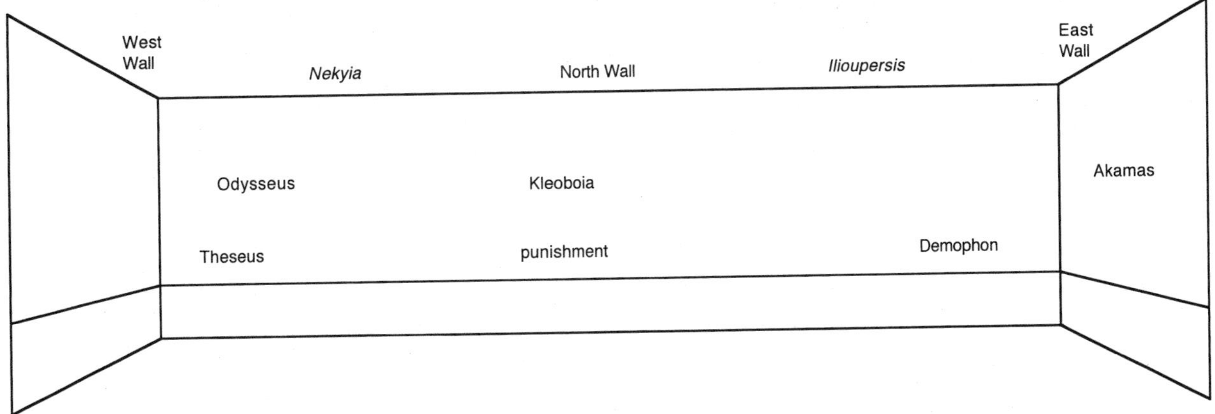

FIGURE 7.5. *Plan of the arrangement of figures along the north wall of the Lesche of the Knidians at Delphi, by M. D. Stansbury-O'Donnell.*

the renegade Aias, emphasizing their virtue in punishing wrongdoing while at the same time highlighting through the captive Trojan women the Greek triumph over Trojan hubris.[54]

However, the description of these figures at Delphi by Pausanias is noteworthy for conveying a sense of their *pathos:*[55]

> After Helen comes the mother of Theseus with her hair shorn and Demophon, one of the sons of Theseus, who, I gather from his attitude, is trying to determine whether it will be possible for him to save Aithra.

From Pausanias' subsequent recounting of the story of Aithra's rescue, it seems that in the painting Eurybates is presenting a petition from Agamemnon to Helen, who is to make the decision regarding Aithra's fate. Demophon's doubt about the outcome and Helen's command of the situation, now that she has returned to her role as queen of Sparta, paints a very different picture from that of Athenian prominence. Indeed, in this light and with a date of 460 or after, the Delphi painting may rather reflect the struggles of the first war between Athens and Sparta. It certainly does not seem to reflect Athenian self-assuredness.

The same undercurrents can also be seen in the representation of Theseus in the Lesche. While Odysseus states in the *Odyssey* that he did not have time to see the glorious hero Theseus, Polygnotos has made room for Theseus and Peirithoös in the painting, directly below Odysseus sacrificing. Again, it is Pausanias' description of pathos that is striking about the figures:[56]

> Lower down than Odysseus are Theseus and Peirithoös seated on chairs; the former holds both Peirithoös's sword and his own, while Peirithoös stares at the swords. And you would guess that he was angry with the swords because they were useless and of no avail in their adventures.

While Peirithoös is specifically described as being angry, his companion must at the very least be passive in expression, if not saddened or angry himself.[57] Pausanias goes on to explain the reason for their situation in the Underworld: that Theseus had accompanied Peirithoös to take Persephone as the latter's bride. Given that Kimon had triumphantly returned the bones of Theseus to Athens and commissioned the Theseion and its paintings, it is interesting that at Delphi Polygnotos showed Theseus in a failed adventure, imprisoned in the Underworld.[58]

Considering the Lesche paintings in the light of the siege of Thasos, we can turn to another figure that Polygnotos included in the *Nekyia.* At the very beginning of the painting, on the boat of Charon, is the figure of Kleoboia. Pausanias says that she is still a virgin and that she "holds a chest on her knees of the type they usually make for Demeter."[59] Pausanias goes on to tell us that "they say that Kleoboia first brought the rites of Demeter from Paros to Thasos."

Given Polygnotos' continued connection with Thasos, it is understandable that he would include a reference to his homeland in such a large composition. In contrast to Theseus and Peirithoös, however, Kleoboia is remembered for a pious act and is shown as a *kore* and devotee of Demeter. The other figure in the boat, the *ephebe* Tellis, was the grandfather of Archilochos, who like Kleoboia came from Paros but also lived part of his life on Thasos. Thus, in the very center of the wall and at the beginning of the *Nekyia,* we see two figures who have Thasian connections set equidistant from the Athenian contingent (Fig. 7.5).

Given this balance, it is also noteworthy that directly below Kleoboia and Tellis is a father choking his son, who had treated the father unjustly. The figures resemble those of *dike* and *adikia* on the Chest of Kypselos, and the theme of punishment continues in a second group next to the pair of men. Here "is a man who is receiving his punishment for having robbed sanctuaries."[60] This reflects on the judgment made of Aias in the center of the *Ilioupersis* for violating the sanctuary of Athena, but it is also interesting by being placed vertically in conjunction with Kleoboia. At the top of this axis we have figures who lived pious lives, while at the bottom there is the opposite. On the same lower level, below the sacrifice of Odysseus, we see the entrapped Theseus and Peirithoös. Helen and Aithra with Demophon are also on this same lower level. This horizontal alignment of impiety, hubris, or impotence on the one hand (Theseus, Peirithoös, men being punished, Demophon and Aithra) and pious figures on the other hand (Odysseus, Kleoboia, Tellis), and the vertical alignment of piety over impiety, establish a correlation of impiety and injustice with some of the Athenian elements of the paintings, and of piety and justice with the Thasian elements.

This is admittedly quite speculative, and it would be foolish to go so far as to say that Polygnotos was simply equating Athens with wrong and Thasos with right. It is also too extreme to consider Athens as wrong and Sparta, represented by Helen, as being right, as Charles Dugas proposed in considering the paintings in light of the first war between Athens and Sparta.[61] Akamas, for example, is among the Greek leaders and, more important, is on the same side as Odysseus, a group thought to represent those Greek leaders who favored punishing Aias. This group is also on the top of a vertical axis, on the same level as Kleoboia and Odysseus in the *Nekyia.* Akamas is also on the opposite side of the altar from Agamemnon and Menelaos, who as leaders failed to punish Aias for his actions against Athena.[62] Furthermore, the figures of wounded Trojans above Aithra and Demophon do not offer a pious contrast to Aithra and Demophon, and Demophon's action does not appear impious but only uncertain or hesitant. At the same time, however, Aithra had been enslaved to Helen as punishment by the Dioskouroi for Theseus' attempted abduction of Helen. By placing the recovery of Aithra next to Helen enthroned as the mistress of the household, the painting reminds us of the circumstances of her enslavement through the failed actions of her son and her eventual redemption by her grandsons.

I believe that the program formulated by Polygnotos at Delphi is both subtle and multivalent. Theseus is a hero and deserves respect; he also acted impiously or foolishly in the quests for both Persephone and Helen. By making Peirithoös the angry figure and instigator in the *Nekyia,* Polygnotos avoids giving Theseus primary blame but still makes him endure punishment. Theseus remains heroic but flawed. Similarly, Athens under Kimon can be seen as heroic in pursuing the war against the Persians and in the victory at Eurymedon. It can also be seen as stepping away from that ideal in turning on Thasos and, post-Kimon, in fighting the war against the Spartans. Nor does the painting glorify Sparta, since Menelaos is opposed to Odysseus and Akamas in the punishment of Aias. Helen is hardly a paragon of virtue in most mythological accounts, and a Greek male viewer would not likely have seen the authority of women under the Spartan model as an ideal situation.

Casting Greek heroes in such an ambivalent and multivalent light is not unprecedented. The Greeks on the Naples hydria by the Kleophrades Painter are shown in a distinctly unflattering light.[63] The exception here is the recovery of Aithra by Demophon and Akamas at the end of the composition, a recovery and survival matched by Aineias at the other end of the frieze. I would like to believe that this vase painting represents a sympathetic bond between the painter and the Trojans, who endured the sack of their city as did the Athenians in 480 and the Milesians in 494. The absence of Helen in this Ilioupersis removes the difficult reminder of how Aithra ended up at Troy in the first place.

Edith Hall has examined in more detail such examples of "barbaric Greeks" in tragedy, including the army of the Seven before Thebes. As she comments,[64]

> When the playwrights represent mythical Hellenes behaving like barbarians they are not necessarily referring to any historical individual, but to the abstract principle . . . any behaviour suggesting that someone was breaking the "laws of Hellas," transgressing their socially authorized role, or was in danger of committing hubris, could now be defined as "not Greek."

As she warns, this does not mean that every portrayal of a Greek tyrant was intended as negative: "The presence of any one item in the poets' 'vocabulary of barbarism' is by no means always significant: cumulatively, however, the implications become unmistakable."[65]

In the case of Polygnotos' Lesche paintings, there are multiple indications of barbaric behavior, particularly regarding impiety and hubris, that suggest Polygnotos was ambivalent about Athenian actions generally. Polygnotos was noted as the premier painter of *ethos* in Classical Greek art, and if we think of his art in tragic terms, it is reasonable to think of his portrayals as having the depth and dimension that the characters of Aischylos have, heroic but flawed, making bad decisions that prove to be their undoing.[66] These are still figures who are greater than the average mortal but whose legacy is clouded or tainted by their hubris. In this light, Polygnotos may have reflected on the fortunes of Kimon his patron, who brought Athens to glory but also led it to subjugate Greek city-states, who was eventually expelled from Athens, and who saw Athenian policy take an even more belligerent stand toward Sparta and other Greek states. In the context of the creation of an Athenian empire at the expense of fellow Greeks, the warning of the dangers of barbaric behavior among the Greeks is significant.

NOTES

I would like to express my deepest thanks and appreciation to Jerry Pollitt, who has been my model as both scholar and teacher. His encouragement and support for my work as a graduate student on Polygnotos is only one example of his generosity that I hope to emulate in my career. I would like to thank Kerri Cox, editor of *Hesperia,* for permission to reproduce drawings of the Stoa originally published in that journal.

1. Throughout this article I have italicized the names of the paintings in the Stoa and the Lesche of the Knidians at Delphi, while referring to the historical or mythological events that they represent in Roman type. For a reconstruction of the *Battle of Marathon,* see Robert 1895. Later scholars have preferred a more schematic reconstruction of the *Marathon* composition; see Harrison 1972b; Hölscher 1973, 50–68, Taf. 5; and Stansbury-O'Donnell 1999, 142–144, fig. 62. For a reconstruction of the *Ilioupersis,* see Castriota 1992, 128–130, fig. 12.

2. For a collection of the testimonia, see Wycherley 1957, 31–45.

3. On the excavation of the Stoa, see T. L. Shear 1984, 1–19 and Camp 1986, 64–72. For the interior dimensions, see Shear 1984, 17, n. 24, where he calculates the length as either 42.37 m or 50.362 m, depending on the number of interior columns (9 or 11) that the building had. The axial spacing of columns was 3.996 m. The depth of the building was 11.51 m; the interior depth is derived from Shear, fig. 7.

4. T. L. Shear 1984, 12. See also Coulton 1976, 40–41.

5. Pemberton 1989, 187.

6. T. L. Shear 1984, 18–19. Shear (9, n. 8) states that earlier fragments found in excavations and identified as coming from the Stoa Poikile (see Meritt 1970) cannot be linked to the new discoveries.

7. The evidence for painted panels comes from the letters of Synesios of Cyrene (ca. 370–413), who states (*Epistles* 35) that the Stoa "is no longer poikile, however, because the Proconsul took away the boards"; see Pollitt 1990a, 144–145, and Wycherley 1957, 43–44.

8. Pollitt 1990a, 143–144.

9. For the left to right order of the paintings, see Pfuhl 1923, 660; Boersma 1970, 56; Francis and Vickers 1985b, 106; Stähler 1992, 32. *Contra:* Harrison 1972b, 364, n. 73.

10. For the four paintings along the back wall, see Bollansée 1981, 93; Francis and Vickers 1985b, 106–108, 112; and Francis 1990, 87–88, fig. 32, followed by Krumeich 1997, 103. For placing *Oinoe* on an end wall and the other three paintings along the back, see Wycherley 1957, 40; Boersma 1970, 56; Hölscher 1973, 75 (if *Oinoe* were an addition by Kimon's

allies). For placing *Oinoe* and *Marathon* on the ends, see Pfuhl 1923, 660; Harrison 1972b, 364, n. 73 (where the order of paintings is also right to left); Hölscher 1973, 76 (if *Oinoe* were part of the original program).

11. For the painting as a mythological rendering of the Athenian expedition to retrieve the bodies of the Argive dead following the expedition of the Seven against Thebes, see Jeffery 1965, 50–51. Francis and Vickers (1985b, 101), followed by Castriota (1992, 78–79), identify Oinoe as Marathonian rather than Argive, making the subject the arrival of the Plataians at Marathon. On the Kimonian interpretation, see Hölscher 1973, 75–76. Some scholars speculate instead that the painting might be a later addition to the Stoa; see Jeffery 1965, 42; Boersma 1970, 56; Meiggs 1972, 471–472; Taylor 1998, 238.

12. Paus. 5.10.6–7; tr. Pollitt 1990a, 186. One might also point to the paintings by Panainos on the screen around the statue of Zeus at Olympia: "At Olympia there are fences constructed like walls which serve as barriers. Of these fences the section which is opposite the door is painted with a glaze of blue enamel; the rest of them have paintings by Panainos." See Paus. 5.11.5; tr. Pollitt 1990a, 60.

13. Paus. 1.17.2; tr. Pollitt 1990a, 142.

14. Pausanias does not signal the corners in his description of the Lesche, although there is internal evidence consistent with marking the corners in the reconstruction; see Stansbury-O'Donnell 1989, 207, 210–211; Stansbury-O'Donnell 1990, 224, 226. I would suggest that he does not do so there because there is no physical break in the painting surface, as there would be with the wooden panels of the Stoa, and certainly no change in artist or in subject matter.

15. Pausanias states at the beginning that the Stoa is called "painted because of its pictures" (ἣν Ποικίλην ὀνομάζουσιν ἀπὸ τῶν γραφῶν, 1.15.1), using the plural form. He does the same thing before describing the interior of the Lesche at Delphi, saying that it contains the "paintings of Polygnotos" (γραφὰς ἔχον τῶν Πολυγνώτου, 10.25.1). Further on, however, he refers to the two murals of the Lesche as "the whole portion of the painting to your right" (τὸ μὲν σύμπαν τὸ ἐν δεξιᾷ τῆς γραφῆς, 10.25.2) and "the other part of the painting, the part on the left-hand side" (τὸ δὲ ἕτερον μέρος τῆς γραφῆς τὸ ἐξ ἀριστερᾶς χειρός, 10.28.1); see Pollitt 1990a, 131, 133; Wycherley 1957, 40.

16. For details of the Delphi painting reconstruction, see Stansbury-O'Donnell 1989, esp. 204, 207–211. For a reconstruction of the Stoa *Ilioupersis,* see Castriota 1992, 127–130, fig. 11.

17. For schematic reconstructions, see above, n. 2. Harrison also includes figures of the monuments that may reproduce sections of *Marathon.* On the rhetorical qualities and the tripartite structure of *Marathon,* see S. P. Morris 1992, 314–315.

18. There is literary testimony about other paintings in the Stoa. A scholiast to Ar. *Plut.* 385, mentions a painting of the Herakleidai by Pamphilos ("in the stoa of the Athenians"; see Wycherley 1957, 34, no. 58). The *Life of Sophokles* mentions a portrait of Sophokles with a lyre in the Stoa Poikile; see Wycherley 42, no. 90. See also the general comments in Wycherley 31. It is possible that smaller paintings may also have been hung in the Stoa, perhaps between the larger mythohistorical paintings that Pausanias describes or on the end walls.

19. On Mikon and Panainos as painters of *Marathon,* see Wycherley 1957, 31, and esp. 45, n. 3. Robertson (1975, 244) speculates that the painting may have been started by Mikon but left incomplete with Kimon's ostracism and later completed by Panainos. See also Boardman's essay in this volume on the question.

20. Jeffery 1965, 45–46; see also Castriota 1992, 76–78.

21. On Athenian loyalty, see Hölscher 1973, 76.

22. Jeffery 1965, 47–51. On Herodotos and the five glories, see also S. P. Morris 1992, 314.

23. See Wycherley 1957, 34–35, no. 58; Jeffery 1965, 46–47.

24. Indeed, the description of wives and children coming as suppliants to an altar bears a similarity to descriptions of Polygnotos' *Ilioupersis* at Delphi and perhaps to the *Ilioupersis* at Athens as well. See Stansbury-O'Donnell 1989, fig. 3, and Castriota 1992, fig. 12.

25. Francis and Vickers 1985b; Francis 1990, 86–87. For a variation on this proposal, see Boardman's essay in this volume.

26. Castriota (1992, 79) further suggests that Oinoe must be an integral part of the thematic program, since Pausanias refers to the paintings of the Stoa mostly in the singular.

27. On the narrative structure of the *Battle of Marathon,* see Stansbury-O'Donnell 1999, 142–145, with previous bibliography. On cyclical narrative see Stansbury-O'Donnell 1999, 145–149.

28. Wycherley 1957, 35, no. 62. Francis and Vickers would make this refer to the painting of *Marathonian Oinoe,* but from descriptions of *Marathon,* it is clear that the Plataians were in the first part of the painting where the battle is just beginning.

29. 1.15.3; tr. Pollitt 1990a, 144.

30. See Castriota 1992, 79, and above, n. 25.

31. Taylor 1998. On the question of which Oinoe is shown, see 225–228; on the dating, see 238.

32. See also de Angelis 1996, 165.

33. See Kagan 1974, 218–259.

34. Stähler 1992, 44; Krumeich 1997, 54.

35. Schultz 2003a. See also J. L. Shear 2003, who examines the use of Agora buildings as war memorials during the fifth and fourth centuries with a different interpretation of the *Battle of Oinoe* in the Stoa Poikile. On a new theory regarding the display of some of the shields, see Schultz 2003b.

36. See also de Angelis 1996, 141.

37. T. L. Shear 1984, 13, 18. Several scholars have used the

excavation report to suggest a date between 460 and 450, but Shear suggests that the literary and archaeological evidence "coincide perfectly" for the 460s; see Krumeich (1997) 103–104. Hölscher (1973) 76 also argues for the 450s based on politics and patronage.

38. See Wycherley 1957, 31, 45, n. 1.

39. Dedication and dating of the Stoa: Wycherley 1957, 45, n. 2; Jeffery 1965, 41–42; S. P. Morris 1992, 313. On the Kimonian program generally, see Castriota 1992, 33–133. On the source of funding, see Castriota 1992, 76, and Boersma 1970, 56.

40. Even if Kimon's allies were behind the painting of *Oinoe* as a demonstration of his loyalty to Athens during his exile in the 450s, as Hölscher (1973) 75–76 suggests, they could have added the painting to the side wall as an appendix to the original Kimonian program if the Stoa were built and the paintings begun in the 460s. Connecting *Oinoe* with the later conflicts of 431–421 and the shields, however, is a stronger case.

41. Kebric 1983, 8–13.

42. Badian 1993, 2–11, followed by A. C. Smith 1999, 128. See earlier Meiggs 1972, 79–81.

43. For a recent discussion of the dates of Simonides, see Molyneux 1992, 331, 339–343.

44. Page 1981, 274. Robertson (1975, 242) suggests that the Stoa was earlier than the Lesche and that the inscription, if by Simonides, was written for the Stoa *Ilioupersis* and then copied in the Lesche, which is why no second inscription for the *Nekyia* is recorded at the Lesche. This would, however, push the date for the Stoa to the early 460s, which is probably too early.

45. On the source of funding, see Castriota 1992, 76.

46. On Polygnotos' return to Thasos, see Meiggs 1972, 572–573, and M. J. Osborne 1983, 24. Osborne's speculation that Polygnotos came to Athens in 463 following the sack of Thasos would not accord with the dating of the painting programs in the Theseion and probably the Anakeion; see Pemberton 1989, 185–186.

47. See Paus. 9.4.1–2; tr. Pollitt 1990a, 141.

48. See Meiggs 1972, 82–86; Badian 1993, 101.

49. On Athenian elements, see Kebric 1983, 14–29.

50. See Castriota 1992, 128, 262, n. 102, with earlier opinions.

51. On Demophon's position, see Stansbury-O'Donnell 1989, 207, fig. 3; on Theseus' position, see Stansbury-O'Donnell 1990, 222–223, fig. 3.

52. Kebric 1983, 28–29.

53. On the position of Akamas, see Paus. 10.26.2; Stansbury-O'Donnell 1989, 207. On the inclusion of the son(s) of Theseus in the Stoa *Ilioupersis,* see Castriota 1992, 128, and n. 85, with earlier references.

54. Castriota 1992, 128–130.

55. Paus. 10.25.7; Pollitt 1990a, 131. On pathos and ethos generally, see Pollitt 1985.

56. Paus. 10.29.9; tr. Pollitt 1990a, 138. See also *Od.* 11.631. On this section, see also Robertson 1952.

57. Pausanias does comment on the contrasting moods of some figures, such as Penthesileia and Paris. Simon (1963, 52–53) compares the front figures of the Niobid krater to this subject of Theseus in the Underworld, as does Barron (1972, 42–43). Both see a possible but different Polygnotan painting as the source for the vase.

58. This would be an even sharper contrast if Polygnotos were also involved in the painting program at the Theseion, which is possible although not positively attested; see Pemberton 1989, 184.

59. Paus. 10.28.3; tr. Pollitt 1990a, 134.

60. Paus. 10.28.5, tr. Pollitt 1990a, 134. On dike and adikia, see Shapiro 1993, 39–44.

61. On the pro-Spartan interpretation of the painting, see Dugas 1938. Kebric (1983, 16–25) argues extensively against Dugas' position.

62. On this contrast of the Greek leaders, see Robertson 1967, 11–12; Stansbury-O'Donnell 1989, 212–213. Castriota (1992, 114) would view the *Ilioupersis* more as an assembly by the pious kings to deal with an impious act rather than as a dichotomy.

63. Naples, Museo Archeologico Nazionale 2422. On this vase, see especially Boardman 1976, 15; Pollitt 1985, 113; Castriota 1992, 98–99 and passim; Stansbury-O'Donnell 1999, 21–23, 168–174, figs. 72–74.

64. Hall 1991, 204.

65. Hall 1991, 210.

66. On Polygnotan ethos, see Pollitt 1976; on Aischylos and Polygnotos, see Stansbury-O'Donnell 1999, 186–190.

8

FEMINIZING THE BARBARIAN AND BARBARIZING THE FEMININE

AMAZONS, TROJANS, AND PERSIANS IN THE STOA POIKILE

DAVID CASTRIOTA

Classical Athens, whose history and culture J. J. Pollitt's work has done so much to illuminate, has left us many of the greatest works of Greek literature and visual art. Indeed, the form and aspect of Athens' artistic monuments remain so impressive today that they have almost come to epitomize ancient Greek society. About these much has been written. The fifth-century Athenian monument I would like to discuss here, however, no longer exists beyond its foundations and fragments of its architectural decoration: the Stoa Poikile or Painted Colonnade, which once stood on the north perimeter of the Athenian Agora. Unlike the Parthenon and the other monuments of the Akropolis, the important role that the Stoa once played in ancient Athenian culture cannot be discerned from its physical remains. Nevertheless, this monument has left a strong and lasting impression in the Greek literary and historical record.

At first a hall of victory erected to celebrate Athenian military successes, the Stoa Poikile came to function as a major component of the Athenian civic space, where it provided a locus for political and other public discussion. Serving also as a meeting place for philosophical discourse and learning, it eventually gave its name to a whole genre of Greek thought and argumentation: Stoicism.[1] So lasting was this association that the great hellenophile emperor Hadrian built a large colonnaded monument to honor its memory, the "Poecile," at his villa in Tivoli.[2]

The aspect of the Stoa Poikile that I would like to pursue here, however, pertains more to its original function as a victory monument, and I am especially interested in approaching the Stoa once again as I have in my earlier work, as a visual artistic extension of contemporary Athenian political rhetoric. Like the Stoa, this rhetoric no longer exists in its original form. We know it from the bits recounted in Herodotos' *Histories* and from its reflections in the speeches of Athenian orators of the succeeding fourth century. In much the same way, the Stoa's decoration, especially the paintings that once appeared along its interior walls, is recoverable only at second hand from literary descriptions and from reflections in roughly contemporary Attic vase painting of the second quarter of the fifth century.

Despite the barriers that appear to stand between the Stoa and modern attempts to reconstitute and understand it, this monument and its paintings are worth studying for a number of reasons. First, the Stoa was one of the earliest Athenian monuments to explore what would eventually become a dominant strategy of fifth-century Athenian public art: the use of mythic themes or imagery as a means of celebrating victory over the Persian Empire. As such, it represents the genesis or premiere of an artistic program known better from monuments like the Parthenon or the Temple of Athena Nike.[3] Second, the particular juxtaposition or association of mythic and historical themes in the Stoa's paintings provides explicit evidence that the Greeks conceived of their early myths as analogues or precedents for contemporary military achievements. Finally, the Stoa Poikile is the only monument of its kind whose mythic themes or subjects focused primarily on women as analogues for the Persian enemy. Consequently, it offers a unique opportunity to delve into one of the most revealing aspects of Greek or Athenian attitudes toward the Persians during this period: their equivalence to, or affinity with, women, hence my title.

Historical and archaeological data enable us to situate the Stoa in a highly charged political context. Excavations by Shear have established a reliable chronological horizon for the monument. The foundations contained a pottery fill belonging exclusively to the 460s, dating the building to the end of this decade.[4] Literary sources tell us that it was originally called the "Stoa Peisianaktos," that is, that it was named for Peisianax, the brother-in-law and political partisan of Kimon, the leading Athenian general and politician of the 470s and 460s.[5] The association with Kimon, who spearheaded an aggressive war of retribution against the Persians across the Aegean and Asia Minor, provides a plausible basis for seeing the Stoa as a product or vehicle of his militant ideology.

This was a period of Athenian military ascendancy. As *hegemon* or leader of the Delian League, a confederacy of Aegean Greek city-states organized specifically to harass the Persians, Athens basked in the prestige that followed upon a succession of victories, while the city and its leaders grew rich from the booty and ransom extorted from the defeated Persian nobility of Asia Minor. Consequently, there was money to commission public monuments outfitted with murals by the leading painters of the day, which could celebrate, explain, and give thanks to the gods for what the Athenians had achieved. When we bear in mind that all the Stoa's paintings dealt with the imagery of battle or war, there can be little doubt that the monument was very much a part of these events.[6]

Even on its own terms, the specific array of battle themes depicted in the Stoa has much to tell us about how Kimon and the Athenian elite conceptualized Athenian success and its role within the larger Greek world. Here our source for the painting is the account of Pausanias (1.15.1–3), who composed a travel guide, the *Guide Bleu* of its day, in the second century A.D. The first painting he mentions is supposed to have depicted a recent battle between Athenians and Spartans at a place called Oinoe in the Argolid. This encounter is otherwise unknown in the historical record and may be an error on Pausanias' part or a mistake passed on by his informants, but more of that later. The second painting showed the mythic king/hero Theseus and the Athenians defending the city against invading Amazons. The third painting was a scene of Troy that included the Greek victors among an assembly of prisoners, mostly female, in the aftermath of the sack of the city. The fourth painting depicted the battle of Marathon in 490 B.C., the first battle against the Persians on the Greek mainland, a resounding victory that brought Athens into the center stage of international events (Fig. 8.1).

The presence of the *Marathon* scene here has long convinced scholars that the accompanying mythic themes were meant to serve unambiguously as analogies from ancient times for the more recent victories over Persians.[7] Nor did the Athenians scruple to adjust the myths in the interest of asserting this analogy more forcefully. Traditionally, the battle with the Amazons

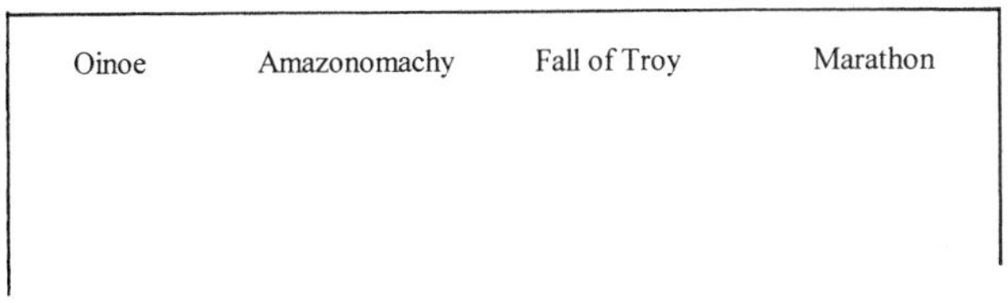

Oinoe	Amazonomachy	Fall of Troy	Marathon

FIGURE 8.1. *Plan of the paintings in the Stoa Poikile, by D. Castriota.*

had featured Herakles, and later Theseus as well, in heroic Greek expeditions against the homeland of the warrior women in Asia Minor. In contrast, the Stoa featured a new version first attested in literature by Aischylos' *Eumenides* 685–690 of ca. 457 B.C. Herodotos 9.27, too, refers to this version in the speech that he attributes to the Athenians before the battle of Plataia in 479 B.C. Here the Amazons attack Athens as a multiethnic hoard from Asia bent on domination of all Greece, a change that was clearly intended to parallel the events of 480–479, when Xerxes invaded Greece with a huge army drawn from all over the Persian Empire to avenge defeat at Marathon a decade before.

In this view of things, where myth served to prefigure contemporary events, and where it could even be refashioned to prefigure those events more effectively, the theme of fallen Troy also assumed a new relevance. In the Stoa painting, Troy appears as a once-powerful Asiatic Empire humbled by a united Greek effort or alliance, in this case paralleling the circumstances of the 470s and 460s when the Delian League under Kimon and the Athenians inflicted defeat after defeat upon the Persians throughout the Aegean and western Asia Minor. Alongside the battle of Marathon, the scenes depicting the Amazonomachy and Troy presented the viewer with a vast panorama through time documenting Athenian leadership in the struggle against Asiatic enemies. Here the defeat of Troy and the Amazons functioned as ancient history, and Marathon as recent history, much as these themes did in fifth-century Athenian rhetoric.

The Athenian speech at Plataia referred to above actually provides the closest rhetorical counterpart for the sort of analogy between past and present that the Stoa's paintings asserted. In the speech, the Athenian commander claims the honor of leading the left wing of the assembled Greek forces against the Persians and their Theban collaborators by citing a catalogue of mythic precedents that document his city's valor and commitment to Greece. Had the Athenians not repulsed the invading Amazons who threatened all Hellas? Had they not done their part in the expedition to Troy? Had they not distinguished themselves in settling affairs in the aftermath of the attack of the Seven Argives against Thebes? Moreover, not to dwell only on the distant past, had they not driven the Persians out of Greece at Marathon? This catalogue of great deeds also appears in the *epitaphios logos,* the standard Athenian funerary speech attested in late fifth- and fourth-century Attic rhetoric. Current opinion places the origin of the funerary speech with its reworked versions of mythic analogues earlier, in the period directly following the Persian invasion.[8]

The parallel between the subjects of the Stoa paintings and the mythic catalogue in this sort of Athenian rhetoric is indeed striking, as scholars have noted.[9] Yet there is one problematic element, the scene of Oinoe in which Athenians were apparently fighting Spartans rather than Persians or mythic Asiatics. It is not unthinkable that an Athenian monument might celebrate victories against fellow Greeks. There was certainly open hostility between Athens and Sparta in the 450s as an initial phase of, or prelude to, the Peloponnesian War. Moreover, as a hall of victories, the Stoa was later decorated with shields taken from the Spartans at the battle of Sphakteria (Paus. 1.15.4). And so perhaps the Oinoe painting, like the shields, was an afterthought, a later addition to the Stoa's program, which originally celebrated Greek victory against Persia.

But, as noted above, a battle of Oinoe is unattested in our historical sources, apart from Pausanias. Consequently, his reference to a scene depicting a battle between Spartans and Athenians at Oinoe was not simply a jarring note in the context of the Stoa's program. More generally, this purported battle posed a problem for understanding the history of the Peloponnesian War, and it had never been adequately explained or explained away by Greek historians until Francis and Vickers advanced an attractive solution some years ago.[10] They proposed that the Oinoe referred to by Pausanias was not a town in the Argolid but another Oinoe located in Attica near the Boiotian border, in

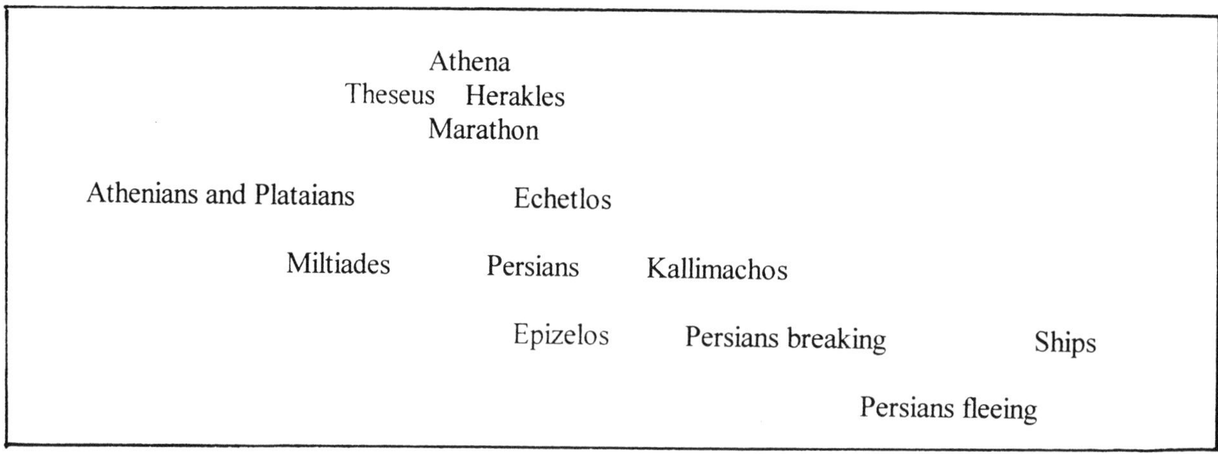

FIGURE 8.2. *Diagrammatic reconstruction of the* Marathon *painting in the Stoa Poikile, by D. Castriota.*

fact, the very site where the Athenians met up with their allies from Plataia before engaging the Persians at Marathon.

In their view, what Pausanias saw was not the scene of a battle but one depicting a rendezvous of allied forces. Pausanias, in fact, remarks upon how the two sides in the painting have not yet begun fighting, that they are only just coming together. Observing a painting some six centuries old, probably worn and faded, Pausanias and/or those who informed him could easily have mistaken a scene of allied solidarity for a battle. They could easily have confused Oinoe in Attika with the Argive town of the same name. With the shields from Sphakteria hanging nearby, he or they may also have concocted or hypothesized a battle against Sparta to make sense of things. Yet Francis and Vickers' thesis does more than explain Oinoe. It now provides an entirely new perspective in which the Stoa's paintings constituted a larger Marathonian epic, with the events leading up to the battle and the great victory itself framing or embracing the mythic themes of the Amazon invasion and Troy's defeat (Fig. 8.1).

This then is the updated conventional wisdom on the Stoa's program of painting: a coherent, effective analogy of past and present, rich in geographic and political overtones that only the imagery of Asiatic Amazons and Trojans could provide. Still, I think that there was something more here at stake and at work that transcended the cultural and geopolitical theme of Europe versus Asia. Ultimately, the paintings confronted the spectator with a concentration of female enemies in the very midst of the Stoa: the Amazon invaders, soon to be defeated, and the captive Trojan women emblematic of their city's destruction. To get at the underlying sense of all this, one needs to consider what we know about the *Marathon* painting more closely, for I believe that in the end, it was the *Marathon* painting that really set the ideological tone or agenda for the Stoa's imagery.

The testimonia for the *Marathon* painting in the Stoa are extensive, comprising data from the Attic orators to Pliny or Pausanias and even including later works of art, and they are far too numerous to go through here. Moreover, they have been carefully studied, most notably by Harrison, Hölscher, and Francis and Vickers.[11] For the purpose at hand, I want to concentrate on Pausanias (1.15.3), who gives a concise but coherent overview of the painting's content and structure. From his account, there appear to have been three main sections, which are sketched out here roughly in diagrammatic form (Fig. 8.2). The painting began with the Athenians and their Plataian allies engaging the Persians more or less on equal terms. By the middle of the painting, the Persians have turned to flight and confusion. At the end of the scene, the Persians have taken to scrambling madly into their ships, hoping only to escape with their lives. Amidst all this, certain figures stood out. There was one of the Greek commanders, Miltiades, the father of Kimon, urging his men on against the Persians. The other commander, Kallimachos, stood riddled with Persian arrows like a pincushion, but miraculously he was still fighting. Similarly the warrior Epizelos was blind, but he too fought on. Echetlos, personifying the people of rural Attika, battled the Persians armed only with a humble plow. Other characters functioned on a more lofty level. Theseus' spirit was shown rising to encourage the men of Athens, corresponding to a popular rumor that circulated in the aftermath of the battle (Plut. *Thes.* 35). The painting also included Herakles, who had a shrine at Marathon, as well as the eponymous hero of the site, and, of course, Athena herself.

The prominence of all these figures and the qualities that they embody suggest that what we have here is not simply a visual account of the battle but rather a composition whose narrative structure was meant to disclose and project the conflict of opposing national characters. In other words, the painting depicted more than the details of the event; it strove to explain the battle and its outcome by giving graphic form to the ethical opposition of Greek vs. Persian—the Hellene/Barbarian antithesis—in terms that closely paralleled the literary imagery conjured up so dramatically at various points in Aischylos' *Persians* or in more prosaic terms by Herodotos.[12] On the Persian side, we have an image of *hybris* incarnate: overbearing, arrogant greed for power and domination, fueled by boundless wealth and superior numbers. The Persians exemplify an agenda driven by unquestioned obedience to the authority of a monarch eager to expand his rule and unwilling to accept any limitations. On the Greek side, we see, in contrast, a collective image of selfless discipline dedicated to protecting the Hellenic homeland, the citizens' political freedom or autonomy, and the restrained moral order handed down to them by the gods. Athena's presence in the painting, alongside the mythic heroes whom she aided, leaves no doubt as to the issue of divine support for the Greek cause. Their inclusion recalls the scene in Aischylos in which the Persian messenger can explain his nation's defeat only through divine intervention:

> Do we seem to you to have been lacking (in numbers) for this battle? No, it was as if some divine power (*daimon*) destroyed the host, weighing down the scale with unequal fortune. Gods safeguard the city of the goddess Pallas (Athena).[13] (lines 454–455, 532–533)

We can no longer see the monumental depiction of Marathon on the Stoa's wall, but we can get a better idea of how Greek painters of the Early Classical period may have communicated this sort of "ethography," a visual representation of character, by recalling the conversation of Sokrates and the painter Parrhasios recorded by Xenophon in the *Memorabilia* (3.10.4–5). There, Sokrates asserts that in pictorial representations, the countenance and features of a man, how he moves or carries himself, may serve to demonstrate his noble attributes—freedom and self-control or *sophrosyne*—just as his physical qualities and bearing may disclose a base and arrogant character lacking in restraint (hybris). This exchange between Sokrates and Parrhasios illustrates a point that Pollitt has rightly emphasized: the ethographic interest of Early Classical painters involved the portrayal not only good *ethos,* good character, but of flawed or weak character as well.[14]

In contrast to the Persians, whose timorous bearing and tendency toward flight was meant to give visual form to a character driven by monarchy and hierarchic obedience to a single mortal authority, the Greeks in the *Marathon* painting provided a graphic illustration of spontaneous dedication to laws and values ordained and protected by gods and heroes. Even though a number of Athenian defenders figured prominently in the painting, they apparently served to emphasize the action, not to dominate it; they still functioned as part of a collective group motivated by common resolve. Within such a system of contrasts we are hardly meant to wonder why, for all their numerical advantages, the Persian *ethos* cracks and collapses before the Greek defense. Most immediately, this appears to be a contrast of national, political, and moral character set against the geographical opposition between Greece or Europe and Asia. But when we look at the Amazons farther down the wall, it becomes clear that something more is at stake.

In the case of the Amazon battle, which was apparently produced for the Stoa by the painter Mikon, we can get some idea of its original appearance from the Attic vase paintings of the 460s and 450s that seem to have imitated the large-scale original of the Stoa Poikile or perhaps the one also depicted by Mikon in the Theseion, shrine of Theseus (Paus. 1.17.2). Alternatively, we can try to combine these vase adaptations in a graphic reconstruction to get some general idea of the original painting (Fig. 8.3).

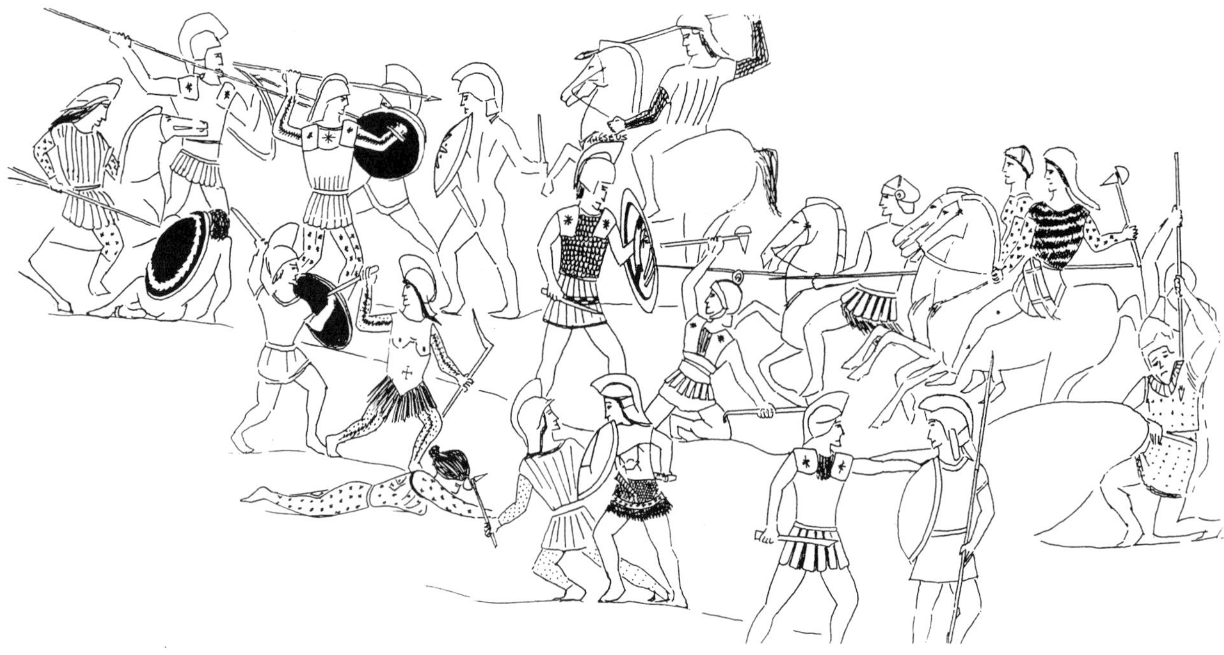

FIGURE 8.3. *Reconstruction of the* Amazonomachy *by Mikon in the Stoa Poikile.*

Yet the best indication of the ideology that the painting originally conveyed comes from the version of the Amazon invasion recounted by Athenian orators such as Lysias (2.4–6). There, the Amazons emerge very much like the Persians. They rule a vast empire in Asia dominating many peoples whom they assemble as an invading horde bent on conquering Athens and Greece. Spurred on by arrogant self-assurance based on wealth and numbers, they expect an easy victory. But like the Persians at Marathon, and especially during Xerxes' massive invasion of 480/79 B.C., the Amazons come to a shocking realization when they clash with the men of Athens, that is, with "real men." They find, as Lysias puts it, that their spirit is commensurate with their female nature.

Various Early Classical Attic vase paintings of the Amazonomachy seem to attempt to convey this by depicting the warrior women with facial expressions of dazed shock.[15] Others, however, suggest flight or timidity; the Amazons cringe as they struggle, or they seem to turn and run, in some cases enough of them do so to suggest panic or rout. The krater by the Painter of Bologna 279, despite its mediocre draftsmanship, may well reflect the spatial-compositional and gestural effects of a more sophisticated original (Figs. 8.4–5).[16] Here, most of the Amazons turn to defend themselves as they run from their Greek opponents. I suspect that these qualities derive from Mikon's large-scale original in the Stoa, and if so, these timorous, panicky Amazons would have posed a striking and explicit analogy to the fleeing Persians in the nearby *Marathon* painting

Here we begin to see the true dimension of the strategy of mythic analogy presented by the Stoa's paintings. It was not simply to project the notion of Asiatic aggression and imperialism into a remote barbaric past. Nor was it merely to claim that Asiatics had always lacked tenacity and courage. The real purpose and sense of the Amazon analogue was to assert a specifically gendered conception of the Persian character. It was deliberately intended to assert a "feminized" image of the Asiatic barbarian. But feminine in what way? Were the Persians being vilified here as effeminate weaklings? Perhaps to some degree, but I suspect that there is much more going on, indeed, something rather different, that goes to the whole root of the Greek indictment of Persian imperialism. What Persians and Amazons, that is, Asiatics and women, really shared was uncontrollable appetite, immoderation, and insatiable desire.

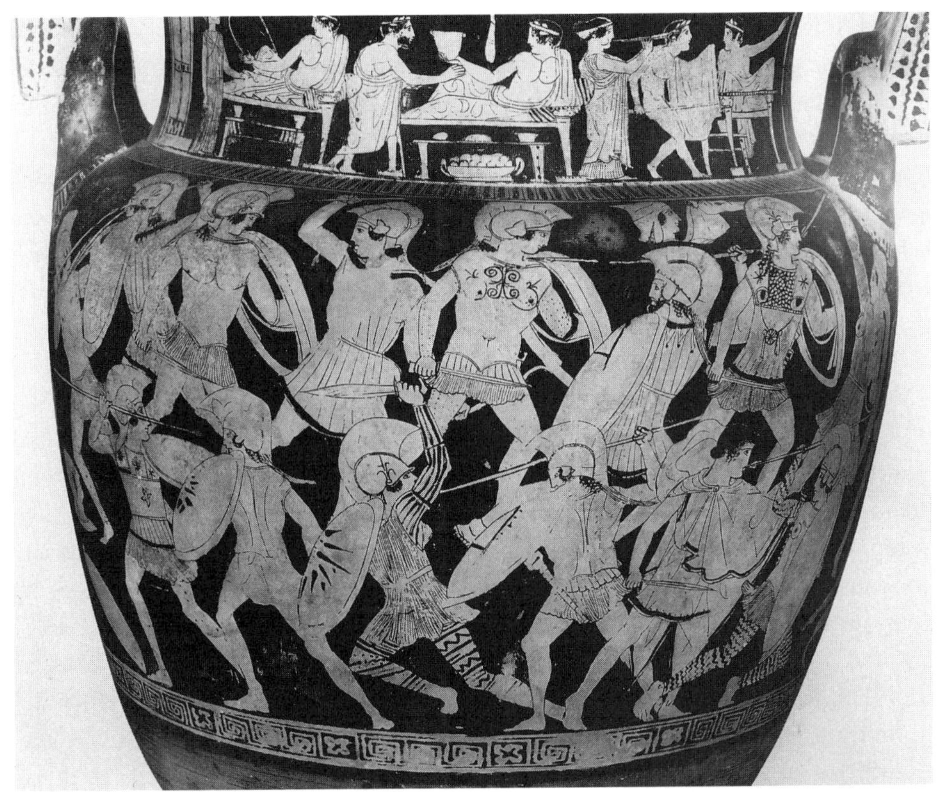

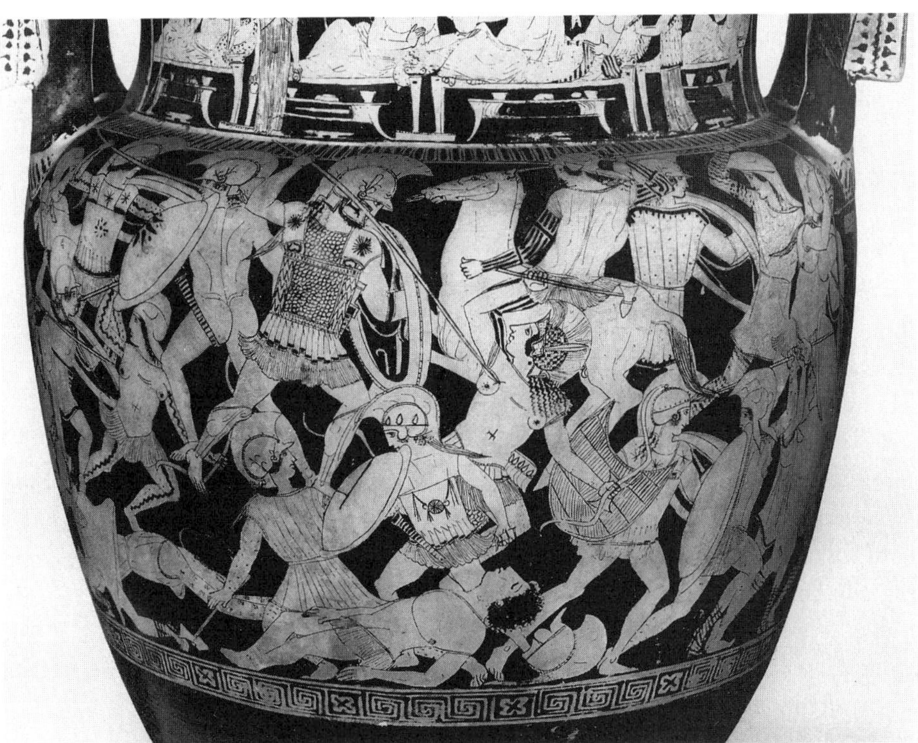

FIGURES 8.4–5. *Attic red-figure krater by the Painter of Bologna 279. Antikenmuseum Basel und Sammlung Ludwig, inv. BS 486. Photos: Claire Niggli.*

There is no need to rehearse this at length. Classical Greek sources are replete with evidence that women were regarded as essentially wild, untamed, even bestial, until "broken in" under the care or control of husbands. Gould has nicely summarized the evidence of Greek language itself in this regard. Unmarried girls or maidens were routinely referred to with the noun *polos,* young mare or "filly." The adjective for unmarried was *adzugos,* "unyoked" or "unhitched," and *admetos,* "unbroken." Nowadays this comes off as uncouth cowboy talk: "Me and my filly are gonna get hitched." But in Classical Greece or Athens, this was typical and acceptable parlance.[17]

The confrontation between the women and the old codgers in Aristophanes' *Lysistrata* vividly exemplifies the fundamental equivalence of women, Amazons, animals, and Persians in the Athenian view:

> Is the hybris of these deeds not enormous? . . . If anyone should give them [the women] just a little hold over us, they will not be lacking in persistent skills. They will build ships to sail against us and wage naval battles, just like Artemisia. And if they turn to horsy matters, write off the [Athenian] cavalry. For a woman is a most horsy thing, with a good seat that will not slip in the gallop. Just look at the Amazons Mikon painted fighting men from horseback. No. Rather we should grab them all by the neck and harness them into collars of wood.[18]

Since the scene in the play is set between the edge of the Athenian Agora and the northwest slope of the Athenian Akropolis, the old-timer would literally have been understood as pointing to Mikon's *Amazonomachy* in the nearby Stoa Poikile. Moreover, the Artemisia to whom he refers was a real-life Amazon of sorts. She was the queen of Halikarnassos, who put on armor and served as Xerxes' ally during his Greek campaign. The Athenians put an enormous price on her head, so horrified were they that a woman should arm herself and fight against them (Hdt. 8.87.93).[19] Ultimately, this scene from *Lysistrata* illustrates a basic tenet of Athenian male-centered culture: the belief that there was a fundamental equivalence between the external barbarians and women inside the *polis.* Both presented the same threat to the polis: wild, unrestrained behavior, one without and one within, and both needed to be contained or repressed to preserve the male Greek ideal of order.

But there is even more to this comparison of Persian and Woman. It is not simply that women were held to be insatiable and overbearing by nature; they also lacked the tenacity, nerve, or staying power to carry through their grandiose desires. Athenian literary sources ascribe to women a lack of fortitude and a tendency to panic, in contrast to the male ideal or attribute of *andreia* (manliness).[20] No wonder that the Amazons collapsed before the spirited Athenian defense in Lysias' account and, no doubt, in the Stoa painting as well. The image of Persians in the nearby *Marathon* painting, initially haughty and overconfident but degenerating into panic and rout, was then entirely consistent with female behavior, especially as it would have appeared down the wall in the *Amazon* painting.

For one last level of nuance in this comparison, we may turn to Pausanias himself (1.15.2) who, in describing the painting, parenthetically notes how women fail to learn by their mistakes. He reminds us how Herakles defeated the Amazons, and still they returned to invade Attika. After that defeat, they returned yet again to fight the Greeks as allies of the Trojans. Here Pausanias describes a reckless, intransigent appetite for danger or destruction, *ate,* again a trait ascribed to the Persians in Aischylos' play and in Herodotos' *Histories.* The Persians lost at Marathon, and still they returned under Xerxes to lose at Salamis and Plataia, and yet again in the many battles waged against them subsequently by Kimon and the Delian League.

Pausanias' little *parekbasis* or digression on the female appetite for trouble is revealing. Some may feel that he is reflecting male attitudes of his own time, and that one should not assume that these were necessarily identical to those of Classical Athens. But I suspect that this is beside the point, because it is probably the painting that is speaking here. These comments take up far more space in the discussion than what Pausanias actually has to say about the painting of the Amazonomachy itself. In a certain sense, he is describing the painting, or rather the impression that the

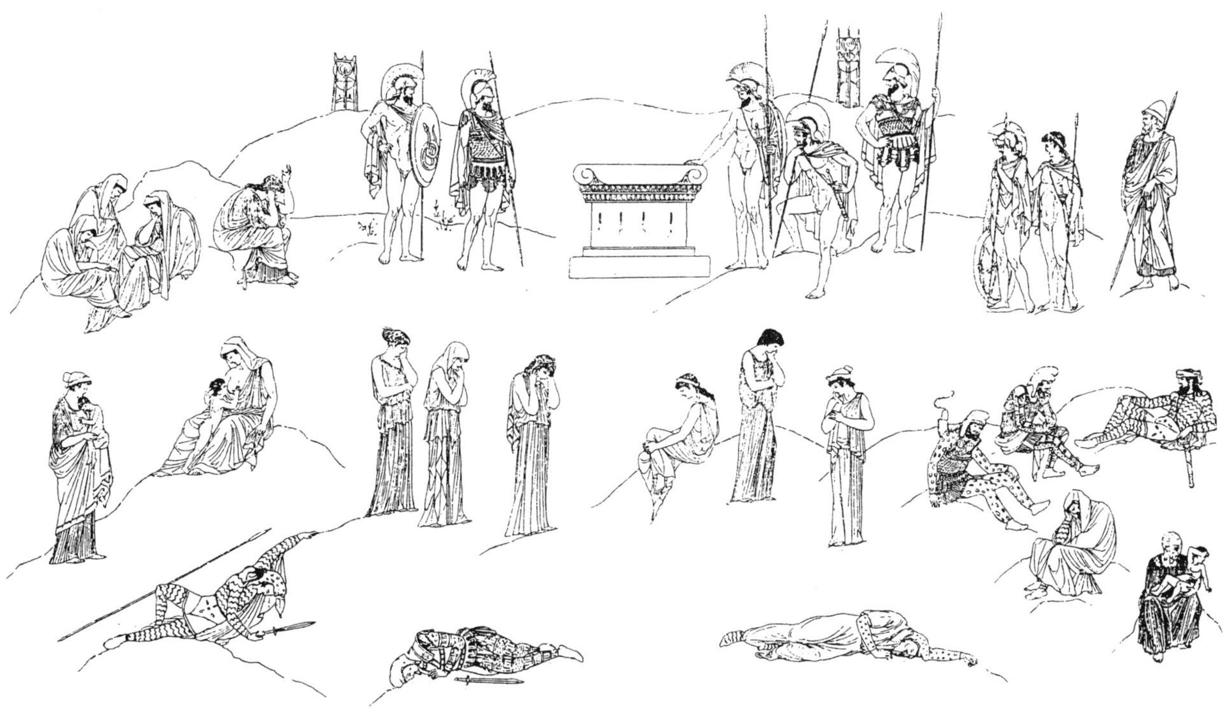

FIGURE 8.6. *Reconstruction of the* Ilioupersis *by Polygnotos in the Stoa Poikile, by D. Castriota.*

painting made, by digressing in this way. He is passing on to us the rhetorical or ideological impact that the painting still exerted upon observers centuries after it was created.[21]

It is also interesting that Pausanias' observations about female, Amazonian recklessness and intransigence shift suddenly to a description of the scene of fallen Troy (1.15.3), which Plutarch (*Kim.* 4.5) tells us was depicted by the great painter Polygnotos of Thasos. The painting he produced here seems to have little to do with the traditional version of Troy's destruction that had been current in Archaic and Early Classical Attic vase painting. It contained no scenes of rape, savage murder, and the violation of sanctuaries that typified the "Ilioupersis" in Greek pictorial art from the Orientalizing period onward.[22] Quite the contrary, Polygnotos' painting in the Stoa depicted not the battle itself but the aftermath of the sack on the following morning. The Greek kings have assembled to deliberate over Aias, who stands accused of raping Kassandra in the shrine of Athena during the sack. All around them are the captive Trojan women, and, since they are described by Pausanias as "the women among the captives," *gynaikas ton aichmaloton,* some male Trojan prisoners must have been included as well.

It is likely that this painting was an abbreviated version of the more extensive scene of defeated Troy that Polygnotos produced for the Lesche or Clubhouse of the Knidians at Delphi.[23] The reconstruction drawing illustrated here is adapted by the writer from Carl Robert's reconstruction of the related portion of the Delphi painting (Fig. 8.6).[24] At the center we see Aias and Kassandra near an altar whose presence is plausible but unattested. They are flanked by Agamemnon, Menelaos, Odysseus, and Theseus' sons Akamas and Demophon, who are all specifically mentioned by Pausanias in the Delphi version, although he refers to them only briefly as the assembled kings in describing the Stoa painting. I have modified Robert's figures to show the Trojans here in Persian or Oriental costume, as I believe that they appeared in the corresponding Troy painting at Delphi, largely on the analogy of contemporary Attic drama and Attic vase painting of the later fifth and fourth centuries, where the Trojans had come to appear almost exclusively as Asiatic barbarians.[25] If this is correct, it would have greatly reinforced the analogy that they posed to the nearby Amazons and Persians, who were similarly dressed.

To some extent, the relatively novel or anomalous aspect of Polygnotos' version of fallen Troy at the Stoa Poikile corresponds to the introspective psychological approach for which the great painter was famous. As Pollitt has also emphasized, Polygnotos preferred to depict not the action of the event but the contemplative aftermath, prompting the spectator to consider and weigh the ethical or moral issues treated in the narrative.[26] Still, it seems that Polygnotos' motive for reworking the theme of Troy's fall was more immediately thematic, if not overtly political.[27] I have argued elsewhere that here in the Stoa, as in the version at Delphi, Polygnotos produced a new treatment of Troy's fall that made it more effective as a mythic analogue for just victory over Persia. He invented a highly expurgated version of the Ilioupersis that largely bypassed the savage and impious excesses committed by the Greeks during the sack of the city. There was virtually no action or violence. Instead, the painting focused on the rectitude of the Greek conquerors. Aias' impiety is not denied, but it is isolated, exceptional. The kings have assembled to judge or purify Aias, thereby distancing themselves from his crime. The theme of Troy's fall has been adjusted to the programmatic requirements of the Stoa. In this highly politicized context, the contrast of Greek and Trojan has become a more strident, polarized opposition in which the Greeks were meant to be seen as positive.[28]

In keeping with fifth-century literary sources, Troy is now an Asiatic city, an analogue for the defeated Persian Empire, so here it is primarily the Trojan crimes that are emphasized. As in Aischylos' *Agamemnon* 355–402, the Trojans are impious and arrogant. They supported Paris' abduction of Helen, flouting the laws of Zeus regarding hospitality and marriage. They resisted all efforts to negotiate Helen's return peacefully. In the end, through their immoderation and reckless *ate,* they have brought down on themselves the righteous retribution of the Greek host. Perhaps the best support for this more polarized, pro-Greek interpretation of the war against Troy appears in a nearly contemporary dithyramb by the poet Bakchylides entitled "The Demand for the Return of Helen." Here Menelaos addresses the Trojan people in one last attempt to avoid the war, admonishing them with the ominous choice between female personifications of goodness and evil:

> Menelaos, son of Pleisthenes spoke; Counseled by the fair-robed Graces, He enchanted them with speech. "O men of Troy, favored by the god of war, Zeus who rules on high and sees all things is not the cause of the great wailings of mortals. The way lies open for all men to attain straightforward Dike [Justice], the attendant of holy Eunomia [Good Order] and prudent Themis [Right]. Children of blessed men have her as a dweller among their homes. Whereas she who is burgeoning forth with shifty wiles and lawless follies, yes, irreverent Hybris, she quickly gives you the wealth and power belonging to another, but then leads into the depths of ruin. And that one [Hybris], she destroyed those arrogant sons of Gaia, the Giants."[29]

In his *Eleventh Epinician Ode,* Bakchylides ends by praising the Greeks at Troy after they had made good the warning of Menelaos:

> When, in time by the will of the blessed gods
> they sacked Priam's well-built citadel
> along with the bronze-chested sons of Atreus,
> whoever keeps Dike [Justice] in his breast will achieve
> measureless feats of Achaian strength.[30]

The attitude toward the Trojans in works like this is clear, and when cast in such a light, Priam and his people fit eminently well into the program of paintings in the Stoa Poikile. Like the Amazons and Persians, the Trojans coveted the possessions and prestige of others despite the wealth and power they already possessed. Like the Amazons and Persians, the Trojans recklessly disregarded the experience of the past. They could not see the wisdom of allowing Helen's return in order to avoid bloodshed and disaster. Like the Amazons, the Trojans too were defeated by Herakles in the wars of the preceding generation, but still they took on the Greeks once more. How fitting it was that the Amazons should become allies of the Trojans later in the war.

In essence, the uncontrolled appetites and reckless misjudgment of the Trojans branded them as feminine, like the Amazons and Persians depicted to either side of them in the Stoa. Consequently, the idea of representing the Trojans primarily as female captives was a highly effective narrative strategy. But framed or surrounded by the larger cycle of the events leading up to Marathon and the battle itself, the central pairing of Amazons and Trojans would have presented the spectator with a kind of duality and a closure of sorts for the imagery as a whole. Ultimately, both the *Amazonomachy* and the scene of the *Ilioupersis* projected a blend of female and barbarian. In the *Amazonomachy* we have what appears more as a feminized barbarian, Mikon's nightmarish image of women on horseback out of control fighting men. They will ultimately be contained, but the battle still rages. The *Troy* scene, on the other hand, presents us with the aftermath of battle. All is resolved. Instead of wild warrior women, we are confronted with an array of female prisoners now totally under control.

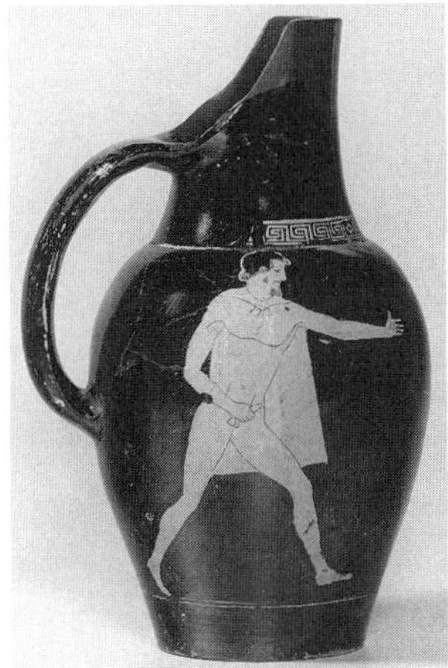

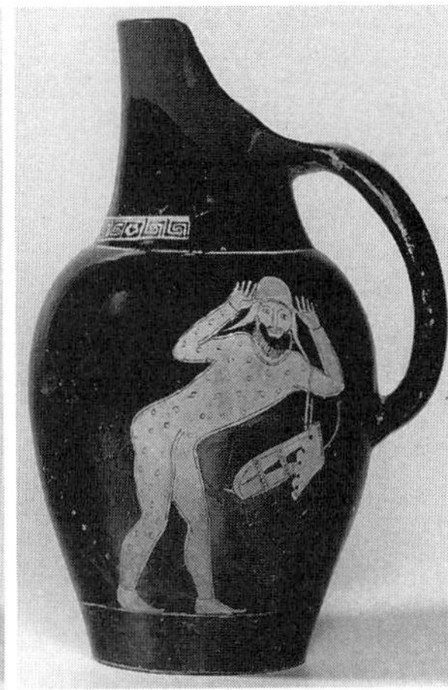

FIGURES 8.7–8. *Attic red-figure oinochoe. Museum für Kunst und Gewerbe Hamburg, inv. no. 1981.173. Photos courtesy of Museum.*

Polygnotos chose to embody defeated Troy not only as captive men but most immediately in the form of its captive wives and mothers. Essentially the inverse of Mikon's feminized barbarian, we now have the Asiatic wife, the barbarized female. Unlike the *Amazonomachy*, the *Ilioupersis* scene shows us women who are again fully domesticated, indeed doubly domesticated, first as Trojan wives and then as concubines, who will soon be allotted as spoils for the sexual gratification of the Greek victors. The feminine immoderation of their Trojan husbands has been crushed, and the actual female contingent of Trojans that remains is remarkably tame. Moreover, the visual juxtaposition or transition from Amazon to Trojan wife here essentially reasserts Greek social practice regarding the proper management of women within the household.

To sense the underlying relevance of all this to the adjacent painting of the defeated Persians themselves, one need only recall the closing scenes of Aischylos' *Persians* (909–1076), where Xerxes becomes similarly feminized. He arrives tattered and bereft of his army, no longer a warrior or force to be reckoned with, but an overgrown child, lost in lamentation and tearing his clothes like a woman. Now he is fit only for the soothing company of his mother, Queen Atossa, and the other Persian women who wail like their king. It is likely that many of the original spectators of the Stoa's paintings had seen Aischylos' *Persians* or that they were at least familiar with the cultural and ethical views it embodied. If we read the weeping Trojan women of Polygnotos' painting as mythic counterparts to the Persian women of the play, as I suspect mid-fifth-century Athenians did, it is possible to recapture something of the impact that this work would originally have made upon informed spectators in the Stoa, alongside the scene of ruined Persians at Marathon.

One other piece of evidence would appear to corroborate this reading of the *Marathon* painting, or at least to parallel it: the well-known Attic oinochoe inscribed "I am Eurymedon. I stand bent over" (Figs. 8.7–8).[31] The vessel shows a mature, bearded, fleeing Persian who suddenly stops and bends over with his hands held to the side of his head in a gesture of panic. Like other Attic vases of this period depicting fights with Persians, he is pursued by a young naked Greek (cf. Fig. 8.9).[32] However, the Greek chasing Eurymedon brandishes in his hand not a sword or a spear but his penis. Given the Greek's gesture, and the bent posture of the nearby Persian, the imagery of the vase is obviously homosexual, and it is obviously meant to denigrate the terrified Persian, whose name refers eponymously to Kimon's greatest victory over the Great King's armies at the River Eurymedon in western Asia Minor. In the most immediate terms, the Athenians are saying, "We've buggered the Persians!" as Kenneth Dover has put it.

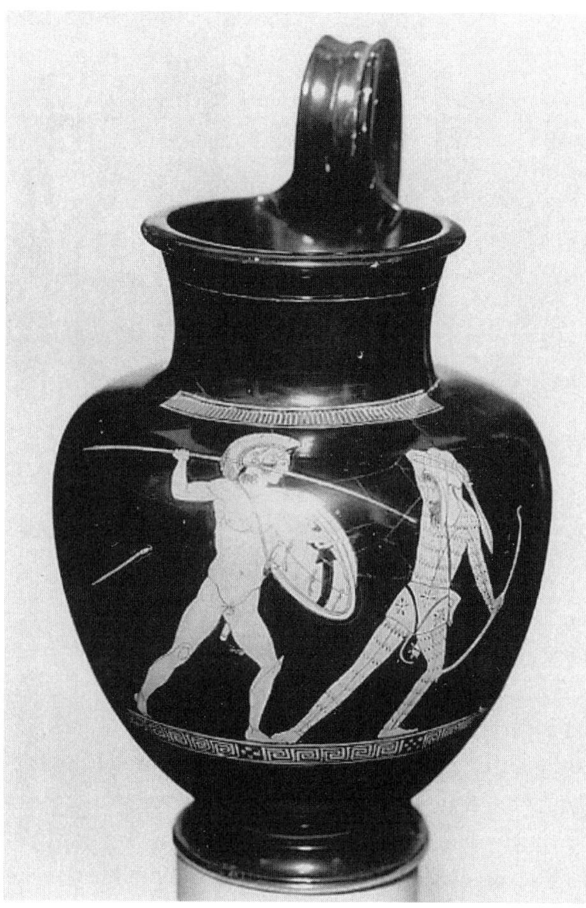

FIGURE 8.9. *Attic red-figure oinochoe attributed to the Chicago Painter. Boston, Museum of Fine Arts 13.196. Francis Bartlett Donation of 1912. Photo © 2003 Museum of Fine Arts, Boston.*

Dover emphasizes, moreover, that the term "bugger" has been used regularly in many languages, ancient and modern, as a vulgar synonym of defeat.[33]

But the sense of the insult was not antihomosexual, that is, it did not mean to denigrate the Persians specifically as homosexuals, which would, of course, have made no sense in Classical Athens. Rather, it sought to denigrate the Persians as passive recipients of the Athenian phallus. The mature, bearded Persian on the vase is too old to be an *eromenos,* a "beloved." Only a boy or adolescent should assume the passive role of penetration appropriate to women in sexual intercourse; male homosexual etiquette would require a man of his years and stature to take the active role as *erastes* or lover. Yet on the vase, it is the youthful Greek who is doing this, while the older Persian is on the receiving end. He is therefore analogous to a woman in physical sexual terms, and that is the real, fifth-century Greek sense of the humorous insult intended by the vase. This is supported by the Persian's gesture of panic, which is also a female trait.[34]

Still, we have not yet really gotten the joke. The term commonly applied to passive male homosexual recipients in Attic comedy is *euryproktos,* which may be translated approximately as "wide ass."[35] It is, of course, fortuitous that Kimon's greatest victory took place at a river named Eurymedon. Most immediately, Eurymedon means "wide-ruling." It is at the very least a humorous irony that the Persian on the vase should be named "wide-ruling," since the battle at the Eurymedon effectively curtailed the power of the Great King in Asia Minor. *Medon,* however, alliterates with the adjective *medos,* "Mede" or "Persian," and so Eurymedon becomes a kind of pun also meaning "wide Mede" or "wide Persian." By now, the comic implication of a "wide Persian" bending over should be evident. If this could be reduced to a simple one-liner as Dover has suggested, one might come closer with something like "Open wide, O wide ruler."

While a number of Attic vases of this period depicting Greeks and Persians could be excerpts or adaptations of the *Marathon* painting (cf. Fig. 8.9), I do not think that the Eurymedon oinochoe is one of them.[36] The humorous tone of the vase seems out of place for *Marathon.* But insofar as the vase provides an independent documentation of a feminized Persian adversary with sexual overtones, it supports a general interpretation along these lines for the nearly contemporary *Marathon* painting. The humor of the Eurymedon oinochoe preserves an attitude toward Persians that was part of the popular mentality of Athens in the glory days of Kimon. Moreover, it is clear that the victory at the Eurymedon was one of the events that the *Marathon* scene and the other paintings of the Stoa were meant to celebrate. What is so striking and effective about the Stoa paintings, however, is the way that they develop the sort of feminized conception of the Persian enemy on the oinochoe even further, even more relentlessly, through the mythic analogies of weak-spirited, panicky Amazons and captive, powerless Trojan women about to be made sex slaves.

Of course, the interpretation of the Stoa paintings that I have advanced here implies or assumes the closest cooperation among Polygnotos, Mikon, and whoever executed the *Marathon* painting. Pausanias (5.11.16) and Pliny (*HN* 35.57) both attribute the *Marathon* scene to Panainos, the brother of Pheidias. Aelian (*NA* 7.38) seemed to think that it might have been by one of the artists who did the other paintings, Mikon or Polygnotos. Some have suggested that the *Marathon* painting was a collaborative effort involving all three painters.[37] In this connection, it may well be significant that Pausanias (1.15.1–3) refers to the Stoa's painted decoration in the singular. Thus he describes the *Marathon* scene as "the end of the painting." This suggests that some six centuries after it was made, the Stoa's decoration still impressed viewers as a unity with one scene or portion eliding continuously into the next, and this in turn indicates that the content of the paintings was meant to be seen as closely interwoven.

Consequently, it seems very clear that the reciprocity of feminized barbarian and barbarized female in the Stoa's imagery was thoroughly intentional or calculated. Indeed, this reciprocity was essential to the visual rhetoric that the paintings collectively projected in the very heart of the Athenian civic space. The artists who realized the Stoa's program strove in concert to establish a rich network of resonance and analogy that could prompt the interpretive involvement of viewers as their attention moved from scene to scene. The image of barbarian Amazons in Persian dress being repulsed as they vainly attempted to invade Attika established a broad chronological context in which viewers were encouraged to understand the events of 490 B.C. as part of a longer, greater, more profound struggle. The image of the women of fallen Troy embodying a defeated barbarian empire carried the implications of this mythic-analogic construct further, given the similarities it posed to the punitive campaigns that Kimon and his Greek allies waged against the Persians in the aftermath of Xerxes' defeat.

But by now it should be evident that this comparison of myth and actuality involved far more than Asiatic ethnicity or geography; it also focused on those qualities of character that Greeks or Athenians of this period saw as a unifying trait between the Asiatic foreigners and the women in their very midst. Thus, the female aspect of the barbarian enemies in the *Amazon* and *Ilioupersis* scenes was absolutely central to their function as analogues to the Persians at Marathon. This aspect announced to spectators that it was an insatiable womanish appetite for power and domination that lead the Persians to attack Greece, just as this womanish nature ultimately prevented the Great King and his slavish lackeys from pursuing their grandiose plans with courage and tenacity. Now in the new order of things, the victors of the Delian League would take the prizes won in war as a reward for upholding Hellenic law and justice. They would have their way with their defeated, passive Asiatic enemies, once again following the precedent of the heroic forebears at Troy.

NOTES

1. See most recently Erskine 1990, esp. 2, 5, and 102.

2. SHA *Hadr.* 10–16.5; Ward-Perkins 1983, 206; Macdonald and Pinto 1995, 4, 7, 218.

3. For the program of the Parthenon metopes, see Castriota 1992, 134–174, and esp. nn. 4 and 15, with references to the extensive earlier bibliography. For the program of the Nike Temple, see E. B. Harrison 1972b; Hölscher 1973, 92–93; Stewart 1985.

4. T. L. Shear, 1984, esp. 13–15 and 18; Camp 1986, 64–72, figs. 40–44.

5. For historical sources on the Stoa, see Plut. *Kim.* 4.5; schol. on Dem. 20.112; Diog. Laert. 7.1.5; Suda, s.v. Zenon; Overbeck 1868, nos. 1055–1056. On the patronage of Peisianax, see Jeffery 1965, 41–42; Boersma 1970, 55–56.

6. For the interpretation of the Stoa Poikile within the context of Kimonian politics, see Castriota 1992, 76–89, with references to the large body of earlier scholarship.

7. See Castriota 1992, 77–78 with n. 89 for references.

8. For the funerary speeches and their innovative approach to mythic analogy, see K. R. Walters 1980, 1–27; Tyrrell 1980, 13–19; Loraux 1986; Castriota 1992, 47–51, with references to earlier scholarship.

9. See esp. Jeffery 1965, 51–52, but also Castriota 1992, 80 with n. 96, for additional references. For the catalogue of mythic precedents in fifth- and fourth-century Athenian rhetoric, see K. R. Walters 1980.

10. Francis and Vickers 1985b.

11. Robert 1895, 1–4 and 16; E. B. Harrison 1972b; Hölscher 1973, 50–68; Francis and Vickers 1985b.

12. For further discussion of the Hellene/Barbarian antithesis with additional bibliography, see Castriota 1992, 19–32; Castriota 2000. See also T. Harrison 2000; Rosalind Thomas 1998, ch. 3.

13. Tr. Castriota 1992, 19–20. On the ethical rationale for Greek victory over Persia, see also Castriota 1992, 17–32.

14. Pollitt 1976.

15. See, e.g., the Amazons on the krater by the Niobid Painter, Palermo, Museo Nazionale G1283; *ARV*[2] 599, 2; or Bologna, Museo Civico 289; *ARV*[2] 891; Castriota 1992, 83–85, figs. 3–4. For a different view of the Amazons in Athenian art and culture, see Stewart 1995, esp. 580–585.

16. Basel, Antikensammlung Ludwig BS 486; *ARV*[2] 612, 2; Castriota 1992, fig. 6, 84, n. 113.

17. For a general discussion of the use of such animal terminology, see Gould 1980. For a list of specific examples from primary sources, see Castriota 1992, 53, n. 35.

18. *Lys.* 658–659, 672–680, tr. Castriota 1992, 52, with n. 32.

19. On Artemisia's male dress, see Philostr. *VA* 4.21. Also see Weil 1976.

20. Dover 1974, 99–102; Just 1989, 154–157.

21. Some scholars have questioned how much this public rhetoric of male/female opposition reflects the realities of gender relations in Classical Athens. See Blok 1995, esp. ch. 5; Stewart 1995; Goldberg 1998, 89, 95. For a detailed discussion of gender relations and female status in Classical Athens, also see Schnurr-Redford 1996.

22. For a discussion of the traditional iconography of the Ilioupersis, see Castriota 1992, 96–100 with nn. 3–8 referring to the earlier scholarship. Also see S. P. Morris 1995; M. J. Anderson 1997, esp. chs. 11–13.

23. For earlier scholarship on the connections between Polygnotos' Troy paintings in the Stoa and at Delphi, see Castriota 1992, 127–130, and 81, n. 102. For the most recent work on the Troy scene at Delphi, also see Kebric 1983; Stansbury-O'Donnell 1989; Stansbury-O'Donnell 1999, 177–183.

24. After Castriota 1992, 129, fig. 12.

25. See Castriota 1992, 102–108. On Asiatic Trojans in drama, see Bacon 1961, 18–19, 27–28, 32, 34–36, 39–41; Francis 1990, 34–35; Hall 1991, 68–69, 119–121, 131–133, 136–137, 155–159. For Asiatic Trojans in Late Attic vase painting, see Castriota 1992, 102–108. On the possibility that the Trojans were dressed as Orientals in Polygnotos' paintings, see also M. C. Miller 1995, 449–465, esp. 453–459.

26. Robertson 1975, 251–252; Pollitt 1976, 52.

27. See, e.g., Leahy 1974, 8–9; Kebric 1983, passim.

28. Castriota 1992, 96–118.

29. First dithyramb, lines 48–63, tr. Castriota 1992, 234.

30. Ode 11 (10) 119–126, tr. Castriota 1992, 87.

31. Fehling 1974, 103; Schauenburg 1975; Hölscher 1989, 19; Kilmer 1993, 22; M. C. Miller 1997, 13; McNiven 2000, 88–89. For alternative interpretations of the vase and the inscription with which the writer does not concur, see Pinney 1984, 181; A. C. Smith 1999, esp. 135–141. I am indebted to Alan Shapiro for reminding me of the relevance of this vase to the Stoa paintings.

32. Attic red-figure oinochoe attributed to the Chicago Painter, Boston Museum of Fine Arts 13.196; *ARV*[2] 631.38; *Addenda*[2] 272; Castriota 2000, 444–445, fig. 17:1.

33. Dover 1978, 105.

34. Dover 1974, 99–102; Dover 1978, 105, 139–143; Just 1989, 154–157; Castriota 1992, 82–83.

35. Dover 1978, 105, 139–143.

36. For Persians in Greek art of the fifth century, see Bovon 1963, 597–600; Hölscher 1973, 40, 44–45; Schauenburg 1975; Raeck 1981, 101–103, 111; Sparkes 1997; Lissarrague 1997.

37. Thompson and Wycherley 1972, 92.

9

NOTES ON THE SUBJECT OF THE ILISSOS TEMPLE FRIEZE

RANDALL L. B. MCNEILL

Little remains of the small Ionic temple that once stood on the banks of the Ilissos river on the outskirts of Athens. It is a frustrating and tantalizing loss, especially since the temple very nearly survived into the present day. Converted for use as an Orthodox church, it was preserved essentially intact for more than two thousand years, only to be abandoned and dismantled in the late eighteenth century. All that exists now in situ is a battered marble foundation tucked between a water main and a highway. Indeed, virtually all trace of the Ilissos temple would have vanished were it not for a careful study of the building made in 1762 by the British architects James Stuart and Nicholas Revett.[1] It was on the strength of their drawings that the German scholar Franz Studniczka first established a connection in 1916 between the temple and a set of fragmentary slabs from a sculptural frieze preserved in Athens, Berlin, and Vienna.[2] His identification has been universally accepted, but uncertainty persists as to the subject matter of this enigmatic frieze. The poor condition of the slabs, the lack of epigraphical evidence, and the small proportion of original sculpture extant have meant that although several readings of the Ilissos temple's sculptural program have been proposed over the past century, none has won widespread scholarly approval.

Nevertheless, it would appear that the answer to the mystery has already been found and simply overlooked. This paper presents compositional, stylistic, and historical arguments in support of one early interpretation that has received scant attention in recent years: namely, that the Ilissos temple frieze originally consisted in large part of a representation of the sack of Troy and its aftermath. It will be argued that such a subject would have had enormous symbolic resonance in Athens between 440 and 430 B.C., the most likely period of the temple's construction, and that the Ilissos temple may in fact have been intended to carry a crucial political and diplomatic message at a time of increasing tension both inside and outside the Athenian Empire.

The core set of accepted fragments of the Ilissos frieze consists of four small slabs known as "B" through "E," which were first studied as a unit by Brueckner before being tied to the Ilissos temple by Studniczka.[3] The four pieces agree in their dimensions and are executed in a recognizably similar style, with individual figures separated from each other within a rocky landscape; dowel holes and traces of the original attachments on the backs of the slabs provide further evidence of a shared origin. On slab B (Figs. 15.1–2), two draped figures sit facing each other on rocky outcroppings amid piles of objects; another draped figure stands to the left, looking away. On the first segment of C (Fig. 15.3), a seated and semidraped man turns to his left with arm upraised; the remainder of the slab shows two standing figures similarly clad, one leaning on a staff. Slab D (Fig. 15.4) depicts a scene of *Frauenraub,* or the pursuit and abduction of women; a man hoists a resisting woman up by her waist, while a second man reaches for another fleeing woman, lunging past a smaller female figure to do so. The *Frauenraub* apparently continues on E (Fig. 15.5): a nude man steps up onto an outcropping and pulls at a draped figure; in the fragmentary central pairing, a man clad in a tunic and carrying a small child in the crook of his arm turns back to pull the hair of a kneeling woman; to the right, a third man, unclothed except for a cloak, leans over another woman who kneels clinging to a low column.

To slabs B through E we may safely add "A," a roughly triangular fragment in Athens that depicts two sacks or bundles similar to those represented on B (Fig. 15.6). "F," an eroded corner block whose two external sides portray a seated figure and two embattled warriors, also demands serious consideration as it was discovered near the temple site in the Ilissos riverbed (Figs. 15.7–9).[4] Möbius offered a plausible reconstruction incorporating F, in which four such blocks would have been placed at the corners of the temple, with thin slabs composing the remainder of the frieze.[5] Although Picón warned that such a combination of blocks and slabs on a single monument is otherwise unattested in Greek temple architecture, most scholars accept F's authenticity.[6]

Other sculptural pieces often associated with the Ilissos temple are more problematic. "G" denotes a frieze represented in one of Stuart and Revett's engravings of the temple's entablature, which shows a number of figures whose dress, manner, and composition are quite unlike those of the figures on the other slabs. Their incongruously togate and Roman appearance may be due in part to stylistic conventions followed by the eighteenth-century engraver, but Stuart and Revett themselves were unsure of the accuracy of their attribution, having simply copied a sculptural fragment found elsewhere in Athens that fit into the Ilissos frieze space.[7] Supported by no evidence beyond their tentative defense, "G" is usually omitted from discussion. Some have argued that the marked resemblance of the figures on slabs B and C to certain figures on the sarcophagus from Torre Nuova (Fig. 15.11) indicates that this piece can be used to interpret the Ilissos frieze as a whole. The private funerary function of the sarcophagus, however, stands in sharp contrast to the public context of the temple; the Torre Nuova images are likely to be free adaptations rather than strict copies, which limits their usefulness for any reconstruction of the missing Ilissos scenes.[8] Instead, fragment A, slabs B through E, and block F remain the only elements that can be securely associated with the frieze.

Studniczka's original dating of the temple to 450–448 B.C. continued to be accepted until scholars in the late 1970s began to argue on stylistic grounds for a later date in the 430s or 420s B.C.[9] Indeed, the composition and spacing of the scenes on the frieze strongly suggest a post-Parthenon construction. The sculptural groupings are sharply demarcated, with the various forms spaced well apart from each other. There is almost no contact between figures, much less the sort of intricate overlapping that one finds on the Parthenon frieze. At the same time, certain individuals bear a close resemblance in their drapery, forms, and movements to figures on the Parthenon. On C (Fig. 15.3), for example, the figure jauntily leaning on his staff strongly echoes one of the leading officials of the procession on the Parthenon's east side (East IV.22).[10] The postures of various Ilissos figures also call to mind those of the assembly of gods on the east frieze: the rightmost figure on B (Figs. 15.1–2) resembles Hermes (East IV.24) as he sits with his hands placed loosely in his lap, while the man clasping his knee on F (Fig. 15.7) openly recalls Ares (East IV.27). These individuals are surely to be read as later imitations of the Parthenon sculptures; figures originally in close proximity have here been reproduced as separated forms in a new composition.

The Ilissos frieze seems to be roughly contemporary with the Hephaisteion and to prefigure many of the features of the frieze of the Temple of Athena Nike. Certainly their compositional styles demonstrate a certain resemblance, particularly in the emptiness of the spaces, the stylized postures and movements of the drapery, and the deployment of landscape details throughout. Individual forms on the Ilissos frieze also match figures from both of these other Athenian reliefs: the right figure on C (Fig. 15.3) and middle figure on B (Figs. 15.1–2) with strikingly similar, indeed nearly identical images on the east frieze of the Nike temple (block b, Fig. 15.17); the seated figure on C with the god on the east frieze of the Hephaisteion (slab 2, fig. 8, commonly identified as Zeus); and the crouching warrior of F (Fig. 15.8) with several counterparts on both works (the comparable poses and rendering of details, such as the shields, are especially noteworthy here). On the strength of such stylistic similarities, combined with a careful review of the archaeological and architectural evidence, including the plan of the temple and the design of its capitals, Miles has argued convincingly that the Ilissos frieze and temple should be dated to between 435 and 430 B.C.[11] Such a dating, if accurate, would make this the first wholly Ionic temple ever to be constructed in Attika, and the only one to be completed within the lifetime of Perikles.

In interpreting the subject matter of the frieze, it is best to approach the various slabs individually rather than attempt to identify the surviving figures as participants in a single unified scene. Kerenyi's suggestion that the frieze represented the ritual sacrifice of the Hyakinthides is questionable precisely because he neatly identifies each and every figure on B through E with a corresponding character in the myth, without making allowance for the figures who must have occupied the remainder of the field.[12] In light of the fact that only about one-tenth of the original sculpture survives from the Ilissos temple, it is unlikely that all the key components of the narrative would have been so preserved. We are on firmer ground if we envision the various sides of the temple as having once portrayed separate but thematically related scenes. This was, after all, standard practice on architectural friezes in the Classical period. The only frieze for which a single-subject composition can be posited with any confidence is that of the Parthenon, itself a highly unrepresentative structure. Indeed, if the Parthenon frieze does in fact represent a conflation of separate and unrelated Athenian civic festivals into one continuous episode, it becomes the exception that simply proves the rule.[13]

As we turn to consider the individual slabs, we can see that the activities they depict fall into three basic categories: seated and standing figures on B, C, and part of F; *Frauenraub* on D and E; and combat on the other face of F. Much attention has been focused on the strange objects piled at the feet of the seated figures on B (Figs. 15.1–2). Sources such as Aristophanes' *Frogs* and Late Classical vase paintings have been employed to support their identification variously as wine sacks and bundles of clothing. Scholars cite the slumping shoulders and listless air of the two men as signifying that they are travelers who have just completed a long journey and are resting beside their luggage.[14]

There are, however, certain difficulties associated with such an interpretation. The conical headgear of the left figure far more closely resembles a *pilos*-style cap or helmet than it does the wide-brimmed *petasos* that is the usual mark of the traveler in Greek art of this period.[15] The wooden object beside the pilos has often been interpreted as a baggage pole of some sort, but Möbius observed that it is far too thick and knobby to be a plausible carrying pole, and resembles more a club than a pole.[16] In the absence of obvious visual cues such as *petasoi* or carrying poles, the items on the right cannot safely be assumed to be travelers' bags as opposed to sacks or bundles of some other sort. Most importantly, neither of the two figures is dressed for a journey; they have no discernible boots or cloaks, and their half-draped himations suggest instead their identity as gods or more probably older men.[17]

For these reasons, I suggest that something more than simple fatigue is rendered here. The left figure cups his chin in his hand, while the one on the right conveys a palpable mood of dejection. *Mutatis mutandis,* their postures and setting bear a striking resemblance to images of captured prisoners on Roman coins: a forlorn Gaul or Dacian hunched over with his head in his hand and perched on a rock strewn with the weapons and accoutrements of his people. It is not inconceivable that the figures of B represent prisoners, perhaps the elders of a defeated city or town surrounded by the spoils of war. The group may then have extended onto other slabs of the frieze, including the one to which fragment A (Fig. 15.6) originally belonged.

The identity of the figures on C (Fig. 15.3), in turn, is suggested by the aforementioned resemblance of the seated figure on the left to that of "Zeus" on the Hephaisteion east frieze. The scepter or staff that this figure must once have held as an attachment in his left hand, his regal bearing, sweeping drapery, and twisting posture are all reminiscent of standard representations of the god.[18] It is unnecessary to attempt to connect him with the seated figures on B (Figs. 15.1–2), since the two slabs are not obviously contiguous; nor does he possess the bags or equipment of the other two. Instead, if we accept his identity as Zeus, a straightforward reading presents itself: C is a segment from a much larger assembly of gods, perhaps originally located on the east side of the temple directly over the entrance to the cella and comparable to those on the Parthenon and the Nike temple. The central figure with his arm raised becomes one of the more youthful and energetic gods—perhaps Apollo—while his neighbor leaning upon a staff can be read as a representation of Hephaistos, since by the 430s B.C. the god's crutch had long since become an identifying token rather than a means of accurately portraying his lameness.[19] The other slabs on this side of the Ilissos temple would have depicted the remaining gods and goddesses of the pantheon, including the relaxed figure on block F (Fig. 15.7), who would then occupy the rightmost space in the scene. Perhaps he can be identified as Ares, which would provide a nice enjambment with the battle scene that begins on the other side of the block (Fig. 15.8).

The *Frauenraub* that encompasses D and E requires careful consideration (Figs. 15.4–5). Robert has read it as a ritual mock abduction, but to treat this scene purely as an Athenian cultic ritual is to ignore its pervasive atmosphere of genuine tension and violence.[20] Nor is it viable to see here Hades' abduction of Persephone or the rape of the daughters of Leukippos by the Dioskouroi, despite ingenious attempts to make the latter story fit through the interpolation of references to Artemis Agrotera.[21] There is no sign of the chariots that constitute indispensable elements in the iconography of either myth. Moreover, too many women already appear even on the extant slabs for these suggestions possibly to be valid. With at least five pairs of men and women involved in the original abduction scene, an incident on a much larger scale is portrayed here.

Of the limited number of mythical *Frauenraube* involving multiple participants, few can be made to fit the available evidence. The absence of Centaurs makes a reference to the Lapiths impossible. No ships or nautical motifs are represented, and the action takes place in a continuously rocky landscape, which would seem to preclude interpretation of D and E as the abduction of Argive women by Phoenician pirate-traders described in Herodotos 1.1. Studniczka used the evidence of Herodotos 6.137–139 to suggest that the frieze depicts Pelasgians attacking the young women of Athens during the festival of Artemis at Brauron, but his proposal is similarly weakened by the lack of any maritime imagery.[22] Herodotos emphasizes throughout his account that this was a seaborne raid, and indeed he introduces the anecdote solely to explain the significance of Miltiades' capture of the island of Lemnos. Nor was the Pelasgian story widely popular as a decorative motif in Athens; the tale begins badly with the Athenians failing to protect the women from attack and ends tragically when the Pelasgians murder the captive women and their Attic-speaking children. Some versions even blamed the Athenians for originating the conflict by treacherously breaking an oath and expelling the Pelasgians from Attika. It seems improbable that such a squalid and unflattering event would have been included on a temple frieze at a time when the Athenians under Perikles' leadership were working to celebrate the greatness, uniqueness, and ethical superiority of their *polis*.

The one mythical *Frauenraub* that seems satisfactorily to match the subject matter on these two slabs is the Ilioupersis or sack of Troy. Certain elements of the composition become readily intelligible when viewed in this context. The woman who clings to the column on E, for example, can be read as the Trojan priestess Kassandra, with Aias son of Oileus bending down to pull her away.[23] The figure to her left who carries a small child while dragging a kneeling woman behind him may be identifiable as Neoptolemos, tormenting

Andromache as he heads off to throw her son Astyanax from the walls of the city.[24] The other elements would then stand as further images of the violence that accompanied Troy's fall, including the little girl on D (Fig. 15.4), who stands motionless amidst the chaos, perhaps to be read as already having been taken captive or else frozen with fear.[25]

Although the basic identification of a Troy scene was first offered as early as 1879, before the four slabs had even been associated with each other or with the Ilissos temple, the proposal was rejected in the early twentieth century on the grounds that none of the male figures on D or E is shown armed, with no weapons or shields to indicate a martial setting.[26] This was taken at the time to be conclusive evidence against the hypothesis, which as a result has been sadly neglected; only Florens Felten has continued to argue on its behalf.[27]

There is, however, no great obstacle to placing an Ilioupersis on one side of the frieze. The warriors of block F (Fig. 15.8) indicate that scenes of combat were included on the Ilissos frieze and perhaps originally extended across one entire side of the temple.[28] As for the apparent *Waffnunglosigkeit* of the men on D and E, it should be remembered that original metal attachments and painted details may have been lost. Furthermore, the nudity of the male figures can be explained as an indication of their heroic status. Greek fighters were conventionally shown clad only in *chlamys* and helmet in this period, except in portrayals of battles with Amazons or other Greeks (in which case, more realistic armor and equipment might be depicted). The rightmost figure on E appears to be wearing something pushed back on his head, possibly a Corinthian-style helmet, and such a detail would have been a sufficient signal of his identity as both a heroic warrior and a Greek.[29]

The great advantage to reading these panels as a representation of the Ilioupersis is that it points the way towards a straightforward, coherent, and plausible interpretation of the Ilissos frieze as a whole, one that allows for the inclusion of scenes and figures that are no longer extant. If we accept C (Fig. 15.3) as part of a separate rendition of the assembly of gods, we can then approach each of the remaining slabs as isolated fragments within a larger series of connected scenes related to the fall of Troy. In the following tentative reconstruction, the *Frauenraub* becomes part of a grand depiction on the south frieze of the city's final night, which might originally have incorporated other familiar images such as Aineias with Anchises or Helen and Menelaos. Block F (Figs. 15.7–9), now placed on the northeastern corner of the temple, closes off the pantheon scene on the east side and initiates a battle sequence on the north, where Greeks fight Trojans in a complementary composition to the Ilioupersis scene (Fig. 9.1).[30]

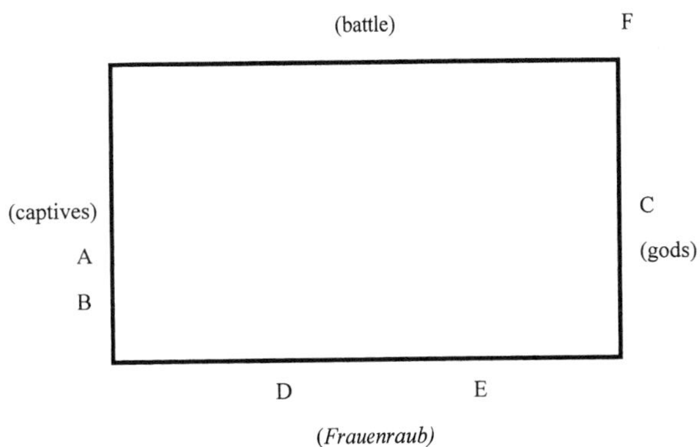

FIGURE 9.1. *Reconstruction by Randall L. B. McNeill of sculptural slabs on Ilissos Temple.*

Regarding the function of the dejected figures on B (Figs. 15.1–2) within this proposed sculptural program, a clue is suggested by the similarity of their poses and melancholy air to those of the heroes on the reverse side of the Niobid krater (Fig. 6.1). It has often been suggested that this vase painting may have been inspired by, or even copied from, the famous wall painting of the *Nekyia* by Polygnotos in the Lesche of the Knidians at Delphi, which Pausanias informs us portrayed an array of heroes seated on rocks in the underworld. Significantly, Pausanias records that this painting formed a pair with another work by Polygnotos: a depiction of the aftermath of the sack of Troy, including representations of the plunder that the Greek warriors loaded onto their ships, images of children sitting or standing near the adults, and portraits of several injured and despondent Trojan captives—all of which find their echoes as motifs on the Ilissos frieze:[31]

> Beyond Helen sits a man wrapped in a purple cloak, in a state of great sorrow; you would guess that he was Helenos the son of Priam even before reading the inscription. Close by Helenos is Meges; Meges is

> wounded in the arm. . . . Lykomedes the son of Kreon is also painted next to Meges, with a wound in the hand. (Paus. 10.25.5–6)

It is tempting to see some interaction between the Ilissos frieze and these Polygnotan paintings, to find among the captives of B the forlorn Helenos slumped in despair, and Lykomedes nursing his hand as he stands awaiting his fate.[32]

One compelling reason for interpreting the Ilissos frieze as a large-scale treatment of the sack of Troy is that such a sculptural and architectural program would match very well with the contemporary political situation in Athens. Miles' dating of the Ilissos temple to 435–430 B.C., if correct, places its construction in the middle of a period of worsening diplomatic tensions within the Athenian Empire, as well as beyond Athens' sphere of influence in the Greek world. In 440, the tributary state and key ally of Samos attempted to break away from Athenian control, secretly seeking (and nearly receiving) assistance for this revolt from Sparta and other members of the Peloponnesian League. Athens managed to quell the Samians and put down a separate rebellion in Byzantium, but the member states of the Athenian Empire remained potentially restive and a constant source of internal distraction.[33] The year 435 saw the beginning of the Epidamnian crisis, an escalating conflict in the far northwest that by 433 would involve the navies of Corinth and Athens on opposing sides. It was widely expected that war would soon break out between the great powers of Sparta and Athens, despite attempts by Perikles as the political leader of Athens to send subtle signals that his state was committed to the balance of power and a policy of peace through deterrence rather than appeasement.[34]

Perikles therefore faced the enormous challenge of reaching separate audiences with very different messages: to encourage his fellow-citizens to hold to the policies he had persuaded them to adopt; to soothe and control the member states of the Athenian Empire; and to discourage Sparta and Corinth from taking drastic action against Athens. At the same time, work was continuing on the Akropolis. These same years saw the completion of the pediments of the Parthenon, the great realization of Perikles' vision of Athens as the cultural model for the rest of Greece. In these years Perikles would assuredly have been involved in the planning of any further public projects; at the very least, it is inconceivable that a new construction such as the Ilissos temple would have been initiated without his approval.[35] In such a context, it becomes possible for us to appreciate the larger significance of the Ilissos temple as a work of sophisticated and multifaceted symbolism, one very much in tune with that curious mixture of pro-Athenian celebration and panhellenic idealism that characterized the Periklean age as a whole.

The first true Ionic temple to be built on Attic soil, the Ilissos temple would have visually reaffirmed the ethnic bond of the Athenians to the Ionian Greeks, who made up the majority population of their empire. This may have been intended as a diplomatic signal to the allies of Athens, an indirect plea for their loyalty and support in any coming conflict. By the same token, the temple's modest size and careful placement outside the city walls minimized any sense of Akropolis-style triumphalism in this latest addition to the Athenian building program and would have helped to obscure the imperialistic nature of Athens' hegemony at a time when suspicion of the Athenians was running high throughout the Greek world.[36] On the frieze itself, portrayals of Greeks fighting Trojans would celebrate the notion of panhellenic triumph over the enemies of the East in a thinly veiled allusion to the days when Sparta and Athens had been allies defending Greece against invasion by the Persians.[37] At the same time, the accompanying scenes of Troy's final agony would serve as a powerful reminder to citizens and visitors alike of the sorrows and tragedies of war, especially those of an unwanted and senseless war in which there could be no true victors, only different forms of defeat.[38]

At a moment when bitter conflict seemed to lie just over the horizon, such a complex of messages and images would have carried an extraordinary emotional and intellectual resonance. Viewed in this way, the Ilissos temple frieze becomes a highly ambivalent and anxious work, yet one that is admirably suited to its times. Should the current crisis be allowed to progress any further, it seems to warn, the fate of the Trojans and the Greeks who defeated them will befall not only Athens but Greece as a whole. The Ilissos temple, in other words, may have represented another subtle, daringly intellectual, and ultimately fruitless attempt by the Athenians to forestall the coming of the Peloponnesian War. Even today something continues to be felt in its few remaining slabs and fragments—ghostly traces of urgency, uncertainty, and fear. Although any interpretation of the Ilissos temple frieze must of course remain purely speculative in the absence of further evidence coming to light, it seems likely that these mysterious and strangely haunting images would thus reflect the turbulent conditions of the world in which they were carved so many centuries ago.

NOTES

The ideas presented here originated in an independent study project under the direction of Jerome J. Pollitt when I was a graduate student at Yale University. An earlier version of the paper was delivered at the colloquium *Genre and Innovation in the Classical World,* held at Yale in the fall of 1994. I would like to take this opportunity to thank Jerry once again for all the advice, encouragement, guidance, and friendship that he has given to me over the years. My thanks go also to Judy Barringer, Jeff Hurwit, and the anonymous readers for the University of Texas Press for their many valuable suggestions for the improvement of this paper and to Olga Palagia for her kindness and generosity in sharing with me her excellent illustrations of the Ilissos frieze.

1. Stuart and Revett 1762, vol. 2.

2. Studniczka 1916, 169–230.

3. Brueckner 1910, 50–62.

4. By A. Skias, who also excavated the Ilissos foundation and uncovered fragment A (Skias 1897, 73–85; 1894, 133–192).

5. Möbius 1935–1936, 262–263. Note that the corner block is here identified as "G." Möbius' arrangement of elements is very different from the one suggested in this paper; the general accommodation of block and slabs, however, is quite successful.

6. Picón 1978, 57. Cf., e.g., F. Felten 1984, 72; Childs 1985, 221.

7. "The figures on the frieze are copied from a fragment found at Athens, which so exactly agreed in dimensions with the place assigned to it, that there is no improbability in supposing them to have been originally in combination." Stuart and Revett 1762, 24.

8. See Hauser 1910, 280–281; Curtius 1923, 47–48. Cf. Picón 1978, 60.

9. E.g., Picón 1978; Krug 1979.

10. But see an even more direct comparison on the Hephaisteion frieze, as noted below.

11. Miles 1980, 313–321. Miles does not discuss the warrior on block F, but she suggests (Miles 1980, 315) that the male abductors on E resemble warrior figures on both the Hephaisteion and the Nike Temple frieze. It should be noted that Childs (1985) has taken issue with Miles' conclusions, suggesting instead a dating of 445–440 B.C. However, there are a number of problems with Childs' proposal, inasmuch as his argument depends upon a questionable stylistic and compositional linkage of the Ilissos frieze to the "less accomplished" metopes of the Parthenon (through perceived similarities in the drapery), as well as a downplaying of the far more obvious parallels—in drapery, three-dimensional rendering, and open composition—to the Hephaisteion and Nike Temple. Childs himself acknowledges some of these weaknesses (see, e.g., Childs 1985, 221, 231, 236), and his overall defense of his position remains unconvincing.

In any event, such a revised dating of the Ilissos temple would only confirm the building's importance as the first fully Ionic temple in Attika. Indeed, a construction date of 445–440 B.C. would place the temple in the years immediately following the end of the so-called First Peloponnesian War, which would lend further urgency and emotional impact to the warning images of war and suffering that I argue are presented in the frieze.

12. Kerenyi 1961.

13. As noted by Pollitt 1992b, 40.

14. This has led to conjectures that they are ancient Pelasgians in Attika or, conversely, visitors newly arrived for the Lesser Mysteries at Agrai. See Studniczka 1916, 173, 193–194. Cf. Möbius 1935–1936, 241.

15. As first noted by von Schneider 1903, 92. Cf. discussion by Chamay 1977.

16. Möbius 1935–1936, 241–242.

17. Krug 1979, 10.

18. See also relevant discussion and reconstructions in Harrison 1967.

19. Boardman 1975a, 225.

20. Robert 1923, 58, 60–61. Cf. discussion by Childs, who calls attention (1985, 221–224) to the dynamism and "very real sense of tension" in this scene.

21. Most recently in von Eickstedt 1994.

22. Studniczka 1916, 191–197.

23. To be sure, the figure is clutching a column and not

the Palladion, which one would expect to have been represented in the scene. Picón (1978, 65), however, notes that the iconography of the Ilioupersis is much in evidence here, and speculates that the Palladion itself might have appeared on a lost slab.

24. Neoptolemos is usually depicted in Ilioupersis scenes not as carrying Astyanax but as swinging him through the air by one foot; variations are evident, however, in representations of the scene during this period. Certainly the tableaux of Aias and Kassandra and Neoptolemos and Astyanax (in conjunction with the death of Priam) were regularly depicted in close proximity as central images of the narrative. See *LIMC* 8.1, s.v. Ilioupersis, 650–657 [M. Pipili].

25. Or engaged in lamentation; suppliant women and girls are commonly included in representations of the death of Priam (slain by the Astyanax-wielding Neoptolemos) to "help to give something of the atmosphere of the sack." See *LIMC* 8.1, s.v. Ilioupersis, 650–657 [M. Pipili]. For discussion of the girl's identity as a child rather than a statue, see Picón 1978, 65, although I disagree that either she or the leftmost woman on D are "undisturbed or unaware" of what is happening to them. There is nothing in the rendering of the figures to suggest a lack of concern.

26. The suggestion was advanced separately by Heydemann 1879, 19, n. 111d; and Visconti 1880, 36, n. 1066. Visconti also suggested the Kassandra-Aias identification for the rightmost pair on E. For the *Waffnunglosigkeit* counterargument, see, e.g., Studniczka 1916, 190–191, following von Schneider 1903.

27. F. Felten 1984, 74–75. Felten cautiously identifies four different subjects, one on each side of the frieze, as an Amazonomachy; a Gigantomachy or a Trojan War combat; the Sack of Troy; and a scene of voyagers, perhaps the Argonauts, Odysseus, or the Herakleidai. I follow some of Felten's proposals but would suggest that all four sides of the frieze were related to each other and showed various scenes associated with the fall of Troy, including its aftermath. The Ilioupersis is also offered as an alternative explanation of E's subject matter by Kunze (1992) without further discussion.

28. Möbius 1928, 3.

29. I am indebted to Jerome J. Pollitt for this observation.

30. Cf. the placement of F on the northwestern corner by Schrader 1932, 179 and 187, followed by Möbius 1935–1936. See also discussion by F. Felten 1984, 76.

31. Paus. 10.25–28.

32. Faint sculptural traces on "Lykomedes" show that his right arm originally jutted out from his body, thereby calling visual attention to his hand. The Ilissos frieze as a whole may be viewed as representing in part an amalgamation or pastiche of Polygnotan elements, with one of its subjects identical to that of the Delphi *Ilioupersis,* but with several of its component figures drawn from the matching Delphi *Nekyia.* For new reconstructions of the Delphi paintings, see Stansbury-O'Donnell 1989; Stansbury-O'Donnell 1990. Note that Stansbury-O'Donnell (1989, 208, fig. 3) offers very different reconstructions of Helenos and Meges from the ones proposed here.

33. Kept in check only by the vigilance of the Athenian navy, as is evidenced by the sudden rise of problems with the collection of imperial tribute following the troubles of 433/432. See Meiggs 1972, 247, 252–253.

34. These included the novel initiatives of a defensive-only alliance with Kerkyra; the imposition of the Megarian Decree, effectively the first trade embargo in recorded history; and a sort of policing action against the city of Potidaia, within the Athenian sphere of influence. Sadly, all three acts merely precipitated the onset of the war. For strategic and political analysis of these moves, see Kagan 1969, esp. 237–242, 261–285.

35. Donald Kagan, personal communication. For discussion of Perikles and his supervision of public building programs in Athens, see, e.g., Pollitt 1972, 65–67.

36. For placement and orientation of the temple, see Miles 1980, 318. See also pertinent discussion in Meiggs 1972, 289–290.

37. See related discussion in Erskine 2001, 113–122. I am indebted to Jeff Hurwit for this reference.

38. For discussion of the peculiar moral and ethical ambiguities of the Trojan War as it was perceived by fifth-century Greeks, see Stansbury-O'Donnell 1989, 214.

10

"PERIKLEAN" CULT IMAGES AND THEIR MEDIA

BRUNILDE SISMONDO RIDGWAY

I cannot possibly hope to tell Jerry Pollitt anything new about Periklean Athens, a subject in which he is far better versed than I. But in my wish to participate in a volume in his honor, I shall make bold to present a few comments on a minor topic that, if not new, has at least not been sufficiently investigated from this specific angle: the appropriateness of media for cult images in fifth-century Athens in the light of preceding and contemporary examples.

Even this brief statement of purpose raises the question, can we possibly say that certain materials—and not others—were considered appropriate for cult images? Even more to the point, Was there such a thing in antiquity as a "cult image" in the current sense of the term? I shall begin with this second issue.

It has recently been argued that the concept of cult image is a modern construct with no true equivalent in Greek culture, either in terminology or in practice. With respect to cult, images at crossroads, in open-air sanctuaries, and even within private habitations could be the recipients of offerings given with the same devotion as those directed at a statue within a temple or the official sacrifices at a public altar.[1] Indeed, ritual did not always need a cult image, and practices varied from place to place and from cult to cult. In addition, manifestations of worship and propitiation were not limited to Olympian or chthonic deities but could be addressed to heroes and even to mortals and their statues, when specific circumstances dictated it.[2] Finally, a temple could house more than one statue through time, and no clear distinction was made, in either the nomenclature or the ritual, among such images. A clear case is provided by the later (fourth-century) temple at the Argive Heraion, where a chryselephantine Hera and a Hebe by Polykleitos (the Younger?) and Naukydes respectively were housed together with a small seated Hera in pear wood and some "ancient" statues of the Charites, according to Pausanias (2.17.3–5). In the Hellenistic period, when honors to mortals were increasing in frequency and quality, ruler portraits could share space with a divine image as σύνναοι and even a Gaulish woman had her statue set up within the Temple of Hera at Pergamon.[3]

I would refine the definition by focusing not on the reception of worship or the number of images but on whether the divine statue occupied a specific location within a temple: axial, central, and permanent, therefore, a position of preeminence. The Pheidian colossi immediately come to mind: the Athena Parthenos, with her dramatic backdrop of two-tiered columns, or the Zeus at Olympia, so big that it could have removed the roof, had he stood up (Strabo 8.3.30). Such masterpieces, with their size and iconographic richness, filled up the cella and dominated their respective space; they were conceived for it and could not have had independent existence outside it, since their construction did not allow for easy removal, and their medium prevented outdoor display. They can therefore be rightly called "temple images." Yet the fifth century does not mark the inception of this "genre." Even when the statues themselves are lost, archaeological evidence shows that, at least as early as the beginning of the sixth century B.C., divine images could be strategically placed within a cella, supported by permanent pedestals on axis with the doorway and thus immediately visible to the ancient visitors who crossed the threshold.

The typical example is provided by the Temple of Hera at Olympia, where a stone base still stretches from inner colonnade to inner colonnade, across the central aisle. Although Pausanias (5.17.1) does not specify their location, he mentions a seated statue of Hera and one of Zeus standing beside her, and this description, coinciding with the honorands of the building, would fit the elongated dimensions of the extant pedestal. Pausanias lists many other divine images within the same cella (5.17.2–3), but their alleged makers are also cited, which may imply that those works, despite their definitely Archaic masters, were not as early as the unattributed Zeus and Hera. Pausanias' wording, moreover, suggests that several among these additional sculptures were votive offerings, and others may have been placed there for safekeeping when the Heraion seems to have been turned into a museum or a repository for sacred antiques. None among them would have occupied the position of honor held by the Hera and the Zeus.

The idea of a temple image appears to fit well with a theory widespread in modern literature: that a Greek temple was the veritable house of a god, so that a sort of "chicken and the egg" game exists among archaeologists. Was the first temple built to protect a preexisting, venerable image, or was the idea of creating permanent statues of the gods sparked by the availability of permanent, monumental housing?[4] Yet the very conception of a specific structure as habitation for a deity, in turn embodied within a tangible image, may be a non-Greek idea derived from contemporary and earlier Oriental religions, specifically Mesopotamian and, to some extent, Levantine.[5] Nonetheless, an unspoken assumption would still envision a "temple image" (in our sense of the term) inside the cella of each Greek temple, regardless of its geographic location and date.

According to a new study,[6] however, some claim can be made that not all temples housed a "temple statue," at least until the Classical period. Material remains are not always helpful, in that centered pedestals can provide positive evidence only when they survive, but their absence cannot be taken as definitive proof that they never existed. The regularly shaped blocks that served as support for sculpture could certainly be, and often were, more easily removed and reused than the masonry and column drums of the temple itself. But to assume that no cella lacked the central focus of an image of its "inhabitant" is a misconception based on Hellenistic and Christian practices.

To cite a few possible examples: no ancient idol seems to have stood in the Temple of Zeus at Olympia before Pheidias made his chryselephantine Zeus after 438 B.C., although the building was completed some twenty years earlier. No temple image is ever mentioned for the Temple of Poseidon at Sounion, and none may have existed in the Temple of Zeus at Nemea and that of Apollo at Delphi, where the specific layouts of the cellas, with their subterranean chambers, did not allow for centrally placed pedestals. At Delphi, moreover, Apollo was not the only "inhabitant" of the building, since he ceded it to Dionysos during the winter months, and the Wine God seems to have had his tomb there, but not his statue.[7] In terms of geographic preferences, the Magna Graecian temples appear not to have housed temple images, and some temples in Asia Minor had specific arrangements that differed from those of the Greek mainland.[8]

Against this more nuanced background, the great role played by temple images in Periklean Athens and its demes is striking. Perhaps the city was already predisposed to the reception of divine statues in their temples: on the Akropolis alone, the Temple of the Polias housed an Athena of olive wood of such great antiquity that it was said to have fallen from the sky (Paus. 1.26.7), and the Temple of Athena Nike, even in its fifth-century version, held an earlier wooden image that may have gone back to the beginnings of the cult.[9] But a virtual flourishing of temple images occurred under Perikles and his immediate successors: not only the chryselephantine Athena Parthenos by Pheidias in the Parthenon but also the gold-and-ivory Dionysos by Alkamenes for a temple near the theater and the marble Nemesis by Agorakritos at Rhamnous, to name only those that can be attributed to a structure with certainty.[10] For the city, Pheidias is also credited with a statue of Aphrodite Ourania in Parian marble (Paus. 1.14.6), although the building that has come to light so far, at the northwest corner of the Agora, is of Augustan date.[11] Outside Attica, Pheidias is said to have made a chryselephantine Aphrodite Ourania for Elis (Paus. 6.25.1), an Athena in the same medium for the same town (Paus. 6.26.3), a similar Athena for Pallene, in Achaia (Paus. 7.27.2), and, perhaps earliest of all, an akrolithic Athena Areia for Plataia (Paus. 9.4.1).[12]

To be sure, many gold-and-ivory images, or the akrolithic, less costly versions of that technique, may have been attributed to the great Athenian master and his pupils to enhance their prestige, even if other sculptors unrelated to the Pheidian circle had actually made them. The fact remains, nonetheless, that Pausanias, with his antiquarian penchant, could record a great number of temple images somehow connected with Athens and its masters, suggesting that a specific interest in such statues was sparked by the great impact produced by the Parthenos in her spectacular setting. Those of us who have seen the modern recreation of this colossus that Alan LeQuire has made for the Parthenon in Nashville, Tennessee, realize its awe-inspiring effect, even without the full gilding of its immense expanses of drapery. Jerry Pollitt was one of the speakers at the Athena's unveiling[13] and can attest the truthfulness of my statement.

On that occasion, Pollitt emphasized that Pheidias was a member of a selective circle, in which philosophers, theoreticians, and dramatists around Perikles were beginning to challenge the established religion and the meaning of the gods. He pointed out that Metrodoros of Lampsakos, a pupil of that Anaxagoras who belonged to that circle, could even interpret the Olympian deities as "personifications of contemporary philosophical ideas" and visualize Athena as the embodiment of *Tekhne*. This is an enlightening comment, if we accept that a chryselephantine statue, with its enormous size and the difficulty of its media, must have appeared indeed a highly "technical" work, in both the ancient and the modern sense of the word[14] and its maker was a man everyone knew, not some unknown master shrouded in the fogs of a past that people could not remember!

The temple images that Pheidias made could not be said to have fallen from the sky or to have appeared mysteriously in bushes or by the seashore. These were creations carefully planned in advance and properly paid for—the ancient equivalent of seeing "your taxes at work." Whatever magical aura was lost through these mundane details, however, was more than counterbalanced by the results. If people could accept that a temple statue had a contemporary maker, then obstacles could no longer be raised to filling structures with these symbols not only of divine power but also of a city's wealth and religious beliefs.

To be sure, as Pollitt pointed out, a work like the Parthenos could be read at various levels: from the most traditional, for the masses, to the most sophisticated perceived only by the few. Yet I am convinced that the primary requirement for these temple images had to be a sort of religious faithfulness that made them recognizable and acceptable, through the centuries, by all people, regardless of ethnic distinctions. This "orthodoxy" may have inspired the anecdotes about the Zeus at Olympia: that the god himself signaled his approval of the image by striking the floor in front of it with a thunderbolt; that Pheidias, according to Strabo, claimed to have derived his inspiration from Homer's description in the first book of the *Iliad*.[15]

Gold and ivory as materials for a divine statue require no explanation. Their costliness and physical properties made them specifically appropriate: the ivory, with its organic nature and its texture was closest to human flesh, the subject of many poetic similes; the gold, with its gleaming within the darkened temple, recalled the luminous epiphanies of the "blond" gods.[16] Although in Athens the materials of the Parthenos may also have alluded to Oriental luxury and therefore to the recent victory over the Persians, the existence of chryselephantine statues in earlier times shows that the technique was not invented ad hoc for the Parthenon.[17]

Marble too requires no explanation. It was the material most abundant in Greece, available even in large blocks, easiest to work to a high finish, capable of being tinted with a coating of wax (*ganosis*) and paints, and best suited for rendering the delicate complexion of female figures. Wood, as already mentioned, was the material of some early idols, and it continued to be used down to the Imperial period for specific rituals involving divine images. It too could carry symbolic meaning, the olive wood of the Polias being particularly appropriate for the goddess who had "created" the olive tree.[18]

One other temple in Athens received its "temple statues" during the fifth century but in a different medium: bronze. Among all other religious buildings in the city, the Hephaisteion may have been the only one with its main images in that material, and I believe that choice was made not out of tradition or developed technical capabilities but for a specific religious reason: because bronze was appropriate for the smith god. This point has been obscured by an awareness that statues of the gods in bronze were well known from earlier times; witness, especially, the colossal Athena on the Akropolis, the so-called Promachos, by Pheidias himself.[19] We also have assumed implicitly that no restriction on the materials of temple statues existed. This may be so, but a cursory check through the literature suggests that bronze "temple statues" were very rare. I shall first review the evidence for the Hephaisteion images and then that for earlier "temple statues" in bronze.

Whether or not the building on the hill to the west of the Athenian Agora is the Hephaisteion or a temple to another divinity is immaterial to my point. Equally irrelevant are the dimensions and even the pertinence to the base of the blocks in dark Eleusinian limestone at present in the cella of that temple. What matters is that a fragmentary inscription datable between 421 and 415 B.C. records the purchase of bronze, lead, and tin for "a pair of statues for the Hephaisteion." The official inventory implies that this was a public commission, not a private enterprise. Pausanias (1.14.44) states that he was not surprised to find an image of Athena in that sanctuary, given "the story about Erichthonios," and therefore the "temple statues" are thought to have been Athena and Hephaistos. It is also generally assumed that Alkamenes made them, but this theory is based on Roman sources that do not specify the location of the work. Again, attribution of the images to a master is not necessary, since the inscription already places them within the climate of Periklean and post-Periklean Athens.[20]

No record survives, however, of any ancient restriction on materials to be used for specific purposes, and therefore the subject has not been investigated in depth. In her survey of early Greek cult statues, Irene Romano takes it as a given that some were in bronze, whether as metal sheets over a wooden core or hollow cast, as soon as the technical difficulties of casting were mastered. Yet the examples she gives are not entirely in keeping with my own definition of "temple statue." Several of them were *sphyrelata* that clearly did not stand in a temple—for instance, the Apollo at Amyklai (Paus. 3.19.2)—and the *sphyrelaton* technique seems to me simply a form of adornment for a core in a lesser medium, like an akrolith whose drapery is covered with gold foil.[21] Others had a reputation for being dedications or booty, and although the antiquity of the offerings may have been exaggerated, their status as "temple statues" is again questionable.[22]

Finally, some material evidence is open to different interpretations: the bronze Apollo found within a cache in the Peiraieus may not be Archaic, and there is no assurance that it was a temple image; the molds for the casting of a sizable *kouros* recovered by the excavations of the Athenian Agora may be for a votive offering rather than for the temple image of Apollo Patroos.[23] One more divine statue possibly in bronze, the Zeus Ithomatas by Ageladas (who allegedly was Myron's teacher and worked mostly in metal), moved from year to year to the house of the priest who was annually chosen (Paus. 4.33.2). The specific political circumstances of the Messenians and Naupaktians may have determined this itinerant practice, but the fact remains that the idol must have been small for easy transport and not anchored to a permanent base.

Three statues, however, seem definitely to fit our definition: a bronze Apollo from Thessaly; a Poseidon for a shrine near Naupaktos, by the sea (Paus. 10.38.6); and the Athena in the Temple of Athena Chalkioikos in Sparta (Paus. 3.17.2). Only literary evidence exists for the last two cases. In both instances Pausanias specifies that the image was made of bronze, but he does not attribute the first one to a master, and so no date can be ascertained for it. On historical grounds, we can perhaps assume that the Poseidon was from the fourth century or later, when religious practices may have become more diversified.[24] The Spartan Athena was made by a local man, Gitiadas, which gives it an Archaic date. But this may be a case that proves the point, since Athena's epithet called her "of the bronze house" and Pausanias' description of the temple (made by the same master) suggests elaborate bronze reliefs revetting the walls. As was the case for the Hephaisteion, the choice of medium may have been dictated by the specific cult.

The third case, from Metropolis, in Thessaly, cannot be easily explained away. It consists of a rather large (ht. 0.802 m with plinth) image of a bronze warrior wearing a conical helmet and arm-guards; weapons were probably held in the (now empty) fisted hands; and traces of a curved inset on the abdomen may suggest a separately added "mitra" as body protection for an archer. The figure's bare feet were individually attached to a rectangular plinth, which in turn was fastened to a stone pedestal by pins at two corners. The pedestal itself stood in the center of an Archaic Doric peripteral temple, which inscriptional evidence attributes to Apollo; the statue is stylistically dated to the third quarter of the sixth century and may depict the god, although its pointed chin implies the presence of a beard. This unusual version of the youthful god and the peripheral location of the temple, I would argue, make them less compelling as precedents for practices in fifth-century Athens.[25]

To be sure, a bronze statue is less likely to have survived through time than a marble one, since the reuse of metal was even more thorough than that of pedestal blocks. As for the literary evidence, Pausanias' account is both selective and cryptic, in that he mentions only what interests him and often does not specify the medium of the works. If this apparent penury of bronze "temple images" could be substantiated, however, we might gain some insight into Greek practices in general[26] and, more specifically, the religious attitudes of Periklean Athens.

It still seems strange to think of restrictions by type in Greek art, but perhaps a case can be made also for freestanding funerary monuments, which may have been exclusively in marble (or, for a brief period, in wood with metal attachments?).[27] Bronze seems not to have been used, perhaps because it was reserved for votive and athletic sculpture. The few examples that are mentioned by the ancient sources either are not strictly Greek or consist of elements that may be considered decorative, like finials for structures.[28] Greek architectural sculpture, as far as we know, was always in stone, with metal used solely for attachments and minor details. Once again, only the Hellenistic period may provide some examples, like the Tritons on the Pharos at Alexandria and the weathervane on the Tower of the Winds in Athens. Chryselephantine statues were reserved for the gods, until Philip of Makedon commissioned statues of himself and his family for the Philippeion at Olympia, in a clearly hubristic vein.[29]

Practices in other ancient cultures may also be significant. In Etruria, despite the lack of written testimonia, it is assumed that architectural sculpture was always in terracotta, funerary monuments were in stone, and bronze was the medium for votive offering. In Rome, the early statues of the gods were also in terracotta, and only under Greek influence were they made of more costly materials, especially in the akrolithic technique and even in gold and ivory. Votive and honorary images were in bronze, and the medium, according to Pliny, was first used for a statue of Ceres, in 484 B.C.[30]

I cannot claim to have thoroughly surveyed the topic, but I believe I can raise the question, Was bronze generally unacceptable for "temple statues" in Classical Athens? Perhaps Jerry Pollitt, with his impressive knowledge of the ancient sources, can provide either confirmation or rebuttal.

NOTES

I wish to thank Judith Barringer for inviting me to contribute to what I consider a most appropriate and well-deserved recognition for a great scholar and a good friend. The scholarly limitations of my contribution in no way reflect the intellectual limits of my admiration for the honorand.

1. For this point of view, although expressed in somewhat different terms, see Donohue 1997b, 31, where the basic defi-

nition is "an image of a god that is the focus of worship." See also Donohue 1997a.

A somewhat similar definition is given by Pemberton (1990, 2): ". . . a statue (never a painting) that in some way embodies the meaning of the cult, or is the focus for the cult. . . . Not every cult has an image, nor does every image stand inside a temple. But most cults do have a cult statue, and some have several."

2. Besides the examples cited by Donohue 1997b, 36–37, see also S. C. Jones 1998.

3. Pergamon, Temple of Hera, dedicated by Attalos II: Dörpfeld 1912, esp. 260–261 and pl. 17 for the plan (on which Adobogiona's base is marked "d"). The base within the cella is T-shaped and meant to support three statues: probably a central, seated Hera, flanked by Zeus and (Dörpfeld suggests) Dionysos; an inscribed base structurally connected with the main pedestal held the statue of Adobogiona, wife of the Gallic Tetrarch Brogitaros (65–40 B.C.). See also Schmidt 1995, 384, cat. no. IV.1.147. A well-known marble statue found within the Heraion, Istanbul, Arch. Mus. 2767, and usually called the "Zeus/Hero," probably stood on the T-shaped base; it is considered a portrait of Attalos II by, e.g., Himmelmann 1989, 142; an image of Zeus by, e.g., Pollitt 1986, 108, fig. 112. I agree with this latter interpretation: Ridgway 2000, 149–150. Damaskos 1999, 137–149, has the most extensive discussion of both base and statues; he reconstructs a central seated Hera, flanked by a standing Zeus/Attalos I and a standing, veiled Aphrodite/Apollonis/Stratonike, from which an arm with armlets and with traces of drapery survives.

For the sharing of temples, see Nock 1930, esp. 44–48 for Greek (as contrasted with Roman Imperial) practices.

4. See, e.g., Burkert 1977, 148: "Der Tempel ist die 'Wohnstätte', *naós,* der Gottheit, er beherbergt das menschengestaltige Kultbild. Die Anfänge des Tempelbaus überlagen sich darum mit der Entwicklungsgeschichte der Götterbilder." (Cited by Donohue 1997b, 32 n. 5). Dinsmoor 1975, 40: "It was not until the gods had become personified and embodied in statues of considerable size that they would have required specially built shelters."

5. See Wilson 1997. The Levantine practices were explored in 1995 by J. Griffin Miller in her original Ph.D. dissertation for Bryn Mawr College, "Temple and Statue: A Comparative Study of Practices in the Ancient World." The official, abridged version of her text (Miller 1995) focuses on the Greek evidence.

6. J. G. Miller 1996, 1997.

7. Philoch. fr. 7a–b, who mentions also a gold statue of Apollo, "probably cast soon after 346": Levi 1971, 468, n. 141. (Note that, in citing Pausanias, I use Levi's numbering, which occasionally does not correspond to that of other editions.) See also Paus. 10.24.4, who adds that two statues of the Moirai with Zeus and Apollo Moiragetes stood within the Delphic cella, but obviously these are not "temple images" according to my definition: cf. *LIMC* 2, s.v. Apollon, no. 794 [G. Kokkorou-Alewras].

8. Various examples of "empty" temples and their geographic distribution have been collected by J. G. Miller (1995); see also J. G. Miller 1997.

9. For more details on these two statues, see, e.g., Ridgway 1992, esp. 120–127 (Athena Polias), 135–137 (Athena Nike).

10. The Dionysos attributed to Alkamenes by Pausanias (1.20.3) seems to have stood in a fourth-century temple, and various conjectures have been advanced to explain this chronological discrepancy. See, e.g., Delivorrias 1994, 177. We could perhaps add the Aphrodite "in the Gardens" to Alkamenes' list, since a temple of the goddess stood in the area, but Pausanias (1.19.2) is not explicit in locating the Alkameneian creation within the building and does not specify its medium, although we can assume it to have been marble because of the appropriateness of that stone for female images.

11. For a recent plan of the area, see, e.g., *JHS-AR* 44 (1998) 4–5, fig. 4. It was probably in this temple that Pausanias saw the image, evidently transported from an earlier location. We cannot therefore be sure that it was originally a "temple statue." See also Camp 1986, 57, for the altar of Aphrodite Ourania, and the statement that the temple, if it existed, should be within the still unexcavated area to the west of the altar.

On three possible temple images of Aphrodite (at Daphni, on the north slope of the Akropolis, and in the Ilissos area), all in marble and datable to the fifth century, see Dally 1997.

12. Given their materials, all these statues are bound to have been sheltered by a structure (as contrasted with votive offerings set up in the open air), and in many cases Pausanias specifies the existence of a temple. The ancient sources on Pheidias' works and those of his pupils are conveniently collected in Pollitt 1990a, 53–68. For a recent discussion, see E. B. Harrison 1996, esp. 34–38, on the Athena Areia at Plataia. See now also Lapatin 2001 for a thorough treatment of technique, actual examples from the Bronze Age to Late Roman Imperial, literary mentions and his appendix on the Athena Areia (198–199).

13. Pollitt 1990b, 22. During summer 2002 the Nashville Athena was fully gilded and tinted, to approximate more closely the appearance of the original in antiquity.

14. For the complex meaning of *Techne* in antiquity, both "art" and "skill"/"craft," see Pollitt 1974, 32–37.

15. The ancient sources of the anecdotes are Paus. 5.11.9 and Strabo 8.3.30 respectively. See also Dio Chrys. *Or.* 12.50–52, cited by Pollitt 1990a, 62.

16. See, e.g., the comments by Stewart 1990, 36.

17. See, e.g., Lapatin 2001, and the works cited in Lapatin 1997, esp. 664–665.

18. This point is forcefully made by Pemberton 1990, 4–5. Donohue (1988) objects to the translation of the term *xoanon* as "a *primitive* wooden statue" (my emphasis), especially in connection with the origins of Greek sculpture, which, as she correctly maintains, did not evolve from crude wooden forms to shapely and refined stone renderings. But she does not deny the existence in antiquity of statues in wood, often quite detailed and aesthetically appealing. For the making of wooden "*daidala*" at a Plataian festival honoring Hera down to his own time, see Paus. 9.3.1–4. Woods used to fashion divine images are the cultivated trees (olive, fig, vine, pear) and some wild ones (cypress, ebony, cedar, oak, juniper); cf. Romano 1982, 360.

19. For the latest discussion of the Promachos, see Lundgreen 1997; for a different position, see E. B. Harrison 1996, 28–34.

20. I happen to believe that the temple on the hill is indeed the Hephaisteion, but several scholars hold opinions to the contrary. See, for a helpful summary, Thompson and Wycherley 1972, 140–149, esp. 142 and n. 123 for different identifications; add E. B. Harrison 1977, esp. 139–141 and n. 15, for a discussion of the inscription (*IG* I^2 370–371). Although she rejects the current identification of the temple, she accepts attribution of the statues to Alkamenes; she also points out that we only have the end of the inscription and that the amount of bronze there specified is not sufficient for two large statues. She therefore assigns it to the making of the *anthemon* that seems to have accompanied the sculptures; but she does not doubt that the Athena and the Hephaistos were in bronze (cf. her p. 175). For cautious comments on the attribution of the statues to Alkamenes, see Ridgway 1981, 174 and n. 14. More positive, Delivorrias 1994, 176–177.

On the alleged base, see Dinsmoor 1941, 105–109, fig. 38 (in favor); Delivorrias 1994, 176, and Delivorrias 1997 (contra). It is perhaps relevant that much evidence for bronze casting was found in the vicinity of the Hephaisteion, including one pit, ca. 10 m southwest of the temple, containing fragmentary molds for two large statues: Thompson and Wycherley 1972, 145.

21. Romano 1982, 364–367; the early examples I cite are culled from her work, unless otherwise indicated. Romano's discussion includes the sphyrelata from Dreros, which may not be "temple images" since Cretan buildings were not Greek temples in the accepted sense of the term. In a more recent paper, Romano suggests that only the male figure was the "temple image" originally standing on an altar (in the "later decades of the eighth century"); the two females were probably independent votives, perhaps even supports for tables, added later (first quarter of the seventh century): Romano 2000.

Other nonqualifying sphyrelata are the Apollo at Thornax, which, according to Pausanias (3.10.8) was like the one at Amyklai and does not seem, from his wording, to have stood in a temple; and the Zeus Hypatos at Sparta (Paus. 3.17.6), which stood in the vicinity of the Temple of Athena Chalkioikos. Romano 1982 includes also the statue of Athena Kranaia at Elateia, in Phokis (Paus. 10.34.4; material unspecified), but that image was made by the sons of Polykles and is therefore of second-century B.C. date. Extant fragments show moreover that it was of marble: Despinis 1995, esp. 339–347, 347–349 (attributed head, Athens, National Archaeological Museum 4817), 363 and n. 180 (date).

22. See, e.g., the bronze Apollo Argeotas "dedicated by the crew of the *Argo*" (perhaps to explain the epithet): Paus. 4.34.7; the temple, however, which lies ten miles beyond Korone in Messenia, belongs to Apollo Korythos, and the Periegete states explicitly that its statue is wooden. Another possible dedication is the Poseidon Hippios at Pheneos, although Pausanias (8.14.5–7) argues against it being an offering by Odysseus because it was in cast bronze, a technique not known in Odysseus' time; that Apollo, moreover, just stood on the akropolis and not in a temple. A bronze Athena at Amphissa (Paus. 10.38.3) stood in a temple but was said to have been looted from Troy and set up by Thoas. Again, the Periegete disbelieves this account on technical grounds, but he does not state clearly whether this was *the* temple image.

The Apollo Philesios by Kanachos is mentioned by Romano 1982 as a cult image, but additional work at Didyma has shown that it must have been a votive offering of the city: Tuchelt 1986; the article considers votive also the "copy" of that Apollo mentioned by Pausanias at Thebes (Apollo Ismenios in wood: 9.10.2). Tuchelt (1986, 78 and n. 23) mentions a bronze Artemis Soteira by Strongylion at Megara (Paus. 1.40.2) and a similar one at Pagai (Paus. 1.44.7) but takes both to be city offerings.

23. Peiraieus Apollo, doubted as a sixth-century image: Palagia 1997b, esp. 180–183 (second century B.C.). See also Mattusch 1996, 138. For a first-century B.C. date, see Fuchs 1999, 18–21, with conclusions on p. 22. I continue to believe that the Apollo may be Late Archaic or Early Severe, but there is no way to ascertain whether it ever stood in a temple; the thickness of its bronze walls, especially if later than Archaic, may imply an open-air setting.

Bronze molds for a kouros or Apollo from area of Temple of Patroos: Mattusch 1977; Mattusch 1988, 54–59, esp. 59. Hedrick (1988, esp. 190–191, figs. 4–5) believes that the molds were just for a votive kouros. In Ridgway 1997, 357, n. 25, I thought the bronze would have been too sizable for a dedication at that early a date, but, with further thought on the media of "temple statues," I am beginning to reconsider the point, especially since the later images of Apollo within the Agora temple were in marble.

24. A selective listing of statues of Poseidon is given in *LIMC* 7, s.v. Poseidon, nos. 1–9 [E. Simon]; none of the items mentioned qualifies for our definition of "temple statue," and in many cases the material is unspecified or the

date is assumed to be post-Archaic. If material evidence, such as bases, is included, as well as images of the god with other figures (nos. 10–18), the few temple statues mentioned are in marble and late. One more bronze statue (Paus. 10.36.4) showed Poseidon with a foot on a dolphin, hand on hip, and holding a trident; it was therefore of the so-called Lateran type, no earlier than the early Hellenistic period. Moreover, the shrine in which it stood, at Antikyra, is described as being made of field stones, which implies that it, and therefore also the statue, were small. It could be argued, to be sure, that size would not dictate whether or not a sculpture could be considered a "temple image" by our definition.

25. Bronze Apollo: Intzesiloglou 2000. The statue was found in two pieces: its lower half was still fastened to the stone base; its upper half was found nearby. The excavator considers it the temple image.

At Kalapodi, in ancient Phokis, one more Apollo, a bronze statuette, was found fastened to the front left corner of a stone pedestal; a second, now missing, statuette once stood on the opposite (right) corner. For a convenient illustration and account, see *EAA* Suppl. 2:3 (1971–1994), 159–161, fig. 187. The stone pedestal is described as a "cultic bench" within a small temple built after the destruction of a previous structure in 480. Given the off-center placement and the relative insignificance of the figure in relation to its support, I believe that this Apollo does not qualify as a cult image.

26. Damaskos 1999, 201–202, states that only one case of bronze cult images can be demonstrated for the Hellenistic period: a group of Sarapis, Isis, and Anubis in Naiskos F of the Sarapeion on Delos, mentioned in the temple inventories; Egyptian influence and probably form are suggested. Two other instances are uncertain; one (an Asklepios on Delos) is postulated on the uncertain reading of an inscription, another (in the agora temple at Priene) on the attachment traces on a block, which, however, may not belong to the cult-statue base. During the Hellenistic period, the preferred medium was marble, but examples in wood, gilded wood, akrolithic technique, and marble and gold are also attested.

27. For this theory, albeit unsubstantiated and primarily based on depictions on Attic white-ground lekythoi, see Ridgway 1970, 44 and n. 1. My statement refers primarily to Attic gravestones during the period ca. 490–450 B.C., when production elsewhere is, however, attested. To be sure, some burials used sarcophagi, either in clay or wood, often decorated with terracotta plaques added to the exterior.

28. Bronze not used for funerary monuments: Ridgway 1997, 166, n. 36; the same observation was made by Schmaltz 1983, 66–69. Kurtz and Boardman 1971, 240, cite some Hellenistic epitaphs for bronze statues on non-Attic territory, but during the Hellenistic period, the line between honorary and funerary must have been very thin. The tumulus of Auge at Pergamon seems to have been surmounted by the bronze image of a naked woman (Paus. 8.4.9), but the deceased is legendary, and her importance was enhanced by the Attalids who wanted to claim descent from Herakles through her son Telephos. A bronze "*kore*" was said to stand over the tomb of Midas, perhaps the Phrygian king (*Anth. Pal.* 7.153). Finally, a bronze siren seems to have crowned Sophokles' funerary monument: *TrGF* 4, 36–37; cf. Hofstetter 1990, 26; her n. 202 on p. 318 mentions the lack of bronze for funerary monuments, but she does not doubt the possibility and suggests that even the figure on Midas' tomb was a siren. We can perhaps visualize Sophokles' siren as crowning a precinct wall like that of Dexileos' plot in the Athenian Kerameikos (see, e.g., Ridgway 1997, 4, ill. 1).

29. Pharos at Alexandria by Sostratos of Knidos (ca. 280 B.C.; four bronze Tritons with conch shells at corners of first stage, bronze statue of Zeus Soter on roof): Clayton and Price 1988, 138–157, esp. 149 and fig. 74. Horologion (Tower of the Winds) by Andronikos of Kyrrhos (Triton on roof; first century B.C.): Vitr. *De arch.* 1.6.4. Philippeion statues (Philip, his parents, his wife, and his son Alexander, ca. 336 B.C.): Paus. 5.20.10.

30. Bronze use in Rome: Plin. *HN* 34.15. Cf. also *HN* 35.157, about statues of the gods in terracotta, and see Pollitt 1966, xiii, for comments on what he calls the "lament over decadence." Surprisingly, Artemidoros of Ephesos (mid/late second century A.D.), *Oneirocritica* 2.39, believes that statues made "from terracotta, clay, plaster or wax, those that are painted and the like are less auspicious, often even inauspicious." Pemberton 1990, 4, who quotes him, suggests that clay may have been an inappropriate material because man was thought to be made of earth and water. Artemidoros seems to think that divine statues in bronze (as well as gold, silver, ivory, stone, amber, or ebony) are auspicious because their substance is hard and incorruptible. Is he speaking as a Greek or as a Roman?

For temple images in Late Republican Rome, see H. G. Martin 1987. For second-century B.C. examples, in both Greece and Rome, see Ridgway 2000, 230–246.

11

ATHENA AT PALLENE AND IN THE AGORA OF ATHENS

EVELYN B. HARRISON

Jerome J. Pollitt has bravely defended the right of classical sculptors to be known in Art History by their own names and characterized according to perceivable qualities of their works. It may not be inappropriate in a volume in his honor to identify, however conjecturally, a work of Lokros of Paros, who is otherwise known to us only from Pausanias.

In this essay I shall propose that the Athena Giustiniani type, whose pose, drapery, and ethos have much in common with those of the Nemesis of Rhamnous, a securely identified work of Agorakritos of Paros, actually represents the Athena by Lokros of Paros that was seen by Pausanias together with a statue of Ares by Alkamenes in the Temple of Ares in the Athenian Agora. As it has now been established that this temple was moved from Pallene in the time of Augustus, this identification helps to support the long-proposed but not always accepted identification of the Ares Borghese type with the Ares of Alkamenes.

THE TEMPLE OF ARES IN THE AGORA

Pausanias states (1.8.4) that there was a sanctuary of Ares near the statue of Demosthenes in the Athens Agora: "The statue of Ares was made by Alkamenes and the Athena by a Parian named Lokros." The American excavations of the 1930s uncovered the foundations of the temple and enough blocks of its marble superstructure to permit a tentative reconstruction of the plan (Fig. 11.1).[1] The style of the architecture served to date the temple in the second half of the fifth century B.C., as one of a series of Attic temples with related plans,[2] but it was clear that this temple had been dismantled and moved from its original site into the Agora during the Early Roman period, almost certainly in the time of Augustus.[3] Votive statues, two of Aphrodite and one of the war goddess Enyo, seen by Pausanias inside

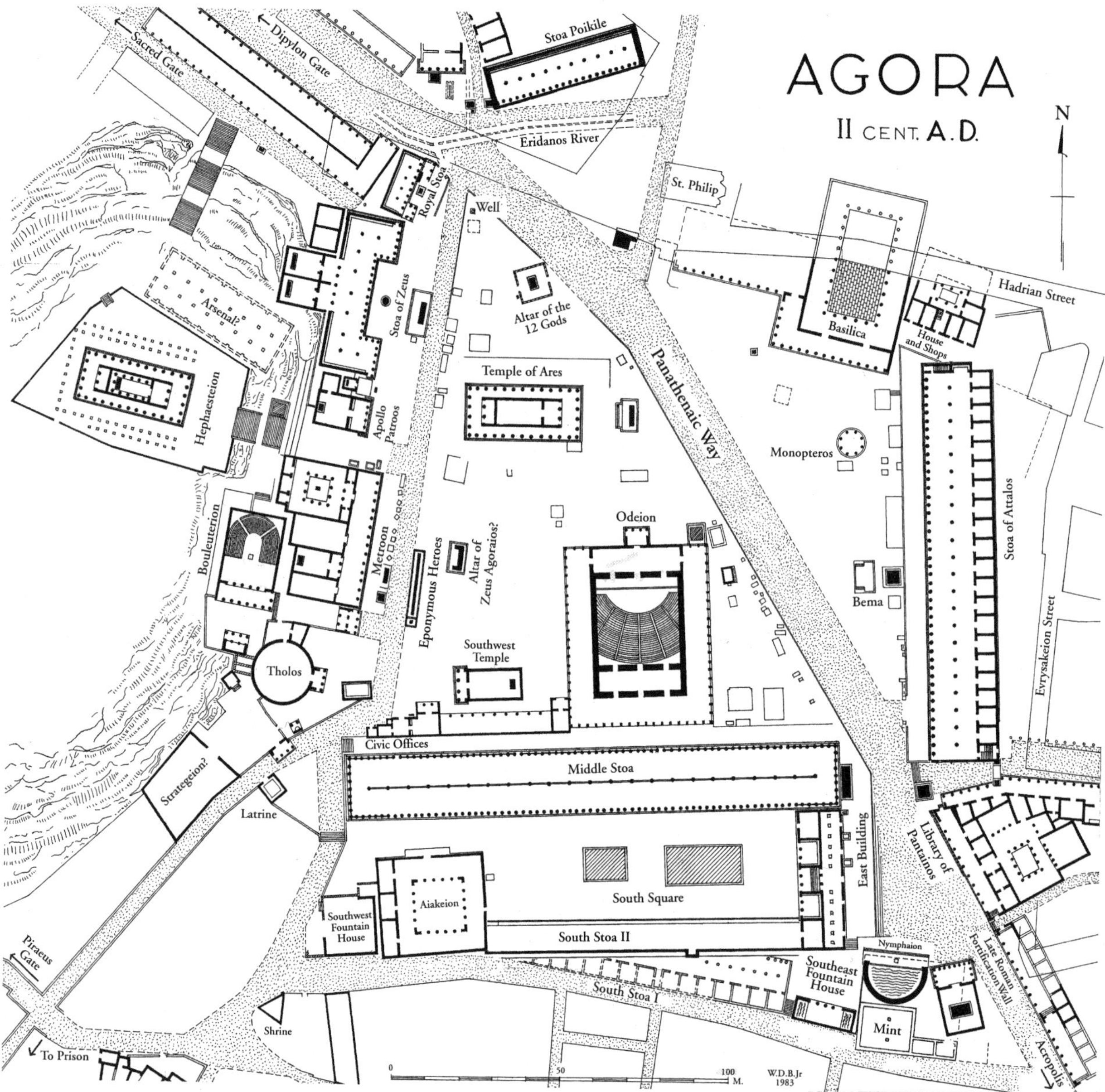

FIGURE 11.1. *Plan of the Agora in the second century* A.D. *by W. B. Dinsmoor Jr. Photo courtesy of the American School of Classical Studies at Athens, Agora Excavations.*

the temple, seem to reflect the association of Mars and Venus as ancestors of the Romans, but the joint cult of Ares and Athena was evidently the principal one.[4]

It has usually been assumed that the Ares and Athena were designed as a pair, although made by different sculptors, and were transferred along with the fifth-century temple in which they had originally stood. Alkamenes was a fifth-century sculptor. The date of Lokros is unrecorded. Enyo, however, was by the sons of Praxiteles, about a century after Alkamenes.

Cults of Ares are rare in Classical Greece. Ares is linked in mythology with the Areopagos, and Pausanias mentions (1.28.5) an altar of Athena Areia on the hill but not one of Ares. The only place in Attika for which we have evidence for Ares and Athena Areia is Acharnai. A decree passed by the Acharnians in the second half of the fourth century specifies that altars be built to Ares and Athena Areia, but there is no mention of a temple. The site of the altars has never been discovered. Nevertheless, until recently this was the most widely accepted conjectural source for the temple and its statues.[5]

This is no longer the case. Manolis Korres has identified and meticulously recorded the surviving foundations of the Temple of Athena at Pallene, and his results, now fully published, leave no doubt that these are the foundations on which the marble temple in the Agora originally stood.[6] This throws an entirely new light on the statues of Ares and Athena that Pausanias saw in the temple.

The statuary type of the Ares Borghese in the Louvre was early proposed and has been widely accepted as copied from the Ares of Alkamenes.[7] In spite of a recent attempt to call the statue a Roman invention, the attribution to Alkamenes seems increasingly convincing as we learn more about this sculptor.[8] It has been more difficult, however, to identify the Athena of Lokros. Most scholars would agree that the Ares was of bronze. On the other hand, there has been an urge to see the prototype of the Athena in a marble statue of which the upper part was found in the central part of the Agora, thus not far from the Temple of Ares. For this reason, Barbara Vierneisel-Schlörb suggested that the original of the Ares Borghese might also have been of marble. This idea has not found favor.[9]

ATHENA PALLENIS IN THE "THESEION" FRIEZE

There is no reason to assume that the Athena of Pallene ever had Ares as a *paredros* in her temple.[10] The cult is an old one and is often mentioned: in Herodotos, in Aristotle, and in inscriptions, as well as in tragedy and comedy. It was at Pallene that Peisistratos, coming from Marathon to retake Athens, fought a battle in which he and his allies defeated those coming from the city to prevent him, and so established his tyranny until his death (Hdt. 1.62–63, Arist. [*Ath. Pol.*] 14.15.3). In the *Herakleidai* of Euripides, Athena of Pallene is mentioned twice: when Iolaos pursuing Eurystheus passes "the holy rock of Athena of Pallene" (lines 849–850) he prays to Zeus and Hebe to make him young again, and his prayer is answered. Later (lines 1030–1031) the captive Eurystheus, condemned to death, reveals an oracle that he is to be buried "in the presence of the divine virgin of Pallene" and lying under the earth will defend Athens from Peloponnesian invaders. Because his prophecy was not fulfilled, we can date the tragedy to the early years of the Peloponnesian War.[11]

Associations with Marathon and the route from the Mesogaia via Pallene to Athens figure also in Plutarch's *Life of Theseus* (13.1–3), in which Theseus, forewarned, destroys an ambush at Gargettos (next to Pallene) and so defeats the sons of Pallas in their attempt to wrest the kingship from Aigeus.

This story is depicted in the east frieze of the so-called Theseion.[12] The figures in the east frieze, although their faces and genitals were mutilated, probably by Christians, are relatively well preserved. All the slabs remain in situ so that the actions can be read consecutively. Following the interpretation as the battle of Theseus against the sons of Pallas, one can distinguish the direction of the battle in time and space. This fits the topography of Plutarch's account.[13]

Six gods in two antithetical groups divide the combatants into scenes. The rocks on which the gods are seated represent mountainous or hilly terrain.

The first scene to the left is preliminary to the attack. A kneeling prisoner, I, 3, is being tied up. Probably he is Leos, who informed Theseus of the ambush at Gargettos. This group is on the side of Theseus. One who rushes forward as if to pass behind the gods, I, 5, signals the start of the attack. Athena seated on her rock, II, 6 (Fig. 11.2) should be the Athena of Pallene.[14] Her companions are generally recognized as Hera, II, 7,[15] and Zeus, II, 8.[16] Zeus is actively interested in the battle, as are the other gods, though in a less dynamic way. All of them favor the part of Theseus. The giantlike sons of Pallas, IV, 16–19 (Fig. 11.3), struggle against a natural catastrophe, which must be the work of the gods. The Pallantids do not pick up the stones to throw them but seem only to be pushing them away. The scene recalls Herodotos' account of what befell the Persians when they invaded the sanctuary of Athena Pronaia at Delphi. Thunderbolts struck them; two peaks broke off the mountain and rolled down on them; two tall heroes pursued and killed them.[17] Zeus throws thun-

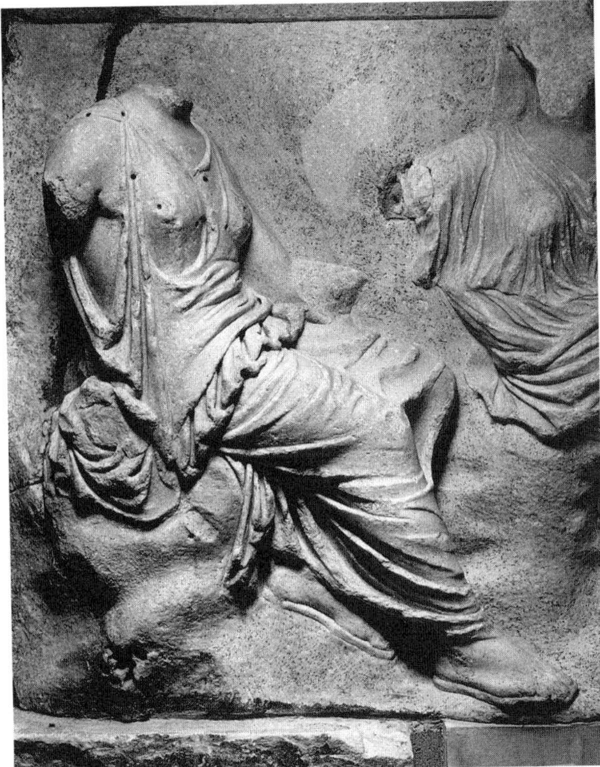

FIGURE 11.2. *Athena in the Theseion frieze, II, 6 (detail). Photo courtesy of the American School of Classical Studies at Athens, Agora Excavations.*

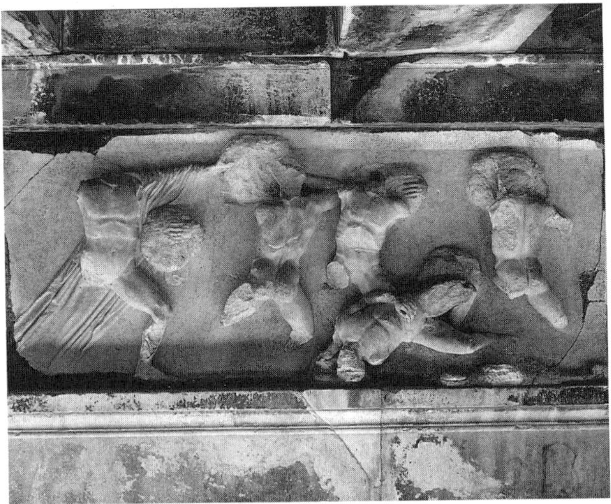

FIGURE 11.3. *Theseion frieze, IV, 15–19. Photo courtesy of the American School of Classical Studies at Athens, Agora Excavations.*

derbolts. Athena makes landslides. Poseidon causes earthquakes.

The one tall hero on the frieze, IV, 15, who must be Theseus, pushes away a boulder with one hand, while with the other he aims a spear at his enemies. The hand pushing the rock recalls the Poseidon of Parthenon east metope 6. This reminds us that Theseus is Poseidon's son. The designer of the "Theseion" east frieze, which was created around 430 B.C., was certainly familiar with the Parthenon metopes, which preceded it in date. In east metope 6, Poseidon has a large cloak draped over his left shoulder and flying out behind him, while he pushes at a rock with his left hand and raises his right arm to strike. Neither the arm nor the weapon has left any traces, but we can assume that Poseidon held a trident.[18]

It would make sense to restore the raised right hand of Poseidon, V, 24, on the frieze with a trident pointed down toward the earth. His left hand was probably braced on a projection of his rocky seat, which is now broken away close to the edge of the slab. The broken area appears in Dörig's photos but is clearest in a photo by Alison Frantz (Fig. 11.4).[19]

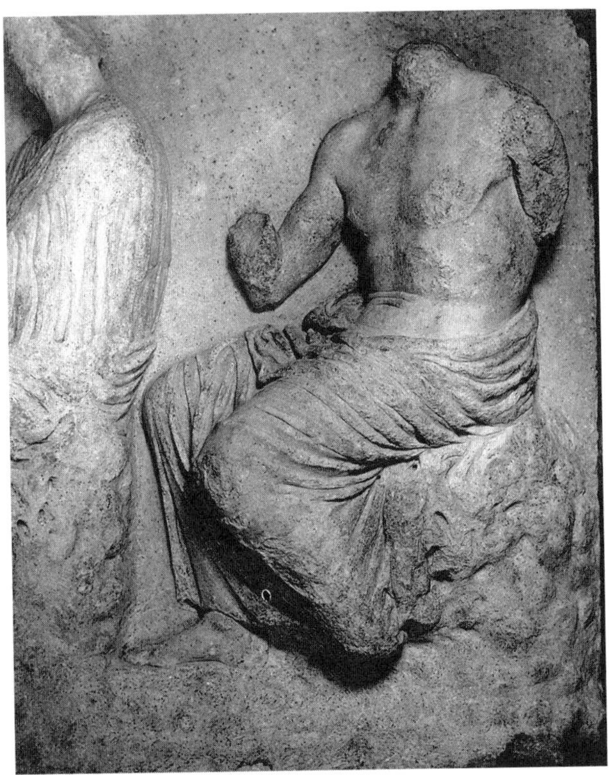

FIGURE 11.4. *Poseidon in the Theseion frieze, V, 24 (detail). Photo courtesy of the American School of Classical Studies at Athens, Agora Excavations.*

Bruno Sauer placed a hammer in the left hand of V, 24 to identify him as Hephaistos. The god is not using this implement: he simply holds it. The hand grasping the handle of the hammer would have touched the broken area mentioned above, and the head of the hammer would have been fastened by two rather large holes in the mass of drapery bunched over the rock, but as Dörig notes, these holes might have resulted from the undercutting of the drapery folds, whose outer surface in this area is all broken away.[20] Sauer restored the right hand with no attribute, simply held open in a gesture of astonishment at the events taking place. Such a passive participation, however, is out of tune with the active roles of the other gods, whose alert seated poses are echoed in the leg positions of V, 24. Though Sauer depicts V, 24 with head erect to match his raised hand, all the photos show clearly that the missing head was bent down and turned to his left. Nowhere did it touch the background. The prominent tendon on the proper right side of his neck shows the turn. The raised right hand projected forward from the background. It must have grasped the trident so that it aimed at the low ground between the rocks, which can have represented the Mesogaia.

Athena, Poseidon's opposite in the frieze, may have signaled her participation by holding out her helmet as if to pour down rain from it. Zeus, the rainmaking god of Mount Hymettos, whose cloak streams down like water from his raised, scepter-holding hand, seems to be preparing to throw a thunderbolt with the lost right hand, swinging it back like a diskos-thrower as he bends forward. Another thunderbolt strikes a Pallantid in the back of the neck.[21] By recognizing the presence of an active Poseidon, we can understand the victory of Theseus as won with the consent and help of the gods of all Attika, not those of Athens alone.

THE STATUE OF ATHENA PALLENIS IN THE FIFTH CENTURY B.C.

The absence of Ares from this action centered at Pallene reinforces the impression gathered from written sources that Athena Pallenis did not share a cult with Ares in the fifth century B.C. The absence of Ares need not, however, exclude the possibility that this Athena Pallenis, like the Athena Areia of Acharnai in the fourth century, had a particular concern for *ephebes.* The *Herakleidai,* with its Marathonian references and its savior roles assigned to Herakles and Hebe (lines 854–857), seems aimed at inspiring patriotism in the youth of Athens.[22]

Rather than supposing that Ares and Athena were already paired at Pallene, or that both statues were taken together from elsewhere, a more likely and less forced solution would be that the Athena of Pallene was a bronze statue made in the fifth century by Lokros of Paros and that Alkamenes' statue of Ares, not originally housed in a temple, came from the Areopagos in Athens.

If the statue of Ares was created for the Areopagos, where the myth of his trial for murder provided the foundation legend of the Court, he would not originally have needed an accompanying statue to hear his defense: the whole court would have been his listeners. The mouth of the Ares Borghese is open as if speaking; he speaks for himself. Alkamenes is said by Pliny to have made a statue of a pentathlete being examined for admission to a competition.[23] The stance of the Ares looks like a forerunner of that of the Diskobolos attributed to Naukydes, a follower of Polykleitos. Ridgway correctly points out that the figure is not literally throwing but carrying the diskos and so cannot be certainly identified with the work ascribed by Pliny to Naukydes.[24] Her opinion of the relationship between the Ares and the diskos-carrier is succinctly stated: "The forward right leg of the Ares is straight, not bent: nonetheless the lateral opening of his composition cannot be denied, and the inclination of his head is comparable to that of the athlete." She would accept that "the Ares is a classicizing creation after Polykleitan prototypes." After viewing copies of the two statues together in the Louvre, Ridgway observed that the Ares looked more static and frontal, while the Diskobolos showed greater fluidity and torsion.[25] Thus the Ares ought to be either earlier than the Diskobolos or enough later to have been produced in a period that harked back to fifth-century style. If we assume that it is really by Alkamenes, it must be earlier. How does the lost *encrinomenos* fit in here?

An athlete awaiting approval to enter a contest and a young war-god awaiting judgment on a murder charge are alike in that both are submitting to authority. The inclined heads of the Ares and the Diskobolos express this submission. Pliny's encrinomenos was a pentathlete. We do not know if the sculpture contained allusions to all five contests or if it depended on the inscribed base for information. In any case, the sculptor would avoid showing extremes in the physique of his pentathlete such as might distinguish the runners from the wrestlers. A versatile body would also suit a young warrior. The innovation of the submissive attitude may well be due to Alkamenes. This expresses the ethos of the figure and ties it to its social situation, while stressing the validity of the concerned authority.

This attitude will have been adopted by the sculptor of the Diskobolos, which may also have been an encrinomenos but specifically for the diskos throw. The innovations noted by Ridgway in this statue—the more open stance, the torsion, and the gripping toes—serve to suggest the movements involved in the actual throw. Thus the statue deserves the name Diskobolos and can well be by Naukydes. A hypothetical succession of the three works would be: (1) Pentathlete of Alkamenes, (2) Ares of Alkamenes, and (3) Diskobolos of Naukydes.

This is not the place for a full discussion of the acceptance of Polykleitan formal schemes in Attic sculpture after the Parthenon. The important thing is to recognize that it happened not only in the case of Alkamenes but also with other, less famous sculptors. A stance with "the left hand holding a spear, the right foot firmly advanced, while only the toes of the left foot were touching the ground" is attested by the attachment holes on the base of the statue of Athena Hygieia on the Athenian Akropolis.[26] The sculptor, Pyrrhos, signs as an Athenian but is otherwise unknown. The dedication was made by the Athenian People (Plutarch erred in ascribing it to Perikles personally).[27] The date of 433 B.C. is given as a terminus post quem in the most recent publication of the inscription *IG* I^3 506.[28] In any case, work must have stopped on the Propylaia before the statue was put in place. The Hope-Farnese Athena type has been proposed and seems to fit the fastenings on the base, although there is some slight variation among the copies.[29]

If the Velletri Athena is, as I have argued, the Athena that was made for the Hephaisteion, the accounts for which run from 421 to 415, we have a still more precise date for the typical "Polykleitan ponderation" in a statue thought to be by Alkamenes.[30] The statues for the Hephaisteion, together with their floral column and figured base, were a major project. The mention of the encrinomenos suggests that this sculptor, occupied hitherto in ongoing major constructions, may have begun to accept commissions for single statues on a lesser scale as conditions in Athens interrupted work on buildings such as the Erechtheion and the Temple of Athena Nike with its parapet. The Polykleitan influence on Alkamenes already evident may have extended to interest in the attitudes and ethos of the athlete.

The Ares may have been as late as the last decade of the century. A dedication for the Areopagos would be in accord with the sentiments that inspired the copy of the Homicide Code of Drakon that was decreed to be set up in front of the Royal Stoa in 409/8 B.C.[31] To make a convincing pair, the statues of Ares and Athena would not need to be of the same date. Certainly they ought to be of similar scale and similar high quality. With a nude Ares and a clothed Athena, the problem of congruence of drapery style would not arise. We already know that the two statues were by different sculptors. Even though they were not designed to stand together, they should turn their heads toward rather than away from one another, and the outer contours of the group should be closed rather than open.

W. B. Dinsmoor Sr. considered all four of the Attic temples that he assigned to the "Theseum Architect" to be part of a Periklean program and dated their plans schematically in a stylistic sequence from 449 to 432 B.C. The so-called Theseion, which he believed was the Hephaisteion, was clearly the earliest in design. His series ran: Hephaisteion 449–445; Temple of Poseidon at Sounion 444–440; Temple of Ares 440–436; Temple of Nemesis at Rhamnous 436–432 B.C. Korres accepts the sequence of the plans, while recognizing that it does not define the periods of actual construction.[32]

None of these temples was finished quickly. The Theseion appears to have made a good start in the 450s but to have been interrupted during the time when work was being done on the Parthenon and the Propylaia, ca. 449–432. It was resumed around 430, when attention shifted to the Agora. The metopes belong to the earlier period; the friezes and pediments, to the later. The program of the friezes was Periklean, but the pediments must have been executed after Perikles' death. The Temple of Poseidon at Sounion was finished, though we do not know how long it took. The same appears to have been true of the Temple of Athena at Pallene, which was to become the Temple of Ares. The Temple of Nemesis, like the Propylaia, never received its final finish, although its statue and its sculptured base were finished and installed.

Since the Nemesis was a colossal marble statue, it is possible that a model was completed by around 430 but could not have been carved and erected in the temple until much later because of enemy incursions into the Attic countryside. That would explain why the style of the sculpture on the base appears later than that of the statue, although the structure of the base shows that the statue cannot have been put in place before the sculptured slabs.[33]

It is natural to think that Lokros of Paros who made the Athena that Pausanias saw in the Temple of Ares was an associate of Agorakritos of Paros, who made the Nemesis. Until 1971, when Despinis published his identification of the type of the Nemesis, the ideas of most scholars about the style of Agorakritos were vague and various.[34] The large group of Late Hellenistic and Roman statues, in many different sizes and some with portrait heads, which, thanks to Despinis, we now recognize as derived from the Nemesis, was generally considered to depend on a classicizing work somehow descended from "the School of Pheidias."[35]

Long before their true source became known, however, an affinity was seen between this group and the Athena Giustiniani. The basic draping of the *himation* is the same as that of the Nemesis, as is the basic stance, which is not Polykleitan. Important differences are not so much stylistic as iconographical. The Nemesis held attributes in both hands, while the Athena holds only a spear, in her right hand. The Nemesis is a mature goddess assimilated to Aphrodite but with some of the attributes of Artemis. The Athena (Figs. 11.5–6) is modestly dressed as a maiden, with minimal modeling of the torso beneath her crinkled linen *chiton*.[36] Her age is appropriate for an Athena especially concerned with the ephebes, the "Parthenos Pallenis" of *Herakleidai*, line 1031. The statue should be dated around 430 B.C.

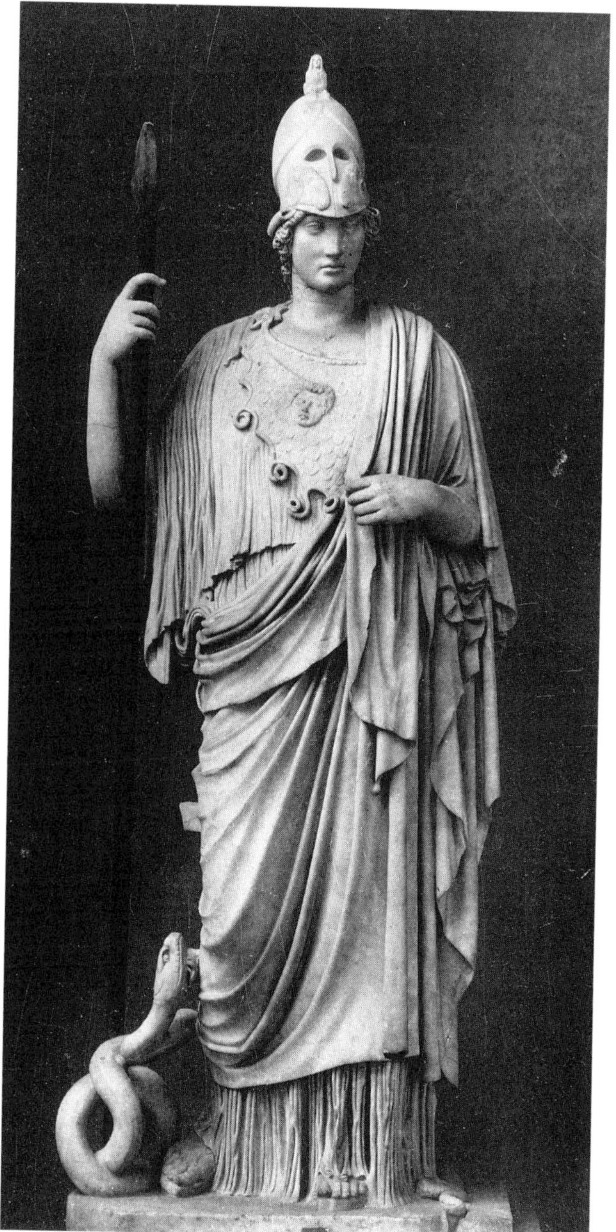

FIGURE 11.5. *Athena Giustiniani, Vatican 2223 (Antonine). Photo © Deutsches Archäologisches Institut, Rome, neg. 42.710 by Faraglia.*

A head of Athena of the Giustiniani type (Figs. 11.7–9) that was found in the ruins of the Stoa of Attalos (Athens, National Museum 3004) has been variously dated. Semni Karouzou and a number of others

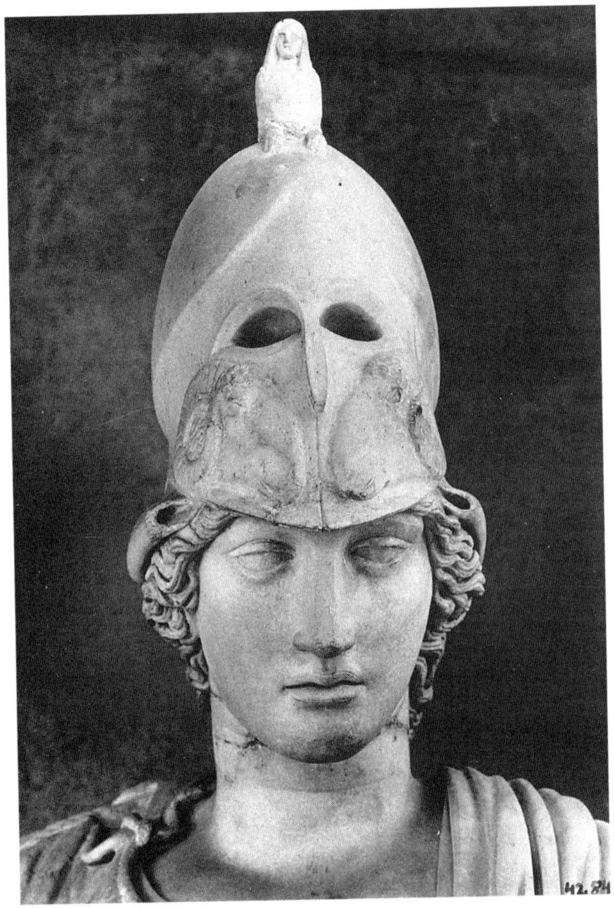

FIGURE 11.6. *Head of the Athena Giustiniani, Vatican 2223 (Antonine). Photo © Deutsches Archäologisches Institut, Rome, neg. 42.711 by Faraglia.*

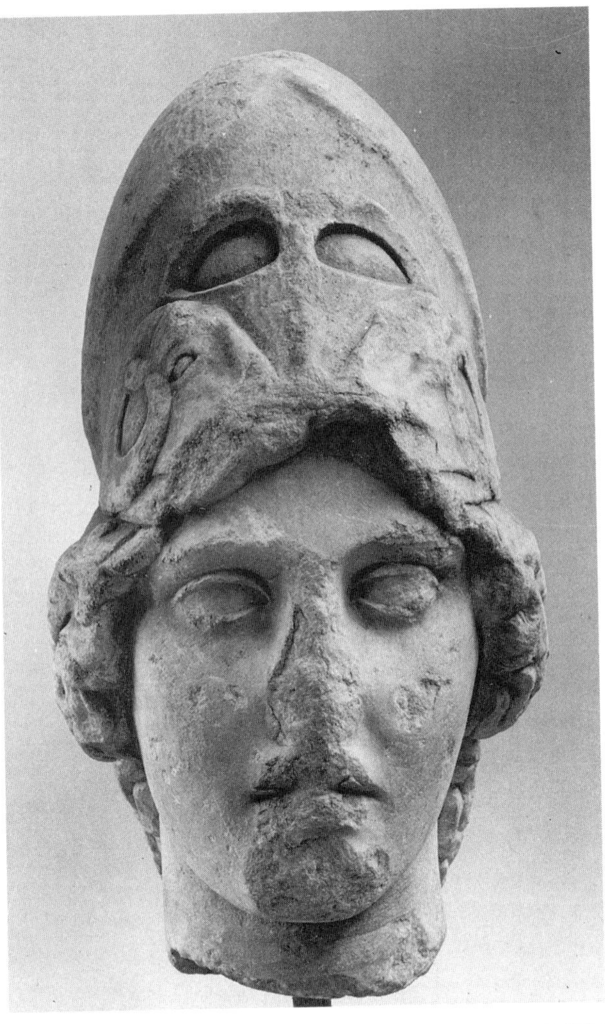

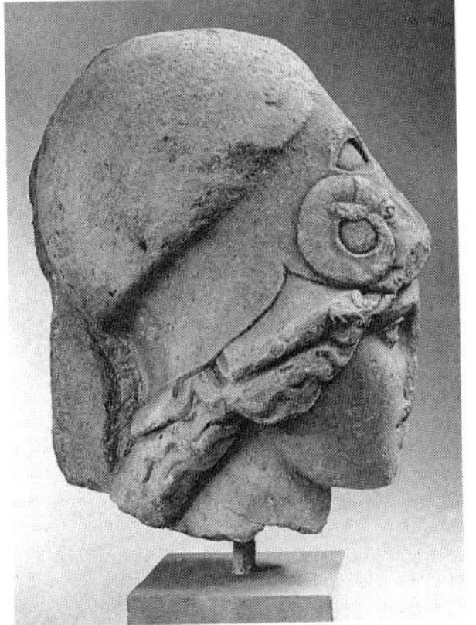

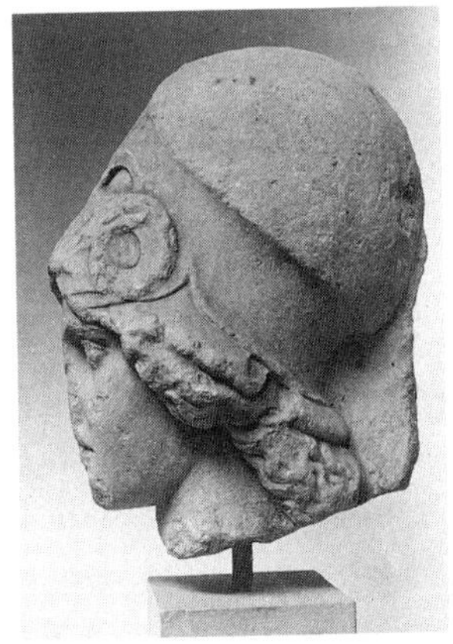

FIGURE 11.7. *Head of Athena Giustiniani, Athens, National Museum 3004, front. Photo: Deutsches Archäologisches Institut, Athens neg. nr. NM 4763.*

FIGURE 11.8. *Right profile of Fig. 11.7. Photo: Deutsches Archäologisches Institut, Athens neg. nr. NM 4764.*

FIGURE 11.9. *Left profile of Fig. 11.7. Photo: Deutsches Archäologisches Institut, Athens neg. nr. NM 4765.*

following her have accepted a date in the second century B.C., while Despinis most recently suggests lowering the date to the time of Augustus.[37] To me the head looks Trajanic, and this dating is supported by a comparison with the Dresden copy of the Athena of Myron, which Daltrop and Bol have dated in the time of Trajan.[38]

The Athena Giustiniani, like the Ares Borghese, is of the size common to statues of gods and heroes, over-life-size but not colossal. There is remarkably little variation in the scale of the copies, unlike those of the Velletri Athena and the Nemesis of Rhamnous.[39] The uncertainty about the original helmet crests of the Athena and the Ares prevents a precise measurement of the overall heights, but the two go well together in photographs of comparable scale (Fig. 11.10).

Athena has her weight on the left foot and her spear in her right hand. Her head turns slightly to her left,

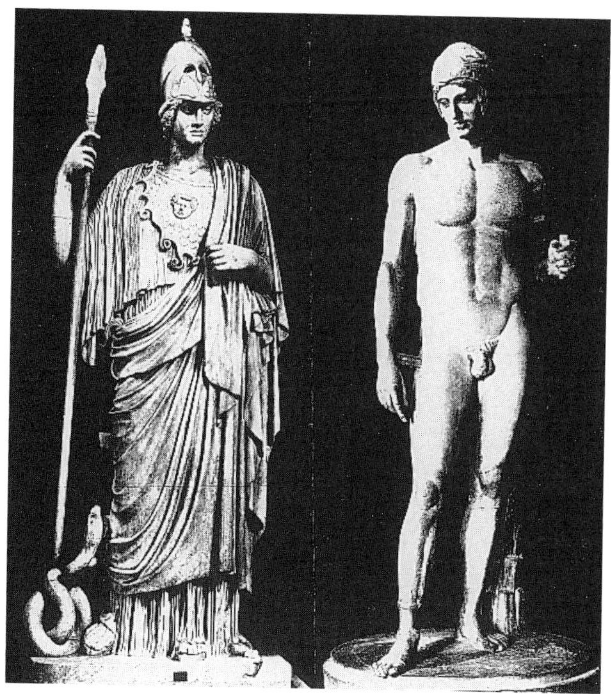

FIGURE 11.10. *Athena Giustiniani, paired with Ares Borghese; collage by E. B. Harrison. Photo: Nita Roberts.*

thus toward Ares who also has his weight on his left foot. He holds his spear in his left hand and a shield on his left arm, while his right hand hangs down. Athena's left hand lightly holds in place the end of her himation that falls over her left shoulder. This closed gesture may denote modesty, but its main function here is to show that the hand is not active. As grouped with Ares, Athena may be thought of as listening to him. In her original place in Pallene, she would have listened to her worshipers.[40]

The Athena Giustiniani wears her Corinthian helmet over a Persian tiara whose flaps are folded back inside. Elfriede Knauer has shown that this device alludes to victory over the eastern barbarians.[41] It is thoroughly appropriate to Athena Pallenis as a reference to Marathon and the defense of Attika. Scholars have noted that the Athena of the Marsyas group had the same motif, but Myron was not the first sculptor to use it. Despinis has recently presented evidence that the fragmentary head of Athena, Akropolis 2338, which also had the tiara under the helmet, is copied from the Athena who crowned Miltiades in the Marathon monument at Delphi attributed by Pausanias to Pheidias and probably set up in the 460s.[42] The Corinthian helmet of the Velletri Athena lacks this lining, perhaps because of her unwarlike role as the foster mother of Erichthonios.[43]

The Athena who sits on the holy rock of Pallene in the east frieze of the Theseion (Fig. 11.2) resembles the Athena Giustiniani in her youthful forms though not in her dress. Instead of wearing the linen chiton and himation of the statue, she imitates the Athena of the Parthenon frieze with her Argive peplos and the V-shaped area of bare flesh below her right armpit.[44] Athena in the Theseion frieze had her hair bound up in back like that of Athena in the Parthenon frieze. The Giustiniani Athena, like the Nemesis of Rhamnous, has her long hair twisted together at the nape and hanging down in back. The hair of the fragmentary Athena head, Akropolis 2338, copied from the Marathon dedication at Delphi was evidently similar.[45]

The Giustiniani Athena has her aegis fastened on her right shoulder, where the snakes seem to be knotted together. This motif occurs also in the so-called Lemnian Athena, but there the aegis hangs to below the waist, leaving the left breast free, and is belted with snakes.[46] The Athena of the Theseion frieze appears likewise to have had a single point of fastening on the right shoulder, but the aegis, whose limits are defined only by the holes for fastening the snakes, fell only to the level of the breasts. In this respect it is closer to the Giustiniani than to other well known Athena types.[47]

The unusual aegis of the "Lemnia" appears to be an innovation of around 450 B.C., perhaps invented for this statue. The statue of Athena in Madrid that Dörig assigned to the Aiginetan school of around 470 to 460 B.C. still wears an aegis with a central hole that can be slipped on over the head. This is an Archaic form that continues into the Early Classical period.[48] Despinis offers the attractive suggestion that the Madrid type copies the Athena crowning Miltiades from the Kimonian Marathon dedication at Delphi.[49] Athena on the Niobid Painter's kalyx krater in the Louvre (*ARV*² 601, 22; Fig. 6.1) has the same aegis.

The inspiration for the costume of the Dresden-Bologna "Lemnia" with the left breast not covered by the aegis and with a girdle around the waist may result from an assimilation to Artemis, who often wears an animal skin fastened on one shoulder and belted at the waist. The assimilation to Artemis, who takes care of the young and insures that they grow up safely, may indicate that this Athena was designated for a *gymnasion* where younger boys were being trained as well as ephebes ready to receive their armor.[50]

The fastening on the right shoulder like a *chlamys* is retained in the Giustiniani Athena and in the Theseion frieze. If both belong to Pallene, we could infer that the cult there was only for ephebes, who received a chlamys along with their first armor.[51] The aegis of the Giustiniani will have covered her left breast under the himation, a corner of which is draped over the left shoulder and held in place by the left hand. That hand gesture seems to imply respectful attention such as should be given by the young. The softer, less boyish face of the Giustiniani shows her as more mature than the Dresden-Bologna Athena, whose androgynous face recalls the Athena of the Lion Metope on the Temple of Zeus at Olympia.[52]

When the Dresden-Bologna Athena is viewed in the context of Athena types from the Early Classical period to the end of the fifth century, it becomes clear that this statue was a significant original creation that fully deserves the admiration it has received. Its innovative aegis inspired both the narrow diagonal aegis of the motherly Athena of the west pediment of the Parthenon, which does not cover either breast, and the aegis tied on the right shoulder of the maidenly Athena Giustiniani. It ought not to be dismissed from Classical Greek sculpture just because it is not the Lemnian Athena of Pheidias. Quite possibly, it was designed by Alkamenes, who seems to have had a leading role in the execution of the Parthenon frieze.[53]

The widespread popularity of the Athena Giustiniani type as a single figure in Imperial Roman art, west and east, may be largely due to the prominence given to it in the time of Augustus by setting it as a paredros of Ares in the temple moved from Pallene to the Agora of Athens. The two figures combined in the Augustan group appealed to Greeks and Romans alike for their youthful seriousness and their beauty.

NOTES

I owe special thanks to Judy Barringer and Jeff Hurwit for their patient and meticulous editing of this multi-authored work. Also to Nita Roberts for photography; to Blair Fowlkes for copying my text onto disk; to Laura Gadbery for measuring and drawing; and to Manolis Korres, Hans Rupprecht Goette, and Ronald Stroud for enlightening consultation. Also to Julia Lenaghan for information on recent finds. All errors are my own.

1. Dinsmoor 1940; McAllister 1959, 1–6.

2. These temples, the so-called Hephaisteion, the Temple of Poseidon at Sounion, the Temple of Ares in the Athenian Agora, and the Temple of Nemesis at Rhamnous, were assigned by Dinsmoor Sr. to the "Theseum Architect," first in Dinsmoor 1940, 44–47, and then in Dinsmoor 1941, 153–154, as well as in Dinsmoor 1975, 179–183. Dinsmoor's precise date of 449 B.C. for the "Hephaisteion" is no longer accepted for the beginning of work on that temple, but the place of the Temple of Ares as third in the list, as well as a general dating in the 430s based on style, still seems probable; see Korres 1998, 91–97.

3. The letters carved on the marble blocks of the temple to enable the rebuilders to assemble them correctly have forms appropriate to the time of Augustus (see Dinsmoor 1940, 47–54). In addition, because the Odeion in the Agora, dedicated by Agrippa, has its axis at right angles to that of the Temple of Ares (Fig. 11.1), it appears that the two structures were parts of one plan (see Camp 1986, 181–187). Note that the Temple of Ares does not take its orientation from the buildings on the West Side of the Agora.

4. Pausanias does not name the sculptor or sculptors of the Aphrodites. Possibly these were the two marble Aphrodites found in the filling of the Post-Herulian Fortification Wall in a section where ceiling beams and coffer blocks of the Temple of Ares were built into the outer faces (see Harrison 1988a). No candidate for the statue of Enyo has been found. Perhaps it was of bronze. Pausanias implies by using the definite article for Ares and Athena that these two were the divinities to whom sacrifice was made on the altar.

5. Daux (1965, 89) points out that at the time of the decree (second half of the fourth century B.C.) there was no temple of Ares in Athens. He suggests that at that time Acharnai was the principal center of Ares worship for all Athenians.

6. Korres 1998 (see p. 83 for a list of the members of the Greek Archaeological Service who directed the excavations and allowed Korres to interpret the temple remains).

7. The most complete lists of those who accepted the identification of the Ares Borghese with the Ares of the Athenian Agora are given by those who question it. Bruneau (1982, 178–180) counts 31 and ends with "etc." I am one of the cetera (see Harrison 1977, 174).

8. Hartswick 1990. This long article contains much valuable information but errs in using certain elements, such as the griffins on the helmet, to support his idea that the type is a Roman Mars. See most recently Ridgway 1997, 244, 280, n. 18. Ridgway discusses the Ares Borghese here because the stance is somewhat related to that of the diskos-carrier that has been attributed to Naukydes. She considers the Ares to be later than the diskos-carrier, "a classicizing creation after Polykleitan prototypes." She does not consider the evidence for Polykleitan influence on Alkamenes himself. For photographs of the Diskobolos, see Arnold 1969, pls. 12–13; Bol 1996.

9. Dinsmoor (1940, 1) reported that a fifth-century marble torso, Agora Inv. S 654 was found "only 16 m. south of the southwest corner of the Temple of Ares." This led to the idea that the torso belonged to the statue by Lokros of Paros, an idea that was taken up by Barbara Vierneisel-Schlörb, who then suggested that the Ares also should have been of marble (see Vierneisel-Schlörb 1979, 181–182). Actually the torso was found reused in a Byzantine wall approximately 50 m south of the temple.

Meanwhile, a copy of the Agora Athena was found in the Temple of Allat at Palmyra (Gawlikowski 1977, 253–274). One need not assume that the head of the Athena Parthenos type on the Palmyra statue copies the head of the Agora statue. The combination of the motherly type of the Athena with the diagonal aegis (derived from the west pediment of the Parthenon) with the warrior-maiden type of the Athena Parthenos can have been chosen to express the dual nature of the Palmyrene goddess.

10. See Goette 1998, 105–118, pls. 21–24, for inscriptions from the region of Pallene. No cult of Ares is mentioned either in these inscriptions or in the literary testimonia.

11. See Wilkins 1993, xxxiii–xxxiv, for dating by metrical analysis; Zuntz 1963, 81–88, for an historical argument for the year 430 B.C. for the *Herakleidai;* Wilkins remarks, "Zuntz is perhaps to be followed."

12. This, of all the interpretations offered over the last two centuries, is the only one that does not conflict in some way with the visual evidence. Dörig (1985) is useful for its excellent photographs, less so for his reading as Erechtheus fighting the sons of Poseidon. Felten (1984) attempts to give Hephaistos a major role, fighting the river gods as in Hom. *Il.* 20, but this does not work because there is continuous ground under the figures. Also, one of the supposed river gods wore a sword (see Harrison 1988b, 346, and pl. 99:IV, 16). In spite of this, Felten's reading was welcomed by Delivorrias (1997, 84) because it would support the identification of the temple as the Hephaisteion. Knell (1990) was persuaded by the logic of Felten's "closed composition."

13. Now Reber (1998) has revived the idea of the Pallantidai. Though he accepts most of the analysis of the action presented by Thompson (1962), Reber does not assume a consistent development of the narrative from left to right. Thus he identifies VI, 27 as Leos the informer rather than the defeated Pallas. The contrary is suggested, however, by a fragment of a red-figure cup from the Akropolis, Graef and Langlotz 1929, no. 412, pl. 30. This shows Lykos laying his hand on Pallas' shoulder in a gesture so like that of VI, 26 that, though the hand itself is hidden on the frieze, it is hard to deny a similar intent. Pallas on the frieze is surrounded by his brothers in their camp. Even as they prepare to march out, they have learned that Theseus has destroyed their ambush.

14. I would differ from Thompson only in naming the three gods on the right as Apollo, Artemis, and Poseidon. Pausanias (1.32.2) mentions an altar on Mount Hymettos to Apollo Proopsios (foreseeing). A boundary stone of Artemis Orthosia was found in the neighborhood of Pallene (see Goette 1998, 107, no. 4). Poseidon on the frieze sits on a solitary rock that could well represent Sounion. Cf. the Poseidon seated on a rock in the east frieze of the Temple of Athena Nike in Harrison 1997, 111, fig. 3.

15. Hera cults are infrequent in Attica, and none is mentioned in the documents from the neighborhood of Pallene. She is appropriate as the companion of Zeus, however. Her dress, a chiton with overfall and a himation pulled over her head as a veil, as well as the rocky seat, recalls the Hera of Parthenon north metope 32. I suspect that both reflect the image of Hera in the *Marathon* painting. Hera's presence could underline that this mythical battle of Theseus is analogous to the battle of Marathon (see Harrison 1972b, 366).

16. Zeus, surprisingly, is not recognized by Felten in any of the figures. Contrast the east frieze of the Siphnian Treasury at Delphi, a Trojan War myth, where Zeus weighs the fates of the combatants.

17. Hdt. 8.37–39. At Delphi there were two heroes, Phylakos and Autonoos, whose shrines were near the sanctuary of Athena Pronaia. The role of Athena in these miracles was signaled first by the sacred weapons leaving her temple under their own power and appearing on the ground in front of it, then by a shout of triumph issuing from the temple when the Persians were hit by the stones rolling down on them.

18. For description and actual state, see Praschniker 1928, 159–161 (the reconstruction on 203, fig. 123 has the trident improbably sticking in the body of the giant) and Brommer 1967, text, 28, pls. 52–54. On the other hand, a small hole in the rock below could have served to attach the lower part of the trident. As Poseidon pushes the rock Nisyros over on top of the giant, he may also be splitting the rock with his trident to make a chasm that will swallow the giant up. See also Schwab 1988, 35–37, pls. 14–16.

19. Sauer 1899, pl. 3. H. Koch (1955) used Sauer's drawn reconstructions and did not attempt his own. Sauer's detailed observations have proved to be very accurate. It is mainly in the reconstructions that one can differ from him. Dörig

(1985) also relies on Sauer's drawings and comments on his observations.

20. Dörig 1985, 55, with fig. 57.

21. Harrison (1988b, 346, no. 17 and pl. 100) describes the cutting behind the head of IV, 17, in which a metal thunderbolt could have been fastened. Beside it are traces of fingers clutching the back of the Pallantid's neck in a gesture like that of a giant hit by a thunderbolt on the kalyx krater in Ferrara, Museo Archeologico Nazionale di Spina T300; *ARV*^{2} 1041, 6: Alfieri and Arias 1958, pl. 67. Next to the group of Zeus and Porphyrion on the krater is Poseidon pushing Nisyros down on a giant, while between them flies the eagle of Zeus. In the crowning molding of Slab V above figure 20 are two large holes for an attachment. See Harrison 1988b, pl. 93. A flying eagle in this place could have served to show the connection between Zeus in the left-hand group of gods and the gods on the right. In 1953 when I took notes transcribed in Harrison 1988b, I wrongly assumed along with others that the stone behind this stricken Pallantid had hit him in the back. It may simply have passed behind him.

22. Wilkins 1990.

23. Plin. *HN* 34.72: *Alcamenes Phidiae discipulus et marmorea fecit et aereum pentathlum, qui vocatur encrinomenos* (Alkamenes, the disciple of Pheidias, made marble statues and also a bronze statue of a winner in the *pentathlon,* known as the *enkrinomenos* [tr. J. J. Pollitt]).

24. Ridgway 1997, 243–244.

25. Ridgway 1997, 270, n. 18.

26. *IG* I^3 Fasc. II, 1995, no. 506, "paullo post 433." For full description, see Raubitschek 1949, 185–188. For a photo of the base set against the lower step of the Propylaia, see Travlos, *Athens,* 126, fig. 170.

27. Plut. *Per.* 13.

28. Above, n. 26.

29. I thank Laura Gadbery for providing me with a tracing of the cuttings on the top of the base and Patricia Butz for measuring the distance between the feet of the Hope Athena. Subsequently Leventi (1991) set forth in detail the stylistic arguments for dating the Hope-Farnese type early in the decade 430–420 and made further comparisons of the dimensions of the statue and the cuttings on the base. Thus an attribution suggested by Studniczka before 1900 but not carried further by him has gained a high degree of probability.

30. Harrison 1977. My effort to find a place for the fifth-century Hephaisteion on the north slope of Kolonos Agoraios is now out of the question, since the remains of the Hellenistic Arsenal have been thoroughly explored. It is clear that the structure was destroyed in the first century B.C. and never rebuilt (see Pounder 1983). See also Korres (1998, 100–104) for the reuse of stones from the Arsenal in the foundations of the transplanted Temple of Ares and other Athenian buildings.

It now seems more likely that the fifth-century temple for which statues of Athena and Hephaistos were made lay west of the Painted Stoa and north of the street leading to the Dipylon. It may have suffered a fate like that of the Arsenal, damage in the time of Sulla and dispersal and reuse of its elements. Pausanias (1.14.6) makes no mention of the "anthemon" or the base for the statues mentioned in *IG* I^3 472. Perhaps the anthemon was melted down, and the sculptured slabs were carried off to be copied. The statues will have been rescued and placed in a modest temple of their own. The small temple of Roman date above the altar now ascribed to Aphrodite Ourania is directly across the street from the north end of the Royal Stoa and at a slightly higher level, thus fitting Pausanias' location above or beyond the Kerameikos and the Royal Stoa. I would no longer suggest that the shield of Athena was suspended from the anthemon. The "shield" below which leaves (or petals) were attached at the time the anthemon was installed must have been an ornamental round plaque masking the junction of the chimney and the ceiling, like the ornamental disks at the base of door knobs.

31. *IG* I^3 104, 102–124. For general discussion, see Camp 1986, 104–105.

32. See above, n. 2.

33. Petrakos 1981; Petrakos 1986.

34. E.g., Schlörb 1964.

35. Despinis 1971. See the catalogue of copies of the type on 28–32 and 148–149, with bibliography, also pls. 35–38. Despinis there mentions the Athena Giustiniani frequently and is firm in denying that it could be a work of Agorakritos himself. He does not discuss the problem of Lokros.

36. Ridgway (1997, 324, 352–353) does not take into account the age difference between the Athena and the Nemesis. For a similar contrast between the draped renderings of the "complete woman" and the virgin, see the Aphrodite M and the Hestia K of the east pediment of the Parthenon.

37. Despinis 1999, 179–180. The same article provides an update of his bibliography on the Athena Giustiniani. He there suggests that the original of the type was made for the Temple of Athena at Sounion. A fragment of the marble copy of the statue was found at Sounion, though its precise provenance is unrecorded.

38. See Daltrop and Bol 1983, 25, figs. 17–19, for the Dresden head. They consider the Frankfurt head of the Myron Athena to be an Augustan copy.

39. A "small," i.e., life-sized Athena of the Giustiniani type was placed in the same building at Kremna with a "large" Athena of the usual heroic size. See Inan 1970, 52–73, pl. 19, figs. 1–2. The "head at colossal scale" in Ostia mentioned by Ridgway (1997, 352, n. 3) is one of the Velletri at its usual scale.

40. See Korres (1998, 97–98 and pls. 16–17) for the possibility of placing a base slightly over one meter in depth in

front of the interior columns at the back of the cella. He outlines a base two meters wide, but there is no limiting factor for this dimension.

41. Knauer 1986, 121–126, pls. 20–21.

42. Despinis 1998. This disproves the pessimistic remark I made in Harrison 1996, 28, that "no visual document exists that can be taken seriously." I gladly retract it.

43. Harrison 1977, 153–154, n. 67.

44. Hera in the east frieze of the Parthenon shows the same motif. See Boardman and Finn 1985, pls. 45–46.

45. In addition to Despinis 1998, 59–64, see Trianti 1998, pl. 417, and Despinis 2001.

46. For the most detailed description of the aegis of the Dresden-Bologna type, the so-called Lemnia, see the publication of the Kassel replica in Bieber 1915, 5–6. For a back view of Torso B in Dresden, see Protzmann 1984, 21, fig. 19.

47. Because the Athena of the Theseion frieze is presented in profile, though in high relief, neither the fastening of the peplos nor any fastening of the aegis on the left shoulder is depicted. The snakes that were fastened in two holes in the arm behind the left breast would have been visible only in their upper parts. Sauer's reconstruction errs in showing the coiled lower parts of the snakes, which would have been hidden. Also mistaken is his indication that the aegis was fastened between the breasts by the gorgoneion. There is no central drill hole below the gorgoneion, only the one above.

48. Boardman, Dörig, Fuchs, and Hirmer 1967, pl. 169 left.

49. Despinis 2001.

50. Though a helmet in the right hand of the Dresden-Bologna Athena is not certain, it is visually and iconographically satisfying. It would refer to the ephebe who received his armor, while the Artemis motif of the aegis would refer to Athena's care for the younger boys. Since no representation of this statue has been identified on coins, we have no indication of its original setting. The figure of Thetis holding the new helmet for Achilles on a red-figure bell krater from Gela (*ARV*[2] 1054, 45) is comparable in its stance and simple beauty. See Barringer 1995, pls. 15–19 and appendix no. 24, with full bibliography. A copy of the Bologna head type was discovered along with other sculptures in modern fill of ancient cryptoportici in Rione Terra-Pozzuoli. I owe to Julia Lenaghan photocopies from the exhibition guide, *Nova Antiqua Phlegraia,* Naples: Electa 2000, frontispiece, p. 26. Compared with the Bologna head and the fragmentary head in Dresden, the face of the new copy looks like that of a young boy. Like the Bologna head, it was made to be inset, in this case perhaps into a herm. This could well have served a gymnasion that trained younger boys.

51. See Daux 1965, 79–80, pl. I.

52. Ashmole, Yalouris, and Frantz 1967, pls. 143–151. In the second metope, pls. 154–159, Herakles is a grown man with a beard, and Athena has a softer, more feminine face.

53. Patricia Lawrence remarked in a letter of March 1983 that the Dresden-Bologna Athena "looks more like an elder cousin of the Velletri" than like works of Pheidias. An attribution to Alkamenes would explain the similarity of Athena's coiffure to that of Athena in the east frieze of the Parthenon (Boardman and Finn 1985, pls. 46–47).

THE PERIKLEAN AKROPOLIS

12

THE PARTHENON AND THE TEMPLE OF ZEUS AT OLYMPIA

JEFFREY M. HURWIT

Whenever the precursors of the Periklean Parthenon (447–432 B.C.) are discussed, attention focuses, as it well should, upon the Older Parthenon, that very late Archaic marble temple begun after Marathon (490) upon a massive limestone foundation that extended and leveled the southern part of the Akropolis summit. The Parthenon not only stands upon the podium built for its aborted predecessor (the Older Parthenon had not risen very high when it was destroyed in the Persian sack of 480), but, as many commentators have noted, the Periklean building is also in essence an expansion and widening of the Older Parthenon. Indeed, it consists in large part of recycled marble originally quarried and worked for that earlier structure.[1] In addition, the Periklean Parthenon can be seen as the culmination of a local Akropolis architectural/sculptural workshop tradition older and broader than the Older Parthenon alone. Its "double cella" (with two rooms separated by a solid wall between two unusually shallow porches) was anticipated not only by the plan of the Older Parthenon but also by that of the *Archaios Neos,* the Old Temple of Athena Polias constructed in the late sixth century on the north side of the summit (also destroyed by the Persians in 480).[2] Moreover, the insertion of Ionic elements into the Parthenon's otherwise Doric fabric (for example, the four Ionic columns in its western chamber, the continuous frieze around the top of its cella walls, and various moldings) was anticipated not only on the Akropolis itself by the Archaios Neos (whose porches were likely topped by a continuous frieze) and the Older Parthenon (which had at the very least a large Ionic base molding and conceivably was intended to carry a continuous frieze of its own)[3] but also below in the Agora, where the Doric Stoa Poikile (ca. 470–460) had interior Ionic columns, and elsewhere in Greece by such composite temples as the late sixth-century Temple of Athena at Paestum.[4]

The Parthenon was thus the product of both local Athenian and wider Greek traditions, even as it transcended them (its octastyle peripteral plan, with a hexastyle double-prostyle cella, is unique).[5] Yet there is one building that has only rarely been mentioned in discussions of possible influences upon the Parthenon, a temple that had just become the largest temple ever built on the Greek mainland (a prestigious title) and that was decorated with the most grandiose sculptural program that had yet been seen anywhere in the Greek world. This was the Temple of Zeus at Olympia, a quintessentially Doric building that dominated the greatest of all panhellenic sanctuaries and that was completed (it is too infrequently appreciated) less than a decade before the start of work on the Parthenon itself. It is inconceivable that Pheidias, Iktinos, and Kallikrates—the reputed masterminds behind the Parthenon—designed and executed their project without ever looking over their collective shoulders at it. The plan and composite nature of the Parthenon owe most to Late Archaic predecessors atop its own Akropolis. But the Temple of Zeus was the immediate precursor that Pheidias, Iktinos, and Kallikrates (and of course Perikles, who clearly hoped to catapult Athens to the cultural and ideological forefront of Greece with his building program) most consciously sought to rival and surpass. It was the new, sculpturally loaded Temple of Zeus that exerted the greatest creative pressure upon the makers of the Parthenon.[6]

The Temple of Zeus, designed by the local Libon of Elis, was begun, we surmise, in the years just after Elis' destruction of Pisa around 470 and was architecturally complete (we surmise again) by the time the Spartans fixed a gilded, gorgon-faced shield to the peak of its east gable sometime after the battle of Tanagra in 457.[7] The notion that the managers of Olympia wanted the temple to be ready for the 81st Olympiad (456) is plausible enough. But although it took the fourteen years between 470 and 456 to build, the Temple of Zeus was not in all respects complete. It is likely, as Paul Rehak has suggested, that the pedimental sculptures were installed in haste before final details could be executed to make the Olympic deadline and that work was intended to continue on some sculptures while they were in place in the gables, in years even closer to the inception of the Parthenon.[8] Whether such post-installation carving actually took place—and some sculptures did remain unfinished—it is now agreed that the temple cella did not acquire its cult statue until the 430s or its roof its gilt bronze *akroteria* until the 420s, a good date for the floruit of their sculptor, Paionios.[9]

In short, the dust had barely settled around the Temple of Zeus when the Parthenon was begun in 447, and there was still sculptural work to do even as work on the Parthenon progressed (and even after it was complete). If the Greek world had just acquired a brand new masterpiece—a sculpturally rich Doric monument that must have generated considerable temple-envy in Athens—the elaboration and adornment of the Temple of Zeus and the creation of the Parthenon to a degree overlapped.[10] In this essay, offered to a teacher and scholar who has done so much to elucidate the Classical style and temper, I briefly survey the points of contact between what are arguably the two finest monuments of Classical Greece and suggest that in crucial respects each building acknowledged the other. The two buildings—one set in the middle of the most important panhellenic sanctuary, the other atop Greece's most important Akropolis—engaged in a competitive "dialogue," a kind of *agon* in the second half of the fifth century.

THE TEMPLE OF ZEUS AND THE ART OF EARLY CLASSICAL ATHENS

It is first necessary to rehearse the Temple of Zeus' indebtedness to Athens and Athenian iconography. Pausanias says the sculptor of the east pediment (Fig. 12.1) was Paionios of Mende (in Thrace), and he is certainly wrong about that. He also says the sculptor of the west pediment (Fig. 12.2) was Alkamenes, and if he means the Alkamenes who was the pupil or younger contemporary of Pheidias, he is probably wrong about that, too.[11] The origin of the temple's sculptors remains a famously open question, with various scholars favoring local Peloponnesian, Spartan, Parian (the marble of the pediments, metopes, simas, and roof tiles is Parian), or Attic masters, schools, or workshops.[12]

Wherever the sculptors came from, it is commonly accepted that Athenian influences pervade at least the pediments of the temple. The east pediment displayed a local myth (preparations for the fateful chariot race between Pelops and Oinomaos) that nonetheless

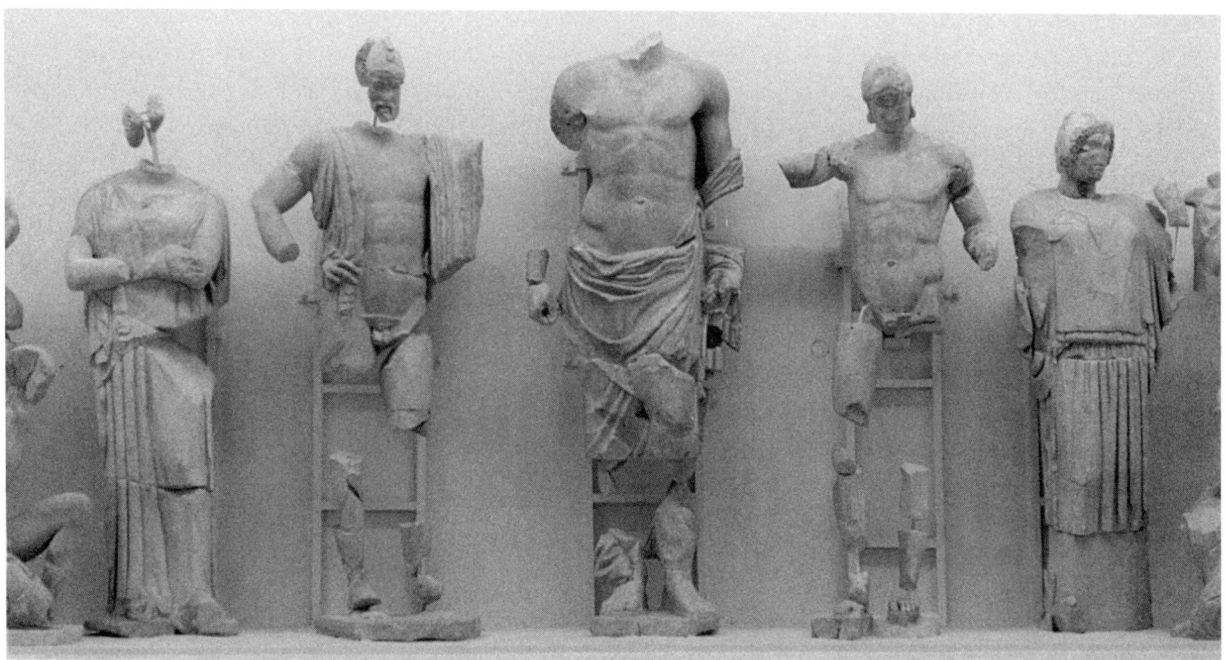

FIGURE 12.1. *Temple of Zeus at Olympia. Central figures of the east pediment. Olympia, Museum. Photo: J. M. Hurwit.*

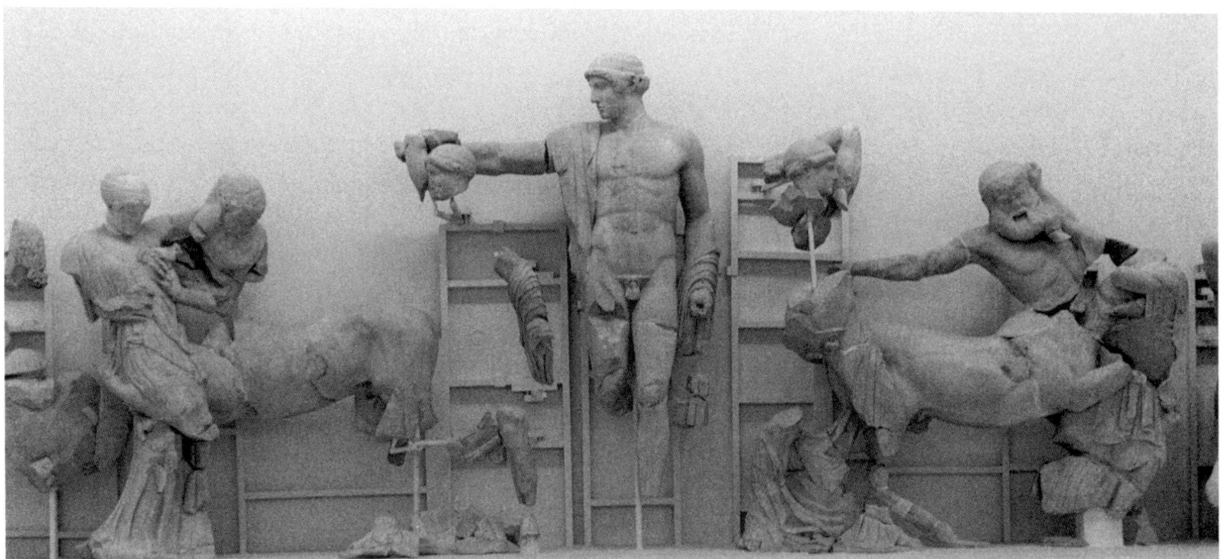

FIGURE 12.2. *Temple of Zeus at Olympia. Central figures of the west pediment. Olympia, Museum. Photo: J. M. Hurwit.*

may have borne some relation to Sophokles' lost tragedy, *Oinomaos,* possibly performed around 468, just in time to make an impact on the designer of the sculptures.[13] The west pediment, displaying the brawl between the Lapiths and the Centaurs, displays a new and peculiarly Athenian version or stage of the story, with the action taking place at the wedding feast rather than out-of-doors afterward, with Theseus (whose iconography is of course overwhelmingly Attic)[14] playing a leading role, and with Peirithoös (the groom) posed like Harmodios, the younger Tyrannicide set up by Kritios and Nesiotes in the Athenian Agora in 477/6. As a number of scholars have stressed, the west pediment is in some respects a monumentalization in marble of a wall painting, possibly by Mikon, in the Theseion in Athens (dated to ca. 475) that also inspired such red-figure artists as the Painter of the Woolly Satyrs.[15] Moreover, the Apollo at the pediment's center bears so strong a resemblance to such works as the Blond Boy (ca. 480) and the Euthydikos *kore* (ca. 490) from the Athenian Akropolis that, Barron has plausibly argued, it was indeed the work of an Athenian, an elder Alkamenes, sufficiently practiced and known to be awarded the Olympic commission around 470.[16]

Where the sculptors of the Temple of Zeus went after they completed their work in the years around or just after 456 we do not know. But if an Athenian or an Athenian team was responsible for the design or execution of one or both pediments, they would have been ready to work on the next big thing when it came along: they had the skill and they had the experience. The next big thing was, of course, the even more ambitious sculptural program of the even larger Parthenon, and there is no reason to doubt that some of the same sculptors who had worked at Olympia in the 460s and 450s were already working in, or were drawn to, Athens in the early 440s.

THE PARTHENON AND THE TEMPLE OF ZEUS (I)

By 447 Athenians already knew the Temple of Zeus well. Athenian sculptors likely worked on the project, and the Olympic Games were, despite intermittent states of war in the late 450s and early 440s, still open to Athenian athletes and pilgrims (three Olympiads—those of 456, 452 and 448—passed between the completion of the Temple of Zeus and the inception of work on the Parthenon). There is circumstantial evidence that Athenian visitors to Olympia were duly impressed, and several features of the Parthenon can be considered responses to the Temple of Zeus.

It is, perhaps, not so strange that the ratio of the number of façade columns (8) to flank columns (17) on the Parthenon follows the classic ratio or "principle of commensurability" of 2:1 plus 1 canonized by the Temple of Zeus (6 × 13).[17] But it is remarkable that the height of the peristyle columns of both temples, and the height of the temples themselves, are virtually identical, despite the Parthenon's greater width and length, narrower column diameters, and smaller axial spacings.[18] The typical column at Olympia is 10.43 m tall (there is actually a range between 10.42 and 10.44); the Parthenon's columns are 10.43 m tall, too, and, as Wilhelm Dörpfeld noted in the still fundamental publication of the Temple of Zeus, that "ist gewiss kein Zufall"[19] ("is certainly no coincidence"). Iktinos seems to have wanted to match certain critical dimensions of the Temple of Zeus, and that he did so under the constraint of having to reuse hundreds of column drums already carved for the Older Parthenon, makes his *homage* to the Temple of Zeus even more striking.[20]

The theme and representation of the Centauromachy provide another link between the two temples. The battle of Lapiths and Centaurs had never been represented in Athenian architectural sculpture before, so far as we know, and it is possible, as Burkhardt Wesenberg has argued, that metopes depicting the brawl at the banquet, represented monumentally in the west pediment at Olympia, were originally planned for two Doric friezes above the front and back porches of the Parthenon but were then moved to the relatively inconspicuous south side of the building (with additional reliefs added to complete the series) when it was decided to place a continuous Ionic frieze around the top of the cella walls.[21] If so, the original arrangement (ten metopes above each porch) mimicked but outdid the disposition of the metopes showing the labors of Herakles (six above each porch) on the Temple of Zeus. In any case, the metopes of the Parthenon were undoubtedly the earliest sculptures carved for the building—they needed to be ready to go when construction of the Parthenon reached the frieze level and can be dated to c. 447–442—and on the south there are stylistically many echoes of Olympia.

Some echoes are, it is true, stronger than others. South metope 27, for example, with its great V-shaped composition of a Lapith about to deliver a fatal blow to an overmatched Centaur (Fig. 12.3), seems an elaboration of the X-shaped composition seen on the metope of Herakles and the Cretan Bull from Olympia (Fig. 12.4). The way the Lapith's body is set off against drapery has also been considered a variation on the way the human body and cloth sometimes play off each

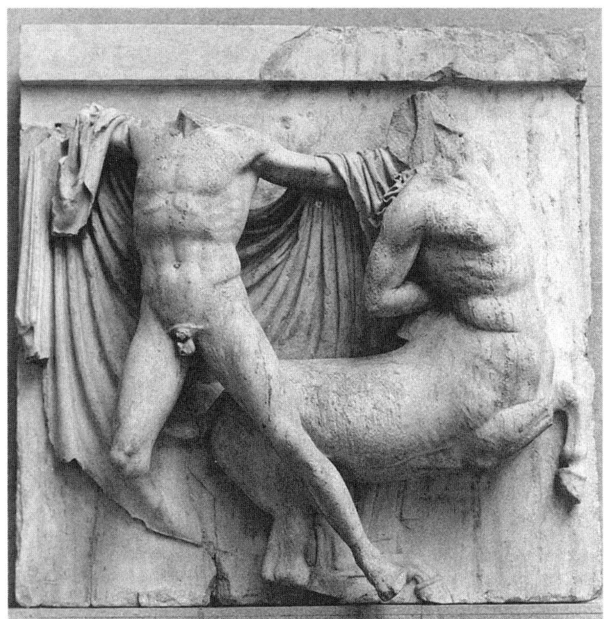

FIGURE 12.3. *Parthenon, south metope 27. London, British Museum. Photo: J. M. Hurwit.*

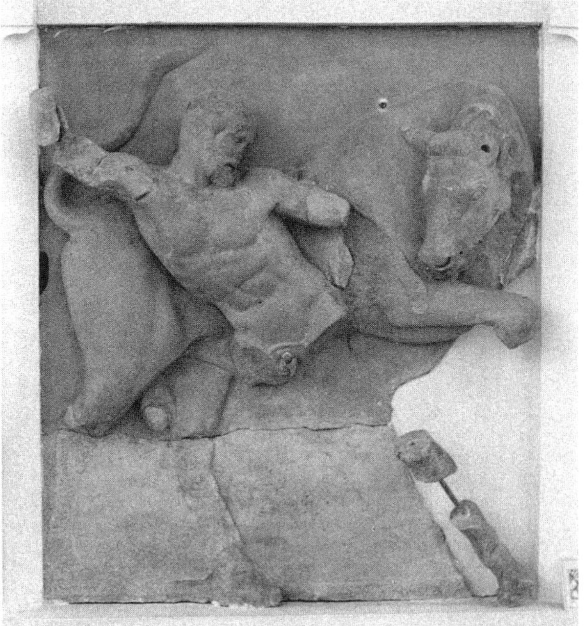

FIGURE 12.4. *Temple of Zeus at Olympia. Metope of Herakles and the Cretan bull. Olympia, Museum + Paris, Musée du Louvre. Photo: J. M. Hurwit.*

other in the Olympia pediments.[22] It is also unlikely to be coincidental that the Harmodios-like stance of Peirithoös in the Olympia west pediment (Fig. 12.2) is reproduced by the Lapith (is he Theseus?) in south metope 32: both are dependent upon the same source, but the Olympia pediment made the Tyrannicide pose appropriate for a Centaur-battling hero.[23] Moreover, the grotesque, masklike faces of some of the Centaurs on the south metopes (for example, south 31) recall the wrinkled scowling faces of the beasts in the Olympia west pediment. The south metopes are so stylistically heterogeneous, it is often said, because Pheidias was at this early stage in the project assembling sculptors from a variety of places, with a variety of experience. He would have been practically negligent if he did *not* hire sculptors who had recently contributed to the grandest architectural sculptural program Greece had to that point ever seen, and it is not implausible that the sculptors of the more "old-fashioned" metopes on the south had gained the experience Pheidias sought at Olympia.

More generally, there may be a connection in the nature of the pediments of the two temples, specifically in the way the pediments on each temple relate to one another. One pediment of the Temple of Zeus (the west, Fig. 12.2) shows a wildly violent scene, with turbulent lines undulating from the center to the angles, while the other (the east, Fig. 12.1) shows a calm, quiet (if ominous) tableau dominated by five heavy verticals. This is not an uncommon relationship between two pediments on a building or, for that matter, between two sides of the same vase (the Early Classical Niobid krater, for example, has the violent destruction of the children of Niobe on one side, and the calm gathering, somewhere, of Athena, Herakles, and assorted heroes on the other).[24] The west pediment of the Parthenon certainly showed a scene of violent action, as Athena and Poseidon—two great diagonals—almost collided as their chariot teams reared up behind them. The nature of the lost center of the east pediment, however, is unknown. Popular reconstructions by Harrison and Berger show another active (if not terribly violent) V-shaped scene, with Athena, having been born from the head of a seated Zeus, veering off at an angle to the (spectator's) right and Hephaistos forming a counter diagonal to the left. Recent studies by Olga Palagia and others, however, favor a central static composition of at least three standing vertical figures (Athena, Zeus, and Hera; Fig. 12.5). If they are right, the central tableau of the Parthenon east pediment would bear a striking compositional similarity to the Olympia east pediment, and there would be on east and west façades the same juxtaposition of calm and violent compositions.[25]

Finally, there is Figure D in the south angle of the Parthenon's east pediment. The identity of this long-haired nude youth reclining on an animal skin remains problematic, but the choice is between Dionysos (who, however, had never before been shown completely nude or youthful in Attic art, and so might have been hard to recognize here) and Herakles (who, however, does not usually sport the long braided hair D wears, and whose presence at the birth of Athena would be anachronistic).[26] The problem is not likely to be resolved completely, though Dionysos is the choice favored by most analysts (it looks as if D could have been holding a kantharos in his lost but raised right hand). Still, if D is Herakles after all, there would be in the east pediment a link between hero and goddess recalling that so sympathetically expressed in the Olympia metopes.[27]

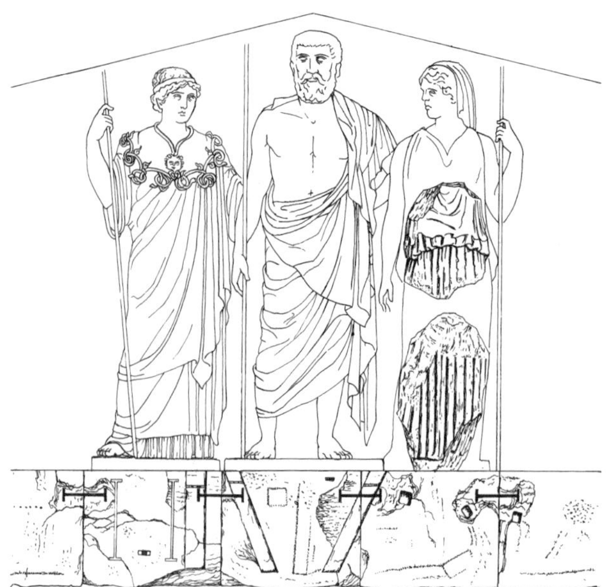

FIGURE 12.5. *Reconstruction of the central figures of the east pediment of the Parthenon. After Palagia 1993, pl. 20. Reproduced by permission of author.*

THE STATUE OF ZEUS AND THE ATHENA PARTHENOS

The Parthenon seems to have been structurally complete by the Greater Panathenaia of 438, when Pheidias' chryselephantine statue of Athena Parthenos was likely dedicated within it. With this event, the Parthenon began to exert creative pressure back upon Olympia: the direction of influence began to flow the other way.

It is not clear what sort of statue, if any, stood or sat within the cella of the Temple of Zeus between the completion of the building around 456 and Pheidias' arrival in Olympia, after a supposedly unpleasant exit from Athens in or shortly after 438.[28] But it is clear, first, that Libon did not design the temple with Pheidias' statue in mind (based on the finds associated with Pheidias' workshop, his Zeus was, again, not created until the 430s, thirty years or more after the temple was begun)[29] and, second, that the cella Libon had built was dramatically remodeled because Pheidias wanted it so. A part of the stylobate was reconstructed of Pentelic marble, which necessitated undercutting some of the interior columns of the cella; a large pavement of dark Eleusinian limestone was sunk into the floor in front of the statue and was enclosed by a raised sill of Pentelic marble (this formed an almost square reflecting pool filled, Pausanias tells us, with olive oil intended to mitigate the damaging effects of Olympia's relatively thick humidity upon the statue); stone and metal screens were set both across the width of the cella and between the columns of the interior; and wooden stairways were added at the corners to give access to the architrave separating the two storeys of interior columns, so that it could serve as a gallery from which to view the statue in greater detail.[30] As it was, the statue of Zeus, about forty feet high, seemed crammed into its setting: "[Pheidias] seems to have failed to take into account the question of proportion," Strabo sniffs, "for although the god is seated, he almost touches the peak of the roof, and thus gives the impression that, if he were to stand up straight, he would take the roof off the temple."[31]

The powers at Olympia clearly, even blatantly, asked Pheidias to outdo himself, to create a statue to eclipse the one he had just made for the Akropolis and so seize the sculptural field for Olympia. If we can trust our sources, that is precisely what he did: as impressive as the Athena Parthenos was, the Zeus had no rival, according to Pliny;[32] its beauty added something to received religion, according to Quintilian;[33] and it (not the Parthenos) was counted among the seven wonders of the ancient world. The statue itself had less gold but more ivory than the Parthenos and, since it was as high as the Parthenos sitting down, was on a larger scale. What Borbein calls its *Inszenierung* ("staging")[34] was richer, too, boasting a far more complicated thematic program.

Like the Athena Parthenos, the Zeus held a chryselephantine Nike in his hand, though his Victory would have been even larger than Athena's. Moreover, just as Athena's base was decorated with the *genesis* of Pandora, her shield with a Gigantomachy and an Amazonomachy, and her sandals with a Centauromachy, so Zeus' pedestal, throne, its screens, and stool were covered with myth, both sculpted and painted. The *kanones,* or bars, connecting the four feet of the throne even bore dozens of statuettes representing athletes and Herakles' battle against the Amazons.[35] There is no question that Herakles, son of Zeus, was the single most visible hero of this program: he appeared not only in three dimensions on the throne's bars but also in paintings by Panainos (Pheidias' brother or nephew) on the screens blocking access to the space beneath the throne, showing him with Atlas, the Nemean lion, and Prometheus; he appeared on the pedestal as well. Although Herakles plays the leading role in the iconography of the program, however, and though its content may in this and other ways be said to be predominantly Peloponnesian, there are still echoes of Pheidias' work on the Parthenon, and the *Inszenierung* of the Zeus to some degree acknowledged or promoted Theseus and Athenian ideology.

The base of the Zeus showed the Birth of Aphrodite from the sea, flanked by gods (including Herakles, standing with Athena as he does on the metopes), the entire scene framed by Helios in a chariot and Selene on horseback. The theme of birth, the assembly of the gods, and the cosmic setting are all motifs Pheidias had just used on the base of the Athena Parthenos and elsewhere in the sculptural program of the Parthenon.[36] Theseus, the Athenian hero par excellence, appeared three times: once in statuette form on a *kanon* as an ally of Herakles in his fight against the Amazons, once in a screen painting (he was shown with Peirithoös, but it is unclear what they were doing), and once in relief on the footstool, fighting his own battle against the Amazons. Pausanias calls this "the first brave deed of the Athenians against those of a different race,"[37] and it may be a mythological prefiguration of Marathon, where the Athenians were the first Greeks to face the Persians on Greek soil. Another Athenian-inspired victory over barbarians was commemorated with a screen painting of the personified Hellas and Salamis holding a ship's prow. To be sure, Hellas, not Athena, stood beside Salamis: the naval victory in Attic waters is thus projected as a broader panhellenic one. Still, the multiple presence of Theseus and the reference to Salamis gives the mythological program of the statue of Zeus "a definite Attic cast."[38]

Moreover, the mythological program of the statue of Zeus reveals an approach Pheidias developed or refined in the Parthenon: its iconography and themes are closely integrated with the architectural sculpture of the temple. The myths adorning the shield and sandals of the Athena Parthenos repeated the myths of the east, west, and south metopes of the Parthenon itself, and even the birth of Pandora on the base, with its assembly of gods, can be thematically tied to the east pediment (with the birth of Athena in the presence of the gods) and the east frieze (with the gods seated, awaiting the arrival of a procession, or something). The image within reprised the images without, just as the Athena within stands as the full epiphany of the goddess just born in the east pediment, and so the experience of the interior reinforced or amplified the experience of the exterior.[39]

It is much the same at Olympia: Theseus and Peirithoös, fighting Centaurs together in the west pediment, were shown together again in a screen painting; Hippodameia and Sterope, who stood apart in the east pediment, appeared together on a screen; Herakles appeared with Atlas and killed the Nemean lion on the screens, as he does in the metopes; he fought the Amazons on the throne *kanones,* just as he clubs an Amazon in another metope. Zeus himself sat in full majesty, the epitome of power and victory, having already made his epiphany at the center of the east pediment (Fig. 12.1). It is likely that the tactic of correlating the content of the cult statue within the cella and the architectural sculpture without is something that Pheidias brought with him from Athens.

The tactic was put to use one more time, with the akroteria of the Temple of Zeus. It is now accepted that the roof of the Parthenon was adorned with heavy marble akroteria in the form of off-balance Nikai alighting at the four corners.[40] There was nothing new about this, of course: Nike akroteria adorned the late sixth-century Temple of Apollo at Delphi, to cite only one example.[41] But the distribution of Nike akroteria was not particularly broad, and their presence on the new Parthenon could have inspired the managers of Olympia, sometime in the 420s, to commission Paionios (a Thracian who was nonetheless probably Athenian, perhaps even Pheidian-trained) to create Nike akroteria in gilt bronze (materially one-upping the marble of the Parthenon akroteria) for the Temple of Zeus.[42] Victory was an obvious choice of theme at the home of the Olympic Games, but just as the Parthenon akroteria were recalled in the Nike held in the palm of the hand of Athena Parthenos, so did the Nike akroteria on the Temple of Zeus and the Nike in the hand of Pheidias' Zeus echo each other at Olympia. One last addition to the Temple of Zeus brought its sculptural program in line with the Parthenon's: cult statue and architectural sculpture were correlated once more and in the same way.

THE PARTHENON AND THE TEMPLE OF ZEUS (II)

Pheidias' statue of Zeus may have been complete by 432, the traditional but, frankly, unreliable date for Pheidias' death.[43] Whenever it was dedicated, the Zeus, itself created in response to the Athena Parthenos, evidently had an impact upon the Parthenon and Parthenos in turn. The olive-oil reflecting pool placed in front of the Zeus was judged an aesthetic success, adding mysterious, shimmering, animating light to the *Inszenierung* of a statue said to have been inspired by Homer's portrait of a dark-browed god able to make Olympos quake with a mere nod of his head.[44] Sometime later, the architects of the Parthenon—whether they were still Iktinos and Kallikrates we do not know—tried for a similar effect.

At some point after the installation of the Athena Parthenos, an almost square area (roughly 9 m × 9.5 m) in front of it was surrounded by a rim of marble rising about 4 cm above the pavement (the bands of dressing for the rim stop at the pedestal of the statue, indicating that they were cut into the floor after the pedestal was already in place).[45] This area was filled with a shallow pool of water, which Pausanias thought, or was told, alleviated the extreme dryness of the Akropolis and so helped preserve the ivory of the statue (the evaporation of the water would in fact have improved the atmosphere of the cella only slightly, but what little additional humidity there was might have helped keep the glue holding the ivory plates pliable).[46]

It is in any case not clear when the water basin was added to the floor of the cella: all we know is that it had to have been sometime between the dedication of the Athena Parthenos in 438 B.C. and Pausanias' visit to the Akropolis around 160 A.D.[47] It is probable, however, that the basin was added before the end of the fifth century, in the immediate aftermath of the dedication of the Zeus, not so much as an "afterthought" as a calculated attempt to make the cella of the Parthenon as visually rich, grandiose, and dramatic as that of the temple at Olympia.[48] The setting of the Athena Parthenos—a statue that had inspired the managers of Olympia to commission Pheidias to surpass himself with the statue of Zeus in the first place—was in turn altered in response to the setting of the statue of Zeus. And so the addition of the water basin was the last entry in a progressive dialogue—one last round in a competition—between the Temple of Zeus, on the one hand, and Athenian art and the Parthenon, on the other, that had lasted half a century or more.

NOTES

1. See, for example, Hill 1912; Korres 1994a, 56–58; Hurwit 1999, 165–166.

2. Korres 1994a, 92; Hurwit 1999, 121–123. Similarly, the Classical successor to the *Archaios Neos,* the Erechtheion (designed and begun, it now seems, in the 430s), was yet another "double temple," another expression of what Korres calls "a tradition belonging only to the temple-building of Athens."

3. Ridgway 1999, 199.

4. For the Stoa Poikile, see Camp 1986, 66–72; for the Temple of Athena at Paestum, see Pedley 1990, 54–59. That temple had eight Ionic columns in its porch and was, according to Pedley, "the first building, known to us, in the whole history of architecture, to incorporate both Doric and Ionic together; as such, it is the clear precursor of developments in Attica some fifty years later" (55). For the Parthenon as a blend of Doric, Ionic, and Cycladic elements, see Korres 1994a, 84–88.

5. Korres 1994a, 59.

6. Among those who have briefly noted the interplay or competition between the two temples is R. Osborne 2000a, 234. Osborne, however, mistakenly cites Snodgrass 1986, as another: although Snodgrass argues that temple building was "a medium of rivalry between peer polities" (55) as early as the eighth century and discusses the Temple of Olympian Zeus at Akragas, he does not discuss the interaction between the Temple of Zeus at Olympia and the Parthenon.

7. The date for the beginning of the project is deduced from Paus. 5.10.2 and Diod. Sic. 11.54.1; the date for its end from Paus. 5.10.4.

8. Rehak 1998.

9. For the date of the statue of Zeus, see Mallwitz and Schiering 1964; Schiering 1991; for the chronology of Paionios, his marble Nike, and the date of the gilt bronze akroteria, see, for example, Barron 1984, 200, and Stewart 1990, 89–91, 142–143, 271 (T 81).

10. Cf. E. B. Harrison 1996, 59: "It is hard to believe that there was no overlap between the last stages of Pheidias' work in Athens and the beginning of his work on the Olympia project."

11. Paus. 5.10.8; Robertson 1975, 284–285.

12. For the problem generally, see Herrmann 1987. See also Ashmole 1972, 15–20; Robertson 1975, 290–291; Barron 1984; Dörig 1987 (esp. 6 for a review of prior opinion). As for the roof tiles, Pausanias (5.10.3) says they were of Pentelic marble, but Pentelic was used only for later repairs; see Dinsmoor 1975, 151. At all events, the use of marble tiles is a Cycladic architectural characteristic (see Korres 1994a, 84) and suggests a link to a broader Ionic tradition. The practice, as well as the marble, was perhaps imported by Parian stoneworkers.

13. Calder 1978.

14. *LIMC* 7, s.v. Theseus [J. Neils], 922–951. Theseus appeared not only in the west pediment at Olympia but also on the Corinthian Chest of Kypselos (ca. 570) on view in the Temple of Hera; he was shown playing his lyre beside Ariadne (Paus. 5.19.1).

15. Ashmole 1972, 50; Robertson 1975, 256, 259; Barron 1984, 201–202.

16. Barron 1984, 205–206. Richter 1930, 123–124, 237–238, first suggested the existence of an Early Classical Alkamenes.

If the pediments were Athenian products, the political meaning of the Spartan dedication of a shield from the battle of Tanagra would have been even clearer: the trophy commemorated a great Spartan victory over Athens, and, set atop the east gable, would have argued for Spartan superiority. The next riposte was the Nike of Paionios, set up by the Messenians and Naupaktians (Athenian allies) before the east façade of the temple around 421 to commemorate a joint victory over the Spartans; see Stewart 1990, 89.

17. Pollitt 1972, 72. The 8 × 17 plan had already appeared at Selinous, in the even larger but never finished Temple G (or GT, ca. 500); Dinsmoor 1975, 78, 160. The 6 × 13 plan had itself already appeared in the precocious Temple of Athena at Paestum; Pedley 1990, 54–59. See also W. Sonntagbauer, "Einheitsjoch und Stylobatmass: Zu den Grundrissen des Zeustempels in Olympia und des Parthenon," *BA Besch* 78 (2003), 35–42, which appeared after the completion of this article.

18. The Temple of Zeus measures 27.68 × 64.12 m at the stylobate; the Parthenon, 30.88 × 69.503 m. The lower diameters of the columns of the Temple of Zeus range between 2.21 and 2.25 m; the Parthenon's are 1.91 m. The normal axial spacing on the Temple of Zeus is 5.22 m; on the Parthenon, 4.29 m. Both temples were approximately 20 m high (to the apex of the pediments, minus akroteria). For comparison plans and elevations drawn to scale, see Coulton 1977, 112–113, figs. 45–46.

19. Curtius and Adler 1892, 6. See also Coulton 1977, 114: the columns of the two temples "are so similar in height as to suggest that a comparison was intended." Carpenter 1970, 48, also believes that the identity of the height of the exterior columns is no coincidence, but he sees it as the result of the architect of his "Kimonian Parthenon," begun between 468 and 464, deliberately imitating the almost exactly contemporary Temple of Zeus. Mallwitz 1972, 214, however, gives the column height at Olympia as 10.53 m.

20. The columns of the Older Parthenon would have been shorter by one drum than those of the Periklean Parthenon (which in all but two cases consisted of 11 drums), but their lowest diameter would have been the same (1.91 m); Korres 1994a, 59; Korres 1994b, 176; Hurwit 1999, 166.

21. Wesenberg 1983; Korres 1994b, 176, concurs; also Hurwit 1999, 174. Ridgway 1999, 197, 200, disagrees, rejecting Wesenberg's political rationale for the change in plans (that the ostracism of Thukydides son of Melesias in 443 gave Perikles a free hand in redesigning the Parthenon to his own liking). I agree that this particular interpretation of events is unlikely, but I find stylistic and architectural evidence, such as the uneven lengths of blocks and metopes, for the replacement more compelling than she.

22. Ashmole 1972, 102.

23. If Theseus is not to be found in south metope 32, he may be the hero in south metope 27 (Fig. 12.3); see Boardman 1985, 105; Berger 1986, 95, 98; *LIMC* 7, s.v. Theseus, no. 274 [J. Neils].

24. The east pediment of the Late Archaic Temple of Apollo at Delphi, to cite another example, was dominated by a frontal chariot and six standing, quiet maids and youths, while the west façade, though also centered on a frontal chariot, represented a violent Gigantomachy; see Robertson 1975, 276; Stewart 1990, fig. 200; R. Osborne 2000a, 233. For the Niobid krater, see, for example, Robertson 1992, 180–182.

25. Palagia 1993, 27–30.

26. Palagia 1993, 19–20. Interestingly, there is a similarly minor question concerning the identity of the seated male god, E25, on the Parthenon frieze, with the majority of scholars seeing Dionysos, but a small minority seeing Herakles; see Neils 2001, 164.

27. See Ashmole 1972, 60–89.

28. The helmeted and presumably Archaic Zeus that Pausanias (5.17.1) saw standing beside a seated Hera within the Heraion might have been moved to the new temple after 456, only to be returned to its original position in the Heraion after the installation of Pheidias' Zeus; see Dinsmoor 1975, 153. Or, possibly, between 456 and the 430s there stood a statue of Zeus that had no chance of being remembered after its replacement by Pheidias' monumental chryselephantine god and, supposedly, Zeus' own approval by thunderbolt (Paus. 5.11.9). E. B. Harrison 1996, 60, citing the Temple of Apollo at Bassai as a parallel, raises the possibility that no permanently fixed statue was originally intended for the cella at all, and, as Brunilde Ridgway notes elsewhere in this volume, there are other examples of temples that lacked cult or "temple statues"; cf. J. G. Miller 1997. Given the importance of the Temple of Zeus in the greatest of all panhellenic sanctuaries, however, and especially given the unprecedented grandeur of its metopal and pedimental program, it seems unlikely to me that the cella of the building was originally intended to be Zeus-less.

29. Mallwitz and Schiering 1964; Schiering 1991. Ashmole and Yalouris 1967, 30, suggest that Pheidias may have received the Olympic commission even before finishing the Athena Parthenos in 438. E. B. Harrison (1996, 63) suggests that Pheidias made several trips to Olympia between 444 and 438, even as he worked on the Athena Parthenos, to begin the planning for the Zeus. She also speculates that double-charging Olympia and Athens for the same ivory led to his trial and supposed execution.

30. Dörpfeld, in Curtius and Adler 1892, 12–13, and for the reflecting pool, pls. II, VIII, IX, XI–XII; Dinsmoor 1975, 153; Borbein 1989, 103. See also Mallwitz 1972, 228–229, where the dimensions of the reflecting pool are given as 6.54 m × 6.40 m. Pausanias mistakenly says the raised rim around the olive-oil pool was made of Parian marble (5.11.10). The change from Parian (the material of the Olympia metopes and pediments) to Pentelic marble (the material of the Parthenon, architecture and sculpture alike) again testifies to Athenian influence. In any case, the olive oil in the pool would not in fact have improved the condition of the ivory or reduced the humidity of the cella. Intended as a reflective surface, its purpose must have been primarily aesthetic; see Gaugler and Hamill 1989.

Korres (1994a, 65) has found evidence for a stairway to the roof built within the thickness of the east cella wall of the Parthenon. Perhaps this stairway inspired those inserted at Olympia, though there were similar stairways earlier elsewhere (e.g., in the Temple of Athena at Paestum; Pedley 1990, 54–59). Similarly, the folding gates that screened the spaces between the columns and antae of the pronaos, and the doors that were fitted to the opisthodomos, may have been inserted later in emulation of the Parthenon, whose grilled front and back porches served as treasuries; see Dinsmoor 1975, 152; Ashmole and Yalouris 1967, 7; Hurwit 1999, 164. Like the Parthenon, the Temple of Zeus became something of a strongbox.

31. Strabo 8.3.30; tr. Pollitt. For the statue in general, see now Lapatin 2001, 79–85.

32. Plin. *HN* 34.54.

33. Quint. *Inst.* 12.10.9. The Athena Parthenos, in contrast, certainly inspired wonder and admiration in its viewers but not necessarily religious feeling. It may not have even been, technically, a cult statue: see Hurwit 1999, 163–164; also Preisshofen 1984.

34. Borbein 1989, 103.

35. See Paus. 5.11.1–9, for a full description of the statue.

36. Hurwit 1999, 170, 229; Ridgway 1999, 198; also Palagia 2000.

37. Paus. 5.11.7; E. B. Harrison 1996, 62.

38. Ridgway 1999, 199; see also Himmelmann 1977, 86. E. B. Harrison (1996, 62–63) minimizes the promotion of Athens in the iconography of the statue, believing that it emphasizes the role of the Peloponnesians in the Persian

Wars; its message, she argues, is that "Athens must keep her place" as but one *polis* among many, just as Theseus merely assists Herakles in his Amazonomachy. But it is well to keep in mind that both Herakles on the north side and Theseus on the south are shown fighting Amazons in the metopes of the Athenian Treasury at Delphi (now generally regarded as a post-Marathon monument) and that their two battles seemingly fused on the east metopes; see, for example, Stewart 1990, 132–133.

39. Hurwit 1999, 187; Ridgway 1999, 196, 199.

40. Korres 1994a, 61–64; Hurwit 1999, 169, 230; Ridgway 1999, 91–92.

41. Boardman 1978b, fig. 204; Ridgway 1993, 152, 177, 304–305, 322, 330–331.

42. At least one Nike was set atop the peak of the east gable, surmounting and politically trumping the Spartan shield set there after Tanagra; see above, n. 9. It is the inscription on the triangular base of the Nike of Paionios, installed in front of the Temple of Zeus' east façade around 421, that tells us Paionios was also responsible for the akroteria of the temple, which included Nikai and *lebetes* (cauldrons). Misreading the inscription, Pausanias (5.10.8) attributed the sculptures of the east pediment to Paionios. See Meiggs and Lewis 1988, 223–224.

43. Some believe Pheidias continued to work at Olympia into the 420s; see Stewart 1990, 89, 257–259.

44. Strabo 8.3.30, citing Hom. *Il.* 1.528–530.

45. Stevens 1955, 267–270.

46. Paus. 5.11.10; Gaugler and Hamill 1989. Evaporation from such a large, shallow pool would of course have been rapid in the summer, but the water would have been unnecessary in the Athenian winter (a rainy season).

47. Stevens 1955, 267, indicates that the shape and size of an iron dowel securing the rim are not typical of fifth-century dowels yet seems ready to credit Iktinos with the design of the basin (269).

48. Stewart 1990, 157; Hurwit 1999, 363–364, n. 35.

13

THE PARTHENON FRIEZE AND PERIKLES' CAVALRY OF A THOUSAND

IAN JENKINS

The more the frieze is studied the greater will be the admiration of the genius displayed in plan, invention, drawing and execution.

W. WATKISS LLOYD

The enduring idea of the Parthenon frieze is that it represents the procession of the Panathenaic festival,[1] but even those who fully accept this interpretation have had to question the role of the horsemen who feature so prominently.[2] No direct literary evidence records that horsemen actually took part in the procession, whereas hoplites, who are reported as having marched in it, are omitted from the frieze.[3] On the basis of circumstantial literary evidence, not least the role of horsemen in other contemporary festival parades, it is possible to make the case that they also participated in the Panathenaic festival.[4] Yet, there remains the burden of proof.[5]

Adolph Michaelis explained the absence of hoplites on aesthetic grounds.[6] Whether or not horsemen actually participated in the procession, they make a better show than would have been the case with serried ranks of marching soldiers. Besides, it could be argued, the hoplites are present in the picturesque scenes of the chariot race. Michaelis also sought to define the actual role of the horsemen in the frieze. He made much of differences between the cavalcades of the south and north sides. Although working with an imperfect reconstruction of the south frieze,[7] he nonetheless saw that some at least of the horsemen fall into orderly, similarly dressed groups. These he attributed to the democratic organization of the Athenian cavalry under *phylarchs* and *hipparchs*.[8] The horsemen of the west and north friezes are not so uniformly composed. These he saw as emblematic of the legendary fame of Athens' horsemen, "The pride of the people who follow Theseus the king," as they are celebrated in Sophokles' *Oedipus at Colonus*.[9] At the same time, the contrast between the formality of the south cavalcade and the informal atmosphere of the west and north friezes reflects that combination of respect for the law on the one hand, and the freedom of the individual on the other, that is to be found in Perikles' Funeral Oration.[10]

Although few cite him, many have followed Michaelis in justifying the presence of the horsemen as part of an idealized and artistic representation, rather than a documentary record of the procession.[11] There is, however, by no means a consensus on how exactly this idealization is conceived. John Boardman has responded to the presence of horsemen and absence of hoplites by arguing for a special case, namely, a commemoration of 192 Athenian hoplites who fell at the battle of Marathon in 490 B.C.[12] They are raised to the status of heroes by their placement on horseback. The Panathenaic peplos, therefore, and the procession must be seen as incidental to the real message of the frieze, which is to heroize the Marathonomachoi.[13]

Robin Osborne has sought an explanation of the horsemen that is concerned less with heroizing the past than with promoting the present.[14] Osborne sees the frieze as a document of Athens' contemporary self-image.[15] He seeks a correspondence between the civic values of the *polis,* expressed in Perikles' Funeral Oration, and the values he finds implicit in the horsemen of the frieze. In both, "citizens are soldiers and soldiers are young men." These are not the common hoplite, however, but the "quintessential soldier"; "the very aristocratic image of Athenian democracy at its most elitist."[16] The Athenian military is shown on horseback not so much as a representation of a specific cavalry, but more as an icon of how Athenian males liked to think of themselves. The obvious parallel here is with the horsemen in idealizing funerary sculpture.

Jerome Pollitt takes a different view again.[17] For him, the horsemen are not an indirect reference to a heroic past nor are they emblematic of the contemporary Athenian *demos.* They are simply a literal representation of Perikles' horsemen on Perikles' Parthenon. Pollitt sees the horsemen of the frieze as a deliberate advertisement of Perikles' own military reforms by which the Athenian cavalry was substantially expanded from 300 to 1,000.[18] To the question as to what the cavalry is doing in the Panathenaic procession of the frieze, he would answer that the frieze "has little or nothing to do with the *procession.*"[19] Rather it is seen as a "general and collective picture of certain cultural institutions in Classical Athens."[20]

Pollitt's "picture" is inspired by the civic ideology of Periklean Athens, set out in the Funeral Oration of 431 B.C. It has been a commonplace for scholars to seek reflections of this text in the Parthenon frieze.[21] Pollitt's attempt is exceptional in finding specific institutions singled out for praise in the speech: *thusiai* (sacrifices), *agones* (competitions), and *polemike melete* (military training), all pervaded by a sense of *deos* or reverence.

> We should understand the frieze not as a kind of documentary picture of a single event but as an evocation of all the ceremonies, contests, and forms of training that made up the cultural and religious life of Classical Athens. Such an interpretation means that far from being a repository of ambiguous myth or a veiled vision of history, the Parthenon frieze represents contemporary Athenians and is one of the most explicit expressions that we have of the cultural ideology of Perikles.[22]

Pollitt's generalized and synoptic view of the frieze will not satisfy those who seek in it a single message commemorating myth or history. No theory, however, that has claimed a single message for the frieze has ever enjoyed lasting or universal appeal.[23] Nor should such a theory, when it comes invariably and perhaps inevitably without the support of secure documentary evidence. In the absence of any clear epigraphic or literary text to identify the intended meaning of the frieze, it is the presence of the blanket of cloth at the heart of the east frieze that offers the most tangible clue. If there is any consensus, it is for the notion, which Pollitt himself does not reject,[24] that the central scene of the east frieze represents the sacred peplos dedicated at the Panathenaia. It is sometimes argued that, being isolated from the rest of the frieze by the gods, this scene has no direct bearing on the procession.[25] It is surely inevitable, however, that participants in the real-life Panathenaic procession, passing along the north side of the Parthenon, should connect with this nearest pictorial paradigm of their own experience.[26] As "the ideal embodiment of a recurrent festival," the frieze will have had lasting appeal for successive generations of participants in the Panathenaia.[27]

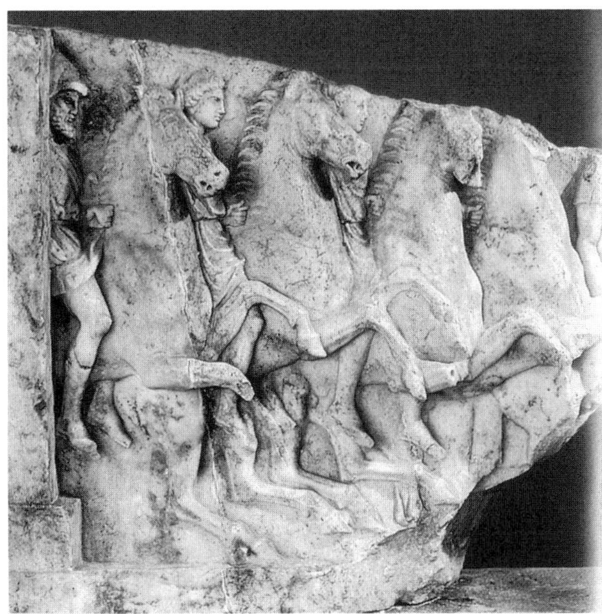

FIGURE 13.1. *Fragment of a marble relief commemorating the victory of the tribe Leontis in the* anthippasia, *ca. 400 B.C. Athens, Agora Museum I7167. Photo courtesy of the American School of Classical Studies at Athens, Agora Excavations.*

I should go further and argue that, if the frieze served to fix a permanent idea of the Panathenaia, then it also transcended it to present a larger idea, that of the polis itself. The frieze presents a microcosm of Athens, past and present.[28] It epitomizes the physical city in the movement of the procession between the outskirts and its sacred heart. It defines the social makeup of the city in a portrayal of the procession as young and old, male and female, citizen and noncitizen. It creates a hierarchy of Athenian life: of beast serving man, and of man and woman serving god. In portraying the essential elements of the festival, it presents a paradigm of the religion by which mortal communicates with the divine: contest in the horse parades; pomp in the pedestrian figures; sacrifice in those leading victims and carrying sacrificial apparatus.[29] It moves between present time and the past by representing images of contemporary cult that were resonant with associations of the heroic age. At the very heart of the frieze was the peplos woven with scenes of the Gigantomachy, an emblem therefore of the struggle by which the gods came to power. Thus the community of the city was set against the community of Olympian gods commanding the cosmos.[30]

Horsemen are prominent in this picture of a city. They fill all sixteen blocks of the west frieze, and, of forty-seven blocks of the north and south friezes, they occupy nineteen and twenty-four blocks respectively.[31] One of their striking features is their youth. With others I have been misled into calling them *ephebes.*[32] It is now clear that the ephebes trained as hoplites.[33] The horsemen of the frieze are presented in a manner entirely consistent with other representations of Athenian cavalrymen. In literature, for example, besides being aristocratic and rich, they are young.[34] In art they are also young, and so they are found in the fragment of a relief commemorating a tribal victory in the *anthippasia,* a mock battle in the hippodrome. The exceptional bearded figure here is usually seen as the phylarch (Fig. 13.1).[35] In life a cavalryman's career was over by his early thirties, at the latest.[36] While not so universally young as most pictorial representations suggest, therefore, the cavalryman's was nonetheless a young profession.

PERIKLES' CAVALRY REFORM AND THE DATE OF THE FRIEZE

Perikles' reform of the cavalry has long been linked with the horsemen of the frieze.[37] The precise nature and date of the reform is not explained by any one source, however, and has been much discussed.[38] The basic fact appears to be, as Thukydides informs us, that by the year 431 B.C., the cavalry numbered 1,200 and that this included 200 mounted archers, *hippotoxotai.*[39] They are not to be confused with the famous Skythians who provided Athens' police force and are a popular motif with archaic vase painters.[40] The hippotoxotai were citizens but drawn from a class inferior to the elite corps of 1,000.[41] Before this change, the elite corps numbered only 300, and Perikles is thought to have increased it to 1,000, not only as a military but also as a political measure. It is probably too much to say that the increase resulted in a more "democratically disposed" cavalry, but Perikles will have reinforced his political position by cementing further his relationship with the cavalry class, not least by opening up new positions for them to serve as commanders.[42]

Opinion varies as to when Perikles' reform came into operation. It is thought to have been part of an increase in stages after the Persian Wars. Perhaps following the battle of Tanagra (458/7), or perhaps Koroneia in 447, the corps numbered 300.[43] Connecting Perikles' reform directly to the frieze, Martin and Spence both set a terminus ante quem of 438, which is the received date for completion of the main structure of the temple, in time for the dedication of Pheidias' statue at the Great Panathenaia of that year.[44] Bugh, by contrast and following Robertson and Frantz,[45] places the completion of the frieze in 440 B.C. and is inclined to see the horsemen there as representing the corps of 300.[46]

If with Martin and Spence and contra Bugh a link between the horsemen of the frieze and Perikles' cavalry is accepted, then the date of the frieze would be critical for dating the cavalry reform.[47] The date of the frieze is, however, far from certain. The suggestion that it was completed by 438 is only one of three possibilities. The other two are that none of it was carved then or that it was only partially carved. All that we can say for certain is that the blocks into which the frieze is carved had to be in place earlier than 438. In that Panathenaic year, Pheidias' gold-and-ivory statue of Athena was dedicated. For this to happen, it must be assumed that the roof was on, and for that to happen, the frieze blocks had to be in place but not necessarily carved. The frieze was set as a course of masonry, its face worked rough. It has sometimes been suggested that the frieze blocks were lifted into place ready carved, but William B. Dinsmoor Sr. put the fact of the frieze having been carved on the building beyond doubt.[48] He also dated its carving to between 443 and 439 B.C., which is less certain. In fact, the procession could have been carved into the rough-worked surface of the frieze blocks at any time between its construction as an architectural member and 432 B.C., when the finishing processes seem to have been completed.[49]

The frieze may not have been completed until the year before Perikles delivered the Funeral Oration in 431 B.C., but the critical question in the attempt to establish a link between the horsemen of the frieze and the cavalry of Perikles' reforms is not so much when it was carved as when it was designed. That the frieze is the product of a single master plan is beyond doubt. Without such a scheme, the complexity of the north frieze cavalcade alone could not have been attempted. The design, however, could have been drawn up by Pheidias (if it was he) well before it was executed.[50] The question of when a decision was made to feature horsemen so prominently in the Ionic frieze of the Parthenon cannot be answered with any precision. If a proposed link with Perikles' reform is to be sustained, therefore, we must ask whether there is anything distinctive in the Periklean cavalry that can be found in the representation of the horsemen in the frieze.

A QUESTION OF ARITHMETIC

Perikles' reforms established a corps of 1,000 *hippeis*. These were divided into ten units (*phylai*) each led by a phylarch, one chosen from each tribe, under overall command of two hipparchs. Each phyle formed a block of 10 files of ten men, that is to say a 10 × 10 square (Figs. 13.2–3). The files were fronted by *decadarchs*, ten in all, of which the phylarch was presumably also one.[51] This system of ten phylai determined basic order in festival parades, state inspections (*dokimasia*), and battle order alike. One Panathenaic event, for example, was the *anthippasia*, the mock battle in which the hipparchs divided the cavalry into five phylai apiece, and the phylai then rode through each other at a charge.[52]

How far can the horsemen in the frieze be identified with the military and parade order of the actual cavalry at such events as those described by the historian Xenophon in his accounts of Greek horsemanship? A proper understanding of the intended manner of representing the horsemen of the frieze must depend upon proper understanding of the original sequence of frieze blocks and upon an agreed reconstruction of the figures shown in them.[53] Until relatively recently, scholars have been working with faulty sequences, which had their origins in that of Michaelis.[54] The first to attempt a thorough overhaul was Dinsmoor.[55] His great book on the Parthenon was never published. We are therefore indebted

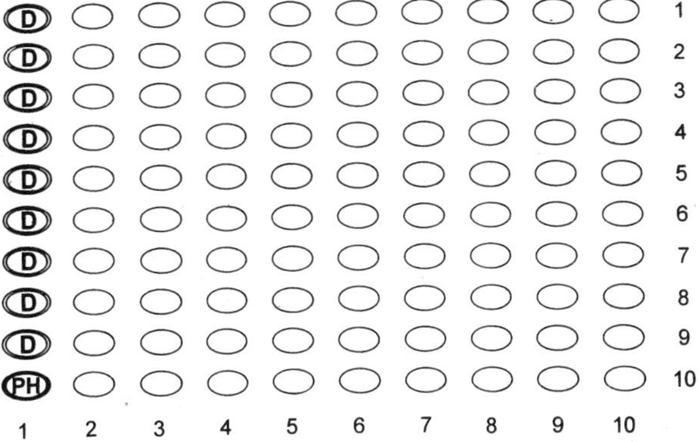

FIGURE 13.2. *The formation of a tribal unit of a hundred horsemen in the Athenian cavalry, commanded by a phylarch.*

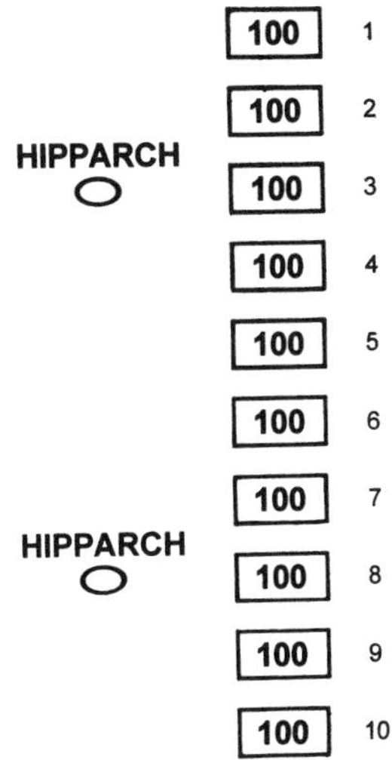

FIGURE 13.3. *The Athenian cavalry arranged in ten tribal units commanded by two hipparchs.*

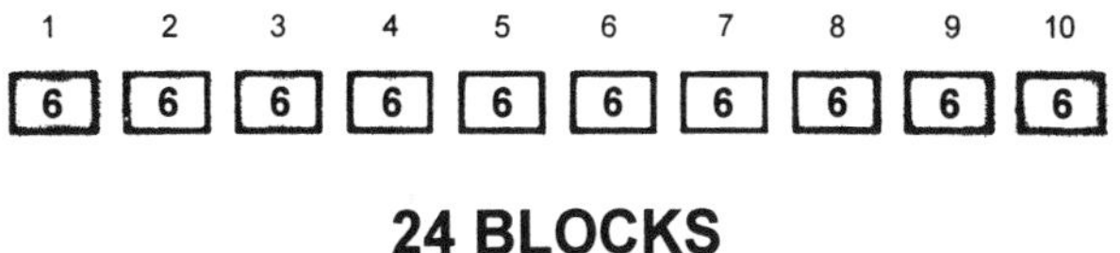

FIGURE 13.4. *The division of the horsemen of the south frieze of the Parthenon into ten groups of six, carved over twenty-four blocks.*

to Evelyn Harrison for extracting and publishing the relevant parts of Dinsmoor's manuscript to illuminate understanding of the arrangement of blocks in the north and south friezes.[56] She has also demonstrated once and for all that the south cavalcade comprises sixty horsemen, who can be divided into ten groups of six riders, each distinguished by its dress, and carved over twenty-four blocks (Fig. 13.4).[57]

This clearer picture of the south frieze invites speculation as to whether or not the north frieze cavalcade can be similarly divided, and there have been attempts to do so. As with the south, so with the north cavalcade, any attempt at finding meaningful divisions must depend upon a satisfactory reconstruction of block sequence. My own sequence[58] and that published by Berger and Gisler-Huwiler[59] both build on Dinsmoor's. Both sequences agree in allowing sixty riders spread over nineteen blocks. Harrison employing Dinsmoor's sequence has sixty-one,[60] while Luigi Beschi has sixty-two.[61]

In analyses of the groupings of figures in the procession as a whole, preferred divisions have been into groups of four, into groups divisible by four, or into groups of ten. Four are sought by those who would like to see evidence of a conscious effort to represent the four Ionian tribes of archaic Attika.[62] Ten are sought by those who seek representation of the Kleisthenic tribes of democratic Athens. John Boardman, for example, suggested that not only the south frieze cavalcade but also that of the north falls into ten "ranks or clusters, which can only represent the tribal organization of democratic Athens."[63]

For the most part, the desire to see the Ionian tribes in the north frieze cavalcade is the prevailing one. Harrison shares it and points out the frequent occurrence of four or numbers divisible by four in the participants in the procession elsewhere in the north frieze: four cattle and four sheep being led as victims; four hydria-bearers, four *auletai* (flute-players), four *kitharistai* (kithara-players), sixteen elders.[64] But she acknowledged the difficulty of three *skaphephoroi* (tray-bearers) and eleven chariots. Nor did she attempt to force the sixty riders of the north frieze into uniform groups. Instead she saw in their looser arrangement a reflection of an earlier age, suggesting the phratries or old tribal divisions of pre-Kleisthenic Athens. Harrison accepted that no division could be discerned by order of dress; she does speak of "ranks" but does not indicate where the divisions might fall.

Beschi took up the challenge in a closely argued paper with many valuable insights.[65] Working with sixty-two figures in the north frieze, he devised ten groups of six in the north to match those of the south. His divisions are, however, hard to follow and lack the clarity of those seen in the south. Moreover, his count of sixty-two riders meant that he had two too many. He argued them away by saying that the first two horsemen of the north actually belong to the preparation scenes of the west frieze and, dividing sixty by six, achieved ten groups of six, as on the south frieze. This, if true, would seem to have indicated a Kleisthenic cavalry, but that did not fit his theory that the twelve phratries of the pre-Kleisthenic order should somehow be represented. So Beschi argued that the north frieze horsemen should be taken with the west, and there he found twenty-two horsemen, excluding servants, marshals, two hipparchs, and a herald. These twenty-two, with the two borrowed from the north frieze, make up a total of twenty-four, a number that, divided again by six, gives four groups. The arithmetic thus yields a grand total of fourteen groups on the combined north (10 × 6) and west (4 × 6) friezes. Now this number did not fit his theory either, and so, by what can only be described as a sleight of hand, Beschi detached two groups from his fourteen on the west to arrive at the preconceived twelve.[66]

More recently, Ernst Berger, while accepting Beschi's basic thesis, rejects his reasoning.[67] He is surely right to reject such "arithmetical contortions." Berger, however, went on to present his own brand of arithmetical acrobatics. Reluctant to give up the quest for the number four, Berger extracts four groups of fifteen out of his *sixty* riders. The criteria for judging where the divisions should fall are riders with a naked torso, whose horses are not overlapped, and/or who look back. The principal difficulty here is that this fourfold division omits to take account of several figures in the cavalcade who fulfill his criteria and should themselves mark divisions.

Pollitt is rightly skeptical of some of Beschi's reasoning, but he accepts part at least of the argument and employs the ten groups of Beschi's north frieze cavalcade as evidence to support his own thesis that in both the north and south friezes we should think in terms of the Periklean cavalry.[68]

Wesenberg too accepts the Periklean nature of the horsemen and sees the combined north and west frieze as comprising one of the ten tribal units and the south as representing another. He does not attempt any close analysis of the composition, but his account is exceptional in seeking to locate a specific part of the Periklean cavalry in the frieze, to which question we shall return.[69]

A PROBLEM SOLVED

In 1994 I published a plan showing the relative positions of the horses in the north cavalcade (Fig. 13.5).[70] The plan demonstrates that the horsemen of the north frieze can be divided into ten ranks, but not in equal numbers and not by costume. The division between ranks is clearly and simply marked by a horse shown nearest the spectator and therefore not overlapped by any other figure in that rank. At the time, I took this to be concrete and irrefutable demonstration that, with ten front horsemen, the north frieze cavalcade must comprise ten ranks. Berger has dismissed it, however, as "having produced no clear results," and Neils has suggested an alternative reading.[71] It seems the case must be restated so as to make the results clear.

The horsemen of the north and also, as we shall see to some extent, the south frieze can be simply divided once the key device for distinguishing them has been identified. It was first recognized in print by a scholar who, in the nineteenth century, made several important contributions to our understanding of the Parthenon sculptures, but whose name is rarely mentioned now. William Watkiss Lloyd pointed out that the horsemen are advancing in ranks. He also observed how "the broad smooth surface of the outer horse gives rest to the eye and marks the sequence." He goes on, "There seems scarcely any limit to the number of superimposed masses which the sculptor was able to comprise within the relief of his rigorous two inches." Watkiss Lloyd thought he could detect groups of six, eight, and even ten.[72]

Watkiss Lloyd made his discovery, not while in the Elgin Room of the British Museum, but while looking up at the Athenaeum, a Gentleman's Club in London (Fig. 13.6). There the replica frieze carved by John Hen-

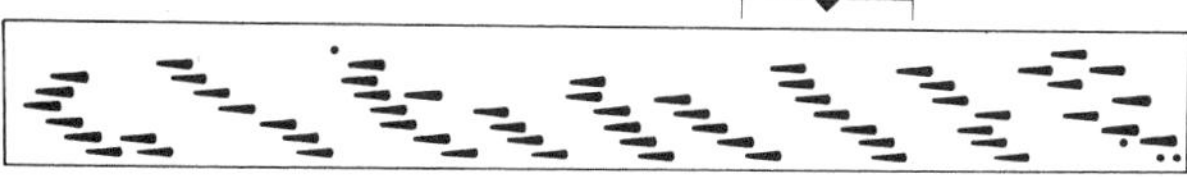

FIGURE 13.5. *The arrangement of the horsemen of the north frieze, divided into ranks.*

ning and his two sons was the nearest one could get in the modern age to seeing the effect of the frieze on the eye of the ancient spectator.[73] Although I know of no written account by them, the Hennings must be credited with having first resolved the problem of seeing how the horsemen were laid out. The method is illustrated here by Figure 13.7, which shows a drawing of a rank of horsemen in the north frieze. Below, their positions have been mapped in diagram form, and we see how the rider placed nearest the viewer marks the rank. He is deliberately made conspicuous by his striking nudity and the three-quarter view of his back. Ahead, another horseman placed nearest the viewer marks the next rank. He too is conspicuous by virtue of his nudity and his turning to look back. Between these two are six other riders. Each one occupies a new plane in the depth of field. The nearest to the spectator, therefore, is six places away from the furthest. Watkiss Lloyd's description of what happens between these two figures cannot be bettered:

> We are thus, in effect, presented with an oblique view of the long front of the rank. But the perspective conditions of such a view are disregarded. The heads of all the riders near or remote are on the same level, as if on that of the spectator's; but, nevertheless, the hoofs of the remoter horses touch the base line of the slab as distinctly as those of the nearest.[74]

In the frieze, then, the illusion of a ride-past is an entirely artificial one. The idea of a cavalcade is suggested, without any direct attempt at realism. The pictorial effect is nonetheless a highly successful simulation of what it would be like to stand on the sidelines of the parade ground in the Athenian marketplace and watch the cavalry go by. The designer knew, as we know, that it would be impossible to see the individual horsemen as he has shown them. He invites us, however, to join a game of make-believe, and we willingly accept.

The eye accepts this illusion without analyzing what it sees. The process of seeing and understanding the

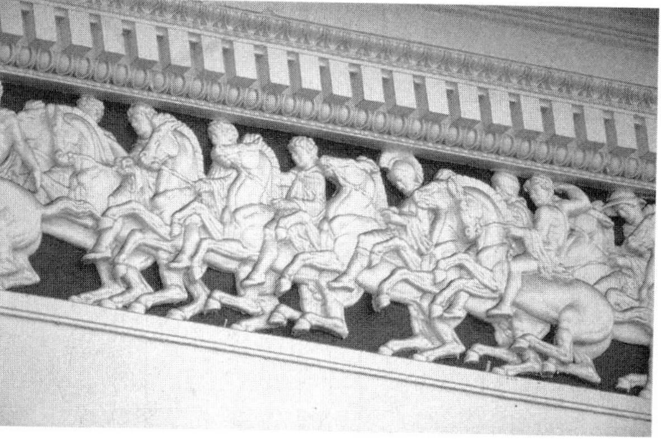

FIGURE 13.6. *Detail of the north frieze of the Athenaeum Club in Waterloo Place, London. John Henning senior and junior, ca. 1828–1830.*

cavalcade of the frieze in its present condition is, however, impaired by losses in the sequence and, where it survives, by mutilation and discoloration of the stone. If the background of the frieze were painted blue and contrasted with the color(s) of the horsemen, this will certainly have assisted the spectator's comprehension of the figures in antiquity. It is also possible to speculate that the figures placed nearest the spectator and marking each rank were distinguished with color.[75]

To demonstrate all the more clearly how the cavalcade was designed and meant to be seen, Figure 13.8A–D shows images that have been especially generated in a computer. "A" shows the north frieze rank of Figure 13.7 restored as a complete image. "B" shows the same rank as it would look if the horsemen had been represented in three-point perspective. Because this approximates more to modern Western traditions of pictorial representation, the image suddenly becomes more accessible. "C" shows the same rank converted into wire-frame figures and turned through space. "D" turns the rank a full 90 degrees. The line of figures is straight, with the riders abreast. Thus it would appear if the spectator were to stand in the path of a line of horsemen moving along, say, the *dromos* of the Agora. Art has been converted back into life.

The frieze was by no means the earliest use in Greek art of such devices for representing figures in a depth of field. Its designer was able to draw on a long tradition of pictorial representation reaching back through Archaic Greek to the art of Persia, Assyria, and Egypt. Two Greek examples will suffice. The first is an Attic red-figure cup painted a couple of generations before

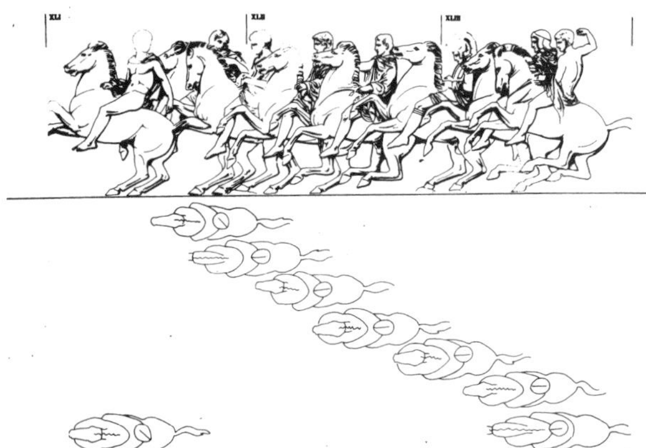

FIGURE 13.7. *"Elevation" and "plan" of a rank of horsemen of the north frieze. Drawing: Susan Bird.*

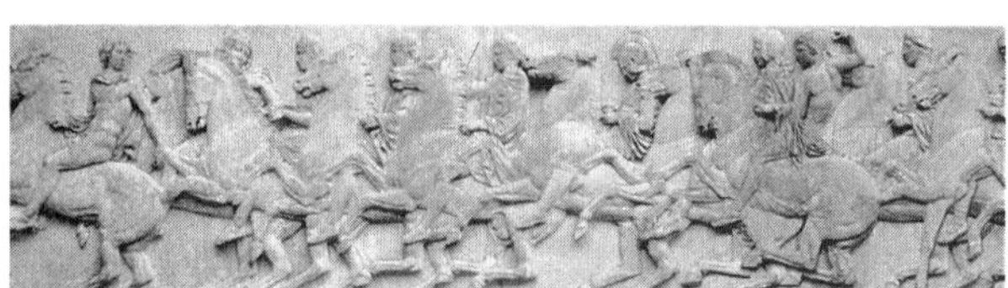

FIGURE 13.8A. *Rank of horsemen in the north frieze, restored. Rendition: John Redfern Animation.*

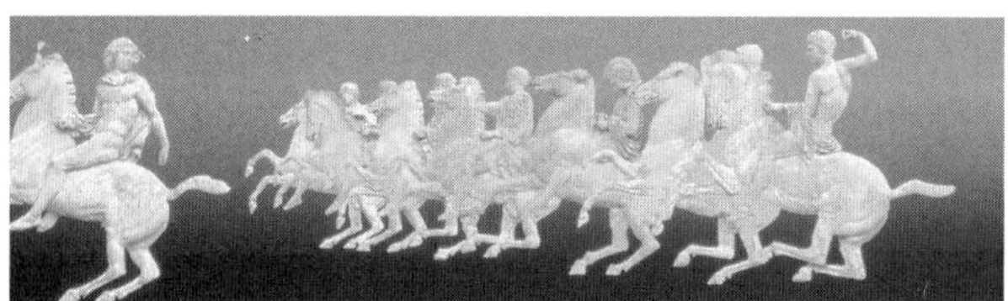

FIGURE 13.8B. *The same rank as it would appear rendered in three-point perspective.*

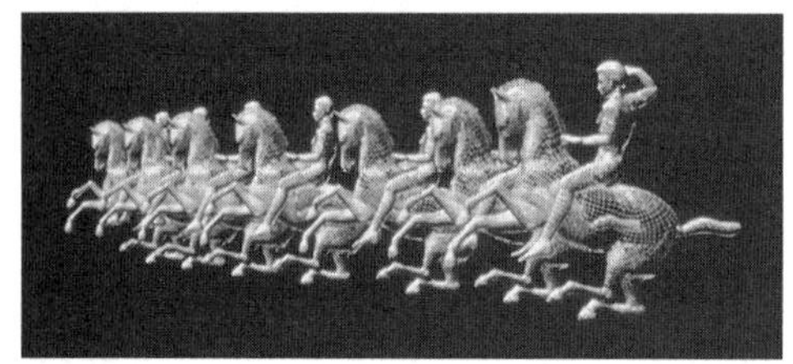

FIGURE 13.8C. *The same rank rendered in a wire frame and turned to suggest an advancing line.*

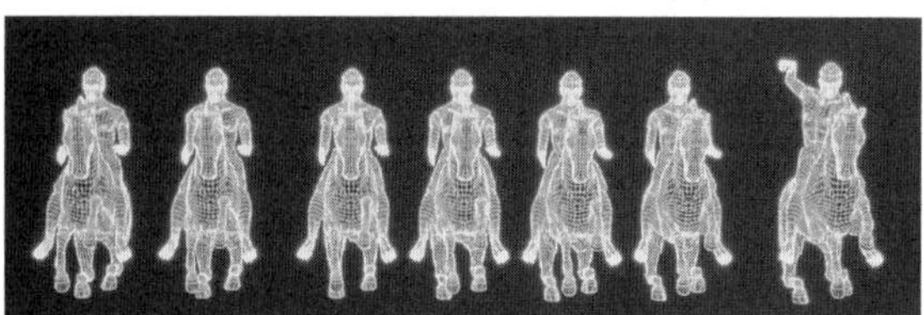

FIGURE 13.8D. *The rank as it would appear in life to a spectator standing in its path.*

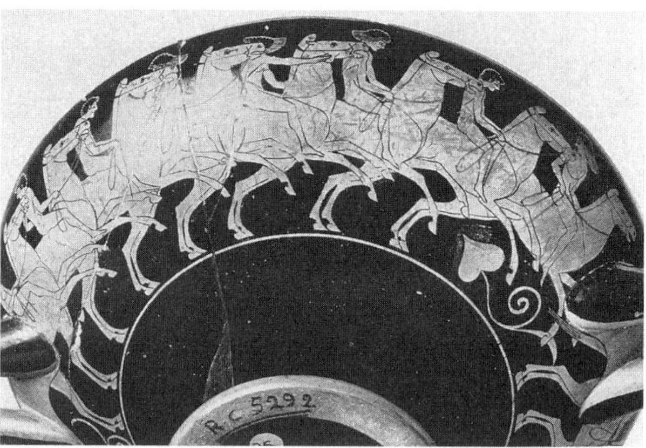

FIGURE 13.9. *Attic red-figure cup, name-vase of the Pedieus Painter, ca. 490 B.C. Rank of eight horsemen. Tarquinia, Museo Nazionale Tarquiniense RC 5292. The image is deliberately reversed.*

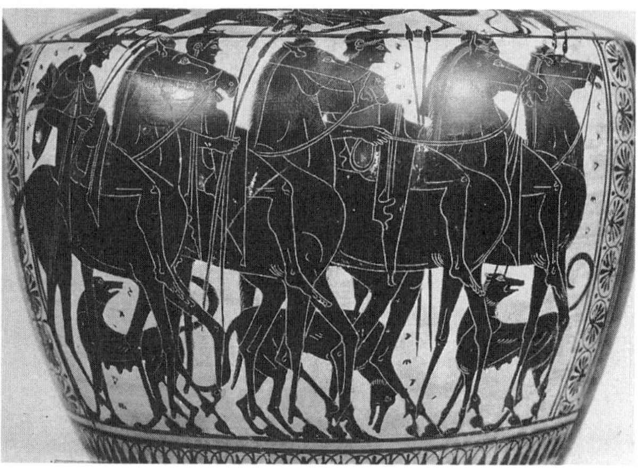

FIGURE 13.10. *Attic black-figure hydria, Leagros Group, ca. 530 B.C. Rank of four warriors. London, British Museum B306. Photo courtesy of the Trustees of the British Museum, © Copyright The British Museum.*

the building of the Parthenon (Fig. 13.9).[76] It shows a surging wave of horsemen, which, when the image is reversed as it has been deliberately reproduced here, is strikingly similar to the rank of horsemen of the north frieze. A horseman partially obscured by the handle of the vessel is placed nearest the viewer. Seven places away from this figure is an eighth horseman, whose head is turned over his shoulder. It is interesting to remark how the rider in the equivalent position in the rank of the north frieze also looks over his shoulder. In the vase painting, the direction of this glance appears to be back, but according to our analysis of horsemen in the frieze, this may in fact be across the breast line of his companions. As in the frieze, the rear hooves of the horses touch one base line, while the heads of the horsemen meet another line. Again, as in the frieze, fore-hooves are raised off the ground to suggest—rather than represent realistically—a surge of forward movement.

A generation earlier still, the painter of an Attic black-figure hydria drew four huntsmen, or as one has a shield perhaps warriors, in a line abreast (Fig. 13.10).[77] We see across the troop, where each horse flexes one leg to paw the ground in nervous anticipation of the start. As before, hooves touch the ground line, while the hunters' heads meet the same top line. The pattern of the horses' legs is rendered the more fascinating by three dogs. They are placed on the far side of the horses, but their paws stand on the same ground line.

A BLUEPRINT FOR THE FRIEZE

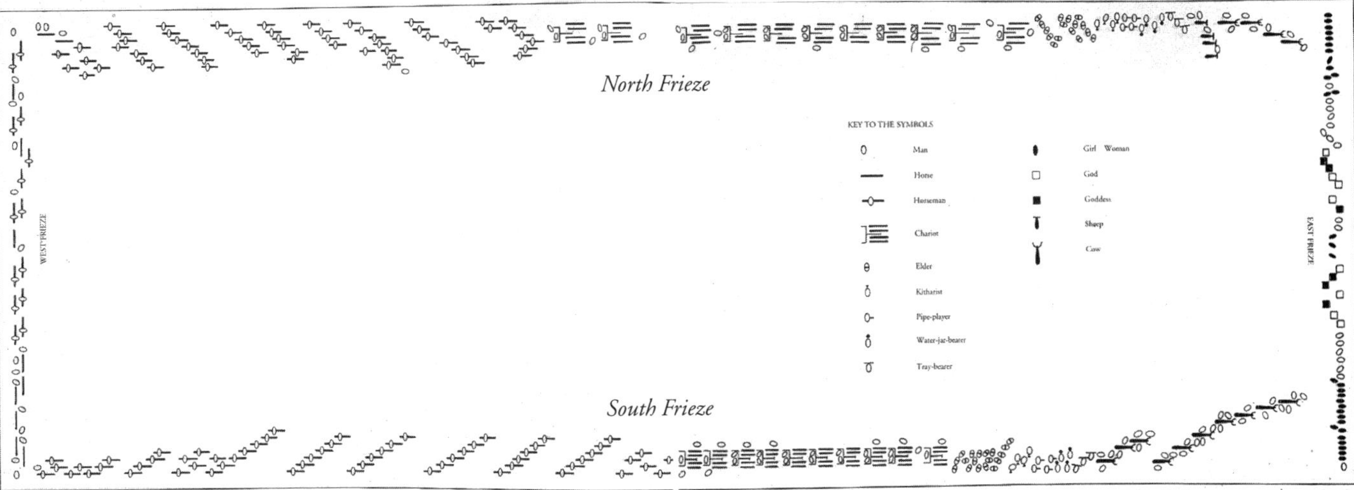

FIGURE 13.11. *Reconstruction of the original "blueprint" design for the arrangement of the entire procession of the Parthenon frieze. Drawing: Susan Bird.*

Watkiss Lloyd's original observation has implications for reading not only the frieze but all such complex figured compositions in Greek art. Few, however, have pursued its significance, even for the frieze. Where his lesson has been applied it is without acknowledgment. In 1910 Arthur H. Smith published a ground plan illustrating the formation of the cavalry of the north frieze showing the ranks of horsemen.[78] This is based on an erroneous reconstruction and allows for eleven figures marking the groups. Smith's diagram in turn inspired Maxime Collignon to publish in 1912 his own version, mapping the horsemen not only of the north frieze but of all the procession, based on his inaccurate reconstruction of it.[79] Subsequently, in preparing his book on the Parthenon, Dinsmoor sought to improve on Collignon's plan of the procession, but his sketches were to go unpublished.[80] In 1998 Susan Bird and I produced our own schematic plan of the procession, based on the reconstruction of it that we published in 1994 (Fig. 13.11).[81]

Seeing how the riders are articulated into ranks brings us closer to the original design. It is reasonable to think that the designer of the frieze drew just such a plan to instruct the team of carvers in how to achieve the remarkable degree of pictorial depth exhibited in the frieze. As many as eight horsemen are carved abreast in a depth of relief that is never more than about two and a half inches. In this blueprint it is possible to see at a glance how the composition is conceived. To take the south first: the horsemen set out in disorderly array, jostling for space. They have yet to find the pace and rhythm of those that ride ahead. Divisions of six defined by dress, which I have distinguished by calling "groups," have yet to coincide with compositional divisions or "ranks," as they have been defined in the north frieze cavalcade. Marking the divisions of the ten groups of six by alternate black and white, it is possible to see how the first three groups do not correspond with the ranks (Fig. 13.12). The fourth group, however, nearly coincides with a rank, except that it

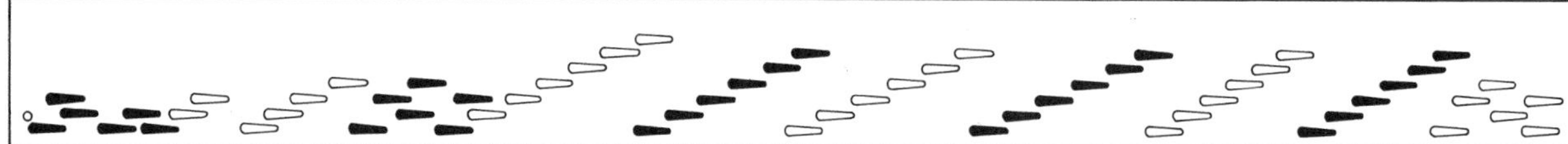

FIGURE 13.12. *The division of the horsemen of the south frieze into groups by dress. Each group is here distinguished by alternate black and white. Drawing: Kate Morton.*

contains seven instead of the usual six riders. The next five groups all contain six riders arranged in regular ranks. The tenth group again coincides with a rank, but in broken formation, as the riders slow to a halt in anticipation of stationary chariots ahead.

A synopsis of the drama of the south frieze cavalcade is revealed in this plan, proceeding from confusion through order to the incipient disintegration of that order. The plan of the cavalcade in the north frieze is no less revealing (Fig. 13.11). With the same number of sixty riders carved over nineteen blocks as the south cavalcade has carved over twenty-four, the composition of the north cavalcade is more compressed and apparently more numerous. There is here none of the measured regularity of the south. "When your object is to make the number of your cavalry look large . . . ," writes Xenophon, "you must know that horses look many when crowded . . . but are easily counted when scattered."[82]

There is no apparent dress code for horsemen in the north frieze and therefore no separation of "groups" from "ranks." By remarking on the rider placed nearest the viewer, the ranks can be readily seen. Of these marker riders, there appear to be ten. These indicate ranks with as many as eight horsemen in the greatest rank and two in the smallest. The apparent rank of eight serves to bunch the riders at the beginning of the parade and is composed of both mounted riders and two others who have yet to mount their horses. Ahead, the ranks of riders fall wave upon wave in a great stream flowing down the north frieze, until the leading rank is reached. This is shaped like the head of an arrow, the leading rider being the tip. He has got ahead of his neighbors and is reining back hard so as not to appear to run into the back of a stationary chariot ahead.

To reduce the procession of the frieze to plans of this kind, resembling an architect's blueprint, is to see it in essence. It is not unlikely that in seeking to instruct the foreman of the team of carvers, the designer of the frieze drew just such a plan. He will also have drawn sketches of how the frieze should appear to the eye, as it were, in elevation. These original sketches have not survived, but vestiges of them can be detected in the compositional framework upon which not only the cavalcade but the entire frieze is constructed.

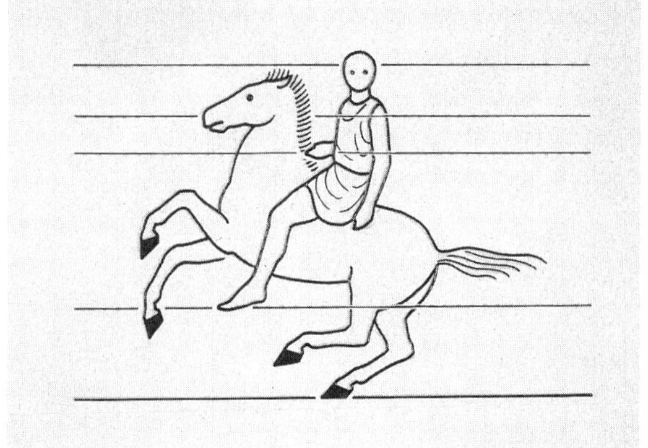

FIGURE 13.13. *Horizontal lines of construction for the cavalcade of the Parthenon frieze. Drawing: Susan Bird.*

No matter where the figure occurs in the depth of field, the heads of the horsemen and the rear hooves of the horses meet the top and bottom limit of the sculpted area. Between the lines of these two limits, others flow horizontally through the cavalcade (Fig. 13.13): the line comprised of the horses' heads; the line formed by the rein hands of the riders; the line of hanging feet of the riders coinciding with one of the rearing fore-hooves of the horses. They can be detected when the frieze is viewed front on (Fig. 13.8A) but are even more noticeable when it is seen at an angle (Fig. 13.14). Here the individual elements seem to hang like notes on a musical score. These lines almost certainly reflect the planning of the original design and its transfer to the stone. Their role, however, is more than merely mechanical. Together they bring rhythm to the composition, giving it structure and balance. The eye is guided along the frieze by these lines of energy. They play across the surface of the composition in a two-dimensional counterpoint to the three dimensions of the depth of field. These devices, which seem not to have been noticed before, represent self-conscious attempts in the origi-

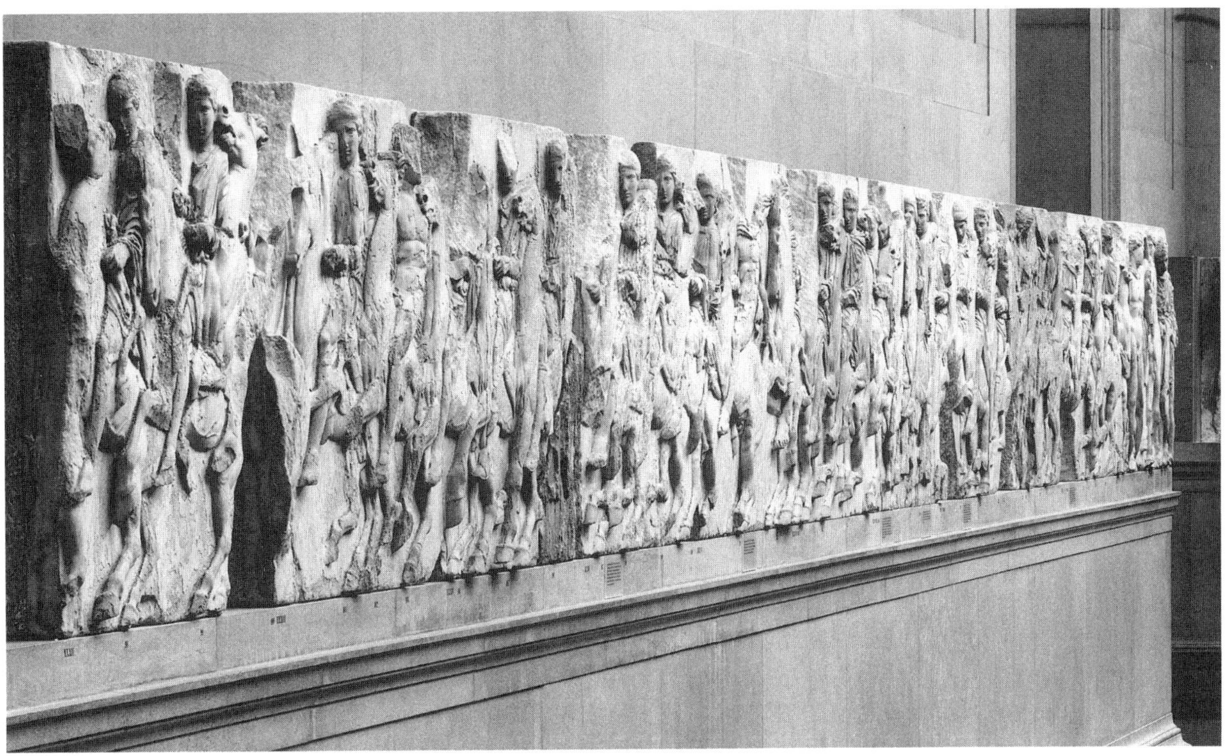

FIGURE 13.14. *Oblique view of the cavalcade of the north frieze revealing the horizontal lines of composition. Photo courtesy of the Trustees of the British Museum, © Copyright The British Museum.*

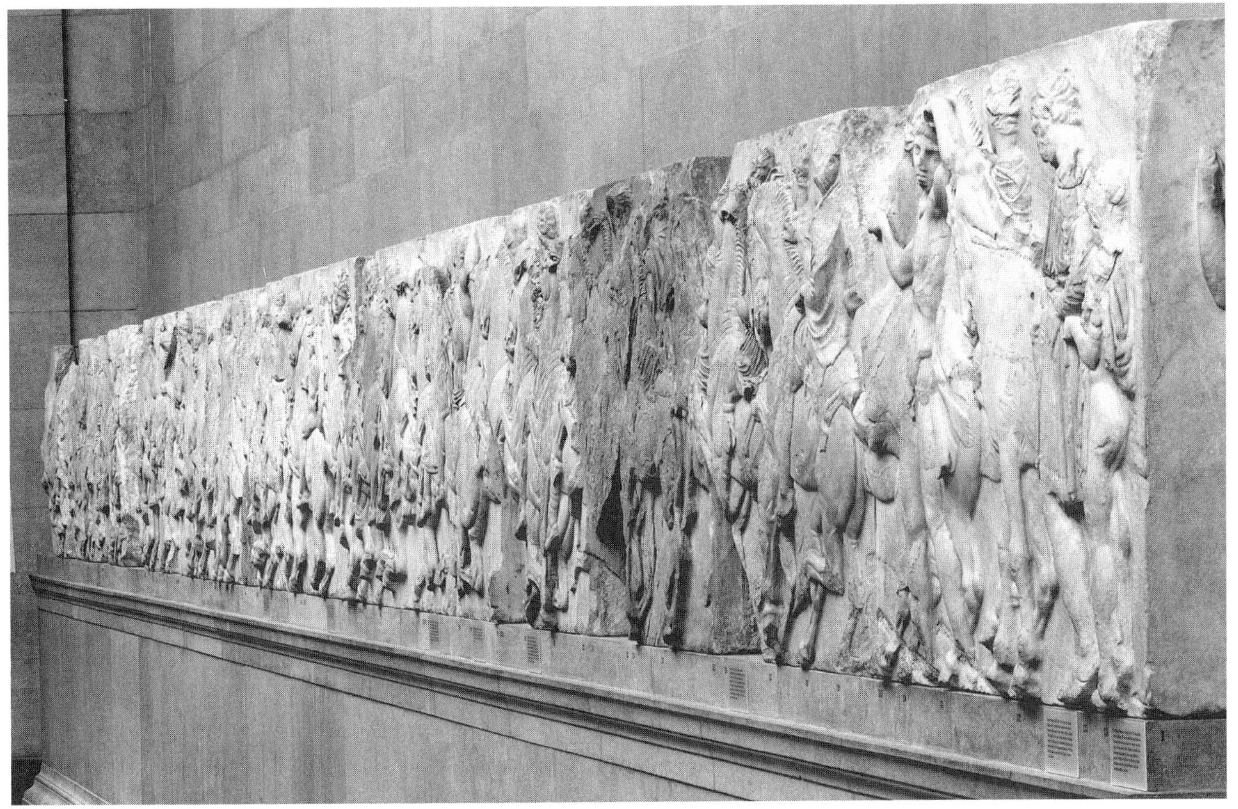

FIGURE 13.15. *Reverse view of the cavalcade of the north frieze. Photo courtesy of the Trustees of the British Museum, © Copyright The British Museum.*

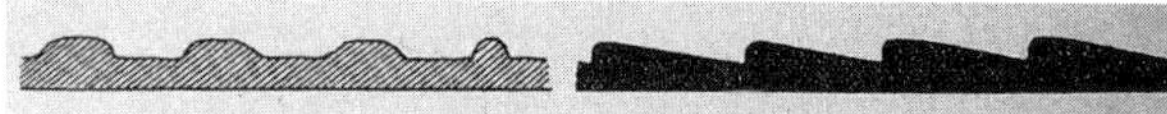

FIGURE 13.16. *Diagram to show the contrast between (left) the projection of carving of figures in the pedestrian processions and (right) the cavalcade. After A. H. Smith 1910.*

nal design to facilitate the viewing of the frieze on the temple. As such, they may be compared with such optical refinements as the curving of straight lines and the swelling of corner columns that so famously enhance our viewing of the architecture.

Viewing the cavalcade at an angle looking into the face of the oncoming riders serves, as we have seen, to bring out an intrinsic property of the relief. The same would not be true if we were to look at the cavalcade from an angle in the opposite direction (Fig. 13.15), that is, if our gaze follows the same direction in which the riders are moving. The reason for this has to do with the manner of accommodating so many riders in such shallow relief. A plan of the top bed of the frieze blocks shows how the horses are accommodated by cutting them in towards the rear, so that the foreparts project in higher relief (Fig. 13.16).[83]

One of the fascinating features of the frieze is an apparent tension between, on the one hand, the desire to achieve depth in its pictorial illusion of three dimensions and, on the other, the desire to achieve harmony in the play of pattern across its two-dimensional surface. In attempting to reconcile these complementary aims, the masons responsible for carving the frieze did not always follow the blueprint exactly. A number of anomalies occur in both the north and south cavalcades. The two most notable instances are in the north frieze (Fig. 13.17).[84] Here two of the horses that were placed furthest from the spectator do not appear quite as they should. In both cases the muzzle should have been "clipped" by the cloak of the next rider on the left—that is, the figure placed nearest the spectator at the beginning of the next rank. This Procrustean reduction of the horse's nose, however, was deemed too ugly, and so the head is shown entire and partially obscures the cloak instead of being obscured by it. This results in an impossible contortion. Three-dimensional veracity has been compromised for the sake of more pleasing surface effect.

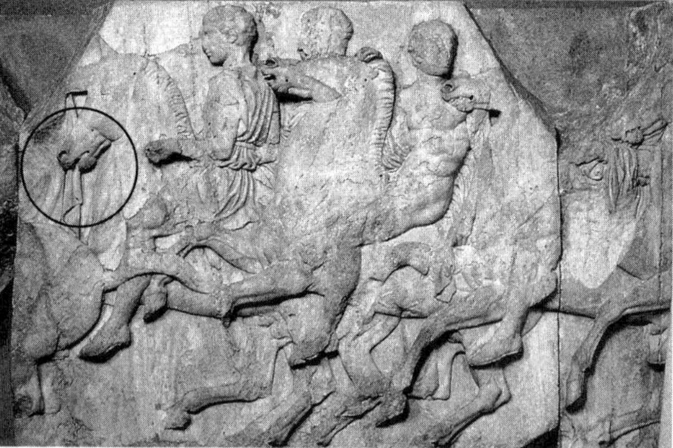

FIGURE 13.17. *The muzzle of the horse of rider 103 of the cavalcade of the north frieze overlapping (impossibly) with the cloak of the horse of 104.*

CONCLUSION

Close analysis of the mechanics of representation shows that the designer of the frieze employed certain artistic devices for carving in shallow relief a credible idea of the ride-past of horsemen, which for all who had seen this real-life spectacle must have been a marvelous and unforgettable experience. We may now turn to the question of whether there is anything in his pictorial strategy that suggests the designer had the Periklean cavalry specifically in mind.

The sixty riders of the south cavalcade can be divided into ten *groups* of six figures, each group distinguished by its dress, while the same number in the north cavalcade can be divided into ten *ranks* of unequal numbers of figures, divided according to the system of marker riders who are placed nearest the viewer. This division of horsemen into ten gives no support for those who have seen here a representation of four pre-Kleisthenic tribes. Can the argument be taken a stage further to show that the cavalcade is democratic and, furthermore, Periklean? More specifically, is the cavalry of the frieze arranged in Xenophonian parade formation? The distinctive feature of the south frieze, absent in the north, may point in that direction, namely, the deliberate arrangement of ten groups identified by dress, which surely represents the tenfold division of the democratic, if not Periklean cavalry. This division into groups in the south frieze cuts across the division into ranks. In the south frieze as a system of articulating the riders into meaningful parts, the groups are visually more pronounced than the ranks, especially if each group was differentiated further by added paint.

Given the emphasis on groups in the south frieze, the rank divisions in both the south and north cavalcades may be no more than what they appear, namely, the designer's device for accommodating so many horsemen in such long strips of stone. It may, however, be asked whether the total of 120 horsemen, 60 in the north and 60 in the south, is significant. It is reasonable to speculate that the total number of 1,200 cavalry was intentionally represented by this tenth of that number. Just so, the hecatomb of cattle led to sacrifice at the Panathenaia is perhaps represented in the ten cattle shown on the south frieze. The full complement of the Athenian cavalry included 200 archers, and we look in vain for these in the frieze. Arms are almost totally excluded, however, and we should not expect to find specific attributes of this kind.

Professor Wesenberg has other arguments in favor of seeing the Periklean cavalry in the frieze. He finds that by sheer numbers alone, the combined horsemen of the north and west frieze are too many to be other than a representative part of the cavalry augmented by Perikles.[85] He sees the two bearded horsemen of the west frieze as likely hipparchs and therefore "signs" of the Periklean cavalry.[86] He also argues that the unmounted clean-shaven figure 12 of west frieze block VI is by virtue of his sword a phylarch. This appears to be the only horseman of the frieze who carries a sword, and comparison can be made with the anthippasia relief from the Athenian Agora, where the phylarch carries a sword (Fig. 13.1). A difficulty here is that in this last and in other Classical representations of phylarchs, the face is bearded.[87] In the combined north and west cavalcades, Wesenberg sees a representation of one of the ten tribal units of the Periklean cavalry. It may, however, be objected that the west frieze, although connected with the north by the predominant right-left directional flow, is pictorially independent of the north and south friezes and should be seen as separate.

In the final assessment, the problem of defining the cavalry of the frieze is that of defining the frieze as a whole. We seek the Panathenaia in it but do not find the documented record we know from other sources. Just so the horsemen: we seek Perikles' cavalry but find a version that escapes documentary proof. That it is there, I have no doubt. The horsemen of the frieze are not, however, a mechanical record of Perikles' model cavalry. Rather, as we should expect of Athenian art of this period, they transcend the particular to present a gloriously universal image that defies narrow definitions and the petty theories of scribbling scholars.

NOTES

The quotation of W. Watkiss Lloyd that began this essay is from Lethaby (1927). A version of this paper was read at Yale University and many other meetings of the Archaeological Institute of America across the United States during my Samuel H. Kress Lectureship in Ancient Art, Fall 1998. I should like to thank all those who participated in the meetings and especially friends in Ithaca, New York, who hosted the visit.

1. Stuart and Revett 1787, 12: "It represents the Panathenaic Procession, as will be evident on comparing the following Plates with the accounts yet remaining of that splendid solemnity." For recent reflections upon the problem of its interpretation, see Wesenberg 1995, 149–150; Hurwit 1999, 222–228.

2. The first detailed discussion of the problem is Michaelis 1871, 214.

3. For hoplites in the procession, see Parke 1977, 43, n. 23.

4. The evidence is surveyed by Spence 1993, 187–188, who concludes on the strength of it that the cavalry were a part of the procession; see also M. A. Martin 1886, 134.

5. It could be argued that the mounted horsemen on the Niarchos cup, albeit in the sixth century, provide proof that horsemen participated in the Panathenaic procession: Marangou 1995, 88–89.

6. Michaelis 1871, 214–215.

7. Jenkins 1995, 447.

8. Michaelis 1871, 214–217.

9. *OC* 1066.

10. Michaelis 1871, 217; Thuk. 2.37.

11. E.g., Corbett 1959, 23; Robertson and Frantz 1975, 9.

12. Boardman 1977.

13. The follow-up article is Boardman, 1984c. Many have sought to challenge the thesis; see, for example, bibliography collected by Wesenberg 1995, 150, n. 10. And Boardman (1999) himself has withdrawn his Marathon thesis.

14. Osborne 1987.

15. Wesenberg 1995, 150, n. 6, collects references to a few of them.

16. R. Osborne 1987, 103–104.

17. Pollitt 1997.

18. Pollitt 1997, 53, in company with M. A. Martin 1886, 130–131; Bugh 1988, 77; Spence 1993, 15; Stewart 1997, 78–79.

19. Pollitt 1997, 51.

20. Pollitt 1997, 61.

21. Michaelis 1871, 217; M. A. Martin 1886, 133–134; Dohrn 1949.

22. Pollitt 1997, 63.

23. See, e.g., Spence 1993, 267–271, on Boardman 1977; and Hurwit 1999, 223, on Connelly 1996.

24. Pollitt 1997, 61.

25. Hurwit 1999, 227.

26. Fehl 1961, 9: "In the contemplation of the frieze the source of 'animation' is the locomotion of the spectator. I have tried to show that his trip was really a double one, his actual walk along the Parthenon, and his fancied journey along the entire road taken by the procession." See also R. Osborne 1987, 99–103.

27. Robertson and Frantz 1975, 11; Brommer 1979, 34: "a timeless representation of a recurrent event."

28. Jenkins 1994, 35–42.

29. For this three-part analysis, see Beschi 1984, 191–192. It is adopted by Jenkins 1994, 32.

30. Jenkins 1994, 39–40.

31. Jenkins 1994, 54–63, 95–102.

32. Jenkins 1994, 33; Spence 1993, 269.

33. Picked up by Stewart 1997, 145. Stewart 1997, 80–81, sees the deliberate "youthening" of the horsemen in terms of their status as potential *eromenoi* (objects of desire) under the gaze of a rapacious demos.

34. Spence 1993, 180–198.

35. Agora 17167, for the tribe Leontis: Camp 1998, 28–29.

36. Bugh 1988, 64–65.

37. Michaelis 1871, 217; M. A. Martin 1886, 131–132, 151.

38. Bugh 1988, 74–78; Spence 1993, 10–16; Wesenberg 1995, 173; Pollitt 1997, 53–54; Hurwit 1999, 233–234.

39. Thuk. 2.13.8.

40. Vos 1963.

41. Bugh 1988, 39–40, appendix D.

42. Bugh 1988, 75–76.

43. M. A. Martin 1886, 121–134; Bugh 1988, 41–52. Cf. Spence 1993, 9–17.

44. M. A. Martin 1886, 131–132; Spence 1993, 10–15.

45. Robertson and Frantz 1975, 9.

46. Bugh 1988, 77.

47. Wesenberg 1995, 144.

48. Dinsmoor 1954, 145. See also Korres 1988.

49. Brommer 1977, 171–172.

50. E. B. Harrison 1996, 39.

51. Xen. *Eq. mag.* 2.2–6; Bugh 1988, 53–54; Spence 1993, 10, 16; Worley 1994, 75–76.

52. Xen. *Eq. mag.* 3.11–12; Vanderpool 1974, 311 (cf. Thompson 1961); Bugh 1988, 59–60; Camp 1998, 28–30.

53. Jenkins 1995, 447–449.

54. E.g., Brommer 1977, 253, fig. 47; Beschi 1984, pls. 1, 6.

55. Dinsmoor 1954.

56. E. B. Harrison 1979c, 490.

57. E. B. Harrison 1984, 230–232.

58. Jenkins 1994, 51–111; Jenkins 1995, passim.

59. Berger and Gisler-Huwiler 1996, passim.

60. E. B. Harrison 1984, 230.

61. Beschi 1984, 186, 194. He has one too many in his block xxvii and another in his block xxix.

62. The problem is surveyed by Jenkins 1994, 30.

63. Boardman 1977, 40.

64. E. B. Harrison 1984, 233.

65. Beschi 1984, passim.

66. Beschi 1984, 186–188.

67. Berger and Gisler-Huwiler 1996, 87.

68. Pollitt 1997, 55.

69. Wesenberg 1995, 175.

70. Jenkins 1994, 99.

71. Berger and Gisler-Huwiler 1996, 87; Neils 2001. Below, n. 81.

72. He is quoted by Lethaby 1927, 897. Watkiss Lloyd gives another version of the same observation in 1893, 4–5.

73. For the Athenaeum frieze, see now Jenkins 2000.

74. Watkiss Lloyd 1893, 4.

75. The question of whether or not the frieze was actually colored in antiquity is an open one. See Jenkins 2001, 16.

76. *ARV*[2] 86.4; *Para* 330; *Addenda*[2] 170, name-vase of the Pedieus Painter. Ferrari 1988, 34–39, no. 6, pls. 11–13.

77. London, British Museum B306, *ABV* 45.47, Leagros Group.

78. A. H. Smith 1910, 59, fig. 113. Smith allocated to the sequence a block xxix* (his fig. 15) and put into it the fragment formerly in the Villa Cataio, now in Vienna. The Vienna fragment is now, however, put into Smith's xxx, and xxix* is eliminated.

79. Collignon 1912, pl. 75.

80. Unpublished manuscript in the library of the American School of Classical Studies at Athens.

81. Bird, Jenkins, and Levi 1998, 18–19. Neils 2001, 54, does not cite this publication in her attempt to argue for eight against my ten ranks in the north frieze. Nor is her

argument accurately or consistently presented. Her figure 41 is a redrawing of Collignon's plan of the horsemen of the north frieze. Neils' draftsman, however, has left out one of Collignon's figures and so achieves a count of fifty-nine and not the sixty of the original source. Moreover, this use of Collignon's plan is not compatible with Neils' apparent agreement with my reconstruction of the horsemen of the north frieze (Jenkins 1994), which is at odds with Collignon's long discredited arrangement of the frieze. That is to say, her plan (an inaccurate rendering of Collignon) is not consistent with her elevation (a redrawn version of Jenkins'). Neils herself appears to have erratic conviction in her own case. In spite of the previous assertion that there are only eight ranks represented in the north frieze, on page 132, she writes: "As we have seen in Chapter 2, they [the horsemen] are divided into two lines of ten ranks each."

82. Xen. *Eq. mag.* 5.5–6.

83. A. H. Smith 1910, 51.

84. Jenkins 1994, block XXXVIII, 103, and XLV, 128.

85. Wesenberg 1995, with bibliography at n. 147.

86. Wesenberg 1995, 173, n. 147.

87. Bugh 1988, 78, n. 135; Spence 1993, 200. The principal monuments are the Agora *anthippasia* relief and the inscribed base, Athens, National Museum 1733, commemorating a victory in the anthippasia honoring three phylarchs of the same tribe and showing a bearded rider approaching a victory tripod.

14

ALKAMENES' PROKNE AND ITYS IN CONTEXT

JUDITH M. BARRINGER

The statue group of Prokne and Itys (Athens, Akropolis Museum 1358) initially caught my attention in my first semester of graduate school at Yale University, when I wrote a paper about the sculptor Alkamenes for my advisor, Jerry Pollitt. This graduate student effort was devoted to sorting out Alkamenes' oeuvre using written and stylistic evidence. As my studies progressed, I became more interested in iconography and iconology and less so in matters of connoisseurship. Here, many years later, I revisit Prokne in a contextual reading, a methodology pioneered by Jerry Pollitt and taught to his students with exemplary patience and good humor. I dedicate this essay to him with admiration, gratitude, and affection and absolve him from all responsibility.

The marble group on the Athenian Akropolis, identified as Prokne and Itys on the basis of Pausanias' brief mention (1.24.3) and stylistic evidence, has been the subject of scholarly controversy since its discovery in 1836 (Figs. 14.1–6). To judge from the extant remains, ancient artists rarely took up the myth of Itys' death at the hands of his mother Prokne, and this sculptural group has elicited an amount of scholarly speculation inverse to what little is firmly known about it. Previously, scholars have discussed whether the group is an original or a Roman copy,[1] its stylistic properties and whether the group is by Alkamenes,[2] its use as an index of Alkamenes' style,[3] its date, its marble type,[4] the original position of the hands and arms, its technical features, whether a head that has been restored to the group belongs, and what may have motivated the dedication of this group. Detailed stylistic analyses have already been made, and so I will not rehearse that issue here.[5] This paper assumes that the marble group is an original work created and dedicated by Alkamenes ca. 430–410 B.C.,[6] offers a new interpretation for the motivation of the dedication, and explores how a contemporary Athenian might have experienced the sculpture. Critical to this reading is the method, which concentrates on the group's physical, mythological, and religious context.

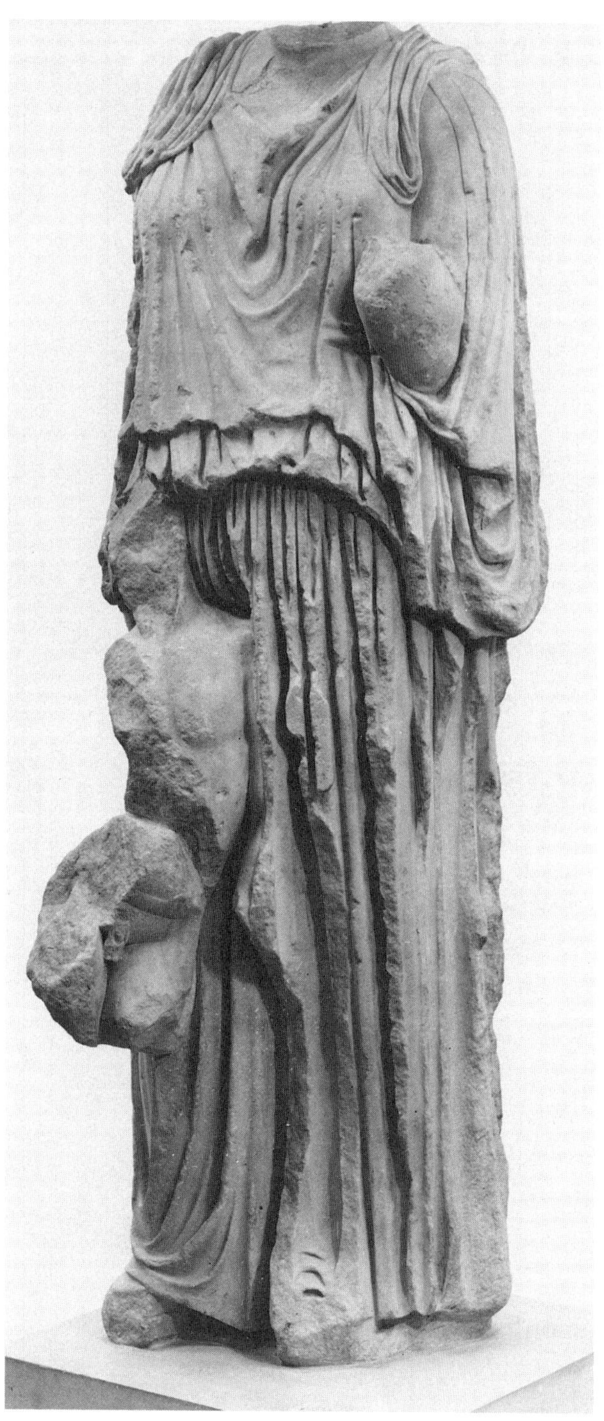

FIGURE 14.1. *Prokne and Itys, by Alkamenes, ca. 430–410. Athens, Akropolis Museum 1358. Photo: Deutsches Archäologisches Institut, Athens, neg. nr. 75/421.*

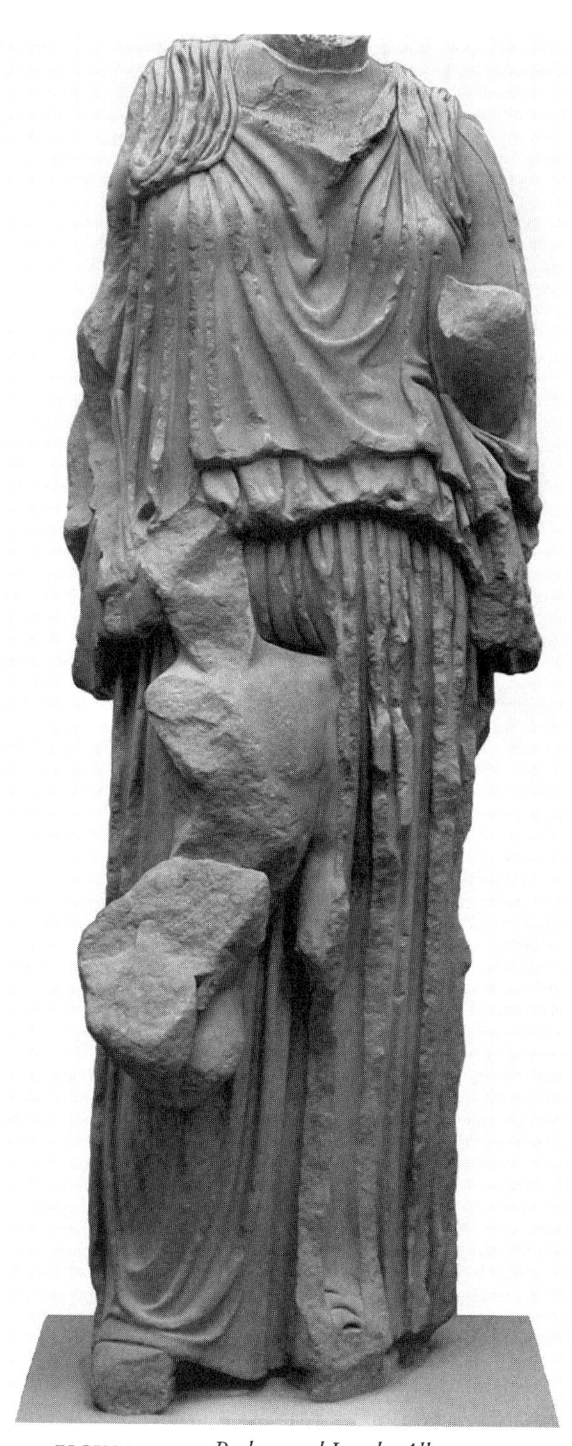

FIGURE 14.2. *Prokne and Itys, by Alkamenes, ca. 430–410. Athens, Akropolis Museum 1358. Photo: Deutsches Archäologisches Institut, Athens, neg. nr. 2001/864.*

PROKNE AND ITYS: THE MYTH

The myth of Prokne and Itys was recounted by Sophokles in his *Tereus,* surviving now only in fragments; Apollodoros 3.14.8; and Ovid *Metamorphoses* 6.424–674, and it is alluded to more briefly elsewhere, including *Odyssey* 19.518–523; Hesiod *Works and Days* 568; Pausanias 10.4.8; and Hyginus *Fabulae* 45. Common elements of the myth include the following: Pandion, king of Athens, gave his daughter Prokne or Aedon (nightingale) or even sometimes Chelidon (swallow)[7] in marriage to King Tereus, a foreigner,[8] as a thank-offering for Tereus' help in a war, and the couple subsequently had a son, Itys. Prokne's husband seduced Prokne's sister, Philomela (sometimes named Chelidon or "swallow" in visual representations), then cut out her tongue so that she could not reveal what had happened. But Philomela thwarted her brother-in-law's plans by weaving the event into a garment, which she showed to Prokne. In revenge, Prokne killed her son and served him as dinner to her husband. When her husband discovered what had transpired, he pursued the two sisters. The three figures were transformed into birds: Prokne became a nightingale or a swallow;[9] Philomela, a swallow (Apollod. 3.14.8); and Tereus, a hoopoe[10] or hawk.[11] Ovid, in *Metamorphoses* 6.587–674, adds that the murder of Itys took place during Bacchic rites.[12]

The earliest account, that in the *Odyssey,* refers to a wife named Aedon or nightingale, daughter of Pandareos, wife of Zethus, and mother of Itylus, but most later authors identify the wife as wedded to Tereus and the mother of Itys.[13] Sophokles is the first to name the wife Prokne. The location of the myth varies.[14] Sophokles portrays Tereus as a Thracian king,[15] but Daulis in Phocis,[16] and Megara[17] are other frequently mentioned settings.[18]

With the exception of *Odyssey* 19.518 mentioned above, nearly all the ancient testimonia recount that this murderous mother was the daughter of Pandion,[19] king of Athens and one of the eponymous heroes. Pandion is also the son of Erichthonios[20] and the father of Erechtheus (Apollod. 3.14.8; Paus. 1.5.3) and Boutes (Apollod. 3.14.8). The Pandion who fathered these two sisters, Erechtheus, and Boutes is the older of two Attic kings of this name,[21] and Pausanias 10.4.10 clearly refers to Prokne as an Athenian. Suffice it to say that Prokne or Aedon was a member of one of the oldest royal families in Athens, that her brother founded one of the most venerated aristocratic priestly families, the Eteoboutadai, that her marriage was to a foreign king, and that the myth takes place in foreign territory.

PROKNE AND ITYS: THE SCULPTURE

Few now would dispute that the marble group in the Akropolis Museum (1358) is the Prokne and Itys referred to by Pausanias in his traversal of the Akropolis as a dedication by Alkamenes (Figs. 14.1–6). Heiner Knell, in a careful and thorough physical examination of the group, asserts that the two figures were carved from a single block of marble.[22] Prokne's still, monumental form contrasts strongly with that of Itys, who twists his body as the small figure turns into his mother's skirts (Figs. 14.1–2). Itys' face does not survive, though a portion of his head does, and the head (Athens, Akropolis Museum 6460) attributed to Prokne by Praschniker was recently removed and dissociated from the group.[23] Prokne's now lost left hand was raised toward her face (Fig. 14.3), and her right arm, which survives in part and the outline of which is clearly visible, is held by her side with the right hand close to Itys' head (Fig. 14.4).

Sheila Adam believed that the weapon, presumably a knife, was held in Prokne's left hand,[24] while she grasped Itys by the hair and pulled his head back with her right. Others, however, think the raised left hand was empty and poised in a gesture of distress[25] or contemplation. More commonly now, the posited knife is placed in the lowered right hand.[26] I think we might go further and consider the possibility that Prokne actually held the sword to her son's throat, rather than simply gripping the knife, while Itys, anxiously pressing into his mother's skirts and drawing this drapery toward him

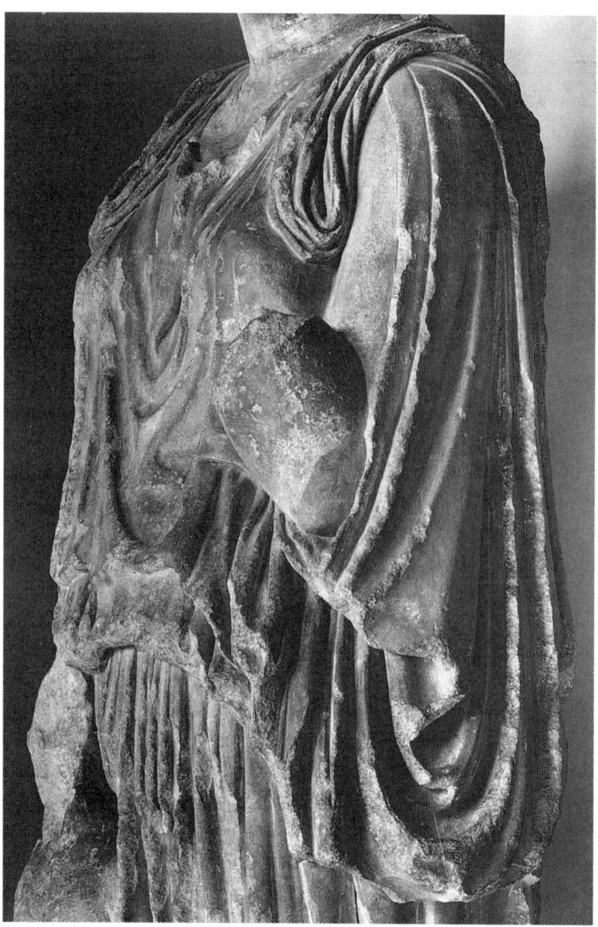

FIGURE 14.3. *Prokne and Itys, Athens, Akropolis Museum 1358. Detail of left side. Photo: Deutsches Archäologisches Institut, Athens, neg. nr. Akrop. 1481.*

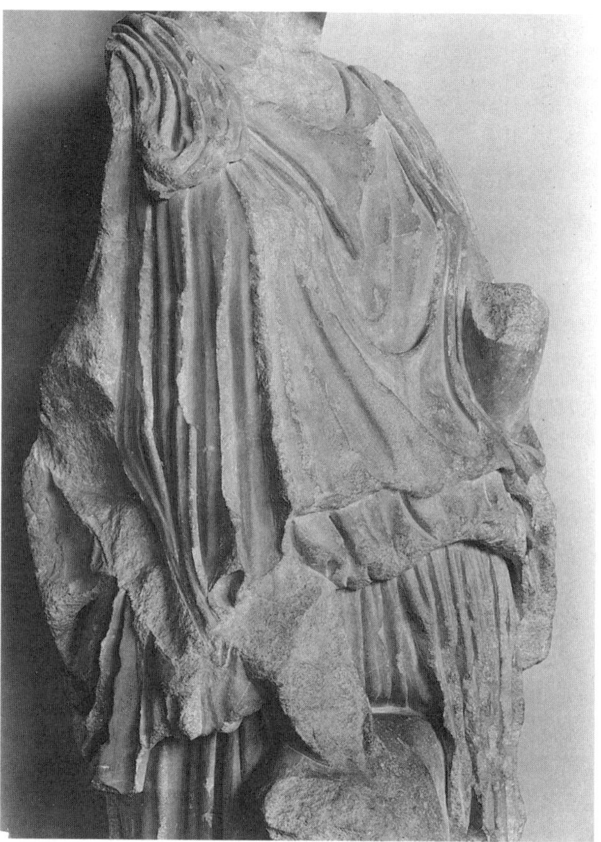

FIGURE 14.4. *Prokne and Itys, Athens, Akropolis Museum 1358. Detail of right side. Photo: Deutsches Archäologisches Institut, Athens, neg. nr. Akrop. 1482.*

with his left hand,[27] gazed up at his mother. What we would see then would be the moment of greatest tension and conflict as Prokne struggles with the decision to slaughter her child, who looks appealingly at her.

As noted above, Ovid sets the murder of Itys during Bacchic rites, and the statue group suggests that Alkamenes knew of this scenario earlier.[28] Holes for attachments to Itys' head have prompted suggestions that he wore a metal crown or band,[29] perhaps a "festive crown," presumably as part of Bacchic rites (Figs. 14.5–6).[30] Furthermore, the earliest surviving vase painting of this myth, on an Attic red-figure kylix tondo of ca. 510–500 by the Magnoncourt Painter,[31] is complemented by Dionysiac scenes on the exterior of the kylix, perhaps suggesting a Bacchic context for the murder that takes place within the cup.

That Pausanias singles out this group is somewhat remarkable since Pausanias is, if nothing else, a capricious travel guide, citing some things while ignoring others (like the Parthenon frieze, upon which modern scholars are fixated). Either the Prokne and Itys group enjoyed some renown in antiquity or the group was arresting to Pausanias and was identified for him because, to judge from the extant evidence, this subject was strikingly uncommon in ancient art (Greek, Etruscan, or Roman) and would have been difficult to identify without help. Other than our marble group, the only certain depictions of this myth in antiquity are the painted metope of ca. 650–625 B.C. from Thermon, a handful of Attic red-figure vases ranging from ca. 510 to 430 B.C. and possibly as late as 380/370, a bronze Etruscan mirror of the fourth to third century B.C., a cinerary urn from Praeneste, and a second-century A.D. Roman sarcophagus.[32]

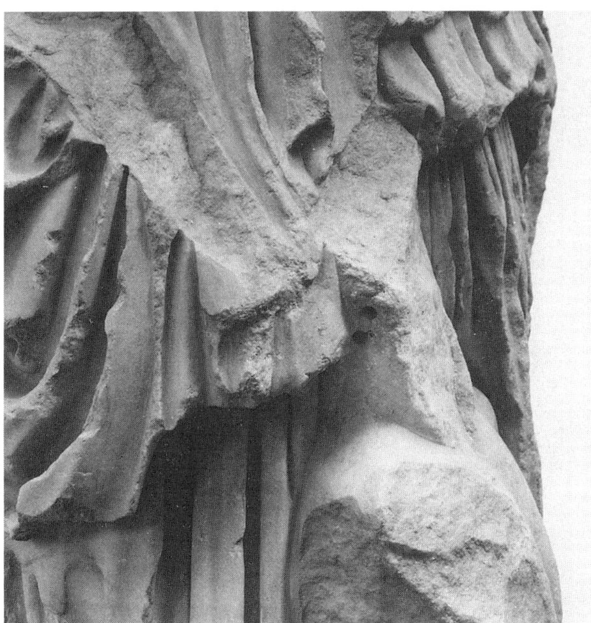

FIGURE 14.5. *Prokne and Itys, Athens, Akropolis Museum 1358. Detail of Itys' head. Photo: Deutsches Archäologisches Institut, Athens, neg. nr. 75/427.*

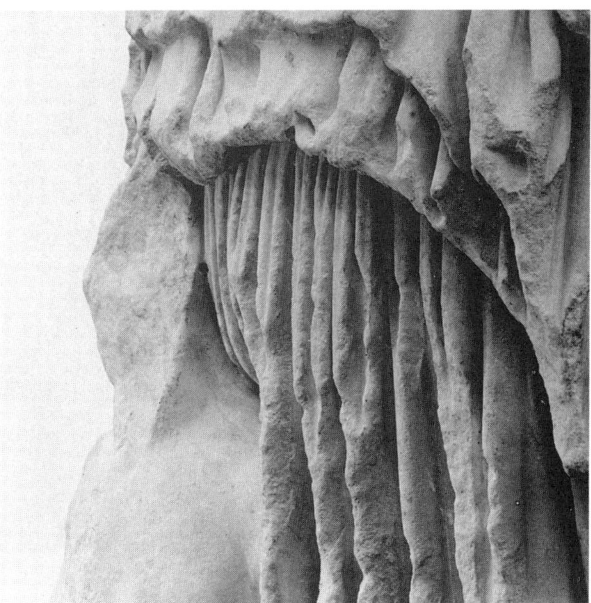

FIGURE 14.6. *Prokne and Itys, Athens, Akropolis Museum 1358. Detail of Itys' head. Photo: Deutsches Archäologisches Institut, Athens, neg. nr. 75/439.*

Even if Pausanias knew the myth, he would have been hard pressed to identify this sculpted manifestation without some assistance, since this group marks a sharp contrast to the other known depictions of Prokne and her son. All other identifiable images portray Prokne in the act of murdering her child and his resistance to her, or the husband's pursuit of the two sisters; that is, action and/or violence mark these scenes. In some instances, both sisters carry out the murder; in others, Prokne acts alone. The sculptural group atop the Akropolis, however, is restrained, quiet, and still as Prokne mentally prepares to dispatch her son; Pausanias' (1.24.3) use of the perfect participle βεβουλευμένη indicates that Prokne has made up her mind but that she has not yet begun the task. This contemplative moment, focused only on the most essential figures, finds contemporary resonances in Sophoklean and particularly Euripidean drama.

The group of Prokne and Itys has been dated ca. 440–410 on the basis of style, with present opinion placing it ca. 430–420. But this posited date is also bound up with the date of Sophokles' aforementioned *Tereus*. Scholars have suggested that the sculpted group was erected in conjunction with Sophokles' play,[33] and thus the sculpture, according to this line of thinking, should date just after the play.[34] Although the play has usually been dated ca. 431, David Fitzpatrick points out that the terminus ante quem for Sophokles' *Tereus* is 414, not 431.[35] Thus, if the sculpture relies on the play at all, its date is less certain than previously supposed.

While Sophokles seems to have invented the name Prokne, and his play may have inspired the sculptural dedication on the Akropolis referred to by Pausanias, we have seen that the myth certainly was known in some more rudimentary form long before Sophokles. The myth centers on an early royal family in Athens, and its themes include a daughter married to a barbaric foreigner, rape, weaving, infanticide, and the transformation of the eternally mourning mother—and sometimes sister or child or husband—into birds. Literary and vase-painting evidence underscore some of these elements. For example, Tereus' foreignness as conceived by contemporary Athenians is apparent on an Attic red-figure bell krater of ca. 460 by the Achilles Painter (New York, Metropolitan Museum of Art 07.286.81), where the figure identified as Pandion, whose face is now missing, is clearly designated as "Athenian" by his mantle, partially undraped chest, staff, and carefully coiffed hair, while Tereus (inscribed ΤΕΛΕΩ), who

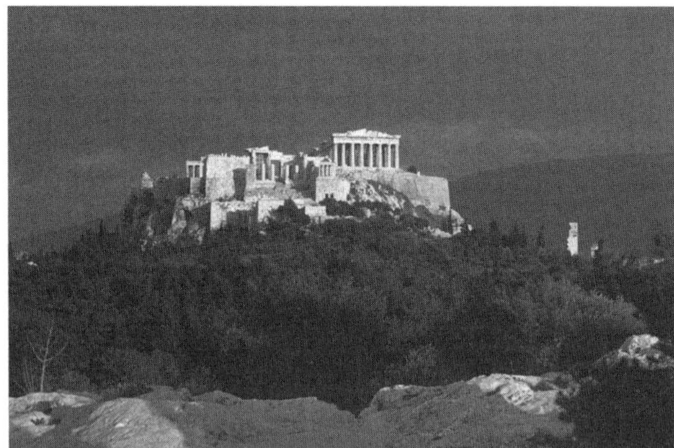

FIGURE 14.7. *Athenian Akropolis, view from the west. Photo courtesy of Hans Rupprecht Goette.*

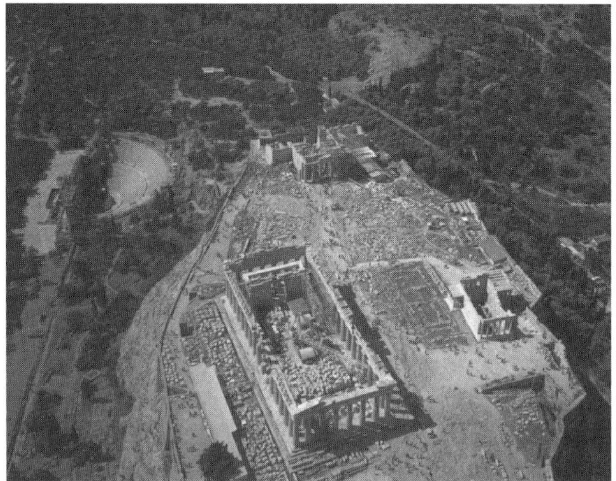

FIGURE 14.8. *Athenian Akropolis, aerial view. Photo courtesy of Hans Rupprecht Goette.*

extends his hand out toward Pandion, is marked as non-Athenian by his shaggy hair and beard, furrowed brow, crooked nose, and deep-set eyes.[36] Furthermore, the fragments of Sophokles' play reveal that Prokne makes repeated references to her sad fate as living in a foreign land and being married to a foreigner.[37] We shall see that the sculptural group by Alkamenes, by means of its physical context and the associations manifested by it, refer to other aspects of the myth.

Although the remains of the Prokne and Itys group were found during the dismantling of the west bastion of the Propylaia,[38] Pausanias' description suggests that the group originally stood somewhere between the Propylaia and the east façade of the Parthenon. Stevens more definitively placed the group along the north flank of the Parthenon, perhaps close to the northeast corner of the temple near the third column along the flank (Figs. 14.7–9).[39] The group's placement on the Akropolis, especially along the north face of the Parthenon, is particularly apt because Prokne claims an important place in early Athenian legend and on the Athenian

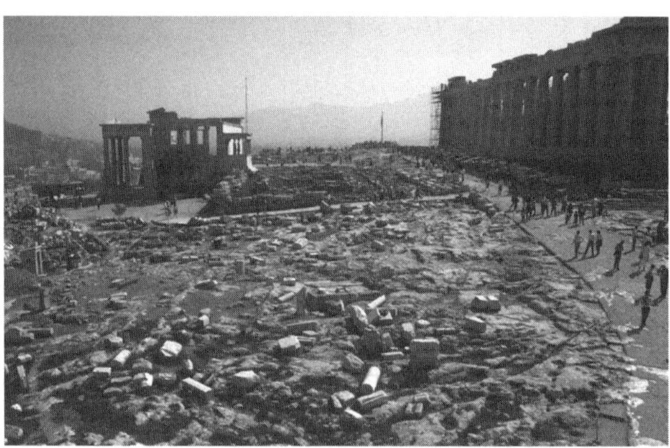

FIGURE 14.9. *Athenian Akropolis, view between the Parthenon and the Erechtheion. Photo courtesy of Hans Rupprecht Goette.*

Akropolis, where her father ruled and her brother and father were worshiped. If we consider Prokne in her physical context, we learn that the image is charged with associations, and it finds and fosters resonances with other images and structures on the Akropolis.

PROKNE AND ITYS ON THE AKROPOLIS

Images stimulate thought and associations in their viewers, and the group of Prokne and Itys was part of a play of resonant images on the Periklean and post-Periklean Akropolis.[40] Rather than a carefully orchestrated program designed to elicit certain reactions in the viewer, the experience was less choreographed than this. Nevertheless, a consistent emphasis on certain themes was a significant and intended experience for the Periklean viewer. The associations range from the simple and direct to the more indirect and layered. Such associations were not complex, but one must assume that various viewers experienced different levels of understanding. It is difficult to define the average ancient viewer of the Prokne group, much less to guess what might have been on his or her mind. If, however, we restrict our definition of the viewer to a participant in the Greater Panathenaia during the period when the Prokne was produced, that is, ca. 430–420 (perhaps as late as 410), we can narrow the scope considerably, describe much of what would have been seen, and therefore talk plausibly about what a viewer might have experienced at a particular moment along the route.

This is not groundless speculation, a kind of anachronistic mind reading or free association. For we know that the human experience and reading of images depends on cultural and historical context, as Jerry Pollitt brilliantly demonstrated in his ground-breaking *Art and Experience in Classical Greece* several decades ago, and as many others have done since.[41] Careful analysis of material and visual remains can yield insight into this experience. When an Athenian aristocrat of the 430s–410 looked at Prokne and Itys as he or she participated in the Panathenaia, this viewer saw not an isolated figure but one of the key players in the early history of their city, a history that was visually manifested, recounted, and celebrated in the very landscape in which the Prokne group appears.

Both males and females, aristocrats and metics (and sacrificial animals), participated in the Panathenaic procession, and there were many of them. After passing through the gateway of the Akropolis, the crowd walked past the sanctuary of Artemis Brauronia to their right, then moved toward the north flank of the Parthenon. Immediately above to the right was the contest between Athena and Poseidon for the patronage of Athens in the west pediment of the Parthenon. Tucked into the pediment's corners were the early kings of Athens, including Erechtheus, Kekrops,[42] and perhaps Pandion. One then had the choice of moving along the north flank of the Parthenon, which was the more direct route toward the object of the procession, the wooden *xoanon* of Athena housed either in the Erechtheion or in the Archaios Neos, or one could pass across the west of the Parthenon, then down its south side, and around the eastern end.

As the participants filed along the north side, perhaps bunched together in groups rather than single file, they would have walked past the Prokne and Itys group, which stood directly across from the imposing Altar of Athena Polias,[43] and just beyond the Old Temple to Athena[44] and perhaps the Erechtheion, whose construction may have commenced in the 430s.[45] To the left of the procession in the old temple of Athena (if it was indeed still there) and in the Erechtheion (if it was already standing) were the cult sites of Athens' early legendary figures, including Kekrops, Boutes, and Erechtheus, relatives of Pandion and his daughter Prokne. As the procession reached the end of the Parthenon, the hero shrine of Pandion, identified in Building IV of perhaps the 440s, lay just ahead at the southeast angle of the Akropolis.[46] A participant who strayed from the procession to the east façade of the Parthenon was greeted on the frieze above by, among others, the eponymous heroes of Attika, including Pandion.[47] In short, the viewer would have filed past buildings and images immediately connected to the family of Prokne and Itys.

Similarities between elements of the Prokne myth and aspects of the sculpted group's immediate visual landscape may also have struck the viewer. The animal victims led to the Altar of Athena Polias during the Panathenaia found a poignant human counterpart in the sculpted figure of Itys, standing opposite, whose ivy wreath marked him as Bacchic participant but also perhaps as sacrificial victim. Along the north side of the Parthenon, the well-placed spectator could have looked up at any point and seen the north metopes of the temple (those too close to the Parthenon would not have enjoyed an advantageous angle), which depict the Ilioupersis, the tale of a war brought on by a foreign prince who took away a Greek woman, a situation analogous to Prokne's. Athena's xoanon, the goal of the procession, stood on the north side of the Akropolis[48] and was echoed by the Trojan palladion in Parthenon north metope 25, to which Helen clings for safety; the knowledgeable viewer may have recalled that Prokne herself was credited with bringing a wooden xoanon of Athena to Daulis (Paus. 10.4.9–10).[49]

Philomela's weaving, her use of the quintessential female task as a form of communication, is one of the most striking aspects of the Prokne myth and one that has a real counterpart on the Athenian Akropolis. The culminating event of the Greater Panathenaia was the presentation of a new peplos to the venerated xoanon of Athena Polias. The weaving of this peplos was initiated several months before, at the festival of the Chalkeia in honor of Hephaistos and Athena, the dual gods of arts and crafts. A group of women, the *ergastinai,*[50] set up a loom and, together with two or four Arrhephoroi, young aristocratic girls, worked on the peplos until the festival of the Arrhephoria (see below).[51] The Arrhephoroi themselves lived on the Akropolis in the House of the Arrhephoroi (Building III?), constructed in the second half of the fifth century.[52]

The decoration of the peplos was always the same: the myth of the Gigantomachy in which Athena played a critical part (the same subject appears on the Parthenon east metopes and on the interior of the shield of the statue of Athena Parthenos housed within the Parthenon). Robert Fowler has recently argued that the draping of the peplos, a symbolic aegis, on the ancient xoanon at the Panathenaia was a type of magic designed to insure the protection of the city.[53] In any case, weaving formed a critical aspect of ritual on the Athenian Akropolis and, as is well documented, is the mark of domestic skill and female *metis,* which can be used both for good and ill. In the case of Philomela, her weaving announces the great injustice done to her and leads to the punishment of a brutal, duplicitous foreigner. While the Prokne and Itys statue group makes no direct allusion to Philomela's weaving, the attentive viewer would not need the prompt, since Itys' imminent death is the result of this action.

While the weaving of the peplos benefits the goddess and, by extension, the city, it also trained and prepared the young Arrhephoroi for adulthood and the domestic tasks of a married woman, and the Arrhephoria marked the conclusion of the Arrhephoroi's service on the Akropolis. Pausanias 1.27.3 provides the only surviving account of the Arrhephoria, a nocturnal festival in which the two Arrhephoroi transported objects unknown to them in baskets on their heads from the Athenian Akropolis to, or past, a sanctuary of Aphrodite, where they deposited the baskets and retrieved new similar burdens, which they carried on their heads back up the Akropolis. After their return to the summit, the two girls were dismissed from their duties to the goddess. The ritual apparently reenacts the myth concerning the daughters of Kekrops, who were entrusted with the care of the baby Erichthonios, who was kept inside a covered chest.[54] The girls were warned not to peer inside, but curiosity got the better of two of the three daughters, who, frightened by what they saw within the chest, jumped from the Akropolis to their deaths. The sole obedient sister, Pandrosos, was honored with a shrine on the north side of the Akropolis (Paus. 1.18.2), and one of the disobedient siblings, Aglauros, was worshiped on the east slope of the Akropolis.[55] Some scholars construe the ritual, together with a brief mention in Aristophanes (*Lys.* 641), as a rite of passage designed to promote the girls to a marriageable state, since they pass from the realm of Athena the virgin to that of Aphrodite.[56] Thus, the Arrhephoria may serve as a rite of passage in which weaving prepares young girls to take up their adult domestic duties as wives.

Philomela's weaving is a perverse parallel: sexually initiated by her brother-in-law, she uses the art of weaving, the technique of the wife, to communicate her plight and spur her sister, the true wife and mother of Itys, to vengeful action. Burkert goes so far as to describe Philomela's weaving as belonging "to the realm of Athena Ergane."[57] We might pause to ask ourselves: would the viewer of the late fifth century have linked the weaving implied by the Prokne group to the weaving of the Arrhephoroi? On any given day, the answer may be negative. Yet the woven peplos of the Panathenaic procession, a textile that also relates a story, was central to the festivities, and its transport along the north side of the Akropolis, with the house of the Arrhephoroi in the distance off to the left, then past the images of Prokne and Itys, surely would have prompted an association between the early history of Athens, woven garments, and their importance to the city.

Our heroine Prokne and the Arrhephoroi, who reenact the myth of the daughters of Kekrops, who themselves were charged with caring for the baby Erichthonios, are not the only wives and mothers or potential wives and mothers on the Akropolis. To reach the north flank of the Parthenon, one would have passed by the sanctuary to Brauronian Artemis, which was established on the Akropolis by the Peisistratid period.[58] Much has been written about the *arkteia* celebrated in honor of Artemis Brauronia, and only the barest essentials are necessary for the present discussion.[59] Young girls (their age is disputed) "played the bear" (Ar. *Lys.*

645) or *arktos* in honor of Artemis, chiefly at her sanctuary in Brauron but also elsewhere in Attika, including at her sanctuary on the Athenian Akropolis. Dancing and footraces comprised part of the activities, which seem intended to promote the arktoi to a marriageable state.[60] Thus, the physical setting of the Prokne group was charged in multiple ways with the ideas of female preparation for marriage and motherhood.

Were a participant of the Panathenaic procession to wander around the south side of the Parthenon, he or she might have encountered the drama of Prokne and Philomela again on the temple's south metopes, which also included the well-preserved Centauromachy and perhaps also episodes concerning Kekrops and Erechtheus.[61] South metopes 19 and 20, known from the Carrey drawings and surviving fragments,[62] have been nominated as depictions of Philomela displaying her woven account to her sister Prokne.[63] Although this is merely one of numerous identifications proposed for metopes 19 and 20,[64] a double occurrence of Prokne around the Parthenon, on opposite sides of the temple, would be a less than remarkable coincidence, given the number of repeated themes on the Athenian Akropolis. Such a circumstance would place this myth—with its emphasis on weaving—on the Akropolis before Sophokles' play, the hypothetical inspiration for Alkamenes' dedication and artistic interest in the myth. Moreover, the Carrey drawings depict the figure in south metope 19, purported to be Prokne, with her left hand raised to her chin, in precisely the manner in which Alkamenes' Prokne, created somewhat later, holds her left hand (though the right arm is crossed over her waist on the metope).[65] If south metopes 19 and 20 depict Prokne and Philomela, it would be noteworthy that south metope 21, the last metope before the Centauromachy resumes in south metope 22, depicts two women flanking a female xoanon, which, as others have noted, would bring to mind other xoana, most immediately that of Athena Polias on the Akropolis.[66] One might recall Prokne's bringing the wooden xoanon of Athena to Daulis and suggest that south metope 21, usually given to the Centauromachy,[67] belongs to the history of Prokne. In any case, if we can recognize Prokne and Philomela in metopes 19 and 20, the theme of Philomela's rape would have found an immediate echo in the rape of the Lapith women by the barbarian Centaurs in the adjoining metopes.

Thus far, we have constructed an astute viewer, keen to nuance and subtlety and observant of visual and thematic parallels ricocheting across the Akropolis from one image to another. This viewer may be so ideal as to be implausible, yet certain basic themes reiterated on the Periklean Akropolis are beyond denial. Athens' legendary early history and cult and the emphasis on the eponymous heroes and their histories figure prominently. Given this context, one can consider the motivation for Alkamenes' dedication. We have noted the suggestion that Sophokles' play may have inspired the sculptural dedication, and some scholars have proposed that Alkamenes and perhaps also Sophokles were driven by contemporary political events. Such claims revolve around the location of the myth and the traditional date for the group of ca. 430–420.

La Rocca, for example, accepts the account of Pausanias 1.49.8, which locates Tereus and the myth in Megara, and thinks that the gruesome tale metaphorically expresses the poor relations existing between Megara and Athens.[68] But if we accept that Tereus was thought to be Thracian—at least by the time of Alkamenes' dedication—then, according to Capuis' line of thinking, Alkamenes may have erected this group after the assassination of Sitalkes in 424 (recounted by Dem. *Philippics* 12.9, although Thuk. 4.101 says he died in battle) to underscore the familial killing involving a Thracian king. Alkamenes, Capuis posits, would have been especially sensitive to these events since he was from the island of Lemnos in the Thracian Sea.[69] Starting from precisely the same point but moving in the opposite direction, Tsiaphake suggests that the group demonstrates and underscores approvingly the close relations between Athens and Thrace between 430 and 420.[70] Athenian vase painting may provide some evidence for a positive Athenian view of Thrace: the popularity of Boreas' pursuit of Oreithyia in vase painting of the second quarter of the fifth century may be attributable to the perceived beneficence of the northern Boreas, often depicted in Thracian dress, in the Greek victory over the Persians at Artemision.[71] While Athens certainly had close ties to Thrace in the fifth century,[72] scholars rightly note that Athens clearly had an ambivalent view of their northern, barbarian neighbors.[73] Thukydides 2.29 suggests that Athens was trying to curry favor with this region in ca. 430,[74] yet the story of Prokne and the brutal Tereus would hardly be the myth that one would choose to emphasize chummy relations.[75]

This leaves us with various possibilities: that the group alludes to Thrace but perhaps makes a negative comment, which is difficult to accept considering the prominent placement of the group; that the group alludes to another location—perhaps Megara, as La Rocca suggests, or Daulis, where Prokne served as priestess to Athena; that the group makes an entirely different political statement; that the group makes no reference to the political world at all; or that the group refers to vengeance taken on barbarian foreigners.[76] This last explanation may be the most plausible, considering the sculptural program of the adjacent Parthenon, whose metopes, it is generally agreed, metaphorically refer to the defeat of barbarians by civilized Greeks.

The Alkamenes Prokne and Itys group is one of many instances of renewed interest in the early heroes and history of Athens in art and literature just before and during the Peloponnesian War.[77] We have already noted some of these manifestations on the Akropolis, such as the possible appearance of eponymous heroes on the Parthenon frieze; the Erechtheids and Kekropids in the west pediment of the Parthenon, which also recounts the ascendancy of Athena as the city's patron goddess; the construction of the hero shrine to Pandion in ca. 440; and the building of the Erechtheion, whose fragmentary frieze surely represents some aspect of Athens' legendary history.[78] Elsewhere, one might recall the construction of the Eponymous Heroes Monument, which included an image of Pandion, Prokne's father, in the Athenian Agora ca. 430–420,[79] the date posited for the erection of the Prokne and Itys group. It also is noteworthy that Pandion enjoyed a special position as the eponymous hero of Perikles' and Phormio's tribe,[80] and both Sophokles and his contemporary Philokles wrote dramas entitled *Tereus,* the first full treatments of the myth (as opposed to brief references) known to us. The interest in Athens' legendary past in the second half of the fifth century may be a patriotic response to the hardships and challenges of the lengthy Peloponnesian War.[81]

Moreover, the image of Prokne and Itys may provide a more particular and direct visual expression of the need for personal sacrifice and hard decisions when faced with a foreign threat. This sentiment is enunciated in Perikles' funeral oration as it is reported in Thukydides 2.34–46, which was delivered in 430 after the first year of the Peloponnesian War. After referring to Athens' ancestors fighting against opponents, both Greek and foreign (2.36), and describing the worthiness of sacrifice for the city of Athens (2.42–43), Perikles comforts the bereaved, particularly parents (2.44), whom he encourages to have more children if they are still of the age to do so. In the final section of his speech (2.45.2), Perikles advises and exhorts the Athenian women to be not inferior to their natures (τῆς τε γὰρ ὑπαρχούσης φύσεως μὴ χείροσι γενέσθαι ὑμιν μεγάλη ἡ δόξα). Although he singles out widows in this passage, Perikles clearly directs his advice to all Athenian women,[82] including the mourning mothers addressed in 2.44.3. As has been recently argued, each portion of the oration is addressed to the individual in an effort to encourage behavior that is good for the city,[83] and Perikles particularly crafts his funeral oration so as to "fashion . . . the kind of women he needed for success" in the ongoing war.[84]

While Perikles' Funeral Oration may not have been the immediate inspiration for Alkamenes' image, the sculptural group captures the same tension between individual loss and duty, with its emphasis on contemplation. In contrast to prior depictions of this myth, the sculptor emphasizes Prokne's suspension of action, her momentary indecision and painful resolve, rather than the killing itself. The painful choice to sacrifice one's child for the sake of duty, in this case vengeance against a foreigner who not only has betrayed Prokne but who has also done violence to, and dishonored, the Athenian royal family, forms the subject of the group.[85] Itys' childlike pose and, as I reconstruct it, his appealing gaze emphasize his vulnerability, and the close bond between mother and child heightens the weightiness of the decision and underscores the magnitude of the loss.

Rather than a gesture of appeasement toward Thrace, an explanation particularly difficult to reconcile with its placement on the Akropolis, the sculptural group of Prokne and Itys, erected in ca. 430–410, may have offered a subject of contemplation and inspiration to contemporary Athenians as they processed among images and monuments recounting and celebrating the history of their city and its legendary past. Unlike the foreign sorceress Medea, portrayed in Euripides' play of the same name in ca. 431,[86] who murdered her children in vengeance for her husband's abandonment, Prokne was an Athenian sent to a foreign land, betrayed by a foreign husband, and forced to make a wrenching decision of self-sacrifice to remove the stain of dishonor from herself and her family. The image of Prokne may have had special resonance for Athenian wives and mothers, many of whom were faced with the catastrophic loss of a male family member in the first years of the Peloponnesian War. With no end to the war in sight, the prospect of further loss and self-sacrifice on behalf of the city must have been vivid. As part of a physical landscape of monuments and images that glorified the city's origins, history, and divine favor, the group of Prokne and Itys may have especially appealed to women, who featured so prominently in rites, such as the Arkteia and Arrhephoria, celebrated on the Akropolis and who, as wives and mothers, were essential to the city's continuity. Perhaps Alkamenes' group of Prokne contemplating the sacrifice of her own child provided some measure of inspiration, and perhaps even comfort, to Athenians as Athens endured some of its greatest travails.

NOTES

I am grateful to Aileen Ajootian, who spent a great deal of time examining and talking about the Prokne and Itys group with me in Athens in May 2001. Our enjoyable discussions greatly enhanced my understanding of the group, and some of the ideas presented here arose from those conversations. I also wish to thank my coeditor, Jeff Hurwit, for his careful reading and suggestions for bettering this text. Any errors, of course, are solely my responsibility. I am also indebted to Hans Goette at the Deutsches Archäologisches Institut and Marie Mauzy at the American School of Classical Studies at Athens for help in obtaining photos.

1. Ridgway 1981, 175–176, briefly summarizes the arguments. Copy of original in bronze: Schuchhardt 1977, 21–22.

2. Not by Alkamenes, the student of Pheidias: Stevens 1946, 10–11. Original but not necessarily by Alkamenes: Stewart 1990, 164. Original of Alkamenes: Adam 1966, 92; Capuis 1968, 68–71; Knell 1978; Ridgway 1981, 176. Robertson 1975, 286, thinks it is an original and probably by Alkamenes.

3. Ridgway 1981, 175.

4. Stevens (1946, 10) identifies it as Pentelic; and Knell (1978, 9) bases his claim that the marble is Pentelic on a comparison with Parthenon sculpture fragments. Trianti (1998, 396) and Tsiaphake (1998, 196, n. 898) designate the group as Parian. Capuis (1968, 60) provides a summary until 1968 of various opinions and concludes that the marble is Parian.

5. E.g., stylistic affinities with Erechtheion caryatids: Robertson 1975, 345; Schuchhardt 1977, 11, 14, though Schuchhardt also indicates important points of distinction; Trianti 1998, 396; with the Parthenon frieze: Capuis 1968, 70; Robertson 1975, 286; Stewart 1990, 164; with leaning figures on the Erechtheion frieze: Robertson 1975, 345–346. Knell 1978, 14–17, draws other stylistic comparisons.

6. Date of ca. 430–420 B.C.: Knell 1978, 17; Stewart 1990, 28. Harrison (1980, 71) would date it earlier. On the issue of Alkamenes as both donor and maker of the group, see La Rocca 1986, 155–157, 165–166. Alkamenes received Athenian citizenship in thanks for this public monument.

7. Aedon: Hom. *Od.* 19.518. Chelidon: Hes. *Op.* 568; Sappho fr. 135. Ant. Lib. *Met.* 11 recounts that the daughter of Pandareos, Aedon, married Polytechnus of Colophon with whom she had a child, Itys. An act of *hybris* sets the tale in motion when the couple declares that their love for each other surpasses the love they possess for Zeus and Hera. The husband still seduces the sister-in-law, but in this telling, the weaving belongs to Aedon, and she eventually pities her husband when he is punished for his crime. Later commentators report that Aedon mistakenly killed Itys instead of another child: Eustathius on Hom. *Od.* 19.518 and scholia *ad loc.*

8. Aisch. *Supp.* 60–62; Thuk. 2.29.3; Apollod. 3.14.8; Ov. *Met.* 6.428; Paus. 1.5.4, 1.41.8.

9. Nightingale: Hom. *Od.* 19.518; Aisch. *Ag.* 1142–1145, *Supp.* 60–62; Thuk. 2.29.3; Apollod. 3.14.8. Swallow: Hes. *Op.* 568 and Sappho fr. 135. March (2000, 128–129) thinks Aisch. *Supp.* 62 implies that Tereus was transformed into a hawk. On the literary image of the mourning nightingale, see Loraux 1998, 57–65; I thank Corinne Pache for bringing this to my attention.

10. Soph. fr. 581; Ov. *Met.* 6.674; Paus. 10.4.8.

11. Aisch. *Supp.* 62.

12. Burkert 1983, 181, n. 11, claims that the Dionysiac aspect is already present in Sophokles' text.

13. Cf. also Pherek. *FGrH* 3 F 124. March (2000, 124–125) points out that the scholia to the *Odyssey* passage indicate that the myth recounted in the epic is Theban in origin and distinguishes a Theban Aedon myth, in which the mother mistakenly kills her son, from the Athenian Prokne myth recounted by Sophokles. She argues that Sophokles altered the myth under the influence of Euripides' *Medea,* produced in 431.

14. See *LIMC* 7, 527, s.v. Prokne et Philomela [E. Touloupa]; Zacharia 2001, 97, for summaries.

15. Tsiaphake (1998, 268) and Hall (1989, 104) argue that Tereus' Thracian origin is a fifth-century invention, inspired by the similarity in names between Tereus and Teres, the father of the Thracian king Sitalkes at the time of Perikles. Hall adds that the Thracian origin is a Sophoklean invention, but Archibald (1998, 100) is more cautious, pointing out that it is impossible to know if Sophokles invented the Thracian connection or if he was using preexisting material. To be sure, Hes. 312 MW mentions disorder caused by Aedon and Chelidon at a feast in Thrace. Although Tereus may have been shown as "foreign" in fifth-century depictions, his first visual manifestation as "Thracian" only occurs in the early fourth century B.C., according to Tsiaphake (1998, 268). See, e.g., Simon 1968, who discusses a Gnathia bell-krater fragment in Würzburg (H4600) of ca. 340–330 B.C., which she identifies as a depiction of an actor holding the mask of Tereus.

16. Thuk. 2.29.3, who says Phocis was occupied by Thracians at the time; Paus. 1.41.8, 10.4.8. But Apollodoros (3.14.8) writes that Tereus pursued the two sisters to Daulis in Phocis.

17. Paus. 1.41.8, which says that the Megarians made an annual sacrifice to Tereus. Kron (1976, 105) believes Megara to be the original location of the myth. On Tereus' Megarian origin, see Hall 1989, 104.

18. Schefold and Jung 1981, 318 intriguingly compare the myth of Boreas, the north wind, raping Oreithyia to Tereus of Thrace raping Philomela.

19. Hes. *Op.* 568; Sappho fr. 135; Thuk. 2.29.3; Apollod. 3.14.8; Ov. *Met.* 6.427, 634, 666; Paus. 1.41.8; Hyg. *Fab.* 45.

20. For ancient sources, see *LIMC* 7, 162, s.v. Pandion [A. Nercessian].

21. Kron (1976, 104–106) explains the doubling of Pandion. Contra: March (2000, 127), who argues that Pandion, father of Aedon or Prokne, is not necessarily Athenian. She makes no mention of Kron's work.

22. Knell 1978, 9.

23. E.g., Trianti 1998, 396.

24. Adam 1966, 90.

25. Ridgway 1981; Stewart 1990, 164.

26. Knell 1978, 13; Stewart 1990, 164.

27. Itys' grasp on the drapery is also noted by Adam 1966, 90.

28. Sophokles may allude to a Bacchic context in fr. 586. See Zacharia 2001, 93. Contra: Burnett 1998, 182 n.16.

29. Adam 1966, 90; Stewart 1990, 164.

30. Knell 1978, 13. Such a band or fillets might indicate that Itys is about to be sacrificed as if he were an animal; cf. the description of the sacrifice of Iphigeneia in Aisch. *Ag.* 231–247 in which Iphigeneia is compared to an animal sacrifice. Interestingly, a festival honoring Pandion, the Pandia, took place just after the City Dionysia. See Deubner 1932, 176–177; Kron 1976, 111–112. Kron (above) dismisses the possibility that the Pandia honors Selene or Zeus. Apollodoros (3.14.7) reports that worship of Dionysos began in Athens during Pandion's rule. March (2000, 131) accepts the veracity of Apollod. 3.14.7 and makes the intriguing suggestion that in early mythical accounts, Itys was sacrificed as a victim to Dionysos. This would assume that the myth takes place in Athens, contrary to March's claims, but March (2000, n. 35) argues that Apollodoros conflates an earlier, non-Athenian version of the myth with the Sophoklean version. This seems like special pleading. Why is March willing to accept Apollodoros' authority on one point but not the other?

31. Munich, Antikensammlungen 2638; ARV^2 456, 1; *Addenda*^{2} 243; *LIMC* 7, s.v. Prokne et Philomela, no. 2 [E. Touloupa]. Here, the murderous female is inscribed as Aedonai. March (2000, 125) believes the vase may depict the Theban Aedon, not the Athenian mother, but is unwilling to declare with certainty that the painting is a depiction of Itys' death at the hands of his mother in spite of the presence of Itys' inscribed name and his being the target of a weapon aimed by one woman while another holds him. This seems perversely argumentative to me.

32. See *LIMC* 7, s.v. Prokne et Philomela [E. Touloupa], and also Tsiaphake 1998, 189–197, who includes objects not mentioned by Touloupa.

33. Robertson 1975, 286–287; Schuchhardt 1977, 17, raises the possibility; Ridgway 1981, 174–176; Stewart (1990, 164) is guarded.

34. Capuis (1968, 80) places the sculpture between 431 and 424 on the basis of dates for Euripides' *Med.* (431) and *Herak.* (424–423), the latter of which is now dated ca. 414 (*OCD3* 571, s.v. Euripides); Knell 1978, 17; La Rocca 1986, 159. Adam (1966, 90) dates the play slightly before 414 and thus the sculpture ca. 415 and attributes both the work and the dedication to Alkamenes (92).

35. Fitzpatrick 2001, 90, n. 3.

36. ARV^2 991, 61; *Para* 437; *Addenda*^{2} 311; Schefold and Jung 1988, 73, fig. 78; *LIMC* 7, s.v. Pandion, no. 13 [A. Nercessian]. Cf. also the Attic red-figure column krater of ca. 470–460 in Rome, Villa Giulia 3579 (ARV^2 514, 3), illustrated in Schefold and Jung 1988, fig. 80, where Tereus, who

is menacing the two sisters, is portrayed with a long, bushy beard.

37. On Sophokles' play, see most recently Burnett 1998, 180–191; Fitzpatrick 2001; Zacharia 2001.

38. Knell 1978, 9.

39. Stevens 1946, 10–11, fig. 3; La Rocca 1986, 154.

40. For another look at resonant images on the Akropolis with a different focus and results, see Hurwit 1999, 228–232.

41. See, e.g., Zanker 1988; Freedberg 1989; Hurwit 1999, esp. 228–232; Barringer 2001, passim.

42. E.g., see Pollitt 2000.

43. On the altar, see Hurwit 1999, 192.

44. See now Ferrari 2002, who argues that the *Archaios Neos,* which stood on the Dörpfeld foundations, was still standing throughout the fifth century.

45. See Hurwit 1999, 206.

46. Stevens 1946, 21–25; Kron 1976, 110; Hurwit 1999, 188–189. Inscriptions attesting the Pandion heroon: *IG* II^2 1138, 1140, 1144, 1148, 1152. Kron (1976, 109–111) places the earliest of these inscriptions at the end of the fifth century B.C. but indicates that the shrine to Pandion existed much earlier. Kron (1976, 110) also posits that the Athenians located Pandion's grave at this heroon.

47. The identity of these bearded, standing men is controversial, but many scholars, including the author, believe them to be the eponymous heroes. See Neils (2001, 158–161), who summarizes the various identifications, including marshals, magistrates, and eponymous heroes, and concludes that the best identification may be that they are embodiments of Attika's *phylai* (161). In favor of eponymous heroes: Kron 1976, 202–213; Mattusch 1994, 74.

48. Ferrari 2002, 16.

49. Burkert (1983, 182) claims that in doing so, Prokne behaves as a priestess of Athena. Although no trace of Astyanax survives in the badly damaged north metopes—Jeppesen 1963, 44, fig. 10:c, posits Neoptolemos and Priam in north 22, which is where we would expect to see the child; his presence would provide a meaningful counterpoint to Itys. I thank Jenifer Neils for this suggestion.

50. M. Dillon (2002, 58) identifies the ergastinai as *parthenoi.*

51. Brulé 1987, 102.

52. See Hurwit 1999, 199–200.

53. Fowler 2000, 325.

54. Burkert 1966.

55. See Shapiro 1995 for a discussion of the myth and its visual manifestations; and Hurwit 1999 for the cult sites.

56. Contra: Fowler 2000, 326, who argues for the ritual's magical properties, designed to "secure the prosperity of the city and (in olden days) its king"; M. Dillon 2002, 60.

57. Burkert 1983, 182. Burkert takes the parallel between Philomela and the Arrhephoroi even further (perhaps too far) when he claims that both experience sex, either literally or metaphorically; according to Burkert, the Arrhephoroi encountered a snake at the end of their service.

58. Goette 2001, 24.

59. For discussion and bibliography, see Barringer 2001, 144–146.

60. See Barringer 2001, 144–146, for a summary of scholarship and bibliography.

61. Brommer (1967, 230–231, 233–240) summarizes the numerous possibilities for the south side; Dörig 1978.

62. Brommer 1967, 106–108; Mantis (1997) presents more recent finds.

63. Becatti (1951, 38–40) sees Prokne reading Philomela's woven account in South 20 while Philomela stands next to her, holding a shuttle in her hand; Jeppesen (1963, 34) definitively endorses Becatti's opinion that 20 depicts Prokne and Philomela but refuses his reading of the other middle metopes; Dörig (1978, 226–228) accepts 19 as Prokne and Philomela but thinks that 20 shows Zeuxippe, mother of the two sisters, and Chthonia, wife of Boutes, who turns to the cult statue in South 21; Schefold 1988, 71, 75; *LIMC* 7, s.v. Prokne et Philomela, no. 12 [E. Touloupa].

64. E.g., Becatti (1951, 17–41) summarizes variously championed views until the time of his publication and argues that the 20 is one of a group of metopes concerning the family of Pandion. Brommer (1967, 233–240) summarizes previous work on the middle metopes and favors the myth of Erechtheus. Simon (1975) proposes that the central metopes are devoted to the myth of Ixion. Robertson (1984) argues that the central eight metopes on the south side of the Parthenon are devoted to the myth of Daidalos. Robertson also notes that south metope 20 portrays a woman holding "woven cloth from a loom" and that the adjacent 19 may depict a woman spinning while another watches (207).

65. Dörig (1978, 226–227) notes the similarity between the torso of the freestanding Prokne and that of the left figure on Parthenon south metope 20, which survives in fragments and is also known from the Carrey drawings. Dörig identifies the metope figure as a female servant and posits that south metopes 19 and 20 were carved by Alkamenes (227). Mantis 1997, 75, notes that the so-called Prokne of south metope 19 holds her hand to her chin but would restore a distaff in the upraised left hand and a spindle in the lowered right.

66. Robertson 1984, 208. Dörig (1978, 228) accepts the cult statue both as a reference to that of Athena Polias on the Akropolis and also as a point of refuge for the Lapith women in the Centauromachy in the following metopes, i.e., the statue has a dual function, one tied to Athens, one tied to Thessaly.

67. Jeppesen 1963, 33; Brommer 1967, 230.

68. La Rocca 1986, 161–164.

69. Capuis 1968, 79–80. Capuis points out that Sitalkes so wanted to underscore an Athenian connection that he banked on the identification of his father, Teres, with Tereus

when the Athenians wished to forge a Thracian-Athenian alliance. Thukydides' (2.29) emphatic distinction may be in response to this effort at identification. Dörig (1978) also emphasizes Alkamenes' Lemnian/Thracian connection and posits his authorship of Parthenon south metopes 19 and 20, which, together with south metopes 13–21, Dörig interprets as referring to the early myths of Athens, especially those concerning Thrace.

70. Tsiaphake 1998, 190, 196. Pache (2001, 5) also shares this view and cites Xen. *An.* 7.2.31 and 7.3.39 as evidence. Tsiaphake (190) allows the possibility that Sophokles may have intended his play as anti-Thracian but ultimately seems to decide on a positive reading of the statue group, analogous to depictions of the myth of Boreas abducting Oreithyia after the Persian Wars.

71. Pollitt 1987, 13–14.

72. Tsiaphake (1998), for example, discusses this at great length, pointing to the popularity of images of Boreas abducting Oreithyia after the Persian Wars.

73. E.g., Parker 1996, 174–175; Archibald 1998, 94–102; Pache 2001; Zacharia 2001, who suggests that Sophokles' version of the myth reflects Athenian colonization of Thrace (105).

74. Archibald (1998, 99) rightly points out that Thukydides' protestation of any relationship between Teres of Thrace and Tereus of Daulis is in response to some contemporary attempt to establish one.

75. Cf. Hall 1989, 105, for a similar view: "Teres' son Sitalces, who was probably the king on the Odrysian throne when the play was produced, could hardly have construed Tereus' treatment of his wife's sister as a compliment."

76. Goette 2001, 47. Zacharia 2001, 106, notes that Dem. 60.28 singles out the story of the daughters of Pandion as a patriotic example of how the hybris of barbarians did not go unpunished.

77. Cf. Shapiro 1995, 47.

78. E.g., Brommer 1967, 238; Hurwit 1999, 207–208.

79. On the Eponymous Heroes Monument, see Mattusch (1994, 75–80), who proposes an earlier date. Kron (1976, 228–236) considers a date at the beginning of the Peloponnesian War to be plausible.

80. Zacharia (2001, 105) makes this observation.

81. On the emphasis on Pandion as eponymous hero in the last decades of the fifth century, see Kron 1976, 119.

82. Tyrrell and Bennett 1999, 46.

83. Tyrrell and Bennett 1999, 46.

84. Tyrrell and Bennett 1999, 46.

85. Cf. Burnett 1998, 190, who comes to a similar conclusion by way of Sophokles' play.

86. Above, n. 13.

15

INTERPRETATIONS OF TWO ATHENIAN FRIEZES

THE TEMPLE ON THE ILISSOS AND THE TEMPLE OF ATHENA NIKE

OLGA PALAGIA

The small Ionic temple that once stood on the hill above the banks of the Ilissos River was a virtual twin of the Athena Nike temple on the Akropolis: both were built of Pentelic marble and are attributed to the same architect, Kallikrates.[1] Their friezes are here considered together, even though created by different sculptors: they were both designed to be viewed close to eye level, and the elucidation of their subject matter was evidently dependent on the figures being named by painted inscriptions. The planners of the twin Ionic temples were clearly being innovative not only in their architectural design but also in the sculpted decoration, which explored new means of expression.

THE ILISSOS TEMPLE

Only a handful of slabs of the Ilissos temple frieze survives, whereas the best part of the friezes of the Athena Nike temple is still extant. Three of the Nike temple friezes represent battle scenes; the fourth carries a divine gathering of uncertain purpose. The question arising from the fragmentary nature of the extant material from the Ilissos temple is whether these slabs belong to the same side and, if not, whether all friezes formed part of a single theme. The present study explores the iconography of the friezes of the twin Ionic temples.

Manolis Korres pointed out that this pair of temples did not stand alone in Athens: there was a similar Ionic temple, the remains of which are now stored by the church of Agioi Pantes on Tsocha Street.[2] Another such temple may have stood on the Areopagos.[3] There were additional temples at Ambelokipi, Acharnai, Gerakas, and Penteli.[4] The fragments of an Ionic frieze in Pentelic marble, of a size and style similar to that of the Athena Nike temple, were found on the south slope of the Akropolis, providing further evidence of the existence of such temples.[5]

It is generally thought that the temple of Athena Nike was completed ca. 424/3 B.C., on the evidence of the decree *IG* I^3 36 regulating the priestess' salary.[6] There is no consensus as to the date of its twin on the Ilissos, which ranges from the 440s to the 420s.[7] A date after the completion of Pheidias' cult statue of Zeus at Olympia in the late 430s, however, is suggested by the dependence of the fleeing woman in slab D (Fig. 15.4) and the kneeling woman in slab E of the Ilissos frieze (Fig. 15.5) on two of the Niobids from the throne of Zeus.[8]

The Ilissos temple was drawn by Stuart and Revett in 1751–1753 and published in 1762, before being demolished in 1778.[9] Their drawings indicate that the temple had an exterior Ionic frieze. The slimness of the slabs suggests that the contractors were being economical; it is therefore assumed that they used imported Parian marble rather than local Pentelic. As the frieze had vanished by 1751, Stuart and Revett restored the entablature with a relief they found nearby:

> . . . the cymatium of the cornice is destroyed, as are likewise the ornaments of the frieze, which was composed of slabs about an inch and a half thick [= 3.81 cm]. These were probably decorated with sculpture, and added after the temple was built. . . . the figures here represented on it are copied from a fragment found at Athens, which may possibly have belonged to this place, since its height and thickness is such as exactly supplies the space designed for this ornament.[10]

This relief has since disappeared.[11] Though Stuart and Revett's drawing is evidently restored, we can make out a procession of men, women, and children. The adult figures recall the style of the Parthenon frieze (note especially the *himatia* with selvages), but the presence of marching infants is hard to accommodate in a narrative frieze. It is remarkable that the relief has a ground line like the actual Ilissos frieze (Figs. 15.1–9) that Stuart and Revett never saw. Their restoration is now rejected by general consensus. Nearly everyone who discusses the Ilissos frieze suggests that they inadvertently drew a votive relief showing a family of worshipers. This, however, does not explain the children's nudity since children are invariably draped in all processions in votive reliefs. Nor does it account for the ground line, which is not a normal feature of votive reliefs. On the other hand, the slab could not have belonged to a corner of the frieze as drawn by Stuart and Revett, plate 6, because the corners here consisted of blocks, not thin slabs.[12] In addition, the dimensions of this slab are reduced compared to the measurements of the frieze given in Stuart and Revett, plate 8.[13] Since the subject of the Ilissos frieze is still *sub judice,* however, it may be wiser to reserve judgment on Stuart and Revett's choice.

It has been calculated that, assuming that it ran around the building, the Ilissos frieze would have contained thirty-two to thirty-four slabs.[14] Three slabs in Berlin, B (Figs. 15.1–2), C (Fig. 15.3), D (Fig. 15.4), along with slab E (Fig. 15.5), plus a fragment of C in Vienna (Fig. 15.3 [left]) were recognized by Studniczka on the basis of their height, width, and thickness, which match the measurements in Stuart and Revett, plate 8.[15] All slabs are of Parian marble. Studniczka's attribution was based on fragment A (Fig. 15.6), excavated near the foundations of the Ilissos temple in 1897.[16] It shows a sandaled foot in motion near a pair of wineskins, a theme related to slab B (Fig. 15.2); the ground line is characteristic of the Ilissos frieze. Slabs B, C, and E carry anathyrosis all around the back and were fastened to their backers by means of double-T clamps.[17] The lack of anathyrosis at the left vertical edge of D suggests that it was not adjacent to E.[18] The slabs in Berlin were acquired via Venice, those in Vienna via Padua, and it is now known that Morosini's men carried them away in 1688.[19] Because of its height and marble quality, which match those of the thin slabs, Möbius attributed to the Ilissos frieze a corner block of Parian marble (Figs. 15.7–9), found in 1893 in a cistern near the church of Agia Photeini by the Ilissos River, down the slope from the Ilissos temple.[20] It carries reliefs on two sides, anathyrosis on the other two, and a dowel hole on top. The architect of the Ilissos temple was evidently compelled to use corner blocks for structural reasons.

Slabs B (Figs. 15.1–2) and C (Fig. 15.3), and fragment A (Fig. 15.6) presumably come from the same side of the building and are usually considered together. Unlike common practice in architectural friezes, the figures here are widely spaced and mostly frontal. These compositional devices are akin to the statue bases of Pheidias and his school.[21] At the extreme left

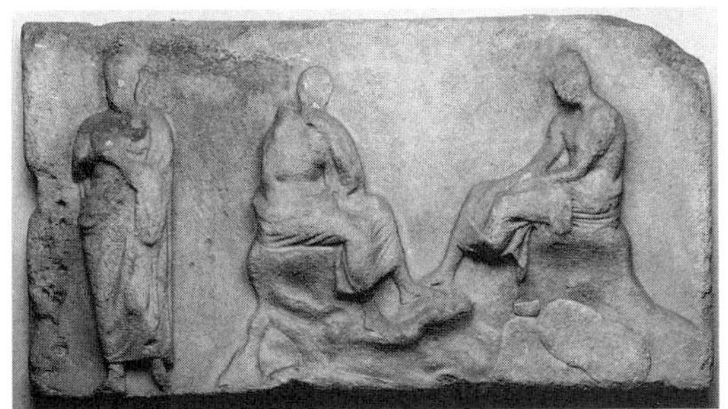

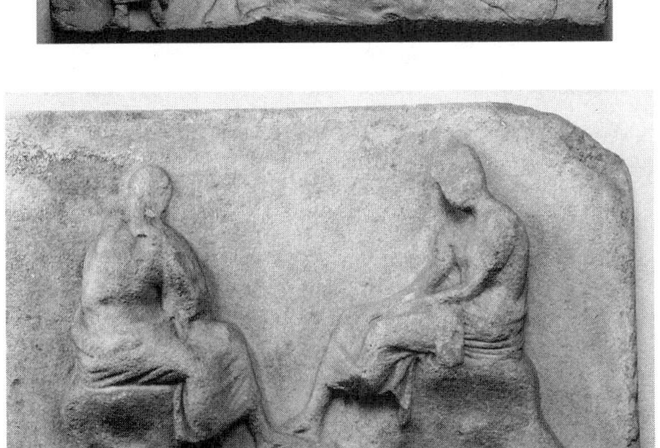

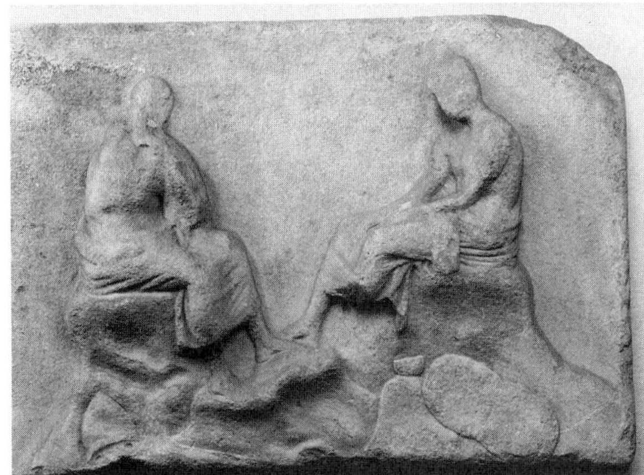

FIGURES 15.1–2. *Ilissos frieze B. Berlin, Antikensammlung, Staatliche Museen–Preussischer Kulturbesitz Sk 1483. Photos by and courtesy of Hans Rupprecht Goette.*

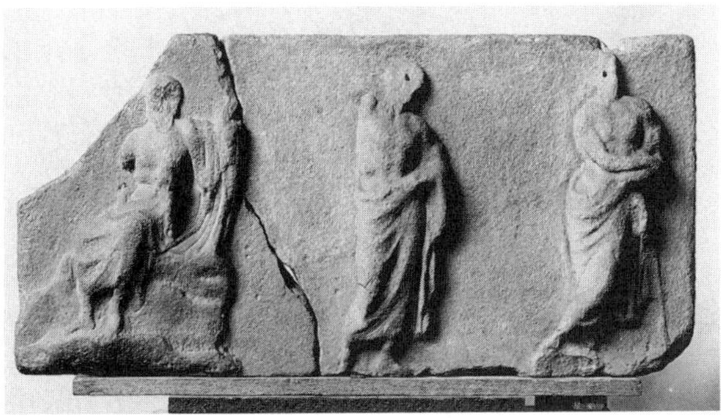

FIGURE 15.3. *Ilissos frieze C. Vienna, Kunsthistorisches Museum I 1094 (cast) + Antikensammlung, Staatliche Museen zu Berlin–Preussischer Kulturbesitz Sk 1483. Photo: Staatliche Museen zu Berlin.*

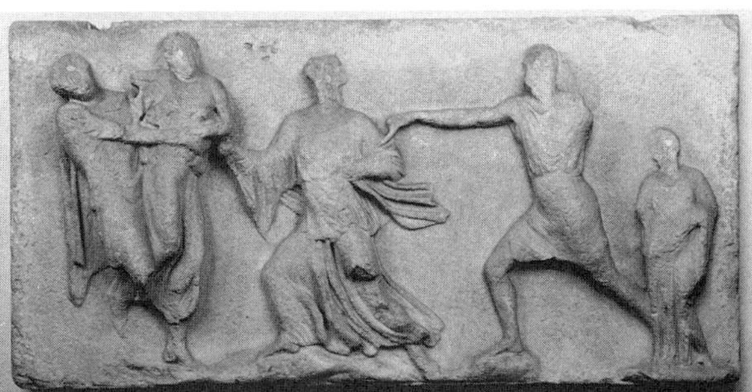

FIGURE 15.4. *Ilissos frieze D. Berlin, Antikensammlung, Staatliche Museen–Preussischer Kulturbesitz Sk 1483. Photo by and courtesy of Hans Rupprecht Goette.*

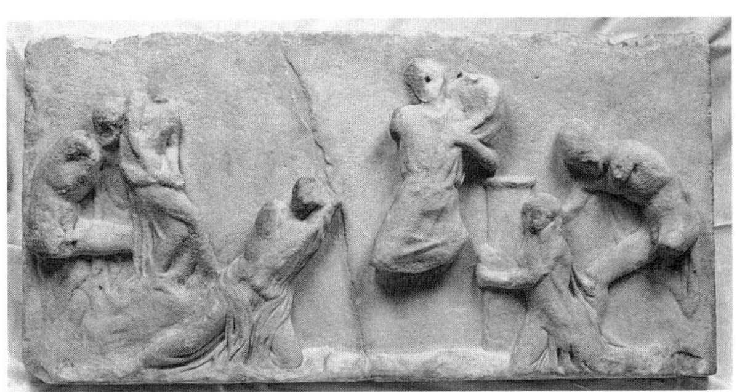

FIGURE 15.5. *Ilissos frieze E. Vienna, Kunsthistorisches Museum I 1093. Photo by and courtesy of Hans Rupprecht Goette.*

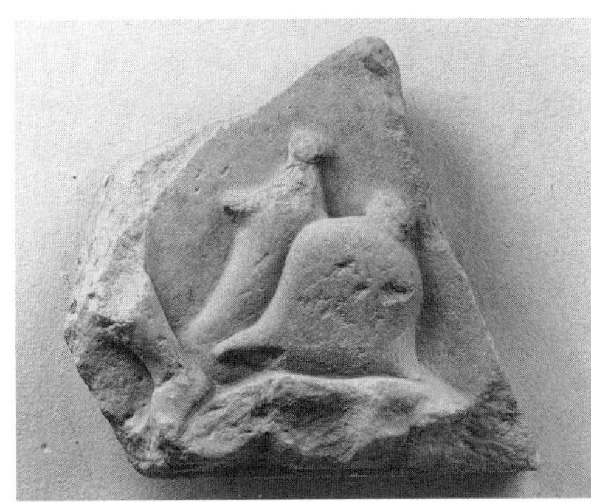

FIGURE 15.6. *Ilissos frieze A. Athens, National Museum 1780. Photo by and courtesy of Hans Rupprecht Goette.*

of C (Fig. 15.3), a bearded man sits on a rock, his left arm raised, presumably once holding a staff or scepter. He grasps an edge of his himation in his right hand as if draping himself. His left flank is bare. He looks over his right shoulder. Two men stand at the right, one making the gesture of a wine-pourer, the other leaning on his staff, legs crossed. In B (Figs. 15.1–2), a frontal, standing man is accompanied by a pair of men sitting opposite one another on rocks. A bundle of bedding and a sack of food rest against the rocks on the right (Fig. 15.2).[22] These are complemented by the wineskins in A (Fig. 15.6). The pilos-like object on the left of B (Fig. 15.2), with two holes in its bottom, a crooked stick at the viewer's right leaning against it, has

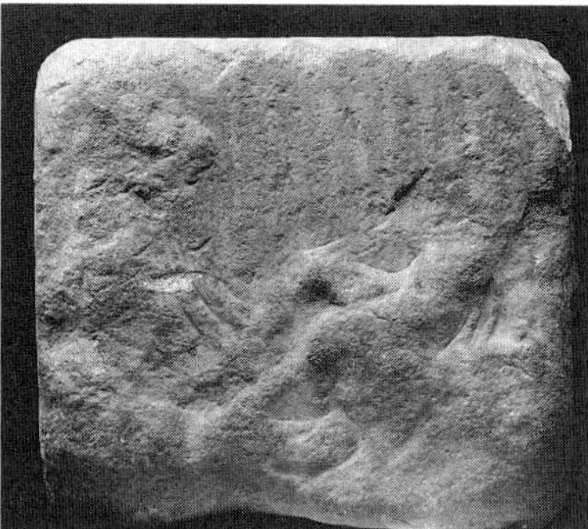
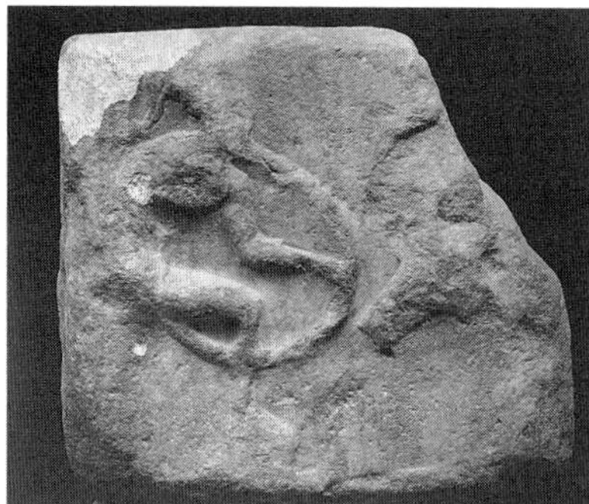
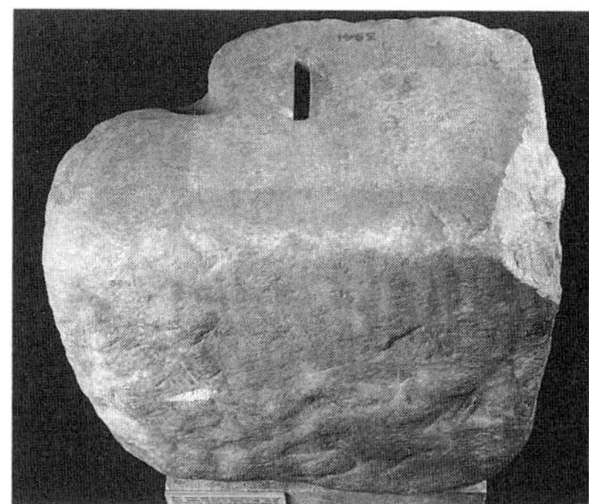

FIGURES 15.7–9. *Corner block of Ilissos frieze. Athens, National Museum 3941. Photos by and courtesy of Hans Rupprecht Goette.*

been variously interpreted as a pilos helmet or a traveling hat with a club. This interpretation would suggest that the man is a warrior, even though he is dressed in a simple himation. But a helmet has no place among men not dressed for war, who are moreover laden with baggage implying travel or pilgrimage. In addition, it is far too large for this man's head. It appears not to be a hat but an upturned bucket with holes for inserting the handle, which is clearly missing.[23] The holes are too shallow for fastening a metallic handle, and there is no room to paint one. The stick would have served for carrying it over one's shoulders along with the food and bedding bags.[24] The bucket was necessary for drawing water from wells. Its bottom here ends in a flat base, partly obscured by the stick, and is comparable to the upturned bucket on a Kabeirion skyphos in Berlin.[25] A similar bucket in sculpture can be found in a Roman relief from Lakonia in London.[26]

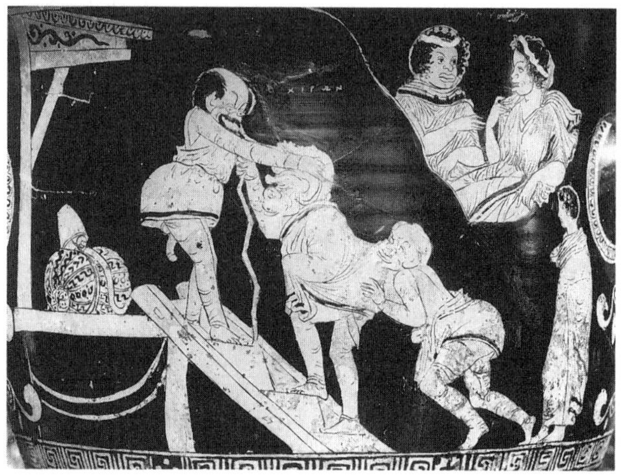

FIGURE 15.10. *Apulian bell krater. Cheiron visits an Asklepieion. London, British Museum F151. Photo courtesy of the Trustees of the British Museum, © Copyright The British Museum.*

Pilgrims were normally accompanied by a slave carrying all sorts of baggage (e.g., Dionysos visiting the Underworld in Ar. *Ran.* 12 or the family offering sacrifice to Pan in Men. *Dys.* 402–404). The baggage contained offerings to the gods as well as equipment for the convenience of the pilgrims. Illustrations of such scenes from drama are common on South Italian vases of the fourth century.[27] A good example of a slave's bag and bucket hanging from a crooked pole is offered by Cheiron's pilgrimage to Asklepios on an Apulian (phlyax) bell krater in London (Fig. 15.10).[28] A similar scene of a visit to an oracle of Zeus is found on an Apulian bell krater in Bari.[29] The large bag in slab B is also reminiscent of a sack of grapes on an Attic red-figure cup in Munich.[30]

Slab B (Figs. 15.1–2) not only is one of the earliest extant representations of a traveler's or pilgrim's baggage but also has the peculiar distinction of associating the baggage with the master, not the slave. Bucket and bags clearly belong to the citizens in himatia. The only example known to me of masters carrying their own baggage are the three initiates on their way to celebrate the Mysteries at Eleusis shown on the Ninnion tablet. Their sacks, probably containing offerings to the two goddesses, hang from sticks over their shoulders.[31] Other initiates carry sticks only, having deposited their sacks in the sanctuary.

The owner of the bucket lacking handles in slab B (Fig. 15.2) rests his chin on his hand in a gesture of despair and frustration. The other man, seated with head bowed, is reflected in the narrow side of the Torre Nuova sarcophagus in Rome (Fig. 15.11), which shows an Underworld scene:[32] the young man sits on a rock under a plane tree, indicating the proximity of water.

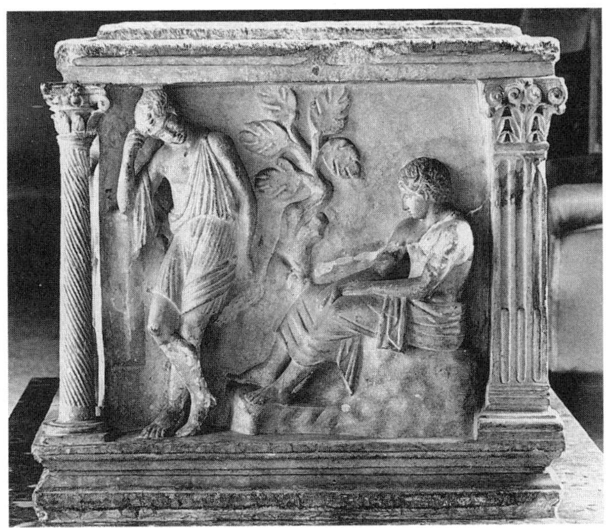

FIGURE 15.11. *Asiatic sarcophagus. From Torre Nuova, perhaps originally from Ephesos. Rome, Palazzo Borghese. Photo: Deutsches Archäologisches Institut, Rome 58.2001, photo by Bartl.*

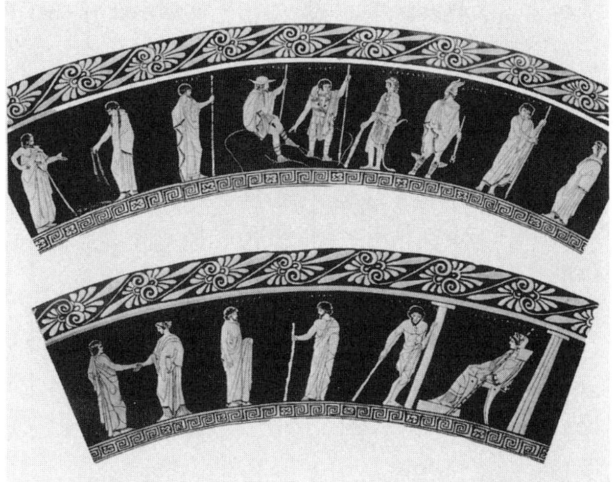

FIGURE 15.12. *Attic red-figure kalyx krater.* Nekyia. *New York, Metropolitan Museum of Art 08.258.21, Rogers Fund 1908. Photo after Richter and Hall 1936, pl. 135.*

The rock may be an allusion to the banks of the Acheron River.

The composition of dejected men sitting on rocks or standing around evokes Pausanias' (10.28–31) description of Polygnotos' painting of the Underworld (*Nekyia*) in the Lesche of the Knidians at Delphi, dating from the late second quarter of the fifth century.[33] The painting was inspired by Odysseus' visit to the entrance of Hades to consult Teiresias about his homecoming, as told in Homer's *Odyssey* 10.510–541 and 11. Polygnotos painted the shades of the heroes in Hades in poses similar to those we see in slabs B and C (Figs. 15.1–3): Agamemnon leaning on a scepter under his armpit and holding up a staff; Hektor sitting, clasping his left knee with both hands in an attitude of dejection; Memnon sitting on a rock; Orpheus sitting under a willow in Persephone's grove. A comparable Underworld scene appears on an Attic red-figure kalyx krater in New York (Fig. 15.12).[34] The heroes stand around in himatia holding staffs (Meleager, Aias) or leaning on a stick (Palamedes). Theseus and Peirithoös sit on a craggy ground line, Peirithoös in traveler's garb, Theseus in armor. Odysseus sitting on the crag at the mouth of Hades, sword in hand, guarding the sacrificial victims, as described by Homer, is represented on an Attic red-figure pelike in Boston[35] and a Lucanian red-figure krater in Paris.[36] On the pelike in Boston, the figures sit or move up and down a rocky ground line, with Elpenor emerging from the reeds on the banks of the Acheron River. The figures in Ilissos A and B (Figs. 15.1–2, 15.6), arranged in a rocky landscape with supplies resting on the ground, recall Dionysos' journey to the Underworld in Aristophanes' *Frogs,* complete with a slave carrying equipment.

Since 1910, even before the frieze was attributed to the Ilissos temple, the scene in B–C (Figs. 15.1–3) has often been interpreted as a Nekyia, thanks to Brueckner's identification of the two seated men (Fig. 15.2) as Theseus and Peirithoös in Hades, and to Hauser's association of the man on the right with the Torre Nuova sarcophagus (Fig. 15.11).[37] Studniczka (1916) and Curtius (1923) accepted the Nekyia theory, and they additionally suggested that the standing men are the three judges of the Underworld. The usual iconography of Theseus and Peirithoös in Hades, however, does not bear out Brueckner's identification. At least one of the heroes should be armed. In Polygnotos' fresco, Theseus carried the swords of both heroes, while on the kalyx krater in New York (Fig. 15.12), Theseus holds a spear, and on one of the three-figure reliefs of the late fifth century, both are armed.[38]

If the scene in A–C (Figs. 15.1–3, 15.6) is set in Hades, different heroes must be meant here. The useless bucket may in fact be an allusion to the punishment of the uninitiated in Hades, condemned to carry water in broken vessels.[39] In his *Nekyia* Polygnotos painted a pair of women attempting to fetch water in broken pitchers, identifying them by an inscription as uninitiated (Paus. 10.31.9). The Eleusinian Mysteries were probably meant here. The wineskins and sacks in A and B may allude to a failed pilgrimage, either to Eleusis or to Hades. The landscape and flora of the Underworld, the crags, the reeds of the Acheron River, and Persephone's grove as described in Homer's *Odyssey,* which also inspired Polygnotos' *Nekyia,* the Boston pelike, and the Torre Nuova sarcophagus (Fig. 15.11), may account for the wide spacing of the figures in B and C. The rocks are modeled in relief, but the trees and reeds may have been painted in the background between the figures, thus giving a pictorial dimension to the composition.

Because the owner of the baggage is reflected in the Torre Nuova sarcophagus (Fig. 15.11), which carries an initiation rite on its face, Möbius associated slabs B and C with Herakles' initiation in the Eleusinian Mysteries. He consequently identified the Ilissos temple with the sanctuary at Agrai or Agra, where the Lesser Eleusinian Mysteries were held.[40] As most of our sources merely locate the Lesser Mysteries in Agra, the name of the sanctuary is elusive.[41] Möbius later came to realize that the rite represented on the face of the sarcophagus of Torre Nuova does not derive from Eleusinian imagery.[42] This, however, need not have stopped the sculptor of the sarcophagus from adapting single figures from disparate scenes to decorate the sides.

An alternative interpretation to the Nekyia was offered by Krumme (1993), who saw the depiction of a local myth in A–C (Figs. 15.1–3, 15.6). The Athenians believed that they had in their possession the palladion carried from Troy by Diomedes. On their way home from Troy, the Argives landed in Phaleron, not knowing they were in Attika, and were defeated by the Athenians, led by Theseus' son Demophon. The Athenians obtained possession of the palladion, which they housed in the sanctuary of Zeus and Athena *epi palladio.* The location of this sanctuary is uncertain; it has been tentatively placed at the end of the Phaleron Road, near the Ilissos River, but the evidence is inconclusive.[43]

According to Krumme, slabs A–C show the Athenians and the Argives negotiating after the battle. He suggested that the bags at the feet of the seated heroes carried the treasures of Troy by analogy with the bags of tribute money depicted in a record relief of 426 B.C.

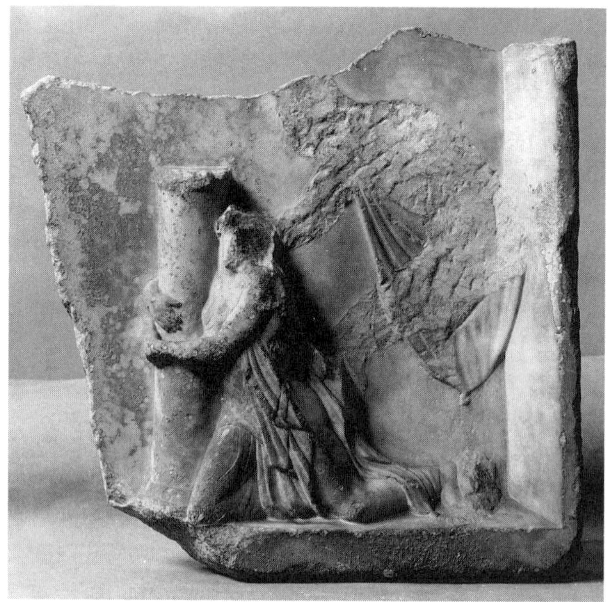

FIGURE 15.13. *Neo-Attic relief. From Ephesos. Vienna, Kunsthistorisches Museum I 868. Photo: Museum.*

in the Epigraphical Museum in Athens.[44] The tribute, however, is stored in pots and sacks of quite another shape from those in slabs A and B. Krumme's view entailed the identification of the Ilissos temple with another elusive candidate: the temple of Zeus and Athena of the Palladion.[45] Finally, by interpreting the seated men with the bags as travelers at rest, Felten restored here another episode from the *Odyssey.* He did not favor the Nekyia but the encounter with Aiolos, and he suggested that the bags are full of winds.[46]

Slabs D (Fig. 15.4) and E (Fig. 15.5), showing assaults on women, are usually grouped together, though this was contested by von Eickstedt (1994), who allocated them to different sides of the building. This episode too was copied in the Roman period. A Neo-Attic relief found at Ephesos (Fig. 15.13) reproduces the group at the extreme right of slab E (Fig. 15.5).[47] The adjacent figures are omitted, indicating that the Ephesos relief was not a straight copy of E.

Slab D (Fig. 15.4) depicts the abduction of a woman on the left and the pursuit of another woman in the center, while a little girl looks on. The men here are dressed in short *chitons,* and the one at the left wears a *chlamys.* The figures move on a rocky ground line, indicating an open-air location. The ground line is probably a pictorial element introduced for stylis-

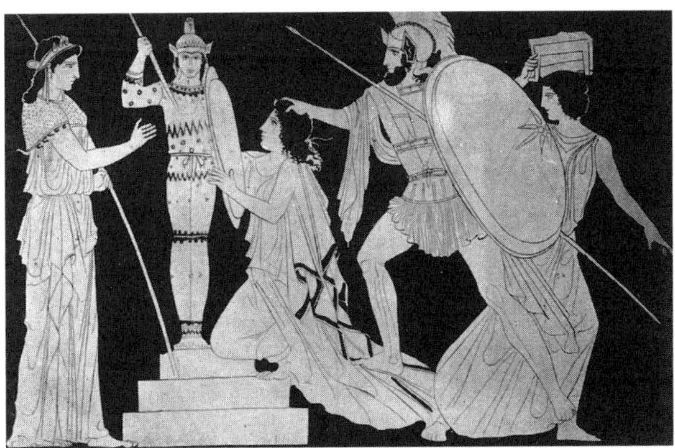

FIGURE 15.14. *Attic red-figure amphora. Aias and Kassandra. Cambridge, Corpus Christi College. After J. Davreux,* La Légende de la prophétesse Cassandre *(Paris 1942), fig. 49.*

tic rather than iconographical reasons. Slab E (Fig. 15.5) retains the irregular ground line, even though set in a shrine. The kneeling woman on the right clasps a columnar statue base, seeking sanctuary. She wears an ungirt *peplos,* leaving her left side bare. The base has lost its statue, presumably already plundered. A warrior wearing a pilos helmet and a chlamys is about to drag her away from the base. At the other end, a bareheaded warrior in chlamys seizes a woman who has climbed a rock to escape. In the center, a woman kneels with hands raised, being dragged by a striding man in short chiton, who carries a little girl, perhaps the woman's daughter. The striding man's lower legs were freestanding and are now broken off. The background of the relief between his legs is smooth, indicating that no drapery is missing here. The outer legs of the men at either end were freestanding, and the head and neck of the woman on the rock were carved separately and attached. Slabs D and E may be grouped with one side of the corner block Athens, National Museum 3941 (Fig. 15.7), depicting a fleeing figure on the left, while another figure sits precariously on a rock on the right, perhaps being attacked by someone from behind. This scene may be interpreted as another assault.

Von Schneider (1903) identified slab E (Fig. 15.5) with the Ilioupersis, recognizing Kassandra in the woman taking refuge at the column. Felten (1984) and Krumme (1993) also favored the Ilioupersis motif. The obvious difficulty here is that the men carry no weapons, although outrages against women and children are indeed the main motif of the Fall of Troy. The group by the empty statue base has a pictorial parallel on an Attic red-figure amphora of the mid fifth century in Corpus Christi College, Cambridge (Fig. 15.14).[48] Their poses and Kassandra's half-open peplos are strikingly close to slab E. Kassandra taking refuge at an empty columnar base, pursued by Aias, is a frequent motif on Roman glass ringstones.[49]

Von Schneider thought that slab D represents the rape of the daughters of Leukippos by the Dioskouroi. Even though only one of them wears a pilos, this interpretation was revived by von Eickstedt (1994), who, following in the footsteps of Travlos, attributed the Ilissos temple to Artemis Agrotera.[50] During her annual festival, the Athenians commemorated the defeat of the Persians at Marathon.[51] Von Eickstedt detected political connotations in the Leukippids episode, attributing the choice of the Dioskouroi motif to the Athenian conservatives, who did not wish to downplay Sparta's contribution to the final expulsion of the Persians from Greece.

The Dioskouroi motif also appealed to Brueckner (1910), who suggested that slabs D and E tell the story of Tyndareos, Helen, and the Dioskouroi. He reversed the traditional order, setting E first, and suggested that it represented Tyndareos and his family fleeing Sparta on account of Hippokoon. He placed Tyndareos in the center, with little Helen in his arms and pulling his wife Leda, and the Dioskouroi at either end, coercing their wives to follow them. He interpreted slab D as the Dioskouroi liberating Helen from Aphidna, where Theseus held her captive. The running woman he identified with Aithra, whom Theseus had asked to look after Helen. Since he also believed that slab B shows Theseus and Peirithoös in the Underworld,[52] he tried to associate all sides of the frieze with the Athenian hero Theseus.

Studniczka (1916), followed by Möbius (1935–1936) and Beschi (2002), offered another variation on the theme of the abduction of women. According to Herodotos (6.137–139), the Athenians exiled the Pelasgians to Lemnos, whence they eventually returned to take their revenge by abducting the Athenian women at Brauron. Möbius arbitrarily associated the abduction of women with the Lesser Eleusinian Mysteries at

Agrai. According to Delivorrias, the abduction in slab D (Fig. 15.4) represents the rape of Oreithyia by Boreas, whose altar was in the area, but he did not try to make sense of the rest of the frieze.[53]

Finally, the other side of the corner block Athens, National Museum 3941 depicts two hoplites charging to the right (Fig. 15.8). The hoplite on the left steps on a rock, carrying a round shield and wearing a crested helmet. There is not enough evidence to identify the battle scene, but we have gained a third theme for the Ilissos frieze.

All interpretations of the Ilissos frieze are bound to sound arbitrary since only a fraction of the material has come down to us. If we discount the slab drawn by Stuart and Revett, we are still in the dark about the subject of the fourth side of the frieze. The composition of the extant slabs seems indebted to pictorial prototypes, and the inspiration probably came from the epics. On the present state of the evidence, it seems to me that two sides of the Ilissos frieze deal with the aftermath of the Trojan War: Troy Taken and Odysseus' Visit to Hades. Slabs A–C (Figs. 15.1–3, 15.6) are decorated with an Underworld scene reminiscent of Polygnotos' *Nekyia,* while the assaults on women in D, E (Figs. 15.4–5), and possibly in Athens, National Museum 3941 (Fig. 15.8), may well belong to an Iliouperis. Polygnotos' *Iliouperis* indeed formed a pendant to his *Nekyia* in the Lesche of the Knidians.[54] The Trojan theme, which was the mythological equivalent of the Persian Wars, might imply that the owner of the Ilissos temple was Artemis Agrotera, whose annual festival celebrated the Athenian victory at Marathon.[55] In addition, if the dating of the Ilissos temple to the late 430s and early 420s is correct, a war theme, combined with a descent into the Underworld, is appropriate to a temple built in the opening years of the Peloponnesian War and seems to match the martial iconography of the Athena Nike temple to be discussed below.

THE NIKE TEMPLE

Even though the friezes of the temple of Athena Nike are better preserved, their iconography is a vexing question. All four friezes of the Nike temple need to be studied together as part of a single iconographic program.[56] Meanwhile, it is good to reexamine the problems and perhaps add a few observations on the iconography of the east frieze (Figs. 15.15–18). If it has defied a generally acceptable interpretation, that is mainly because it consists of a row of figures, facing the spectator. There is no action. Scholars tend to look to the friezes on the other sides for inspiration. All three are battle pieces, each having a character of its own. The south frieze is the most straightforward, showing a battle between Greeks and Persians, therefore, an historic event.[57] The west and north friezes represent battles between Greeks. Blümel reached the conclusion that the south side evokes the Persian Wars, whereas the west and north allude to the Peloponnesian War.[58]

The question arises, Does the south frieze show the battle of Marathon, Athens' greatest moment of glory? Or does the presence of horses preclude that, and are we looking at the battle of Plataia instead, as is sometimes argued? There is nothing in Herodotos about the Persians not using their cavalry, and Pausanias (1.32.4) records an ancient tradition that every night, a ghost battle could be heard at Marathon, which included the sound of horses. The theory that the Athenians attacked the Persians at Marathon after the bulk of their cavalry had been shipped off to Phaleron is a modern construct based on Suda, s.v. χωρὶς ἱππεῖς (without cavalry).[59] Considering that the frieze of the Nike temple was carved during the Peloponnesian War, why would the Athenians wish to commemorate the Spartan contribution to a joint victory? One would expect them to celebrate their own exploits, both mythical and historical.

Hölscher tried to avoid the issue by suggesting that the south frieze represents a generic battle between Greeks and Persians.[60] Harrison argued that the Persian cavalry joined the action at Marathon, based on the Persians' remark recorded by Herodotos (6.112) that the Athenians must be mad to charge them without cavalry or archers.[61] This she took as an implication that the Persians had both. Her attempt to name the figures on the south frieze by comparison to Pausanias' (1.15.3–4) description of the Marathon painting in the

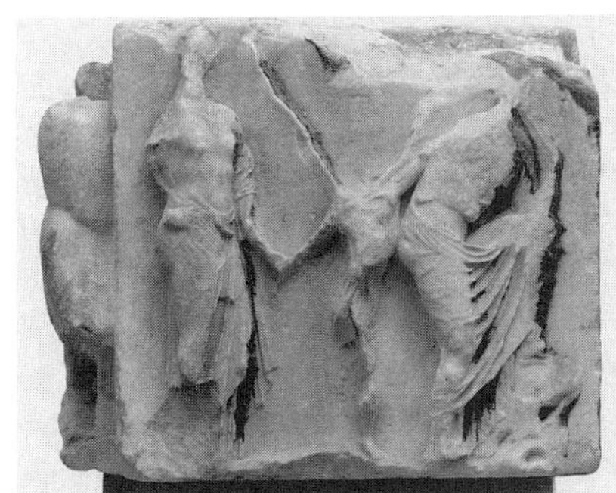

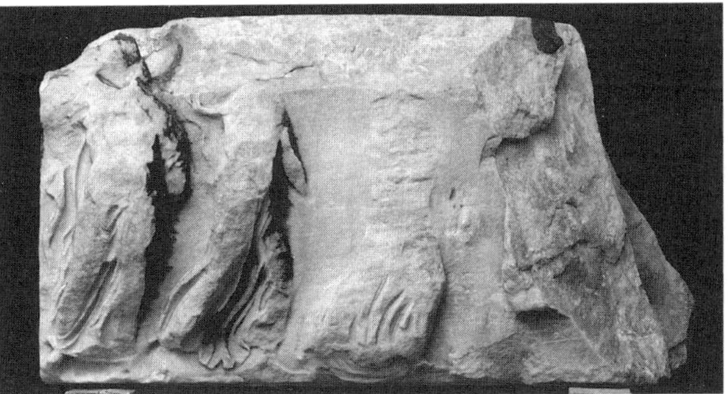

FIGURE 15.15 (LEFT). *East frieze of the temple of Athena Nike. Peitho, Eros, Aphrodite. Akropolis Museum 18135. Photo: Sokratis Mavrommatis.*

FIGURE 15.16 (RIGHT). *East frieze of the temple of Athena Nike. Three Graces, Eurynome. Akropolis Museum 18136. Photo: Sokratis Mavrommatis.*

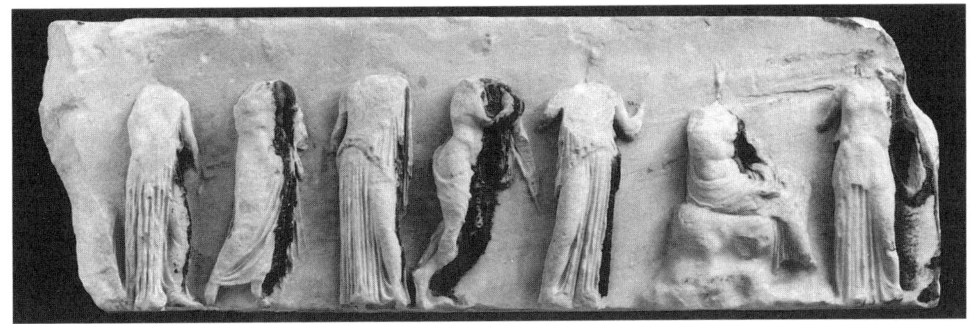

FIGURE 15.17. *East frieze of the temple of Athena Nike. Leto, Apollo, Artemis, Dionysos, Amphitrite, Poseidon, Athena. Akropolis Museum 18137. Photo: Sokratis Mavrommatis.*

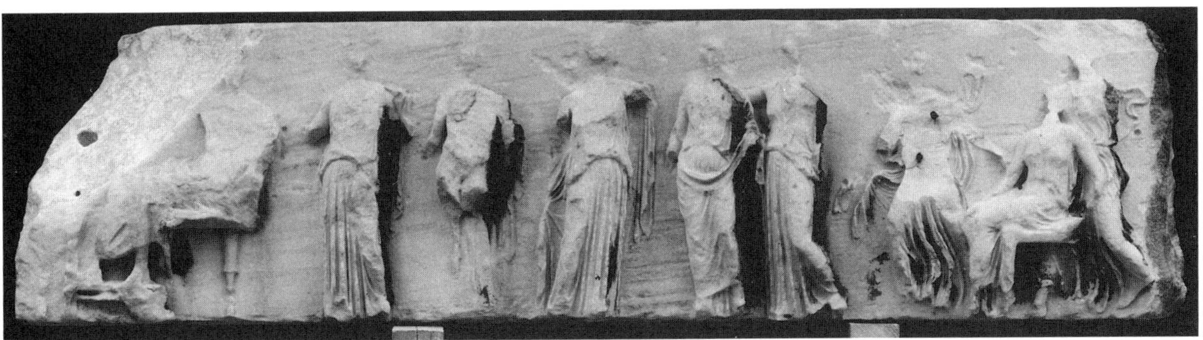

FIGURE 15.18. *East frieze of the temple of Athena Nike. Hephaistos, Zeus, Hera, Hermes, Hygieia, Kore, Demeter, two Horai with Themis. Akropolis Museum 18138. Photo: Sokratis Mavrommatis.*

Stoa Poikile in Athens, however, stretches the evidence and weakens her argument. Nevertheless, this is still the only frieze that can be confidently associated with an historic war.

The battles raging on the west and north sides have been variously labeled mythical or historical. It has been argued that the historic relief had not yet been invented in the Classical period. If, however, there are paintings of historic battles in the fifth century,[62] why not friezes?

Little survives of the north frieze of the Nike temple. The bottom of a fragmentary slab includes an enigmatic scene of men surrounding a large stand, which has been interpreted as the foot of a large vessel.[63] It is,

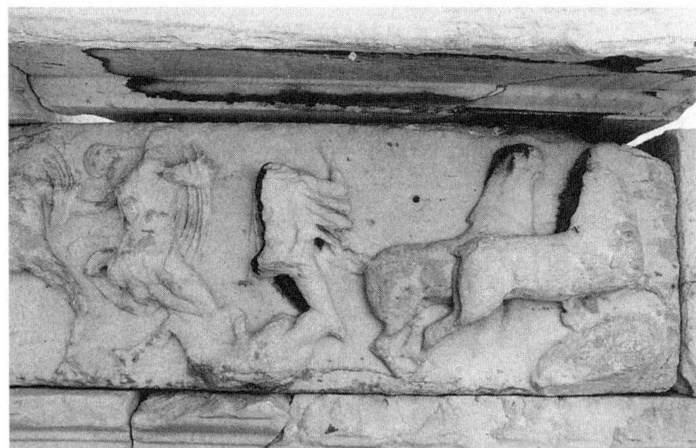

FIGURE 15.19. *North frieze of the temple of Athena Nike. Akropolis Museum 18140. Photo: Deutsches Archäologisches Institut, Athens, neg. nr. 89/277.*

however, too damaged to allow identification. So much is missing here that one suspects that the figures were largely freestanding. The only complete slab represents a fight raging over a pile of bodies, as well as the pursuit and capture of a bearded hero who sheds his Corinthian helmet in his flight.[64] Two riderless horses gallop away over a fallen shield. A hole in the background above the rear horse may have served for the attachment of separately carved baggage (Fig. 15.19).[65] The impression is of a fugitive hero intercepted. The presence of horses suggested to Hölscher a battle between the Athenians and the Boiotian cavalry.[66] Furtwängler associated all battle friezes with Plataia, placing the conflict with the Boiotian allies of the Persians on the north side.[67] Felten argued that the team of horses was harnessed to a chariot, once painted in the background.[68] As the chariot implies Homeric combat, he reached the conclusion that all three sides represent the Trojan War.[69] There is, however, no room behind the horses for a chariot, painted or not. One cannot visualize it on top of the horses, either.

According to Felten, the Persians in the south frieze should be the followers of Memnon, the last great opponent of Achilles, who was based at Susa. He identified Memnon with the owner of the Corinthian helmet. Memnon, however, was king of Aithiopia, and Attic iconography always portrays his followers as black.[70] In describing Polygnotos' *Nekyia* in the Lesche of the Knidians, Pausanias (10.31.7) points out that Memnon was accompanied by a black slave, being king of Aithiopia. He had, nevertheless, he says, made his way to Troy via Susa, thanks to his conquests. Harrison, on the other hand, believed that the north and west friezes represent the heroic exploits of Theseus. She, too, saw the hero with the Corinthian helmet as a fugitive, identifying him as Eurystheus, killed by Theseus and the Athenians near the Isthmus of Corinth. She associated the hypothetical large vessel on the fragmentary slab with a fountain-house scene, pointing out that Eurystheus was buried beside the Makaria fountain.[71] It seems to me that the safest way to argue in favor of a mythical episode is to point to the Corinthian helmet: as it became obsolete after the Persian Wars, its appearance in Classical art was an indication of times past.[72]

The west frieze represents hoplite combat between Greeks.[73] It is remarkable for the many corpses scattered in the field and for the trophy set in the middle of the battlefield. Pemberton attempted an historical interpretation, associating the west frieze with the victory of the Athenians, led by the Marathon veteran Myronides, over the Corinthians at Megara in 458.[74] As they fought over the same battleground twice in a short period of time, she assumed the existence of a trophy in the field. Harrison preferred to see here another exploit of Theseus.[75] She believed that the key to the interpretation lies in the slain warriors, and, calculating that the frieze contained seven corpses, she suggested that it represents the retrieval of the corpses of the Seven against Thebes. It is more likely, however, that a hoplite battle punctuated by a trophy refers to an historic Athenian victory against the Spartans. As the west frieze greeted visitors ascending the Akropolis, one would expect the Athenians to have used the space to glorify themselves with a topical allusion to a significant historic event. If the enigmatic battle between Athenians and Spartans at Oinoe, commemorated by a painting in the Stoa Poikile (Paus. 1.15.1), which formed a pendant to the battle of Marathon, was an historic event of the Archaic period, it may well have been depicted here.

The divine assembly in the east frieze (Figs. 15.15–18)[76] tends to be interpreted in the light of the action in the other friezes. Advocates of the view that all battle scenes belong to a single war also maintain that the gods are debating its outcome. Furtwängler saw the gods as supporting the Greek cause against Persia,[77] whereas Jeppesen thought of them deliberating over the fate of Troy.[78] Kardara read the scene as an assembly celebrating Athena's victory over Poseidon, their contest over Attika forming a divine counterpart to the war of Erechtheus against the invading Eleusinians and their Thracian allies in the other three friezes.[79] According to Felten, the east frieze shows the judgment of the souls of Achilles and Memnon, who are fighting a duel on the north side.[80] Simon[81] and Harrison[82] suggested that the divine gathering glorifies the martial qualities of Athena, who presides over the Athenian victories on the other sides.

There is general consensus over the figures at the extreme left of the east frieze (Fig. 15.15). Second from the left stands Eros with his mother Aphrodite. She rests her foot on a rock, perhaps a topographical allusion. The sanctuary of Aphrodite Pandemos was situated on the south slope of the Akropolis, not far from the Nike bastion.[83] As she shared her cult with Peitho, this goddess is placed on the other side of Eros. Aphrodite Pandemos played an important role in the unification of Attika under Theseus, and Peitho's gifts of persuasion were crucial to the democracy.[84]

The dancing triad that follows (Fig. 15.16) has been variously identified as the Horai[85] or the Graces, with the evidence pointing more in the direction of the Graces.[86] They had a sanctuary in the vicinity of the Athena Nike temple, perhaps directly to the east, and often served as personal companions to Athena.[87] Simon identified the adjacent seated figure as Eurynome, mother of the Graces.[88] Felten preferred to see here Eos, Memnon's mother, attending the weighing of his soul.[89] Harrison suggested Hestia because she is usually shown seated.[90] If the frieze depicted the weighing of souls, one would expect the mother of the victor to sit to the left of the axis, and so Eos is ruled out. The divine triad (Fig. 15.17) of a man standing between two women is generally thought to represent Leto, Apollo, and Artemis, though Artemis carries no bow.[91] Jeppesen is alone in thinking that the triad depicts Triptolemos between Kore and Demeter.[92]

Next comes a slim youth resting on a rather flimsy, knobbly stick (Fig. 15.17). Its bottom was probably freestanding and is broken off. He leans far out of balance, legs crossed, his himation slipping off his body in a nonchalant attitude, which starkly contrasts with the rather formal appearance of the assembly. His left hand rests on the stick, while he holds out a bunched part of his himation in his right. His nature is rather different from that of the other gods. But how different? Several commentators focused on him as a key to the composition. Already in the nineteenth century, Furtwängler identified him as Theseus.[93] He was followed by Simon,[94] who pointed out, however, that the scene cannot be an introduction to Olympos since Theseus never attained divine status. Harrison believed that Theseus' presence here is related to his role in the battle of Marathon and in the mythical battles of the west and north sides.[95] On the other hand, Jeppesen argued that the stick signifies the lameness of Hephaistos.[96] Felten suggested Ares instead.[97] If so, why is he unarmed? Theseus has no place in a divine assembly. If this figure is a maverick, it must be that he is a non-Olympian god. Dionysos, usually relegated to the missing portion of the frieze, would be better placed here. His unstable pose and seminudity imply a drunken reveler. A very similar Dionysos appears on a Paestan bell krater of the fourth century in London (Fig. 15.20).[98]

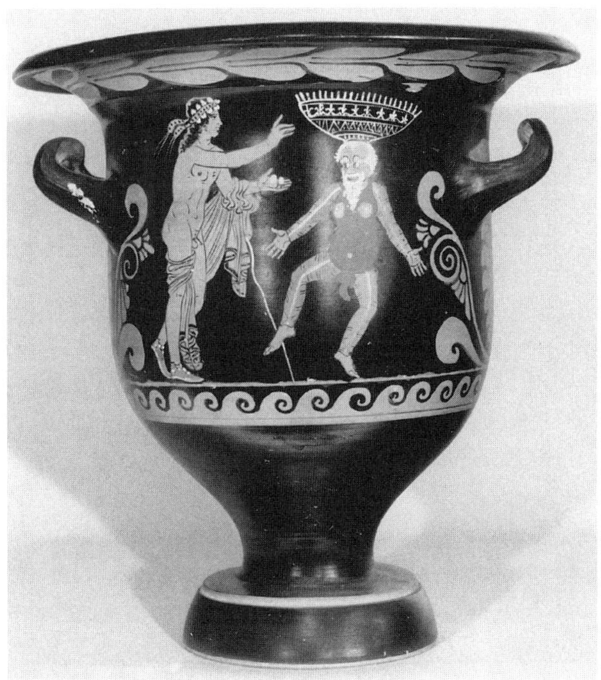

FIGURE 15.20. *Paestan bell krater. Dionysos and phlyax. British Museum F 188. Photo courtesy of the Trustees of the British Museum, © Copyright The British Museum.*

Athena dominates the center of the scene (Fig. 15.17). She was presumably fully armed, even though only her aegis and shield survive. Poseidon sits on a rock to the (spectator's) left of the goddess, with his wife Amphitrite standing behind him. The rock is an attribute of the chthonic fatherly god, while heavenly Zeus to the (spectator's) right of Athena sits on a throne, with his wife, Hera, standing behind him (Fig. 15.18).

The battered remains of a figure between Zeus and Athena have been the subject of controversy. Is it animal or mineral? Furtwängler thought he could see a table of offerings;[99] Kardara[100] and Simon[101] believed it to be a trophy. Close inspection of the stone reveals a naked left leg disappearing behind Zeus' footstool.[102] The outline of the right lower leg can also be made out on the stone. Felten attributed the leg to Hermes, whom he envisaged as holding the scales weighing the souls of Achilles and Memnon.[103] Such a scene would have much in common with the east frieze of the Siphnian Treasury.[104] Both Jeppesen[105] and Harrison[106] placed Ares here to reinforce the martial aspect of Athena, who would thus become Athena Areia. There is, however, no such cult of Athena on the Akropolis. It should also be pointed out that the Greeks did not love Ares and consequently tended not to give him pride of place in their art. The naked leg precludes Nike. The figure next to Athena must have been male. A new suggestion as to his identity will be put forward at the conclusion of this paper.

The god and goddess standing to the right of Hera are among the most uncertain figures in the frieze (Fig. 15.18). Kore and Demeter are usually recognized as the pair, embracing one another to their right. The unidentified god wears a himation hanging down his back and has lost his attributes, while the goddess wears an Argive peplos and seems to be revealing herself by lifting the left edge of her himation. Felten named them Hephaistos and Hekate because they are flanked by Hera and Demeter.[107] Simon thought they are Ares and Nemesis and connected them with the battle of Marathon, where Nemesis played a seminal role by punishing the *hybris* of the Persians.[108] Harrison argued that the male figure would have worn a now-missing lion skin on top of his cloak and could therefore be Herakles, accompanied by his wife, Hebe.[109] But no trace of the putative lion skin can be detected on the stone.

I think that Hermes is as good a candidate as any for the male god.[110] He is strategically placed facing the entrance to the Akropolis, which housed the sculpture of Hermes Propylaios, guardian of the gates.[111] The goddess revealing herself is clearly not paired with him but stands alone. Her gesture, often made by brides, also implies divine epiphany. Her iconography recalls Hygieia on two contemporary votive reliefs of Hygieia and Asklepios, one probably from Athens, now in Copenhagen,[112] and the other from the Athenian Asklepieion.[113] Before the advent of Asklepios to the south slope in 420/19, Hygieia was worshiped on the Akropolis as a manifestation of Athena (Athena Hygieia).[114] A number of Meidian vases of the final decades of the fifth century include Hygieia in the retinue of Aphrodite, often in wedding and courtship scenes, symbolizing good health for the bride. On two Meidian vases in London, Hygieia is characterized by the bridal gesture of lifting the edge of her drapery over her shoulder: a hydria depicting the Garden of the Hesperides[115] and a squat lekythos, on which Hygieia herself is the bride.[116] Her appearance in the Garden of the Hesperides is an intimation of immortality. If the figure in the Nike temple frieze is Hygieia, then she seems to be facing her sanctuary, located within the Propylaia. But what is Hygieia doing in the east frieze of the Athena Nike temple? This of course depends on the theme represented.

The final triad in the frieze, consisting of two dancers flanking a seated figure, has been variously interpreted. Jeppesen identified the figures to the right of Zeus as Apollo, Artemis, Leto, and the Muses.[117] Felten recognized the seated figure as Thetis, the mother of Achilles, whose soul was being weighed in the central scene.[118] He suggested that she is flanked by a pair of Nereids. According to Simon, the dancers could be the Horai with their mother Themis.[119] Harrison identified the triad with the Aglaurids and went so far as to suggest that the missing figures on the right would have represented the birth of Erichthonios, with Ge holding the infant in the presence of his father, Hephaistos, and Hermes.[120] She did not try to connect the birth scene with the central theme of the frieze, which according to her, amounts to a celebration of Athena Areia.

The time has come for an alternative view of the east frieze. The key lies in the composition, which consists of an array of widely spaced frontal figures. This compositional device seems to have been introduced in Classical sculpture by Pheidias, who adopted it for the statue base of his Athena Parthenos. He represented the birth of Pandora by means of a row of quietly standing figures bestowing their gifts on her.[121] A similar composition may be postulated for the birth of Aphrodite, depicted by Pheidias on the statue base of his Zeus.[122] Agorakritos employed a similar schema on the statue base of his Nemesis, which contained the equivalent of a birth scene.[123] Despinis has convincingly connected the style of the east frieze of the Nike temple with Agorakritos on the basis of its similarities to the Nemesis base.[124] A parallel can readily be drawn between the iconography and style of the bases of the Pheidian school and the east frieze. As the bases were decorated with birth scenes, could the frieze too depict a birth scene?

The iconography of the birth of Athena was revolutionized by the east pediment of the Parthenon, which would have barely been installed when the Athena Nike temple was begun. The novelty introduced by the sculptor who designed the pediment is the full-sized Athena standing on Zeus' side rather than springing from his head in miniature form, as was the norm in Attic vase painting.[125] Whether Zeus was standing or seated is a question still unresolved.[126] The Olympian and other gods, including Hera, who is usually restored in a prominent position beside Zeus, even though she was not Athena's mother, attend Athena's birth. Hephaistos is, of course, the other key figure in this event, since he split open Zeus' skull with his axe. He is therefore always depicted near the main characters, though he does not seem to have occupied a specific position. The Classical iconography of Athena's birth is so limited that it is hard to establish a canon. We do not know where Hephaistos stood in relation to Athena and Zeus in the east pediment of the Parthenon because the central scene is lost. In the birth scene on the Madrid puteal, probably after a fourth-century prototype, Zeus is placed between Athena and Hephaistos.[127] Assuming that the archaistic Four Gods base on the Akropolis also depicts the birth of Athena, then Hephaistos stands between Athena and Zeus.[128]

If we take another look at the east frieze of the Nike temple, what do we see but an armed Athena to the (spectator's) left of a seated Zeus, who is accompanied by his divine consort? The crucial figure here is the missing god between Athena and Zeus. I believe that his identity would resolve the issue. If we restore Hephaistos in this position, then it would be possible to interpret the scene as a birth of Athena. His nudity is no obstacle. Hephaistos is nearly naked on an Attic red-figure stamnos of the second quarter of the fifth century with the birth of Erichthonios[129] and on the Madrid puteal.[130] The appearance of the Graces and the Horai near the two edges of the frieze may well point to a birth scene.[131] The Graces, the Horai, and Peitho all attended the creation of Pandora, while Peitho was present at the birth of Aphrodite on Pheidias' base of Zeus.[132] Hygieia too would be welcome in a birth scene, bestowing the gifts of good health and immortality. What of the missing figures at the north end of the frieze? A third dancing Hora could be restored here, perhaps accompanied by Ares, as a counterpart to Aphrodite at the other end,[133] as well as Hekate, who had a cult on this side of the Nike bastion.[134] The presence of deities with cults in the vicinity of the Nike temple (Aphrodite, Peitho, the Graces, Hermes, Hygieia, and Hekate) would add a topical flavor to the scene, thus setting it off from its immediate precursor in the east pediment of the Parthenon.

CONCLUSION

The Ilissos and Nike temples, along with the Parthenon, are the only Classical temples with continuous friezes known to us from the 440s to the 420s. Having no precedents, they would have set the rules. It may well be argued that each adopted a different schema for its iconographical program. For if Athena's birth was depicted in the east frieze of the Nike temple, it could have no immediate bearing on the iconography of the west, south, and north friezes, except in driving home the message that Athena Nike had crowned Athenian ventures, past and present, with victory. If the friezes of the Ilissos temple illustrated the Trojan cycle, on the other hand, they would have followed the opposite pattern by conforming to a unified theme. Both temples provided alternatives to the Parthenon, which adopted a single subject for its entire frieze. Nothing but variety would do. Finally, assuming that both the Ilissos and the Athena Nike temples were built during the first phase of the Peloponnesian War, their attitudes to the conflict were remarkably different. The sad introspection (atrocities to civilians, the gloom of the afterlife) of the Ilissos friezes forms a sharp contrast to the triumphal mood of the sculpted decoration of the Athena Nike temple.

NOTES

I am grateful to Judy Barringer and Jeff Hurwit for the opportunity to offer a small tribute to a good friend and a great master of style, who has opened up new avenues in the study of ancient art.

Thanks are due to Kurt Gschwantler for facilitating inspection of two parts of the Ilissos frieze while it was in storage in the Kunsthistorisches Museum in Vienna. I am grateful to Manolis Korres for his assistance with matters technical and chronological and for examining the fragments Athens, National Museum 1780 and 3941 with me, dispelling all doubts that they belong to the Ilissos temple. Kevin Clinton gave essential advice on questions relating to the Eleusinian Mysteries, and John Boardman, on the iconography of Memnon. Hans R. Goette kindly provided new photos taken especially for this article and discussed the Ilissos frieze in Vienna with me. Last but not least, I am grateful to Helmut Kyrieleis for the hospitality of the German Archaeological Institute in Berlin and to Christina Vlassopoulou of the Akropolis Ephoreia for the photos that are Figures 15–18.

1. First attributed to the same architect by Ross et al. 1839, 10–11. See also I. M. Shear 1963, 389; Giraud 1994, 38–43. That the Ilissos temple was built of Pentelic marble is attested by Stuart and Revett 1762, ch. II.

2. Korres 1996, 104–109.

3. Korres 1996, 112–113, n. 70, fig. 35.

4. Korres 1996, 112–113, nn. 72–74; Korres 2000, 30, figs. 29–30.

5. Vlassopoulou 2002. Not only do the dancing figures on this frieze recall the dancers on the east frieze of the Athena Nike temple but there are instances of piecing of projecting members similar to the west frieze of that temple.

6. Schultz 2001, 1, n. 2, with earlier references.

7. For various views on the date of the Ilissos temple, see Picón 1978; Krug 1979; Miles 1980; Wesenberg 1981; Childs 1985; Giraud 1994, 40; von Eickstedt 1994; Korres 2000, 30.

8. The similarity is explained and illustrated by Schrader 1932, 175–178, figs. 19–22. The Ilissos temple dated to the decade 430–420: Picón 1978; Krug 1979; Korres 2000, 30. For the date of Pheidias' Zeus, cf. Palagia 2000, 53, n. 2.

9. Stuart and Revett 1762, ch. II; Judeich 1931, 420–421; Travlos, *Athens,* 112–120; Picón 1978, 47–48; Wycherley 1978, 171.

10. Stuart and Revett 1762, pl. 6.

11. Studniczka 1916, 188–189, fig. 1; Krug 1979, 15, figs. 3–4.

12. Möbius 1928, 1–6, fig. 1.

13. Stuart and Revett 1762, pl. 6, incorporating the lost relief: slab Ht., 44.87 cm; Th., 3.81 cm. In Stuart and Revett 1762, pl. 8, the measurements of the slabs are Ht., 46.8 cm; Th., 5.8 cm.

14. Möbius 1935–1936, 262; Krumme 1993, 214; Beschi 2002, 16.

15. The dimensions of slabs B–E are Ht., 46.6–46.8 cm; W., 90–95 cm; Th., 5.1–5.7 cm. For the dimensions in Stuart and Revett 1762, pl. 8, see above, n. 13. See also Picón 1978, 49, with n. 10. For illustrated catalogues of the slabs and fragments, see Studniczka 1916, 171–186; Blümel 1966, 88–90, no. 107; Picón 1978, 51–59; Krug 1979, 8–17.

16. Athens, National Museum 1780. Parian marble. Ht., 24 cm; W., 23 cm; Th., 6.5 cm; scamillus, 1 cm; Ht. of leg, 7.1 cm. Skias 1897, 82, pl. A; Studniczka 1916, 171–172, fig. 2; Krug 1979, 8–9, pl. 7:b.

17. Blümel 1966, 88–89; Picón 1978, 51–55, fig. 4.

18. Studniczka 1916, 183.

19. Dinsmoor 1975, 185, n. 1; Blümel 1966, 88; Picón 1978, 49–50, with n. 11. The heads and other parts of the figures on these slabs were restored in the seventeenth century. The restorations were removed in the early twentieth century. Beschi 2002, 14, with n. 21, fig. 4.

20. Athens, National Museum 3941. Ht., 46 cm; W., 47 cm; Th., 43 cm. Skias 1894, 140–142, pl. 8:B–C; Möbius 1928, 1–6; Krug 1979, 15–17, pl. 9:a–b.

21. Palagia 2000.

22. For a discussion of the baggage, see Studniczka 1916, 174–178; Beschi 2002, 17; cf. comparanda in Chamay 1977.

23. Picón 1978, 64.

24. Cf. the examples cited in Chamay 1977.

25. Staatliche Museen 3284; Bieber 1961, fig. 207; Chamay 1977, 59, fig. 3.

26. British Museum GR1861.5–23.1; Walker 1989b, 138, pl. 51.

27. Collected in Chamay 1977.

28. British Museum F151; Studniczka 1916, 175–176; Trendall and Webster 1971, IV, 35; Green and Handley 1995, 53, fig. 28; Boardman 2001, 116, fig. 152.

29. Museo Archeologico 2970; Trendall and Webster 1971, IV, 20.

30. Staatliche Antikensammlungen 2592; Immerwahr 1992, 124, pl. 31a.

31. Athens, National Museum 11036; Mylonas 1961, 213–221, fig. 88; Clinton 1992, 67–68, 73–75, 136, frontispiece. Clinton (1992, 74, n. 60) suggests that the sacks contained the piglet offered to the goddesses.

32. Rome, Palazzo Borghese (Spanish Embassy). From Torre Nuova; said to be originally from Ephesos. Mid second century A.D. Studniczka 1916, 174, fig. 4; Krug 1979, 10–11, fig. 10; Koch and Sichtermann 1982, 501–502, fig. 484; Clinton 1992, 137, no. 6; Krumme 1993, 216, fig. 4. See also below, n. 37.

33. On Polygnotos' paintings in the Lesche of the Knidians, see Robertson 1975, 266–270; Kebric 1983; Stansbury-O'Donnell 1999, 178–190.

34. Metropolitan Museum of Art 08.258.21; *ARV*[2] 1086, 1; *Addenda*[2] 327; Richter and Hall 1936, no. 135; W. Felten 1975, 83–84, fig. 27; Boardman 1989a, fig. 184; *LIMC* 8, s.v. Nekyia, no. 13 [F. Felten and I. Krauskopf].

35. Museum of Fine Arts 34.79; *ARV*[2] 1045, 2; *Addenda*[2] 320; Caskey and Beazley 1954, no. 111, pl. 63, suppl. pl. 1; Touchefeu-Meynier 1968, no. 227, pl. 21:1; W. Felten 1975, fig. 18; Boardman 1989a, fig. 150; *LIMC* 6, s.v. Odysseus, no. 149 [Touchefeu-Meynier].

36. Cabinet des Médailles 422; Touchefeu-Meynier 1968, no. 228, pl. 21:2; W. Felten and Krauskopf 1997, no. 2.

37. Brueckner 1910; Hauser 1910, 281. Beschi (2002, 20) noticed the travelers' equipment and interpreted the scene as the Pelasgians on their way to exile.

38. Boardman 1985 (rev. 1991), fig. 239:3; *LIMC* 7, s.v. Perithoos, no. 83 [E. Manakidou]. For further representations of the pair in Hades, see *LIMC* 7, s.v. Perithoos, nos. 73–84 [E. Manakidou].

39. Pl. *Grg.* 493c; Pl. *Resp.* 2.363d. Keuls 1974, 25–41; Albinus 2000, 133–134.

40. Möbius 1935–1936. For the topography of Agrai, see Judeich 1931, 420–421.

41. Plut. *Demetr.* 26.2; Suda, s.v. Agra. See also Chantraine 1956; Mylonas 1961, 240. Möbius (1935–1936) placed the Lesser Mysteries in the Metroon at Agrai, for which very little evidence exists. This view goes back to Spon 1678, 210, and was criticized by Stuart and Revett 1762, ch. II.

42. Möbius 1964, 38–39. The Eleusinian connection is also rejected by Clinton 1992, 137, no. 6.

43. For the location of this shrine, see Judeich 1931, 421; Krumme 1993.

44. Athens, Epigraphical Museum 6595; *IG* I[3] 68; Lawton 1995, 81, no. 1, pl. 1.

45. Also suggested by Studniczka 1916, 171.

46. F. Felten 1984, 78.

47. Vienna, Kunsthistorisches Museum I 868; Picón 1978, 59–60, figs. 12–13; Krug 1979, 14–15, fig. 11; Krumme 1993, 215, fig. 2.

48. *ARV*[2] 1058, 114; *Addenda*[2] 323; Touchefeu-Meynier 1981, no. 54; Mangold 2000, 55, 173, cat. II 61, fig. 33.

49. Brandt 1972, no. 3216, pl. 309.

50. Travlos, *Athens,* 112–120.

51. Celebrated in Boedromion: Deubner 1932, 209. Cf. also Pemberton 1972, 307–308.

52. Above, pp. 180–182.

53. Delivorrias 1974, 131, n. 566.

54. Paus. 10.25–27. See also above, n. 33.

55. Above, n. 51. On the attribution of the Ilissos temple to Artemis Agrotera, see also Beschi 2002, 30–35.

56. A doctoral dissertation on this topic by Peter Schultz was accepted by the University of Athens in 2003.

57. London, British Museum and Athens, Akropolis Museum; F. Felten 1984, pl. 47:2; Trianti 1998, figs. 398–400.

58. Blümel 1950–1951, 154.

59. A. R. Burn 1984, 247–248; P. Green 1996, 34–35.

60. Hölscher 1973, 91–98.

61. E. B. Harrison 1972b, 353–354.

62. See Boardman, Castriota, and Stansbury-O'Donnell in this volume.

63. Athens, Akropolis Museum 18143; F. Felten 1984, pl. 47:3; Trianti 1998, fig. 395.

64. Akropolis Museum 18140; E. B. Harrison 1997, figs. 16–17; Trianti 1998, fig. 394.

65. For a warrior leading a mule with baggage, see the central frieze on the west wall of the heroon of Trysa; Oberleitner 1994, 36, fig. 81.

66. Hölscher 1973, 91–98.

67. Furtwängler 1895, 446–449; followed by Giraud 1994, 263, n. 27.

68. F. Felten 1984, 126; followed by E. B. Harrison 1997, 119.

69. F. Felten 1984, 123–133.

70. Lissarrague 1990b, 21–22; *LIMC* 6, s.v. Memnon, 448–449, 460, nos. 5–10, 14, 61, 93 [A. Kossatz-Deissmann]; Bérard 2000, 395–402.

71. E. B. Harrison 1997, 119–120.

72. Implying a heroic or mythological era: cf. E. R. Knauer 1992, 394–395; Ridgway 1997, 72, n. 69.

73. London, British Museum and Athens, Akropolis Museum; F. Felten 1984, pl. 47:4; E. B. Harrison 1997, figs. 18–19, 21–22; Trianti 1998, figs. 396–397.

74. Pemberton 1972, 304–307.

75. E. B. Harrison 1997, 120–122.

76. Athens, Akropolis Museum 18135, 18137, 18138; Trianti 1998, figs. 386–393.

77. Furtwängler 1895, 448–449.

78. Jeppesen 1963, 91–96.

79. Kardara 1961, 84–90.

80. F. Felten 1984, 123–133.

81. Simon 1985–1986, 30–31.

82. E. B. Harrison 1997, 116.

83. Paus. 1.22.3. Wycherley 1978, 180; Pirenne-Delforge 1994, 26–34; Stafford 2000, 121–122.

84. Pirenne-Delforge 1988, 151–154; Pirenne-Delforge 1991, 399–403; Shapiro 1993, 186–187; Stafford 2000, 122–129.

85. F. Felten 1984, 130.

86. Pemberton 1972, 309; Simon 1985–1986, 19; *LIMC* 3, s.v. Charis, Charites, no. 22 [E. B. Harrison]; E. B. Harrison 1997, 110.

87. Paus. 1.22.8, 9.35.2–3 and 7. *LIMC* 3, s.v. Charis, Charites, no. 22 [E. B. Harrison]; Palagia 1990, 350–355.

88. Simon 1985–1986, 19.

89. F. Felten 1984, 130.

90. E. B. Harrison 1997, 114–115.

91. So Simon 1985–1986, 18, n. 37. There is no trace of bow on the stone.

92. Jeppesen 1963, 95.

93. Furtwängler 1895, 449.

94. Simon 1985–1986, 17–18.

95. E. B. Harrison 1997, 111.

96. Jeppesen 1963, 94.

97. F. Felten 1984, 130.

98. London, British Museum F 188; Bieber 1961, fig. 536; Trendall 1987, 68, 26, pl. 22:c.

99. Furtwängler 1895, 449.

100. Kardara 1961, 85.

101. Simon 1985–1986, 17, n. 32.

102. F. Felten 1984, 129, n. 433; E. B. Harrison 1997, 112–113; Schultz 2001, 40, n. 136.

103. F. Felten 1984, 129.

104. Boardman 1978b, fig. 212:2; Brinkmann 1994, 139–153.

105. Jeppesen 1963, 93.

106. E. B. Harrison 1997, 113.

107. F. Felten 1984, 130.

108. Simon 1985–1986, 19–20.

109. E. B. Harrison 1997, 113–114.

110. Also suggested by Pemberton 1972, 309.

111. Paus. 1.22.8. *LIMC* 5, s.v. Hermes, 374, no. 345 [G. Siebert]; Chamoux 1996.

112. Ny Carlsberg Glyptotek 1430. Boardman 1985, fig. 171; *LIMC* 5, s.v. Hygeia, no. 53 [F. Croissant]; Moltesen 1995, 132–133; Leventi 2003, 129, R1, pl. 7.

113. Athens, National Museum 1388. Krug 1979, fig. 6; *LIMC* 5, s.v. Hygeia, no. 140 [F. Croissant]; Leventi 2003, 129, R3, pl. 9.

114. Athena Hygieia on the Akropolis: Travlos, *Athens,* 124, fig. 170; Shapiro 1993, 125–128; Parker 1996, 175; Stafford 2000, 151–153; Leventi 2003, 39–45.

115. London, British Museum E224; *ARV*[2] 1313, 5; *Addenda*[2] 361; L. Burn 1987, 36–37, 97, M5, pl. 2:b–3; *LIMC* 5, s.v. Hygeia, no. 1 [F. Croissant]; Shapiro 1993, no. 63, fig. 79; Stafford 2000, 160, fig. 17; Leventi 2003, 156, V1, pl. 50.

116. British Museum E698; *ARV*[2] 1316; *Addenda*[2] 362; L. Burn 1987, P1, pl. 20:c; *LIMC* 5, s.v. Hygeia, no. 52 [F. Croissant]; Shapiro 1993, no. 18, fig. 84; Stafford 2000, 161, fig. 18; Leventi 2003, 156, V4, pl. 51. For other Meidian vases with Hygieia, see Shapiro 1993, 127–131; Stafford 2000, 161–162.

117. Jeppesen 1963, 95.

118. F. Felten 1984, 130.

119. Simon 1985–1986, 19.

120. E. B. Harrison 1997, 114–115.

121. Paus. 1.24.7; Plin. *HN* 36.18. Palagia 2000, 60.

122. Paus. 5.11.8.

123. Paus. 1.33.7–8. Palagia 2000, 63–68.

124. Despinis 1971, 167–169.

125. On the iconography of Athena's birth, see Brommer 1961; *LIMC* 2, s.v. Athena [H. Cassimatis].

126. Palagia 1993, 27–30; Palagia 1997a.

127. Madrid, Museo Arqueológico Nacional 2691. *LIMC* 2, s.v. Athena, no. 373 [H. Cassimatis]; Palagia 1993, 27–30, fig. 8; Palagia 1997a, fig. 4; Sauter 2002, 158–159, figs. 17, 23–24.

128. Athens, Akropolis Museum 610; fourth century B.C. Brahms 1994, 88–96, figs. 9–12; Palagia 1997a, 31, 45, figs. 5–6.

129. Munich, Staatliche Antikensammlungen 2413; *ARV*[2] 495, 1; *Addenda*[2] 250; Boardman 1975a, fig. 350; *LIMC* 4, s.v. Hephaistos, no. 217 [A. Hermary and A. Jacquemin]; Reeder 1995, 255–256, no. 68.

130. Above, n. 127.

131. Graces at birth scenes: *LIMC* 3, s.v. Charis, Charites, 193, nos. 2–4 [E. B. Harrison]. Horai at birth scenes: *LIMC* 5, s.v. Horai, 503 [V. Machaira].

132. Graces, Horai, and Peitho at the birth of Pandora: Hes. *Op.* 73–75. For the Graces with Pandora, see also *LIMC* 3, s.v. Charis, Charites, no. 2 [E. B. Harrison]; Palagia 1990, 356, fig. 18; Palagia 2000, 60, fig. 4:5. Peitho at the birth of Aphrodite: Paus. 5.11.8 (base of Zeus); white-ground pyxis at Ancona, Museo Archeologico Nazionale 3130, *ARV*[2] 899, 144; *Addenda*[2] 303; Shapiro 1993, 199, fig. 160. Peitho at the creation of Pandora: Pirenne-Delforge 1991, 398.

133. So Pemberton 1972, 309.

134. Paus. 2.30.2. Fullerton 1986; Palagia 1990, 349, n. 7, 353–354; *LIMC* 6, s.v. Hekate, no. 112 [H. Sarian].

THE LEGACY OF PERIKLEAN ATHENS

16

ALPHEOS TO THE ORONTES

AN UNUSUAL ECHO OF THE PHEIDIAN ZEUS AT THE SYRIAN PORT OF SELEUKIA PIERIA

CORNELIUS C. VERMEULE III

The theme of this essay is to show how the Zeus of Pheidias, created around 430 B.C., and a similar, standing Zeus at Athens, Delphi, or a contiguous Greek sacral area in the first golden age of Greek sculpture could develop into an unusual divinity in the Hellenistic East. From Pamphylia (the Artemis of Perge) to Emesa in Syria (the conical stone of Bal), gods and goddesses took on forms very unusual in Olympian human terms.[1] The artistic legacy of Pheidias at the grand old cult centers of Greece was applied to turning these ancient Anatolian Hittite and Syrian Mesopotamian "pet rocks" back into orthodox divinities, most notably Zeus, the father of the Olympian pantheon.

The example discussed here, one of several possibilities, is the Zeus Kasios of Seleukia Pieria, gateway to Antioch-on-the-Orontes, one of the two great Hellenistic urban centers and one of four mighty metropolises of the Late Roman world. Around 1937 or 1938, a large statue in Asia Minor marble was unearthed at Samandağ, in the area of Seleukia Pieria, the principal port for Antioch-on-the-Orontes. The statue is now on exhibition in the Hatay Archaeological Museum (Fig. 16.1).[2] Discovery after completion of the Princeton-Antioch excavations, and at the time when Hatay (Antakya) was being united with the Republic of Turkey, has kept this curious figure out of the modern history of ancient Greek and Roman sculpture.

The bearded Jovian statue was first identified as a personification of the river Orontes, seated with a large urn at his left side. The left hand was originally on the urn, and the urn was tipped forward to spill out water. The river-god Orontes, however, was too well known, too fixed iconographically, as the young, beardless swimmer at the feet of the Tyche of Antioch, by the sculptor Eutychides of the family of the great Lysippos about 300 B.C.[3] The Seleukia Pieria god in Pheidian pose and ample *himation* is the Syrian Zeus, the watery urn reflecting the fluvial richness of the wider region, from the Orontes to the Euphrates and the Tigris.

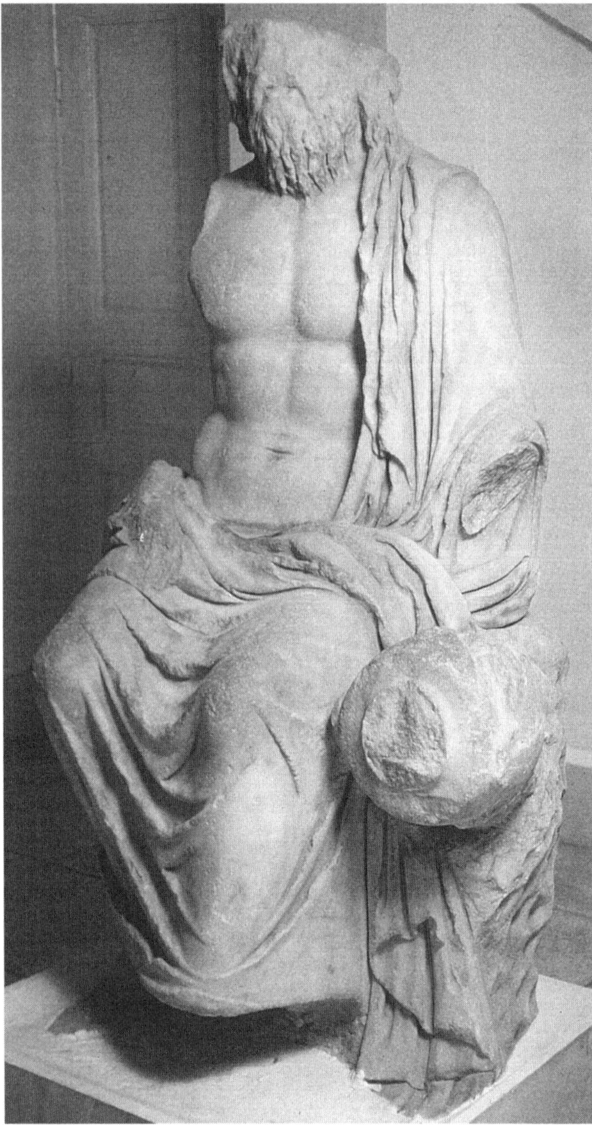

FIGURE 16.1. *Syrian Zeus. Archaeological Museum, Antakya, inv. no. 8498. Photo by John Dean, courtesy of Worcester Art Museum, Antioch exhibition project.*

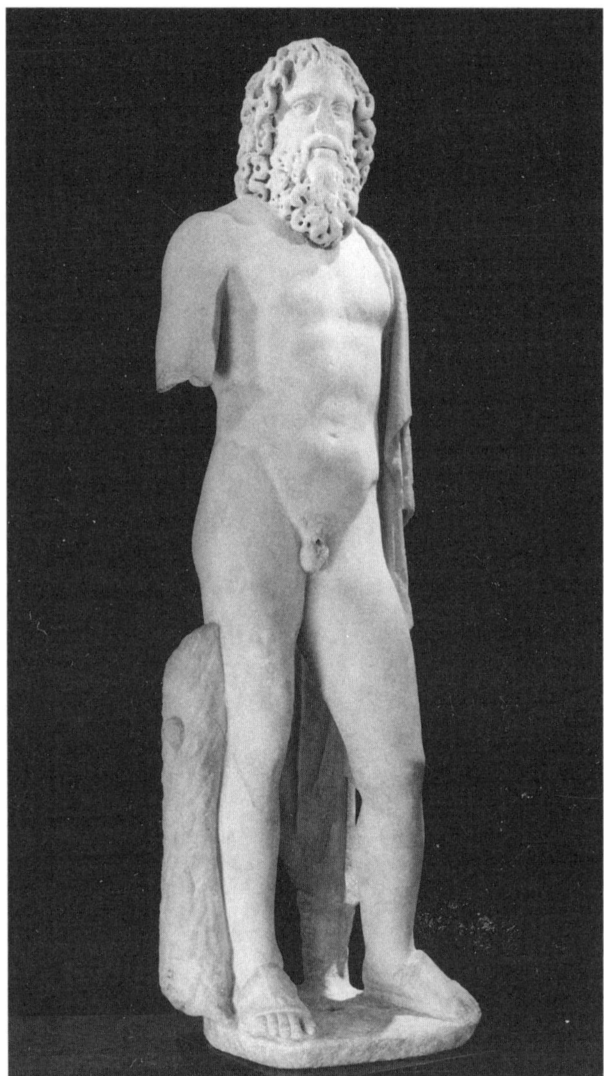

FIGURE 16.2. *Zeus. Private collection, Spain. Photo courtesy of Royal Athena Galleries, New York.*

This statue echoes a temple image, which, like the great gold-and-ivory statue undertaken by King Seleukos I Nikator (312 to 280 B.C.), represented the Zeus of Olympia in Elis brought to the banks of the Orontes. This statue was probably an urban symbol, akin to a personification rather than an object of veneration. The Zeus worshiped at Seleukia Pieria, as will be shown, took the popular Eastern Mediterranean form of a conical, indeed pyramidal rock.

The style and substance of the Syrian Zeus in marble are paralleled by a standing Zeus, also in marble, of slightly smaller size and said to have been brought to France in the nineteenth century, from Byblos by way of Berytus (Beirut; Figs. 16.2–3).[4] This standing Zeus serves to complete the head of the seated figure from Seleukia Pieria (Fig. 16.1). Both marbles were probably carved in the first or early second centuries of the present era. Like the seated Zeus, the standing Zeus finds its way back through the fourth century B.C. to the age of Pheidias. Leochares, who made the cuirassed Ares of Halikarnassos around 350 B.C., has been mentioned as the creator of the standing Zeus, perhaps also for a temple known to have existed at Halikarnassos.[5]

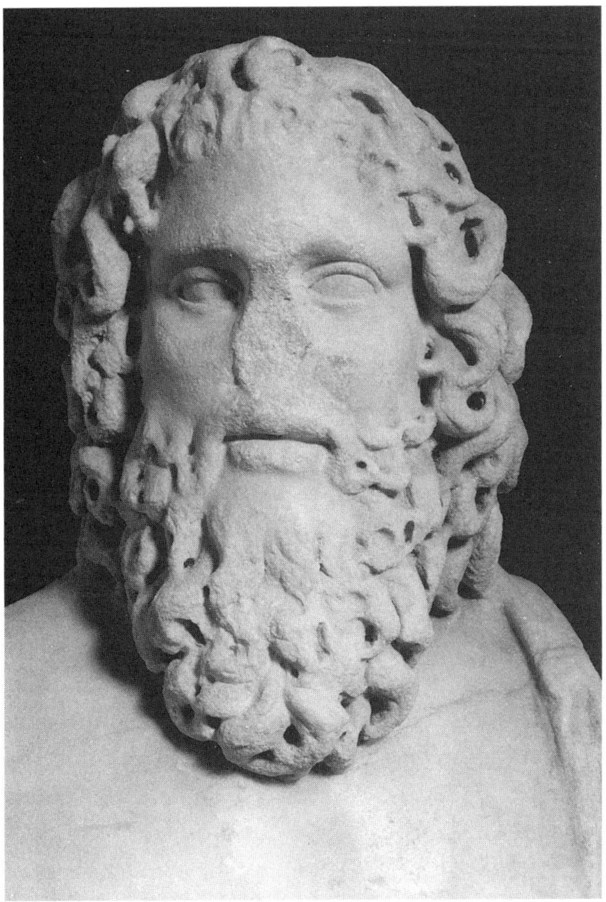

FIGURE 16.3. *Zeus. Detail of 16.2. Photo courtesy of Royal Athena Galleries, New York.*

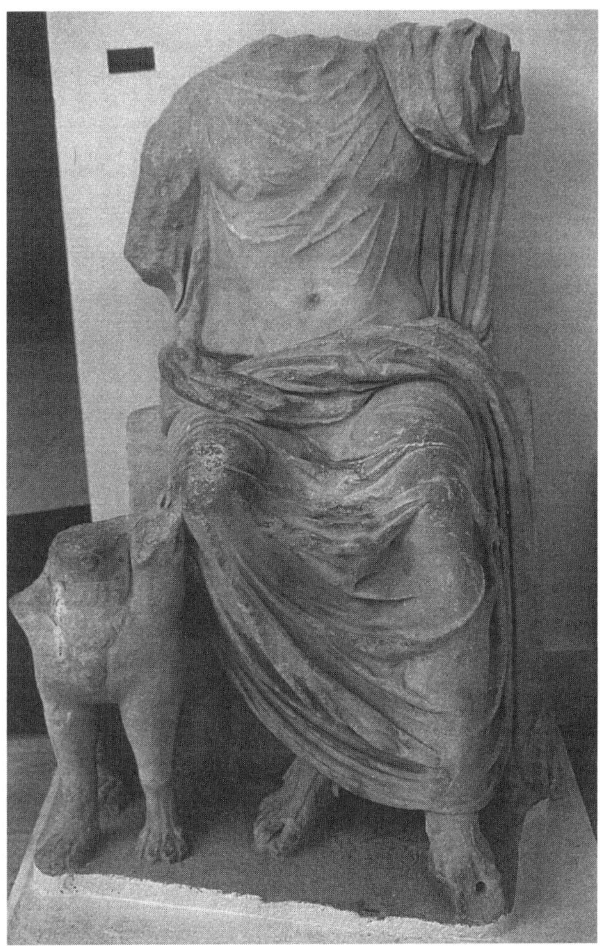

FIGURE 16.4. *Sarapis. Archaeological Museum, Antakya, Inv. no. 10799. Photo by John Dean, courtesy of Worcester Art Museum, Antioch exhibition project.*

The Seleukid temple-image of the seated Zeus at Antioch, progenitor of the signature Zeus on all the later Seleukid tetradrachms of Antioch-on-the-Orontes and beyond, may have been the work of Bryaxis the Younger. It is generally agreed that this Bryaxis was commissioned to carry out the seated statue of Sarapis for the Sarapeion at Alexandria in Egypt.[6] It is perhaps more than a coincidence that a seated Sarapis, with Kerberos, in marble and of size nearly identical with the seated Syrian Zeus was also, it seems, excavated, by private enterprise, at Samandağ (Fig. 16.4).[7] It, too, is on exhibition in the Hatay Archaeological Museum (inv. no. 10799), having been purchased by the museum authorities.

The styles and details of carving of the seated Zeus and the seated Sarapis are sufficiently identical as to suggest the two images were carved at the same time for Seleukia, the port of Antioch. The first statue reflected and recalled the Seleukid past of the region. The second statue stood in recognition of the long-standing and strong Ptolemaic Egyptian presence in the area of Seleukia Pieria, port of the metropolis of Antioch and hinter Asia, and complemented by Alexandria, the port of the Nile from the Delta to Nubia.

In a 1988 catalogue I identified a large bronze statuette of a seated Zeus, acquired over thirty years ago by the Museum of Fine Arts, Boston, as the Zeus of Cappadocia because of the attribute, a small rectangular pyramid held on the outstretched right hand (Fig. 16.5).[8] The left arm and hand were raised, doubtless to hold a scepter and staff, and an ample himation is wrapped around the lower limbs and draped down from the left shoulder, in a manner generally similar to the two seated marble statues from Seleukia Pie-

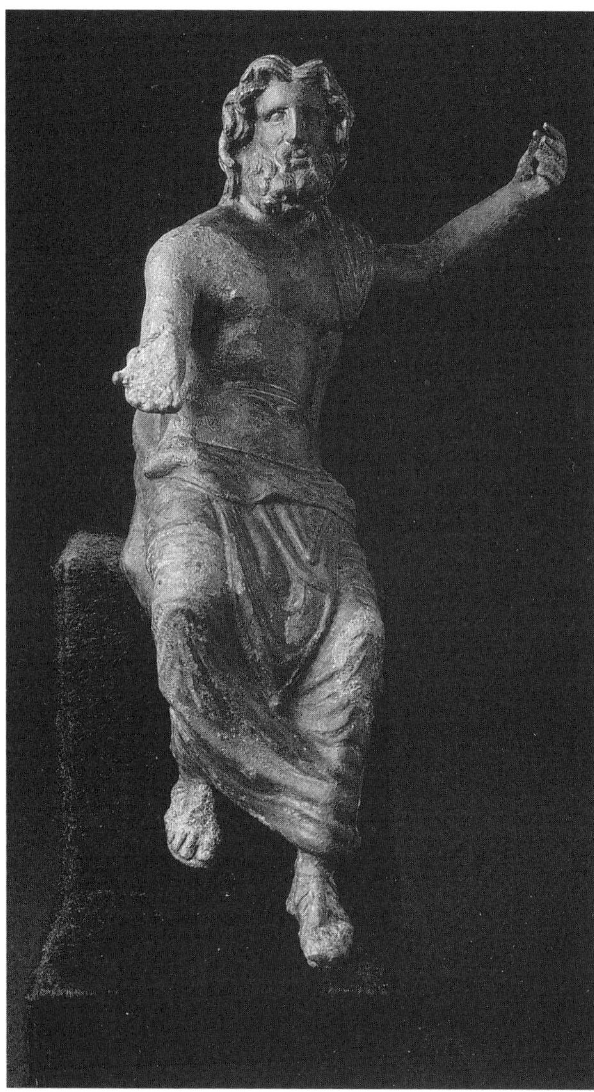

FIGURE 16.5. *Zeus Kasios of Seleukia Pieria. Museum of Fine Arts, Boston. Edwin E. Jack Fund, no. 1972.920. Photograph ©2004 Museum of Fine Arts, Boston.*

ria. The association with Caesarea in Cappadocia was made because the pyramid suggested the stylization of the sacred Mount Argaios (modern Egedağ) on bronze coins of the city under the emperor Trajan (98 to 117 A.D.). This, it might be remembered, is roughly the date suggested for the Seleukia Pieria Zeus and also appears to be the date of the Zeus in bronze.

Identification of the bronze as the Zeus of Cappadocia was made before study of a bronze coin of Trajan from Seleukia Pieria in which a sacred stone of Zeus Kasios has been set in a pyramid under a tetrapod

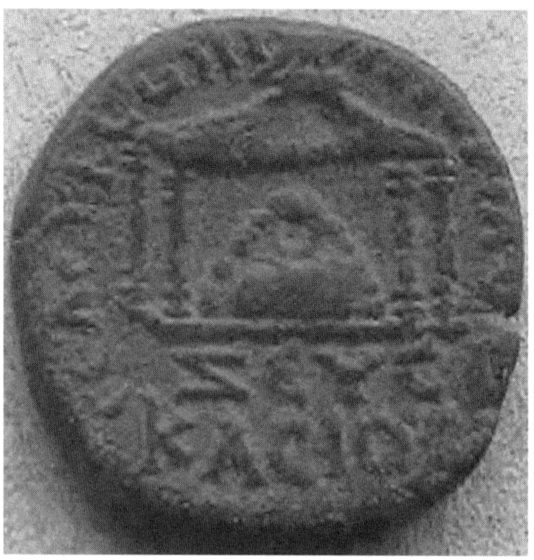

FIGURE 16.6. *Shrine of Zeus Kasios. Reverse of a bronze coin of Seleukia Pieria, Emperor Trajan, 98–117 A.D. Photo courtesy of Classical Numismatic Group, Inc.*

shrine, with the four Corinthian columns supporting a pyramidal roof surmounted by the god's eagle, whose wings are half spread (Fig. 16.6).[9] Thus, it seems more likely that the bronze Zeus identified on more slender grounds with a Zeus of Cappadocia is instead the traditional human form of the Zeus Kasios of Seleukia Pieria, southeast of Cappadocia on the coast of Syria.

Because of all these associations, it would also seem that the seated, bearded, himation-clad divinity with the flowing urn (Fig. 16.1) is another human form of the Zeus Kasios of Seleukia Pieria. We do not know about the standing Zeus also in marble (Figs. 16.2–3), but most likely he is an ordinary traditional Zeus, derived from the Greek sources already mentioned and found in various forms, with various names all over the Roman imperial world.[10] In Rome itself, on the Capitoline Hill, he is Jupiter Stator, Jupiter Tonans, and even Jupiter Ultor, Stayer, Thunderer, and Avenger, as various Roman imperial coins of the first and second centuries A.D. tell us. He went wherever Roman colonies were established, and a number of cities along the eastern Mediterranean coast enjoyed this status. Again, it was natural for the port of Antioch in Syria to host Sarapis, just as the city had on occasion been occupied by the Ptolemies and was linked commercially and militarily with Roman imperial Egypt.

NOTES

Dean and Professor Jerome J. Pollitt has shown and taught me many things over the past forty years, and I am indeed proud to reflect his thoughts, albeit in ever so pale a fashion, in this essay, one inspired by his writings on cultural centers and their achievements in his books on Hellenistic art.

I wrote this just after preparing "The Sculptures of Roman Syria" for Kondoleon 2000. The exhibition was shown in Worcester, Cleveland, and Baltimore. Christine Kondoleon and Rebecca Molholt prepared the photographs and statistics on the two marbles from Seleukia Pieria on visits to the Archaeological Museum in Antakya. Kevin Cahalane, Jerome Eisenberg, Cathy England, Susan Matheson, and Florence Wolsky have also made this contribution possible.

1. For example and in addition, the reverse of a sestertius-sized (32 mm) bronze coin of the empress Tranquillina, wife of Gordianus III (238–244 A.D.), 241–244 A.D., presents the veiled "aniconic" statue of Artemis Eleutheria standing in a distyle temple or shrine. Beside her right foot is a round attribute, a votive stone with a hole in the center, like the image of Zeus Kasios. This attribute must be another mercantile "anchor" for the divinity of an important port complex where grain was stored and shipped to Italy. The coin was struck for the Mediterranean coastal city of Myra in Lykia. See Triton IV, Classical Numismatic Group, etc., Auction, New York, Dec. 15, 2000, 82, no. 364 = Münzen und Medaillen A.G., Auction 64, Basel, Jan. 30, 1984, no. 175. Also Sear 1982, 369, no. 3848, and references. Zeus Heliopolitanos of Baalbek was tree-trunk shaped, like Artemis Eleutheria, Aphrodite of Aphrodisias, Kore of Sardis, Zeus of Milasa, and most celebrated, Artemis Ephesia. Images that were purely rocklike anchors or populated mountains, like Zeus Kasios and the Zeus of Cappadocia, needed Pheidian images to keep their far-flung faithful flocking to the shrines. Zeus of Milasa (Labrandos) had a perfectly Pheidian (Olympian) head on his tree-trunk body, as the over-life-sized marble in Boston demonstrates (acc. no. 04.12), with the addition of a Karian *polos* on top. See Comstock and Vermeule 1976, 70, no. 44, and many references, 1976 to 1988; Comstock and Vermeule 1988, 108, no. 44. Finally, why would the Hellenistic and Roman people of Seleukia Pieria turn a stone anchor into a local Zeus? The anchor could have come from a Minoan or Mycenaean (Bronze Age) ship found in the harbor and been treated as a semidivine link with Seleukia's prehistoric past. The stone lintel of a Mycenaean tholos tomb set up in Classical times in a hall of the Athenian Agora became an object on which sacred oaths of office were affirmed. See Camp 1986, 101–104.

2. Inv. no. 8498. Ht.: 1.80 m = 70⅞ in. The figure is based on an enthroned Zeus, such as the statue in Florence: *RSGR* 5:1 1898–1930, 7, no. 1; and most particularly, the Syrian Jupiter found in Rome: *RSGR* 6 1898–1930, no. 1. A statue from Tebessa, similar in pose and style, bears a dedication to Kronos-Saturn. See *RSGR* 2 1898–1930, 24, no. 5.

3. The young beardless river-god Orontes, swimming at the feet of the Tyche of Antioch, has been associated with athletes by Lysippos and his atelier. See Frel 1978, 20, 22, 38–39, pls. 12–13.

4. Brought from the old French collection to the New York art market, Royal-Athena Galleries. Ht.: 1.194 m. See *Art of the Ancient World, Greek, Etruscan, Roman, Egyptian, and Near Eastern Antiquities* 11 (New York 1999) 7, no. 10.

5. See Vermeule 1984. On the standing Zeus as shown on a denarius from Spain of 18/19 B.C., see Zanker 1988, 108–109, fig. 89:a. On Leochares, see Stewart 1990, 283–285.

6. E.g., Stewart 1990, 202–203. *Contra:* Ridgway 1990, 95–97 with further references.

7. Ht.: 1.55 m = 63 in. From the Kapisuyu district of the port area. The head is broken off and was originally of a piece with the body. The god was seated on a chair with turned legs. Compare the statue, with head, from Egypt via the Dattari Sale, no. 337: *RSGR* 5:1 1898–1930, 9, no. 1. Also the relatively complete marble in the Musei Vaticani: Amelung 1903, 38, no. 74; *RSGR* 3 1898–1930, 227, no. 8 (also 226, no. 5 = Amelung 1903, 50, no. 255, without Kerberos). Hades-Pluto, rather than Sarapis may have been the subject, because of the arrangement of the *chiton* over the chest and stomach, and the heavy end of the cloak on the left shoulder. The chiton is definitely not the short-sleeved, V-necked tunic of the Sarapis identified with Bryaxis in Alexandria. A Hades in Cherchell has a similar cloak on the shoulder but appears to lack the chiton. See *RSGR* 2 1898–1930, 19, no. 8.

8. Edwin E. Jack Fund no. 1972.920 from the Eastern Mediterranean. Ht.: 0.192 m. Vermeule and Comstock 1988, 70, no. 73.

9. Reverse of the bronze coin of Seleukia Pieria under Trajan (98 to 117). Diam: 25 mm. G. Hirsch Auction 187, Munich, 19–23 September 1995, lot 1224. Wroth 1899, 274, no. 44, no. 50. Zeus Kasios ("Encased," "Boxed") is a perfect divine patron of a cargo port.

(Zeus) Kasios was also the local mountain (Samandağ, the modern name for Seleukia Pieria) and a source of flowing water (Kapisuyu, the precise spot where the marble Sarapis was discovered). The emperor Hadrian (117–138 A.D.) worshiped the rising sun on top of Mount Kasios, and the cult of the pyramidal rock (with a hole through the top to make it like the ancient merchant-ship anchor appropriate to a seaport) spread with Egyptian cults through the Aegean to select locations in the Latin West. See Turcan 1996, 133, 171–172, in a chapter titled, after Juvenal, "The Orontes Flowing into the Tiber."

10. At Maeonia in eastern Lydia in the time of Hadrian, a head of Zeus like the example in marble from Byblos is identified as Zeus Olympios. See Classical Numismatic Group, Inc., Auction 43, September 24, 1997, p. 101, no. 978. Price and Trell 1977, 212, fig. 445, Septimius Severus (193–211 A.D.). See also Lindgren and Kovacs 1985, 180, no. A2129A, pl. 132.

17

KOSMETAI, THE SECOND SOPHISTIC, AND PORTRAITURE IN THE SECOND CENTURY

EVE D'AMBRA

I dedicate this essay to Jerome Pollitt as a teacher and scholar whose work anticipated several tendencies of the "new" Archaeology and Classical Art History. Although he may be reluctant to take credit for some of the recent developments in the field, his insistence on the broad cultural horizon preceded current interest in "recontextualization" of works of art and material culture (and makes us reconsider how we conjure up context), and his curiosity about Roman art was rarely exhibited by scholars of Classical Greece who accepted conventional attitudes about Roman art being second-rate. Set against his independence of mind, his appetite for painstaking historical inquiry, and his elegant simplicity of expression, this essay serves only as a dim reflection of the luminous powers of Jerome Pollitt's work.

The topic of this essay catapults us six centuries forward to the period of the Roman High Empire when Athens was living in its past, so to speak. Its theme, however, is rooted in the culture of the fifth-century *polis* and, in particular, *paideia,* defined not only as the curriculum of great authors but also as the elite sphere of high achievements and well-rounded excellence, which is synonymous with Periklean Athens. The revival of high Attic culture in the second century A.D., promoted by Hadrian's philhellenic program and the phenomenon of the Second Sophistic, has been well documented; it has also been linked to the emergence of a Greek cultural identity as a means to assert the difference and superiority of the children of *Hellas.*[1] The vigorous revival of the Greek tradition came in reaction to Roman culture with its Latin, military might, and mass spectacles. Above all, the Roman Empire showcased a society marked by expansion and the inclusion of foreigners, whereas the traditional polis maintained a more exclusive society in which membership was based on a common language and heritage.[2] It is all the more poignant that this swan song, this reprise of the golden age, came at a time when Greece was in economic and political decline.

The subject of this essay, portraits of the *kosmetai,* allows us to consider the self-fashioning of the leading men of Athenian society in this period of renewed Hellenic pride. The portraits have defied easy interpretation as a group: some appear to resemble emperors in their physiognomy, while others recall the otherworldly aspect of Plato and other Greek intellectuals. Rather than attributing stylistic inconsistencies to alternating phases of Romanization and resistance to Imperial control, we should look more closely at what was enshrined as Greek and what was assumed to be Roman in the first half of the second century A.D. in the reigns of Trajan and Hadrian.[3] Given the attraction of Hellenism to elite Romans and the complicated procedure of acculturation in the course of the empire, it may be that Rome itself had a stake in keeping the Greek past alive.

The kosmetai were senior administrators of the *gymnasion,* an institution that began, before the Classical period, as the training ground for citizen-soldiers to acquire both physical fitness and mental acuity, and then developed into a military college and, finally, into a quasi-university in the Imperial age.[4] As the institution at the heart of the polis by the very nature of its mission in educating and training youth, upholding standards, and transmitting the Athenian heritage, the gymnasion played a crucial role in programs of cultural revival and renewal. Admission was only for the sons of the elite, *ephebes* with the requisite aristocratic lineages carefully documented in civic records (usually about three hundred per year were enrolled).[5]

The kosmetai, literally meaning "order-masters" and described as members of the board or as governors, performed as administrators rather than as intellectuals.[6] They typically held other high public offices, such as *archon* or *strategos* and enjoyed the respect of the community as local notables while they served the gymnasion.[7] The annual president of the Athenian gymnasion was honored with a sculpted portrait mounted on a herm; a long file of these adorned the *palaistra,* rather like the painted portraits of founders and presidents in the conference rooms or dining halls of our colleges and universities. The extant herm portraits of the Athenian kosmetai are displayed in the National Archaeological Museum in Athens.[8]

Testifying to the importance of its institutional history, the gymnasion maintained a dense sequence of kosmetai portraits from the second and third centuries; we will examine only three of the earlier portraits for the purposes of this brief essay. The three portraits entail problems current in the study of Roman portraiture: the relationship of portraits of private citizens to the images of emperors, the combination of features from different types (e.g., plain, unassuming faces with elaborately coiffed hair) that defy conventional methods of dating, and the meaning of beards as attributes of a philosophical vocation. It is also instructive to look at portraits of philosophers, such as Theon of Smyrna, and sophists, such as Herodes Atticus, to get a sense of the range of possibilities available for portraits of the kosmetai (and how well-documented personalities chose to represent themselves). Herodes Atticus, millionaire sophist, friend of emperors, and patron of Athens, stands out as the archetypal cosmopolitan linking Roman and Greek elites, and disrupting the usual compartmentalization of Greek wisdom and Roman mass culture.

In method, this essay leans on the important article by R. R. R. Smith on honorific portrait statues in the Greek East in the second century.[9] Smith brushes away assumptions about private portraits assuming the look of emperors and, instead, asserts the independence of private portraits that cannot fit into any neat evolutionary schemes of stylistic development. He also cautions against assuming that portrait statues always represent the subject in a role that effectively characterizes his vocation or reputation. According to Smith, statues can project an image not completely consonant with the status and role of the subject, or the patron may select one aspect of the subject's career to single out for praise (e.g., a sophist commemorated as a patron of his city rather than as a celebrated performer of high-flying orations). The "styled self" of the portraits is one that bears an ambivalent relationship both to the biographies of great men and to the daily lives of those forgotten by history.

I would take Smith's thesis one step further and suggest that many of the private portrait styles following the shopworn Augustan Classicism of the first century A.D. were stock types, templates distinguished by gender, age, and social role that were modified by the features of the individual subject. Stock types establish the subject's identity according to his peer group and also provide a likeness that may give the illusion of realism—of capturing the visceral qualities of a personality caught in a specific place and time—by manipulating styles and technical devices (this also allowed sculptors to produce funerary portraits with little or no warning—surely a benefit given the mortality rates of the young and funerary practices).[10] Assumptions that portraits faithfully transcribe their subjects' features in a transparent manner unhindered by the requirements of artistic styles or social conventions ignore the patterns of similarities and common features in the corpus of Roman private portraits, which have allowed scholars to classify them according to types.

That metropolitan Roman and Greek portraits developed somewhat separately in this period is no doubt correct, as Smith posits, but the persistence of similar styles suggests a cosmopolitan style for the elite, for example, the Greek city fathers who also served in the Roman Senate, that cannot be defined as either particularly "Greek" or "Roman" on the basis of cultural allegiances or public roles (especially considering that "Greek" traits had been long assimilated by the Romans and filtered through their portrait types).[11] Those who loitered by the statues in the *agorai* of their towns may not have recognized "Greek" and "Roman" types as contemporary art historians and archaeologists have classified them (it should be added that the ancient viewer did not have the opportunity to study the portraits, originally mounted on statues on tall bases, as closely as scholars poring over detailed photographs of widely dispersed portraits).[12]

One portrait style, that of clean-shaven, aging men with plain hairstyles or balding heads, was popular throughout the empire in the second century. Although Smith ascribes distinct meanings to the appearance of this style in the Eastern provinces and metropolitan center, it may be that the style conveyed a simple meaning: conservatism and adherence to tradition, although these revered qualities evoked rather different ideas to Eastern and Western viewers.[13] The nuances of the style, its responses to changing political climates and shifting elite identity that Smith observes, may not have registered with local audiences at large, particularly those of the lower social orders (the elites, of course, staked their reputations on the semiotics of their statues).

In Smith's analysis the driving force behind Greek portraiture is conservatism, and, certainly, a desire to reclaim the past looms large in second-century Athens. Portraits produced in the city of Rome, however, are seen to be motivated by fashion, although it is not clear how fashion "works" in a traditional society, especially when many subjects do not feel compelled to copy the Imperial model in their portraits.[14] The three portraits of kosmetai under discussion involve a dialogue between Greek identity and Roman styles, which allows us to reconsider the cultural imperatives of honoring the past and keeping up appearances at the same time. Also of interest is Smith's notion of the "styled self," the cultivation of appearances expressed by intricately curled coiffures and well-groomed beards, which appear in both East and West as a sign of the urbane and sophisticated citizen, a subset of the elite male that was previously subordinated to types of military heroes or political statesmen in Rome.[15]

THE PERIOD-FACE

The annual president of the Athenian gymnasion was commemorated with a portrait mounted on a herm erected by the ephebes, who assumed the expenses of the commemoration; honors were also decreed, golden crowns issued, and *elogia* inscribed on the shafts of the herms. The herm portrait of the *kosmetes* Heliodoros offers an example with, at first glance, a strikingly Roman countenance and a fully extant inscription of note (Figs. 17.1–2).[16] The herm portrait, dated to the Trajanic period, has been compared to portraits of the emperor Vespasian because they share features: the wide cranium, heavy-lidded eyes, lined skin, and square jaw.[17] The similarities have been attributed to the concept of the *Zeitgesicht,* the period-face, the

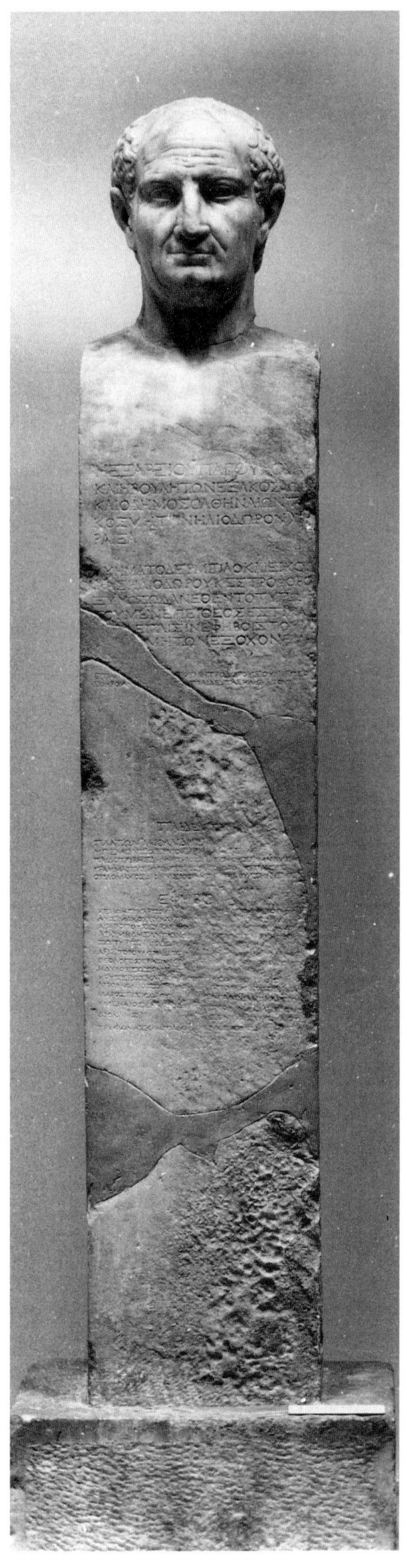

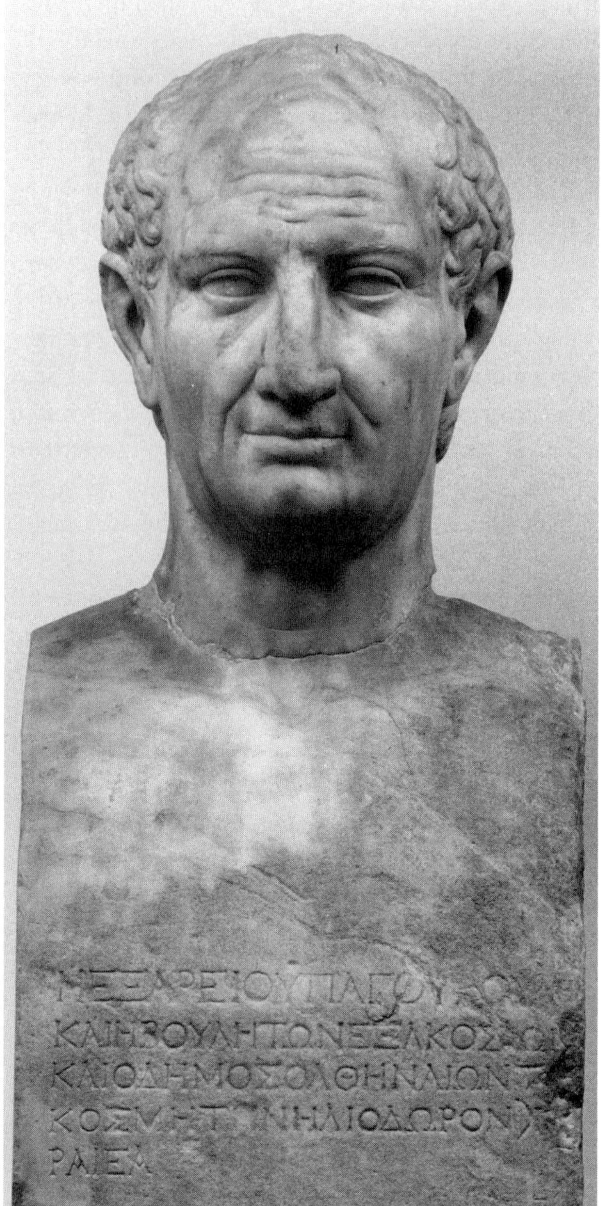

FIGURE 17.1 (LEFT). *Herm portrait of Heliodoros. Athens, National Museum 384. Photo courtesy of the National Archaeological Museum, Athens.*

FIGURE 17.2 (ABOVE). *Herm portrait of Heliodoros. Athens, National Museum 384. Photo courtesy of Hans Rupprecht Goette.*

phenomenon by which the public image of the reigning emperor sweeps the portraits of his subjects in its wake by inspiring imitation.[18] Against this interpretation note the approximate forty-year gap between the first portraits of Vespasian and Heliodoros' portrait and the significant differences between the two portraits:

Heliodoros' face is less wide, the eyes are not deeply set nor have hooded brows, the nose is high-bridged, the chin is longer, and hair more plastically modeled on the sides of the head.[19] The representation of an elder with a receding hairline generally recalls Vespasian's portraiture; however, the apt comparison is with private portraits (see below), works that are not well studied, although there has been some recent interest in the self-representation of elites in the Greek East.[20]

As a subject of study, the portrait often invites unwarranted speculation about the personality of the subject, especially when a name and career can be retrieved, and scholars interpret portrait features in light of the character the subject ought to have had or, conversely, supply a biography based on indelible marks of virtues and vices expressed by the arch of a brow or the downturned corner of the mouth, if the subject is unknown.[21] At the risk of making too much of the looks of Heliodoros, I would like to consider a few salient points of the physiognomy of the portrait. First, the age of the subject is characterized in later middle life, that is, for the ancients, over forty years of age, which corresponds to the requirement for kosmetai.[22] Age is defined by the lines on the skin, with furrows on the forehead, vertical notches at the bridge of the nose, wrinkles forming parentheses from the nostrils to the mouth, and an underchin. This calligraphic treatment of flesh losing its form is standard, but the furrows extending to the dome of the receding hairline, delineating a hump at the crown of the head, are distinct.

Heliodoros' egg-shaped crown may reflect his actual appearance, although the demands of verisimilitude could have been met by the repertory of stock types, in particular the type of the beardless elder, characterized by Smith as portraying a conservative democratic image in Greece.[23] Yet this type, which remained popular through the mid second century, was inflected with various meanings in a metropolitan Roman context: moral fortitude, aristocratic honor, and perhaps a conservative reaction to the new Antonine styles with abundant hair and full beards.[24] Any or all of these meanings evoked the profile of the ruling elite in Rome, and I would suggest that the first two also worked well for stately men, such as Heliodoros, who were pillars of their community; that these portraits have a Roman hard-edged look may have added to their prestige and afforded their subjects no discomfort since Hellenic identity did not seem to be threatened by the adoption of these particular Roman forms.[25]

Portraits of the type of the balding and shaved elder, similar to that of Heliodoros, are found in metropolitan Rome and the Greek East.[26] A brief indication of their common features will suffice: the Roman examples share the squared jaw and broad, balding cranium in busts from the Lateran[27] and the Braccio Nuovo in the Vatican Museums[28] and in a relief on a stele in the Capitoline Museums.[29] The works from the Greek East display deeply engraved wrinkles on the brow, the naso-labial lines, and downward-turned mouths in the herm portrait of Moiragenes[30] from the Athenian Agora, the herm portrait from the Levant in the British Museum,[31] the portrait head possibly from Athens and now in the Ny Carlsberg Glyptothek,[32] and the wreathed portrait head from the Athenian Agora.[33]

In many aspects (such as the square shape of the head, the treatment of the retreating hairline, the taut wrinkles), the portrait of Heliodoros resembles the Roman busts more than those from the Greek East, although this similarity does not necessarily suggest that Heliodoros was a *philorhomaios* (friend of Rome); it could indicate the extent of the distribution of portrait types and their utility in honoring the Athenian elite. That many of these works tend to be later in date (that is, dating to the mid second century) than the portrait of Heliodoros does not disqualify them from comparison; rather, private portraits in the second century cannot be arranged in a linear sequence of development, and types seem to stay current with minor modifications.[34]

Whether specific features were identified as Greek or Roman is difficult to say due to the written sources' silence on most aspects of personal appearance, except for beards and clothing.[35] Art historians and archaeologists, naturally, have tended to invest significance in features that allow them to date the portraits or, more recently, that have ideological meaning as expressions of social or cultural identity. An ancient observer informs us of some of the difficulties associated with the latter. In his thirty-first oration, Dio of Prusa takes the people of Rhodes to task for being too willing to honor notable citizens with statues and accommodating them by merely replacing the inscriptions on old statues, that is, relabeling statues originally intended to represent someone else. Dio describes the statues of the Rhodians as being like actors in that they take on different parts—one statue may appear as a Greek, then as a Roman at another time with a new inscription.[36] Cast as actors, degraded Imperial subjects on the bottom social rungs (who lacked moral integrity by their ability to slip in and out of character),[37] the statues actually deceived no one because their clothing or footwear revealed their true origins. It is interesting, however, that Dio did not mention the portrait features that connoisseurs and art historians find crucial in determining the identity of the statues' subjects. If inscriptions provided the key to identity, then were portrait features less important in representing cultural affiliations?

Heliodoros' portrait also expresses both difference from and similarity to a type (i.e., types provided templates through which sculptors filtered the individual's features). That it has been characterized as Roman rests on the stereotypical notion of the severe, authoritative, and dominating imperialist. The features are blunt with a strong nose, slightly hooked in its profile, thick throughout its course and with large nostrils. The eyes are narrower and bean shaped, unlike the almond-shaped eyes of many other second-century portraits. The modeling, from the shapely contours of the large ears to the snaking locks at the side of the head and the bulbous chin, shows the care taken to enliven surfaces. The right ear, however, appears larger and thicker than the left and may have been depicted as such to indicate Heliodoros' athletic youth, his roustabout days as a *pankratriast* or boxer, activities that rounded out the ephebe.[38] The carved face of Heliodoros, therefore, subscribes to a type in its depiction of the age and strong features of a man of honor individualized with the high dome of the cranium, the narrowing of the eyes, and the battered ear, features that may reflect either Heliodoros' looks or a physiognomy that projected the appropriate intellectual and athletic accomplishments.

The careers of such local notables were awash in Roman honors that did not compromise their Hellenic background.[39] That the portrait of Heliodoros stood in the gymnasion, the heart of Hellenic culture, and honored its administrator did not require that it had to bear a Greek pedigree; the herm format already exemplified that.[40] Other portraits of civic benefactors in the Greek East are scarcely different from Imperial portraits; in fact, the wreathed and cuirassed portrait statue of Ti. Julius Celsus Polemaeanus from his library in Ephesos appears more ostentatious than some Imperial statues.[41] This adoption of the Roman signs of power and prestige may be explained as a way in which the leading men of the city elevated themselves above their peers. That they held Roman offices does not mean that they had forsaken a Greek cultural identity; rather, it goes hand in hand with a heightening of their status as men of the world.[42]

Granted that portraits had different inflections for their viewers in West and East, the consistency and uniformity of aspect in these heads, their reliance on common types, may have dovetailed with the political realities of the "empire of honor."[43] That is, the portrait type served as a professional perquisite for those who were aristocratic and wealthy enough to participate in the system of priesthoods, magistracies, and offices that allowed them to accrue honor and influence, rather than power per se. Yet the Roman Empire was rather loosely run, with opportunities for local notables to take the stage—the similarity of portrait types is all the more striking given the cultural autonomy of cities and must have conveyed a flattering and suitably dignified image of the elite throughout the empire.[44] The image evidently "spoke" to its audience, even if we cannot quite clearly hear its message now.

THE HERM

The preserved inscription on Heliodoros' herm dates the portrait to between 100 and 110–111.[45] It begins with a formula, "The council of the Areopagos and the Boulè of 600 and the people of Athens honor the kosmetes Heliodoros, son of Heliodoros of the Peiraieus. . . ." It continues by stating that the ephebes dedicate this image, at the same time a representation of Hermes and a portrait of Heliodoros, no doubt, as a pedantic gloss on the origins of the herm and flattery for Heliodoros. The compact Hellenic form of the herm, a pillar (often ithyphallic) surmounted by a sculpted head of the bearded god, stood in files to decorate courtyards or colonnaded gardens in the Imperial period, although it guarded entrances and crossroads in the Classical period and earlier. The notorious incident in 415 B.C., when the herms at the doorways of Athenian houses were damaged in the middle of the night, has been attributed to civic unrest on the eve of the Sicilian expedition.[46] It was taken as a warning that Athenians were vulnerable in the core of the polis, at the hearth of the citizenry. The passage across boundaries strictly maintained in Greek society—from the interior of the polis to the hinterlands beyond its walls—was governed by Hermes, the god of shepherds and travelers, of trade and contact.[47] As an intermediary between the gods, men, and the Underworld, he is always in motion. Ephebes, youths in transition to adulthood, would find Hermes a benevolent deity as the inscription duly notes.

Yet there may be more to the relationship than merely rites of passage and liminal states because Hermes also possesses *metis*. In myth, Hermes begins his adventures as a child, only to be fully vested as a divinity by contract when he exchanges his lyre for the cattle he stole from his brother Apollo.[48] The exchange of goods sets up Hermes as the protector of traders, while the charms of the lyre evoke the persuasive power of Hermes' words, full of deceit and trickery, which ultimately seduce Zeus. Hermes the sophist may be the aspect that is evoked in the inscription of Heliodoros' herm. Young men studied forensic oratory to succeed in lawcourts and in the city council, but their imaginations were captivated by the sophists, performance artists such as Favorinus and Polemon, who won fame, fortune, and glamour from the theatricality of their epideictic displays.[49] By erecting the sculpture, the ephebes paid tribute to both their kosmetes and to Hermes; the cunning intelligence of the latter may have been also attributed to the former. That the herm was appropriate for portraits of intellectuals, benefactors, and administrators in the Roman period does not militate against the thematic relevance of Hermes for young men, who had to make their way in the world with their wits.

PHYSIOGNOMY, CULTIVATION, AND APPEARANCES

Two other herm portraits (Figs. 17.3–4) from the mid second century reflect types that were also produced in both the West and the East. The portrait of an unidentified kosmetes (Fig. 17.3), from the Trajanic and Hadrianic periods, depicts a subject with casually handsome features that suggest a refined and urbane milieu. The portrait is composed of a combination of types, the first depicting a clean-shaven face and the second showing a cap of attractively tousled curls.[50] In fact, the portrait is distinguished by the hair forming thick coils of curls atop the head in a couple of layers, giving the head some height and décor in the form of the artful arrangement of crescent-shaped locks, which only take on their swirling, looping form in the front (from the side they appear doughy and less shapely). Despite the abraded surface, the face displays the sleek features, heavy-lidded large eyes and full lips of a man in early middle age with a fleshy jaw and chin.

The mannered appearance of the portrait, evinced not only by the styled hair and the overripe features but also by the projecting lower lip and slight downward tilt of the head, demonstrates the *cultus* (cultivation) of a man of means. Care taken to maintain one's appearance and to distinguish oneself from the *hoi polloi* by grooming was an essential prerequisite for a man of honor. Attention to appearances was only one-half of the equation: the second century, according to Foucault, was one in which the elite male monitored his appetites and regulated his desires in the formation of an internally constructed and disciplined self. In Foucault's account, the self-control practiced by individuals was an ethical act.[51] Although much criticized by classicists, Foucault's theory remains influential and has been corrected by forays into complementary discourses, such as physiognomic theory and the rhetorical performances of the Second Sophistic.[52] Physiognomists understood that externals, such as gait, gestures, and facial expressions, reflect the subject's interior, that is, moral worth, upbringing, and sexual desires.

The handbooks of the period rather predictably support the established hierarchies of power in their obsession with ferreting out imposters (i.e., men who are not "real" men, and social climbers). Authorities, such as the highly successful and competitive soph-

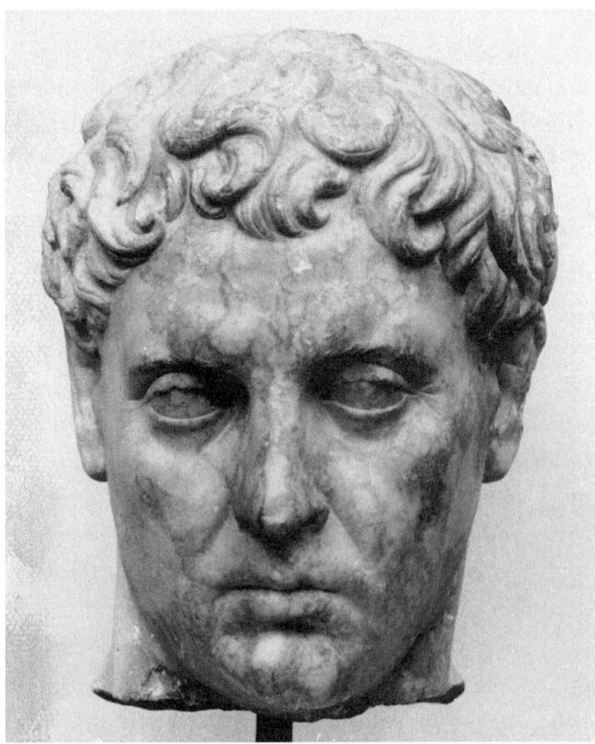

FIGURE 17.3. *Herm portrait of unidentified kosmetes. Athens, National Museum 392. Photo courtesy of the National Archaeological Museum, Athens.*

ist Polemon of Laodicea (Asia Minor), list the telltale signs for detecting manliness or its opposite: flashing eyes and a straight gaze convey conviction and valor; drooping eyelids, a tilted head, a high-pitched voice, and a swaying gait suggest effeminacy, and so on.[53] Polemon showed off his techniques of detecting base or deceitful characters in marketplaces or at wedding parties as a public service (and as an entertainment using the dramatic devices out of the sophists' bag of rhetorical tricks).[54] Besides the policing of character, the physiognomists also evinced the spectacles of civic life in accounts of the physical bearing of the elite: a magistrate should walk straight through crowds in a slow and stately manner without looking from side to side so that the crowd will part for him.[55] The social order depends upon the performance of such rituals with familiar cues.

The staging of public life, with its choreographed entrances and scrutinized wardrobes, exceeds the physiognomist's interest in comportment. A corollary of the "scientific" practice of the physiognomists is the Second Sophistic, with its public oratory of Greek themes, mythological narratives, reworkings of classical literature, or reenactments of the speeches of Perikles and Demosthenes. The sophists, best exemplified by Polemon, were itinerant orators who performed in grand public recitals to wildly appreciative audiences. Although the Second Sophistic has practically come to stand for the Greek Imperial period in its performances of archaic Greek, Attic dialects, and historical subjects (at least, in the minds of those who are the proponents of this rapidly growing field), the melodramatic and histrionic style of its performers clashes with their heroic themes of manly virtue.[56]

One anecdote suffices to convey a sense of its highly self-conscious theatricality (a quality deemed unmanly and suspect in Roman eyes): in 144 A.D. the dying Polemon, after he had arranged to be buried alive in order to pass away with voice intact, pleaded to his assembled friends, "Give me a body, and I will declaim!"[57] Sophists identified themselves as Greeks and lived up to it by indulging in excesses—in dress, jewelry, perfume, and flamboyance of all types—that signaled stereotypical Greek (and effeminate) customs to Romans. Joy Connolly has analyzed this contradiction as a "point of resistance" to the dominant practices, the culture of self-control and moderation.[58] Maud Gleason has interpreted the sophists' self-presentation as performances that, paradoxically, uphold traditional codes of conduct by pushing them to the limits of decency and beyond.[59] However we choose to interpret the intriguing epideictic performances of Polemon and Favorinus, it is striking that their age ushers in portraits of men displaying a heightened elegance in both the East and West, a cultivation of appearances with well-coiffed hair and beards that seems to have no precedent in the plain and unassuming portraits popular in the Roman West in the late first and early second centuries.[60]

The curls of the anonymous kosmetes (Fig. 17.3) suggest a milieu that preferred the artificial, the styled, and the precious. Although the face is clean shaven, it bears little resemblance to the type of Heliodoros (Fig. 17.1), for example, with its hardened and objective description of age.[61] The fine wrinkles at the outer corners of the mouth and the nose of the unidentified kosmetes are barely visible, in contrast to the high cheekbones, the shapely turn of the cheeks, and the delicate cleft of the chin. Although there is nothing in particular to link the kosmetes with the sophists, the refinement and sophistication of the portrait may have been attributed to the Greek revival, with its taste for overt stylization and finesse.

Not having the marks of the drill in the irises and pupils of the eyes, the portrait of the unidentified kosmetes may be dated before 140 A.D. (with the earliest date being 110).[62] A group of portraits depict luxuriantly curling locks capping the head, along with heavy-lidded eyes, full lips, and mostly clean-shaven chins: two busts displaying heroic nudity, one in the Vatican Museums,[63] and the other in London;[64] two works in the Terme Museum;[65] a head in Boston, reportedly from Tralles;[66] a head from Nikaia in the museum in Bursa;[67] a wreathed head in the Capitoline Museums;[68] and a head in Munich.[69] The Roman, London, Bursa, and Munich heads are Trajanic in date, but the others belong to the Hadrianic period; several depict men older than the well-preserved example of early middle age of the kosmetes.

The geographic distribution of the heads with curled coiffures, both old and young, shows that this type was current in both the East and West. If we accept the hypothesis that the style accompanied the Second Sophistic,[70] then does it also signal Greek identity? Is the Western occurrence of the type with short curls a phenomenon with a different connotation? The sophists had a wide appeal across the empire: Philostratus claims that Marcus Aurelius was moved by the orator Aelius Aristides' account of earthquakes at Smyrna, and the Senate disbanded in excitement when the sophist Hadrian came to Rome.[71] The cultivated style may have been one style adopted by the elite who identified as Greek in the East, and it was also embraced by Romans as a mark of sophistication that overrode the taint of effeminacy or otherness attached to extreme displays of cultus in the first century. Antoninus Pius, after having been scolded by the sophist Alexander Peloplaton for losing interest in his performance, retorts, "I am paying attention, and I know you very well. You are the fellow who is always arranging his hair, polishing his teeth, buffing his nails, and smelling of myrrh."[72] The ironic exchange underscores the tensions underlying an epideictic display—the overpaid and arrogant performer unmasked by the emperor who is, if not enthralled by the act, at least still complicit with it.[73] Rather than situating Hellenism as the opposite of Roman culture, we should perhaps understand it as a set of characteristics selected by members of the elite; some aspects of Hellenism had long made themselves at home in Rome, while the value and acceptance of others shifted with the changing composition and ethnic origins of the elite in the late first and early second centuries.[74]

For Roman precedents of the elegant male, one need only recall Domitian's pristine tiara of comma-shaped locks, along with his contribution to the literature on baldness and hair care in a manual that he wrote, and Nero's earlier crested coiffure.[75] It is telling that both emperors also were smeared with the taint of excessive Hellenic sympathies by the senatorial elite and were subsequently brought down. Although Smith dismisses these emperors and their styles as not being good models for their subjects, there are private portraits with crested or tiered coiffures and evidence that, as Smith acknowledges, subjects of the lower orders adopted the Imperial styles in the orbit of the Zeitgesicht.[76] Self-fashioning with an eye to an urbane and cosmopolitan appearance played a role in the life of the Roman elite male.[77] The flamboyance of the sophists, active from the first through the third centuries, may have given a new impetus to this tendency towards cultus.

The third portrait (Fig. 17.4) to be discussed depicts the kosmetes Onasos and is dated to 129–138 A.D. on the basis of the inscription.[78] Its physiognomy and sculptural technique suggest how Roman artistic practice accommodated the Greek renaissance of the second century. With its tousled, loosely flowing locks and the full moustache and beard, the portrait of Onasos appears to assert a Hellenic identity. The light touch of the drill in the hair and beard reflects Hadrianic advances in portrait production but the higher cheekbones, the smooth brow, and finely chiseled nose seem to recall portraits of fourth-century B.C. intellectuals and public figures.

The age of Onasos as depicted in his portrait, with its firm unlined skin, appears younger than that of the other two kosmetai portraits of decidedly older-looking men; Onasos' beard, along with his position as chief kosmetes, indicates that he was at least forty when the portrait was erected, yet his features register an elegant and simply beautiful aspect of maturity attained, so it seems, without the exertion and pressures afflicting his colleagues. In its graceful proportions, slightly elongated through the cheeks and chin, and sensitive modeling, particularly at the raised cheekbones and in the delicacy of the tip of the nose and nostrils, the face of Onasos recalls the style of Greek portraits in the fourth century B.C.

Smith points out that the hallmarks of the portraits of Hellenistic intellectuals (e.g., beyond beards, the furrowed brows and strained postures) are absent in the portraits of the kosmetai. This should not be surprising because, after all, they were not intellectuals but administrators and benefactors.[79] The portraits of the kosmetai also cannot be compared to those of the sophists because not one of the portraits of the orators has been conclusively identified (it is likely that they were commemorated for their other roles, such as civic benefactors).[80] The stylization of portraits discussed above may have been popularized by virtue of the cultural climate that fostered the Second Sophistic, which has also been implicated in the popularity of Greek mythological subjects in statuary and on sarcophagi.[81]

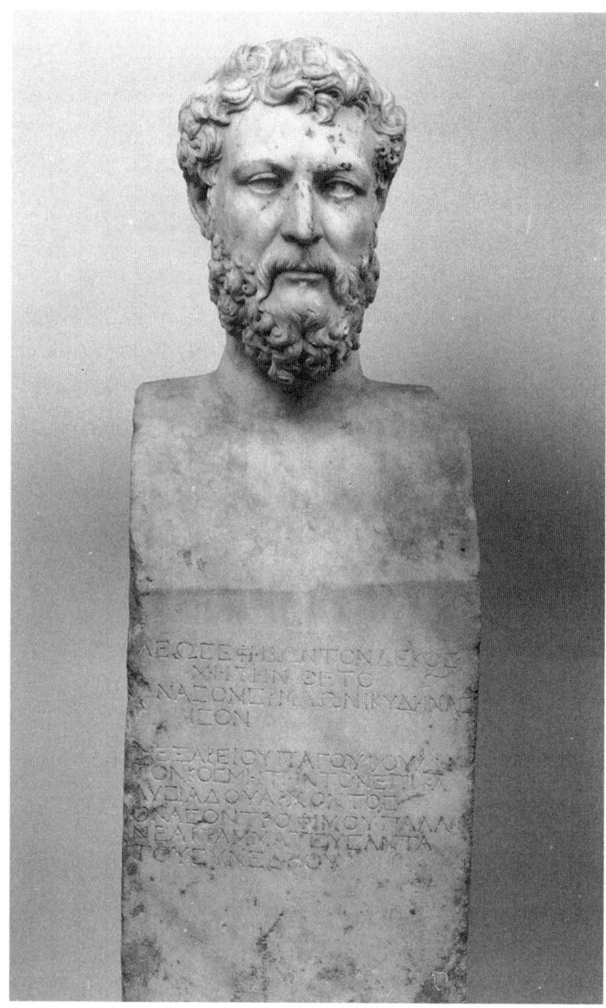

FIGURE 17.4. *Herm portrait of Onasos. Athens, National Museum 387. Photo courtesy of Hans Rupprecht Goette.*

BEARDS

Sources for the portrait of Onasos have been sought in portraits of thinkers and philosophers, such as Sophokles and Metrodoros.[82] Yet it is only the long, full beard that creates this resemblance (otherwise, the Roman copies of the philosophers lack the visceral appeal and sensitivity of the portrait of Onasos). Closer to the type is the Hadrianic bust of Theon of Smyrna, a noted mathematician and Platonic philosopher, who is represented with shorter and straighter hair but with a full beard of corkscrew curls (Fig. 17.5).[83] The physiognomy of Theon's portrait emphasizes the length of the face and the (restored) nose, as does that of Onasos, but with an expression of mental concentration with creases across the forehead and rounded eyes under a hooded brow instead of the unmarked and highly polished surface of Onasos' skin. The profiles of both are also comparable, although Onasos' portrait shows a hooked nose, large ear, and slightly receding chin. The bust of Theon extends to show the nude chest draped with a mantle in the Greek manner of intellectuals and public speakers, and the inscription below states that "the priest Theon [dedicated this bust to] his father Theon, the Platonic philosopher."[84] It is not known if the bust was erected in Theon's tomb or commemorated him in another setting, such as a garden or portico associated with his school.

Another bearded type that invites comparison with Onasos' portrait is that of Herodes Atticus (ca. 101–

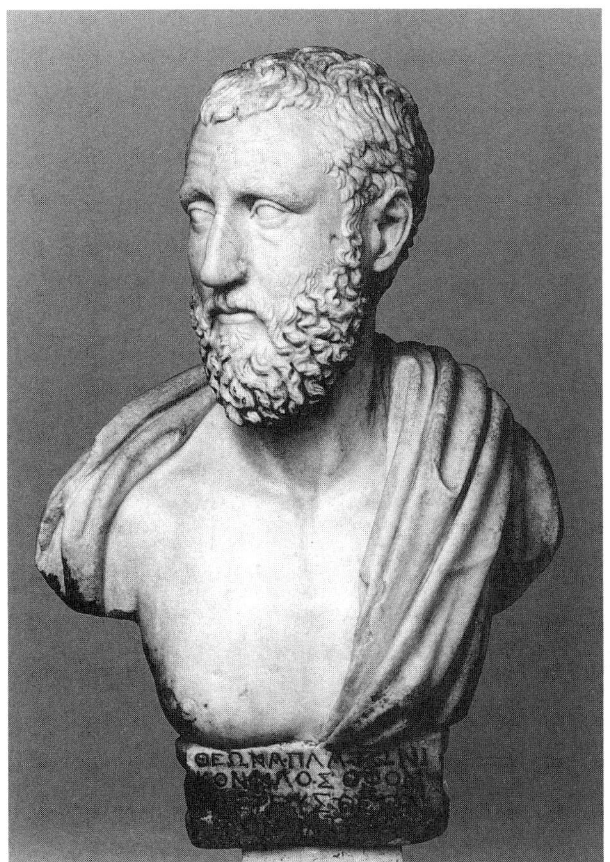

FIGURE 17.5. *Portrait bust of Theon of Smyrna. Rome, Capitoline Museum 529. Photo courtesy Archivio Fotografico dei Musei Capitolini. AC/MCn.1022.*

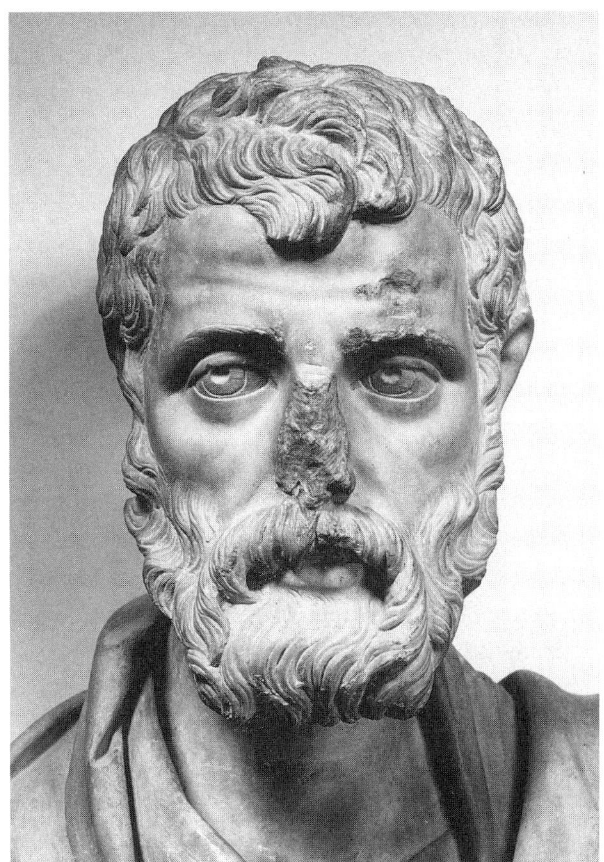

FIGURE 17.6. *Portrait bust of Herodes Atticus. Paris, Musée du Louvre MA 1164. Photo: M. and P. Chuzeville. Courtesy of the Louvre.*

177), the enormously wealthy and influential Athenian who taught Marcus Aurelius philosophy and suffered reversals of fortune in both his political career and personal life (Fig. 17.6).[85] Extraordinary in the consistency of the physiognomy, the series of portraits of Herodes Atticus is as recognizable as Imperial portraits and is compelling in the sense that they *seem* to summon a personality and the life lived.[86] The portrait has been described as casting Herodes Atticus as a city-father, a patriot, and defender of the polis, rather than as a sophist or philosopher (roles that Herodes clearly reveled in) because of the modest demeanor conveyed by the downward tilt of the head, the creased brow, the complete costume (tunic and *himation*) and the full beard. In particular, this last male attribute is instrumental to notions of self-fashioning and cultural identity.[87]

Herodes' facial hair consists of an untrimmed moustache and a fuller, brushy beard, in contrast to those of the portraits of Onasos and Theon, which have neater moustaches and beards composed of individual spiraling locks. It is curious that such an effortlessly cosmopolitan figure would choose to be depicted (simply) as a Greek, as an elder of the polis. Smith interprets the busts as reflecting fourth-century B.C. models and purposefully rejecting Antonine portrait styles (the Roman look also adopts the beard as well as flamboyant hairstyles, clouds of curls or manes of rippling locks).[88] The beard in second-century A.D. portraits has been thought to evoke the philosopher or intellectual, yet Smith has punctured this assumption with the observation that there are many distinct types of beard, and not all of them indicate a scholarly profession or bookish air.[89]

What does a beard say about a man? For Greeks, the beard signified the attainment of maturity and wisdom.[90] Shaved cheeks, on the other hand, suggested youth or profligacy. Alexander the Great shaved while some conservatives clung to their beards. Until the mid second century A.D., Romans preferred their men to be without beards, except while in certain stages of their lives or in mourning; yet lightly bearded soldiers and officers appear on state reliefs of the late first and early second centuries (e.g., the Cancelleria Reliefs, the Column of Trajan, and some portrait heads or busts).[91] When Hadrian is bearded in his official portraits, he flaunts his philhellenic leanings, his infatuation with the Greek past, and his patronage of Athens.[92]

Smith attributes Hadrian's portrait style to fashion and to an account that the beard covers unsightly blemishes.[93] Yet there is nothing to suggest that fashion motivates change in the ancient world as it does in postmodern consumer cultures, with their over abundance of goods, instant communication, and marketers with the ability to spot and promote trends (i.e., novelty for novelty's sake and for the sake of profit making in global markets). Against this explanation recall how little costumes change in portrait sculpture in the Greek and Roman periods (and the relative poverty of material culture on every social level, except for that of the elites, makes fashion irrelevant).[94] Other aspects of personal adornment, such as coiffure and facial hair, were less conservative, yet it seems unlikely that the ancients altered their habits of grooming purely for their self-improvement or to appear stylish as an end in itself.[95]

Susan Walker has observed that the wearing of a beard is "rather more than a question of fashion or personal taste."[96] Besides their role in male grooming, beards have long served as contrarian markers, as badges of political dissidence or revolt. More recently, the Greek junta in the late 1960s and early 1970s banned beards (because of their Classical pedigree and evocation of democracy?). In Afghanistan under the Taliban regime, men were required by law to wear untrimmed beards as a sign of their spiritual growth. Note also the Rastafarian belief that their dreadlocks are "God's antennae," to support this notion that hair, as well as beards, connotes the otherworldly.[97]

Even in antiquity, beards (often accompanied by long hair) expressed identity in terms of political and cultural orientation: traveling on the north coast of the Black Sea in ca. 98 A.D., Dio tells of an assembly of citizens, long-haired and bearded "like the ancient Greeks described by Homer," except for one man who was clean shaven, "to curry favor with the Romans."[98] The fellow, scorned by his peers for his appearance and his politics, stood out in the crowd, and it is precisely the difference, his lack of a beard, that marks his Roman allegiance amidst the Hellenic looks of long hair and flowing beards, a sight that would have pleased a philosopher, according to Dio. This passage, one among many that draws a distinction between Greek and Roman identities, evokes the dignity of the long beard, which could signal the high-mindedness of the philosopher or the nobility of a Hellene but had little to do with fashion. Smith is no doubt correct in his assessment that beards can have different meanings (and the beard as an intellectual attribute may have been overplayed),[99] but to assign Hadrian's image merely to an ill-defined and anachronistic view of fashion is not useful.

For the theory that the beard serves as a cover-up, we should consider the source: the *Lives of the Later Caesars* written in the fourth century A.D., possibly by six unidentified individuals who had a taste for fiction.[100] The story has the familiar ring of invective used to deflate the vanity and pretensions of an emperor like Hadrian by faulting him on his looks. To a world attuned to physiognomic theory, looks count: spotty skin points to a blemished character. Domitian scored a frontal attack on his critics, who must have made fun of his bald head, by penning a treatise on the subject that was allegedly sparkling with wit and humor.[101] These anecdotes reinforce the idea that hair and beards had moral connotations. Surely it is wrongheaded to discount Hadrian's beard as too short to be a philosopher's beard and, therefore, conclude that his philhellenic programs had no bearing on his public image.[102] Rather, we may see Hadrian's trimmed beard as assimilating Roman conventions of grooming, that is, expressly avoiding the connotations of decadent Greek habits and evoking the noble modes of the Greek revival at the same time.

Furthermore, Hadrian's version of Hellenism was grounded in his intellectual and religious interests, which were focused on Athens as the center of the Panhellion, the league of Greek cities drawn together by common descent in 131–132 (lineage and purity of heritage being an obsession of the Second Sophistic). The Panhellion appears to have had one important function: to administer the Imperial cult.[103] It was, perhaps, a clever political move of Hadrian to link worship of the Imperial house with an organization drawing the often fractious Greek cities together.[104] It also benefited Athens by means of building programs and urban renewal projects that reclaimed the city's position as a cultural capital: the library of Hadrian, the arch, and gymnasion were among the gifts of the emperor.[105] Hadrian's repeated visits to the city—he spent more time in Athens than anywhere else besides Rome—beginning with his archonship in *absentia* in 112–113 before he was emperor and continuing with his celebration of the Eleusinian Mysteries in 124 and 128, and the dedication of the Temple of Olympian Zeus in 131–132 in which Polemon gave the address, indicate his vocation as a student of Hellas, an aspect not to be dismissed lightly in the zeal to rid portraiture of facile biographical interpretations.[106]

CONCLUSIONS

Finally, Hadrian's beard may have provoked a reaction in a manner markedly different from the imitation spawned by the emperor's image in the phenomenon of the period-face. Rather than copying the Imperial portrait as a model (or, conversely, rejecting it out of Hellenic pride), the leading men of the Greek East may have desired to correct it, to take back the image of the wise man, and to restore it to its full-bearded grandeur. Public citizens, whether kosmetai or other city elders, were motivated to reclaim their heritage with more authentic-looking features, such as curlier or longer hair and beards of varying lengths (as seen in the portraits of Onasos, Herodes Atticus, and Theon of Smyrna). The Second Sophistic, after all, aimed to restore the past glory of the Greeks not only by keeping its culture alive but also by purifying and refining its language and identity.

As the Greeks returned to their roots, some members of the metropolitan elite in Rome adopted the Hellenic features of longer wavy manes and flowing beards that define the Antonine style with its elegant and soigné looks.[107] These men, apparently not satisfied with the discrete Hellenizing aspects of Hadrian's portraits, sought more sophisticated effects in their adaptations from Greek portraiture and the new Roman marble-carving techniques. A minority of the many portraits sporting tousled locks and well-groomed beards probably represents intellectuals, as Smith has suggested.[108] This style has been attributed to fashion, although the luxuriant growth of hair accompanied a quest for authenticity and origins in the Greek East, a phenomenon with greater repercussions than fashion. In Rome and the West, it is likely that this masculine adornment evoked an urbane and worldly milieu shaped by the cosmopolitan attitudes of men who risked charges of effeminacy or permissiveness in order to play their part on a wider stage. The portraits mark the cultural aspirations of Romans who desired the high gloss of the Hellenic heritage without necessarily living the lives or upholding the values evoked by the imagery.[109]

To say that fashion changed under Hadrian does not begin to explain the radical shift in self-representation and cultural identity in the second half of the second century. Roman attitudes toward Hellenism or, better yet, the redefinition of acceptable forms of Hellenism under Hadrian and the Antonines was responsible.[110] The fascination with the sophists and their quasi-transgressive behavior in flamboyant performances may have provided an opening in the West for reconsideration of the Greek heritage. Yet we should also look to Hadrian's Hellenism as a more conservative reformulation of the standards of high culture with his scholarly tours of Athens and his imprimatur on a personal image that exuded Hellenic sophistication and a concern for appearances.

To return to the beginning, the portraits of the kosmetai indicate the standards of self-representation in the late first and early second centuries with portraits that appear superficially Roman but cannot be easily categorized as Roman or Greek upon closer inspection. Instead, they indicate a cosmopolitan type for men who governed Athens but were, in turn, governed by Rome. By the mid second century A.D., however, the civic leaders of Athens and other Greek cities decked themselves out as revered philosophers and patriots as a paean to the past. Their retreat to the world of bucolic reverie and myth was countered by the metropolitan Roman portraits that adapted aspects of the Greek style to suggest their subjects' worldliness and savvy, their mastery of the older culture, at least in the external forms of style. That the Roman portraits outdid their Greek models in their elegant stylization seems to indicate that these cultivated effects were less about the substance of Hellenism (i.e., the philosopher's beard) than about a new cosmopolitan image, which flourished as never before in the empire.

NOTES

I thank Judy Barringer and Jeff Hurwit for their care and patience in editing my essay. I also thank Lynn LiDonnici for help in translating modern Greek. The Salmon Fund from Vassar College covered the cost of travel and photographs.

1. The literature on the Second Sophistic is growing exponentially: Bowersock 1969; Bowie 1970; Brunt 1994, against the exaggeration of the movement and its effects; Anderson 1993; Swain 1996; Goldhill 2001. On Hadrian: Walker and Cameron 1989; Woolf 1994; C. P. Jones 1996; Boatwright 2000.

2. Woolf 1994, 128–130.

3. Elsner 1998, 117–126.

4. Lattanzi 1968, 17–18; Marrou 1982, 105–108, 110–111.

5. Lattanzi 1968, 17.

6. R. R. R. Smith 1998, 79–80, on the annual president of the Athenian gymnasion as the "vice-chancellor of Athens University."

7. Lattanzi 1968, 18–19.

8. Rhomiopoulou 1997, nos. 38–65, 49–67.

9. R. R. R. Smith 1998, 56–61.

10. Borg 1996, 194–195, on this process in the production of painted mummy portraits in Roman Egypt.

11. The interpretation of the iconography of portraits may benefit from advances in the study of so-called Roman copies, Classical statuary in the Roman world; see Gazda 1995, 121–156; Gazda 2002.

12. Zanker 1995, 74, on our seeing the faces "too close up."

13. R. R. R. Smith 1998, 83–87. I would recalibrate Smith's analysis of Greek and Roman features to give more credit to the Roman character of the beardless elder type, the looks of which appeared sufficiently neutral by this time to appeal to the leading men in the Greek East. Other features are so deeply embedded in the elite system of honors that to distinguish between Greek and Roman aspects is beside the point. On the other hand (Zanker 1995, 220–224), some have noted the self-conscious Classicism (and rejection of Roman styles) of the portraits of the kosmetai and their identification with their ancestors.

14. R. R. R. Smith 1998, 90–92.

15. Smith 1998, 59–60, on the period-face as "the default setting" for private portraits.

16. Graindor 1915, 292–300, no. 2, fig. 10; Lattanzi 1968, 34–35; Rhomiopoulou 1997, 50–51, no. 39.

17. Daltrop, Hausmann, and Wegner 1966, 9–17, 72–84, pls. 1–9.

18. Bergmann 1982; Zanker 1982.

19. Daltrop, Hausmann, and Wegner 1966, pls. 2–9.

20. S. Dillon 1996; Hallett 1998.

21. D'Ambra 1998, 96–97; R. R. R. Smith 1998, 60.

22. Lattanzi 1968, 18–19.

23. R. R. R. Smith 1998, 83–87.

24. R. R. R. Smith 1998, 85–86.

25. Woolf 1994, 128–129, on the primacy of language and descent for Hellenic identity, whereas material culture was not central to questions of identity; *contra* R. R. R. Smith 1998, 86–87, and the discussion of Dio of Prusa 36.17 (see below, n. 90, on the meaning of the beard). Hellenic identity could also be shored up by the statue's *himation* or the herm format (R. R. R. Smith 1998, 80 and 86), as in the kosmetai portraits.

26. Contra Smith (1998, 83–92), who emphasizes differences among portraits of the Roman West and Greek East along cultural allegiances and public roles.

27. Daltrop 1958, Abb. 11, Lateran, no. X 583 (ca. 100 A.D.).

28. Daltrop 1958, Abb. 40, Braccio Nuovo, no. 81 (ca. 120–130 A.D.).

29. Daltrop 1958, Abb. 41, Museo Nuovo, vi, 5 (ca. 120–130 A.D.); D'Ambra 1998, 39–40, fig. 19.

30. E. B. Harrison 1953, 35–37, pl. 17, but there are grounds for a later Antonine date; R. R. R. Smith 1998, 83, 85.

31. Inscribed for Rhoummas; Walker 1985, 61, fig. 49 (before 150 A.D.); Smith 1998, 84, pl. 12:2 (mid–later second century).

32. R. R. R. Smith 1998, 84, pl. 12:3 (mid second century).

33. E. B. Harrison 1953, no. 43 (ca. 235–245 A.D.); R. R. R. Smith 1998, 84, pl. 12:4.

34. R. R. R. Smith 1998, 59, 61–63.

35. R. R. R. Smith 1998, 63–70, 86–87, 90–92.

36. Dio. Chrys. *Or.* 31.155. The date of the Rhodian Oration is usually given as Vespasianic (or slightly later in the reign of Titus), but Swain (1996, appendix C, 428–429) proposes a Trajanic date.

37. Edwards 1997, 79–80.

38. E. B. Harrison 1953, 26, n. 1, and 37: indicating "a respectable mark of gentlemanly interest in athletics."

39. Veyne 1990; Woolf 1994; Swain 1996, 65–100; Lendon 1997, 78–89, 176–236; many of the portraits wear the crowns of Imperial priesthoods.

40. See below, n. 46.

41. Rose 1997, 114–117, figs. 3, 4; R. R. R. Smith 1998, 73–75, pl. 5:2; pl. 8:4, on the likely identification of the statue with Celsus.

42. Wallace-Hadrill 1990, on the Republican period and concluding that "the idioms of Greek culture were taken over as part of the process of forming new relations of power within Roman society" (169). For cultural identity in the Greek East, see also Bagnall 1997.

43. Lendon 1997.

44. Saller and Garnsey 1987, 20–40.

45. Lattanzi 1968, 24–25.

46. E. B. Harrison 1953, 124–129; R. Osborne 1985.

47. Vernant 1983, 127–175.

48. Detienne and Vernant 1975, 41–42, 120, 281–283, 286, 301–303.

49. Gleason 1995, 3–54.

50. Graindor 1915, 304–306, no. 4, fig. 11; Lattanzi 1968, 35–36; Rhomiopoulou 1997, 51, no. 40. There may also be a reflection of the Polykleitan style in the pose of the head, turned downward and slightly to one side, and the large, simplified features. I owe this observation to Jeff Hurwit.

51. Foucault 1986. For criticism of his method, see Goldhill 1995, xi–xii, and Richlin 1998.

52. Connolly 2001.

53. Gleason 1995, 55–81; Williams 1999, 125–159.

54. Connolly 2001, 83.

55. Gleason 1995, 61–62, on the walk of the lion as a paradigm for nobility.

56. Connolly 2001, 88–95. The period of the sophists ranges from the mid first through the third centuries, although the second century is under consideration here.

57. Philostr. *VS* 544; cited in Connolly 2001, 75. Polemon also lived large, traveling with a retinue of slaves, pack animals, dogs, and horses in a Phrygian or Gaulish chariot decked out with silver adornments (*VS* 532).

58. Williams 1999, 72–82; Connolly 2001, 93–94.

59. Gleason 1995, 162: "And there may also have been a temptation to appropriate characteristics of 'the other' as a way of gaining power from outside the traditionally accepted sources." See Gleason 1999, 77–79, on grooming, comportment, and *cinaedi* who affect a more virile appearance to avoid suspicion (*Anonymous Latin Physiognomy 74 Förster*).

60. R. R. R. Smith 1998, 91; the types best exemplified by the portraits of Vespasian or Trajan and, of course, by the type of Heliodoros in the East.

61. R. R. R. Smith 1998, 91.

62. R. R. R. Smith 1998, 62 and 83, on the introduction of drilled and engraved eyes in the portraits of Hadrian in the 130s and the wider adoption of the technique by about 140; Fittschen 1992–1993, 448, n. 10, on the portraits of Antinous with pupils and irises engraved between 130–138 (about half of the total number produced).

63. Daltrop 1958, Abb. 26, Chiaramonti VII, 12 (ca. 110–120 A.D.).

64. Daltrop 1958, Abb. 32, British Museum 1975 (ca. 120 A.D.).

65. Felletti Maj 1953, nos. 151 and 170.

66. Comstock and Vermeule 1976, no. 357; Inan and Alföldi-Rosenbaum 1979, no. 215 (late Hadrianic; J. Inan); Fittschen 1992–1993, 460, figs. 7:3–4; R. R. R. Smith 1998, 85, pl. 14:1, for the later Antonine date.

67. Inan and Rosenbaum 1970, nos. 74, 93, Nikaia, Bursa Museum (period of Nerva): pl. 45:3–4.

68. Fittschen and Zanker 1985, II, no. 103; Fittschen 1992–1993, fig. 7:1.

69. Fittschen 1992–1993, figs. 4:1–2.

70. Smith (1998, 63) sees the Second Sophistic as an "attendant circumstance" of the phenomenon.

71. Philostr. *VS* 582, 589.

72. Philostr. *VS* 571 cited in Connolly (2001, 89–90).

73. The sophists tested limits: Favorinus of Arles described himself as a Gaul who lived like a Greek, as a eunuch who had been tried for adultery, and as one who quarreled with the emperor and was still alive (Philostr. *VS* 489).

74. Woolf 1994, 133–135.

75. Suet. *Dom.* 18; Cain 1993, 58–73; Morgan 1997.

76. Cain 1993, 58–78, 81–104; R. R. R. Smith 1998, 88–89.

77. Richlin 1995, 201–206.

78. Graindor 1915, 313–318, n. 7, pl. 17; Lattanzi 1968, 39–40; Rhomiopoulou 1997, 52–53, no. 42.

79. R. R. R. Smith 1998, 79–81, on the kosmetai.

80. R. R. R. Smith 1998, 80.

81. Elsner 1998, 17–85, 145–152, on ideal sculpture and sarcophagi; above, n. 70.

82. Lattanzi 1968, 40, on the Sophokles statue in the Lateran and the Metrodoros portrait in the Capitoline and Athens; see also Pollitt 1986, 65, fig. 60, on a portrait of Epicurus (from a third-century original) that bears some resemblance to Onasos (thanks to Judy Barringer for suggesting this comparison); and Richter and Smith 1984, 205–209, and 164–166, on the Sophokles and Metrodoros types. The classification of Greek and Roman portrait types is also complicated because Classical portraits are known almost exclusively through Roman copies of fourth-century B.C. works (see above, n. 11). Our access to these works depicting statesmen, philosophers, and orators is filtered by Roman sculptural traditions and taste. The domination of *Kopienkritik,* the method by which (it is thought) the original sculpture can be retrieved by carefully comparing the copies to determine authentic features and later deviations, in modern scholarship has been tested recently by

approaches that emphasize the creativity of Roman sculptors who, inspired by Greek masterpieces, freely adapted works for Roman patrons and audiences. So much of the Greek sculptural tradition has been studied and assimilated by Roman craftsmen who either emulated it or chose to sidestep its practices. To define Greek as opposed to Roman features in portraiture denies the intense, and often conflicted, relationship between the two cultures in which contradictory elements resided without clashing.

83. Stuart Jones 1912, 229–230, n. 25, pl. 57; Inan and Alföldi-Rosenbaum 1979, 162–164, no. 115, pls. 95, 105 (K. Fittschen).

84. Stuart Jones 1912, 229; Richter 1984, 55.

85. Ameling 1983; Tobin 1997. Herodes was a Greek aristocrat and Roman senator, a patron of Athens and imposing orator. For the portrait in the Louvre, which was found in a tomb in Probalinthos near Marathon and is dated to about 160, see de Kersauson 1996, 290–293, no. 132.

86. The portrait type is represented by nine copies and versions; see R. R. R. Smith 1998, 78. The facts of Herodes' life do not provide an interpretative framework for the portrait, just as reading a personality from the features of an anonymous portrait is illusory.

87. Walker 1989a; R. R. R. Smith 1998, 59, 78–79.

88. R. R. R. Smith 1998, 79, except for the techniques of engraving the eyes and texturing the hair (see also 62 on the advanced technology of marble portraits).

89. R. R. R. Smith 1998, 86–87.

90. Walker 1991, for much of what follows on customs of shaving and growing beards; also on Dio's Borysthenic oration (*Or.* 36.17; ca. 98 A.D.) about Greek identity and beards and the idea that shaving, interpreted as selling out to the Romans, has less to do with Roman habits than with Greek (and Greeks residing in Olbia, southern Russia) anxieties about identity, as Walker notes (272).

91. Cain 1993, 100–103.

92. R. R. R. Smith 1998, 90–91, on Hadrian's beard as representing metropolitan fashions for elegance and sophistication.

93. SHA *Hadr.* 26; R. R. R. Smith 1998, 90–91.

94. R. R. R. Smith 1998, 66, for the representation of the himation and tunic over the course of five centuries as equivalent to the wearing of Elizabethan costume in portraits today.

95. *Contra* Ov. *Ars am.* 3.149–152.

96. Walker 1991, 265.

97. Walker 1991, 265. An unshaved journalist is commended by a Taliban immigration inspector for showing signs of spiritual growth (*New York Times,* International News, May 6, 2001, A40); a short beard is claimed as evidence that a Pakistani businessman is not involved with the Taliban (*New York Times,* International News, Oct. 14, 2001, B3). Ryle (2000, 18) on the Rastafarians in the 1970s.

98. Dio 36.17; also cited by Walker 1991; Zanker 1995, 220; R. R. R. Smith 1998, 86–87.

99. Zanker 1995, 198–266.

100. Birley 1976, 7–22.

101. Suet. *Dom.* 18; Morgan 1997.

102. R. R. R. Smith 1998, 91: Smith asserts that if the beard signaled Hellenic tastes, then it would have been criticized as such by the authors of the *Historia Augusta.* But it is risky to assign too much meaning to the source's silence on that account. Could it simply be that the beard did not bother its audience? On Hadrian's sexuality (as another example of Hellenic tastes), see Williams 1999, 60–61.

103. Woolf 1994, 134–135; C. P. Jones (1996) thinks that the impulse for the Panhellion came from the Greeks, with modifications by Hadrian.

104. Spawforth and Walker 1985.

105. Boatwright 2000, 144–157.

106. Geagan 1979. Contra R. R. R. Smith 1998, 60, 90–91. Although Smith's model is astute in removing imitation of the period-face as the only motivation for stylistic developments, I think his discussion of the portraiture of Hadrian goes too far in correcting the problem.

107. Ryle 2000, for a methodological model in Old and New World cultures.

108. R. R. R. Smith 1998, 78, 90–91.

109. R. R. R. Smith 1998, 91–92, on the portraits as expressing the refinement brought about by a Classical education although I think that the range of associations is wider.

110. Contra R. R. R. Smith 1998, 63 on Rome coming to some sort of negotiated deal with Hellenism.

18

A RHETORICAL PERIKLES

W. MARTIN BLOOMER

Periklean Athens appealed as a subject of study at Yale University for the last thirty years in part because the imperial democracy of Athens refracted the anxieties and ambitions of an elite American youth about its own imperial democracy. In particular, study of Periklean Athens thrived for reason of the excellent teaching of J. J. Pollitt with his masterly proposal of an integrated study of a brilliant culture. The allure of Athens involved, too, lament for the perceived loss of a confident, integrated American culture. Whether art and politics could have a relation that was not combative or not propagandistic may seem a question somewhat naïve and schematic, but it was nonetheless real, especially to the undergraduate.

Related was the question of whether not simply Art History but especially Classics was a connoisseur's preserve. Professor Pollitt's synthetic view of what scholarship entailed and what a culture had been did not provide the reassuring message that Athens would live again under the leadership of a new political elite. His interpretation of this culture and his demands on students were always more nuanced and more critical. Still, he challenged students to understand the commonalities of culture and of cultural expression in ways that did not cede explanatory authority to the political or to narrow, disciplinary expertise.

In this paper I discuss a different moment in the reception of the image of Perikles and Periklean Athens. The rhetorical understanding of Perikles by Greek and Latin speakers in the Roman Empire has not, I believe, been sufficiently appreciated. While the importance of Plutarch's *Life* as a historical source has rightly been recognized, the conceptions of Plutarch's *Perikles* have often been attributed to the schematic frame of source criticism. This drifts toward a polar understanding with positive portrayals of Perikles credited to Thukydides, negative to Plato and the invective of Old Comedy.[1] I stress not that his composition is pastiche nor even that a descriptive moralism guides his pen (so well described by Pelling)[2] but that a rhetorician's understanding of political leadership underlies his life.

PERIKLES AMONG THE SCHOOLMEN

Roman and Greek declamation, including the portrayals of Perikles in Valerius Maximus and the Greek rhetors, reveals a cluster of uses of Perikles.[3] For the rhetoricians and thus for the educated imperial Greek or Roman, Perikles figured the problem of tyranny. Declaimers spoke upon the question of whether he differed from Peisistratos. In general, declamatory themes involve issues of bribery, treason, and tyranny. Professor Russell in his book on Greek declamation judiciously coined the term "Sophistopolis" for the imaginary world of declamation where, through the fantasies of pirates and rapists, military heroes and the ungrateful friend, the young speakers imagine how service to the city collides with service to family, gods, friends.

In particular terms, Perikles is not celebrated so much as the great general or visionary statesman but as a type for self-control; he displays the virtue of *prāotēs* (self-control), for example, by never giving way to tears (except at the end, amid the plague, he weeps for the last of his children).[4] The rhetorical exercises exploit and replicate the inscrutability of Perikles: he is the master of himself, wielding words against emotion and violence; he is also the historical subject difficult to read, his motives and even his emotions, especially sexuality, hard to know. He is the perfect Aristotelean, giving way neither to joy nor to anger. Schoolboys consider through historical fantasy what constitutes the tyrant and how to read tyrannical behavior from the imperturbable face. Was Perikles a crypto-Lakedaimonian bribe-taker or true Athenian? Was he Peisistratid or democrat?[5] (Perikles here follows the strong model of Themistokles, whose allegiances—Medizer or true Greek—also inspired spirited and repeated treatment.) In Plutarch's logic, both questions are related to whether he ever wept, and their answers can be known not by scrutiny of inscriptions and ostraka, nor by the careful study of the prosopography of the age, but by seeking a rhetorical synthesis of the literary and artistic accounts that time had deemed authoritative. At any rate, the sort of textual approach that seeks to represent a consistent character in a consistent composition informs Plutarch's text and the reception of it by his contemporaries.

Writing the life of Perikles was for Plutarch an encounter with vulgarity, with rumor and slander (which quite often centers on the body, physically deformed or lustful). The Old Comic poets and numerous anecdotes, transmitted or embellished by the rhetorical schools, preserved slanderous reports of his family life, his sexuality, his political opportunism, even his physical appearance.[6] Plutarch writes to contain this slander: he does not ignore it but, rather like the story he tells of Perikles suffering a vociferous critic all day long and then sending him home with a servant (5.2.3), the author exhibits the same virtue of prāotēs. Self-control is a rhetorical and personal as well as political virtue. Plutarch presents Perikles as one who could rule the *demos,* while as an author he contains the libel so that he can argue Perikles was not a tyrant, not a Peisistratid, not a Medizer, nor a deformed, hypertrophic egghead.

Declamatory exercises in which stories critical of Perikles were posed, decided, and, with that typical iterability of the school and of scholarship, reopened the next day, helped enshrine Perikles as the test case for tyrant-in-hiding. This need not mean that Perikles provided a straightforward fantasy about Greek citizens' relations to the Roman emperor; rather, imperial citizens in their education used the inscrutability of Perikles and the corresponding conflict of characterization in the sources of the slanderous charges, as an opening by which to speak and think of the ideal governor. One direct connection is the epithet "Olympian" itself, applied to Perikles in what the rhetoricians called "a *topos* from the name" and which would become the most common epithet of the emperor Hadrian in the East.[7]

More abstractly, the development of Perikles from democratic orator to imperial tyrant replayed the passage of Rome (and the once independent Greek cities) from republic or autonomy to empire. In addition, by plumbing the problematic identity of the emperor, the tyrant in republican clothing, whose *vultus* is immobile (as Tacitus makes Tiberius into a fixed mask), Perikles offered an academic fantasy on empire and its justification.[8] A more popular and no doubt appealing role for the schoolboys was to speak as Alkibiades, the adolescent whose sexuality, ambition, and fidelity to father figure (Perikles) and fatherland was far more suspect and thus productive of categorical impasses, the difficulties of identity that were opportunities for the declaimers. Here, too, the young could face Perikles and with an impertinent remark prod him from his one moment of *aporia* to action.[9] Thus the declamatory Perikles came to be a familiar stand-in for the impassive emperor or even the authoritative father, with the all important difference of the school subject: the *nous* of this dead and distant father, which signifies the consistency of his character, his ability to compose all, and the alleged moral rightness of his composed actions, invited play and contestation.

I begin with a reminder of the Perikles current in the ancient schools not to slight the authority of Plutarch's *Life of Perikles* but to suggest a context for understanding his biographical writing. Historians are far more used to employing Thukydides, Plato, or the scant Ephoros to measure the context and methods of Plutarch. Where there is good historical detail and no parallel from Plato or Thukydides, Ephoros is brought forward as a source, unless the information seems too unworthy. I exaggerate the procedures of the source critics, and Philip Stadter's commentary presents a review of source criticism for this life (and adds valuable new insights, e.g., the suggestion that a series of scandalous and scurrilous details might arise simply from Plutarch taking the comic poets too seriously).[10] Consequently, Plutarch must be made to admit another charge against his method of historical writing: he has not only relied on the fictions of the declaimers, he has taken the old poets' farce at face value. I resist carving up the biographer as if one could savor the historical bones, sinew, and muscle after trimming away the declamatory and comic fat. His anecdotal material and his use of the comic poets are not simply a failure to follow Thukydides or an uncritical eclecticism but an essential part of what he took to be his charge as a historian.

Plutarch's anecdotal treatment of art and artists and his hostile and uncritical use of the poets as sources contribute to a severe esthetics, which subordinates poetry and art to the historian's prose. Both "unreliable" tendencies in his composition, the use of traditional stories and the antipathy toward or lack of understanding of the poet contemporaries of Perikles, derive from a historiographical and biographical imperative. Plutarch is driven to contain slander and in particular to demonstrate the inconsistency (and hence unreliability) of the tales that circulate about the body of Perikles. For the ancient rhetorical historian seeking the best matter for praise and blame, the figure of Perikles appealed especially since he, like Fabius Maximus, was the great man maligned by his contemporaries, whom history, of course, has shown to be right.

But perhaps in calling for a rhetorical understanding of the processes and aims of Plutarch's composition, I, too, am trying to evade slander directed at my author. Plutarch's *Life of Perikles,* while quite useful for the professional historian, shows Plutarch at his worst. Plutarch the iconoclast cares little for the grand building project that continues to enthrall us; Plutarch the snob further belittles artists, artisans, and workers—all unimportant in contrast to the directing mind of Perikles; finally, Plutarch the biographer is antihistorical, showing disdain for chronology in particular and a lack of understanding of the aristocratic politics and civic institutions of Perikles' day. These three "faults," however, arise from Plutarch's chief challenge: how to stem the slander that attends this greatest man of Greece and so to lead the reader to a right apprehension of the merit of Perikles. In short, Plutarch must present a life that constitutes an *imitandum,* a worthy subject for replication. It has been said that Plutarch achieves such an end by a species of abstraction: the historical figure is reduced to a moral type. Here Perikles embodies the self-composure and restraint known as prāotēs.[11]

While it is true that Plutarch is a moralist, moralism hardly captures his method. One ready means to the end of praising famous men is to bowdlerize. Notably, Plutarch does not suppress damaging information. Rather, he crafts the story of Perikles so that we readers may be instructed not simply into the virtue of restraint but into the scholarly virtue of proper assessment of contradictory evidence. This project required that Plutarch face the visible legacy of Perikles—art and architecture, since the authentic speeches had been lost—and argue that the physical legacy was only a sign of what was truly important about Perikles: his self-composition.

THE *Chreia* ORIENTING READERS

The life opens, rather oddly, with a story told of Caesar (probably Augustus).[12] On seeing some foreigners carrying puppies in the folds of their cloaks and making a great fuss of them, the emperor asked, "Don't the women of your land bear children?" There is a rationale for beginning thus, and it is not simply, as some rhetorical criticism maintains, that a rhetorical figure is used here for a general purpose, that is, an anecdote captures the reader's interest. This anecdote's subject is important philosophically and thematically for the topic. Stadter notes that no section of the *Perikles* is devoted to anecdotes.[13] Quite true, but several anecdotes treat Perikles' interpretation of signs. Here Augustus' interpretation of a foreign practice prepares for the series of signs where Perikles' interpretation stands at odds with the popular one. In technical terms Plutarch has begun not simply with an anecdote but with a *chreia*—a sayings story that differs from the saying (*gnōmē*) in that it is not a free-floating truism but the very words of a particular speaker in a specific context.[14] Often, these building blocks of ancient education move from silence and sight to speech: for example, when Sokrates or Diogenes or the emperor saw something, he said. . . .

For the ancient, the chreia was a familiar opening, since it had been his or her early educational exercise and since it had a form as familiar as the formulas of a joke. Plutarch here uses the chreia to good purpose. The verbal castigation of errant popular opinion anticipates Perikles' customary virtue. The Athenian demos, like these wealthy foreigners, is smitten with emotion, but Perikles' prāotēs restrains him from such excess. In addition, the chreia anticipates a dichotomy important for Plutarch's understanding of Perikles. In his opening story the foreigners have taken the *allotrion* for the *oikeion,* the other as one's own.

The oikeion will prove to be an important, recurring term and concept. It can be a rhetorical term, a synonym for the *prepon,* the fitting, a term that describes the perfect relation of form to content but that is also an ethical term for the man who knows himself, his body, his family and friends, his city and people—so well embodied by Perikles who allows no foreign invasion of any of these. In military strategy, Perikles resists the people's confusion of mine and thine; he knows what is proper to the *polis* and so opposes military adventurism in Egypt, Sicily, Etruria, and Africa or keeps the people bottled up in the city when they wish to spill out and engage the Lakedaimonians.[15] Perikles will consistently exhibit a well-defined sense of what is oikeion. He will be particularly finicky about keeping to himself and himself shaping himself, not attending others' banquets, not allowing his body to be subject to others. In the end, Perikles will prove the proper subject for Plutarch—he will be *oikeios* to his readers, not a long dead, difficult-to-understand foreigner or other but a ready model whom his readers can make their own.

Plutarch may well then be leading his imperial reader back from a story of Augustus to his great paradigm for the leader, but he has a philosophical point as well. The chreia recording Augustus' censure has oriented the reader to the familiar task of the rhetorician: praise and blame.[16] Plutarch plays the scholiast or schoolmaster to a chreia of Augustus, but a diction drawn from esthetics and philosophy makes clear that his is also an essay into proper (literary) criticism.[17] The structures undergirding Plutarch's language are often so familiar that criticism of his style tends to present him as the master of pastiche. Since he is a rhetorical writer who follows distinguished sources, analysis of his prose tends to put as conclusions what are in fact observations of detail: the identification of the source(s), a description of the reworking (or combination), and the naming of rhetorical figures.

The ornamentation or stylization of the chreia with philosophical language, however, has a hermeneutic purpose. The pet owners made the mistake of the wayward souls of the *Phaedrus:* they are mistaken about the proper object of affection and desire. Plutarch does not voice the connection to Plato here, nor does he intimate how the speech act of Augustus anticipates the saving words of Perikles. This is one of Plutarch's great virtues: he is so readable because on the immediate, minute level of phrasing, he restates and repeats himself in a way far more colorful than, say, Cicero. Just as he is fond of pairs of synonyms or draping a participial phrase on the end of his sentences, he has that more oral, less implicit habit of stringing anecdotes and events without directly announcing that the succeeding phrase or story may be connected, even explanatory.[18] This allows a certain thematic redundancy, which, given a recognizable rhetorical landscape of organization, carries his reader along.

Without much overt marking of the connection of ideas, this sort of style encourages a swiftness of reading. The easy movement of Plutarch, with his tendency toward the paradigmatic and paratactic, exerts a sort of magnetism on analysts of Plutarch, imperceptibly and irresistibly drawing them to describe his texts in terms of rhetorical division. Certainly, an ancient reader would have recognized the topography of encomium, but seeing it merely as an encomium is a sterile criticism, which only enumerates the bones of a piece. Rhetorical structure easily permits a flow of themes, images, and motifs without strictly requiring connection to be argued or even articulated. Plutarch provides his own philosophical exegesis of the puppy lovers and Augustus: he states that in works of non-*aretē,* an impulse toward action does not immediately arise from gazing at the work but rather quite often the opposite: we take pleasure in the work and disdain the worker as with cloth dyers.[19] He does not range puppy with dyer as the false object of wonder, nor directly equate son with tapestry or objet d'art as the proper object, but he is working his associative route from opening chreia to his point, and that point will be to establish Perikles and not Pheidias (or any artist) as the proper object of our wonder.

In outline, Plutarch's teleological rhetoric may seem heavy-handed, but these opening sections, besides preparing the reader for a proper estimation of the great man, revalue work and the agents of work in a hierarchy of values that favors the intellectual and the textual over the banausic and the plastic arts. The method is heavy-handed and rhetorical in that Plutarch brings forward dyers and artisans to incite his readers' contempt, rather than the sculptors and architects who in fact compete with Perikles for renown, and he delays Perikles' entrance until we have granted his premise on the proper object of admiration. It has been argued that Perikles was not a culture figure, that in fact nineteenth-century scholarship (and ultimately romanticism) is responsible for the picture of Perikles as a cultural leader animating a circle of intellectuals and the cultural glories of Classical Athens. Voltaire had selected from all human history four periods worthy of his readers' special attention: the Age of Perikles, the Age of Julius and Augustus Caesar, the Age of the Medici, and that culminating moment and title of his own book, *The Age of Louis XIV* (1751).

Contemporary scholars may be correct in limiting Perikles' program and so differentiating him from illustrious political sponsors of culture (for example, Frederick the Great) but, unwittingly, they are following Plutarch's lead in denying his connection to the artists of the day. Plutarch was not denying connection of friendship; rather, by means of a philosophizing exegesis of a series of anecdotes, he presents a conception of human agency that divides society and work into a hierarchy where the virtues of Perikles, the virtues of government, those of intellect, indeed of reading, hold sway over the "lesser" arts.

Perikles must be alienated from art and artistic works for a series of reasons, including Plutarch's rather restricted view of the virtue and purpose of art, but also because if we look in awe on the Parthenon, we are misappraising Perikles (and by extension, Greek achievement).[20] In the string of colorful stories that pepper this work, Plutarch has next a pair that (like the story of the puppies and Augustus) consider popular misapprehension, here again of the nonverbal arts, not in this case vision and sculpture but music and dancing. These, too, are chreiai: "Antisthenes, when it was reported to him that Ismenias was a really good flautist" finished the sentence "but not a good man. Otherwise he would not be a good flautist." Plutarch offers a fuller explanation for the second chreia: Philip's rebuke to his son. Alexander had been dancing to his own delight and with considerable expertise at a symposion. His father said, "Aren't you ashamed to dance so well?"

Many chreiai target errant youth; the sayings tale was after all a staple of preliminary education. Both these chreiai, moreover, reflect Greek social biases against professionalism and professionals. Plutarch does not include an intriguing aspect recorded by Aristotle in which the philosopher rationalizes the social bias against the flautist (Plato had also excluded the flautist): in the *Politics* (1341b) flute playing is said to have fallen into disuse because it distorted the face and had no voice accompaniment. (Plutarch also records in the *Alk.* 2.5–7 that Alkibiades as a boy would not play the flute since he did not wish to distort his face.)[21] The cautionary tale probably needed only the slightest allusion. Athena herself had rejected the flute for the same reason; the satyr Marsyas picked it up, but then he and his ugly hide came to no good end. The nonverbal arts and the uncomposed body serve as the foil to one who is a great master of himself and of words.

DENIGRATING ARTISTS, PROMOTING WRITERS

Plutarch continues to denigrate artists by stating that no noble youth on seeing the statue of Zeus in Pisa desires to become Pheidias. Plutarch worries on with a list of artists one should not wish to be. He cites Polykleitos, but he then diverges from the plastic arts with Anakreon, Philemon, and Archilochos. Philemon has struck some as an odd choice (and so editors have read Philetas or, abandoning the manuscript evidence, suggested that writer of barbed iambs, Hipponax). The passage does make a difficult juncture (although music, dancing, poetry are all *mousikē*), for Plutarch has been talking of the objects of vision and their effect upon human beings.

After underscoring the point of his mention of the poets—there is no need to admire and be keen to imitate the maker if one finds the work attractive—he continues this theorizing immediately. The argument resumes: for this reason, such works that do not arouse a mimetic urge or a sprouting that stirs a desire and an impulse toward imitation do viewers no good (the Greek diction is redundant, a bit colorful, even vaguely medical in *anadosis,* but the point the reader has already read: works of art that Plutarch defines as without aretē offer no good imitandum).[22] The poets seem forgotten: Plutarch writes not of readers but of viewers (θεωμένους, 2.2; θεατήν, 2.4). This is all a bit muddled, as if Plutarch wished to make an argument by definition that certain works of art produce wonder alone, unaccompanied by an urge to reproduce them.[23] Perhaps. The passage is difficult in part because Plutarch uses discussion of *mimēsis* as an argument (without much preparation or development) and because at the same time he adduces as proof what are in essence social biases against the banausic arts and artists. Theory and ideology may not fit well here.

Yet the poet Philemon belongs in Plutarch's text. This New Comic poet is remembered, chiefly by Seneca, for an act of political slander. His play provoked the stepson of Ptolemy I, Magas, who in time relented of his intention to kill the poet and sent him instead a child's toys, a ball, and some dice.[24] For Plutarch, Philemon figures well the slander of a prince or statesman (as Magas displayed Perikles' great virtue, self-restraint, although Plutarch neither narrates the episode nor does he make explicit the connection). Philemon is then of a piece not simply with his fellow mordant and risqué poets, Archilochos and Anakreon, but also with the other artists, the dancing Alexander and the cheek-puffing Ismenias. Alexander's dancing was inappropriate for a king: such virtuosity risked diminishing his status. Similarly when the philosopher Antisthenes was told that Ismenias was good, the Platonist had to draw the line between being good at a *techne* and being good at life. The minor arts consistently work toward slander, a diminution of status, a confusion of the ends of art, and an elevation of the artist (and the body) into the imitandum.

Dancing, flute playing, and satiric poetry disturb the composure of the prince or statesman. Yet the reader may well ask, How does a noble youth looking on Pheidias' Zeus commit slander? On the sting of the accusations current in the declamatory schools that alleged Pheidias had pocketed funds for the Parthenon or provided women for Perikles, has Plutarch, in his search to redeem Perikles, imported Plato's censorious remarks on poets and art? Plutarch's position disagrees strongly with Dio Chrysostom's, who held that this statue of Zeus, and the plastic arts more generally, could inspire men to the divine (12.44–46).

What should be the effect of viewing the Zeus? Plutarch writes that works of aretē cause a double reaction: wonder at the work and zeal to imitate the worker (to anticipate: Perikles' actions will cause Plutarch's readers wonder and move them to imitate, not naively and literally the exact deeds of a long dead statesman but the moral virtue, the prāotēs, figured in such deeds). The work of slanderous poets has been disqualified. They do not arrive at aretē. Again the reader may object, Is Pheidias' sculpture not a work of aretē? It produces wonder and apparently, like all art, an impulse to imitation. The apposite question may then be, Who is the worker? Plutarch's implied answer is, not Pheidias but the mind behind him: Perikles in the case of the famous Athena Parthenos. Gazing on the statue of Zeus at Olympia, the well-born youth should want to become not a sculptor but Olympian, an epithet that Zeus must share with Perikles (and with Hadrian).[25] The role of the maker of art is reduced to insignificance, damned by association with those arts that produce deformity of the body—the sensuousness of dance, the deformity of the face of the flautist, the laughing sneer of the slanderer. Plutarch's text promises the young viewer, in place of the artist and of the plastic arts, written directions to decide upon proper imitanda and to achieve the serenity of a Perikles.

It is as if the opening of the *Perikles* were a different, lost Plutarchan tract, a *De signis videndis* to accompany his other educational works such as *De poetis audiendis*. The treatment of the plastic arts, however, does not spring from the strict demands of a treatise "On the proper appreciation of sculpture" nor even from abstract questions of esthetics; praising Perikles seems to have driven Plutarch to this topic. Indeed, the answer for that ideal reader, the well-born youth Plutarch summons up, was not to gaze at the gold-and-ivory statue by Pheidias but the words, the prose that Plutarch prefers to remember as "Perikles." In his developing devaluations of the arts and of sculpture in particular, Pheidias' sculpture recedes from view, leaving the viewer to contemplate Perikles. Plutarch's diction in particular maintains the theme of viewing and wonder while the subject is changed.

Perikles' effect on his viewers as described by Plutarch is curiously statuesque. When Perikles enters the political scene, the effect is that of the sudden revelation of a new work of art: he struck wonder into the Athenians (θαυμαστῶς ἐξέπληττε, 5.1). Plutarch uses the same verb for the wonder felt by the Athenians on seeing the eclipse, "as if a great sign," ὡς πρὸς μέγα σημεῖον, 35.2). With his strict, almost sculptural control of language (πλάσμα φωνῆς, 5.1) and of his drapery (καταστολὴ περιβολῆς also apposite for sculpture), Perikles is represented as making himself into a statue. Plutarch had just related the wonder felt by the Athenians for the philosopher/scientist Anaxagoras and especially of Perikles for Anaxagoras (4.6, 5.1). The course of marvels continues, for the next generation has its own particular wonder in Perikles himself. Perikles' unemotionalism can be read from the composition (σύστασις) of his forehead. Indeed, he is much like a well-born youth, but one long dead: the old men are struck by his physical similarities to Peisistratos (οἱ σφόδρα γέροντες ἐξεπλήττοντο πρὸς τὴν ὁμοιότητα, 7.1), as if a statue had come to life.[26]

Plutarch's imagination of Perikles' self-control and self-presentation as processes of self-composition and self-sculpture recurs in other passages. Plutarch attributes Perikles' epithet "Olympian" to his oratory, although he concedes others connected it to the buildings with which he adorned the city. Another tradition also contrasts with Plutarch's interpretation, for Valerius Maximus derived Perikles' Olympianness from his calmness. Plutarch consistently displaces building and stone with oratory and words. This he generalizes at *Praec. ger. rep.* 802b: the statesman adorns the city like an architect a building; his speech is an *organon.* In Plutarch's portrait of Perikles, Perikles seems himself to share Plutarch's reevaluation of his achievement: he is made to say that his accomplishment can be measured not from his nine trophies but from no Athenian having gone into mourning on his account (38.3).

Plutarch's self-composed Perikles reflects that author's own valorizing of the verbal and the textual. Comedy, uncomposed speech, and sculpture—all tainted as banausic signs—stand as foils to Perikles' oratory and his biographer's prose.[27] The reaction of the Athenians on first seeing the young Perikles should be contrasted to the effect of Perikles' building program, which "gave greatest pleasure and ornament (κόσμος) to the Athenians and greatest shock (ἔκπληξις) to other men" (12.1). Architecturally induced shock brings on slander. The Athenians are delighted except for those

Plutarch calls Perikles' enemies. Plutarch quotes their reaction: "They said Greece was outraged, openly tyrannized seeing her treasury removed from Delos and used to ornament Athens like a shameless woman (ὥσπερ ἀλαζόνα γυναῖκα, 12.2)." These viewers have impaired vision and esthetics because they do not know to what they should compare the buildings. Unlike Plutarch, they are smitten with the physical qualities and expense of the stone. Perhaps when they compare the monuments to a wanton woman and not to Olympian man, they err in the composition and interpretation of metaphor.

THE GENRES OF SLANDER

Similarly, Perikles recognizes Aspasia as *sophē* and *politikē;* the comedians see a whore, a *pornē* (24). Plutarch terms their remarks slander (ἐβάσκαινον οἱ ἐχθροὶ καὶ διέβαλλον ["his enemies engaged in slander and abuse"], 12.1). Comic and satiric poetry are the genres least to be trusted in the writing of Perikles' life and the genres antithetical to Periklean composure and composition. Plutarch's rhetorical censure consistently associates the corporal, the emotional, the sensual with verbal excess. It is not simply that the libidinous talk too much or prefer the nonverbal (dancing, sculpture) for the verbal. The libidinous man, the dancer, the critic quick to see Perikles as a sensualist, and the enthusiast of the plastic arts have all misobserved the proper end of their desire. In their faulty estimations, they share a pathology that consistently prefers the physical to the intellectual. The slanderer does not understand what he sees. The statues of Pheidias are not worthy in themselves; the statuesque self-composition of Perikles is the true wonder. Those who censure Aspasia or Athens, in drawing false likenesses, have missed appropriate expression, which, in the argumentative mode typical of Plutarch, restores Perikles to the reader as the master of the apt phrase and proper judgment.

In those sources and stories that draw Plutarch's express disavowal and disapproval, the conception of slander may seem an all too convenient argument: all that the writer does not agree with is slander. Even if Plutarch does not appreciate the sleight of hand in dismissing critical stories as slander, the critical reader of Plutarch may take the principles of censure as an illuminating window into the composer's attitudes and method. A survey of notices of slander in the text reveals that (1) Plutarch's sources presented much that was difficult for the encomiast; (2) Plutarch recognized slander as a problem faced by the historical Perikles; (3) he saw slanderous reports as a fundamental problem for the historiographer; finally, (4) slander is expressed preeminently in and through, and perhaps is an intrinsic feature of, two media: poetry and statuary. The principal challenge to the researcher and reader is not to discover new material (Plutarch almost always seems to have an abundance of stories and indeed of versions) but to evaluate the received literary records.

Plutarch sees slander not as an occasional vexation of this particular individual or even as an attribute, long passed, of Athenian democracy but as an essential part of Perikles' chief virtue and of the historian's method. He tells his reader that he has paired Perikles and Fabius Maximus because of their prāotēs and because of their ability to endure the disrespect (ἀγνωμοσώνας) of the people and their fellow rulers (2.5). Plutarch himself, and perhaps his reader, can emulate the restraint under slander by cultivating a disposition to disbelieve the scandalous. This restraint was most memorably depicted by the story of the man who abused Perikles loudly throughout the day, trailing him home from the Agora until the great man sent him a torchbearer to see him safely home (5.2). The reader might assume this virtue of self-control by following the narrator's lead.

All the stories that attribute venality, deformity, and lust to Perikles are cautionary tales against credulity: invariably, Plutarch chastises the poets, especially, who tell these tales (Plutarch does not excuse all Perikles' actions, but he refuses to credit the stories of embezzlement, bribery, and lust). Plutarch explicitly guides his reader both with a general caveat and by the repeated warning that such and such a story is slander (he chiefly labels these βλασφημία).[28] Plutarch writes that the interval of time and the slander of contemporaries complicate the task of the historian (13.16). In fact, he prefaces his remarks about the difficulties of writing history with an indignant rhetorical question, "Who could be amazed at men of such debauched lives (σατυρικοὺς τοῖς βίοις) who are forever sacrificing to the evil god Envy of the People the offerings of their slander against their betters?"[29] He has nicely transferred the object of wonder from the alleged adultery of Perikles with his daughter-in-law, reported by Stesimbrotus, to those who utter such slander. Once again, the satiric and the poetic, not Perikles himself, have produced slander.[30]

On one occasion Plutarch cites the orators, partisans of Thukydides, son of Melesias, who cried out against Perikles (14), and once he notes that a historian, Idomeneus, was censured for accusing Perikles of Ephialtes' murder. Plutarch again leaves the reader in no doubt of the proper explanation of the attack: Idomeneus is said to collect accusations "like bile" and merits another rhetorical question of disbelief from Plutarch. High rhetorical dudgeon and metaphor may do for Idomeneus; the more customary treatment is to disparage the poets and poetry. The tragedian Ion receives a notable treatment. Plutarch records that Ion found Perikles arrogant and aloof; in fact, he considered Perikles' set and society bastardly and arrogant (μοθωνικήν and ὑπότυφον, 5.3) and much preferred the genial, cultured company of Kimon.

Plutarch does not appreciate the contemporary political jab of Ion's characterization: Perikles was no doubt acting in a public, visible fashion that put him at variance with the aristocratic display of Kimon. Plutarch sees Ion not as a political commentator or political agent but exclusively as a literary man. Thus to overturn Ion's judgment, Plutarch resorts to generic analysis of Ion's criticism and then caps his point with a *gnōmē* (aphorism) from the philosopher Zeno. Both these tactics of denigration are highly rhetorical: the first takes the form of *praeteritio:* "let us pass over in silence" (ἐῶμεν) or as Stadter translates: "However, let us leave Ion to one side, who thinks that *aretē,* like a tragic production, should always have a satyric portion."[31] After this *aposiopesis* with simile, Plutarch turns to a chreia of the founder of Stoicism: "When some men termed the solemnity of Perikles a hankering after fame and affectation, Zeno advised them to have the same ambition, in the hopes that the pretense of this virtue might imperceptibly bring about a zealous practice of it" (5.4).

Plutarch has thus indulged in his characteristic censure of what he takes to be slander: the remarks are poetic, comic/satyric, and a mixture of genres that cannot fit the nature of Perikles; the seal on the question at issue is some authoritative gnōmē. According to Plutarch, to believe such slander would not only be credulous but would also involve an error in reading: we would be crediting the improbable and the indecorous, that which is not *prepon* (not fitting), and we would be ignoring the succinct and unalloyed words of an Augustus or a Zeno. Plutarch's presentation and reinterpretation of slander provide a corrective, which, through its rhetorical form, returns his subject to a certain prosaic consistency. Indeed, Plutarch's reiteration of the point of the opening sections seems a form of ring composition that his audience would have understood: a Stoic close responds to the Platonic opening; Zeno's chreia answers Caesar's.

When Plutarch identifies the source of slander (though he never plumbs the compulsion toward it), Pheidias appears. Plutarch writes that Pheidias was put in charge of all the workmen because of Perikles' friendship for him, that this led to envy, and in turn to insult (blasphemy), which the comic poets took up. This is the series that elicits Plutarch's rhetorical closure of the indignant rhetorical question. To counter such slander, Plutarch does have more sustained techniques. Certain attacks upon Perikles seem to require a corrective story, chiefly, the anecdote or the omen and explanation, which is a similar, discrete small narrative. Between the inclusion of the poets' barbs about squill-head Perikles (13.10) and the series of slander that leads from the complaints of the orators of Thukydides (14) and more quotations from the comic poets (16), Plutarch has set an anecdote that bears on the immediate issues of the slander arising from the building program.

This is one of the series of anecdotes in the *Life* that contrast Perikles' reading of signs to that of his enemies or simply of the many. Confronted with a unicorn or a man spouting abuse all day long, Anaxagoras and his student Perikles respond unexpectedly. The story Perikles tells amid the accounts of slander does not quite have the scientific and intellectual detachment of Anaxagoras' refusal to credit a supernatural explanation or Perikles' refusal to be insulted, for it is a dream story, one of those all too convenient fictions, of which even the teachers of declamation disapproved.[32] The most active and enterprising worker fell from a height (13.13).[33] The doctors' help is of no use. Athena, however, reveals to Perikles in a dream the appropriate (easy and fast acting in effect) remedy, which Perikles administered. This handy *dea ex machina* proved, Plutarch had maintained in his introductory sentence, that the goddess favored the building of the Propylaia.

According to Plutarch's understanding, Perikles' grand building provoked the envy of the people and the raillery of the poets;[34] Plutarch has a full rhetorical panoply for remedy. Indeed, when he writes of the grandeur of the buildings, his prose is at its most monumental.[35] Criticism of the critics and stylistic emulation of the artistic and architectural monuments help guide the reader's interpretation of Perikles' most famous and visible legacy. In addition to these overt rhetorical techniques, anecdotes of Perikles' own encounter with physical signs model for the reader a proper hermeneutics of the physical. The story of the workman's fall, interpreted by Perikles' detractors as proof of the goddess' anger, is the second time Perikles' interpretation must come as a corrective to the apparent or obvious interpretation.

Perikles is presented with his first wonder in the story of the unicorn and its exegete. A one-horned ram is brought from the country (6.2). The seer Lampon gives what seems a traditional and literal reading of this phenomenon: of the two political factions in the city, all power will come to one. As reported by Plutarch, this seems traditional in its form (λέγεται introduced the story)[36] and in its interpretation: the physically abnormal has a political, even dynastic, interpretation (like the vine that grew from Mandame's womb, which signaled the coming transfer of all power to Cyrus, Hdt. 1.108) and the interpretation has a certain Delphic vagueness (like the response to Kroisos that should he continue, he would destroy an empire, Hdt. 1.53). The interpreter approved by the narrator and, by Perikles, will have none of this quaint, Herodotean, political symbolism, for here Anaxagoras, by refusing to credit a supernatural explanation, plays the same part that Perikles will to the doctors. This sure interpreter dissects the head and reveals the internal cause of the deformity.

One can imagine the traffic in signs and their interpretation with competing claims of religious authority that made Athens an opportunistic, volatile, propagandistic political stage. Indeed, one wonders if Plutarch has not misunderstood the political dynamics. Lampon might well have been the agent of Thukydides (the son of Melesias), another voice intimating that Perikles was the new Peisistratos aiming at absolute power, whereas the rationalist Anaxagoras treats this sort of political mantics as superstition mongering.[37] In any case, Plutarch presents Anaxagoras as the foil to the critics of Perikles. He has just related Ion's preference for Kimon's civilized and sociable company and then returns (6) to the benefits Perikles gained from Anaxagoras' company. The story of the ram is told to illustrate the freedom from superstition learned from this teacher of the meteorologic (celestial science and religion compete as explanatory systems—the shape of Plutarch's story champions the scientific). An unstated connection is that an oddly shaped head is not to be a source of wonder, whether that head is a bust of Perikles, the ram's, or even the likeness, obliquely set, of Perikles and Pheidias that Plutarch wrongly believed the sculptor had put on the shield of the statue of Athena.[38] Plutarch will deal soon with the poets who gawked and jeered at Perikles' squill-shaped head.

Three other stories of interpretation cast Perikles in the same, approved role where the interpreter is not misled by the surface, by the physical, or by the emotional. Once again, Plutarch will make the moral of Augustus and the puppies: the people mistake the physical (even the illegitimate, the bastard) for the spiritual and the genuine. Repeating a story told in the schools of the philosophers (and decidedly not told in Thukydides' history), Plutarch tells that an eclipse delayed Perikles from setting sail with the Athenian fleet (35.2). This is the sort of story so familiar to readers of Livy, where yet another Roman magistrate has to endure a squealing mouse or chickens that will not eat and so must restart his ceremony or even abort the expedition. Roman historians have been prompt to imagine the *prodigium* (the sign that nature is displeased) as the machination of political factions.[39] Plutarch's audience might well share some of this skepticism, and Plutarch is not vouching for the historical accuracy of the tale. He reports simply that he has heard the story in the schools of the philosophers. Perikles, of course, plays the scientific rationalist here, but he does so by a sort of pantomime. To his helmsman fearful to proceed against this ominous sign, Perikles acts out a materialist explanation: he blocks the man's sight with his cloak. The helmsman and the army seem to be good readers of Perikles' physical exegesis, and so off they go.[40]

Perikles, then, in philosophical fashion, like Thales in Herodotos (1.74), where the armies of the Lydians and the Medes do not understand an eclipse, explains a celestial event in physical rather than in religious terms. A statue or an eclipse or a one-horned ram is no wonder but a physical object, which can be understood by inquiry into its physical makeup. Plutarch has patterned his stories not to give lessons in physical science but with an epideictic flare to demonstrate the right interpreter, that solitary figure who must lead the people from delusion by means of a rhetorical proof. In showing the inside of the ram's head or enacting the eclipse with his cloak, the interpreter has not given precise meteorologic, scientific proof. Instead, he performs a proof as an orator must, working from what the people understand, just as the orator must use *enthymeme* and not scientific syllogism.

ARGUING WITH SIGNS

As an author, Plutarch himself performs a similar popular argumentation through physical signs in, for example, his detailed accounts of how the statue of Athena and the building projects of the Akropolis were executed. To mistake the physical for the spiritual is the act of the superstitious and, one must add, the scandal seekers. Perikles' eldest son falls into the latter category, for he disparages his father for discussing with Protagoras the situation so well known from Antiphon: the case of the young man accidentally slain in a javelin accident at the *gymnasion.* Xanthippos derides his father for wasting a day talking about a hypothetical case with a sophist. The day is spent, however, in an essentially Periklean (Anaxagorean) mode: the determination of the cause of a physical action. Plutarch says simply that Perikles and Protagoras considered who was responsible: javelin, the unfortunate thrower, or the gymnasion supervisors. The positions of Perikles and Protagoras are not discussed.[41]

Plutarch has included the story ostensibly as an instance of the family discord now afflicting Perikles. Perhaps the story appealed to Plutarch not simply as slander that needed refutation but because slander of Perikles consistently reflects a misunderstanding of the hermeneutic method of the great man. One can imagine Perikles arguing that the javelin that strikes the boy is not guilty nor is the thrower tainted by religious guilt: neither is *aitios* in that sense, just as the unicorn was not an *aition.* Plutarch, however, is not such a strict rationalist. He points out the deficiencies of Anaxagoras' method, for Plutarch believes in something like double causation or double exegesis of the physical record.[42]

Plutarch objects that by positing material causes for signs exclusively, men ignore the fact that signs are created by gods—Plutarch here offers in place of proof the analogy that artificial signs are likewise created by men—and so miss the final cause (signification).[43] Again, they are like the readers of meteorological events above or the puppy petters who mistake the thing, the material object, as the source of wonder. Perikles himself is customarily a strict scientist. He takes the material for the final cause and so does not entertain an openness to double causation. Only once does he deviate from his rigorous materialist position, and it is significant that his slip, which sees the physical as an object of wonder in itself, occurs with a religious amulet, a charm hung about his neck to ward off the plague, which Plutarch says has weakened his *phronema,* that characteristic, remarkable self-reliance and self-composure.[44]

In the story of the slander from Perikles' son, Plutarch has given the first hint of the breakdown of Perikles' control. The statesman's failure to govern his son may have been of far longer standing than the slander, but Plutarch puts it here at the start of the series of catastrophes that lead to Perikles' death. Plutarch clusters the failures to good effect. Certainly, he has judged a few prior actions as failures—Perikles' stumbling with the people for reason of his friendship with Pheidias, losing sea battles to the philosopher Melissos [26.2], perhaps being too Anaxagorean in not crediting divine causation as another level of signification—but whenever Perikles has seemed to be smitten with the physical, Plutarch has assured his reader: this is slander. Although the highest authorities had thought the fascination with meteorological events idle chatter, Plutarch has championed such thinking as Olympian by showing its connection to Perikles' essential moral quality, self-composure.[45] Now the failure to control the boy's spending and his speaking prepares for the sorrows of the deaths of friends and family.

Even here, Perikles almost remains the same; then come two signs of the change in his constitution. First, he weeps openly at the funeral of his youngest son (36.8–9, where Plutarch notably departs from the biographical tradition). Perikles is softened (καμφθείς). Here Plutarch, like Perikles, seems to become a bit poetic, breaking away from the strict restraint of prose style with another metaphorical expression: "break into speech," ῥῆξαι φωνήν, a touch of Sophokles perhaps, who used the expression of tears at *Trachiniai* 919. Then Plutarch retells an episode from the *Ethics* of Theophrastos: to a friend visiting him at his sick bed, Perikles showed an amulet that the women had hung about his neck. Perikles is at his perigee when he indulges in nonverbal (and superstitious) communication. He is now a trafficker in objects as signs in themselves, thus playing the sort of emotional politics and semiotics that Plutarch believed he had resisted all his life.

As the grand building projects have been reduced to one physical sign of the nous of Perikles, Plutarch's *Life* as a whole schools the reader in the proper objects of wonder. The lessons of bad reading are clear: Perikles' enemies thought the Parthenon and the statue of Athena had made Athens a shameless woman; misled youth are infatuated with the glamour of sculpture; comic poets likewise are stuck at the physical level. The corrective comes through Perikles' words, that singularly genuine legacy that sets the statesman as a reader of σημεῖα. Indeed, subject, author, and reader seem to draw close together, as the hermeneusis of statesman, historian, and young reader involves the avoidance of slander through a strict self-composition that takes the stories presented and rinses them of any fascination with the physical. The physical challenges the hermeneusis of the historian in a way that we should not simply lay to Plutarch's Platonism.

To mistake the physical (unicorn, eclipse, slanderous story of Perikles' sexual appetite) as an object of wonder in itself is to wonder at the surface structure. We would be like Ion or Archilochos or the superstitious if we were struck by the egghead and wanted to know how the egg was made or wanted to praise the maker of the egghead. The physical is but a sign of the intellectual, without power or virtue in itself. Such a hermeneusis, acted out by the subjects of anecdotes, rigorously pursued by the main character, presented as historiographic and readerly method by the author, makes an appealing mode of essay. In this strongly rhetorical, guided reading, Plutarch has written lessons of, and for, the good reader and the bad reader, where, were we to credit the comic poets, we would be like that harasser of Perikles who needs the forbearance of the true intellectual and the light provided by him to take him home.

The plastic representations of Perikles—from his alleged squill-shaped head to the oblique portrait (and that of Pheidias) on the shield of Athena (so Plutarch thought)—consistently tempt the reader to misappraise the orator. Plutarch has learned the outlines of his esthetics from Plato; he seems to have had an especially strong sense of the rhetorical power of a dichotomy of true versus false objects of wonder and an allied hermeneusis that disparages the surface and valorizes the interior. The plastic Perikles distressed Plutarch because the misshapen form realized the slander of deformity, demagoguery, and vice, where Plutarch chose to see only noble words. Perhaps the sculptors of those busts of Perikles, with the battle helmet raked back, sought to deflect the slander of their subject. Plutarch, however, seems to have seen only a reminder of the poets' insulting jibes.[46] Like Anaxagoras with the ram, Plutarch has delved into the elongated head of Perikles. This dissection reveals the verbal or textual Perikles as an incorporeal imitandum. Challenged by the nameless boor in the street, by the comic poets, or the noble Elpinikē (the sister of Kimon, free-spoken in her criticism), the textual hero responds with words alone.[47]

There is a price to this understanding. The intellectual connections of contemporary literature, art, and politics recede from view as the biographer sketches a solitary individual intent on self-composition (with the implication that this self-control sympathetically produces civil control). An unfortunate consequence for the writing of history is that critical testimony and ambiguous reports are decocted to "slander." The author strives to segregate the slanderous by means of his own denigration of art and artists. Here there is some novel thinking, for Plutarch actually must theorize the banausic arts and their place in society not simply to counter the association of Perikles with architecture and sculpture but also to counter Perikles' contemporaries for censuring him because he courted the people by employing the artisan classes (12.1).

The historian, however, may wish to say that Perikles was a political son-of-a-bitch, a puppy on whom the Athenians and Thukydides misspent their affections. Laughter is harder to send packing than the rhetorician allows. Periklean composition, however, remains a form of esthetic exclusionism. On Plutarch's reckoning, lives demand the asking of questions, especially the question, Is this or that event consonant with the virtues of character of the subject at hand? The writer of a life need not inspect the material record, but just as Plutarch veers close to slander in treating the slanderous poets, he seems attracted by the stone and gold and ivory of Pheidias. The material record, like unsavory stories, calls out to the historian for displacement and reinterpretation.

In form, the queries that the historian must put to this most intractable of his materials arise from rhetorical categories. The credible, the likely, the consistent form the principles to be brought to bear on the scandalous. These rhetorical questions tend to conflate the literary and the lived, the textual and the personal. The proper body of study looks like and behaves like a text of consistent and persuasive construction. Experience or anecdote can be given credence in so far as it fits the character.[48] The questions that will direct his presentation arise from categories that themselves arise from story structure and the rules of story telling, that is, the rules of rhetoric, whereby the biographer must found his *ethopoiia* on the *prepon*.

At its extreme, we might say that that which is not consistent is not verisimilitudinous. Of course, Plutarch finds fault with some of his characters or some of their actions (e.g., *Per.* 10.7). In the *Life of Perikles,* Plutarch composes his scenes much like the novelist Walter Pater (to reverse the order of influence). Like Pater, Plutarch's writing performs an encounter with a lost classicism. The authors bring their readers into an ancient room and estheticize all that they have their reader see. Thereby, issues of politics, violence, oppression, and bodily desire take their place on the Procrustean bed of literary motif and reminiscence. The lived experience of the past, like its reanimation, is a bookish business where the characters' actions and even perceptions of actions are literary gestures. This mentality of composition is profound, deformative, and tidy. One consequence is to perpetuate a blindness to the ugliness that characterizes the use and rule of others' bodies. More positively, the literary mode and Olympian intellectualism are the real story. Plutarch does not bring moralism or allegory as some additive to the facts of history. His rhetorical understanding of character, of historiography, and of argument and composition exert a chastening influence on his subject and help create a quite un-Platonic desexing of the scene where Perikles becomes a statue, and his words are the only lasting, marvelous signs of Periklean Athens.

NOTES

I gratefully acknowledge the help of the editors, and for his valuable discussion and suggestions, my colleague Chris McLaren.

1. This stems from an ancient understanding: like Plutarch, Aelius Aristides balances the complaints of Plato and the Old Comic poets with the positive portrayal from Thukydides (*On the Four*). Plutarch is more creative: he uses Plato against Plato; see Stadter 1989, xlii–xliii. Plato's criticisms were, for Plutarch, significant; e.g., the statement at *Grg.* 515E that Perikles had corrupted the *demos* through jury pay. Of course, Plutarch's sources presented a more complex record, see Stadter 1989: lviii–lxxxv (with bibliography). De Romilly (1988) treats Plutarch's rewriting of Thukydides (on Perikles in Thukydides, see also Westlake 1968, 23–42). The search to define the genre or generic affinities of Plutarch's biographical writing stems from Leo (1881), whose conclusions about two strains of biographical writing, with an origin in the Peripatos, are not now accepted (he had posited a nonchronological treatment for men of the mind, a chronological treatment for men of action). Geiger (1985) provides a useful corrective. For Plutarch as a rhetorical-ethical historiographer, see the brief remarks and survey of bibliography in Scardigli 1995, 13–18.

2. Pelling 1979; Pelling 1988, 15.

3. See the discussion of rhetorical sources in Stadter 1989, lxxxi–lxxxiii. Russell (1983, 111) notes that the schools had put into circulation speeches of Perikles, which were generally recognized as spurious. On the charge of treason against Perikles (and others) as a declamatory theme, see Russell 1983, 121. For another concocted, ahistorical attack on Perikles, see ibid., 127 (an interesting case, the rhetorician Sopatros misread Plutarch; see *Rhetores Graeci* VIII.11.17 and Plut. *Per.* 2.2). Valerius Maximus closes his exemplum of the similarity of Peisistratos and Perikles with this rhetorical question (and *comparatio personarum*): "What else is the difference between Peisistratos and Perikles other than that the one founded his tyranny on arms and the other did not?" (8.9.ext.2). Perikles' presence in the schools and his popular reception can also be gauged by his appearances in the paroemiographers. Under Zenobius' name (von Leutsch and Schneidewin 1965, Z III 91 and cf. Macarius 3.62 and Apostolius 6.74) was listed a saying recalling the story of Perikles bribing Pleistoanax, the Spartan king, to withdraw from Attika. Plutarch's contemporary Zenobius lies (ultimately) behind the collection of these proverbial sayings. Stobaeus' collection has included two of Perikles' *gnōmai,* that to Sophokles (3.17.18, a general must keep his hands and his eyes chaste, recorded by Plutarch at 8.8) and a lightly modified version of another saying from Plutarch's *Life,* namely, that he thought his greatest deed that none of the Athenians went into mourning on his account (4 praef. 15). For a story of Pheidias probably from the schools (told only by Valerius Maximus), see Val. Max. 1.1.ext.7. Similarly at 2.6.5 Valerius is the sole source to relate that the Athenians gave Perikles a crown.

A great expert on Plutarch, D. A. Russell, disagrees with the degree of importance of this rhetorical aspect: "It is not often that Plutarch descends into the shades of *le monde rhétorique,* where Lucian, Aelian, Valerius Maximus, and the rest move and have their being" (in 1995, 80). Prof. Russell is quite right that Plutarch's range of reading and method of composition distinguish him. His use of oral sources: Pelling 1988, 29.

On the charges of tyranny against Perikles in Plutarch, see Stadter 1995, 159.

4. The weepy Perikles: Plut. 36.9; cf. Val. Max. 5.10.ext.1. Stadter 1989 *ad loc.* 36.8 notes the resonance for the ancient reader: not giving way to tears is a mark of the philosopher.

5. Plutarch himself is as fickle as the declaimers: in *Kim.,* Perikles' motives and sympathies are far more suspect; he is more clearly pro-Spartan (see *Kim.* 16.1–17.3), a contrast in treatment pointed out by Stadter (1989, 1).

6. See Stadter 1989, lxxxiii, with references for the rhetoricians' critical stories and (lxiii–lxix) for Old Comedy. Plutarch makes his disapproval clear. The comic poets are responsible, for instance, for "the worst explanation" of the outbreak of war (31.2).

7. Stadter 1989, 347. Aelius Aristides also has this topos in his work *On the Four.*

8. On Tacitus' careful handling of Tiberius' face and expression, see Bloomer 1997, 154–195. The motif of the immobile (but serene) public face of the emperor recurs in the grand and static image of Constantius II's entry into Rome (Amm. Marc. 16.10.10).

9. Alkibiades is an interesting case, since he can be the *aristeus,* the hero of declamations, but also the traitor, the sexual profligate, and potential tyrant; see Russell 1983, 121–128.

10. On Ephoros in particular, see Stadter 1989, lxxi–lxxii.

11. The πρᾶος man is he who can control his emotions, especially, it would seem, anger, lust, and grief. See Stadter 1989, xxx–xxxii; Stadter 1995, 160–164.

12. Stadter 1989, *ad loc.* 1.1.

13. Stadter 1989, xxvi, n. 7.

14. The ancient rhetoricians provide definitions of the chreia: Theon 202.20; Quint. 1.9. These texts (and others, e.g., Hermogenes, Priscian, Aphthonius) are given with translation and notes in Hock and O'Neill 1986. Plutarch discusses his own technique of collecting chreiai at *De ira cohibenda* 457D–E. Collections of sayings are attributed to him, e.g., *The Sayings of the Spartans, The Sayings of Kings and Commanders* (see Fuhrmann 1988). Barrow (1967, 153) reconstructs Plutarch's typical mode of composition: asked by a friend for some help, he would consult his notebooks and begin his treatise with a quotation from them. For the *Lives,* of course, he had different sources and materials, but to frame the work and to insert comparisons, he might well have turned to his commonplace books, if memory failed. Simon Swain (1990, 77) has pointed out the connection of the opening of the *Per.* to the *lalia,* the popular genre of the rhetors. *Quest. Rom.* 270c indicates that Plutarch began the *De glor. Ath.* with a chreia about Themistokles.

15. See Plut. *Per.* 20 and Stadter 1989, xxxi and 221 *ad loc.* 20.4, where he suggests Perikles' restraining the expeditions is simply an overly generous interpretation of Thuk. 2.65.11–12.

16. Not only does Augustus, like many a speaker of a chreia, censure what he has seen or heard, but Plutarch also draws the moral for his readers: "Since the human soul has a natural tendency to love learning and spectacle, it is reasonable to blame (λόγον ἔχει ψέγειν) those who squander this on frivolous arts and entertainments and neglect those which are beautiful and profitable" (1.2). On the relation of encomium and invective to Plut. *Vit.,* see Leo 1881, 148–149 and the brief remarks of Russell 1973, 104. Plutarch's sensitivity to invective in his sources: Pelling 1988, 35.

17. Plutarch's philosophizing exegesis of the chreia abounds in a Platonic vocabulary of the soul, its nourishing by visions of the beautiful, its turning and pursuit, the zeal and impulse toward mimesis (1.2–1.3). Plutarch has taken specific vocabulary from Pl. *Symp.,* the esthetic theory of vision from Pl. *Ti.* (see Stadter 1989 *ad loc.*), and, from Pl. *Resp.,* such diction as φιλοθέαμον. We need not imagine him checking these texts.

No doubt he knew them by heart and had heard and read hundreds of variations and recapitulations of these philosophical commonplaces.

18. On the virtues of Plutarch's style, see Russell 1973, 20–23; and for a useful overview with bibliography, Stadter 1989, liii–lvii, who at lvi describes and analyzes Plutarch's reliance on participles to create "long, loosely constructed sentences." Lasserre (1979, 140) connected Plutarch's use of synonyms to Demosthenes' practice.

19. Amid artisans, cloth dyers seem to have attracted literary criticism: Hdt. 3.22, Dio Chrys. 7.117 (cited by Stadter 1989, *ad loc.* 1.4, who notes Greek contempt for perfumers and dyers). Social prejudice against the banausic arts is indisputable; see D'Arms 1981. Nonetheless, literature often seems to have a vested interest in disparaging other arts. The prejudice is well exploited by Sokrates with his questions about cobblers and their *aretē.* The dyer or perfumer makes an easy target: he engaged in manual labor, counterfeited nature, and served women, in sum, a useful trinity for the literary writer celebrating the work of the mind and seeking (male?) approval for his "work." Dyeing was, however, not a marginal or foreign activity but a profitable and important part of ancient Greek and Roman society. See Rostovtzeff 1941, 564, on the textile industry and mining of materials for dyes in Pergamon, and Rostovtzeff 1941, 1225–1226, for its importance in the Hellenistic world, including given scientific treatment in the treatise of Bolus Democritus Mendus. Plutarch's Roman audience would have thought of the corporations of dyers, see Rostovtzeff 1957, 226, and Brunt 1974, 43–46. See now Rogers, Jørgensen, and Rast-Eicher 2001.

20. For Plutarch's views of art, see the passages cited by Stadter (1989, *ad loc.* 2.1–4) and the article there cited: Svoboda 1934. The thesaurus of ancient attitudes to art is Pollitt (1965, rev. 1990); see also Pollitt 1974; Pollitt 1983. Lucian (second century A.D.) offers a most interesting parallel comparison of sculpture and literature in his (purportedly) autobiographical *Dream.*

21. Aristotle characterizes the *aulos* as the instrument of professionals (*Pol.* 1341a17). Aelian in the *Miscellany* tells a story of a flautist Satyrus who was smitten with the lectures of the philosopher Ariston and draws the moral that the musician deprecated his own art in comparison to philosophy.

22. 2.2. I have translated ἀνάδοσις as "sprouting up," although the LS&J lexicon cite this passage under II2 as a metaphorical use meaning "digestion" of knowledge, thus associating the passage with other usages concerning the distribution or assimilation of food. Plutarch is using the word as a synonymous doublet for the mimetic zeal that causes an eagerness and impulse toward imitation. Theophrastus had used it of the sprouting of plants (*CP* 2.14); Aristotle of the "issuing forth" of fire and water (*Mu.* 395a9). Plutarch in his search for doublets seems to have sought a scientific, biological expression, but one more energetic and generative than "digestion."

23. H. Martin (1992, 229) faults Stadter's translation of this passage and certainly offers a more coherent version (than the original?).

24. Sen. *De ira cohibenda* 458A. Discussion of the passage with further references in Stadter 1989, 59.

25. Eusebius thought that Hadrian had appointed Plutarch as (some sort of) governor of Greece in 119 A.D. Eusebius may well be in error; see C. P. Jones 1995; Barrow 1967, 48–49.

26. Val. Max. 8.9.ext.2 has the same story. Stadter (1989, 89) believed both derived from Theopompos, although the tale may well have been a commonplace of the schools. Further, Valerius does not seem to have used Theopompos, despite 8.13.ext.4 and 8.14.ext.4, and Plutarch may simply be adapting Valerius. Plutarch's use of Theopompos: Stadter 1989, lxxii–lxxiii, and Connor 1968. Valerius' use of Greek sources: Bloomer 1993b, 62–64, 78–99.

27. On Plutarch's disapproval of Old Comedy, see Russell 1973, 53–54.

28. Plutarch uses βλασφημία three times in the *Perikles* (5.2, 13.15.2, 13.16.3), βασκαίνω once (12.1).

29. I slightly mistranslate the phrase so as to communicate Plutarch's metaphor; he says more literally "they sacrifice to the envy of the people, as if to an evil god."

30. The comic poets are also blamed for slandering Perikles' friends as the new Peisistratids (16.1). *Satyra* and *satira* are a Latin pun, perhaps not meant by Plutarch, who puns on satyr drama and men whose morals are like satyrs. Still, it is possible he means to suggest satiric poetry as well. Plutarch's knowledge of Latin: Barrow 1967, 150–151; see also Russell 1973, 54; C. P. Jones 1971, 81–87.

31. Stadter 1989, *ad loc.* 5.3.

32. Seneca the elder disapproved of Junius Otho's book of *colores,* which had so many dreams and introduced claims that could not be argued (*Contr.* 2.1.33); see Fairweather 1981, 167, 173. The rhetoricians may have disapproved of the dream as an element of composition, but this does not mean such dream cures were disbelieved. Aelius Aristides spent ten years at the temple of Pergamon, where he waited to be cured; he relates the dream cures in the course of his life, 130 in number, in his *Sacred Tales.*

33. For the story, see Plin. *HN* 22.44 and also Stadter's note on the course of this story in the schools in Stadter 1989, *ad loc.* 13.13. On the folkloric quality of the use of superlatives in such anecdotes, see Bloomer 1993a.

34. Russell (1973, 60) nicely characterizes Plutarch's attitude: "What we think of as tendentiousness in history, Plutarch tends to think of as malice: a more, emotional, subjective and rhetorical way of looking at it."

35. Stadter 1989, 154, 156 (*ad loc.* 12.5: "The words are as grand as the projects").

36. On such indirect references, see Pauw 1980, 83–95.

37. In this anecdote, Plutarch seems to understand Lampon as friendly to Perikles. Stadter (1989, *ad loc.* 6.2) points out the thin grounds for believing this.

38. A story believed in antiquity but without evidence before the third century: Stadter 1989, *ad loc.* 31.4. Plutarch believed that Pheidias had sculpted his own and Perikles' heads in three-quarter view.

39. MacBain 1982.

40. Such scenes of visual parables might have struck Perikles and his audience as old fashioned as they seem to us: cf. the tyrant Thrasybylos, who knocked the heads off the tallest of the grain as he walked with the envoy of Periander and so communicated a message it takes a Periander to appreciate (Hdt. 5.92). In the *De liberis educandis,* a work perhaps from Plutarch's school, the venerable lawgiver Lykourgos stages a visual parable with two puppies (3A, where the Spartans have to have the point explained).

41. See Stadter 1989, *ad loc.* 36.5, who directs the reader; for the connection of this accident to Protagoras' thinking, see Untersteiner 1954, 30–32.

42. The motif of false beliefs and their correction is not, of course, limited to the figures of Perikles and Anaxagoras. In his essay on *Superstition* (*Deisidaimonia*) Plutarch vividly describes two sources of false belief, superstition and atheism, as hyper-religiosity and hyper-rationality. See Barrow 1967, 91–95. Atheism comes off rather better than superstition, as Russell (1973, 80) says, it is "a less serious thing, an intellectual error not aggravated by . . . emotional trauma."

43. *Per.* 6.5. Plutarch distinguishes between the immediate cause that interests the scientist from the seer's interest, the purpose (*aitia* from *telos*). His final examples are illustrative: "Those who believe the discovery of the immediate cause eliminates the purpose of the sign do away with divine and with artificial tokens, such as the sounding of gongs, signaling by fire and the shadow lines of sundials." These instances of non-verbal communication contribute to the minor motif of the proper interpretations of signs, statues. The reader will come to appreciate that all art stands in need of verbal exegesis. Works of art (Plutarch's term here is τεχνητά), like the sounding gong of the statue of Pheidias, do not seem to have a language of their own but point to the higher realm of signification, words.

44. On amulets, approved by the high authority of Galen, see Ferguson 1970, 164–166; and Scarborough 1969, 120. Pliny approved of amulets; the far less credulous Lucian did not (C. P. Jones 1986, 47).

45. Stadter 1989, *ad loc.* 39.2.

46. Pliny admired Kresilas' statue of Olympian Perikles (34.74), but Plutarch (3.2) does not mention this. The extant busts are all of the slanting-helmet type: the Vatican herm (Rome, Vatican Museums 269); London, British Museum 459. For further bibliography, see Richter 1955, 173–175. Cohen (1991, 465–502) compares the statues found off the coast of Riace to the four existing Perikles herms to argue that the elongated head reflects a sculpting method by which helmets were affixed to the heads of statues in bronze and were not a deformity. See Revermann 1997, 197–200, for additional evidence of ancient belief in Perikles' deformity.

47. Elpinikē's challenges are met with slander: 10.5 "you are an old woman." At 28.5, Perikles chooses verse to answer the woman's complaint that the fine sounding words of his funeral oration hide an ugly reality: he quotes Archilochos and again calls Elpinikē γραῦς.

48. Stadter (1989, *ad loc.* 38.2) gives a succinct account of Plutarch's view of change in character. He notes, "Several other lives consider apparent changes in character at the end." Perhaps it should be added that such changes do not seem to interest Plutarch, aside perhaps from signaling the coming of death.

19

ON SOME MOTIVES SUPPOSED PRESENT IN SELF-PORTRAITS OF PHEIDIAS AND OTHERS

CREIGHTON GILBERT

The starting point of this small query is far from the Akropolis, in the general phenomenon of the self-portrait. In the twentieth century, it has been a familiar category of works of art; one need only recall Picasso or Warhol. Looking at them, we are induced to speculate about the artist's personality and his own attitude about it. Is the self-portrait a boast to the viewer, a confession, a self-analysis, a mere convenience? Many more possibilities might be claimed. In any case, they give art historians a fine tool in their efforts to explain individual artistic personalities.

It was not always so. Picture books collecting self-portraits through the ages tend to begin in the early Renaissance.[1] Only a few can be assembled from earlier eras. Then around 1500, a further step seems to occur. Dürer and Raphael, both at that time, seem the first to repeat the theme a number of times. Another sort of self-portrait multiple is the unique engraving by the lesser figure Israel van Meckenem of himself and his wife. Since engravings seek a broad market, it does not seem obvious why he would have made it, nor does the question seem to have been asked. Perhaps it was for distribution to friends, in the way today printmakers create small works as Christmas cards.

Dürer's and Raphael's self-portraits are of two types: the autonomous images, which are the usual form today, and the ones included in the corner of a many-figured composition, standard up to that time. Raphael's *School of Athens* and Dürer's All-Saints altarpiece, both of 1511, show famous examples. Their marginal position, often in the background or small in scale, evokes an analogy with written signatures. They do not seem boastful or analytical. While in the case of modern art specialists rightly appeal for explanations to cultural factors shared with the artist and the reader, needing only a quick citation, there is difficulty for anyone focusing on the era when the self-portrait emerges. General remarks on the status of the artist and on the rediscovery of nature and man are not wrong but seem inadequate.

Besides this larger problem, a narrower one for this earlier era is in deciding whether a given image actually is a self-portrait. Vasari was only the most obvious of those who hopefully claimed to see self- and other portraits in many images. They projected their interests on a not very compliant past. If that is understandable, it is less so that many of Vasari's dubious claims, often involving faces that probably are not portraits at all, survive little challenged today. Though his general unreliability about previous centuries is notorious, on this point one finds remarkable credulity.

Help on that problem, it is here suggested, might be available from finding the self-portraits in large compositions recurring in works on the same subjects. In general, they turn out to be random in this respect, but enough of them are attached to one subject matter to suggest a meaningful convention. That is the Last Judgment, a theme whose composition shows exceptional stability through the centuries that interest us here, throughout Western Europe. One of its recurrent segments shows the blessed, the people whom Christ is sorting, at his right, after all the dead have been lifted out of their tombs. Among these, self-portraits appear often enough to seem significant. For the first two examples I am indebted to Walter Cahn. The sorting of the blessed and damned souls in an English illumination of about 1250 includes a man who is holding a scroll inscribed with an artist's signature: *W. de Brail me fecit.*[2] (The figure, unlike all the others to be discussed, appears among the damned, but an angel is lifting him out of that group. Other Last Judgments show similar groups of single souls on the wrong side being relocated by angels. Here it might be felt to suggest the artist's sense of vulnerability.)

The second example, about 1340, is in a Last Judgment sculpture over the door of the Church of Our Lady in Rottweil, Germany. The study of medieval portraits of craftsmen in Germany by Gerstenberg presents it well; of his two hundred illustrations, it is the only one where the portrait is within a large scene.[3] Here the sculptor holds the hammer, the tool of his craft, found in several other cases in the volume.[4] He is emerging from his tomb, wearing contemporary costume, while the other dead emerge naked. These factors make his identification as the sculptor sufficiently plausible, in combination with the analogy in the manuscript.

Two Italian examples from the same years again include one that is firm and a second that is plausible. The latter appears in the carved relief of the Last Judgment on the façade of the Cathedral of Orvieto, linked to documents of 1330. All the saved wear generic robes, except for three men at the edge, in contemporary dress. Two are younger, while the more mature one holds an L-shaped measuring form, another tool of the craft, one carried by a number of the masters shown in Gerstenberg's illustrations.[5] Among these, the well-known self-portrait of Anton Pilgram in Vienna Cathedral is notable.

As to the firm example, the earliest brief biography of Giotto, produced about 1395 by Filippo Villani, considered trustworthy by all specialists, states that a fresco by him in the Bargello, Florence, included a self-portrait.[6] He does not report the subject of the fresco, but a partial ruin of it survives showing a Last Judgment. Among many other later analogues, it may suffice to recall the one by Michelangelo in his Last Judgment, famously painted on the skin of St. Bartholomew. It is an oddity that the large literature on that image seems not to observe that it belongs to a long tradition.

To be sure, Last Judgments provide only a small fraction of the self-portraits in this era. As noted in the case of the many assembled by Gerstenberg, most are in isolation, such as Peter Parler's famous one in Prague Cathedral, in a series of identifiable portraits. Other, single, instances appear in larger scenes of many subjects, such as the School of Athens mentioned above. It is only the Last Judgment, however, in which they recur. From this it may seem reasonable to infer that there is a meaningful relation, which in turn might help to understand the general phenomenon of self-portraits. What that significance is also seems possible to suggest. It is the only theme that implies, for the culture of Christianity, the inclusion of all humanity. Spectators of Last Judgments are called to find their own position in that event and feel a strong urge to claim membership among the saved rather than the damned. The artist then takes his opportunity to locate himself in the favorable way. His motivation is not primarily to show off to the viewer of his work, nor is he following instructions from a patron. To the contrary, he would seem to be letting his private advantage intrude in his public work.

No verbal correlative for this phenomenon has emerged, but that is hardly a surprise. In that era, such texts may not have existed and may, if they exist, be hidden in brief lines of other contexts, only retrieved by chance. One is then glad to have them, not least because they may alter one's presumptions. In this case, a text that might be applicable has emerged in the context of classical antiquity, and it brings us to the Athena Parthenos.

Several writers, mainly of the first centuries B.C. and A.D., say that there is a self-portrait of Pheidias among the figures shown on Athena's shield. The claim may be unique in the classical period, though the casual form of the comments could also suggest that it was not felt to be remarkable. The most detailed remarks are in Plutarch's *Perikles.* These and four others, which concentrate on points that might be diverting to the general reader, have potential value for the art historian's goal of seeing what the work was like; they have been made available by Pollitt.[7] The other thirty-odd ancient allusions to the Parthenos that have been collected do not lack any such utility.[8] Yet one of these, invoking the self-portrait most briefly of all, with no visual evocation or biographical assertion, is of interest in the present context. Here Cicero, in the *Tusculan Disputations* (1.15.34), in fact poses as none of the other writers does the question why Pheidias would wish to portray himself. The answer is offered as a support of Cicero's broader theme in this part of the work and does not claim any basis in information about Pheidias. Book 1 of the *Disputations,* one of the author's longer treatises in the area of popular philosophy, is devoted to the then lively debate as to whether or not the soul is immortal. Those who believe that it is include great writers, who, he says, would not work as hard as they do if they did not expect fame after death, which would not be possible for them to enjoy, at least, unless the soul were immortal. The same applies to artists:

> Opifices post mortem nobilitari volunt. Quid enim Phidias sui similem speciem inclusit in clipeo Minervae, cum inscribere non liceret?
>
> [Artificers wish to be renowned after death. Why did Pheidias include his own lifelike image in the shield of Minerva, when it was not allowed to write there?]

To our culture, the argument may seem odd in that the desire for fame after death does not implicate an immortal soul. Whether he believed that it did or was giving space to a claim by others is an issue for better-informed discussion.

Of course, Cicero's base was not at all that of the artists who later inserted their portraits in Last Judgments, since for them such immortality was unquestioned. Apart from that, it is unlikely that his idea could have been in the minds of the later artists or of their public. Nevertheless, some counter-arguments should be put on record. His words by no means remained unknown in the context of writings about artists prior to the labors of philologists in the nineteenth century. These are literally anticipated in the best-selling handbook on classical mythology of Natale Conti, first issued in 1551. Near the beginning of his sketch of Pheidias, of 28 lines, he quotes Cicero's remark almost word for word ("in clipeo formam sibi similem insculpsit, cum inscribere non esset licitum").[9] It is also tempting to see as an exception one notable self-portrait within a Last Judgment around 1500, that by Luca Signorelli in his famous fresco cycle in Orvieto. It is, unlike others, filled with imagery from the literature of classical antiquity.[10] The self-portrait is also unique as a grand full length, suggesting a Renaissance concern for fame and an appeal for it to the viewer.

Cicero's lines cannot, apart from such hypotheses, fulfill a hope for a written analogue to the images in Last Judgments. Yet it gives pause to find the similar bracketing of two such independent, and seemingly remote, variables, the self-portrait and the immortality of the soul. If it merits notice, it might best do so along the lines explored by Erwin Panofsky in memorable cases, from Blind Cupid to Father Time, of the ways in which general themes show surprising modifications of imagery and underlying ideas, and of the stimulus we may have from defining the character of such modifications.[11]

NOTES

1. Benkard 1927; Goldscheider 1936; Masciotta 1955.

2. This is well presented by Alexander 1992, 25, with illustration fig. 38, and a discussion of other self-portraits; one of these is also by de Brailes.

3. Gerstenberg 1966, 34, illustration on p. 37. Unfortunately, this valuable assemblage of examples does not explain the reasons why the images are identified as self-portraits of masters, or give any count of their number.

4. See especially the illustrations in Gerstenberg 1966, 164–175.

5. See Middeldorf Kosegarten 1996, frontispiece.

6. F. Villani, *Vite degli uomini illustri fiorentini* in *Croniche di G., M. e F. Villani,* Milan, n.d., 2:450. Villani's added point that the same work also included a portrait of Dante tends to support his accuracy, since a frescoed Last Judgment of about twenty years later by Nardo di Cione, working in Giotto's tradition, includes one.

7. Pollitt 1990a, 53–54, translates the passage from Plutarch in full, and lists the four others cited, in his note 2.

8. Overbeck 1868, nos. 645–690. Maria Georgopoulou kindly helped me in checking these texts with respect to that point.

9. N. Comes, *Mythologiae,* edition of 1637, 416. The book's title does not prepare the reader for its inclusion of 139 entries on Greek artists as a set, in the chapter on Daidalos, and they appear to have remained little noted. Since Comes was a compiler rather than an original thinker, one may leave open the chance that Cicero's text had been similarly cited earlier in the Renaissance. He was of course immensely admired then. The neatest token of the standing of his *Tusculan Disputations* is its use as a model for the *Disputationes Camaldulenses* of the Florentine humanist Landino (dramatic date 1463). Landino also wrote a book on the immortality of the soul.

10. Gilbert 2003, 92–98 (scenes with classical themes), 133–136 (self-portrait).

11. This essay does not address the question of whether or not Pheidias really did include a self-portrait on the shield. For one thing, I have no competence on the matter, and for another, if he did so, no deductions as to his reasons would follow to assist in the concern here. The current consensus, for information on which I am indebted to the editors of this volume, is negative. Thus, Höcker and Schneider 1993, 14, endorse a longer comment by Preisshofen 1974 when they treat the report as "an anecdote which, at least in this form, surely (*wohl*) must count as an invention of a later era." Evidently, the material does not allow one to go further than a strong expression of judgment. These writers oppose the positive view of Metzler 1964, who had suggested that Douris of Samos, writing in the late fourth century B.C., might have been a source for Cicero. Douris, not cited by the other scholars, wrote much on art, and Cicero quoted him often and respectfully, though others denigrated his emphasis on amusing anecdotes as unreliable. It does at least seem plausible that Cicero did not create the story, which then would have an origin earlier to some degree.

20

EARLY PHOTOGRAPHY AND THE RECEPTION OF CLASSICAL ANTIQUITY

THE CASE OF THE TEMPLE OF ATHENA NIKE

PETER J. HOLLIDAY

> The historical discontinuity between Greek culture and our own, the disappearance for so many centuries of any direct influence, made it all the easier, when it was rediscovered, for each nation to fashion a classical Greece in its own image.
>
> W. H. AUDEN[1]

The astronomer Johann Heinrich Mädler coined the term *photography* in 1839, the very moment the modern Greek nation was uncovering and restoring the monumental evidence for its classical past. Mädler combined the Greek words for *light* and *painting* or *writing* to describe the new process by which light and chemical substances produce an image of seeming reality fairly true to the original—a goal shared, if by different means, by modern archaeology and restoration. Although today photographs are taken for granted in archaeological and art historical studies—the authors in this collection use photographs to record or illustrate their diverse subjects—scholars have not always embraced photographic documentation. During the nineteenth century they felt ambivalent about using photographs for such purposes, for early photographers pursued goals other than documentation.

This paper examines issues related to the intersection of the invention of photography, the development of scientific archaeology, and the creation of modern Greece. Its catalyst is a group of nineteenth-century photographs of Athenian sites and monuments collected by the Getty Research Institute. I am not concerned with the technical development of photography and its practical applications in the field of archaeology. Rather, the focus here is on how the practice of the medium in the newly founded Greek state affected the reception of the classical subjects portrayed.

The images adduced here raise questions that transcend any nostalgia evoked by their sepia-toned record of a then near-empty cityscape. Who took photographs like these, and for what purposes? How did contemporary aesthetic doctrines affect photographic practice, and in turn what role did photography play in the interpretation of the subjects depicted? What significance do the images carry for scholars of classical antiquity today?

In investigating these questions, I will focus on a particular example, the temple of Athena Nike, one of the final monuments associated with the Periklean building program.[2] By considering both its early restoration and how that rebuilt artifact was represented and interpreted, we will be able to establish how the Nike temple, and the other monuments of Periklean Athens, became a substitute agent for a past that is continually refashioned in the present.

THE NIKE SANCTUARY

According to the Oath of Plataia, after the Persian Wars, the Greek sanctuaries destroyed by the Persians were never to be rebuilt. Rather, they were to remain as admonitory symbols of barbarian infamy. Although scholars have expressed doubts regarding the oath's historicity,[3] the archaeological evidence attests to how strictly its temple clause was construed: from 479 to mid century the Nike bastion remained unterraced and unrebuilt, with at most a simple altar. Yet by mid century, Athens attained both capital and craftsmen sufficient to re-erect her shrines with the finest materials in unrivaled form.[4] The entire bastion was sheathed in limestone, its lines straightened and its area increased. Two rectangular niches were left open in the rebuilt Nike bastion to reveal the Bronze Age core within. The new naïskos, which provided shelter for the Archaic marble cult statue of Athena Nike that survived the Persian sack[5] was Ionic tetrastyle amphiprostyle (i.e., with four columns in front and four in back). Its architecture demonstrates the same kind of refinements that characterize the other Periklean monuments, and its sculptural decoration was among the richest on the Akropolis. Inside and out, the temple celebrated Athenian *nike,* victory.[6]

In the late third century A.D. the addition of a two-towered gate on the lower stairs connecting the Propylaia and the Nike bastion made the Akropolis a citadel for the first time since the Persian Wars in 480 B.C. (cf. Fig. 20.3).[7] It remained fortified from the Late Roman through the Medieval and Turkish periods (267–1833). The earliest damage to the Nike temple probably dates to the period from the thirteenth through the fifteenth centuries, when the Franks built up the citadel. In the process they walled shut the two main portals of the western ascent, the Beulé Gate and the Propylaia, and drew a new line of fortification from the Nike bastion to the Monument of Agrippa.[8] The monumental altar of Athena Nike lay directly across the new approach and was likely razed at this time; only its prothysis and foundations survive. The temple and sculpted parapet, however, remained largely unharmed.[9] With the sixteenth-century installation of cannon on the Akropolis, the Turks fashioned the Nike temple into a powder magazine.[10]

After the last Duke of Athens, Franco Acciajuoli, delivered the Akropolis to the Turks in 1458, transactions between the East and Europe ceased. Few early Western travelers saw the Nike temple intact, although in 1671/6 the French physician Jacob Spon and his English companion George Wheler visited Athens. Ascending the medieval ramp, they lingered over the view from the bastion, commended the columns and finely carved frieze of the temple, and noted the powder store below.[11] From the "Court of the Guards," Spon and Wheler admired what they thought to be the foundations of the Propylaia or of a superb marble portico; it was actually the southern side of the podium of the Nike temple, which, still in place, retained its marble cornice. To the west of the northern side of this court, the visitors found a third gate, over which they observed an eagle carved on ancient marble with "very fine craftsmanship," probably a piece of the Nike parapet.

Shortly before the Venetian siege in 1686, the Turks razed the Nike temple to the krepidoma and overbuilt the bastion with a battery for cannon. The epistyle, geison, and wall blocks of the temple and four blocks of the figured frieze were built into the inner face of a new fortification wall from the bastion to the Monument of Agrippa; the remaining frieze slabs, column drums and capitals, and several fragmentary slabs of the Nike parapet were set in as packing behind.[12] The powder magazine survived intact within the temple krepidoma, its roof now protected by the battery, the inner face of which crossed just in front of its main chamber.[13] Three low relief sections from the frieze had been built in the battery wall in a way that they remained visible. A 1687 drawing of the Akropolis once in the collection of Gravier d'Ortières shows the Nike temple was missing.[14]

EARLY TRAVELERS AND REPRESENTATIONS

In antiquity the remains of the past provided material for ensuing building projects; if too sacred to discard or reuse, they were buried.[15] The Cyclopean fortifications exposed at the core of the Nike bastion recalled for later generations of Athenians the deeds of hero-ancestors, who were closer to deities than to humans.[16] Although politically meaningful, such remnants lacked the aesthetic significance that they have acquired since the Renaissance: regarding collapsed remains at some remove of space and time, the Renaissance viewer was the first to distinguish "ruins" from mere dilapidation. In addition, Enlightenment savants came to look upon the archaeological remains of classical civilization as markers of a heritage to which they laid claim.[17] Such remains thereby became also objects of science that offered crucial evidence in the effort to understand the history of civilization. Once fragments from antiquity were uncovered, it was assumed that the trained antiquarian could piece them together and even rebuild the past.[18] Archaeological remains, therefore, are effectively the invention of modernism, holding aesthetic and scientific meaning.

Although still remote, at the dawn of the modern era northern European travelers once again visited Athens, which provided new and original material for archaeological exploration. In fact, the very geographical and temporal distance of Athenian monuments added to their appeal. Early modern discourse held that art's primary value lies in its power to assist the viewer to form or to imagine (in German, *bilden*), which benefited humanity by showing a people its ideal image and purpose.[19] The process of elevating and forming an individual's capacities (a process called *Bildung*) consisted in its holding up to the individual an image of the conditions of his or her subjectivity, which meant displaying also the subjectivity of an other. Indeed, the value of "disinterested satisfaction" was that it allowed people to distance themselves from their private interests and purposes and to look at these the way another would see them. Within the ideal of *Bildung,* art's value for forming subjects derives from the artwork's status as a unique object and therefore as a radical otherness perfectly matching the subject's individuality. This otherness may be attributed to the singularity of artistic "genius," or it may result from the artwork's having been made for another place and time (e.g., ancient Athens). What it occasions, above all, is a recognition of art's history, a consciousness not only that past artworks look different from works of the present, and call for other criteria, but that they were also beheld differently in their past, and that their values, like all values, are historically specific.[20] Such concepts profoundly affected the European reception of monuments from antiquity, such as the Nike temple; I hope to suggest how this discourse also mediated the reception of their representations.

As scholars applied more sophisticated technical and interpretive methodologies to the remains of antiquity, the ruins of classical Greece also came to be regarded as paradigms of artistic excellence through which humanistic values—the values of the past revived in the present—were transmitted. At root was the Classical Ideal, which had been ripening in Europe since the Renaissance but which owed its renewed force in the early modern period to the writings of J. J. Winckelmann and the resulting Neoclassical Revival. It is hardly coincidental that Winckelmann argued that freedom is essential for the creation of the best art and that fifth-century Athens was characterized as a paradigm of freedom.[21]

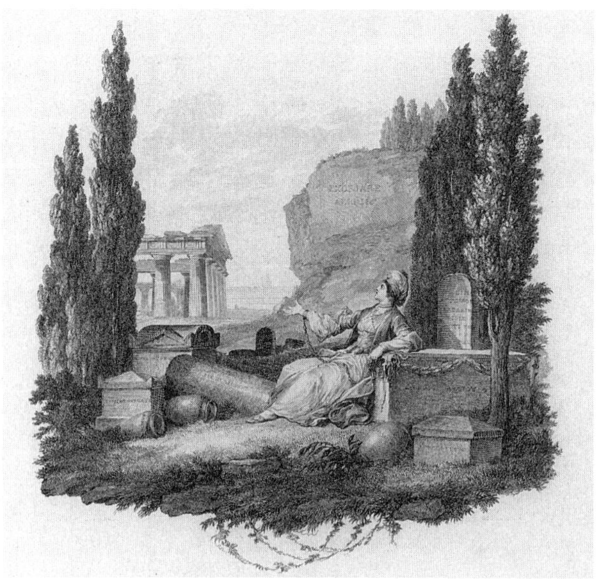

FIGURE 20.1. *"Greece Expiring among the Ruins." Title page of the Comte de Choiseul Gouffier's* Voyage pittoresque de la Grèce, *1782.*

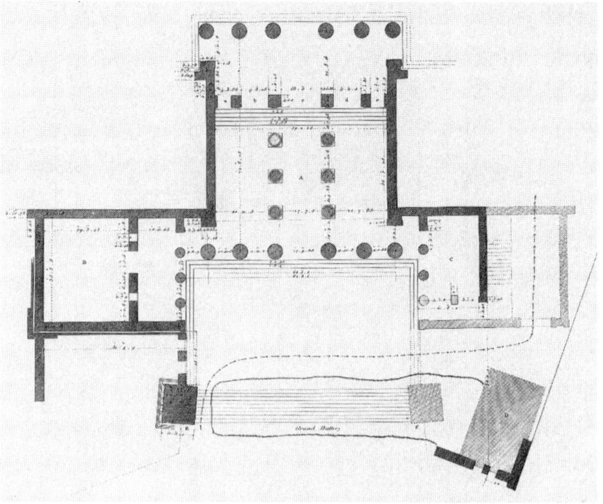

FIGURE 20.2. *Plan of the Propylaia. After Stuart and Revett's* The Antiquities of Athens, *vol. 2, ch. V, pl. II, 1787.*

At the same time, the staunchly philhellenic sentiments exhibited by European savants and travelers coincided with the colonialist agendas of northern European powers and the growing competition among nations eager to "rescue" neglected monuments for display in the halls of national museums. In such a milieu the romanticization of classical ruins in art and literature was accompanied by fierce commitment to the Greek independence movement.[22] Exemplary of this attitude is the personification of Greece collapsed among the devastated monuments of her past on the title page of the Comte de Choiseul-Gouffier's 1782 *Voyage pittoresque de la Grèce* (Fig. 20.1). The inscription carved into the cliff calls for an avenger to arise—*exoriare aliquis*—and break the chains of Eastern oppression.

Working in Athens between 1751 and 1753, James Stuart and Nicholas Revett sought to provide accurate models based on actual historical monuments for the contemporary Greek Revival (a specific aspect within the larger phenomenon of neoclassicism) in architecture and ornament. Their five folio volumes published at intervals between 1762 and 1830 established the tone and method of all later scholarly archaeology.[23] They began by sketching the actual condition of each monument. Portraits of the Turkish inhabitants going about their business then enlivened the scene, on one level giving the pictures documentary value and on another, romantically heightening the exoticism of the locale. Careful drawings with precise measurements provided the basis for accurate restorations of the ruined buildings: for Stuart and Revett, the final purpose was an antiquity freed of medieval alterations and modern accretions. In contrast, artists like J. D. Le Roy (working at Athens in 1755) sacrificed accuracy for picturesque effects that evoke sympathy for the antique past rather than provide architectural models.[24]

Antiquarians of the eighteenth and early nineteenth centuries found the partially exposed steps of the Nike temple and its immured wall and frieze blocks an enigmatic challenge.[25] The drawings of Stuart and Revett document the condition of the site and establish just how rapid and pervasive the loss was. They include the krepidoma on a plan of the Propylaia (Fig. 20.2) and reproduce three of the four visible blocks of the figured frieze.[26] Of the two houses that existed in the Court of the Guards in 1687, only one can be seen on their plan to the west of the second gate of the citadel; the east part of the court is separated by a wall having its entrance to its northern end (Fig. 20.2). Nor do they mention the foundations of the Propylaia or the "eagle" seen by Spon and Wheler from that court.[27] A generation later William Leake reexamined the site and, using Pausanias, reargued its identification as the sanctuary of Athena Apteros ("without wings"). He completed his study with a restored plan and elevation of the temple, wildly incorrect (distyle in antis facing north) but of interest for its use of a drawing made on site (between 1810 and 1817) by Charles R. Cockerell.[28] For the Turks, who had not yet absorbed the Western conception of ruins, the site had little value beyond diplomatic bargaining chips. In 1802 Lord Elgin, responding in his own way to the impulse to collect and record the remains of antiquity, pried four frieze slabs free and shipped them to England, a part of the celebrated Elgin marbles.[29]

By the early nineteenth century the romantic Philhellenes of Europe were able to form a picture of Greece and its people by means of travelers' descriptions, drawings, and engravings. Nevertheless, these materials did not satisfy their yearning for the renewal and enrichment of their own world through the rebirth of an ancient heritage instructed by its monuments. In addition, such vague sentimental nostalgia had little to do with the political reality in Greece after the War of Independence.

THE SITE FOLLOWING INDEPENDENCE

By the end of the Greek War of Independence in 1828, the Turkish settlement of the Akropolis was reduced to a heap of rubble, and the Parthenon, Erechtheion, and Propylaia had also suffered damage.[30] Christopher Neezer, the Bavarian officer to whom the Turks surrendered the city in April 1833, described the devastation:

> I entered the Acropolis and saw heaps of tumbled marbles. In the midst of the chaotic mass of column capitals, fragments of columns, marbles large and small, were bullets, cannon balls, human skulls and bones, many of which were near the slender Caryatids of the Erechtheion.[31]

England, France, and Russia created the modern state of Greece with the Protocol of London (1830). The Western powers imposed a foreign king, Otto, the second son of Ludwig of Bavaria, who arrived with an entourage of German soldiers and diplomats to establish the bureaucratic framework for the new kingdom. These regents, trained in the best classical tradition, helped orient the new state toward the West, which considered itself the heir of the ancient Greek spirit and was a magnet for the Greek intellectual diaspora.[32] Their values also helped determine the subsequent history of the Akropolis.[33]

Greece entered the mainstream of contemporary European thought, and for the first time, efforts were made to protect and display antiquities. With the evacuation of the Turkish garrison on March 31, 1833, plans were formed to free the Athenian Akropolis of Medieval and later accretions, for those centuries represented Greek servitude to the Franks after 1204 and to the Turks after the 1450s.[34] The Byzantine period, although genuinely "Greek," was suspect as part of the long dark hiatus between antiquity and modern times. The new nation sought to identify with the traditions of an antiquity esteemed throughout the West, then captivated by the Greek Revival.[35] With a strong sense of nationalism, the new state was to be Greek, not Frankish or Turkish or Byzantine.[36] The desire to restore and identify classical buildings of the "best" period, the fifth century B.C. (which were held to symbolize the identity of the young state), together with the zeal to discover their original form, caused the demolition of masses of masonry that surrounded them. As these additions were considered barbaric intrusions, offensive to the classical past of the building, little official documentation was made.[37]

The arrival of Leo von Klenze from Munich in July 1834 marked a decisive period for the Akropolis monuments. Von Klenze quickly recognized that with modern warfare, the site was useless as the fortress favored by Otto's military advisers.[38] The Akropolis came under the jurisdiction of the Greek Archaeological Service and began to take on the character of an archaeological site. (Other options for the site, such as a memorial to the revolution or Karl Friedrich Schinkel's plan for a royal palace, were also weighed. For reasons of historical sentiment, it was decided to preserve it as an

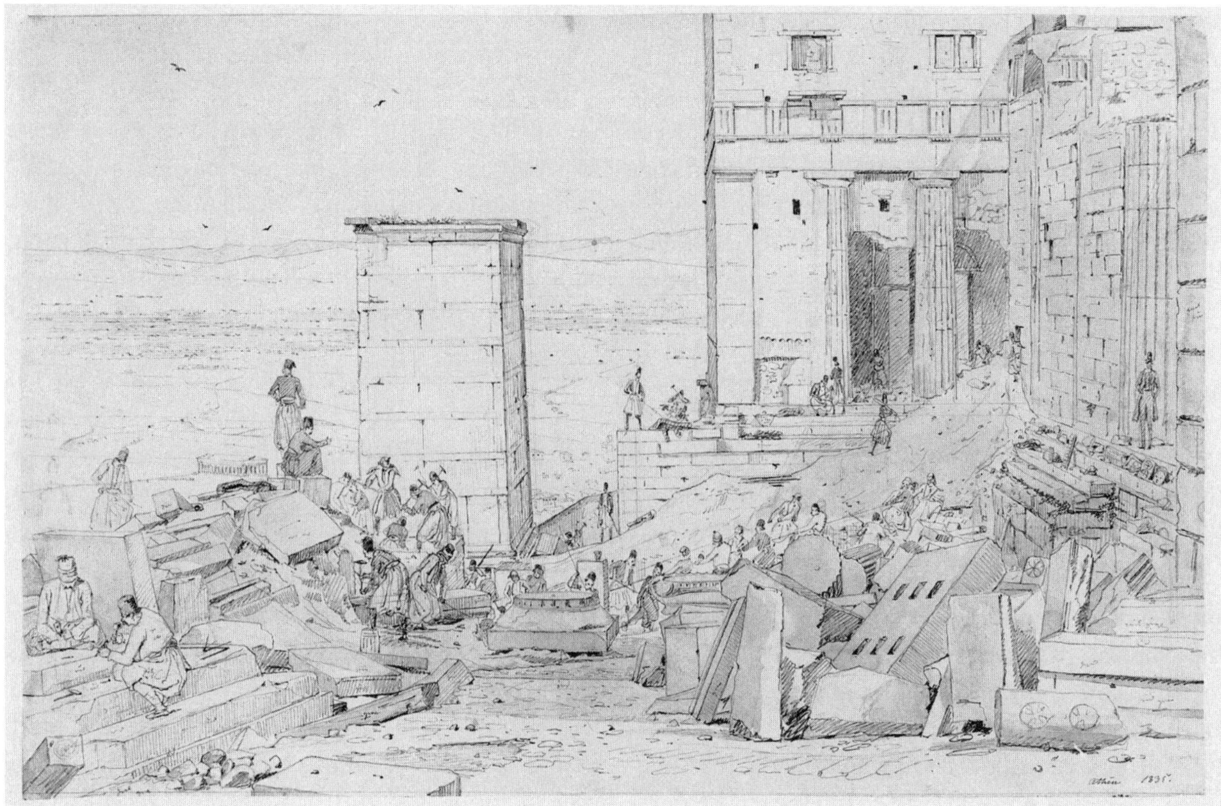

FIGURE 20.3. *Removal of Turkish bastion. M. Rørbye, 1835, pen and ink drawing, 27 × 42 cm. Photo by Hans Petersen, courtesy of the Statens Museum for Kunst, Copenhagen.*

archaeological park or museum.) The designs of von Klenze demonstrate the inherent conflict between his classicist vision of a cleared Akropolis plateau with restored classical monuments and his romantic desire to preserve the picturesque character of ruins.[39] Von Klenze did some excavating and assisted at the ceremony of symbolic inauguration of the restoration of the Parthenon on September 10, 1834.[40] Before leaving later that month, he entrusted the supervision of the work to the young German archaeologist Ludwig Ross, together with the architects Stamatios Kleanthes and Eduard Schaubert.[41]

The first restoration of the Nike temple, undertaken in an atmosphere of romantic yearning, demonstrates how archaeological remains could be made to exemplify the achievements of the past and transmit moral precepts to sustain and promote modern national and ethnic identity.[42] Towards the end of December 1834 work began on the Akropolis, with a fresh impetus under the direction of Ross, Schaubert, and Christian Hansen, who replaced Stamatios Kleanthes. As the first General Ephor (inspector) of antiquities, Ross had sympathies for the later remains but in the end cleared away the "barbarian rubbish." Anything interfering with the recovery of the ancient world was expendable.[43] Thus the despised remnants of the Medieval and Turkish Akropolis were quickly disposed of as soon as the opportunity and funds allowed.[44]

In December 1835 Ross oversaw more than one hundred workmen in the demolition of the battery built in front of the Propylaia connecting the pedestal of Agrippa to the podium of the Nike temple and also of the Frankish fortifications and ramp beneath (Fig. 20.3). In the process they found the krepis of the Nike temple in situ;[45] furthermore, the battery contained practically all the blocks of the temple, largely intact and unreworked, and some fragments of the parapet as well.[46] Work on the foundations was done in June or early July 1835 (soon after clearing the krepidoma), for in a progress report dated July 18, 1835, Ross states that he would begin to re-erect the temple after replacing a few missing blocks of stylobate with newly made ones.[47] He later reported:

> Consequently the work was eagerly continued and by July, 1835, we had pretty nearly all of the remains of the temple together in the area in front of the Propylaia except for a few pieces which seem to be entirely missing as may be easily understood. The reerection of the temple was begun in December 1835, and was almost finished by May 1836. Pentelic marble was used for new column drums which were inserted in the three broken column shafts and for a new column base; poros limestone was used for new blocks replacing missing or fragmentary blocks in the cella wall.[48]

The north and east sides of the temple were re-erected to the height of the architraves. In the bastion, workers also found architectural members of the Propylaia and parts of its staircase in situ. The Greek Kyriakos Pittakis succeeded Ross, who resigned from his post in July 1836; Pittakis followed the same plan and continued work without interruption until 1842.[49] A book on the temple appeared three years later; the text by Ross and drawings by Schaubert and Hansen provide an early landmark in scholarship on the site.

Finally, during the years 1843 and 1844 the restoration of the Nike temple came to an end. The southern and western walls, which had been built up only to half of their height, were completed. All the epistyles of the temple, the beams connecting the cella with the porticoes, the coffers, the southern pier, and the southwestern column were put in their places.[50] In 1845 the British Museum sent four plaster casts of the pieces of the temple frieze that Lord Elgin had removed to London in 1804.[51] The Nike temple became the first monument in Greece to be completely restored, the earliest fulfillment of von Klenze's vision. It was an unprecedented example of the classical style that far exceeded European scholars' hopeful visions.

By contemporary standards, the early excavation and original reconstruction were a matter of unskillful trial and error, extremely detrimental to the ancient material. Excavators purposefully destroyed the Medieval and Turkish past of the temple's site to preserve only fifth-century material, ripping the building from the context that brought it down to modern times. Indeed, all early archaeological activity on the Akropolis was the result of two attitudes: a radical and purist scholarship imported from the West that saw Greek art of the fifth century as the pinnacle of good taste, and a heightened sense of national self-worth on the part of the Greeks.[52] Both perspectives were conditioned by the triumph of neoclassicism, particularly in its philhellenic phase that fashioned Greece, not Rome, as the font of Western civilization. Certainly work on the Nike temple was initiated early on due to the excitement over the finds and the small, manageable scale of the undertaking. Just as important, perhaps, was its ideological significance: in the fifth century the Nike temple had symbolized Hellenic triumph, the victory of Western civilization over barbaric, Eastern oppression, and in the nineteenth century of a newly independent Greece over the Ottoman heirs to the Persian Empire.

The restoration of the Nike temple was one example of a growing practice. During the nineteenth century, Europeans moved beyond the mere contemplation of ruins and undertook the restoration of richly resonant monuments.[53] The practice was controversial. John Ruskin argued that the very act of restoration paradoxically necessitates destruction, for the aesthetic balance that makes an object a ruin is destroyed when the edifice is saved:

> Neither by the public, nor by those who have the care of public monuments, is the true meaning of the word *restoration* understood. It means the most total destruction which buildings can suffer: a destruction out of which no remnants can be gathered: a destruction accompanied with fake description of the thing destroyed. Do not let us deceive ourselves in this important matter; it is *impossible,* as impossible to raise the dead, to restore anything that has ever been great or beautiful in architecture.[54]

The loss of context entailed in restoration was felt to add to the "fakery." Since much of the work on the Akropolis was done before the development in the 1860s and 1870s of careful documentation techniques, we have no recourse to the archaeologist's own records. (For example, in 1835 Pittakis pulled down the encrustations of the Propylaia without recording them.) The invention of photography, however, provided a partial solution to this problem, for the work of early photographers documents this period in the site's history.

EARLY PHOTOGRAPHS OF THE NIKE TEMPLE

It is no coincidence that the invention of photography formed a fundamental requisite for the history of Classical Art, providing the means by which the development of ancient culture (apart from philological and historical studies) could be made visible. The photograph reduces immense three-dimensional landscapes and architecture to a manageable two-dimensional device. Artists and scientists recognized that photography made it possible to capture ever-changing spatial relations (and motion) and, each in its own way, were fascinated by the visual phenomenon. At first antiquarians felt no need for photographic documentation in connection with interpretation or analysis[55] (the archaeologist K. O. Müller, however, did find the possibility intriguing).[56]

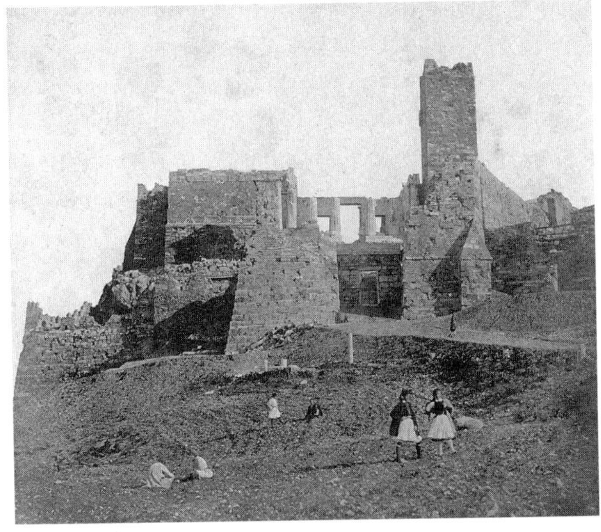

FIGURE 20.4. *Akropolis. James Robertson, 1854, salt print from wet collodion negative, 25.9 × 29.1 cm. Research Library, Getty Research Institute, Los Angeles (92.R.84).*

Although Italy had been the traditional focus of the Grand Tour, during the nineteenth century, disturbances of the Risorgimento made Greece more attractive; in addition, it was a transit station on the way to the East, which had become another popular destination. In Italy the desire for mementos had supported artists (and, more recently, daguerrotypists) for centuries. In Greece photographs, primarily in publications, fulfilled this role, with the album considered the most appropriate presentation. In the beginning an album was a rare luxury item with highly individual artistic content; when the early calotypists chose it as a way of presenting their works, they consciously evoked similarities to traditional albums of drawings and engravings.

Initially the only active photographers in Greece were travelers who came for the sake of the antiquities, driven by a desire to deepen their education and by enthusiasm for the heritage of an heroic past. One significant foreign photographer was the Scot James Robertson.[57] Robertson worked previously as a designer of medals, some of which he exhibited at the Royal Academy in London; later, he was chief engraver to the Imperial Mint in Constantinople, where he also practiced photography. Photographs such as his view of the Akropolis (Fig. 20.4) are distinguished by the dexterity of their composition and their inclusion of human figures at differing distances from the camera so as to provide a sense of scale. (The dumped fillings are from Beulé's excavation of 1852/3.)

Like Robertson, other early practitioners of photography were frequently drawn from lithographers, copper engravers, and draftsmen who had previously been involved in copying artworks and preparing them for printing. Symmetry and axiality, determined by measured fixed points, played an important role in their work. This schematization, conditioned by technical procedures, predestined early photographers of archaeological sites as purveyors of information distanced from their subjects by virtue of mechanical methods and freed photography from subjective coloring. It was this very quality that, in turn, prompted beholders to project their own feelings and thoughts (a kind of *Bildung*) into the photograph. In a related phenomenon, the architects who made measured drawings on the Akropolis and who were thoroughly familiar with the ancient written sources made a surprising discovery.[58] They determined that the Akropolis building ensemble had not been composed according to the laws of axial compositions as they had expected, in conformity with contemporary architectural theory based on Vitruvius, Alberti, and Palladio, and thus opened up a new understanding of classical architecture. They saw that although the individual buildings indeed had canonical symmetry, each building was sited in relation to the whole Akropolis complex in such a way that a variety of sight lines were offered.[59]

In the nineteenth century both photography and painting used the same compositional conventions, although they differed in function (photography was tied to practical purposes). Photography therefore mirrored the controversy throughout Europe over calculated and natural balance in representation. Although photography did not arise to demonstrate one point of view or another, it became an unconscious reflection of current discourse, for the photographers themselves were often architect-artists for whom such questions were one of the legitimate reasons for undertaking a trip to Greece. Pictures of the Nike temple by two Greek photographers who had received Western training demonstrate these differences. Philippos Margaritis studied painting in Rome, and he is cited as the first modern Greek artist to express Western trends; he also opened the first photographic studio in Athens.[60] At the annual exhibition at the National Technical University in 1855, Margaritis displayed the first photographs of the monuments of the Akropolis to have been exhibited in Greece. A few months later he organized the Greek installation at the 1855 World Exhibition in Paris. There he received a medal for his photographic images of various ancient monuments of the Akropolis and the city of Athens (Fig. 20.5). Dimitris Konstantinou was the first photographer to be associated with the Hellenic Archaeological Society, on whose behalf he photographed antiquities in Athens and ancient finds in the society's collection.[61] He sold his systematic studies of the antiquities on the Akropolis and of Athens and its environs (Fig. 20.6) in the form of albums to foreign visitors, signing his work "Demetre Constantin" or "Demetre Constantinidis."

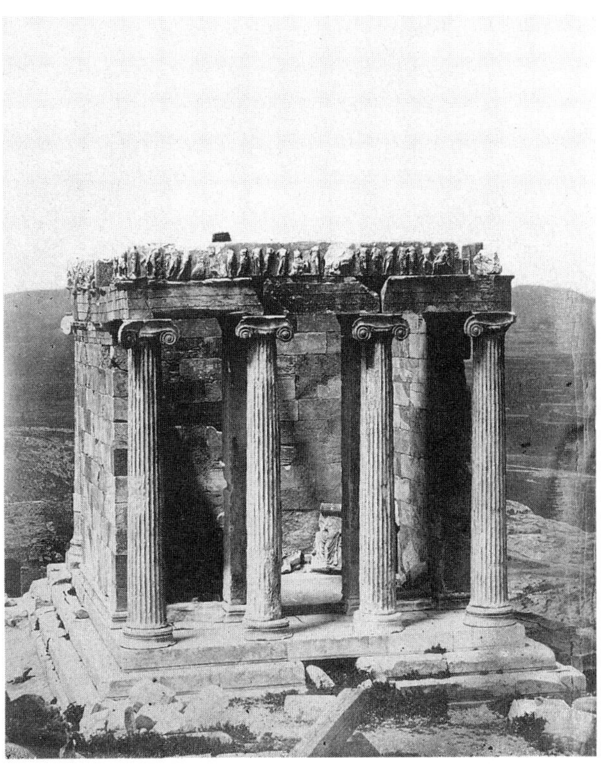

FIGURE 20.5. *Temple of Athena Nike. Philippos Margaritis, 1855, salt print from wet collodion negative, 28.5 × 22.8 cm. Research Library, Getty Research Institute, Los Angeles (92.R.84).*

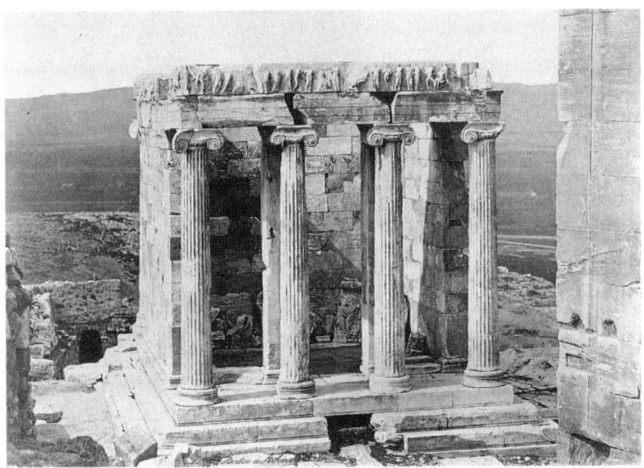

FIGURE 20.6. *Temple of Athena Nike. Dimitris Konstantinou, 1865, albumen print, 27.9 × 36.8 cm. Research Library, Getty Research Institute, Los Angeles (92.R.84).*

Both Margaritis and Konstantinou use near-frontal views; however, the employment of suitable angles indicates the temple's architectural mass and suggests a degree of perspectival diminution into space. But whereas Margaritis composed a tight vertical shot emphasizing the temple as an individual monument, existing only for itself, Konstantinou uses the wall of the Propylaia at the right as a framing device for his horizontal view, giving a greater sense of the temple's immediate and distant surroundings. As in the case of Robertson, other photographers might use figures as props. Although such figures might serve as an indication of scale, Greeks in traditional dress picturesquely draped beside the stones also satisfied the European taste for exoticism and, with ever-greater self-consciousness, the national pride of the Greeks.

After the 1860s more Greeks practiced photography, and their images reveal the pride of Athenians in their city. It was no longer merely a matter of depicting ancient monuments. Instead, photographers sought to bring out the prestige of the new town by using ancient monuments as a background to enhancing the modern. The literal picture of Athens no longer incorporated only foreign longing for Winckelmann's "eine edle Einfalt und eine stille Grösse" (a noble simplicity and silent grandeur); rather, it also embodied the realistic attitudes of its inhabitants living in the present.[62] Nevertheless, photographs of ancient monuments still took precedence, for they were valued as noble artistic creations and the obvious choice for entries in international and national exhibitions.[63]

The works of Gabriel de Rumine reflect this subtle shift. A Russian nobleman and amateur photographer of independent means living in Paris in the late 1850s, Rumine conducted a Mediterranean tour in 1858–1859, accompanied by Grand Duke Constantine, son of Nicholas I. Rumine was dedicated to promoting understanding between France and Russia, and he used newly independent Greece as a model of a nation bridging past and present, East and West. The Grand Duke entrusted him with the task of recording the most remarkable sites and monuments encountered during the voyage. Although today his work is hardly known, his photographic documentation of the trip was extensive and includes a view at close range of the façade of the temple of Athena Nike (Fig. 20.7). Rumine exhibited at the Société Française de Photographie exhibition in Paris in 1859 and at the Amsterdam and London international exhibitions in 1862. Although he may not have shown his photographs of Greece in the first exhibition, he probably showed some at the others.[64] His images are of particular interest because they give an accurate description of the architecture and town planning of Athens in 1859 and stress his interest in the continuity of the classical heritage into the modern age (Fig. 20.8).[65] Images of modern buildings spreading beneath the Akropolis illustrated how the Greek state was taking its rightful place among Western nations.

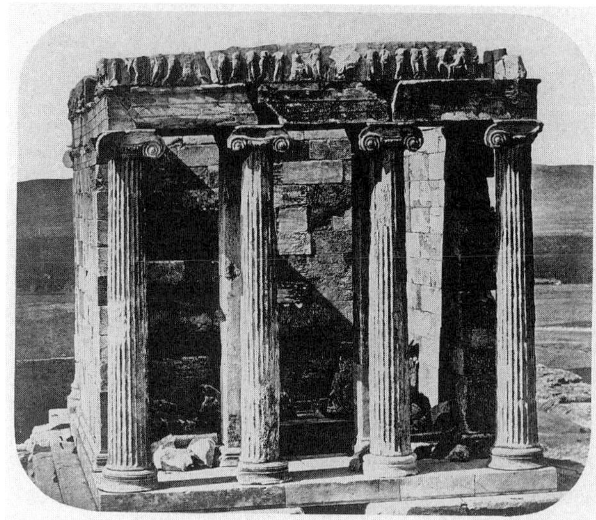

FIGURE 20.7. *Temple of Athena Nike. Gabriel de Rumine, 1859, albumen print, 16 × 22 cm. Research Library, Getty Research Institute, Los Angeles (92.R.84).*

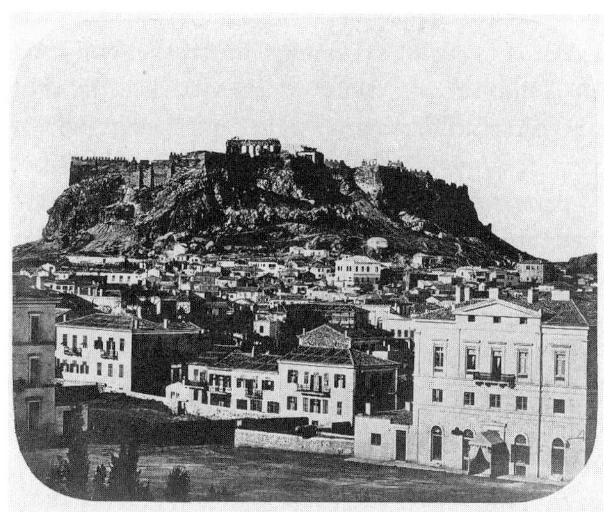

FIGURE 20.8. *View of Akropolis. Gabriel de Rumine, 1859, albumen print, 16 × 22 cm. Research Library, Getty Research Institute, Los Angeles (92.R.84).*

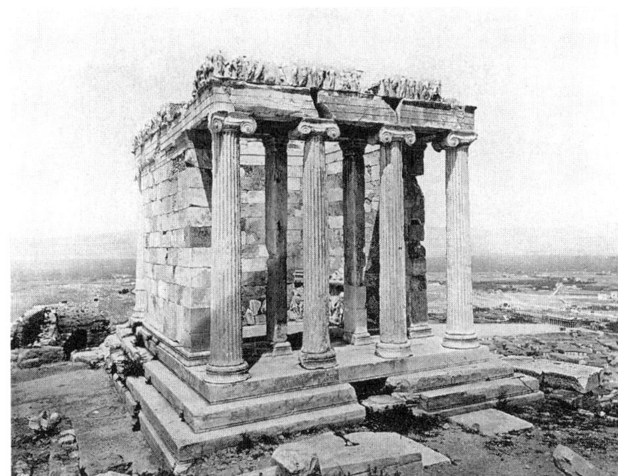

FIGURE 20.9. *Temple of Athena Nike. Francis Frith, 1860, albumen print, 15.6 × 20.9 cm. Research Library, Getty Research Institute, Los Angeles (92.R.84).*

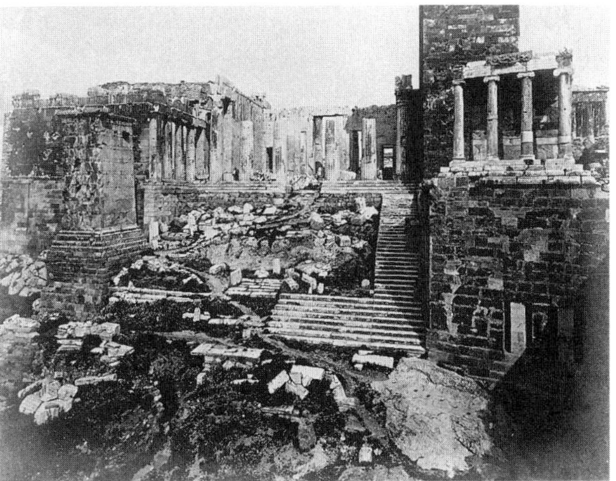

FIGURE 20.10. *Propylaia, particularly the Frankish addition of the eastern wall of the north wing. William James Stillman, 1869, albumen print, 18.3 × 23.4 cm. Research Library, Getty Research Institute, Los Angeles (92.R.84).*

Most of the travelers who photographed Greek subjects in the 1860s and 1870s continued to publish their work in albums of original prints and thus automatically limited the size of the edition. Typical of this practice was Francis Frith (1822–1898). His main purpose—as was true of many other early photographers—was to photograph Egypt and other parts of the Middle East, with the inclusion of Greece being coincidental.[66] Frith's image of the Nike temple (Fig. 20.9) dates from 1860, at the end of his third photographic tour. His horizontal composition shows the temple from a slightly greater degree of angle than the work of his predecessors, thereby setting the temple off against a vista of the stark Attic landscape. Products like these were meant not only for tourists but also for the delectation of those not able to visit the sites for themselves.

One exception to the popular albums was a book printed in folio format by the American William James Stillman, *The Acropolis of Athens,* whose images reveal the lingering tension between architectural training and romanticism. Stillman moved in intellectual and artistic circles on both sides of the Atlantic. In his autobiography he wrote: "As I had given my leisure in Crete to the practice of photography and was provided with everything necessary for correct architectural work, I set about photographing the ruins of Athens."[67] In 1868 Stillman and his family moved to Athens from his assignment as American Consul in Crete, where for the preceding two years they had been under siege owing to Stillman's overt assistance to the Cretans in the face of Ottoman repression. His architectural studies of the monuments show an extraordinary interest in the details in the foreground, seeming to confirm the stylistic relationship between landscape photographers of the albumen-print era and the art of the Pre-Raphaelite Brotherhood. His view of the Propylaia (Fig. 20.10) not only shows the restored Nike temple but it also indicates the progress made in clearing the site in the fifteen years since Robertson's visit (cf. Fig. 20.4). Such images display Stillman's ability to fuse art and document.

Unlike architectural ruins, sculptural remains held little interest for early photographers. Both Margaritis and Robertson had photographed single relief slabs from the Nike temple.[68] They rarely looked upon them as compositions per se; instead, they used them as fragments, which functioned as the primary elements within a larger pictorial design. The images feature arrangements commonly used by Piranesi, with bits and pieces of sculpture filling up the corners. Such compositions were purposeful, not the result of the exigency of the situation. Most pieces were kept out-of-doors at the time and were easily accessible (some fragments are visible just inside the restored Nike temple in Figs. 20.5–7, 20.9).[69] The authorities readily permitted the rearrangement of the reliefs by photographers, and workers gladly helped move them for a small tip, freeing the photographer to organize compositions according to his own taste.

At this time there were two ways of photographing sculpture: an axial view preferred by many Italian photographers (such as Alinari) and an oblique view taken to bring out a piece's three dimensionality. Pascal Sebah used the latter for his photographs of the reliefs from the Nike balustrade in 1870 (Fig. 20.11). The bright Athenian sun provided even illumination for the rendering of plastic qualities. Slightly slanting or three-quarter views present an event in motion, building a sense of drama. Contemporary scholars found nothing of interest in such images, but in 1924, the French archaeologist Henri Lechat bestowed the highest praise on Sebah's works, for he felt they exhibited perfectly the standards he was then formulating for photographing the Akropolis sculpture.[70] More than any line drawing or traditional frontal view, the play of light and oblique angles suggested the effects originally experienced by the ancient viewer.

Although photography had been established as a viable commercial activity in the nineteenth century, it remained only of marginal interest for contemporary archaeologists. Drawing remained the preferred means of recording in publications of archaeological finds, a propensity indicative of the professional training of scholars, who generally were good draughtsmen.[71] Rather than technological innovation and economic potential, other forces lead to the eventual employment of photography by scholars. Thanks to a stream of new finds, Winckelmann's model of ancient Greek art was continuously reviewed and revised, although at first the reaction to finds from hitherto unknown periods was far from enthusiastic. It was not by accident that the first Archaic and Early Classical sculptures to be found in the Persian destruction fill on the Akropolis in 1863 were photographed as mere curiosities.[72] Yet to provide a basis for discussion and promote understanding of the discoveries, there had to be visual documentation that could be internationally communicated. Photographic illustrations eventually began to accompany descriptions of new finds in publications.[73] For example, in 1873 the École Française began excavations at Delos, and in 1876 the German Archaeological Institute started excavations at Olympia with tremendous expenditures for technical aids.[74] Both campaigns were recorded by drawing and photography. Finally, towards the end of the century, the trend towards creating photographic archives penetrated the entire study of antiquity.[75] All the twentieth-century work on the Nike temple possesses full photographic documentation.

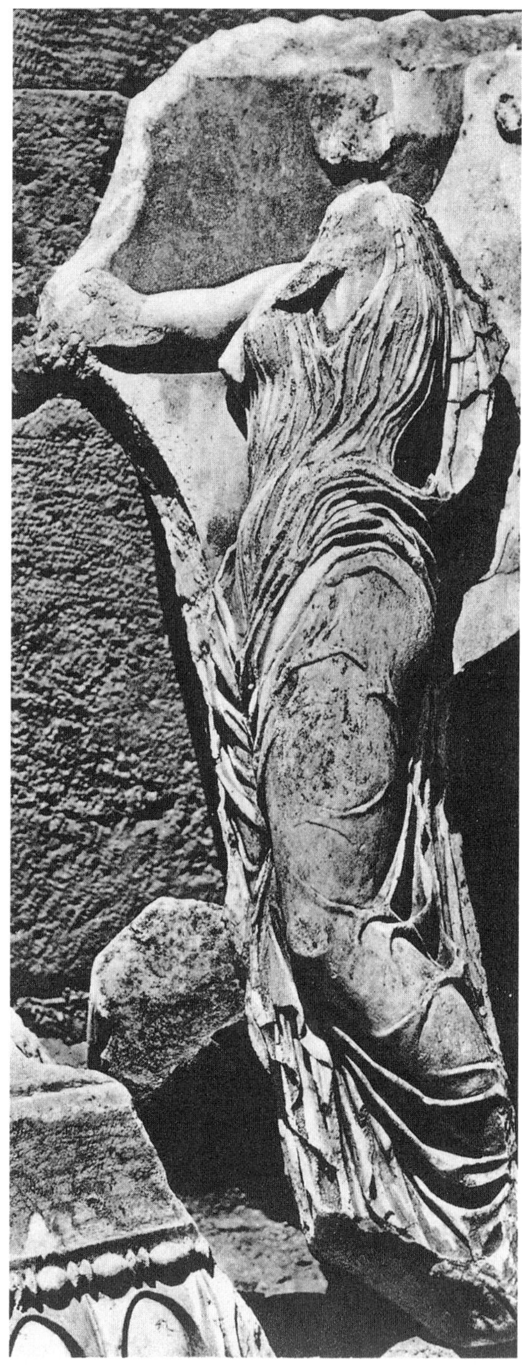

FIGURE 20.11. *Parapet relief from the temple of Athena Nike, Pascal Sebah, 1870, albumen print, 22.5 × 8.5 cm. Private Collection.*

REPRESENTATION AND RECEPTION

This brief survey has shown how photography in Greece proliferated immediately following its invention against the background of the development of the new state and the democratization of the Grand Tour. At the same time, in the early modern era, ever-widening components of society came to consider classical antiquity a birthright, part of their cultural inheritance. It was a short step from this notion to the appropriation of archaeological remains by governments keen to establish national and ethnic identities or to demonstrate the force of empire.[76] Archaeologists have built up knowledge about the topography of ancient sites on the basis of the ruins above ground and through excavation. Then as now, scholarly debate was indispensable for this enterprise. At the same time, the West used any new evidence to fashion a classical Greece befitting its agenda, and photographs played a crucial role in framing and disseminating those constructs.

Like the prints acquired by earlier visitors to Rome, photographs offered a means of collecting and recollecting the past as a souvenir.[77] Indeed, such images—old, brown, preserved, catalogued—are now themselves imbricated within notions of archaeology and antiquity. Their power to frame the historical study of classical sites in Western aesthetic terms, while seeming to present objective documentation, continues to affect our understanding and interpretation of these monuments. Most of the compositions illustrated here are firmly grounded in eighteenth-century conventions of the picturesque. They are part of a process that determined the taste in Europe and America from the mid-nineteenth century until World War I. Certain views (especially those in which the immediate or more distant surroundings could be included and thereby give a sense of place) are considered worthy of photographing, especially the monuments of the Akropolis. In the case of the Nike temple, representing it according to Western pictorial traditions and, with the advent of photography, by means of Western technology, subsumed the monument into the Western tradition. Equally important, its historical significance—the triumph of Greece over foreign oppression—brought the symbolism of the Nike temple into the service of contemporary Western ideology.

Initially a product of ancient Greek workmanship, the Nike temple's current incarnation is a thoroughly modern phenomenon (as of this writing, the temple has been completely dismantled in preparation for another restoration). As Ruskin had argued about other contemporary restoration projects, it represents an attempt to arrest and reverse decay, necessarily resulting in a pastiche, an approximation to historical accuracy rather than an exact reconstruction of the past.[78] Writing at the end of the century, Sigmund Freud distinguished the option of leaving ruins from that of excavating them.[79] He argued that ruins can neither be left alone nor preserved intact because "*saxa loquuntur!*" (Stones talk!)[80] Rather, they must be dug out and worked through, for only by excavating the rubble can we reveal the fragments of a larger story or meaning from the past. Yet Freud also warned that when remnants are uncovered, they are irrevocably changed: they become a part of the present.

Problems of multiple temporality and the construction of reality confronted in archaeology are further complicated in the case of photography. Photographs reveal changes wrought by time, including the physical marks of natural deterioration, disaster, war, urban development, tourism, and looting. These images provide us with crucial—and often unique—evidence documenting the early modern history of classical sites. The photographs we now use as records concerning local costume or the restoration of ancient buildings or changes in the townscape were made by men unknowing of the coming movement of historical documentation. More straightforward views eventually began to replace those structured according to truly picturesque conventions, and the resulting photographs moved from the realm of the souvenir to archaeological documentation, from romance to science.[81] Yet in claiming objectivity, even science serves Western ideology, for the rhetoric of the photograph is to conflate naturalism and realism.[82] Since these photographs possess an aura of objective reality, the narratives Westerners describe for the subjects portrayed will also lay claim to that aura. Curiously, it is sometimes because early photographers used the artistic conventions they did that their products possess historical value today. Certainly, by adhering to the picturesque in composing their views, early photographers permitted their contemporary public to gaze upon the radical otherness of classical Greek ruins. Simultaneously, though, the lens of familiar conventions provided a catalyst to their imaginations—a comprehensible visual avenue toward the otherness of the ancient object.

The photographs illustrated here evoke temporality, especially a sense of melancholy for the past. For the nineteenth-century viewer they depicted objects from the distant past uncovered and restored in the present. But by picturing an Athens that no longer exists, these photographs allow us, too, to form and imagine based on our distance from the nineteenth century. Today the photographs not only depict artworks of another age but they are themselves artworks of another age. They bear witness to the abrasions of time, turning the then present into the now past. According to early modern aesthetic discourse prevalent when they were made, the contemplation of this important temporal component of ruins elevates the viewer's capacities (*Bildung*). They help us recognize art's history, that we behold singular monuments like the Nike temple differently than did Athenians in the fifth century B.C., and that we view it—and even these representations of it—differently than did viewers in the nineteenth century. These photographs underscore Freud's perception that the practice of archaeology also has a multiple temporality involving the past, its decay, and the encounter with remains in the present.

Freud made his reference to archaeology at a time when scholars had already begun to document the archaeological discoveries of classical Athens with photographs. The camera had come to be seen as an instrument that could arrest the passage of time: it actualized a technology that could capture what had come to pass and what remained.[83] The debris of the past, once seen as material remnants connected with legends and myths of origin, was now scientific evidence for the historical past, but a history that could be fashioned to serve various agendas. Crumbling monuments that were built to signify the immortality of civilization had become proof, rather, of its transience. Freud realized that any re-presentation of the past—even a seemingly authentic restoration—is a reworking of it.[84] In its ability to document the modern history of a monument like the Nike temple, photography not only functions as a compensation for transience, for the experience of losing the past; it also frames our reception of that past.

NOTES

I would like to thank Gordon Baldwin, Claire Lyons, and Frances Terpak for their assistance in working with materials in the Getty Research Institute and the J. Paul Getty Museum.

1. Auden 1948, 2.

2. The nature of the association of the rebuilding of the Nike bastion with the Periklean building program is controversial. See Travlos, *Athens,* 148–149, who dates the rebuilding of the temple proper to 427–424; Mark 1993, to 424/3–418; see also Hurwit 1999, 209–215.

3. For a recent discussion of this problem, see Ferrari 2002, 14.

4. Mark 1993, 134.

5. Mark 1993, 124–125. The seated, under-life-sized marble image dated from ca. 580 to 560 B.C. According to Heliodoros, the "wingless *xoanon*" was still on the bastion in the second century B.C., but may have been removed by Sulla in 84 B.C.; it was probably gone by Pausanias' day: see Mark 1993, 93. On Sulla's looting: Ferguson 1974, 55; on artwork carried to Rome: Pollitt 1978.

6. See Stewart 1985; Rhodes 1995, 113–131; Hurwit 1999, 211–215.

7. The Beulé Gate, named for its modern excavator; see Tanoulas 1987, 416.

8. Ross, Schaubert, and Hansen 1839, 2–3; Ross 1855–1856, 74–77, 94, 97–98, 99–102, 108, 112–113, 115–116; Bohn 1882, 5–7; Travlos, *Athens,* 164–166; Tanoulas 1987, 431; Mark 1993, 7.

9. Mark 1993, 7.

10. Ross, Schaubert, and Hansen 1839, 3; Mark 1993, 9.

11. Spon and Wheler 1678, 2:105–106; Wheler 1682, 358.

12. Ross, Schaubert, and Hansen 1839, 3, 17; Bohn 1882, 8; Travlos, *Athens,* 190–192; Tanoulas 1987, 438; Mark 1993, 9.

13. Mark 1993, 9.

14. An engineer who accompanied him on a tour of the Levant probably drew it; see Tanoulas 1987, fig. 7; McNeal 1991, fig. 6.

15. Lyons 1997, 79. For the buried remains on the Akropolis discovered in 1863, see Hurwit 1989.

16. Hurwit 1999, 74–76, 209, and passim.

17. Constantine 1984.

18. Schnapp 1997, passim.

19. Kant's aesthetics, developed in his *Critique of Judgment* (1790), argued that it is in art that the subject confronts objects with a wholly "disinterested satisfaction," elevating art to the link between self and world, ethics and reason, the individual and the collective. According to the reception of Kantian aesthetics, art functioned to reveal to the subject his or her proper image (*Bild*) as subject.

20. According to Hegel, in his *Lectures on Aesthetics* delivered in the 1820s, *Bildung* occurs in the encounter with otherness and, in particular, with the otherness of the art of the past.

21. Winckelmann 1755, part 10, ch. 2, section 1, accepts Pliny's assertion that art ceased after the 121st Olympiad (295–292 B.C.), which supports both his developmental system, which demands decline after Alexander, and his historicism, which connects artistic stagnation with loss of liberty. Kant also held that the best art was the authentic expression of a culture's ideals, conforming to enfranchisement and reason. See Marchand 1996, 3–35, on the fashioning of classical Greece as an artistic and intellectual model.

22. Constantine 1984; Lyons 1997, 90.

23. Actually, Stuart and Revett were directly involved in only the first three volumes of *The Antiquities of Athens* (1762, 1787, and 1795). The fourth volume (1816) was edited by Josiah Taylor, and the fifth (1830) by C. R. Cockerell.

24. McNeal 1991, 58. Nevertheless, Le Roy was one of the first to publish his drawings, and his text is accurate and useful: see Tanoulas 1987, 444. The criteria that apply to the picturesque—and to the sublime and the beautiful, etc.—were formulated in numerous treatises at the dawn of the modern era; for a typical example in English, see Gilpin 1792.

25. The preservation is amazing, for the Turks usually turned marble architectural elements into lime. See Pococke 1743–1754, 2:161; Montague 1799, 61.

26. Stuart and Revett 1787, vol. 2, ch. 5, 39–40, pls. II, XII, and XIII. The remains are also visible in the picturesque view drawn by W. Pars.

27. The immured blocks of the figured frieze, close at hand along the ramp, were repeatedly prey to vandals.

28. Leake 1821, 191–205. In Cockerell's plan we can see in the Court of the Guards the house to the west of the second gate, with an extension along the walls.

29. London, British Museum 421–424. On the consignment of the slabs to London, see A. H. Smith 1916, 215.

30. The Akropolis was twice a site of battle in the War of Independence: in 1821–1822, the Athenians besieged the Turks and drove them out; and in 1826–1827, the Athenians were forced to surrender to the Turks, who kept possession until 1833.

31. Quoted in Papageorgiou-Venetas 1994, 225.

32. Papageorgiou-Venetas 1994, 225.

33. These values are apparent in the correspondence of such advisors as Leo von Klenze and Ludwig Ross; see Kühn 1979; Hamdorf 1985.

34. McNeal 1991, 61.

35. Among the standard sources, see Crook 1972; Wiebenson 1969.

36. This attitude was evident in the very name that the modern Greeks chose to take: "Hellenes" rather than the old Byzantine term "Romii": see McNeal 1991, 61.

37. Tanoulas 1987, 418.

38. Ross 1863, 81–82.

39. For his 1834 memorandum on the procedures to be followed in excavating on the Akropolis, clearing away later structures, preserving and sorting the finds, and restoring the Parthenon, see von Klenze 1834, 392–395; English translation in Papageorgiou-Venetas 1994, 419–420.

40. Tanoulas 1987, 462.

41. Tanoulas 1987, 462; Papageorgiou-Venetas 1994, 228.

42. Two subsequent restorations of the sanctuary undertaken in the twentieth century have provided critical archaeological data for establishing the chronology of building phases on the site. On the site, see Mark 1993, 10–11.

43. The rubble was sold for building material to pay for the cost of further clearance.

44. McNeal 1991, 51.

45. The krepidoma was badly sunken on the east and south; see Mark 1993, 10.

46. Beulé 1853, 252–253; Tanoulas 1987, 462.

47. Ross 1855–1856, 1:100.

48. Quoted in Papageorgiou-Venetas 1994, 229.

49. From 1841, work on the Akropolis was undertaken by the Archaeological Society of Athens, founded in 1837. For Pittakis' work on the Akropolis, see Tanoulas 1987, 461; Papageorgiou-Venetas 1994, 225, 229.

50. The capital of the latter was made new because the original one had not been discovered; see Tanoulas 1987, 465.

51. Tanoulas 1987, 466.

52. By the 1840s the buildings between the Propylaia and Erechtheion (part of the ducal palace) had disappeared. From 1851 to 1853 the outer Turkish bastion of the Akropolis was dismantled, and the Beulé Gate was discovered. In 1874 the Frankish Tower was taken down.

53. Inter alia, we can cite Viollet-le-Duc's restoration of Notre Dame in Paris and the work on the Colosseum in Rome under Pius IX.

54. Ruskin 1849, 134–135.

55. The first attempts to do so were by the pioneer photographer Fox Talbot. In 1844 he brought out the first photograph album in history, *The Pencil of Nature,* which included a piece of ancient sculpture: plates V and XVII show the so-called Patroklos, then in the Lansdowne Collection (now London, British Museum 1860). As a result of showing different aspects of the same object, Talbot revealed

the manifold possibilities of interpretation and different ways of observing.

56. Letter dated May 7, 1840, cited in Papageorgiou-Venetas 1994, 106.

57. Constantinou and Tsigakou 1998.

58. Many others had joined the German scholars who accompanied Otto to Athens, including since 1846 those at the École Française.

59. Cf. Etlin 1987, 268–269.

60. Xanthakis 1988, 68.

61. Xanthakis 1988, 70.

62. Goette and Zimmermann 1995, passim.

63. Papageorgiou-Venetas 1994, 116.

64. Xanthakis 1988, 58–59.

65. These interests also informed his articles in the short-lived *Gazette du Nord,* a weekly periodical of which he was a director dedicated to promoting understanding between France and Russia.

66. Xanthakis 1988, 60.

67. Stillman 1901, 2:454. This fascinating work tells us of his life as a naturalist, artist, revolutionary, spy, diplomat, and foreign correspondent for the London *Times.*

68. Robertson (who was probably acquainted with the work of Stuart and Revett) was motivated by the desire to make available the reliefs that had remained in Athens to the antiquity-loving public in Europe.

69. Once the Akropolis Museum was completed in 1874, the houses used as storage sheds were no longer needed, and they also came down from 1885 to 1890. Significantly, the museum was modeled on von Klenze's Glyptothek in Munich.

70. Lechat 1924, 163–164, n. 1. These aesthetic standards were in full accord with contemporary scholarship: in the 1920s the German Archaeological Institute commissioned the German photographers Walter Hege and Hermann Wagner to photograph the Archaic sculpture of the Akropolis Museum out-of-doors.

71. Ernst Curtius and Adolf Michaelis commissioned photographs for various of their studies, but they used drawings in their publications instead: Papageorgiou-Venetas 1994, 114. With his album of prints of Troy (1874), Heinrich Schliemann, an outsider, was the first to utilize photography in publishing archaeological finds from Greece.

72. Brunn 1864; Conze 1864; Gerhard 1864; see Hurwit 1989.

73. In the course of the 1880s, photographs won acceptance as a means of illustrating sculpture. They are usually starkly hieratic pictures of the whole work, imposing a frontal view on statues, following the rules adopted by firms such as Alinari. In general, photographs of details did not assume key importance until the end of the century, when scholars introduced the practice of *Kopienkritik,* a step-by-step method borrowed from natural science for which photography supplanted plaster casts; see Furtwängler 1893, viii; Pollitt 1996, 1–15.

74. Bismarck drastically cut the German budget a few years later, demonstrating that the failure of governmental bureaucracies to appreciate scholarly endeavor is not unique to our era.

75. Papageorgiou-Venetas 1994 traces this development.

76. Lyons 1997, 93.

77. Lyons 1997, 80.

78. Cf. McNeal 1991, 49.

79. After reading Wilhelm Jensen's novel *Gradiva,* Freud decided Jensen's concept of a past locked in the present provided spatial and archaeological analogies for the procedures of psychoanalysis, which, like archaeological excavation, could reveal what remained but had become invisible. See Freud 1956, 175–176.

80. Freud 1896, 3:192.

81. Not that the conventions of the picturesque have died out, especially in images that strive to give a sense of place: they are manifest today in typical tourist views.

82. Barthes 1977. Although a conventional photograph is usually considered to be realistic, in that it reproduces the familiar space of perspective, it is important to distinguish between naturalism and realism. "Naturalism is an adherence to the appearance of things, a replication of external features": Shanks 1997, 78. Photography can do this very well, but it may not, thereby, provide a realistic picture.

83. Merewether 1997, 26.

84. One might even argue that obliterating the evidence of the Medieval and Turkish periods, a willful but unexamined gesture at the time, invites comparison with Freud's psychoanalytical concept of repression.

THE LEGACY OF JEROME J. POLLITT

21

GREEK ART AND CULTURE SINCE *Art and Experience in Classical Greece*

ELIZABETH A. MEYER AND J. E. LENDON

INTRODUCTION

The study of Greek art in the context of Greek culture is now accepted and established, tenured and cosseted in the universities, as comfortable and complacent as a sherry-sipping vicar in Trollope. But once it was young and unbeneficed, bold and heretical, dangerous and brave. One of the enduring monuments of that exciting time is J. J. Pollitt's *Art and Experience in Classical Greece* (1972), a rare book of ideas as influential among students as among scholars. For although neither handbook nor textbook, *Art and Experience* became—and remains—a leading text in courses on Greek art at American universities. And so it has left its imprint on the collective unconscious of a generation of American undergraduates, a generation from which subsequent cohorts of art historians, classical and otherwise, were drawn. Its arguments have passed into the realm of *communis opinio:* traded hand to hand, from lecturer to student, they are now the comfortable property of many with little idea whence first they came.

This essay traces the firework flight of the scholarship of which *Art and Experience* is a founding document. It begins by trying to place *Art and Experience* in the intellectual milieu of the time of its writing. Then it answers some of the objections soon lodged against the interpretations the book offered, objections grounded in misreadings significant because they prefigured some of the curious byways the cultural study of Greek art would take after Pollitt. The bulk of the essay explores and evaluates some major representatives of these subsequent scholarly trends, trends that have sometimes called into doubt (or have attempted to improve upon) three particular components of the interpretive machinery underlying *Art and Experience:* the concept of culture; the relationship of experience, culture, and art; and the role of the artist, especially in the understanding of change over time.[1]

We—writing as ancient historians rather than as historians of ancient art—have a real investment in looking at the History in Art History, for the larger issues of interpretation of artifacts in cultural context, mechanisms for the transmission of taste, and an understanding of change over time are important to us. From this perspective, we find some of these recent trends in the study of Greek art troublesome. They may broaden the object of inquiry and fire the imagination, but they fail as history. Some of them attempt to investigate the meaning of objects of art in ways only arbitrarily or loosely connected to ancient place or time, or make little effort to explain change over time, a focus of ours as historians that may, to be sure, lend an idiosyncratic coloring to this critique. These trends are also disquieting because they often replicate similar swerves taken, and results achieved, in nonclassical historical fields. For at least two decades we have seen our own colleagues plunging, with cut-short cries of joyous discovery, into these same tarpits, leaving others to peer over the edge and assess the value of the path taken. So historians' current reevaluations of the "cultural turn" in their own field may perhaps offer a little self-awareness to scholars of Greek art. Some of their, and our, pleas for care and balance lead directly back to the more solid ground explored and elegantly explicated by J. J. Pollitt in 1972.

THE CONTEXT AND CRITICISM OF *Art and Experience*

CONTEXT

Pollitt expected that many of the readers of *Art and Experience* had already

> read an introductory text in which the formal development of Greek art, particularly its mastery of an increasingly accurate representation of our optical experience of nature, is seen as its most interesting and noteworthy achievement.[2]

He meant especially Rhys Carpenter's *Greek Art: A Study of the Formal Evolution of Style* (1962),[3] a book we may take as emblematic of the dominant strain of formalist American scholarship against which Pollitt revolted.[4] To Carpenter the history of Greek art was an advance towards more perfect naturalism—"natural truth"[5]—through progress in technique. The slow progress from primitive beginnings to the acme of the school of Lysippos is subject to hardly any exterior influence. The sculptor's wax guards his ears against events outside his studio. He does not hear the terrible cry that carried into the city the news of the loss of Athenian fleet and empire; on that night when no one slept, the artist snored soundly, dreaming of improvements to his claw chisel. To Carpenter there was no point to turning the eye away from a strictly interior account of the development of art, for "it is impossible to tell how much the evolution of artistic style, with its technical determination from within, may be influenced by external human events and moods."[6]

Those who, like Pollitt, in the 1960s found the formalism of Carpenter (and others, like Margarete Bieber and Gisela Richter) narrow and unedifying had two main resorts. German-language scholarship had a tradition, going back to Winckelmann and Goethe, of interpreting Greek art in terms of the spirit of the age, looking to Greek freedom, democracy, individualism, or beauty[7]—and professing an open-mouthed idealism that may come as a surprise to those who associate "German" only with "pedantry." In Karl Schefold's *Classical Greece* (1967),[8] Classical Greek art is a fathomless wonder. And if "wonders can never be explained, nevertheless we can distinguish seven factors that made classical art possible," including the Greek landscape, "where land and sea interpenetrate each other with a clarity of contour whose forms are absolutely inexhaustible in their variety" and the beauty of the ancient Greek body, especially the shape of the Greek eye.[9] Even so, the qualities of culture said to influence Greek art Germans sought less in Greek writings than in their own Romanticism. The dazzled awe consequent on being trampled by the *Urpferd* could be reconciled with German *Wissenschaft* because analysis by *Zeitgeist* was not called upon to do much actual work: it overlay a formalism no less exacting than that of the Anglo-Saxons. High Grecian ideals and circumstances might be the ultimate silent movers propelling the Rolls Royce that was Greek art, but the hills and turns of artistic evolution were negotiated with a white-knuckled grip on the wheel of artistic technique.

A more determined counterpoint to the prevailing formalism was provided by the English scholar T. B. L. Webster, author of a series of studies on the relationship between art and literature from 700 B.C. down through Hellenistic times. In his *Greek Art and Literature 530–400 B.C.* (1939), a set of styles—"the strong style," "the classical style," "the rich style"—coexisted through successive chronological periods. Each style manifested a different ideal of the time, the "strong style," for example, fear of *hybris* and the need for self-control; to serve those cultural "needs," each style was created by "great artistic spirits."[10] The styles rise and fall against one another with the influence of the cultural ideal that drives them: so culture is a force for change, even quite subtle change. But Webster's method pressed his styles too hard to exhibit themselves at once in art and literature, not only through parallel subject matter but also through parallels, often extreme, in form and composition. And in later works even Webster seems to have lost faith in his cultural analysis, reducing the dynamic to a brilliant high-table conversation between *litterateur,* philosopher, and sculptor.[11]

Traces of the influence, direct or indirect, of German Romantics and Webster can easily be detected in *Art and Experience. Art and Experience* is, however, not a predictable elaboration of any strand of previous scholarship in ancient art. What Pollitt did was deduce for each period of Greek art a cultural theme or set of themes. These he found in contemporary literature and philosophical writings, with the help of what were then the best scholarly treatments of the intellectual and religious atmosphere of the periods. He then looked for, and found, those cultural themes in the art of the time: "The same motivating forces which shaped classical Greek art also shaped its literature."[12]

Pollitt's main interest was in style rather than iconography (the "conventional meaning" of images), and in what Panofsky, in a famous essay first published in 1939, called iconology (the "intrinsic meaning" of images).[13] To Pollitt, the formal evolution of Greek art towards greater naturalism was true but not the most important thing about it,[14] its changes in style an expression of specifically historical attitudes and circumstances rather than Webster's generic responses to competing cultural ideals, its stylistic variations manifestations of a response that could be paralleled in other cultural forms. About the prevailing style in late fifth-century Athens Pollitt wrote:

> The development of this flying drapery style has sometimes been seen as part of an inevitable evolution in sculptural technique, an evolution directed toward solving the problem of how to sculpture a draped figure in movement. . . . Technical problems of this sort were no doubt continually of concern to Greek sculptors, but this technical challenge alone cannot explain the prevalence of the florid style in the last three decades of the fifth century. It clearly represents a taste of the age and must have answered an emotional need, both for its users and its viewers. Artistic styles are products of conscious choice, and one may well doubt that there was any irresistible evolutionary force which could have compelled Greek sculptors, robot-like, to create the flying drapery style if they had not wanted to. Cultural conditions must have made it desirable, rather than technical evolution inevitable.[15]

To Pollitt, art changes because the culture that uses it as a method of expression changes, and with it all its forms of expression. As Greek culture changed, in response to experience, so with it did Greek art. "Greek art is an expression of Greek cultural experience."[16]

CARPING DISMISSED

Unsurprisingly, *Art and Experience* was coolly received by the formalists at whom it was aimed. But objections lodged against it in reviews and articles in fact show three common types of misreading and point up the subtlety and sophistication of the argument, the strength of the method, and some of the snares Pollitt avoided into which others (as we shall see) were soon to become entangled.

In *Art and Experience,* Pollitt associated the Early Classical Severe Style with Greek victory in the Persian Wars, which brought on both "a new self-confidence and a new uneasiness," also manifest in tragedy: confidence in a human order rooted in the self-controlled life in the city-state, and a related anxiety that "men were responsible for their own fortunes."[17] Critics complained that elements of the Severe Style could be detected before the great Persian invasion of 480–479, especially on vases whose artists may well have echoed painting on grander media.[18] They noted that two exemplary sculptures of the new style, indeed, the so-called Kritios Boy and the Blond Boy, might have come from the Persian wreckage on the Akropolis and so have predated the sack of 480. So, they concluded, the method must be faulty:

> It is . . . a rash assumption that the evolution of classical art and architecture was spiritually determined by historical events. In the arts the revolutionary changes which began the Classical style can be dated securely around 500, so that they cannot have been the result of a defeat by the Persians in 480–79. . . . Art, after all, has its own momentum.[19]

Yet the claim that the Persian Wars, or any other historical event, conjured into being new techniques was one Pollitt was careful not to make. The turn of the fifth century was a time of great intellectual and artistic ferment.[20] In the years before the Persian invasion, much that was old jostled with much that was new. Success in the Persian Wars gave the Greeks the confidence to adopt the new ways wholesale, creating in a few years a relatively uniform panhellenic style, confining the old to cultural backwaters, witty archaists, and those with a studied taste for the old-fashioned. When Pollitt wrote that "the victory over the Persians . . . was the catalyst which transformed the groping humanism of late Archaic art into the Classical style,"[21] he was pointing to a revolution of taste, not of technique. Pollitt admits that technique by itself has a history of its own;[22] he simply does not think that it necessarily determines the direction of style. Formalists mistook the argument of *Art and Experience* by reading into it their own preoccupation with formal technique. And Pollitt, although relying on formalists' assessments of technique, was wise to confine his analysis to taste: as will be seen, attempting to link changes in mechanical technique to culture is far more difficult.

Pollitt also associated the shift from the Early Classical Severe Style to the High Classical style with Athens, and particularly with Pheidias and Perikles.[23] His critics objected that associating this panhellenic style with Athenian democracy attributed to it too parochial an origin. "Yet conditions at Athens," one noted, "were far from typical for the rest of Greece; indeed, Athens was in many respects unique; however, there is no evidence to suggest that Athens ever had a monopoly on the Classical style."[24] This complaint too is rooted in a misreading: Pollitt's German predecessors did sometimes make the connection between Athenian uniqueness—particularly democracy—and Classical style,[25] but Pollitt did not.[26] Pollitt, in fact, displays an extreme reluctance to associate the High Classical style with Athenian democracy per se (indeed the very word "democracy" appears rarely).[27] Athens simply displays an extreme case of panhellenic "humanistic optimism," driven by "the psychological legacy of the victory over the Persians" and by contemporary theoretical thinking—whose representatives, the sophists, were of course itinerant intellectuals and so the property of the whole of Greece.[28]

The Athenian hypertrophy of this attitude is grounded in the additional boost to Athens' self-confidence given by empire,[29] but the importance of Athens in setting the High Classical style depends not on its constitution but upon the individual genius of an artist, Pheidias, and his like-minded patron, Perikles. To Pollitt, Perikles is a humanist, not a democrat, and the ingredients of humanism were not confined to Athens; nor, indeed, were its artistic consequences.[30] Pollitt's interpretation was cultural, not political: Pollitt sought to account for Athens' clear predominance without making a taste for the Classical style dependent on conditions that could exist only there. But not everyone after Pollitt was to avoid so deftly the fundamental problems that political interpretation poses.

Pollitt argued that the long, terrible, Peloponnesian War, with its escort of disasters natural and man-made, destroyed the supreme humanist confidence of the High Classical moment.[31] Responding to this new anxiety, Greek artists produced a florid ornate style with riots of windblown drapery, which "shows a fascination with technique and exalts ornamental elaboration above subject matter."[32] This is an escapist art, parallel to the show-rhetoric of the Sicilian sophist Gorgias, active in Athens—a retreat, a "refuge in gesture."[33] But Rhys Carpenter complained that

> we should expect, on Prof. Pollitt's theory, that the terrible experience of the plague in 430–29 or the great military disasters towards the close of the century would have produced a gloomy and despairful style at Athens; yet on the evidence of Meidias' vases or the Maenad reliefs an almost frivolous lightness animated the arts. It would be specious to plead that this response to "experience" took the form of escapism.[34]

Yet Pollitt could easily have offered parallels to this escapism from outside the visual arts, in—for example—the *Birds* and *Peace* of Aristophanes. Societies react variously to crisis: Pollitt offers the popularity of Fred Astaire and his ilk during the Great Depression as a parallel to the "frivolity" of the art of the Peloponnesian War.[35] And who would have expected that out of the maelstrom of Paris in 1968 would emerge a novel of over three hundred pages using no word containing the letter E?[36] Pollitt's cultural analysis is not "scientific" or, indeed, robotic, as Carpenter's complaint demands that it be. It is a great strength of Pollitt's method that, allowing for the play of the individual artist, he does not require art merely to be a wax death mask of the mood of the time. In *Art in the Hellenistic Age* (1986), Pollitt was to rely even more on the individual artist as an agent of stylistic change who was responsive to Hellenistic emotional and intellectual currents. As will be seen, attempts to deny or reduce the importance of the artist in the evolution of art exact their own, quite high, price.

RECENT ROADS

We now turn to survey some of the principal approaches to the cultural study of Greek art that have developed since the publication of *Art and Experience.* Virtually all claim as their *raison d'être* the slaying of the old, artist-dominated, technique-oriented formal histories of art, although this crumpled dragon is hardly now fearsome enough to justify the lack of rigor with which these newer cultural approaches are often applied.[37] Formal studies of Greek art have of course continued to appear since 1972, often taking as the dynamic of art's evolution artists' repeated efforts to "solve problems" and noting, not without asperity, that it is upon such painstaking and methodical work that the airier cultural analyses are constructed.[38] Indeed, as Oakley, Palagia, Robertson, and others have all noted, technical expertise as well as close and careful examination of the objects themselves—some of the Art in Art History—tend to impose real and necessary limitations on the cultural interpretation of art, and the practitioners of the cultural approach, by neglecting detailed work with objects, have sometimes wandered into real and mortifying error.[39]

Our perspective is on the History of Art as History, which prompts us to look at the assumptions that underlie, and implications that follow from, the various theories on which the work of cultural art historians so often depends. Literary theory and anthropology in particular have contributed to the kinds of Ancient Art History being written today. These bodies of thought above all lay out wide fields of possibility: in theory, just about anything is possible. Yet the limitation of possibilities is above all the role of historical knowledge. Too often, practitioners of these newer cultural approaches to Greek art are more critics than historians, their minds expanded by theory but not brought back to sober reality by history. Their work therefore has trouble answering a series of historical questions: How does the specifically *Greek* "context" impose limitations on the possibilities posited by various theoretical stances? Do the newer interpretations assume mechanisms and produce results that existed in, or can be reasonably postulated for, *Greek* culture? Can an interpretation explain change over time? All the recent works here examined take culture as significant, but all define culture, its relationship to art, and the activities of the artist within this culture somewhat differently. In short, these approaches can be problematic not only as studies of the art itself, but also as historical studies of art and as historical reasoning: in the worst-case scenario, neither art nor history.

FRENCH CULTURE: STRUCTURALISM AND ITS CRITICS

From France, Structuralism—which has its origins in linguistics and anthropology, and especially the work of C. Lévi-Strauss—and from France, its destroyers. Yet despite the fact that Structuralism in literary criticism was pronounced dead by the early 1980s, it still survives and flourishes—abetted by friends in high places such as Vernant, Detienne, and Vidal-Naquet, with their wonderfully inventive writing on Greek culture—in the French study of Greek art, especially in the study of Greek vase painting, where the imagery is deemed to "reflect" experience and memory, making them images "recognized" by viewers.[40]

Structuralism consists of discerning commonalities of pattern in different human realms—the imagined supernatural order, the layout of the village, and the face-paint of natives miles away—seeing them all as "signs to be read of deep structures of meaning" lying within a culture.[41] These commonalities are expressed with physical metaphors: in François Lissarrague's *The Aesthetics of the Greek Banquet* (1990),[42] the centrality of the great mixing bowl (the krater) to the communal experience of the *symposion* is reflected in its use as a compositional axis in the artistic representation of the symposion and the *komos*—festive procession—on pots.[43] The mental world, this patterning, is constituted in terms of oppositions, the dangerous area between poles of an opposition, and the bridging and dissolution of such oppositions. In the collaborative volume *A City of Images* (1989),[44] Lissarrague, drawing on Vidal-Naquet's celebrated essay "The Black Hunter," takes note of a cup on which deer are pursued by hunters, some of whom are equipped as hoplites. "The rarity of these images, liminal in bringing together hunting and hoplite war, which usually inhabit separate spheres, allows us to grasp the essential opposition between these activities that the city organizes but keeps distinct,"[45] and thus also allows the decipherment of the image. Structuralism thus draws attention to, but also assumes, the centrality of structuring, of oppositions and inversions, in an image, and bases its interpretation on this.[46]

Structuralism at its best was, and is, exhilarating. It suggested ways of looking, and perceiving connection, previously unimagined: the microscope transformed into a kaleidoscope, the image brilliantly re-illuminated, the interpreter forever changed by the experience. Yet even so, this method, which has found non-French imitators,[47] also leads to results that can be uncomfortable to historians, for its objectives do not include explaining why people paint, sculpt, or act in a given way at a given moment, or why any of this, or the art itself, would change.[48] Structuralism instead investigates how the human mind is organized at an abstract level, at a considerable distance from grimy *realia,* and is "essentially," therefore, "unhistorical."[49] This distance could be a problem: Structuralism seeks to understand the human mind on a plane so profound that not everyone may believe it actually exists.

The French have developed a characteristic style for this sort of writing, rather like the Caucus Race in *Alice in Wonderland:* it begins where it likes, stops where it likes, and in between bedazzles the reader with the cleverness and multiplicity of the juxtapositions being made. These juxtapositions often take the form of associations, like that proposed (again in Lissarrague's *Aesthetics of the Greek Banquet*) between the fall of the target in a drinking game, and the fall of falling in love.[50] Looked at closely, such associations often turn out to be not near or distant analogies but, in fact, largely arbitrary, a kind of word play.[51]

The problem with Structuralism, then, is not only that it investigates the architecture of the deepest—some will say nonexistent—sub-basements of the human mind without acknowledging the formative experience of external events, but that it by and large fails to generate reproducible results even in its own terms. Yet even so, the unfettered imaginativeness of Structuralism churns up the mind of readers and sets them thinking their own inventive thoughts, especially about the ways Greek artists could "combine or conceal what might seem contradictory messages."[52] Done well, it is beautiful, as the systems of metaphor unfold with the elegance of *origami.* It works best in French, the natural home of the abstract noun. Written in English with a hefty dose of jargon it is joyless, often baffling, and sometimes absurd.

In contemporary Structuralist interpretations of ancient art the opposition that features most prominently is that between the self and the Other. The Other is not purely Structuralist in pedigree,[53] but it is the most enticing of all oppositions because it emphasizes the centrality and subjectivity of the observer, a stance highly congenial to the postmodern temperament: the Other contributes to contemporary Structuralism a sleek subjectivity that displaces the plodding claims to scientific objectivity of old Structuralism. So at the symposion, according to Lissarrague, "the experience of wine is also the experience of the Other."[54] To Françoise Frontisi-Ducroux in *A City of Images*—drawing on Vernant's "Death in the Eyes: Gorgo, Figure of the *Other*"—faces that stare frontally out of a pot at viewers bring them into contact with the Other personified.

> The mask of Gorgo, by its monstrosity, renders visible to humans the radical otherness of night, which blurs and mixes categories distinguished by the world of the living. The bestial mingles with the human: a leonine muzzle, enormous bovine ears, an animal mane, often bristling with snakes. . . . Thus the masculine is superimposed on the feminine.[55]

Such interpretations imply that the opposition of the Other plays a crucial role in self-definition and therefore in the expression of social norms and their power (and to their challenging as well, of course).[56] This historicizing use of Structuralism, this recasting of it as the polarity of Self and Other, therefore encounters, almost immediately, a second problem: Who are the "selves" or viewers of these pots?[57] Scholars? Athenians? Athenian men or women? Elite or not? Etruscans, the final recipients of so many of these vases?[58] Who is defined through "alterity"? If the interpretation of an object or artifact is shifted decisively to the viewer, whom it simultaneously positions and defines, such a wide range of possible opposites (all potentially self and Other) and possible viewers emerges that the method, by failing to define the viewer, loses its moorings and dissolves into mere opinion.

Belatedly, and largely by English-speakers, the corrosive French attack on the assumptions underlying Structuralism—formerly called Deconstruction, but now one approach among many in the broader category called poststructuralism—has been applied to Greek art. The attack on Structuralism often takes place at a level of abstraction and in a type of language—incomprehensible jargon—that many find impenetrable. In actual use, as exemplified by John Henderson in "*Timeo Danaos:* Amazons in Early Greek Art and Pottery,"[59] the Deconstructionist attack has a great deal in common with Structuralism, only with more "scare-quote" quotation marks and *italics.* The Structuralists' habit of juxtaposition by analogy (at best) or caprice (at worst) is adopted with enthusiasm, and even elaborated by its critics. Yet the yield from these juxtapositions is not, as to a Structuralist, what can be known about the human mind but ultimately a deeper insight into what *cannot* be known, "since, as we know, visual meanings are uncontainably multi-directional and regularly reversible in sense."[60] At best, the investigation tells us about ourselves rather than about antiquity:

> Specifically, figure 28 bids us examine, then reconsider, the views we have of viewing, our ways of "seeing" *seeing.* Images structure *and fracture* identities; their work is to articulate *and blur* processes of transformation, change, assimilation/differentiation; their *raison d'être* is to tell us (how) to debate our own existence, values, "nature."[61]

Like anarchists, Deconstructionists aim only to explode and destroy, leaving readers in fear—the fear that they have been naïve. Since *in theory* anything is possible, *therefore* anything is possible, and *therefore,* also, meaning can only inhere in the subjective process of interpretation itself. Structuralism may have been too abstract to be historical, but Deconstruction is antihistorical; only the critic, existing within his or her own critical consciousness, remains.

With the destructive critique of Structuralism comes a new poststructuralist definition of culture as well. Again, John Henderson:

> Culture: to be discovered, now, not in a sum or set of shared "ideas" or "mentality," but in the specific pro-

> cesses of a series of arguments or conflicts about the boundaries and norms of "relationships," the affirmations and modulations of terms of social "exchange." *These pots* were a "what" and a "where" that "The Greeks" disputed, for goods and for resources, for value and power.[62]

The poststructuralist tears the concept of culture into fragments, like a bacchant at a *sparagmos.* Or, to put it another way, for Henderson, culture is everybody shouting at everybody else. Culture to him is not the sum of the vectors, because there is no mechanism for determining which "discourse" is stronger, who shouts loudest. This is not a definition of culture that will help us to explain very much about ancient art or its evolution, for a wholly incoherent culture is no culture at all: as Pollitt remarked, "diversity is more often a characteristic of chaos."[63] Exploding it completely and forever in this fashion does not respect the fact that cultural coherence can exist, while varying in degree, and from time to time and place to place. Structuralism is therefore, in our view, too simplifying, too generic and timeless, too arbitrary, while its opposite, by dissolving the few supports on which Structuralism rested, is in the end also too simplifying, as well as too self-referential. Neither is primarily concerned with a world that exists in time.

CAMBRIDGE CULTURE

With Cambridge University is associated a school of archaeologists who work in prehistory or early Greece and who busy themselves to a great extent with theory—for when cultural analysis is attempted of times from which we have very little other than artifacts, all types of theory sing like sirens. Structuralism and poststructuralism can be employed, but more often, large categories of analysis are trucked in from New World archaeology, generic Marxism, postprocessual archaeological theory (especially associated with Ian Hodder, at Cambridge), and the even grander theories of culture penned by Bruno Latour and Walter Benjamin.

In these views artifacts "transcend" the epoch of their creation: "time reveals meanings that are accessible *without* a knowledge of the time and condition of [their] making."[64] Knowledge of artifacts' specific context, while admirable, is actually unnecessary; the meaning of artifacts is accessible because one has acquired a general understanding of how and why all societies generate artifacts. In other words, all-encompassing theories of universal process and meaning are called on to do much of the work of interpretation. Structuralists and poststructuralists made seemingly eternal structures of the mind—or of criticism itself—the basis of their interpretations; Cambridge archaeologists instead import into their study of artifacts eternal engines that generate meaning. As a consequence, despite all the methodological sophistication (and the obligatory Cambridge histograms), despite all the boundaries challenged, the answers offered by this scholarship to the question of artifacts' meaning(s) are always the same: power and ambivalence. Could this interpretation be right? Sure. Does this help us to understand the development of *Greek* art at a particular time and place any better? *Can* it? No, for it is fundamentally ahistorical. Does it tell us all something about what Cambridge archaeologists have been reading lately? Absolutely.

James Whitley's *Style and Society in Dark Age Greece* (1991) offers a cultural interpretation of Geometric pottery that appears to proceed from premises, and a sensitivity to context, very similar to Pollitt's:

> Art is responsive to the needs of the society that produces it, and in many ways is congruent with other, contemporary cultural forms. At every stage . . . there is a discernible relationship between the forms that works of art take, the collective mortuary representations of the community, and the general cultural and social climate.[65]

But Whitley's analysis ends in 700 B.C., treating an era for which written evidence—upon which a fine-grained understanding of culture necessarily depends—is very rare. Whitley has only Homer and Hesiod, and as is fashionable now among archaeologists, takes a minimalist view of the value of the former.[66] As a result of the dearth of written evidence, when Whitley sums up some of the features of Late Dark Age society on which a cultural analysis of style might call, they turn out to be rather general:[67]

1. "[T]he integration of men . . . as citizens and the integration of territory within the *polis.*"
2. "The demarcation of space," profane and sacred, that of the dead from that of the living.
3. Influence from the East.
4. "The de-personalization of authority," that is, the rise of loyalty to the state rather than to chieftains.
5. "A new sense of Greek identity," that is, of identity as Greeks.

This list of characteristics is unobjectionable, but imagine if we had to interpret the last four hundred years of Western art on the basis of similar knowledge:

1. The integration of men . . . as citizens and the integration of territory within the nation-state.
2. The demarcation of space, that of public from private.
3. Influence of the West on the rest of the world.
4. The depersonalization of authority, that is, the rise of loyalty to the state rather than to local entities or magnates.
5. A new sense of national identity.

An analysis of the development of art from Rubens to Damien Hurst, via David, Monet, and Picasso, on the basis of such a model of "culture" would be thin indeed. Predictably, Whitley finds the five features of limited use, and since the lack of ancient evidence prohibits a model of culture with analytical bite, he must find culture, and cultural context, elsewhere. He seeks it in the grave particularly ("a social document"), but otherwise from archaeological material in general, from which he hopes to evoke the "spirit of the age," for "archaeology is nothing if not culture history."[68] In this way he comes to conclude that the artistic style of grave artifacts is above all a way of marking social status, of signifying social solidarity and distance. Confusion in the application of style either indicates that a group has not yet formed or that the group is in crisis, an argument so supple that it cannot be disproved.

What Whitley has, in the end, conjured up from his graves and his artifacts is no Greek daemon but the shade of American anthropology, obsessed with "social divisions . . . [and] status symbols, the Dark Age equivalents of Cadillacs."[69] This larger paradigm of competition through symbols into which he fits the production and significance of Dark Age art is a perfectly unremarkable, dangerously straightforward account of the rise and fall of an aristocracy, an off-the-shelf sub-Marxian model applied mechanically, as countless times before, to premodern states. This imported conception, that art has above all a social function, is arid and reductionist. As Michael Shanks complains of Whitley: "Why express society in this way? Why with Geometric amphorae? Why express it at all?"[70] Whitley's social structures are historically generic, the processes that create them and also mandate their expression through art and artifact generic as well. But a generic historical explanation must be adapted to the specific historical society it purports to explain; otherwise, generic explanations produce sadly predictable conclusions.

Yet Whitley deserves our sympathy: he had the right instincts. It was lack of evidence about Greek culture before 700 B.C. that compelled him to go bargain-hunting for a shopworn, generic "culture" and therefore also for an engine to drive change in artifacts and determine their meaning. Others merit less compassion. Michael Shanks's criticism of Whitley, which looked as if it intended to challenge imported ideas of social structure and of obsessions that drove its representation in art, was in fact more concerned that Whitley did not go far enough. For Shanks, Whitley failed because he did not "reference" the appropriate theoretical discussions: Whitley was shopping at Oxfam, not Versace. In his own edgily stylish *Art and the Greek City State* (1999),[71] a study of Archaic Corinthian pottery, Shanks insists that artists are producers, not creators; that art (better called "style and design") is "social production" produced, indeed, by a social or cultural "machine"; and that art "is less about representing particular aspects of the social world than it is to do [*sic*] with principles of order and how order should be."[72] This much, at least, anthropological and Marxist discussions of art have established. Thus, for Shanks, "pots translate interests in a reworking of political discourse"; Corinthian figural scenes clearly communicate "the ideological components of violence, excess and the mediation of the animal in a world of aristocratic masculinity" because a focus on the body is a focus on "a primary site for the aesthetic ethos of violence and war."[73] This masculine sovereignty is "related" by Shanks "to a war-machine—concepts, meanings, powers to do [*sic*] with permanent war and the identities by which it is sustained."[74] And these identities, and the cultural associations of the war-machine, are particularly discoverable in two works of Klaus Theweleit devoted to the interpretation of popular German military literature of the 1920s and after.[75]

Shanks always links the fragments of what we know about early Corinth in this way: the mortar between the bricks of the bricolage, the collagen of the collage, is provided by distant conceptual parallels like that offered by Theweleit, by language (like "to do with") that never dares to make clear what it means, by overarching theories that are only questioned when they seem too straightforward, and by approaches ("the varied intellectual contexts include critical theory, Hegelian Marxism, poststructuralism and constructivist thought")[76] that help the argument to be both itself and its opposite. Thus, for example, the imagery of "masculine sovereignty" appears on aryballoi or perfume jars although, as he himself notes, "most references to perfume in ancient poetry are in association with women, not men,"[77] but this apparent contradiction is not a problem, since "the conceptual space of Korinthian ceramic imagery is one which works upon alterity and in relation to the fields of the domestic and gender."[78] "Masculine sovereignty" on vases whose contents are associated with women is not actually a problem after all. Jargon, vague hand waving, and lamentable prose connect what otherwise cannot be connected, and lead to the conclusion that "Korinthian pottery . . . is an *actualisation of ambivalence.*"[79] Thus, after 213 extraordinarily painful pages, the reader has explored "lifeworlds" and can admire the "creativity like dreamwork" of the interpretation, "seeking and forging links which know no necessary limits;"[80] but the dream world is that of other men's theories and there has been remarkably little to learn about Corinth and its art. In the end, Whitley and Shanks together seem to prove decisively that neither culture nor the meaning(s) of artifacts can be deduced from artifacts alone, even when combined with some scraps of poetry, no matter how avant-garde the theoretical stance and methodological tools brought to bear. Any attempt to do so merely invites on board a whole host of modern assumptions, and sets them to sail in a leaky boat under a false Greek flag.

Those who believe in the "social production" of art, like Whitley and Shanks, stress that it is *product*—in Shanks's image, produced by a machine whose gears and cables are, at a fundamental level, universal. A gentler version of social production looks at time and circumstance in a more flexible, open, and historical way. An example of this is Nigel Spivey's *Understanding Greek Sculpture: Ancient Meanings, Modern Readings* (1996).[81] Yet even in this more historically rooted conception of social production, the individual genius of the artist necessarily comes off second best. As Spivey says, "Foucault is fundamentally right: art belongs to a game of power. And in that game, institutions and customs are more powerful than individuals. That is why the understanding of ancient Greek sculpture rests, essentially, with the understanding of ancient Greek society."[82] The eye is firmly on customers and their expectations, on the "institutions and customs" that serve them, and on the practical limitations that technology and technique impose on the satisfaction of those culturally conditioned desires.

That much may be right; but is the apparently inevitable corollary of the powerlessness of the artist also right? Into the Foucauldian vision few artists can intrude, for in the end "hegemonizing is homogenizing," as Marshall Sahlins put it in a witty little critique of Foucault's ideas and influence. "The dissolution of specific cultural forms into generic instrumental effects"[83] that adulation of Foucault and his obsession with power have promoted leads not only to the abandonment of historical specificity in favor of the Universal Engine of Meaning Production, as was true for Whitley and Shanks, but also to the erasure of individual agency even in Spivey's more historical understanding. So much for Pheidias, even if a chapter is devoted to him.

The most significant problem with discarding the agent is that the activity of the individual artist is often the most natural and most helpful explanation for change, especially sudden change, in artistic style. Even if we no longer exalt the artist as a wholly autonomous entity interested only in aesthetics,[84] and even if we cannot identify many artists for certain,[85] the fact of a sentient artist or maker is a necessary element in any logic by which art is created. The so-called Greek Revolution, for example, the movement from static Archaic statuary to the dynamic sculptures we call Classical, cries out to be explained; even if not the only important question in Greek art, such a stylistic change poses a significant one.

Spivey associates the advancing naturalism of Greek sculpture with institutions and customs, and specifically with the anthropomorphic strain in Greek religion, but not with any individual breakthroughs: the "determination of sculptors to reconcile the ideal with the natural" has its origins in the fact that almost all Greek sculpture was made for religious contexts, that glimpses of the divine were sought in the human body, and that artists were competitive with one another.[86] But so general a cultural explanation, while an improvement on power and ambivalence, can tell us little about why, after centuries of slow evolution towards naturalism, a great change should come over Greek sculpture in the few years around the Persian Wars, about why the Kritios Boy and his kin should appear *just then.*[87]

If the cultural pressure for naturalism were constant, would we not then expect advances in naturalism to follow immediately after the technical advances that made them possible? If "the catalyst for change was the technical empowerment of Greek artists"; if, as Spivey argues, the mastery of the technique of casting life-sized bronze statues "offered sculptors a sort of release,"[88] then should not the results of that release, Classical sculpture, date to the early sixth century B.C., when casting was perfected, rather than to a century later? The problem here is that it is next to impossible to find compelling connections between changes in artistic style (or in any sort of behavior) and changes in the cultural substratum powerful enough alone, without the intervention of pivotal individuals, to propel those changes. A cultural approach that leaves out people is sometimes helpful in understanding the "what does it mean?," but it is usually quite hopeless with the "why at exactly that moment?"

If the old formalism against which Pollitt rebelled minimized exterior influences upon art, conceiving art only as social production denies its interior history, reducing artists to ciphers of their times. Spivey's presentation of the competitive—agonistic—culture of Greek artists reveals that it had such an interior history, and he knows it: drawn together by their competition, artists formed a world apart where they learned from each other, strove to outdo each other, and jeered at each other: to goad a rival, a masterstroke on a pot might be labeled "Euphronios couldn't do this!"[89] This is exactly a world in which great changes in method or style, or possibly even in iconography, might hang on the achievement of a single outstanding performer, a Pheidias or a Polykleitos. This achievement could be quickly copied by jealous rivals, thereby demonstrating how methods and styles that were geographically and chronologically Greek rather than just Athenian could come into being. As a mechanism to explain change, however, this competitive world works only if there *is* a visionary Pheidias, a Polykleitos who dared to be different. Pollitt allows for the significance of the individual artist while simultaneously seeing art as an emanation of culture: the artist, who captures—and uses his art to express—his time (or some aspect of it), is an indispensable link. To understand art strictly as social production and an emanation or expression of power, even if the historical context is more sensitively construed as in Spivey's case, fails as logic and as history. And it is weak and ineffectual at explaining change, and explaining why the rate of change over time may vary.

OUR CULTURE

Faced with such an array of anthropologically or theory-based cultural approaches, it is nearly irresistible to regard them as a smorgasbord, and make up a meal with selections of all. So Robin Osborne proceeds, in his painfully unjudgmental *Archaic and Classical Greek Art* (1998). His point of departure is announced at the beginning: he will not treat "art as having its own history, quite independent of the political, social, cultural, or economic history of the people by whom and for whom the art was produced."[90] J. J. Pollitt and his student "J. J." (!) Hurwit are gently corrected for their narrowness—"they tend to look to political rather than social history, to landmarks in literature and philosophy rather than the humdrum nature of daily life"—while Bérard and Lissarrague, who do (in Osborne's opinion) relate vase painting to the lives of ordinary Athenians, do so "at the expense of consideration of the particular contribution of the artist."[91] So: the defects of previous approaches are to be avoided, and no object and no constituency are to be overlooked.[92]

Osborne's benevolent capaciousness creates two problems. First is the hazard of simultaneously using logically contradictory systems: Structuralism *and* its critics, social production *and* the exaltation of the artist. The second is the danger of building a church so undoctrinaire that judgment is suspended as to whether a given method is in fact of any use. The natural consequence is to let down the guard against anachronism and to allow ancient concerns—and so ancient culture—to be supplanted not just by timeless or generic categories of analysis, which are, of course, covertly modernizing, but by more obvious modern interests as well.[93]

Osborne's 1994 article, "Framing the Centaur: Reading Fifth-Century Architectural Sculpture,"[94] is startlingly direct in its dependence on anachronistic attitudes. It is commonplace that the motif of the battle between man and Centaur—the Centauromachy—can symbolize the struggle between mankind and nature, between order and disorder, between civilization and wildness, between the human excellence of self-control—(*sophrosyne*) and hybris.[95] To Osborne, however, the meaning of Centauromachy programs in fifth-century relief sculpture—at Olympia, on the Parthenon, and at Bassai—is to be understood in terms of their significance to the sponsors of the projects, the men of Elis, the citizens of the Athenian democracy, and the Arcadian mercenaries whose wages erected the Bassai temple to "Apollo of Mercenaries."[96] This is a fair enough position, a possible evocation of an historical patron-consumer model—or it would be, if some coherent shared agenda between patron and art could be discerned. Instead, however, this art does not, in Osborne's view, respond clearly to these consumers' desires; rather, these friezes "pester the viewer with . . . questions."[97] At Olympia, the questions are about the uses of violence;[98] at Athens, about the social exclusion implicit in the democracy;[99] at Bassai, about the value of a career as a sword-for-hire and thus about the moral ambiguity of war: "The forms that dart round and round the dimly lit cella of the temple at Bassai reduce the viewer to a spin: either you reject war, or you turn a blind eye to its atrocities, and pocket the money for fighting."[100] Violence, exclusion, the morality of war: the ancient Greeks seem, astonishingly enough, to have had anxieties identical to those of some late twentieth-century academics.

That the significance of art lies in the questions, even the insulting questions, it provokes is a fashionable but anachronistic position, ubiquitous in the manifestos of late twentieth-century artists whose art schools found it less taxing to teach them drivel than drawing. The odd willingness of patrons to pay for art that insults them is also recent: the unhappy sculptor who "questioned" the source of the bloody drachmas that built the temple of Apollo at Bassai would likely have found himself unemployed, if not thrown off the convenient cliff. In Osborne's *Archaic and Classical Greek Art* (1998), to turn to that work again, these modern hobbyhorses continue to masquerade as ancient concerns. Vase painting as early as the seventh century B.C. is as self-referential and intellectualized as the work of a Turner Prize finalist: "This pot introduces the viewer to some of the issues at stake in seeing pictures in a pot."[101]

Art conveys certain meanings from artist to viewer less than it asks endless questions, forces the viewer to contemplate and "become implicated," or provides extensive, thought-provoking "commentary."[102] Greek artists labor at endowing their works with trendy and aggressive opacity-to-interpretation: "The device of the isolated figure is exploited here to open up gaps in any story that the viewer tries to tell."[103] Art, in short, is not just to be read like a text,[104] but to be read as a poststructuralist critic would read a text, with due sensitivity to silences, gaps, exclusions, and questions. This all makes a virtue out of our lack of knowledge: it makes art that is opaque to us intentionally opaque to its contemporaries. If we are forced to question, Greeks must have been too.

None of this, of course, is really about the Greeks, or the Athenians, at all. Scholarship of this type is about modern academics and their anxieties, as well as their nervous eclecticism. Are the intellectual responses to art in the present appropriate to the art of the past?

Perhaps in art criticism, but, we humbly suggest, not in art *history.* It is hard work for historians to recognize and adjust for their own biases, but it is necessary work; merely to embrace biases on the flimsy excuse that they are impossible to avoid is to avoid work. If we make a virtue of being trapped in our own subjectivity, then we are critics only, rather than historians. It is quite clear that modern obsessions can warp and therefore err in ludicrously obvious ways, as when Osborne suggests that Hermes, in dangling grapes before the infant Dionysos, was "introducing" him "to addiction"[105]—itself an impossibility, since Dionysos was, famously, impervious to the effects of his own gift. Not to struggle against this kind of importation of current attitudes is an abdication of scholarly responsibility.

POLITICAL CULTURE

In the same year as the publication of *Art and Experience,* John Boardman published the first of a series of papers arguing that the appearance of Herakles on pots from Peisistratid Athens reflected the tyrant Peisistratos' identification of himself with the hero, which artists exploited in allegory.[106] Perhaps, he speculated several years later, the vase paintings of Exekias allegorically reflected opposition to Peisistratos.[107] The controversy that erupted over these claims[108] reawakened interest in the political close reading of art, which had been fitful before.[109]

David Castriota's *Myth, Ethos, and Actuality* (1992) can serve as a guide to the main fifth-century exhibits of this political approach to Greek art. Castriota warmly thanks Pollitt for inspiration,[110] for political interpretation—which casts a narrow but intense spotlight on art in its historical context—is a natural sequel to Pollitt's broader cultural conception. Political interpretation is, in principle, a more muscular contemporary method than the ones already surveyed. It can, given some assumptions, assess the meaning of art in time and explain change in iconography and style over time. The weakness of the approach is its dependence upon assumptions about the sophistication of the audience, the conscious or unconscious role of art in Greek politics, and the role of allegory in Greek art. There is also a practical defect: given the different politics of each Greek *polis,* a political interpretation cannot explain international trends in Greece without considerable difficulty (and so Castriota understandably confines his treatment to Athenian and Athenian-influenced art). Finally, there is the danger that political interpretation can be over-ambitious and can press too political an interpretation of too many monuments, monuments that may be more profitably interpreted in terms other than those of the master political narrative.

As applied to fifth-century Athens, Castriota's political approach has two main fronts. Monuments from the 470s and 460s are interpreted in light of the Greek victory in the Persian Wars and the predominance of the Athenian politician Kimon and his aggressively anti-Persian policy. This draws on a skein of—especially German—scholarship extending back sixty years that interpreted the explosion of Theseus imagery in Athenian art as a Kimonian project.[111] In this light Castriota (following others) interprets the paintings in the Athenian Theseion, the Temple of Athena Areia at Plataia, the Athenian Painted Stoa, and the Knidian *lesche* (lounge) at Delphi (in which the Athenians were "silent partners").[112] The paintings are uniformly lost but can be reconstructed through literary descriptions, and one at least possibly approximated through vase painting as well. Understandably enough, it is in light of Perikles' preeminence at Athens, and his political association with the Athenian Empire, that Castriota then interprets the sculptures on the Athenian Parthenon. In both cases, "officially sponsored Athenian monuments of the second and third quarters of the fifth century" are found to be "finely tuned vehicles of an official ideology."[113]

Such political analyses press meager evidence very hard. We are unlikely to reach a decision between Boardman and his critics on Peisistratid art because at the end of the day we know very little about the relations of pot-painters and politics, little about the large-scale art of Peisistratid Athens, and hardly more about the political programs of the Peisistratids and those who opposed them. Alan Shapiro was quite right, in the end, to decline to enter this controversy:[114] it is hopelessly inconclusive. Even the thicker evidence of the fifth century can yield alarmingly contradictory results. Castriota follows Kebric's[115] close reading of the iconography to label the Polygnotan paintings in the Lesche of the Knidians at Delphi a Kimonian hymn to Athenian hegemony over the Delian League. Yet Dugas, who thought no less deeply, deemed it an anti-Athenian monument.[116]

Castriota cites figures in the paintings whose names may allude to Kimon's relations and achievements: a figure named Eioneus, for example, perhaps referring to Kimon's capture of Eion in Thrace.[117] But he cannot at the same time conceal his discomfort that one of the paintings classes Kimon's mythic ancestor, Aias, among the wicked dead.[118] Nimbleness ensues, as it also must when he reinterprets the *Ilioupersis* in the Lesche from what it had always been—a horrifying example of Greek hybris and savagery—to a moderate and justified taking of retribution, not least because all paintings in the building *had* to be "with the program."[119] The presence of too many alternatives and the sense of pushing too hard will cause more than one reader to shrug out a verdict of *non liquet.*

Political analysis of art requires a much finer grain of information about art and history than a broader cultural analysis does. It is unclear whether the information we have about art and politics in ancient Greece can sustain such systematic political analysis, even in relatively well reported Athens. And underneath the mismatch between information possessed and information needed lie more profound issues of method. Castriota is at least interested in how contemporary viewers might have viewed art, and propounds an attractive (and Pollitt-derived) theory of *ethos*- (character-) based depiction and perception that has some basis in what we know of these matters in Athens (even if only in the fourth, not the fifth, century).[120] Even so, however, his focus is very often iconography, the message or ideology of the regime communicated through small tweakings of traditional visual formulae for which the way had been prepared, he suggests in one case, by a painting in a small clubhouse in Delphi. Yet can we be sure that an Athenian audience would "get" it? For a political interpretation to be successful, it must be shown that the audience—how defined?—was expected to be able to interpret the art; authors propounding delightfully complicated political analyses should stop for a moment and consider just how subtle and sophisticated this "interpretive community"[121] could be, how this can be demonstrated, and make an effort to do so.

Other problems also arise. Does public art merely reflect current constellations of power and their interests, rather than seek to serve them? Is it a memorial? Or an honor? Or is this art *intended* to communicate something, to participate in politics, to compel acceptance of a view? A political reading of art implicitly pushes the last point of view, but here there is much to prove, and not just about the receptivity of the audience. First: did the patron intend to communicate, intend to use art as a political tool? Not only do we have no Greek writings that suggest this, but what we do have may imply otherwise: the Goebbels-like Kimon of the art historians, spreading the tentacles of his propaganda[122] to Plataia and Delphi, bears little resemblance to the bluff, jolly, bibulous admiral of the historical sources. An intuition that political intent existed can easily be undermined, moreover, by doubts about the effectiveness of a chosen medium: could a patron expect to communicate successfully through the Parthenon frieze, up so high, or through vases alleged to offer complicated Athenian political allegory but exported, perhaps immediately, to Etruria? Why choose these media?

Even if one banishes the calculating minister of propaganda and speaks instead of a not fully conscious or intentional political manipulation of traditional iconography by which official ideology was conveyed, these problems still remain. Political interpretation requires that there *was* a message, conscious or unconscious, that an audience *was* attuned to it, and that *we* can see it. Some strikingly modern-sounding political interpretations of Athenian art are the result: the monuments of fifth-century Athens were motivated by an Athenian "need for legitimation" of empire,[123] by "a need to reaffirm their collective superiority,"[124] by a need to hide what they were doing.[125] Yet the exercise of power in historical societies is not necessarily illegitimate, apologetic, or self-deceiving: to assume it was always so is an anachronism. And if we cease to assume that power was illegitimate, then art (never identified by ancient politicians or autocrats as effective propaganda anyway) reverts to inert and untroubled glorifying publicity. This is much less surprising, much less political in the modern sense, and much less problematic.

Perhaps most important, however, is the last problem: how can art represent current political situations through mythical allegory? Political interpretations must assume that iconographical representation is ruthlessly consistent (and therefore most likely simple), but is it? Greek art that is claimed to be of political significance usually speaks in subtle code: fights between Greeks and Amazons, say, alluding to the war between the Greeks and Persians. But do Amazons always represent Persians, or can Amazons sometimes just be Amazons? Moreover, it is one thing to suggest that a depiction of Greek self-control in a mythic battle against frenzied Amazons is a prefiguring or analogue in mythical time of the qualities that gave victories to the Greeks in the Persian Wars, and quite another to insist that this artistic analogue is intended to celebrate a specific historical victory achieved for specific reasons.[126] Asserting that we are like our ancestors is not the same as asserting that our ancestors, portrayed as fighting against Amazons, are in fact ourselves, fighting against the Persians yesterday. Indeed, analogies and allegories are more likely to free the viewer from historical contexts and direct them away from their current experiences—encouraging them to see their own virtues as timeless, for example—rather than toward a political understanding of event or circumstance in the present. The contribution of analogy and allegory to a political understanding of art is, therefore, much more difficult than it at first appears.

Art can remain political in one important and ancient sense: art can still be usefully interpreted in the context of the polis or city that paid for it. Perhaps Castriota has introduced some anachronisms, has forced too many monuments into the service of the grand "political" narrative, has attributed too much sly intent to Kimon and Perikles, and did not leave enough room for the experiments of artists or for human creations to be simply human and traditional rather than political; but a relationship with the polis and the men who sponsor the art is still there. In this, Castriota's is the most historically faithful of the contemporary approaches here surveyed.

CONCLUSIONS

The historian's natural joy in the triumph of the cultural study of Greek art must, we conclude, be deflated by several common vices in the way that study is actually carried on. Sometimes the concept of culture is defined from an understanding so universal, abstract, or generic that its relationship to any specifically Greek culture is dubious; sometimes the concept of culture is itself deconstructed out of existence; sometimes "Greek culture," although no doubt intended to be recognizably Greek, is wrongly or anachronistically conceived. In these cases, Greek culture—the tool to be used to interpret Greek art—is awkwardly fashioned. Often, too, Greek culture, however defined, is "applied" to the understanding of art in a clumsy or weak way, with methods ill-fitted to answer important questions, whether of meaning in time, causation within time, or change over time: here the worker does not wield the tool well. In all cases, the possibility of generating historically plausible results, results that have some chance of fitting what else we know about ancient Greece, is reduced. Mundane historical knowledge is needed to restrain the giddy possibilities that the carnival of theory so temptingly offers. But in what specific ways can progress be made?

First, more scholars should recognize that multiple, competing definitions of culture are, at the moment, simultaneously in use in the study of Greek art. Different visions of culture have been especially characteristic of different fields of Greek art, and all see different things. Social structure and social change are emphasized in the document- and art-poor earlier periods; the oppositional Structuralist mind is the frame for vase painting in particular; and religious and political functionalism is especially used to explain the great public monuments, usually of stone. But are Greek, or even Athenian, artifacts products of different "cultures," or of the same "culture"? Do they speak different languages or the same language?

Although each of these approaches—each of these visions of culture—implicitly claims for itself a wider importance in the interpretation of all Greek art, that wider significance must be tested for viability and compatibility in as many types of art as possible. In placing art in context—in reconstructing to the best of our ability the world of the ancient creators and viewers—more rather than fewer types of artifact should be used to evoke that world, and to prove the wide and historic viability of any interpretation.

If scholars facing this challenge decide, upon contemplation, that they do not mean to assert a wider significance for each of their disparate definitions of culture, they then face a different problem: explaining the existence of subcultures, segments of the larger whole with different characteristics, rules, and languages. How could these subcultures come to exist? A fracturing of culture into subsets is not a fact established by a theoretical rejection of the concept of cultural coherence, but is the result of certain historical circumstances. What were they? What was the place of one subculture, and context of interpretation, within the wider society?[127] Either way, the simultaneous use of different definitions of culture for different media has left unfinished business for the field of Greek art as a whole.

One of Pollitt's great strengths was his recognition that culture in the Greek city-state had to have an irreducible core: it had to have a heart and a definition, just as language has to have basic meanings and a group of speakers who can communicate. This is a conclusion that has also been reached by contemporary historians weary of twenty years of their colleagues' frantic searching for "resistance" to dominant culture and attempts to "fracture" culture itself.[128] Pollitt's conception of culture—a more-or-less unified set of ideals and ways of doing things expressed in all media, in literature, philosophy, art, and architecture—worked, and still works, well. He compared visual arts with other arts (literary or philosophical, for example), that is, cultural product with cultural product, and used that comparison to try to understand what that culture was—values, beliefs, ideals, ideas, ways of seeing—in short, a kind of conceptual filter in and through which the "motivating force" of experience could shape them all.[129] He reconstructed Greek culture from the arts of the same time period and often the same place, which is fundamentally more sound than importing a general definition of culture or a theory of what constitutes it from the anthropology of the American Southwest or the rainforests of Brazil.

The comparison of poetry, philosophy, architecture, and art with one another kept the comparison at the level of like with like, while also drawing on Greek assertions that these arts were related.[130] This means that, whatever else Pollitt was doing, he believed in the possibility of a more-or-less unified culture and was rooting his search for it in the arts and artifacts of the time—looking for shared meanings in Greek rather than in French or English, so to speak. His was a broad but historical view that led to broad but historically plausible results.

Understanding culture this way, as a conceptual filter, draws on an older, humanistic way of envisaging culture. This is not the very influential anthropological concept of culture,[131] which aims to assess meaning by collapsing into itself historical event, contemporary views and ideas, and product—Pollitt's experience, culture, and art. This collapse makes the anthropological concept of culture a totalizing, long-view one that is by its nature and focus antithetical to traditional art history (or so Bal and Bryson say),[132] as well as an inadequate tool of historical explanation,[133] for the collapse results in the loss of fruitful friction among art and context and with it all the mechanisms that can help explain change over time.[134] If everything from social structure to war to philosophy embodies "culture," nothing within the body of surviving evidence can account for changes in it: all swirl around together in one big and stagnant lake of meaning, powerless to act upon one another. And so motivators and dynamics must be smuggled in from elsewhere. On the other hand, Pollitt's culture as a conceptual filter is not the fracturing gaze of the poststructuralist. For if experience and culture are not shared at all—if all perceptions of social structure, war, and philosophy are only subjective, as poststructuralists would have it—then the three categories are collapsed into one again, but in a different way: all combine into countless individual, and individually different, drops of water. This turns the study of Greek art and its history into little more than an investigation of what can and cannot be known.[135]

The individual cases examined here show the truth of the general principle: the anthropological concept of culture is too big to explain change, the postmodernist too small to explain anything. By adhering to an older, humanistic concept of culture, broad but not too broad, and by positioning culture between the arts (its expression) and experience (their motivator), Pollitt created an equation with three variables, powerful enough to produce powerful results. But none of his variables is fixed, none determines the results before the investigation gets under weigh: all are rooted, instead, in history with all its unpredictability. His concept is therefore both historical and fruitful.

Next, in applying conceptions of culture in the interpretation of art, it is necessary not to overstate what art does, and how art does it—how art "works" in society. The various approaches surveyed here have different mechanisms and ends in mind. All, in attempting to explain art, reach for characteristic verbs: the Structuralists assume that art *reflects* experience and memory, which means that artists unconsciously convey culture and viewers recognize themselves or their lives in an image. Many of the more theoretically minded approaches assume that art *transcends* specific historical meaning, with artists again the unconscious producers of meaning, or mutterers of a dissonant lack of meaning. The politically minded approach is committed to the idea that art and artists intentionally or unintentionally *disseminate* a position. But where *is* meaning located, and how does art convey it? Does it merely mean something to the private understanding of the ancient viewer, so the viewer does all the work? Or do artists and art work actively as agents, using a specific ancient visual language to convey experience or a message—or at least creating a visual world of viewers through which they will see and understand this and other works of art? The views surveyed here crowd the ends of this spectrum: unconscious artists and very abstract or generic meanings; or much more conscious artists and very specific, political meanings. We must, implicitly, choose between them, between drifting and driving. But these options are unsatisfactory; the mechanisms posited seem too crudely absolute, the results too generic or too specific.

Pollitt again staked out a middle ground: "The visual arts in Greece were vehicles of [the] expression" of "basic cultural experiences."[136] Although apparently vague, this statement denies either excessive intentionality or excessive lack of intentionality to any work of art, and posits a relationship between art and an individual's or a society's historical experiences that allows for balanced interaction among artist, viewer, artifact, and monument. The concept of expression (rather than reflection, transcendence, or dissemination) implies the artist's thoughtful receptivity to experience, his active interest in representation, an incompleteness if there is no response on the part of the viewer, and the creation of new experience through the act of viewing that in turn can become a basis of further artistic endeavor and reception.[137] This is art that has unifying characteristics as well as a "considerable inner diversity"[138] precisely because it may be a personal expression of a wider cultural experience. Pollitt's vision of what Greek art could do and how it did it is open and flexible without being random.

The attempts to go beyond Pollitt surveyed here have generally relied upon uncomplicated, even impoverished notions of how art works. Pollitt's view, even thirty years ago, was more sophisticated because it allowed for more possibilities and remembered, always, that it was dealing with humans, not automata. Here, nonetheless, there is even more work to be done, more careful explication of the relationship between patron (when there is one), artist, and audience needed. Pollitt has pointed the way, in both *Art and Experience* and his important work on Greek views of art itself, but the scholars have not yet come along who will synthesize it all and root the study of Greek art in what can be known about how artists were seen, what freedoms they had, how patrons and artists worked together, and what observers may have seen when they looked at art. With so much of the foundation already laid, we can still hope one day to read the Baxandalls of Greek antiquity who will pull it all together, who can devise historical interpretations that are not only interesting but also possibly—to use an unfashionable word—true.[139]

Finally: does Greek art merely have meanings? Or does it truly have history? Why do art and its meanings change over time? Some of the approaches investigated here do not, and cannot, come to grips with motors and motivations of change in artistic endeavor. By adopting approaches that make an explanation of change both difficult and unimportant, many students of Greek art in its cultural context have missed an important analytical perspective. For even if they aim only to explicate meaning at a specific time, the added dimension of change over time can test or reshape the conclusions about meaning arrived at in other ways, and this dimension is therefore important in the study of anything in the past.

Dissatisfaction with the bland and generalizing conclusions often generated by anthropologically or theory-based cultural inquiry have led contemporary historians of other fields to revive and reemphasize two factors that can help to explain change over time in the cultural sphere: that the degree of cultural coherence is itself an historical variable, and that there is human agency.[140] The first is the observation that the degree to which a culture may be said to have essential characteristics varies over time; the second, to be obvious about it, that nothing beyond natural disasters occurs without someone doing it. Art is not merely produced. Someone imagines and makes it: individuals matter. That the culture this art expresses can be less or more coherent Pollitt recognized, especially in his identification of the fifth century as a highly coherent period and in his understanding that during the Peloponnesian War and the fourth century there was a loss of coherence;[141] that individual artists are important, and influence viewers and other artists, he always accepted.[142] In other words, were the study of Greek art in its cultural context to follow the rebalancing currently occurring in other historical fields, artists would have to come back into the picture, along with a readiness to accept (and look for) variation in the level of cultural cohesion over time, a concept of expression, and, perhaps above all, an historically specific and measured definition of culture. All can be found in J. J. Pollitt's *Art and Experience in Classical Greece,* published in the year 1972.

NOTES

We extend our thanks to the many friends who have read and commented on this paper: M. Bell, J. S. Clay, C. M. Johns, J. F. Kett, S. A. Rosenfeld, H. A. Shapiro, T. J. Smith, and the editors. The attitude, and any remaining errors, are ours—all ours.

1. Constraints of space confine us to works written in, or translated into English; for a wider survey of recent work, cf. Sparkes 1991. Much valuable German scholarship seems to avoid the cultural approach entirely, assuming that stylistic change is autonomous, cf. Whitley 1987; Whitley 1991, 70.

2. Pollitt 1972, xiii.

3. Pollitt (1985, 110, n. 6) also identifies Carpenter 1960 as a target.

4. For a convenient brief history of scholarship on Greek sculpture, Stewart 1990, 29–32. On vase painting, see H. Hoffmann 1979; Sparkes 1996, 34–63: R. M. Cook 1997, 275–311. The formal and technical study of Greek art continues to have an important place in scholarship, but will not be treated at any further length here.

5. Carpenter 1962, 182.

6. Carpenter 1962, 203.

7. Renata Thomas (1981, 15) collects instances; her summary translated by Ridgway 1985, 2.

8. A translation of his *Klassisches Griechenland* (1965).

9. Schefold 1967, 17.

10. Webster 1939, 206.

11. Webster 1956.

12. Pollitt 1972, xiv.

13. These definitions of both iconography and iconology are found in Panofsky 1939, 4–8 (an essay revised and published as Panofsky 1982), and were known to Pollitt (cf. Pollitt 1974, 25–26). Pollitt 1972 seems to aim at an iconological interpretation of Greek style, very close to what Panofsky thought could be done by an iconological interpretation of iconography: Iconology "is apprehended by ascertaining those underlying principles which reveal the basic attitude of a nation, a period, a class, a religious or philosophical persuasion—qualified by one personality and condensed into one work": Panofsky 1939, 7 = 1982, 30. Perhaps it is not coincidental that some of Pollitt's conclusions also parallel interpretations of Renaissance art, one of Panofsky's specialties. "Iconology" as a term has been used somewhat differently since Panofsky; cf. Burke 2001, 34–38.

14. Pollitt 1972, xiii.

15. Pollitt 1972, 122.

16. Pollitt 1972, 140, n. 1.

17. Pollitt 1972, 22, 27 (tragedy), 24.

18. R. M. Cook 1972, 112–115.

19. R. M. Cook 1972, 9; cited in his critical review of Pollitt by Carpenter 1973, 349; see also Cook's own ungenerous review (1974, 149).

20. See now Stewart 1990, 133–136, who notes in particular "the fundamental revaluation of human potential by late sixth-century poets and thinkers."

21. Pollitt 1972, 9.

22. Pollitt 1972, xiii, 122.

23. Pollitt 1972, 64–110.

24. Hallett 1986, 74; cf. Boedeker and Raaflaub (1998a, 11), who conclude that Pollitt "comes close to equating Greek classical art with Athenian classical art, and Athenian clas-

sical art with democratic art"—close enough that he needs to be refuted. But even they concede (1998a, 320) that the "quantity and pace of . . . developments was especially great at Athens."

25. E.g., Schefold 1967, 20.

26. Fans and followers at times did, though; see especially the exhibit "The Greek Miracle" (Buitron-Oliver 1992) and responses to it, summarized by Ridgway 1994, 763–764 and n. 25.

27. In his contribution to the "Greek Miracle" exhibition catalogue, Pollitt (1992b, 32) suggests only that the invention of democracy in Athens contributed to the aura of optimism there, and might explain ("it may not be a coincidence") the "democratization of subject matter" apparent in vase painting after 510 B.C.

28. Pollitt 1972, 68. The recurring theme of psychology and emotion in *Art and Experience* may itself be a borrowing from other cultural histories of the sixties; cf. Barzun 1974, 12–27 and passim, and the turn to historical psychology in the *Annales* School, noted in Burke 1990, 67–71 (although he thinks that the *Annales* School has in general had relatively little impact in North America).

29. Pollitt 1972, 64.

30. Pollitt 1972, esp. 68 and 134; emphasized also in Pollitt 1992b, 43–44.

31. Pollitt 1972, 112.

32. Pollitt 1972, 123.

33. Pollitt 1972, 125.

34. Carpenter 1973; cf. Hallett 1986, 74.

35. Pollitt 1972, 125.

36. Pérec 1969.

37. Attacks on formalist histories, cf. H. Hoffmann 1985–1986, 61–62 and Beard 1991, 16–17 (specifically vase painting); J. Henderson 1994, 94; Whitley 1991, 15–17; Shanks 1996, 164; Shanks 1999, 2, 4; R. Osborne 1998, 1.

38. Problem-solving, e.g., Hallett 1986; foundation-laying, Robertson 1991, 10.

39. Cf. Oakley 1999, on vase painting (and especially Whitley); Palagia 1998, on Spivey, and Palagia 1999, on sculpture; Robertson 1991, 2–4, on vase painting; Boardman 1997, 260–261, on Henderson; Hurwit 1997, on Spivey; Donohue 2001, on Shanks.

40. Lissarrague 1990a, 106 (reflect); approach summarized by Sparkes 1991, 71–73; cf. Lissarrague 2000, 87 (recognition) and 9: vase painting is "the visual way of thinking and experiencing through which many aspects of this society were aestheticized, as though the painters held a mirror to the Athenians themselves."

41. Quotation from Shanks 1996, 163; example from Lévi-Strauss 1955, 203–224, 244–277.

42. Translating *Un Flot d'images: Une esthétique du banquet grec* (1987).

43. Lissarrague 1990a, 19–46.

44. Translating C. Bérard et al., *La Cité des images* (1984).

45. Lissarrague 1989, 43. P. Vidal-Naquet's essay is "The Black Hunter and the Origin of the Athenian *Ephebia,*" in P. Vidal-Naquet, *The Black Hunter: Forms of Thought and Forms of Society in the Greek World.* Trans. A. Szegedy-Maszak (Baltimore 1986), 106–128.

46. Burke 2001, 172–173.

47. H. Hoffmann 1977 was one of the earliest; see also H. Hoffmann 1988, and (a book-length version of the approach) H. Hoffmann 1997.

48. Burke 2001, 172, 175–176.

49. Quotation, Sparkes 1991, 72; cf. Csapo and Miller 1998, 93.

50. Lissarrague 1990a, 84.

51. Cf. Boardman 1984b, 241; R. Osborne 2000b; or the chart at Shanks 1999, 126.

52. Boardman 2001, 301.

53. For a summary of the intellectual pedigree of "alterity," see B. Cohen 2000, 6–12 and M. C. Miller 2000, 413, n. 1 ("fundamental to structuralist and post-structuralist thought . . . even if it is not always articulated").

54. Lissarrague 1990a, 58; cf. Lissarrague 2000, 30.

55. Frontisi-Ducroux 1989, 157–158. She refers to J.-P. Vernant, *La Mort dans les yeux: Figures de l'autre en Grèce ancienne* (Paris 1986).

56. Social norms and their challenging, cf. Beard 1991, 30; Sutton 2000, 180–181 (and see 185 for jokes on otherness, 199 for depiction as "a weapon in a kind of cultural war").

57. An important question, cf. Boardman 2001, 301: the (only?) value of the "sophistry" of the postmodern approach has been to focus our attention back on the ancient viewer, "who is our main concern."

58. For the problem of the viewer, see Beard (1991, 12), who seems to think that we are the most important viewers ("it is more a matter of learning enough about our own culture and patterns of communication to give a meaning to the images we see and to make appropriate connections between those images and our own experiences, values and beliefs"), although this is qualified later as "attempt to reconstruct *in our own terms* (for we cannot do otherwise) what it was like to be an Athenian *viewer*" (1991, 18; her italics). Others, like Shapiro (1994, 10), are less radical, seeing the audience as "Greek" or, indeed, as specifically Athenian: "Athenian vase-painters painted what interested them and their Athenian circle of friends, colleagues, and buyers, without regard to a pot's final destination" (2000b, 318). For Margaret Miller (2000, 438) vase painting was "largely a demotic art." Lissarrague (2000, 54) notes differences in male and female viewpoints. Since there is no agreement on viewer, there can be no agreement on the self defined by viewing the Other. Vickers and Gill (1994, 196–199) have pointed out the problem created for ascertaining viewers by the Etruscan find

spots of so many vases; Webster 1972 suggested that Etruria was a secondary market for vases.

59. J. Henderson 1994.

60. J. Henderson 1994, 105.

61. J. Henderson 1994, 136. About this article, Boardman (1997, 261) comments: "This is a self-indulgent style of commentary more common in critical writing about some of the wilder reaches of modern art. It is made very much easier by knowing as little as possible about the primary evidence, its archaeological and historical contexts, and never looking at it too closely."

62. J. Henderson 1994, 136.

63. Pollitt 1972, 6.

64. Shanks 1996, 124 (his italics).

65. Whitley 1991, 196.

66. Whitley 1991, 34–39, 192.

67. Whitley 1991, 42–43.

68. Whitley 1991, 10, 87.

69. Whitley 1991, 68. Nuristan also provides a parallel; see Whitley 1991, 38, 192–193.

70. Shanks 1996, 142.

71. This is the title that appears on the title page; but note that the title on the spine and the dust jacket is *Art and the Early Greek State.*

72. Shanks 1999, 3, 158–159.

73. Shanks 1999, 6, 167, 129.

74. Shanks 1999, 203.

75. Shanks 1999, 126.

76. Shanks 1999, 7.

77. Shanks 1999, 174.

78. Shanks 1999, 202. Such sovereignty belongs, rather, "in a field of ideological negotiation": Shanks 1999, 174.

79. Shanks 1999, 203 (his italics).

80. Shanks 1999, 3, 34.

81. Limitations, Spivey 1996, 14–15; for a wider discussion of this movement and a list of its major works, see Shanks 1999, 158.

82. Spivey 1996, 15.

83. Sahlins 1996, 16 (he also includes a little ditty: "Power, power everywhere / And how the signs do shrink; / Power, power everywhere / And nothing else to think").

84. Cf. Tanner 1999; at 147, n. 76, he summarizes previous interpretations that valorized the artist and made (modernizing) claims about the function of art. Bal and Bryson (1991, 182) make past examples of the exaltation of the artist an excuse to deny agency to the artist in general, clearly an overreaction.

85. A long-acknowledged problem; cf. Ridgway 1994, 761.

86. Spivey 1996, 17–53, quotation at 53.

87. See Hurwit 1989 on the probable but not provable dating of the Kritios Boy to the decade after the Persian Wars.

88. Spivey 1996, 26, 25.

89. On competition, see also Onians 1999, 57–104; he identifies competition as one of two great themes through which Greek art can be analyzed.

90. R. Osborne 1998, 1.

91. For the reduplication of J. Hurwit's initial, implying perhaps that Pollitt reproduces by cloning, R. Osborne 1998, 249; for his opinions of Bérard and others, see also R. Osborne 1991; quotation, R. Osborne 1998, 249.

92. They can all be found in R. Osborne 1998: the "landmarks in literature" approach on p. 67, French structuralism with the characteristic phrase "good to think with" on pp. 45, 51, and 221 (and also in his other works, e.g., R. Osborne 1994b and 1997); and so on.

93. On avoiding anachronism, see Baxandall 1985, 105–137.

94. R. Osborne 1994a.

95. E.g., Castriota 1992, 34–36.

96. R. Osborne (1994a, 291, n. 25) accepts Cooper's explanation of Apollo *Epikourios.*

97. R. Osborne 1994a, 75.

98. R. Osborne 1994a, 62.

99. R. Osborne 1994a, 75–77; see also R. Osborne 1998, 183–185, 218.

100. R. Osborne 1994a, 81.

101. R. Osborne 1998, 61 and cf. 169.

102. Endless questions: R. Osborne 1998, 66, 103, 108, 154, 173, etc.; become implicated: R. Osborne 1998, 85, 97, 103, 118, 138, 159, and 209; commentary: R. Osborne 1998, 72. This is also a theme in other works of Osborne; cf. R. Osborne 1987, 99–100, 101; 1988, 4 ("as she stares at this pot, makes it an object of her vision, the viewer finds pots staring back at her, making her the object of their gaze. The whole question of who is subject and what is object, of seeing and being seen, is reopened"); R. Osborne 1989, 311–312 ("the vase evokes questions and then insists on answering back"); R. Osborne 1994, 86 (the Nike parapet questions "both what representation is and what Victory is"); R. Osborne 1996, 72, 74 ("the viewer is invited . . . and directly implicated").

103. R. Osborne 1998, 148–149, cf. 79, 81, 101, etc. Also, R. Osborne 1994b, 88: "Like Praxiteles' Knidian Aphrodite and the Nike fiddling with her sandal, Amelung's 'goddess' challenges the viewer to construct a narrative in order to comprehend the image, and like them this statue makes the construction of a definitive narrative impossible and ensures that the act of building a story frames the viewer and exploits and exposes his male desire."

104. R. Osborne 1998, 100–101.

105. R. Osborne 1998, 230.

106. Boardman 1972; cf. Boardman 1975b, 1978a, 1984b, 1989b, and now 2001, 204–208; also Sparkes 1991, 69–70.

107. Boardman 1978a.

108. Criticism is gathered in Castriota 1992, 237–238, n. 4; see also R. Osborne 1983–1984 and Blok 1990.

109. For early scholarship offering political interpretations of archaic art, see Shapiro 1989, 15–16; Pollitt (1997 and 2000) has also tried his hand at political interpretation.

110. Castriota 1992, xi.

111. See Castriota 1992, 238, n. 8, for references. Pollitt has also experimented with this; cf. Pollitt 1987.

112. Castriota 1992, 90.

113. Castriota 1992, 12.

114. Shapiro 1989, 15–16. He is more comfortable with imagery of Theseus reflecting Athenian imperial ambition; see Shapiro 1992.

115. Kebric 1983.

116. Dugas 1938.

117. Castriota 1992, 90–91.

118. Castriota 1992, 123.

119. Castriota 1992, 96–127; the need to include the *Iliou-persis* in the Lesche's glorifying program stressed at 100.

120. Castriota 1992, 8–12, 17–32; cf. Pollitt 1972, 43–50; fourth century, cf. Pollitt (1974, 194–195) for quotations from Xenophon (about *ethos*) and Aristotle (about Polygnotos).

121. A term of Stanley Fish's, used by Castriota, endorsed by Boedeker 1998, 194; its theoretical analogue is Sewell's (1999, 49) "semiotic community."

122. Cf. "these images are thoroughly congruent with the iconography we have come to associate so closely with Cimonian propaganda": Francis 1990, 102. Castriota (1992, 7) also refers to Kimon's "propaganda" and (1992, 16) to the manipulation of the Athenian public by the elite.

123. Hölscher 1998, 182.

124. Boedeker and Raaflaub 1998b, 325.

125. Castriota 1992, 229.

126. As in Castriota 1997 (1998), 199, 212. Pollitt (1972, 81) avoids this problem by not insisting on the necessity of a direct political connection, instead seeing such art as an expression of the cultural experience of victory (no specific Kimonian or Periklean message attached), filtered through a "relatively small number of themes" that were themselves the result of the "tendency to see the specific in the light of the generic."

127. The distinction between commissioned art and art that was not commissioned, both of which may have different relationships to culture and subcultures, could be useful here; see Webster 1972, 42–62, and Boardman 2001, 226–239.

128. As Sewell (1999, 39–52, 55–56) makes clear, one of the results of the new cultural history of the last twenty years is that we have either Culture (a theoretically defined category, an abstract, usually anthropologically defined and contrasted with another large category, like Biology) or resistance and fragmentation. He notes that not enough attention is given to cultures in Ruth Benedict's sense (like "Samoan culture") that achieve coherence (even if only "thin coherence," 49–51 and 53–55, 57). See also Appleby, Hunt, and Jacob 1994, 268; Bonnell and Hunt 1999, 25; and Sahlins, too, is critical (1996, 13–14): "In order for the categories to be contested at all, there must be a common system of intelligibility. . . ."

129. Pollitt 1972, xiv; cf. Pollitt 1992b, 36 (the Persian Wars as a "precipitating factor"); and Pollitt 1997, where the major comparison for the Parthenon frieze is the Periklean Funeral Oration in Thukydides. Stewart (1997, xiii) espouses the same principle by noting that word and image are "like cousins." Pollitt's idea is therefore also wider than Boardman's (1995, 2) suggestion that culture can be defined as "the 'visual experience' of the ordinary citizen of antiquity."

130. Pollitt 1972, 5–6; cf. Castriota 1992, 8.

131. See, e.g., the definitions of Lévi-Strauss ("man . . . in all his aspects") or Malinowski ("culture is an integral whole consisting of implements and consumer goods, of constitutional charters for the various social groupings of human ideas and crafts, beliefs and customs"), quoted in H. Hoffmann 1979, 66.

132. Bal and Bryson 1991, 179 (they criticize the separation of art and context as "a fundamental rhetorical move of self-construction in art history").

133. Hunt (1989, 10–12), Bonnell and Hunt (1999, 1–14), and I. Morris (2000, 9–17) survey the scholarship of cultural history, and explicate the anthropological focus on (ahistorical) meaning rather than (historical) explanation; it was a definition developed for other purposes.

134. Appleby, Hunt, and Jacob 1994, 226–228 (attributed here more to postmodernist theory, but the logic is the same).

135. R. Osborne (1994a, 52) provides an example of the subjectivity of experience by imagining responses to a portrait, but Appleby, Hunt, and Jacob (1994, 237) note the ultimate end of this approach: "In the final analysis, then, there can be no postmodern history."

136. Pollitt 1972, xiii.

137. Expression is a very carefully chosen word, and is not the same as reflection; Stewart (1997, 12) groups the two together to denounce them as not properly respectful of the capacity of art and language to be "socially formative," but that is precisely the kind of quality Pollitt uses "expression" to convey.

138. Pollitt 1972, 2.

139. Pollitt 1974, on views of Greek art; by Baxandall we mean Michael Baxandall, whose 1972 work was subtitled *A Primer in the Social History of Pictorial Style.* His documentary records were better than those for Greek antiquity, but as Tanner 1999 shows, some very basic questions have not been asked of the evidence that does exist. Burke 2001, 179–180, also sees Baxandall's approach (especially when it can correlate with Freedberg 1989) as the one "most valuable"

at the moment for understanding the meaning(s) of images in their own time.

140. Sewell's (1999, 50, 52–58) concept of the fruitful interrelationship of culture as a meaningful system of signs and culture as practice revives the notion of individual agency within a larger cultural system; cf. I. Morris 2000, 17, on the need to recognize "both individual agency and the limits of self-fashioning."

141. Pollitt 1972, 97, 184. See also his observation (Pollitt 1985, 100) that over time, a different range of experience may have an impact on art.

142. The importance he gives to Pheidias is therefore not "special pleading" (Hallett 1986, 74) but part of a larger understanding of agency in context; see also his remarks (1972, 174) on Lysippos: "Wherever . . . mutations occur, they seem to be connected to the activity of the great sculptor Lysippos of Sikyon."

WORKS CITED

Adam, S. 1966. *The Technique of Greek Sculpture.* Oxford.

Albinus, L. 2000. *The House of Hades: Studies in Ancient Greek Eschatology.* Aarhus.

Alexander, J. 1992. *Medieval Illuminators and Their Methods of Work.* New Haven.

Alfieri, N., and P. E. Arias. 1958. *Spina.* Munich.

Ameling, W. 1983. *Herodes Attikos.* 2 vols. Hildesheim.

Amelung, W. 1903. *Die Skulpturen des vaticanischen Museums* 1. Berlin.

Amyx, D. A. 1958. "The Attic Stelai. Part III." *Hesperia* 27: 163–310.

———. 1988. *Corinthian Vase Painting of the Archaic Period.* Berkeley.

Anderson, G. 1993. *The Second Sophistic.* London.

Anderson, M. J. 1997. *The Fall of Troy in Early Greek Poetry and Art,* Oxford Classical Monographs. Oxford.

Appleby, J., L. Hunt, and M. Jacob. 1994. *Telling the Truth about History.* New York.

Archibald, Z. H. 1998. *The Odrysian Kingdom of Thrace: Orpheus Unmasked.* Oxford.

Arnold, D. 1969. "Die Polykletnachfolger." *JdI-EH* 55.

Ashmole, B. 1972. *Architect and Sculptor in Classical Greece.* London.

Ashmole, B., N. Yalouris, and A. Frantz. 1967. *Olympia: The Sculptures of the Temple of Zeus.* London.

Auden, W. H., ed. 1948. *The Portable Greek Reader.* New York.

Austin, N. 1994. *Helen of Troy and Her Shameless Phantom.* Ithaca.

Bacon, H. 1961. *Barbarians in Greek Tragedy.* New Haven.

Badian, E. 1993. *From Plataea to Potidea: Studies in the History and Historiography of the Pentecontaetia.* Baltimore.

Bagnall, R. 1997. "The Fayum and Its People." In *Ancient Faces: Mummy Portraits from Roman Egypt,* edited by S. Walker and M. Bierbrier, 17–20. London.

Bakir, G. 1982. *Sophilos.* Mainz.

Bal, M., and N. Bryson. 1991. "Semiotics and Art History." *ArtB* 73: 174–208.

Barringer, J. M. 1995. *Divine Escorts: Nereids in Archaic and Classical Greek Art.* Ann Arbor.

———. 2001. *The Hunt in Ancient Greece.* Baltimore.

Barron, J. P. 1972. "New Light on Old Walls: The Murals of the Theseion." *JHS* 92: 20–45.

———. 1984. "Alkamenes at Olympia." *BICS* 31: 199–211.

Barrow, R. H. 1967. *Plutarch and His Times.* Bloomington, IN.

Barthes, R. 1977. *Camera Lucida.* Translated by R. Howard. London.

Barzun, J. 1974. *Clio and the Doctors: Psycho-History, Quanto-History and History.* Chicago.

Bassi, K. 1993. "Helen and the Discourse of Denial in Stesichorus' Palinode." *Arethusa* 26: 51–75.

Baxandall, M. 1972. *Painting and Experience in Fifteenth Century Italy: A Primer in the Social History of Pictorial Style.* Oxford.

———. 1985. *Patterns of Intention: On the Historical Explanation of Pictures.* New Haven.

Bažant, J. 1987. "Les Vases athéniens et les réformes démocratiques." In *Images et société en Grèce ancienne: L'Iconographie comme méthode d'analyse, Actes du colloque international Lausanne,* 8–11 février 1984, edited by C. Bérard, C. Bron, and A. Pomari, 33–40. Lausanne.

Beall, E. F. 1989. "The Contents of Hesiod's Pandora Jar: *Erga* 94–98." *Hermes* 117: 227–230.

Beard, M. 1991. "Adopting an Approach II." In *Looking at Greek Vases,* edited by T. Rasmussen and N. Spivey, 12–35. Cambridge.

Beazley, J. D. 1928. *Greek Vases in Poland.* Oxford.

———. 1932. "Battle-Loutrophoros." *The Museum Journal* 23: 5–22.

———. 1943. "Groups of Campanian Red-figure." *JHS* 63: 66–69.

———. 1960. "Some Inscriptions on Vases: VIII." *AJA* 64: 219–221.

Becatti, G. 1951. *Problemi Fidiaci.* Milan.

Bengtson, H. 1965. *Griechische Geschichte*³. Munich.

Benkard, E. 1927. *Das Selbstbildnis vom 15.ten bis zum Beginn des 18.ten Jahrhundert.* Berlin.

Bérard, C. 1974. *ANODOI: Essai sur l'imagerie des passages chthoniens.* Rome.

———. 2000. "The Image of the Other and the Foreign Hero." In Cohen 2000, 390–412.

Bérard, C., et al. 1989. *A City of Images: Iconography and Society in Ancient Greece.* Translated by D. Lyons. Princeton.

Berger, E. 1986. *Der Parthenon in Basel: Dokumentation zu den Metopen.* Mainz.

———, ed. 1984. *Parthenon-Kongress Basel, Referate und Berichte 4 bis 8 April 1982.* Mainz.

Berger, E., and M. Gisler-Huwiler. 1996. *Der Parthenon in Basel: Dokumentation zum Fries.* Basel.

Bergmann, M. 1982. "Zeittypen im Kaiserporträt?" *Römisches Porträt: Wege zur Erforschung eines gesellschaftlichen Phänomenons. Wissenschaftliche Konferenz. Wissenschaftliche Zeitschrift der Humboldt-Universität Berlin* 31: 143–147.

Berman, L. M., and K. J. Bohac. 1999. *The Cleveland Museum of Art Catalogue of Egyptian Art.* New York.

Beschi, L. 1984. "Il fregio del Partenone: Una proposta di lettura." *Atti della Accademia dei Lincei* 39: 173–195.

———. 2002. "I Tirreni di Limno a Brauron e il tempietto ionico dell'Ilisso." *RivIstArch* 57 (III. Ser. 25): 7–36.

Beulé, M. (Charles-Ernest). 1853. *L'Acropole d'Athènes; par E. Beulé. Publié sous les auspices du Ministère de l'instruction publique et des cultes.* Paris.

Bieber, M. 1915. *Die antiken Skulpturen und Bronzen des Königl. Museum Fridericianum in Cassel.* Marburg.

———. 1961. *The History of the Greek and Roman Theater.* Princeton.

Bird, S., I. Jenkins, and F. Levi. 1998. *Second Sight of the Parthenon Frieze.* London.

Birley, A., ed. 1976. *Lives of the Later Caesars.* Harmondsworth.

Blok, J. 1990. "Patronage and the Pisistratidae." *BABesch* 65: 17–28.

———. 1995. *The Early Amazons: Modern and Ancient Perspectives on a Persistent Myth.* Leiden.

Bloomer, W. M. 1993a. "The Superlative *Nomoi* of Herodotus' *Histories.*" *ClAnt* 12: 30–50.

———. 1993b. *Valerius Maximus and the Rhetoric of the New Nobility.* Chapel Hill.

———. 1997. *Latinity and Literary Society at Rome.* Philadelphia.

Blümel, C. 1950–1951. "Der Fries des Tempels der Athena Nike in der attischen Kunst des fünften Jahrhunderts vor Christus." *JdI* 65–66: 135–165.

———. 1966. *Die klassisch griechischen Skulpturen der Staatlichen Museen zu Berlin.* Berlin.

Boardman, J. 1972. "Herakles, Peisistratos and Sons." *RA:* 57–72.

———. 1974. *Athenian Black Figure Vases.* London.

———. 1975a. *Athenian Red Figure Vases: The Archaic Period.* London.

———. 1975b. "Herakles, Peisistratos and Eleusis." *JHS* 95: 1–12.

———. 1976. "The Kleophrades Painter at Troy." *AntK* 19: 3–18.

———. 1977. "The Parthenon Frieze: Another View." In *Festschrift für Frank Brommer,* edited by U. Höckmann and A. Krug, 39–49. Mainz.

———. 1978a. "Exekias." *AJA* 82: 11–25.

———. 1978b. *Greek Sculpture: The Archaic Period.* London.

———. 1984a. "Centaurs and Flying Rocks." *OJA* 3: 123–126.

———. 1984b. "Image and Politics in Sixth Century Athens." In *Ancient Greek and Related Pottery. Proceedings of the International Vase Symposium in Amsterdam 12–15 April 1984,* edited by H. A. G. Brijder, 239–247. Allard Pierson Series 5. Amsterdam.

———. 1984c. "The Parthenon Frieze." In *Parthenon-Kongress Basel, Referate und Berichte 4 bis 8 April 1982,* edited by E. Berger, 210–215. Mainz.

———. 1985. *Greek Sculpture: The Classical Period.* Reprinted with corrections, 1991. London.

———. 1989a. *Athenian Red Figure Vases: The Classical Period.* London.

———. 1989b. "Herakles, Peisistratos and the Unconvinced." *JHS* 109: 158–159.

———. 1995. "Culture and the City." In *Culture et Cité. L'Avènement d'Athènes à l'époque archaïque. Actes du colloque international organisé à l'Université libre de Bruxelles du 25 au 27 avril 1991,* edited by A. Verbanck-Piérard et D. Viviers, 1–14. Brussels.

———. 1997. "Boy Meets Girl: An Iconographical Encounter." In *Athenian Potters and Painters: The Conference Proceedings,* edited by J. H. Oakley, W. D. E. Coulson, and O. Palagia, 259–267. Oxbow Monograph 67. Oxford.

———. 1999. "The Parthenon Frieze: A Closer Look." *RA:* 305–330.

———. 2000a. "Pandora in Italy." In *Agathos Daimon: Mythes et cultes. Études d'iconographie en l'honneur de Lilly Kahil. BCH* Suppl. 38: 51–56. Athens.

———. 2000b. *Persia and the West.* London.

———. 2001. *The History of Greek Vases.* London.

Boardman, J., J. Dörig, W. Fuchs, and M. Hirmer. 1967. *Greek Art and Architecture.* New York.

Boardman, J., and D. Finn. 1985. *The Parthenon and Its Sculptures.* London.

Boatwright, M. T. 2000. *Hadrian and the Cities of the Roman Empire.* Princeton.

Boedeker, D. 1998. "Presenting the Past in Fifth-Century Athens." In Boedeker and Raaflaub 1998, 185–202.

Boedeker, D., and K. A. Raaflaub. 1998a. "Introduction." In Boedeker and Raaflaub 1998, 1–13.

———. 1998b. "Reflections and Conclusions: Democracy, Empire, and the Arts in Fifth-Century Athens." In Boedeker and Raaflaub 1998, 319–344.

———, eds. 1998. *Democracy, Empire, and the Arts in Fifth-Century Athens,* Center for Hellenic Studies Colloquia 2. Cambridge, MA.

Boersma, J. S. 1970. *Athenian Building Policy from 561/0–405/4 B.C.,* Scripta Groningiana. Groningen.

Bohn, R. 1882. *Die Propylaeen der Akropolis zu Athen.* Berlin.

Böhr, E. 2000. "ΑΦΡΟΣΥΝΗ." *AA:* 109–115.

Bol, P. C. 1996. *Der antretende Diskobol.* Liebieghaus Monographie no. 17. Frankfurt am Main.

Bollansée, J. 1981. "The Battle of Oinoe in the Stoa Poikile: A Fake Jewel in the Fifth-Century Athenian Crown?" *Ancient Society* 22: 91–126.

Bonnell, V. E., and L. Hunt. 1999. "Introduction." In *Beyond the Cultural Turn. New Directions in the Study of Society and Culture,* edited by V. E. Bonnell and L. Hunt, 1–32. Berkeley.

Borbein, A. H. 1989. "Phidias-Fragen." In *Festschrift für Nikolaus Himmelmann,* edited by H.-U. Cain, H. Gabelmann, and D. Salzmann, 99–107. Mainz.

Borg, B. 1996. *Mumienporträts: Chronologie und kultureller Kontext.* Mainz.

Bottini, A. 1988. "Elena in occidente." *BdA* 50–51: 1–18.

Bovon, A. 1963. "Les représentations des guerriers perses et la notion de barbare dans la Ire moitié du Ve siècle," *BCH* 87: 587–600.

Bowersock, G. 1969. *Greek Sophists in the Roman Empire.* Oxford.

Bowie, E. L. 1970. "Greeks and Their Past in the Second Sophistic." *PastPres* 46: 3–41.

Brahms, T. 1994. *Archaismus.* Frankfurt am Main.

Brandt, E., A. Krug, W. Gercke, and E. Schmidt. 1972. *Antike Gemmen in deutschen Sammlungen. München* 1:3. Munich.

Braun, L. 1982. "Die Schöne Helena, wie Gorgias und Isokrates sie sehen." *Hermes* 110: 158–174.

Brinkmann, V. 1994. *Beobachtungen zum formalen Aufbau und zum sinngestalt der friese des Siphniensschatzhauses.* Munich.

Brommer, F. 1961. "Die Geburt der Athena." *JRGZM* 8: 66–83.

———. 1967. *Die Metopen des Parthenon.* Mainz.

———. 1977. *Der Parthenonfries.* Mainz.

———. 1978. *Hephaistos.* Mainz.

———. 1979. *The Sculptures of the Parthenon.* London.

Brown, P. 1980. *The Body in Society: Men, Women, and Sexual Renunciation in Early Christianity.* New York.

Brueckner, R. 1910. "Ein athenischer Theseus-Fries in Berlin und Wien." *ÖJh* 13: 50–62.

Brulé, P. 1987. *La Fille d'Athènes: La religion des filles à Athènes à l'époque classique.* Paris.

Brümmer, E. 1985. "Griechische Truhenbehälter." *JdI* 100: 1–168.

Bruneau, P. 1982. "L'Ares Borghèse et l'Ares d'Alcamène, ou de l'opinion et du raisonnement." In *Rayonnement Grec: Hommages à Charles Delvoye,* edited by L. Hadermann-Misguich and G. Raepsaet, in collaboration with G. Cambier, 177–199. Bruxelles.

Brunn, H. 1864. "Scavi dell'Acropoli di Atene da lettere dei sigg. P. Decharme e P. Pervanoglu." *BdI* 36: 83–89.

Brunner-Traut, E., and H. Brunner. 1981. *Die Ägyptische Sammlung der Universität Tübingen.* Mainz.

Brunt, P. 1994. "The Bubble of the Second Sophistic." *BICS* 39: 25–52.

Bugh, G. R. 1988. *The Horsemen of Athens.* Princeton.

Buitron-Oliver, D., ed. 1992. *The Greek Miracle: Classical Sculpture from the Dawn of Democracy.* Washington, DC.

———. 1997. *The Interpretation of Architectural Sculpture in Greece and Rome, Studies in the History of Art* 49. Washington, DC.

Burke, P. 1990. *The French Historical Revolution: The* Annales *School, 1929–89.* Stanford.

———. 2001. *Eyewitnessing: The Uses of Images as Historical Evidence.* Ithaca.

Burkert, W. 1966. "Kekropidensage und Arrephoria." *Hermes* 94: 1–25.

———. 1977. *Griechische Religion der archaischen und klassischen Epoche.* Stuttgart.

———. 1983. *Homo Necans.* Translated by P. Bing. Berkeley.

Burn, A. R. 1984. *Persia and the Greeks.* 2nd ed. London.

Burn, L. 1987. *The Meidias Painter.* Oxford.

Burnett, A. P. 1998. *Revenge in Attic and Later Tragedy.* Berkeley.

Busolt, G. 1904. *Griechische Geschichte* 3. Gotha.

Cain, P. 1993. *Männerbildnisse neronisch-flavischer Zeit. Studien Reihe Archäologie.* Vol. 2. Munich.

Calder, W. M. 1978. "Sophocles, Oinomaos, and the East Pediment at Olympia." *Philologus* 118: 203–214.

Camp, J. M. 1986. *The Athenian Agora: Excavations in the Heart of Classical Athens.* Reprinted 1998. London.

———. 1998. *Horses and Horsemanship in the Athenian Agora.* Athens.

Capuis, L. 1968. *Alkamenes: Fonti storiche e archeologiche.* Florence.

Carpenter, R. 1960. *Greek Sculpture: A Critical Review.* Chicago.

———. 1962. *Greek Art: A Study of the Formal Evolution of Style.* Philadelphia.

———. 1970. *The Architects of the Parthenon.* Harmondsworth.

———. 1973. Review of *Art and Experience in Classical Greece,* by J. J. Pollitt. *AJA* 77: 349.

Carter, J. B., and S. P. Morris. 1995. *The Ages of Homer: A Tribute to Emily Townsend Vermeule.* Austin.

Castriota, D. 1992. *Myth, Ethos, and Actuality: Official Art in Fifth-Century B.C. Athens.* Madison.

———. 1997 (1998). "Democracy and Art in Late Sixth- and Fifth-Century B.C. Athens." In *Democracy 2500? Questions and Challenges,* edited by I. Morris and K. A. Raaflaub, 197–216. Archaeological Institute of America Colloquia and Conference Papers No. 2, 1997. Dubuque, IA.

———. 2000. "Justice, Kingship, and Imperialism: Rhetoric and Reality in Fifth-Century B.C. Representations Following the Persian Wars." In Cohen 2000, 443–479.

Chamay, J. 1977. "Autour d'un vase phlyaque—un instrument de portage." *AntK* 20: 57–60.

Chamoux, F. 1996. "'Hermès Propylaios'." *CRAI:* 37–53.

Chantraine, P. 1956. "ΜΕΤΡΟΣ ΕΝ ΑΓΡΑΣ." *ClMed* 17: 1–4.

Childs, W. A. P. 1985. "In Defense of an Early Date for the Frieze of the Temple on the Ilissos." *AM* 100: 207–251.

Clader, L. L. 1976. *Helen.* Leiden.

Clairmont, C. W. 1983. *Patrios Nomos: Public Burial in Athens during the Fifth and Fourth Centuries BC.* Oxford.

Clark, A. J. 1992. "Attic Black-figured Olpai and Oinochoai." Ph.D. diss., New York University.

Clausewitz, C. von. 1984. *On War.* Edited and translated by M. Howard and P. Paret. Princeton.

Clayton, P., and M. Price, eds. 1988. *The Seven Wonders of the Ancient World.* London.

Clinton, K. 1992. *Myth and Cult: The Iconography of the Eleusinian Mysteries.* Stockholm.

Cohen, B. 1991. "Perikles' Portrait and the Riace Bronzes: New Evidence for 'Schinocephaly.'" *Hesperia* 60: 465–502.

———, ed. 2000. *Not the Classical Ideal: Athens and the Construction of the Other in Greek Art.* Leiden.

Coldstream, J. N. 1968. *Greek Geometric Pottery.* London.

Collignon, M. 1912. *Le Parthénon.* Paris.

Comstock, M., and C. C. Vermeule. 1976. *Sculpture in Stone: The Greek, Roman and Etruscan Collections of the Museum of Fine Arts, Boston.* Boston.

———. 1988. *Sculpture in Stone and Bronze in the Museum of Fine Arts, Boston: Additions to the Collections of Greek, Etruscan and Roman Art, 1971–1988.* Boston.

Connelly, J. B. 1996. "Parthenon and *Parthenoi:* A Mythological Interpretation of the Parthenon Frieze." *AJA* 100: 53–80.

Connolly, J. 2001. "Reclaiming the Theatrical in the Second Sophistic." *Helios* 28: 75–96.

Connor, W. R. 1968. *Theopompus and Fifth Century Athens.* Cambridge, MA.

Constantine, D. 1984. *Early Greek Travellers and the Hellenic Ideal.* Cambridge.

Constantinou, F., and F.-M. Tsigakou, eds. 1998. *Photographs by James Robertson, "Athens and Grecian Antiquities," 1853–1854 from the Photographic Archive of the Benaki Museum.* Athens.

Conze, A. 1864. "Denkmäler und Forschungen." *AZ* 22: 170–173.

Cook, A. B. 1940. *Zeus: A Study in Ancient Religion.* Vol. 3. Cambridge.

Cook, R. M. 1972. *Greek Art: Its Development, Character and Influence.* London.

———. 1974. Review of *Art and Experience in Classical Greece,* by J. J. Pollitt. *CR* n.s. 24: 148–149.

———. 1997. *Greek Painted Pottery.* 3rd ed. London.

Corbett, P. E. 1959. *The Sculpture of the Parthenon.* Harmondsworth.

Coulson, W. D. E., O. Palagia, T. L. Shear, Jr., H. A. Shapiro, and F. J. Frost, eds. 1994. *The Archaeology of Athens and Attica under the Democracy.* Oxford.

Coulton, J. J. 1976. *The Architectural Development of the Greek Stoa.* Oxford.

———. 1977. *Ancient Greek Architects at Work.* Ithaca.

Cousin, C. 2000. "Composition, espace et paysage." *Gaia* 4: 61–103.

Crook, J. M. 1972. *The Greek Revival: Neo-classical Attitudes in British Architecture 1760–1870.* London.

Csapo, E., and M. Miller. 1998. "Democracy, Empire, and Art: Toward a Politics of Time and Narrative." In Boedeker and Raaflaub 1998, 87–125.

Curtius, E., and F. Adler, eds. 1892. *Olympia II: Die Baudenkmäler von Olympia.* Berlin.

Curtius, L. 1923. "Zum Sarkophag von Torre Nova." *AM* 48: 31–51.

Dally, O. 1997. "Kulte und Kultbilder der Aphrodite in Attika im späteren 5. Jahrhundert vor Christus. Zu einem Fragment im Athener Akropolismuseum." *JdI* 112: 1–20.

Daltrop, G. 1958. *Die Stadtrömischen Männlichen Privatbildnisse trajanischer und hadrianischer Zeit.* Munich.

Daltrop, G., and P. Bol. 1983. *Athena des Myron.* Liebieghaus Monographie 8. Frankfurt am Main.

Daltrop, G., U. Hausmann, and M. Wegner. 1966. *Das römisches Herrscherbild.* Vol. 2:1. Berlin.

Damaskos, D. 1999. *Untersuchungen zu hellenistischen Kultbildern.* Stuttgart.

D'Ambra, E. 1998. *Roman Art.* Cambridge.

D'Arms, J. 1981. *Commerce and Social Standing in Ancient Rome.* Cambridge, MA.

Daux, G. 1965. "Deux Stèles d'Acharnes." In *Χαριστήριον εἰς Ἀναστάσιον Κ. Ὀρλάνδον,* edited by D. Zakythenos et al., 78–90. Athens.

———. 1984. "Sacrifices à Thorikos." *GettyMusJ* 14: 145–152.

De Angelis, F. 1996. "La Battaglia di Maratona nella Stoa Poikile." *AnnPisa,* ser. 4, vol. 1: 119–171.

De Kersauson, K. 1996. *Catalogue des portraits romains.* Vol. 2. Paris.

De Romilly, J. 1988. "Plutarch and Thucydides or the Free Use of Quotations." *Phoenix* 42: 22–34.

Delbrück, H. 1890. *Die Strategie des Perikles, erlaütert durch die Strategie Friedrichs des Grossen.* Berlin.

———. 1920. *Geschichte der Kriegskunst, vol. 1, Das Altertum.* Reprint 1964. Berlin.

Delivorrias, A. 1974. *Attische Giebelskulpturen und Akrotere des fünften Jahrhunderts.* Tübingen.

———. 1994. "Alkamenes." *EAA* Suppl. 2:1.

———. 1997. "The Sculpted Decoration of the So-Called Theseion: Old Answers, New Questions." In Buitron-Oliver 1997, 84–107.

Denoyelle, M. 1994. *Chefs-d'oeuvre de la céramique grecque dans les collections du Louvre.* Paris.

———. 1997. *Le cratère des Niobides.* Paris.

Despinis, G. 1971. *Συμβολή στη μελέτη του έργου του Αγορακρίτου.* Athens.

———. 1995. "Studien zur hellenistischen Plastik I: Zwei Künstlerfamilien aus Athen." *RM* 110: 321–369.

———. 1998. "He Kephale tou Mouseiou Akropoles 2344." In *Mneias Charin: Tomos ste Mneme Marias Siganidou,* edited by M. Lilimpake-Akamate and K. Tsakalou-Tzanavare. Thessaloniki.

———. 1999. "Athena Sunias, eine Vermutung." *AA:* 173–181.

———. 2001. "Vermutungen zum Marathon-Weihgeschenk in Delphi." *JdI* 116: 103–127.

Detienne, M., and J.-P. Vernant. 1975. *Cunning Intelligence in Greek Culture and Society.* Translated by J. Lloyd. Atlantic Highlands, NJ.

Deubner, L. 1932. *Attische Feste.* Berlin.

Develin, B. 1993. "The Battle of Oinoe meets Ockham's Razor?" *ZPE* 99: 235–240.

Dillon, M. 2002. *Girls and Women in Classical Greek Religion.* London.

Dillon, S. 1996. "The Portraits of a Civic Benefactor of Second-Century Ephesos." *JRA* 9: 261–274.

Dinsmoor, W. B. 1940. "The Temple of Ares at Athens." *Hesperia* 9: 1–52.

———. 1941. *Observations on the Hephaisteion, Hesperia* Suppl. 5. Princeton.

———. 1954. "New Evidence for the Parthenon Frieze." *AJA* 58: 144–145.

———. 1975. Reprint. *The Architecture of Ancient Greece.* New York. 3rd ed. Rev., London 1950.

Dohrn, T. 1949. "Phidias, Perikles und Athen." *Symbola Coloniensia: Essays in Honor of J. Kroll,* 71–83. Coloniae ad Rhenum.

Donohue, A. A. 1988. *Xoana and the Origins of Greek Sculpture.* Atlanta.

———. 1997a. "The Greek Images of the Gods." *AJA* 101: 382–383.

———. 1997b. "The Greek Images of the Gods: Considerations on Terminology and Methodology." *Hephaistos* 15: 31–45.

———. 2001. Review of *Art and the Greek City State,* by M. Shanks. *CW* 94: 280–281.

Dörig, J. 1978. "Traces de Thraces sur le Parthénon." *MusHelv* 35: 221–232.

———. 1985. *La Frise est de l'Héphaisteion.* Mainz.

———. 1987. *The Olympia Master and His Collaborators.* Leiden.

Dörpfeld, W. 1912. "Die Arbeiten zu Pergamon 1910–1911." *AM* 37: 233–276.

Dover, K. J. 1974. *Greek Popular Morality in the Time of Plato and Aristotle.* Berkeley.

———. 1978. *Greek Homosexuality.* Cambridge, MA.

Driessche, B. van den. 1973. "Fragments d'une loutrophore à figures rouges illustrant une Amazonomachie." *RALouvain* 6: 19–37.

DuBois, P. 1988. *Sowing the Body: Psychoanalysis and Ancient Representations of Women.* Chicago.

Dugas, C. 1938. "A la Lesché des Cnidiens." *REG* 51: 53–59.

Edwards, C. 1997. "Unspeakable Professions: Public Performance and Prostitution in Ancient Rome." In *Roman Sexualities,* edited by J. P. Hallett and M. B. Skinner, 66–95. Princeton.

Elsner, J. 1998. *Imperial Rome and Christian Triumph.* Oxford.

Erskine, A. 1990. *The Hellenistic Stoa: Political Thought and Action.* Ithaca.

———. 2001. "Trojans in Athenian Society: Public Rhetoric and Private Life." In *Gab es das Griechische Wunder? Griechenland zwischen den Ende des 6. und der Mitte des 5. Jahrhunderts v. Chr.,* edited by D. Papenfuss and V. M. Strocka, 113–125. Mainz.

Etlin, R. A. 1987. "Le Corbusier, Choisy and French Hellenism: The Search for a New Architecture." *ArtB* 69: 264–278.

Ewald, B. 1999. *Der Philosoph als Leitbild.* Mainz.

Fairbanks, A. 1914. *Athenian White Lekythoi.* Vol. 2. New York.

———. 1928. *Catalogue of Greek and Etruscan Vases.* Vol. 1. Cambridge, MA.

Fairweather, J. 1981. *Seneca the Elder.* Cambridge.

Faraone, C. A. 1992. *Talismans and Trojan Horses.* New York.

Fehl, P. 1961. "The Rocks on the Parthenon Frieze." *JWarb* 24: 1–44.

Fehling, D. 1974. *Ethologische Überlegungen auf dem Gebiet der Altertumskunde,* Munich.

Felletti Maj, B. M. 1953. *Museo Nazionale Romano: I ritratti.* Rome.

Felten, F. 1984. *Griechische tektonische Friese archaischer und klassischer Zeit: Schriften aus dem Athenaion der klassischen Archäologie Salzburg* 4. Waldsassen.

Felten, W. 1975. *Attische Unterweltdarstellungen des VI. und V. Jh. v. Chr.* Munich.

Ferguson, J. 1970. *The Religions of the Roman Empire.* Ithaca.

Ferguson, W. E. 1974. Reprint. *Hellenistic Athens: An Historical Essay.* Chicago; original edition, London 1911.

Ferrari, G. 1988. *I vasi attici a figure rosse del periodo arcaico.* Rome.

———. 2002. "The Ancient Temple on the Acropolis at Athens." *AJA* 106: 11–35.

Fink, G. 1958. *Pandora und Epimetheus.* Furth.

Fittschen, K. 1992–1993. "Ritratti maschili privati di epoca adrianea: Problemi della loro varietà." *ScAnt* 6–7: 445–485.

Fittschen, K., and P. Zanker. 1985. *Katalog der römischen Porträts in den Capitolinischen Museen und den anderen Kommunalen Sammlungen der Stadt Rom I. Kaiser- und Prinzenbildnisse.* Mainz.

Fitzpatrick, D. 2001. "Sophocles' *Tereus.*" *CQ* 51: 90–101.

Flashar, M. 2003. *Adolf Furtwängler der Archäologe.* Munich.

Foley, H. P. 1992. "Anodos Drama: Euripides' *Alcestis* and *Helen.*" In *Innovations of Antiquity,* edited by R. Hexter and D. Selden, 133–160. London.

Foucault, M. 1986. *The History of Sexuality.* Vol. 3, *The Care of the Self.* Translated by R. Hurley. New York.

Fowler, R. L. 2000. "Greek Magic, Greek Religion." In *Oxford Readings in Greek Religion,* edited by R. Buxton, 317–343. Oxford.

Francis, E. D. 1990. *Image and Idea in Fifth-Century Greece: Art and Literature after the Persian Wars.* London.

Francis, E. D., and M. Vickers. 1985a. "Argive Oenoe." *AntCl* 54: 105–115.

———. 1985b. "The Oenoe Painting in the Stoa Poikile, and Herodotus' Account of Marathon." *BSA* 80: 99–113.

Frangeskou, V. 1999. "Tradition and Originality in Some Attic Funeral Orations." *CW* 92: 315–336.

Freedberg, D. 1989. *The Power of Images.* Chicago.

Frel, J. 1978. *The Getty Bronze.* Malibu.

———. 1983. "Three Notes on Attic Black Figure in Malibu." *Greek Vases in the J. Paul Getty Museum* 1: 35–38.

Freud, S. 1896. "The Aetiology of Hysteria." In *The Standard Edition of the Complete Psychological Works of Sigmund Freud.* Translated under the editorship of James Strachey, 189–221. London, 1953–1954.

———. 1956. *Delusion and Dream, and Other Essays.* Edited by P. Reiff. Boston.

Froning, H. 1981. *Marmorschmuckreliefs mit griechischen Mythen im 1. Jh. v. Chr.* Mainz.

Frontisi-Ducroux, F. 1989. "In the Mirror of the Mask." In Bérard et al. 1989, 151–165.

Fuchs, M. 1999. *In hoc etiam genere Graeciae nihil cedamus: Studien zur Romanisierung der späthellenistischen Kunst im 1. Jhr. v. Chr.* Mainz.

Fuhrmann, F. 1988. *Plutarque, Oeuvres morales, ii. Apophtegmes de rois et de généraux—apophtegmes laconiens.* Paris.

Fullerton, M. D. 1986. "The Location and Archaism of the Hekate Epipyrgidia." *AA:* 669–675.

Furtwängler, A. 1893. *Meisterwerke der griechischen Plastik; kunstgeschichtliche Untersuchungen.* Leipzig.

———. 1895. *Masterpieces of Greek Sculpture.* Translated by E. Sellers. London.

Garland, R. 1985. *The Greek Way of Death.* Ithaca.

Gaugler, W. M., and P. Hamill. 1989. "Possible Effects of Open Pools of Oil and Water on Chryselephantine Statues." *AJA* 93: 251.

Gawlikowski, M. 1977. "Le Temple d'Allat à Palmyre." *RA* 2: 253–274.

Gazda, E. 1995. "Roman Sculpture and the Ethos of Emulation: Reconsidering Repetition." *HSCP* 97: 121–156.

———, ed. 2002. *The Ancient Art of Emulation.* Ann Arbor.

Geagan, D. J. 1979. "Roman Athens: Some Aspects of Life and Culture, 86 B.C.–A.D. 267." *ANRW* 2:7:1, 389–399.

Geiger, J. 1985. *Cornelius Nepos and Ancient Political Biography.* Wiesbaden.

Gerhard, E. 1864. "Allgemeiner Jahresbericht." *AZ* 22: 145–160.

Gerstenberg, K. 1966. *Die deutschen Baumeisterbildnisse des Mittelalters.* Berlin.

Ghali-Kahil, L. B. 1955. *Les enlèvements et le retour d'Hélène.* Paris.

Gilbert, C. 2003. *How Fra Angelico and Signorelli Saw the End of the World.* University Park, PA.

Gilpin, W. 1792. *Three Essays: On Picturesque Travel; and On Sketching Landscape; To Which Is Added a Poem, On Landscape Painting.* London.

Giraud, D. 1994. *Μελέτη αποκαταστάσεως του ναού της Αθηνάς Νίκης.* Athens.

Gleason, M. 1995. *Making Men: Sophists and Self-Representation in Ancient Rome.* Princeton.

———. 1999. "Elite Male Identity in the Roman Empire," In *Life, Death, and Entertainment in the Roman Empire,* edited by D. S. Potter and D. J. Mattingly, 67–84. Ann Arbor.

Goette, H. R. 1998. "O Demos tes Pallenes: Epigraphes apo ten perioche tou naou tes Athenas Pallenidos." *Horos* 10–12: 105–118.

———. 2001. *Athens, Attica, and the Megarid: An Archaeological Guide.* London.

Goette, H. R., and A. Zimmermann. 1995. *Der Wandel archäologischer Denkmäler in historischen und zeitgenössischen Photographien.* Zurich.

Goldberg, M. Y. 1998. "The Amazon Myth and Gender Studies." In Hartswick and Sturgeon 1998, 89–100.

Goldhill, S. 1995. *Foucault's Virginity: Ancient Erotic Fiction and the History of Sexuality.* Cambridge.

———, ed. 2001. *Being Greek under Rome.* Cambridge.

Goldscheider, L. 1936. *Fünfhundert Selbstporträts von der antike bis zur gegenwart.* Vienna.

Gould, J. 1980. "Law, Custom, and Myth: Aspects of the Social Position of Women in Classical Athens." *JHS* 100: 38–59.

Gow, A. S. F. 1914. "Elpis and Pandora in Hesiod's *Works and Days.*" In *Essays and Studies Presented to William Ridgeway,* edited by E. C. Quiggin, 99–109. Cambridge.

Graef, B., and E. Langlotz. 1929. *Die antiken Vasen der Akropolis zu Athen* 2:2. Berlin.

Graf, F. 1981. "Milch, Honig, und Wein. Zum Verständnis der Libation im griechischen Ritual." In *Perennitas: Studi in onore di Angelo Brelich,* edited by H. Rahner, 209–221. Rome.

Graindor, P. 1915. "Les cosmètes du Musée d'Athènes." *BCH* 39: 241–401.

Green, J. R., and E. W. Handley. 1995. *Images of the Greek Theatre.* London.

Green, P. 1996. *The Greco-Persian Wars.* Berkeley.

Hadzisteliou-Price, T. 1974. "Amphoreus Typou 'Nola' en Sikago kai Epanexetasis tou 'Owl-Pillar Group'." *ArchEph* 1974: 168–198.

Hall, E. 1991. *Inventing the Barbarian: Greek Self-Definition through Tragedy.* Oxford.

Hallett, C. H. 1986. "The Origins of the Classical Style in Sculpture." *JHS* 106: 71–84.

———. 1998. "A Group of Portrait Statues from the Civic Center of Aphrodisias." *AJA* 102: 59–89.

Hamdorf, F. W. 1985. "Klenzes archäologische Studien und Reisen, seine Mission in Griechenland." In *Ein griechischer Traum: Leo von Klenze, der Archäologe,* 117–212. Munich.

Hame, J. K. 1999. "Ta Nomizomena: Private Greek Death-Ritual in the Historical Sources and Tragedy." Ph.D. diss. Bryn Mawr College.

Hammond, N. G. L. 1988. "The Expedition of Datis and Artaphernes." *CAH,* 2nd ed., 4, 491–517.

Hampe, R. 1955. "Eukleia und Eunomia." *RM* 62: 107–122.

Harrison, E. B. 1953. *Portrait Sculpture. Agora* 1. Princeton.

———. 1960. "New Sculpture from the Athenian Agora." *Hesperia* 29: 369–392.

———. 1967. "Athena and Athens in the East Pediment of the Parthenon." *AJA* 71: 27–58.

———. 1972a. "Preparations for Marathon, the Niobid Painter and Herodotus." *ArtB* 54: 390–402.

———. 1972b. "The South Frieze of the Athena Nike Temple and the Marathon Painting in the Painted Stoa." *AJA* 76: 353–378.

———. 1977. "Alkamenes' Sculptures for the Hephaisteion: 1." *AJA* 81: 137–178, 265–287, 411–426.

———. 1979a. "Apollo's Cloak." In *Studies in Classical Art and Archaeology: A Tribute to Peter Heinrich von Blanckenhagen,* edited by G. Kopcke and M. Moore, 91–98. Locust Valley, NY.

———. 1979b. "The Iconography of the Eponymous Heroes on the Parthenon and in the Agora." In *Greek Numismatics and Archaeology: Essays in Honor of Margaret Thompson,* edited by O. Mørkholm and N. M. Waggoner, 71–85. Wetteren.

———. 1979c. Review of *Der Parthenonfries,* by F. Brommer. *AJA* 83: 489–491.

———. 1980. Review of *Alkamenes,* by W.-H. Schuchhardt. *Gnomon* 52: 70–73.

———. 1984. "Time in the Parthenon Frieze." In Berger 1984, 230–234.

———. 1986. "The Classical High-Relief Frieze from the Athenian Agora." In *Archaische und klassische griechische Plastik,* edited by H. Kyrieleis, Vol. 2: 109–117. Mainz.

———. 1988a. "Aphrodite Hegemone in the Athenian Agora." In *Akten des XIII Internationalen Kongresses für klassische Archäologie,* Berlin, 346. Mainz.

———. 1988b. "Theseum East Frieze: Color Traces and Attachment Cuttings." *Hesperia* 57: 339–349.

———. 1996. "Pheidias." In Palagia and Pollitt 1996, 16–65.

———. 1997. "The Glories of the Athenians." In Buitron-Oliver 1997, 108–125.

Harrison, J. E. 1900. "Pandora's Box." *JHS* 20: 99–114.

———. 1955 (1922). *Prolegomena to the Study of Greek Religion.* New York.

Harrison, T. 2000. *The Emptiness of Asia: Aeschylus' Persians and the History of the Fifth Century.* London.

Hartswick, K. 1990. "The Ares Borghese Reconsidered." *RA* 2: 227–283.

Hartswick, K. J., and M. C. Sturgeon. 1998. *ΣΤΕΦΑΝΟΣ: Studies in Honor of Brunilde Sismondo Ridgway.* Philadelphia.

Hatzivassiliou, E. 2001. "The Attic Phormiskos: Problems of Origin and Function." *BICS* 45: 113–148.

Hauser, F. 1910. "Der Sarg eines Maedchens: Bemerkungen zum Sarkophage von Torre Nuova." *RM* 25: 273–292.

Havelock, C. M. 1995. *The Aphrodite of Knidos and Her Successors.* Ann Arbor.

Hedreen, G. 1996. "Image, Text, and Story in the Recovery of Helen." *ClAnt* 15: 152–184.

———. 2003. *Capturing Troy.* Ann Arbor.

Hedrick, C. W. 1988. "The Temple and Cult of Apollo Patroos in Athens." *AJA* 92: 185–210.

Hegel, G. W. F. 1975. *Aesthetics: Lectures on the Fine Arts.* Translated by T. M. Knox. 2 vols. Oxford.

Henderson, B. W. 1927. *The Great War between Athens and Sparta.* Reprint 1973. London.

Henderson, J. 1994. "*Timeo Danaos:* Amazons in Early Greek Art and Pottery." In *Art and Text in Ancient Greek*

Culture, edited by S. Goldhill and R. Osborne, 85–137. Cambridge.

Herrmann, H.-V. 1987. "Olympiameister—Olympiawerkstatt—Olympiastil." In *Die Olympia-Skulpturen,* edited by H.-V. Herrmann, 309–338. Darmstadt.

Heydemann, H. 1879. *Mitteilungen aus den Antikensammlungen in Ober- und Mittelitalien.* Halle.

Higgins, R. A. 1959. *Catalogue of the Terracottas in the Department of Greek and Roman Antiquities, British Museum.* Vol. 2. London.

Hill, B. H. 1912. "The Older Parthenon." *AJA* 16: 535–558.

Himmelmann, N. 1977. "Phidias und die Parthenon-Skulpturen." In *Bonner Festgabe Johannes Straub: Zum 65. Geburtstag am 18. Oktober 1977, BJb-BH* 39, edited by A. Lippold and N. Himmelmann, 67–90. Bonn.

———. 1989. *Herrscher und Athlet: Die Bronze vom Quirinal.* Milan.

Hock, R. F., and E. N. O'Neill. 1986. *The Chreia in Ancient Rhetoric.* Atlanta.

Höcker, C., and L. Schneider. 1993. *Phidias.* Reinbek bei Hamburg.

Hoffmann, G. 1985. "Pandora, la jarre et l'espoir." *Etudes rurales* 97–98: 119–132.

Hoffmann, H. 1977. *Sexual and Asexual Pursuit: A Structuralist Approach to Greek Vase Painting.* Royal Anthropological Institute of Great Britain and Ireland Occasional Paper no. 34. London.

———. 1979. "In the Wake of Beazley: Prolegomena to an Anthropological Study of Greek Vase-Painting." *Hephaistos* 1: 61–70.

———. 1985–1986. "Iconography and Iconology." *Hephaistos* 7–8: 61–66.

———. 1988. "Why Did the Greeks Need Imagery? An Anthropological Approach to the Study of Greek Vase-Painting." *Hephaistos* 9: 143–162.

———. 1997. *Sotades: Symbols of Immortality on Greek Vases.* Oxford.

Hofstetter, E. 1990. *Sirenen in archaischen und klassischen Griechenland.* Würzburg.

Hölscher, T. 1973. *Griechische Historienbilder des 5. und 4. Jahrhunderts vor Chr.* Würzburg.

———. 1989. *Die unheimliche Klassik der Griechen.* Bamberg.

———. 1998. "Images and Political Identity: The Case of Athens." In Boedeker and Raaflaub 1998, 153–183.

Houby-Nielsen, S. H. 1995. "'Burial Language' in Archaic and Classical Kerameikos." *Proceedings of the Danish Institute at Athens* 1: 129–191.

Huber, I. 2001. *Die Ikonographie der Trauer in der griechischen Kunst.* Mannheim.

Hunt, L. 1989. "Introduction." In *The New Cultural History,* edited by L. Hunt, 1–22. Berkeley.

Hurwit, J. M. 1989. "The Kritios Boy: Discovery, Reconstruction, and Date." *AJA* 93: 41–80.

———. 1995. "Beautiful Evil: Pandora and the Athena Parthenos." *AJA* 99: 171–186.

———. 1997. "Review Article: The Death of the Sculptor?" *AJA* 101: 587–591.

———. 1999. *The Athenian Acropolis: History, Mythology, and Archaeology from the Neolithic Era to the Present.* Cambridge.

Immerwahr, H. R. 1992. "New Wine in Ancient Wineskins: The Evidence from Attic Vases." *Hesperia* 61: 121–132.

———. 1998. *A Corpus of Attic Vase Inscriptions.* Self-published, preliminary edition.

Inan, J. 1970. "Kremna Kasisi Raporu." *Turk Tarih Kurumu Basimevi,* 51–97. Ankara.

Inan, J., and E. Alföldi-Rosenbaum. 1979. *Römische und frühbyzantinische Porträtplastik aus der Türkei: Neue Funde.* Mainz.

Inan, J., and E. Rosenbaum. 1970. Reprint. *Roman and Early Byzantine Portrait Sculpture in Asia Minor.* 1970. London; original edition, London: The British Academy, 1966.

Intzesiloglou, C. G. 2000. "A Newly Discovered Archaic Bronze Statue from Metropolis (Thessaly)." In Mattusch, Brauer, and Knudsen 2000, 65–68.

Jeffery, L. H. 1965. "The *Battle of Oinoe* in the Stoa Poikile: A Problem in Greek Art and History." *BSA* 60: 41–57.

Jenkins, I. 1994. *The Parthenon Frieze.* London.

———. 1995. "The South Frieze of the Parthenon: Problems in Arrangement." *AJA* 99: 445–456.

———. 2000. "John Henning's Frieze for the Athenaeum." In *The Athenaeum Collection,* edited by H. Tait and R. Walker, 149–156. London.

———. 2001. "Cleaning and Controversy: The Parthenon Sculptures 1811–1939." *BMOP* 146. London.

Jensen, W. 1903. *Gradiva: A Pompeiian Fancy.* Translated by H. M. Downey. Los Angeles, 1993.

Jeppesen, K. 1963. "Bild und Mythus an dem Parthenon: Zur Ergänzung und Deutung der Kultbildausschmückung des Frieses, der Metopen, und der Giebel." *ActaArch* 34: 1–96.

Jones, A. H. M. 1974. *The Roman Economy.* Edited by P. A. Brunt. Oxford.

Jones, C. P. 1971. *Plutarch and Rome.* Oxford.

———. 1978. *The Roman World of Dio Chrysostom.* Cambridge.

———. 1986. *Culture and Society in Lucian.* Cambridge, MA.

———. 1995. "Towards a Chronology of Plutarch's Works." In Scardigli 1995, 100–106.

———. 1996. "The Panhellion." *Chiron* 26: 29–56.

Jones, S. C. 1998. "Statues That Kill and the Gods Who Love Them." In Hartswick and Sturgeon 1998, 139–143.

Jubier, C. 1999. "Les Peintres de Sappho et de Diosphos, structure d'atelier." In *Céramique et peinture grecques. Modes d'emploi,* edited by M.-C. V. Puig, F. Lissarrague, P. Rouillard, and A. Rouveret, 181–186. Paris.

Jubier-Galinier, C. Forthcoming. "De l'usage des pseudo-inscriptions chez le peintre de Sappho, du signe du sens." *Metis.*

Judeich, W. 1931. *Topographie von Athen.* Munich.

Just, R. 1989. *Women in Athenian Law and Life.* London.

Kagan, D. 1969. *The Outbreak of the Peloponnesian War.* Ithaca.

———. 1974. *The Archidamian War.* Ithaca.

Kallipolitis, V. G. 1978. "He Vase tou agalmatos tes Rhamnousios Nemesis." *ArchEph:* 1–78.

Kannicht, R. 1969. *Euripides Helena.* Heidelberg.

Kant, I. 1790. *The Critique of Judgement.* Translated with analytical indexes by J. C. Meredith. Oxford 1952.

Kardara, C. 1961. "Γλαυκῶπις—ὁ ἀρχαῖος ναὸς καὶ τὸ θέμα τῆς ζωφόρου τοῦ Παρθενῶνος," *ArchEph:* 61–158.

Karouzou, S. 1985. "He Helene tes Spartes." *ArchEph:* 33–44.

Kauffmann-Samaras, A. 1999. "Εικονογραφική μελέτη ενός αττικου ερυθρόμορφου θραύσματος από την Πάρο." In *ΦΩΣ ΚΥΚΛΑΔΙΚΟΝ,* edited by N. C. Stampolides, 284–292. Athens.

Kearns, E. 1989. *The Heroes of Attica.* London.

Kebric, R. B. 1983. *The Paintings in the Cnidian Lesche at Delphi and Their Historical Context, Mnemosyne* Suppl. 80.

Kefalidou, E. 2001. "Late Archaic Pottery from Aiani." *Hesperia* 70: 183–219.

Kennedy, P. 1987. *The Rise and Fall of the Great Powers: Economic Change and Military Conflict from 1500 to 2000.* New York.

Kerenyi, K. 1961. "Zum Fries des Ilissostempels." *AM* 76: 22–24.

Keuls, E. 1974. *The Water-Carriers in Hades.* Amsterdam.

Kilmer, M. F. 1993. *Greek Erotica in Attic Red-Figure Vases.* London.

Klenze, Leo von. 1838. *Aphoristische Bemerkungen gesammelt auf seiner Reise nach Griechenland.* Berlin.

Knauer, E. R. 1986. "Still More Light on Old Walls?: Eine ikonographische Nachlese." In *Studien zur Mythologie und Vasenmalerei: Konrad Schauenburg zum 65. Geburtstag am 16. April,* edited by E. Böhr and W. Martini, 121–126. Mainz.

———. 1992. "Mitra and Kerykeion." *AA:* 373–399.

Knell, H. 1978. "Die Gruppe von Prokne und Itys." *AntPl* 17: 9–19.

———. 1990. *Mythos und Polis.* Darmstadt.

Knigge, U. 1975. "Aison, der Meidias Maler?" *AM* 90: 123–162.

Knittlmayer, B. 1999. "Kultbild und Heiligtum der Nemesis von Rhamnous am Beginn des Peloponnesischen Krieges." *JdI* 114: 1–18.

Koch, G., and H. Sichtermann. 1982. *Römische Sarkophage.* Munich.

Koch, H. 1955. *Studien zum Theseustempel in Athen.* Leipzig.

Kondoleon, C. 2000. *Antioch: The Lost Ancient City.* Princeton and Worcester.

Korres, M. 1988. "Überzählige Werkstücke des Parthenonfrieses." In *Kanon: Festschrift Ernst Berger,* edited by M. Schmidt, 19–27. Basel.

———. 1994a. "The Architecture of the Parthenon." In *The Parthenon and Its Impact in Modern Times,* edited by P. Tournikiotis, 56–97. Athens.

———. 1994b. "Recent Discoveries on the Acropolis." In *Acropolis Restoration: The CCAM Intervention,* edited by R. Economakis, 175–183. London.

———. 1996. "Ein Beitrag zur Kenntnis der attisch-ionischen Architektur." In *Säule und Gebälk,* edited by E.-L. Schwandner, 90–113. Mainz.

———. 1998. "Apo ton Stavro sten archaia Agora." *Horos* 10–12: 83–104.

———. 2000. "Κλασική αθηναϊκή αρχιτεκτονική." In *Αθήναι—από την κλασική εποχή έως σήμερα (5ος αι. π.Χ.–2000 μ.Χ.),* edited by C. Bouras, M. B. Sakellariou, K. S. Staïkos, and E. Touloupa, 2–45. Athens.

Kovacsovics, W. K. 1990. *Die Eckterrasse an der Gräberstrasse des Kerameikos, Kerameikos* 14. Berlin.

Kron, U. 1976. *Die zehn attischen Phylenheroen: Geschichte, Mythos, Kult und Darstellungen.* Berlin.

Krug, A. 1979. "Der Fries des Tempels am Ilissos." *AntP* 18: 7–21.

Krumeich, R. 1997. *Bildnisse griechischer Herrscher und Staatsmänner im 5. Jahrhundert v. Chr.* Munich.

Krumme, M. 1993. "Das Heiligtum der 'Athena beim Palladion' in Athen." *AA:* 213–227.

Kübler, K. 1970. *Die Nekropole des späten 8. bis frühen 6. Jahrhunderts, Kerameikos* 6:2. Berlin.

Kühn, M. 1979. "Als die Akropolis aufhörte Festung zu sein: Stimmen der Zeit zur Frage der Errichtung neuer Baüten auf der Akropolis und zur Erhaltung ihrer nachantiken Monumente." In *Schlösser-Gärten-Berlin: Festschrift für Martin Sperlich,* edited by D. Heikamp, 83–106. Tübingen.

Kunisch, N. 1997. *Makron.* Mainz.

Kunze, M. 1992. *Die Antikensammlung im Pergamonmuseum und in Charlottenburg.* Berlin.

Kunze-Götte, E., K. Tancke, and K. Vierneisel. 1999. *Die Nekropole von der Mitte des 6. bis zum Ende des 5. Jahrhunderts: Die Beigaben, Kerameikos* 7:2. Berlin.

Kurke, L. 1992. "The Politics of ἁβροσύνη in Archaic Greece." *ClAnt* 11: 91–120.

Kurtz, D. C. 1975. *Athenian White Lekythoi.* Oxford.

———. 1988. "Mistress and Maid." *AION*(arch) 10: 141–149.

———. 1990. "The Achilles Painter's Early White Lekythoi." In *ΕΥΜΟΥΣΙΑ: Ceramic and Iconographic Studies in Honour of Alexander Cambitoglou, MeditArch* Suppl. 1, edited by J.-P. Descoeudres, 105–112. Sydney.

Kurtz, D. C., and J. Boardman. 1971. *Greek Burial Customs.* Ithaca.

Kyrieleis, H. 1986. *Archaische und klassische griechische Plastik.* Mainz.

La Rocca, E. 1986. "Prokne und Itys sull'Acropoli: Una motivazione per la dedica." *AM* 101: 153–166.

Lapatin, K. D. S. 1992. "A Family Gathering at Rhamnous: Who's Who on the Nemesis Base?" *Hesperia* 61: 107–119.

———. 1997. "Pheidias ἐλαφαντουργός." *AJA* 101: 663–682.

———. 2001. *Chryselephantine Statuary in the Ancient Mediterranean World.* Oxford.

Larson, J. 1995. *Greek Heroine Cults.* Madison.

Lasserre, F. 1979. "Prose grecque classicante." In *Le classicisme à Rome aux I^ers siècles avant et après J.-C.,* edited by H. Flashar, 135–173. Vandoeuvres.

Lattanzi, E. 1968. *I ritratti dei cosmeti nel Museo Nazionale di Atene.* Rome.

Lattimore, R., trans. 1959. *Hesiod.* Ann Arbor.

Lauriola, R. 2000. "Ἐλπίς el la giara di Pandora (Hes. *OP.* 90–104): Il bene e il male nella vita dell'uomo." *Maia* 52: 9–18.

Lawton, C. 1995. *Attic Document Reliefs: Art and Politics in Ancient Athens.* Oxford Monographs on Classical Archaeology. Oxford.

Laxander, H. 2000. *Individium und Gemeinschaft im Fest: Untersuchungen zu attischen Darstellungen von Festgeschehen im 6. und frühen 5. Jahrhundert v. Chr.* Münster.

Le Roy, J. D. 1758. *Les ruines des plus beaux monuments de la Grèce: Ouvrage divisé en deux parties, ou l'on considère, dans la première, ces monuments du côté de l'histoire; et dans la seconde, du côté de l'architecture.* Paris.

Leahy, D. M. 1974. "The Representation of the Trojan War in Aeschylus' *Agamemnon.*" *AJP* 95: 1–23.

Leake, W. 1821. *The Topography of Athens; With Some Remarks on Its Antiquities.* London.

Lechat, H. 1924. *Phidias et la sculpture grecque au Ve siècle.* Paris.

Lendle, O. 1957. *Die "Pandorasage" bei Hesiod.* Würzburg.

———. 1968. "Paris, Helena und Aphrodite: Zur Interpretation des 3. Gesanges der Ilias." *A&A* 14: 63–71.

Lendon, J. F. 1997. *Empire of Honour: The Art of Government in the Roman World.* Oxford.

Leo, F. 1881. *Die griechische-römische Biographie nach ihrer literarischen Form.* Leipzig.

Lethaby, W. R. 1927. "Parthenon Studies IV: The Last Hundred Years." *The Builder,* 3 June: 896–897.

Leventi, I. 1991. "Eikonographia tes Hygeias sta klassika chronia." Ph.D. diss., University of Athens. Publication forthcoming as *Archaiognosia,* Suppl. 2.

———. 2003. *Hygeia in Classical Greek Art.* Athens.

Levi, P., trans. 1971. *Pausanias: Guide to Greece* 1. Middlesex.

Lévi-Strauss, C. 1955. *Tristes tropiques.* Paris.

Lezzi-Hafter, A. 1971. "Ein Frühwerk des Eretriamalers." *AntK* 14: 84–89.

Lindgren, H. C., and F. L. Kovacs. 1985. *Ancient Bronze Coins of Asia Minor and the Levant.* San Francisco.

Lissarrague, F. 1989. "The World of the Warrior." In Bérard et al. 1989, 39–51.

———. 1990a. *The Aesthetics of the Greek Banquet: Images of Wine and Ritual.* Translated by A. Szegedy-Maszak. Princeton.

———. 1990b. *L'Autre guerrier.* Paris.

———. 1995. "Women, Boxes, Containers: Some Signs and Metaphors." In Reeder 1995, 91–101.

———. 1997. "L'immagine dello straniero ad Atene." In *I greci. Storia cultura arte società 2. Una storia greca II. Definizione,* edited by S. Settis, 937–958. Turin.

———. 2000. *Greek Vases: The Athenians and Their Images.* New York.

Loraux, N. 1986. *The Invention of Athens: The Funeral Oration in the Classical City.* Cambridge, MA.

———. 1998. *Mothers in Mourning.* Translated by C. Pache. Ithaca.

———. 2000. *Born of the Earth: Myth and Politics in Athens.* Translated by S. Stewart. Ithaca.

Lubsen-Admiraal, S., and H. Hoffmann. 1995. "The Sotades Painter's Rhyton from Paphos: Reading Athenian Vase Imagery in a Cypriot Context." *Hephaistos* 13: 73–91.

Lundgreen, B. 1997. "A Methodological Enquiry: The Great Bronze Athena by Pheidias." *JHS* 117: 190–197.

Lyons, C. 1997. "Archives in Ruins: The Collections of the Getty Research Institute." In *Irresistible Decay: Ruins Reclaimed,* edited by M. S. Roth, C. Lyons, and C. Merewether, 79–99. Los Angeles.

Maaskant-Kleibrink, M. 1989. "The Stuff of Which Greek Heroines Are Made." *BABesch* 64: 1–49.

MacBain, B. 1982. *Prodigy and Expiation: A Study in Religion and Politics in Ancient Rome.* Brussels.

Macdonald, W. L., and J. Pinto. 1995. *Hadrian's Villa and Its Legacy.* New Haven.

MacDowell, D. M. *Gorgias. Encomium of Helen.* Bristol.

Mallwitz, A. 1972. *Olympia und seine Bauten.* Munich.

Mallwitz, A., and W. Schiering. 1964. *Die Werkstatt des Pheidias in Olympia, Olympische Forschungen* 5. Berlin.

Mangold, M. 2000. *Kassandra in Athen: Die Erhoberung Trojas auf attischen Vasenbildern.* Berlin.

Mantis, A. 1997. "Parthenon Central South Metopes: New Evidence." In Buitron-Oliver 1997, 67–81.

Marangou, L. I. 1985. *Ancient Greek Art: The N. P. Goulandris Collection.* Athens.

———. 1995. *Ancient Greek Art from the Collection of Stavros S. Niarchos.* Athens.

March, J. 2000. "Vases and Tragic Drama: Euripides' *Medea* and Sophocles' Lost *Tereus.*" In Rutter and Sparkes 2000, 119–139.

Marchand, S. 1996. *Down from Olympus: Archaeology and Philhellenism in Germany 1750–1970.* Princeton.

Mark, I. S. 1993. *The Sanctuary of Athena Nike in Athens: Architectural Stages and Chronology. Hesperia* Suppl. 26. Princeton.

Marrou, H. I. 1982. Reprint. *A History of Education in Antiquity.* Madison; original edition, Paris, 1948.

Martin, H. 1992. "Review of Philip S. Stadter: A Commentary on Plutarch's Pericles." *AJP* 113: 297–300.

Martin, H. G. 1987. *Römische Tempelkultbilder: Eine archäologische Untersuchung zur späten Republik.* Rome.

Martin, M. A. 1886. *Les Cavaliers athéniens.* Paris.

Masciotta, M. 1955. *Autoritratti dal XIV° al XX° Secolo.* Milan.

Matheson, S. B. 1995. *Polygnotos and Vase Painting in Classical Athens.* Madison.

Mattusch, C. C. 1977. "Bronze and Ironworking Techniques from the Athenian Agora." *Hesperia* 46: 343–347.

———. 1988. *Greek Bronze Statuary: From the Beginning through the Fifth Century* B.C. Ithaca.

———. 1994. "The Eponymous Heroes: The Idea of Sculptural Groups." In Coulson, Palagia, Shear, Shapiro, and Frost 1994, 73–81.

———. 1996. *Classical Bronzes: The Art and Craft of Greek and Roman Statuary.* Ithaca.

Mattusch, C. C., A. Brauer, and S. E. Knudsen, eds. 2000. *From the Parts to the Whole* 1, Acta of the 13th International Bronze Congress held at Cambridge, MA, May 28–June 1, 1996, *JRA* Suppl. 39.

Mayer, K. 1996. "Helen and the *Dios Boulē.*" *AJP* 117: 1–15.

Mazzaro, V. 1978. "Herodotos' Account of the Battle of Marathon and the Picture in the Stoa Poikile." *AntCl* 47: 458–475.

McAllister, M. 1959. "The Temple of Ares at Athens." *Hesperia* 28: 1–64.

McNeal, R. A. 1991. "Archaeology and the Destruction of the Later Athenian Acropolis." *Antiquity* 65: 49–63.

McNiven, T. J. 1982. "Gestures in Attic Vase Painting: Use and Meaning 550–450 B.C." Ph.D. diss., University of Michigan.

———. 2000. "Behaving Like an Other: Telltale Gestures in Athenian Vase Painting." In Cohen 2000, 71–97.

Meiggs, R. 1972. *The Athenian Empire.* Oxford.

Meiggs, R., and D. Lewis, eds. 1988. *A Selection of Greek Historical Inscriptions to the End of the Fifth Century* B.C. Oxford.

Merewether, C. 1997. "Traces of Loss." In *Irresistible Decay: Ruins Reclaimed,* edited by M. S. Roth, C. Lyons, and C. Merewether, 25–40. Los Angeles.

Meritt, L. S. 1970. "The Stoa Poikile." *Hesperia* 39: 233–264.

Metzler, D. 1964. "Ein neues Porträt des Phidias." *AntK* 7: 51–55.

Michaelis, A. 1871. *Der Parthenon.* Leipzig.

Middeldorf Kosegarten, A. 1996. *Die Domfassade in Orvieto.* Berlin.

Miles, M. M. 1980. "The Date of the Temple on the Ilissos River." *Hesperia* 49: 309–325.

———. 1989. "A Reconstruction of the Temple of Nemesis at Rhamnous." *Hesperia* 58: 131–249.

Miller, J. Griffin. 1995. "Temple and Statue: A Study of Practices in Ancient Greece." Ph.D. diss., Bryn Mawr College.

———. 1997. "Temple and Image: Did All Greek Temples House Cult Images?" *AJA* 101: 345.

Miller, M. C. 1995. "Priam, King of Troy." In Carter and Morris 1995, 449–465. Austin.

———. 1997. *Athens and Persia in the Fifth Century* B.C.: *A Study in Cultural Receptivity.* Cambridge.

———. 2000. "The Myth of Bousiris: Ethnicity and Art." In Cohen 2000, 413–442.

Möbius, H. 1928. "Zu Ilissosfries und Nikebalustrade." *AM* 53: 1–8.

———. 1935–1936. "Das Metroon in Agrai und sein Fries." *AM* 60–61: 234–268.

———. 1964. *Alexandria und Rom, AbhMünchen* 59.

Moltesen, M. 1995. *Catalogue Ny Carlsberg Glyptotek: Greece in the Classical Period.* Copenhagen.

Molyneux, J. H. 1992. *Simonides: A Historical Study.* Wauconda.

Mommsen, H. 1997. *Exekias I, Die Grabtafeln.* Mainz.

Montague, J. Earl of Sandwich. 1799. *A Voyage Performed By the Late Earl of Sandwich Round the Mediterranean in the Years 1738 and 1739 Written By Himself . . . To Which Are Prefixed, Memoirs of the Noble Author's Life, By John Cooke.* London.

Morgan, L. 1997. "Achilleae Comae: Hair and Heroism According to Domitian." *CQ* 47: 209–214.

Morris, I. 2000. *Archaeology as Cultural History: Words and Things in Iron Age Greece.* Oxford.

Morris, S. P. 1992. *Daidalos and the Origins of Greek Art.* Princeton.

———. 1995. "The Sacrifice of Astyanax: Near Eastern Contributions to the Siege of Troy." In Carter and Morris 1995, 221–245.

Mountjoy, P. A. 1999. *Regional Mycenaean Decorated Pottery.* Rahden. Westfalen.

Mylonas, G. E. 1961, *Eleusis and the Eleusinian Mysteries.* Princeton.

Nagy, G. 1990. *Pindar's Homer.* Baltimore.

Neer, R. T. 2002. *Style and Politics in Athenian Vase Painting: The Craft of Democracy, ca. 530–460* B.C.E. Cambridge.

Neils, J. 1983. "A Greek Nativity by the Meidias Painter." *BClevMus* 70: 274–289.

———. 2000. "Who's Who on the Berlin Foundry Cup." In Mattusch, Brauer, and Knudsen 2000, 75–80.

———. 2001. *The Parthenon Frieze.* Cambridge.

Neils, J., and J. H. Oakley. 2003. *Coming of Age in Ancient Greece: Images of Childhood from the Classical Past.* New Haven.

Neitzel, H. 1976. "Pandora und das Fass." *Hermes* 104: 387–419.

Neumann, G. 1965. *Gesten und Gebärden in der griechischen Kunst.* Berlin.

New York Times, Int'l. News, May 6, 2000: 40, and October 14, 2001: B3.

Nilsson, M. P. 1902. *Das Ei im Totenkult.* Lund.

Nock, A. D. 1930. "Σάννασς Θεός." *HSCP* 41: 1–62.

Noica, S. 1984. "La Boîte de Pandore et l'ambiguïté de l'elpis," *Platon* 36: 100–124.

Oakley, J. H. 1987. "A Calyx-krater in Virginia by the Nikias Painter with the Birth of Erichthonios." *AK* 30: 123–130.

———. 1997. *The Achilles Painter.* Mainz.

———. 1999. "'Through a Glass Darkly' I: Some Misconceptions about the Study of Greek Vase-Painting." In *Proceedings of the XVth International Congress of Classical Archaeology, Amsterdam, July 12–17, 1998,* edited by R. Docter and E. Moormann, 286–290. Amsterdam.

———. 2001. "Die Ursprünge der attisch-weissgrundigen Lekythos." In *'Gab es das griechische Wunder?' Griechenland zwischen dem Ende des 6. und der Mitte des 5. Jahrhunderts v. Chr. Tagungsbeiträge des 16. Fachsymposiums der Alexander von Humboldt-Stiftung veranstaltet vom 5. bis 9. April 1999 in Freiburg im Breisgau,* edited by D. Papenfuss and V. M. Strocka, 101–112. Mainz.

———. 2003. "Classical Athenian Ritual Vases." In *The Diniacopolous Collection in Quebec: Greek and Roman Antiquities,* edited by J. M. Fossey and J. E. Francis. Montreal.

———. Forthcoming. *Picturing Death in Classical Athens: The Evidence of the White Lekythoi.* Cambridge.

Oberleitner, W. 1994. *Das Heroon von Trysa.* Mainz.

Ogden, D. 1998. "What Was in Pandora's Box?" In *Archaic Greece: New Approaches and New Evidence,* edited by N. Fisher and H. van Wees, 213–230. London.

Onians, J. 1999. *Classical Art and the Cultures of Greece and Rome.* New Haven.

Osborne, M. J. 1983. *Naturalization in Athens,* Vols. 3–4. Brussels.

Osborne, R. 1983–1984. "The Myth of Propaganda and the Propaganda of Myth." *Hephaistos* 5–6: 61–70.

———. 1985. "The Erection and Mutilation of the Hermai." *PCPS* 23: 47–73.

———. 1987. "The Viewing and Obscuring of the Parthenon Frieze." *JHS* 107: 98–105.

———. 1988. "Death Revisited; Death Revised. The Death of the Artist in Archaic and Classical Greece." *Art History* 11: 1–16.

———. 1989. "A Crisis in Archaeological History? The Seventh Century B.C. in Attica." *BSA* 84: 297–322.

———. 1991. "Whose Image and Superscription Is This?" *Arion* 3rd ser. 1.2: 255–275.

———. 1994a. "Framing the Centaur: Reading Fifth-Century Architectural Sculpture." In *Art and Text in Ancient Greek Culture,* edited by S. Goldhill and R. Osborne, 52–84, with notes on 289–291. Cambridge.

———. 1994b. "Looking on—Greek Style. Does the Sculpted Girl Speak to Women too?" In *Classical Greece: Ancient Histories and Modern Archeologies,* edited by I. Morris, 81–96. Cambridge.

———. 1996. "Desiring Women on Athenian Pottery." In *Sexuality in Ancient Art,* edited by N. B. Kampen, 65–80. Cambridge.

———. 1997. "Men without Clothes: Heroic Nakedness and Greek Art." *Gender and History* 9: 504–528.

———. 1998. *Archaic and Classical Greek Art.* Oxford.

———. 2000a. "Archaic and Classical Greek Temple Sculpture and the Viewer." In Rutter and Sparkes 2000, 228–246.

———. 2000b. "An Other View: An Essay in Political History." In Cohen 2000, 23–42.

Overbeck, J. 1868. *Die antiken Schriftquellen zur Geschichte der bildenden Künsten bei den Griechen,* Leipzig.

Pache, C. 2001. "Barbarian Bond: Thracian Bendis among the Athenians." In *Between Magic and Religion: Interdisciplinary Studies in Ancient Mediterranean Religion and Society,* edited by S. R. Asirvatham, C. O. Pache, and J. Watrous, 3–11. Lanham, MD.

Page, D. L. 1981. *Further Greek Epigrams.* Cambridge.

Palagia, O. 1990. "A New Relief of the Graces and the *Charites* of Socrates." In *Opes Atticae for R. Bogaert and H. Van Looy,* edited by M. Geerard, 347–356. The Hague.

———. 1993. *The Pediments of the Parthenon.* Leiden.

———. 1997a. "First among Equals: Athena in the East Pediment of the Parthenon." In Buitron-Oliver 1997, 28–49.

———. 1997b. "Reflections on the Piraeus Bronzes." In *Greek Offerings: Essays on Greek Art in Honour of John Boardman,* 177–195. Oxford.

———. 1998. Review of *Understanding Greek Sculpture: Ancient Meanings, Modern Readings,* by N. Spivey. *JHS* 118: 245–247.

———. 1999. "'Through a Glass Darkly' II: Misconceptions about the Study of Greek Sculpture." In *Proceedings of the XVth International Congress of Classical Archaeology, Amsterdam, July 12–17, 1998,* edited by R. Docter and E. Moormann, 296–299. Amsterdam.

———. 2000. "Meaning and Narrative Techniques in Statue-Bases of the Pheidian Circle." In Sparkes and Rutter 2000, 53–78.

Palagia, O., and J. J. Pollitt, eds. 1996. *Personal Styles in Greek Sculpture, Yale Classical Studies* 30. Cambridge.

Panofsky, D., and E. Panofsky. 1962. *Pandora's Box: The*

Changing Aspects of a Mythical Symbol. Bollingen Series 52. 2nd ed. New York.

Panofsky, E. 1939. *Studies in Iconology: Humanistic Themes in the Art of the Renaissance.* New York.

———. 1982. *Meaning in the Visual Arts.* Chicago.

Papageorgiou-Venetas, A. 1994. *Athens: The Ancient Heritage and the Historic Cityscape in a Modern Metropolis.* The Archaeological Society at Athens Library 140. Athens.

Parke, H. W. 1977. *Festivals of the Athenians.* London.

Parker, R. 1996. *Athenian Religion: A History.* Oxford.

Patroni, G. 1900. *Vasi dipinti del Museo Vivenzio.* Rome and Naples.

Paul, E. 1995. *Schwarzfigurige Vasen.* Kleine Reihe des Antiken-museums der Universität Leipzig 1. Leipzig.

Pauw, D. A. 1980. "Impersonal Expressions and Unidentified Spokesmen in Greek and Roman Historiography and Biography." *Acta Classica* 23: 83–95.

Payne, H. G. G. 1931. *Necrocorinthia.* Oxford.

Pedley, J. 1990. *Paestum: Greeks and Romans in Southern Italy.* New York.

Pélékides, C. 1962. *Histoire de l'éphébie attique des origines à 31 avant Jésus-Christ.* Paris.

Pelling, C. B. R. 1979. "Plutarch's Method of Work in the Roman Lives." *JHS* 99: 74–96.

———. 1988. *Plutarch. Life of Antony.* Cambridge.

Pemberton, E. G. 1972. "The East and West Friezes of the Temple of Athena Nike." *AJA* 76: 303–310.

———. 1977. "The Name Vase of the Peleus Painter." *JWalt* 36: 62–72.

———. 1989. "The Beginning of Monumental Painting in Mainland Greece." In *Studia Pompeiana & Classica in Honor of Wilhelmina F. Jashemski,* edited by R. I. Curtis, 181–197. New Rochelle, NY.

———. 1990. "*Agalma* and *Xoanon:* Greek Cults and Cult Statues (The Allen Memorial Lecture 1989)." *Iris* (Journal of the Classical Association of Victoria) n.s. 3: 1–14.

Penglase, C. 1994. *Greek Myths and Mesopotamia: Parallels and Influence in the Homeric Hymns and Hesiod.* London.

Pérec, G. 1969. *La Disparition.* Paris.

Petrakos, V. C. 1981. "La Base de la Némésis d'Agoracrite." *BCH* 105: 227–253.

———. 1986. "Provlimata tes Vases tou agalmatos tes Nemeseos." In *Archaische und klassische griechische Plastik,* edited by H. Kyrieleis, vol. 2, 89–107. Mainz.

Pflugk-Harttung, J. von. 1884. *Perikles als Feldheer.* Stuttgart.

Pfuhl, E. 1923. *Malerei und Zeichnung der Griechen.* Munich.

Picón, C. A. 1978. "The Ilissos Temple Reconsidered." *AJA* 82: 47–81.

Pinney, G. F. 1984. "For the Heroes Are at Hand." *JHS* 104: 181–183.

Pirenne-Delforge, V. 1988. "Epithètes cultuelles et interprétation philosophique: À propos d'Aphrodite Ourania et Pandémos à Athènes." *AntCl* 57: 142–157.

———. 1991. "Le Culte de la Persuasion: Peitho en Grèce ancienne." *RHR* 208: 395–413.

———. 1994. *L'Aphrodite grecque. Kernos* Suppl. 4. Liège.

Pococke, R. 1743–1754. *A Description of the East, and Some Other Countries.* 3 vols. London.

Pollitt, J. J. 1972. *Art and Experience in Classical Greece.* Cambridge.

———. 1974. *The Ancient View of Greek Art: Criticism, History, and Terminology.* New Haven.

———. 1976. "The Ethos of Polygnotos and Aristeides." In *In memoriam Otto J. Brendel: Essays in Archaeology and the Humanities,* edited by L. Bonfante and H. von Heintze, 49–54. Mainz.

———. 1978. "The Impact of Greek Art on Rome." *TAPA* 108: 155–174.

———. 1983. Reprint. *The Art of Rome c. 753 B.C.–A.D. 337: Sources and Documents.* Cambridge; original edition, Englewood Cliffs, NJ, 1966.

———. 1985. "Early Greek Art in a Platonic Universe." In *Greek Art. Archaic into Classical. A Symposium Held at the University of Cincinnati,* April 2–3, 1982, edited by C. G. Boulter, 96–112. Leiden.

———. 1986. *Art in the Hellenistic Age.* Cambridge.

———. 1987. "Pots, Politics and Personifications in Early Classical Athens." *YaleBull* 40: 8–15.

———. 1990a. *The Art of Ancient Greece: Sources and Documents.* Rev. ed. Cambridge.

———. 1990b. "The Meaning of Pheidias' Athena Parthenos." In *The Nashville Athena* (symposium sponsored by the Tennessee Humanities Council and the Department of Classical Studies of Vanderbilt University, May 21, 1990), 21–23.

———. 1992a. "Art: Archaic to Classical." *CAH,* 2nd ed., 5, 171–183.

———. 1992b. "Art, Politics, and Thought in Classical Greece." In *The Greek Miracle,* edited by D. Buitron-Oliver, 31–44. Washington, DC.

———. 1996. "Introduction: Masters and Masterworks in the Study of Classical Sculpture." In Palagia and Pollitt, 1–15.

———. 1997. "The Meaning of the Parthenon Frieze." In Buitron-Oliver 1997, 51–63.

———. 2000. "Patriotism and the West Pediment of the Parthenon." In *Periplous: Papers on Classical Art and Archaeology Presented to Sir John Boardman,* edited by G. R. Tsetskhladze, A. J. N. W. Prag, and A. M. Snodgrass, 220–227. London.

Porter, J. 1993. "The Seductions of Gorgias." *CA* 12: 267–299.

Pounder, R. 1983. "A Hellenistic Arsenal in Athens." *Hesperia* 52: 233–256.

Poursat, J. C. 1968. "La Danse armée dans la céramique attique." *BCH* 92: 550–615.

Prange, M. 1989. *Der Niobidenmaler und seine Werkstatt: Untersuchungen zu einer Vasenwerkstatt frühklassischer Zeit.* Frankfurt am Main.

Praschniker, C. 1928. *Parthenonstudien.* Augsburg.

Preisshofen, F. 1974. "Phidias-Daedalus auf dem Schild der Athena Parthenos?" *JdI* 89: 50–69.

———. 1984. "Zur Funktion des Parthenon nach den schriftlichen Quellen." In Berger 1984, 15–18. Mainz.

Price, M. J., and B. L. Trell. 1977. *Coins and Their Cities: Architecture on the Ancient Coins of Greece, Rome, and Palestine.* London.

Pritchett, W. K. 1985. *The Greek State at War.* Vol. 4. Berkeley.

———. 1994. *Essays in Greek History.* Amsterdam.

Protzmann, H. 1984. "Antiquarische Nachlese zu den Statuen der sogenannte Lemnia Furtwänglers in Dresden." *Jahrbuch der staatlichen Kunstsammlungen Dresden* 16: 7–22.

Pucci, P. 1977. *Hesiod and the Language of Poetry.* Baltimore.

Raeck, W. 1981. *Zum Barbarenbild in der Kunst Athens im 6. und 5. Jahrhundert v. Chr.* Bonn.

Raubitschek, A. E. 1949. *Dedications from the Athenian Acropolis.* Cambridge, MA.

Reber, K. 1998. "Das Hephaisteion in Athen—Ein Monument für die Demokratie." *JdI* 113: 1–48.

Reeder, E. D. 1995. "Women and Men in Classical Greece." In Reeder, ed., 1995, 20–30.

———, ed. 1995. *Pandora: Women in Classical Greece.* Baltimore.

Rehak, P. 1998. "Unfinished Hair and the Installation of the Pedimental Sculptures of the Temple of Zeus at Olympia." In Hartswick and Sturgeon 1998, 193–208.

Reilly, J. 1989. "Many Brides: 'Mistress and Maid' on Athenian Lekythoi." *Hesperia* 58: 411–444.

Reiner, E. 1938. *Die rituelle Totenklage der Griechen.* Stuttgart.

Renfroe, W. J., Jr. 1990. Reprint. *Warfare in Antiquity* (translation of H. Delbrück, *Die Strategie des Perikles, erlaütert durch die Strategie Friedrichs des Grossen.* Original edition, Berlin 1890; reprint Westport, CT).

Revermann, M. 1997. "Cratinus' Διονυσαλέξανδρος and the Head of Pericles." *JHS* 117: 197–200.

Rhodes, R. F. 1995. *Architecture and Meaning on the Athenian Acropolis.* Cambridge.

Rhomiopoulou, K. 1997. *Greco-Roman Sculpture in the National Archaeological Museum in Athens.* Athens.

Richlin, A. 1995. "Making up a Woman: The Face of Roman Gender." In *Off with Her Head! The Denial of Women's Identity in Myth, Religion, and Culture,* edited by H. Eilberg-Schwartz and W. Doniger, 185–213. Berkeley.

———. 1998. "Foucault's History: Useful for Women?" In *Rethinking Sexuality: Foucault and Classical Antiquity,* edited by D. H. J. Larmour, P. A. Miller, and C. Platter, 138–170. Princeton.

Richter, G. M. A. 1930. *The Sculpture and Sculptors of the Greeks.* New Haven.

———. 1955. *Greek Portraits.* Brussels.

Richter, G. M. A., and L. F. Hall. 1936. *Red-figured Athenian Vases in the Metropolitan Museum of Art.* New Haven.

Richter, G. M. A., and R. R. R. Smith. 1984. Reprint. *The Portraits of the Greeks.* Oxford; original edition, London 1965.

Ridgway, B. S. 1970. *The Severe Style in Greek Sculpture.* Princeton.

———. 1981. *Fifth Century Styles in Greek Sculpture.* Princeton.

———. 1985. "Late Archaic Sculpture." In *Greek Art. Archaic into Classical,* edited by C. G. Boulter, 1–17. Cincinnati Classical Studies n.s. 5. Leiden.

———. 1990. *Hellenistic Sculpture I: The Styles of ca. 331–200 B.C.* Madison.

———. 1992. "Images of Athena on the Akropolis." In *Goddess and Polis. The Panathenaic Festival in Ancient Athens,* edited by J. Neils, 119–142. Princeton.

———. 1993. *The Archaic Style in Greek Sculpture.* 2nd rev. ed. Chicago.

———. 1994. "The Study of Classical Sculpture at the End of the 20th Century." *AJA* 98: 759–772.

———. 1997. *Fourth Century Styles in Greek Sculpture.* Madison.

———. 1999. *Prayers in Stone: Greek Architectural Sculpture (ca. 600–100 B.C.E.).* Berkeley.

———. 2000. *Hellenistic Sculpture II: The Styles of ca. 200–100 B.C.* Madison.

Ridley, R. T. 1979. "The Hoplite as Citizen: Athenian Military Institutions in their Social Context." *AntCl* 48: 508–548.

Robert, C. 1895. *Die Marathonschlacht in der Poikile und weiteres über Polygnot. HallWPr* 18.

———. 1923. "ΚΥΝΗΤΙΝΔΑ." In *Studien zur Kunst des Ostens, Festschrift J. Strzygowski,* edited by H. Glück, 58–65. Vienna.

Robertson, M. 1952. "The Hero with Two Swords." *JWarb* 15: 99–100.

———. 1967. "Conjectures in Polygnotus' Troy." *BSA* 62: 5–12.

———. 1975. *A History of Greek Art.* Cambridge.

———. 1984. "The South Metopes: Theseus and Daidalos." In Berger 1984, 206–208.

———. 1991. "Adopting an Approach I." In *Looking at Greek Vases,* edited by T. Rasmussen and N. Spivey, 1–12. Cambridge.

———. 1992. *The Art of Vase-painting in Classical Athens.* Cambridge.

———. 1995. "Menelaos and Helen in Troy." In Carter and Morris 1995, 431–436.

Robertson, M., and A. Frantz. 1975. *The Parthenon Frieze.* London.

Robertson, N. 1999. "The Stoa of the Herms." *ZPE* 127: 167–172.

Rogers, P., L. Jørgensen, and A. Rast-Eichler, eds. 1990. *Hellenistic Sculpture I: The Styles of ca. 331–200 B.C.* Madison.

———, 2001. *The Roman Textile Industry and Its Influence.* Oxford.

Romano, I. B. 1982. "Early Greek Cult Images and Cult Practices." Ph.D. diss., University of Pennsylvania, 1980.

———. 2000. "The Dreros *Sphyrelata:* A Re-examination of Date and Function." In Mattusch, Brauer, and Knudsen 2000, 40–50.

Rose, C. B. 1997. "The Imperial Image in the Eastern Mediterranean." In *The Early Roman Empire in the East,* Oxbow Monograph 5, edited by S. Alcock, 108–120. Oxford.

Rosivach, V. J. 1987. "Autochthony and the Athenians." *CQ* 37: 294–305.

Ross, L. 1855–1856. *Archäologische Aufsätze.* 2 vols. Leipzig.

———. 1863. *Erinnerungen und Mittheilungen aus Griechenland.* Berlin.

Ross, L., E. Schaubert, and C. Hansen. 1839. *Die Akropolis von Athen nach den neuesten Ausgrabungen.* Vol. 1, *Der Tempel der Nike Apteros.* Berlin.

Rostovtzeff, M. 1941. *The Social and Economic History of the Hellenistic World.* Oxford.

———. 1957. *The Social and Economic History of the Roman Empire.* Edited by P. M. Fraser. Oxford.

Ruskin, J. 1849. "The Lamp of Memory." In *The Genius of John Ruskin,* edited by J. D. Rosenberg, 131–138. Boston, 1963.

Russell, D. 1973. *Plutarch.* London.

———. 1983. *Greek Declamation.* Cambridge.

———. 1995. "On Reading Plutarch's *Lives.*" In Scardigli 1995, 75–94.

Rutter, N. K., and B. A. Sparkes, eds. 2000. *Word and Image in Ancient Greece.* Edinburgh.

Ryle, J. 2000. "Miracles of the Sacred Grove: Review of Hair in African Art and Culture." *TLS,* April 21: 18–19.

Sahlins, M. 1996. *Waiting for Foucault.* 2nd ed. Prickly Pear Pamphlet no. 2. Cambridge.

Saller, R., and P. Garnsey. 1987. *The Social and Economic History of the Roman Empire.* Berkeley.

Sauer, B. 1899. *Das sogenannte Theseion und sein plastischer Schmuck.* Berlin.

Sauter, E. 2002. "Ein Relief aus Epidauros, Athen Nationalmuseum Inv. 1425 und 142b." *AntPl* 28: 125–162.

Scarborough, J. 1969. *Roman Medicine.* Ithaca.

Scardigli, B., ed. 1995. *Essays on Plutarch's Lives.* Oxford.

Schauenburg, B. 1975. "*Eurymedon Eimi.*" *AM* 90: 97–122.

Schefold, K. 1967. *Classical Greece.* Translated by J. R. Foster. London.

Schefold, K., and F. Jung. 1981. *Die Göttersage in der klassischen und hellenistischen Kunst.* Munich.

———. 1988. *Die Urkönige, Perseus, Bellerophon, Herakles und Theseus in der klassischen und hellenistischen Kunst.* Munich.

Schiering, W. 1991. *Die Werkstatt des Pheidias in Olympia 2: Werkstattfünde. Olympische Forschungen* 18. Berlin.

Schliemann, H. 1874. *Trojanische Altertümer: Bericht über die Ausgrabungen in Troja.* Leipzig.

Schlörb, B. 1964. *Untersuchungen zur Bildhauergeneration nach Phidias.* Waldsassen.

Schmaltz, B. 1983. *Griechische Grabreliefs.* Darmstadt.

Schmidt, I. 1995. *Hellenistische Statuenbasen.* Frankfurt am Main.

Schnapp, A. 1997. *The Discovery of the Past.* New York.

Schnurr-Redford, C. 1996. *Frauen in klassischen Athen: Sozialer Raum und reale Bewegungsfreiheit.* Berlin.

Schöne, A. 1990. "Die Hydria des Meidias-Malers im Kerameikos." *AM* 105: 163–178.

Schrader, H. 1932. "Komposition und Herkunft des Niobenfrieses aus dem 5. Jahrhundert." *JdI* 47: 151–190.

Schreiner, J. H. 1988. "The Battle of Oinoe and the Credibility of Thukydides." In *Studies in Ancient History and Numismatics Presented to Rudi Thomsen,* edited by A. Damsgaard-Madsen et al., 71–76. Aarhus.

Schuchhardt, W.-H. 1977. *Alkamenes.* Berlin.

Schultz, P. 2001. "The Akroteria of the Temple of Athena Nike." *Hesperia* 70: 1–47.

———. 2003a. "History and Image on the Nike Temple Frieze." Paper presented at the annual meeting of the Archaeological Institute of America, January 3–6, 2003, in New Orleans. Abstract retrieved June 2004 from http://www.archaeological.org/webinfo.php?page=10123

———. 2003b. "The Stoa Poikile, Nike Temple Bastion and Cleon's Shields from Pylos: A Note on *Knights* 843–853." *Numismatica e antichita classiche* 32: 43–62.

Schwab, K. 1988. "The Parthenon Metopes and Greek Vase Painting." Ph.D. diss. New York University.

Schwarze, J. 1971. *Die Beurteilung des Perikles durch die attische Komödie und ihre historiographische Bedeutung.* Munich.

Sear, D. R. 1982. *Greek Imperial Coins and Their Values: The Local Coinages of the Roman Empire.* London.

Séchan, L. 1929. "Pandora, l'Ève grecque." *BAssBudé* 23: 3–36.

Sewell, W. H. 1999. "The Concept(s) of Culture." In *Beyond the Cultural Turn: New Directions in the Study of Society and Culture,* edited by V. E. Bonnell and L. Hunt, 35–61. Berkeley.

Shanks, M. 1996. *Classical Archaeology of Greece: Experiences of the Discipline.* London.

———. 1997. "Photography and Archaeology." In *The Cultural Life of Images,* edited by B. Molyneaux, 71–107. London.

———. 1999. *Art and the Greek City State: An Interpretive Archaeology.* Cambridge.

Shapiro, H. A. 1981. *Art, Myth, and Culture: Greek Vases from Southern Collections.* New Orleans.

———. 1986. "The Origins of Allegory in Greek Art." *Boreas* 9: 4–23.

———. 1989. *Art and Cult under the Tyrants in Athens.* Mainz.

———. 1992. "Theseus in Kimonian Athens: The Iconography of Empire." *Mediterranean Historical Review* 7: 29–49.

———. 1993. *Personifications in Greek Art: The Representation of Abstract Concepts 600–400 B.C.* Kilchberg.

———. 1994. *Myth Into Art: Poet and Painter in Classical Greece.* London.

———. 1995. "The Cult of Heroines: Kekrops' Daughters." In Reeder 1995, 39–48.

———. 1998. "Autochthony and the Visual Arts in Fifth-Century Athens." In *Democracy, Empire, and the Arts in Fifth-Century Athens,* edited by D. Boedeker and K. A. Raaflaub, 127–151. Cambridge, MA.

———. 1999. "Cult Warfare: The Dioskouroi between Sparta and Athens." In *Ancient Greek Hero Cult,* edited by R. Hägg, 99–107. Stockholm.

———. 2000a. "Helen Out of Doors." In *Periplous: Papers on Classical Art and Archaeology Presented to Sir John Boardman,* edited by G. R. Tsetskhladze, A. J. N. W. Prag, and A. M. Snodgrass, 271–275. London.

———. 2000b. "Modest Athletes and Liberated Women: Etruscans on Attic Black-figure Vases." In Cohen 2000, 315–337.

Shear, I. M. 1963. "Kallikrates." *Hesperia* 32: 375–424.

Shear, J. L. 2003. "Commemorating Democratic Victory: War Memorials in the Athenian Agora." Paper presented at the annual meeting of the Archaeological Institute of America, January 3–6, in New Orleans. Abstract retrieved June 2004 from http://www.archaeological.org/webinfo.php?page=10123

Shear, T. L., Jr. 1984. "The Athenian Agora: Excavations of 1980–1982." *Hesperia* 53: 1–57.

Siewert, P. 1977. "The Ephebic Oath in Fifth-Century Athens." *JHS* 97: 102–111.

Simon, E. 1963. "Polygnotan Painting and the Niobid Painter." *AJA* 67: 43–62.

———. 1968. "Tereus: Zur Deutung der Würzburger Schauspieler-Scherbe." In *Festschrift des Kronberg-Gymnasiums Aschaffenburg,* 155–167. Aschaffenburg.

———. 1975. "Versuch einer Deutung der Süd-metopen des Parthenon." *JdI* 90: 100–120.

———. 1981. *Die griechischen Vasen.* Munich.

———. 1985–1986. "Τα γλυπτά του ναού και του θωρακείου της Αθηνάς Νίκης," *Arkhaiognosia* 4: 11–28.

———. 1986. *Augustus: Kunst und Leben in Rom um die Zeitenwende.* Munich.

Sissa, G. 1990. *Greek Virginity.* Translated by A. Goldhammer. Cambridge, MA.

Skias, A. 1894. "Ανάγλυφα ἐκ τῆς ἐν τῇ κοίτῃ τοῦ Ἰλισσοῦ ἀνασκαφῆς," *ArchEph:* 133–142.

———. 1897. "Ανασκαφαὶ παρὰ τον Ἰλισσόν," *Prakt:* 73–85.

Smith, A. C. 1999. "Eurymedon and the Evolution of Political Personifications in the Early Classical Period." *JHS* 119: 128–141.

Smith, A. H. 1910. *The Sculptures of the Parthenon.* London.

———. 1916. "Lord Elgin and His Collection." *JHS* 36: 163–372.

Smith, R. R. R. 1998. "Cultural Choice and Political Identity in Honorific Portrait Statues in the Greek East in the Second Century A.D." *JRS* 88: 56–93.

Snodgrass, A. M. 1967. *Arms and Armour of the Greeks.* Ithaca.

———. 1986. "Interaction by Design: The Greek City State." In *Peer Polity Interaction and Socio-Political Change,* edited by C. Renfrew and J. F. Cherry, 47–58. Cambridge.

———. 1998. *Homer and the Artists.* Cambridge.

Sourvinou-Inwood, C. 1985. "Altars with Palm-Trees, Palm-Trees and Parthenoi." *BICS* 32: 125–146.

Sparkes, B. A. 1991. *Greek Art.* Greece & Rome, New Surveys in the Classics no. 22. Oxford.

———. 1996. *The Red and the Black: Studies in Greek Pottery.* London.

———. 1997. "Some Greek Images of Others." In *The Cultural Life of Images: Visual Representation in Archaeology,* edited by B. Molyneaux, 138–158. London.

Sparkes, B. A., and L. Talcott, 1970. *Black and Plain Pottery of the 6th, 5th, and 4th Centuries B.C. Agora* 12. Princeton.

Spawforth, A., and S. Walker. 1985. "The World of the Panhellion, I. Athens and Eleusis," *JRS* 75: 78–104.

Spence, I. G. 1993. *The Cavalry of Classical Greece.* Oxford.

Spivey, N. 1996. *Understanding Greek Sculpture: Ancient Meanings, Modern Readings.* London.

Spon, J. 1678. *Voyage d'Italie, de Dalmatie et du Levant.* Lyon.

Spon, J., and G. Wheler. 1678. *Voyage d'Italie, de Dalmatie, de Grèce, et du Levant fait aux années 1675 and 1676.* Lyon.

Stadter, P. 1989. *A Commentary on Plutarch's Pericles.* Chapel Hill.

———. 1995. "Plutarch's Comparison of Pericles and Fabius Maximus." In Scardigli 1995, 155–164.

Stafford, E. 2000. *Worshipping Virtues: Personification and the Divine in Ancient Greece.* London.

Stähler, K. 1992. *Griechische Geschichtsbilder klassischer Zeit* Münster.

Stansbury-O'Donnell, M. D. 1989. "Polygnotos's *Iliupersis:* A New Reconstruction." *AJA* 93: 203–215.

———. 1990. "Polygnotos's *Nekyia:* A Reconstruction and Analysis." *AJA* 94: 213–235.

———. 1999. *Pictorial Narrative in Ancient Greek Art.* Cambridge.

Stevens, G. P. 1946. "The Northeast Corner of the Parthenon." *Hesperia* 15: 1–26.

———. 1955. "Remarks upon the Colossal Chryselephantine Statue of Athena in the Parthenon." *Hesperia* 24: 240–276.

Stewart, A. 1985. "History, Myth, and Allegory in the Program of the Temple of Athena Nike, Athens." In *Pictorial Narrative in Antiquity and the Middle Ages, Studies in the History of Art* 16, edited by H. L. Kessler and M. Shreve Simpson, 53–73. Washington, DC.

———. 1990. *Greek Sculpture: An Exploration.* New Haven.

———. 1995. "Imag(in)ing the Other: Amazons and Ethnicity in Fifth-Century Athens." *Poetics Today* 16:4: 571–597.

———. 1997. *Art, Desire, and the Body in Ancient Greece.* Cambridge.

Stillman, W. J. 1870. *The Acropolis of Athens, Illustrated Picturesquely and Architecturally in Photography.* London.

———. 1901. *Autobiography of a Journalist.* 2 vols. Boston.

Strauss, B. S. 1993. *Fathers and Sons in Athens.* Princeton.

Stuart, J., and N. Revett. 1762–1830. *The Antiquities of Athens Measured and Delineated by James Stuart and Nicholas Revett.* 5 vols. London.

Stuart Jones, H. 1912. *The Sculptures of the Museo Capitolino.* Oxford.

Studniczka, F. 1916. "Zu den Friesplatten vom ionischen Tempel am Ilissos." *JdI* 31: 169–230.

Stupperich, R. 1977. *Staatsbegräbnis und Privatgrabmal im klassischen Athen.* Münster.

Sutton, R. F. 1997–1998. "The Visual Discourse of Marriage in Classical Athens." *JWalt* 55–56: 27–48.

———. 2000. "The Good, the Bad, and the Ugly: The Drunken Orgy in Attic Vase Painting and the Athenian Self." In Cohen 2000, 180–202.

Svoboda, K. 1934. "Les idées esthétiques de Plutarque." *Mélanges Bidez,* edited by M. R. Werner et al., 917–946. Brussels.

Swain, S. 1990. "Review of *A Commentary on Plutarch's Pericles,* P. A. Stadter," *Ploutarchos* 6: 76–79.

———. 1996. *Hellenism and Empire: Language, Classicism and Power in the Greek World, A.D. 50–250.* Oxford.

Tanner, J. 1999. "Culture, Social Structure and the Status of Visual Artists in Classical Greece." *PCPS* 45: 136–175.

Tanoulas, T. 1987. "The Propylaea of the Acropolis at Athens since the Seventeenth Century: Their Decay and Restoration." *JdI* 102: 413–483.

Taylor, J. G. 1998. "Oinoe and the Painted Stoa: Ancient and Modern Misunderstandings." *AJP* 119: 223–243.

Thomas, Renata. 1981. *Athletenstatuetten der Spätarchaik und des strengen Stils.* Rome.

Thomas, Rosalind. 1998. *Herodotus in Context: Ethnography, Science, and the Art of Persuasion.* Cambridge.

Thompson, H. A. 1961. "The Panathenaic Festival." *AA:* 223–231.

———. 1962. "The Sculptural Adornment of the Hephaisteion." *AJA* 66: 341–347.

Thompson, H. A., and R. E. Wycherley. 1972. *The Agora of Athens. Agora* 14. Princeton.

Tobin, J. 1997. *Herodes Attikos and the City of Athens: Patronage and Conflict under the Antonines.* Amsterdam.

Touchefeu-Meynier, O. 1968. *Thèmes odysséens dans l'art antique.* Paris.

Trancsényi-Waldapfel, I. 1955. "The Pandora Myth," *Acta Ethnographica Académiae Hungaricae* 4: 99–126.

Trendall, A. D. 1967. *The Red-Figured Vases of Lucania, Campania, and Sicily.* Oxford.

———. 1983. *The Red-Figured Vases of Lucania, Campania, and Sicily.* Suppl. 3.

———. 1987. *The Red-Figured Vases of Paestum.* Hertford.

Trendall, A. D., and T. B. L. Webster. 1971. *Illustrations of Greek Drama.* London.

Trianti, I. 1998. *Το Μουσείο Ακροπόλεως.* Athens.

Tsiaphake, D. 1998. *Η Θράκη στην Αττική εικονογραφία του 5ου αιώνα π.Χ.* Komotene.

Tuchelt, K. 1986. "Einige Überlegungen zum Kanachos-Apollon von Didyma." *JdI* 101: 75–84.

Turcan, R. 1996. *The Cults of the Roman Empire.* Translated by A. Neville. Oxford.

Tyrrell, W. B. 1980. *Amazons: A Study in Athenian Mythmaking.* Baltimore.

Tyrrell, W. B., and L. J. Bennett. 1999. "Pericles' Muting of Women's Voices in Thuc. 2.45.2." *CJ* 95: 37–51.

Untersteiner, M. 1954. *The Sophists.* Oxford.

Vanderpool, E. 1974. "Victories in the Anthippasia." *Hesperia* 43: 311–313.

Verdenius, W. J. 1985. *A Commentary on Hesiod* Works and Days, *vv. 1–382.* Leiden.

Vermeule, C. C. 1984. "From Halicarnassus to Alexandria in the Hellenistic Age: The Ares of Halicarnassus by Leochares," in N. Bonasca and A. Di Vita, eds., *Alessandria e il mondo ellenistico-romano* 3 (Studi in onore de A. Adriani), Rome, publ. 1986, 783–788.

Vernant, J.-P. 1974. *Mythe et société en Grèce ancienne.* Paris.

———. 1983. "Hestia-Hermes: The Religious Expression of Space and Movement in Ancient Greece." In *Myth and Thought among the Greeks,* 127–175. London.

———. 1989. "At Man's Table: Hesiod's Foundation Myth of Sacrifice." In *The Cuisine of Sacrifice among the Greeks,* edited by M. Detienne and J.-P. Vernant. Translated by P. Wissing, 21–86. Chicago.

Veyne, P. 1990. *Bread and Circuses: Historical Sociology and Political Pluralism.* Translated by B. Pearce. London.

Vickers, M., and D. Gill. 1994. *Artful Crafts: Ancient Greek Silverware and Pottery.* Oxford.

Vierneisel-Schlörb, B. 1979. *Klassische Skulpturen des 5. und 4. Jahrhunderts v. Chr. Glyptothek München, Katalog der Skulpturen.* Vol. 2. Munich.

Visconti, F. A. 1880. *Documenti inediti per servire alla Storia dei Musei d'Italia* 3. Florence.

Vlassopoulou, C. 2002. "Θραύσματα αναγλύφων του πλούσιου ρυθμού από τη συλλογή του Ασκληπιείου και το Μουσείο Ακροπόλεως." In *Αρχαία ελληνική γλυπτική: Αφιέρωμα στη μνήμη του γλύπτη Στέλιου Τριάντη,* (Μουσείο Μπενάκη, 10 Παραρτημα), edited by D. Damaskos, 143–155. Athens.

Von Bothmer, D. 1985. *The Amasis Painter and His World.* Malibu.

Von Eickstedt, K.-V. 1994. "Bemerkungen zur Ikonographie des Frieses vom Ilissos-Tempel." In Coulson, Palagia, Shear, Shapiro, and Frost 1994, 105–111.

Von Leutsch, E. L., and F. G. Schneidewin. 1965. Reprint. *Corpus paroemiographorum Graecorum.* Hildesheim; original edition, Göttingen 1839–1851.

Von Schneider, R. 1903. "Marmorreliefs in Berlin." *JdI* 18: 91–93.

Vos, M. F. 1963. *Scythian Archers in Archaic Attic Vase-Painting.* Groningen.

Walcot, P. 1961. "Pandora's Jar, *Erga* 83–105." *Hermes* 89: 249–251.

———. 1966. *Hesiod and the Near East.* Cardiff.

Walker, S. 1985. *Memorials to the Roman Dead.* London.

———. 1989a. "A Marble Head of Herodes Atticus from the Winchester City Museum." *AntJ* 69: 324–326.

———. 1989b. "Two Spartan Women and the Eleusinion." In Walker and Cameron 1989, 130–141.

———. 1991. "Bearded Men." *Journal of the History of Collections* 3: 265–277.

Walker, S., and A. Cameron, eds. 1989. *The Greek Renaissance in the Roman Empire. BICS* Suppl. 55.

Wallace-Hadrill, A. 1990. "Roman Arches and Greek Honors." *PCPS* 216: 143–181.

Walters, E. J. 1988. *Attic Grave Reliefs That Represent Women in the Dress of Isis. Hesperia* Suppl. 22. Princeton.

Walters, H. B. 1896. *Catalogue of the Greek and Etruscan Vases in the British Museum.* Vol. 4. London.

Walters, K. R. 1980. "Rhetoric as Ritual: The Semiotics of the Attic Funeral Oration." *Florilegium* 2: 1–27.

Waltz, P. 1910. "A Propos de l'*Elpis* hesiodique." *REG* 23: 49–57.

Ward-Perkins, J. B. 1983. *Roman Imperial Architecture.* Harmondsworth.

Watkiss Lloyd, W. 1893. "On the Central Groups of the Eastern Frieze of the Parthenon." *Transactions of the Royal Society of Literature* 16:1: 1–26.

Weber, S. 2000. "Sappho- und Diosphos-Maler. Studien zur attischen spätest-schwarzfigurigen Keramik." Ph.D. diss., Johannes Gutenberg-Universität, Mainz.

Webster, T. B. L. 1939. *Greek Art and Literature 530–400 B.C.* Oxford.

———. 1956. *Art and Literature in Fourth Century Athens.* London.

———. 1972. *Potter and Patron in Classical Athens.* London.

Weil, R. 1976. "Artemise ou le monde a l'envers." In *Receuil Plassart: Etudes sur l'antiquité grecque offertes à André Plassart par ses collègues de la Sorbonne,* 221–224. Paris.

Wesenberg, B. 1981. "Zur Baugeschichte des Nike Tempels." *JdI* 96: 28–54.

———. 1983. "Parthenongebälk und Südmetopenproblem." *JdI* 98: 57–86.

———. 1995. "Panathenäische Peplosdedikation und Arrephorie: Zur Thematik des Parthenonfrieses." *JdI* 110: 149–178.

West, M. L. 1978. *Hesiod, Works and Days.* Oxford.

———. 1988. *The Hesiodic Catalogue of Women.* Oxford.

Westlake, H. D. 1968. *Individuals in Thucydides.* Cambridge.

Wheler, G. 1682. *A Journey into Greece by George Wheler, Esq., in Company of Dr. Spon of Lyons.* London.

Whitley, J. 1987. "Art History, Archaeology and Idealism: The German Tradition." In *Archaeology as Long-Term History,* edited by I. Hodder, 9–15. Cambridge.

———. 1991. *Style and Society in Dark Age Greece: The Changing Face of a Pre-Literate Society 1100–700 B.C.* Cambridge.

Wide, S. 1893. *Lakonische Kulte.* Leipzig.

Wiebenson, D. 1969. *Sources of Greek Revival Architecture.* London.

Wilkins, J. 1990. "The Young of Athens: Religion and Society in *Herakleidai* of Euripides." *CQ* 40: 329–339.

Williams, C. A. 1999. *Roman Homosexuality: Ideologies of Masculinity in Classical Antiquity.* Oxford.

———. 1993. *Euripides: Heraclidae.* Oxford.

Wilson, K. L. 1997. "Oh, Statue, Speak! Divine and Royal Images in Ancient Mesopotamia." *AJA* 101: 382–383.

Winckelmann, J. J. 1755. *Gedanken über die Nachahmung der griechischen Werke in der Malerei und Bildhauerkunst.* Friedrichstadt. Bilingual edition: *Reflections on the Imitation of Works of Art among the Ancients.* Translated by E. Heyer and R. Norton. La Salle, IL, 1987.

Winkler, J. 1990. *The Constraints of Desire: The Anthropology of Sex and Gender in Ancient Greece.* New York.

Woolf, G. 1994. "Becoming Roman, Staying Greek: Culture, Identity and the Civilizing Process in the Roman East." *PCPS* 40: 116–143.

Worley, L. 1994. *Hippeis: The Cavalry of Ancient Greece.* Boulder.

Wrede, W. 1916. "Kriegers Ausfahrt in der archaisch-griechischen Kunst." *AM* 41: 221–374.

———. 1927. "Kriegers Ausfahrt in der archaisch-griechischen Kunst," rev. ed., Halle 1927, paginated as 222–377, pls. 15–34.

Wroth, W. 1899. *Catalogue of Greek Coins in the British Museum: Galatia, Cappadocia and Syria.* London.

Wycherley, R. E. 1957. *Literary and Epigraphical Testimonia. Agora* 3. Princeton.

———. 1978. *The Stones of Athens.* Princeton.

Xanthakis, A. X. 1988. *History of Greek Photography, 1839–1960.* Translated by J. Solman and G. Cox. Athens.

Zacharia, K. 2001. "'The Rock of the Nightingale:' Kinship Diplomacy and Sophocles' *Tereus.*" In *Homer, Tragedy, and Beyond: Essays in Honour of P. E. Easterling,* edited by F. Budelmann and P. Michelakis, 91–112. London.

Zanker, P. 1982. "Herrscherbild und Zeitgeschicht." *Römisches Porträt: Wege zur Erforschung eines gesellschaftlichen Phänomenons. Wissenschaftliche Konferenz. Wissenschaftliche Zeitschrift der Humboldt-Universität Berlin* 31: 307–312.

———. 1988. *The Power of Images in the Age of Augustus.* Translated by A. Shapiro. Ann Arbor.

———. 1995. *The Mask of Socrates.* Translated by A. Shapiro. Berkeley.

Zeitlin, F. 1995a. "The Economics of Hesiod's Pandora," in Reeder 1995: 49–56.

———. 1995b. "Signifying Difference: The Myth of Pandora." In *Women in Antiquity: New Assessments,* edited by R. Hawley and B. Levick, 58–74. London.

Zettler, R. L., and L. Horne, eds. 1998. *Treasures from the Royal Tombs of Ur.* Philadelphia.

Zuntz, G. 1963. *The Political Plays of Euripides.* Manchester.

ABOUT THE CONTRIBUTORS

JUDITH M. BARRINGER is Reader in Classics at the University of Edinburgh. She is the author of *Divine Escorts: Nereids in Archaic and Classical Greek Art* (1995), *The Hunt in Ancient Greece* (2001), and articles on Greek and Roman painting and sculpture.

W. MARTIN BLOOMER is Associate Professor and Chair of the Classics Department at the University of Notre Dame. He is the author of *Valerius Maximus and the Rhetoric of the New Nobility* (1992), *Latinity and Literary Society at Rome* (1997), and articles on Greek and Latin literature.

Sir JOHN BOARDMAN is Emeritus Professor of Classical Archaeology and Art at Oxford University and a Fellow of the British Academy and of the American Philosophical Society. As an excavator he has published work on Chios and at Tocra (Libya). He has published widely on various aspects of Greek art and archaeology, vases, sculpture, and engraved gems. He has specialized in studies on the role and achievements of Greeks overseas and on the diffusion of their arts in the Old World. His latest books are *The History of Greek Vases* (2001) and *The Archaeology of Nostalgia* (2002).

DAVID CASTRIOTA is Professor of the History of Art at Sarah Lawrence College. He is the author of *Myth, Ethos, and Actuality: Official Art in Fifth-Century* B.C. *Athens* (1992), *The Ara Pacis Augustae: The Imagery of Abundance in Later Greek and Early Roman Imperial Art* (1995), and various articles on the art of Classical Athens.

EVE D'AMBRA is Associate Professor of Art at Vassar College, where she teaches both Greek and Roman art. She is the author of *Private Lives, Imperial Virtues: The Frieze of the Forum Transitorium in Rome* (1993) and *Roman Art* (1998), along with articles on Roman funerary art and portraiture.

CREIGHTON GILBERT is Professor Emeritus of the History of Art at Yale University. His most recent books are *The Saints' Three Reasons for Paintings in Churches* (2001) and *How Fra Angelico and Signorelli Saw the End of the World* (2002).

EVELYN B. HARRISON is Professor Emerita of Greek Art at the Institute of Fine Arts at New York University. She continues to publish sculpture found in the excavations of the Athenian Agora by the American School of Classical Studies at Athens and has written numerous ground-breaking articles in the field of Archaic and Classical sculpture.

PETER J. HOLLIDAY is Associate Professor of the History of Art and Classical Archaeology at California State University, Long Beach. His books include *Narrative and Event in Ancient Art* (1993) and *The Origins of Roman Historical Commemoration in the Visual Arts* (2002). His articles on Greek, Roman, and Etruscan art have appeared in *AJA*, *ArtB*, and other scholarly journals.

JEFFREY M. HURWIT is Professor of Art History and Classics at the University of Oregon, where he has taught since 1980. He is the author of *The Acropolis in the Age of Pericles* (2004), *The Athenian Acropolis: History, Mythology, and Archaeology from the Neolithic Era to the Present* (1999), *The Art and Culture of Early Greece, 1100–480 B.C.* (1985), and many articles on Archaic and Classical Greek art. He was the first of Jerry Pollitt's students to receive a Ph.D.

IAN JENKINS is Senior Curator in the Department of Greek and Roman Antiquities at the British Museum. His many publications about the Parthenon sculptures include *The Parthenon Frieze* (1994).

DONALD KAGAN is Sterling Professor of Classics and History at Yale University. Among his writings are a four-volume history of the Peloponnesian War, *Pericles of Athens and the Birth of Athenian Democracy* (1991), and *On the Origins of War and the Preservation of Peace* (1995). His awards include four teaching prizes at Cornell and Yale Universities, Fulbright and National Endowment for the Humanities fellowships, fellowships to the Center for Hellenic Studies in Washington and to the Center for Advanced Study in the Behavioral Sciences at Stanford, and the Sidney Hook Memorial Award for Distinguished Contributions to the Freedom and Integrity of the Academy.

J. E. LENDON is Associate Professor in the Corcoran Department of History at the University of Virginia. He is author of *Empire of Honour: The Art of Government in the Roman World* (1997).

SUSAN B. MATHESON is the Molly and Walter Bareiss Curator of Ancient Art at the Yale University Art Gallery. Her publications include *Polygnotos and Vase Painting in Classical Athens* (1995) and *Greek Vases: A Guide to the Yale Collection* (1988) and numerous articles about Greek and Roman art. Among her exhibitions are (with J. J. Pollitt) *Greek Vases at Yale* (1975), *An Obsession with Fortune: Tyche in Greek and Roman Art* (1994), and (with D. E. E. Kleiner) *I, Claudia: Women in Ancient Rome* (1996).

RANDALL L. B. MCNEILL is Assistant Professor of Classics at Lawrence University. He received his Ph.D. from Yale University in 1998 and is the author of *Horace: Image, Identity, and Audience* (2001).

ELIZABETH A. MEYER is Associate Professor in the Corcoran Department of History at the University of Virginia. She is the author of *Legitimacy and Law in the Roman World: Tabulae in Roman Belief and Practice* (2004) and articles on Greek and Roman history and epigraphy and Latin literature.

JENIFER NEILS is the Ruth Coulter Heede Professor of Art History at Case Western Reserve University and the author of *The Parthenon Frieze* (2001). She has written extensively on Greek iconography and organized the exhibition "Goddess and Polis: The Panathenaia in Ancient Athens" (1992).

JOHN H. OAKLEY is Chancellor Professor and Forrest D. Murden Jr. Professor in the Department of Classical Studies at the College of William and Mary, Williamsburg, Virginia. The author of several books, including *The Phiale Painter* (1990), *Corpus Vasorum Antiquorum,* The Walters Art Gallery, vol. 1 (1993), and *The Achilles Painter* (1997), he has been a Fellow of the Alexander von Humboldt Stiftung, the National Endowment for the Humanities, and the Metropolitan Museum of Art, and a Visiting Professor at the University of Canterbury at Christchurch and at the American School of Classical Studies at Athens.

OLGA PALAGIA is Professor of Classical Archaeology in the Department of Archaeology and Art History at Athens University. She has authored *Euphranor* (1980) and *The Pediments of the Parthenon* (1993), as well as numerous articles on Greek sculpture. She shares the role of coeditor of several collections of essays, including *Personal Styles in Greek Sculpture* (1996), in which her coeditor is J. J. Pollitt.

BRUNILDE SISMONDO RIDGWAY is Rhys Carpenter Professor Emerita of Classical and Near Eastern Archaeology at Bryn Mawr College, where she taught for over thirty years. She was Editor-in-Chief of the *American Journal of Archaeology* (1977–1985) and has written extensively on Greek sculpture, including seven volumes covering the period from ca. 650 to 31 B.C. Her awards include the Gold Medal of the Archaeological Institute of America, a Guggenheim Fellowship, a Lindbach Award, and several lectureships at American and foreign universities.

H. A. SHAPIRO is the W. H. Collins Vickers Professor of Archaeology and Chair of the Department of Classics at the Johns Hopkins University. He is the author of several studies of Greek iconography, including *Art and Cult under the Tyrants in Athens* (1989) and *Personifications in Greek Art* (1993).

MARK D. STANSBURY-O'DONNELL is Associate Professor of the Department of Art History at the University of St. Thomas. He is the author of *Pictorial Narrative in Ancient Greek Art* (1999) and articles on ancient Greek sculpture and painting.

CORNELIUS C. VERMEULE III is retired as Curator of Classical Art at the Museum of Fine Arts, Boston. He has authored numerous books and articles on many aspects of Greek and Roman art and archaeology, including, most recently, *The Art and Archaeology of Antiquity* (2001).

INDEX

Acharnai, 32, 120, 123, 177
Achilles Painter, 32
Aelian, 101
Ageladas
  Zeus Ithomatas by, 114
Agora, 15, 53, 73, 74, 89, 96, 114, 119, 124, 135, 153, 205
  Eponymous Heroes monument in, 72
  marble frieze from, 42–43
Agorakritos, 125
  statue of Nemesis by, 53, 113, 119, 125, 126, 127, 189
Aischylos, 85
  Agamemnon, 49, 58, 98
  Choephoroi, 15
  Eumenides, 91
  Persians, 93, 96, 99
akrolithic technique, 113, 115
Akropolis, 43, 52, 74, 89, 96, 113, 124, 135, 136, 140, 142, 164, 165, 167–172, 177, 186, 187, 188, 227, 238, 241
  Cyclopean fortifications of, 238, 239
  in early photography, 237–250
  in Medieval and Turkish periods, 238–241
  nineteenth-century excavations of, 241–243
Alkaeus, 49
Alkamenes
  Ares by, 119–121, 123–124
  Athena and Hephaistos by, 114, 124
  Dionysos by, 113
  Dresden-Bologna Athena by (?), 128
  and Olympia sculptures, 136, 138
  and Parthenon frieze, 128
  pentathlete (*enkrinomenos*) by, 123–124
  Prokne and Itys group by, 163–173
Alkibiades, 218–219, 222
allegory, in High Classical vase-painting, 50–52
Altamura Painter, 24, 32
Amazons, Amazonomachies, 64, 66, 94, 141, 269
  See also Stoa Poikile
Anakeion, 74
Anaxagoras, 223, 225–226, 227, 228
Anesidora, 38, 43, 44
anthippasia, 149, 150, 159
Antioch-on-the-Orontes, 195, 197
Antiphon, 227
Aphrodite, 42, 47, 48, 49, 50, 51, 54, 55–56, 60, 119, 170
  birth of, 141, 189
  of Knidos, by Praxiteles, 55
  on Nike temple east frieze, 187
  Ourania, by Pheidias, 113
  sanctuary of A. Pandemos, 187
Apollo
  at Delphi, 112
  and Hermes, 207
  Patroos, 114
  statue of, at Amyklai, 114
  statue of, from Metropolis (Thessaly), 114–115
  in west pediment, Olympia, 137–138
Apollodoros, 165
Apollonios
  Argonautika, 53
Archaios Neos. See Temple of Athena Polias
Archidamian war, 80
Areopagos, 120, 123, 124
  temple on, 177
Ares, 41, 120, 121, 123, 188, 189
  statue of, by Leochares, 196
Ares Borghese, 119, 121, 123–124, 126–127
Aristophanes, 28–29
  Birds, 259
  Frogs, 104, 180, 181
  Lysistrata, 96, 170–171
  Peace, 259
  Ploutos, 78
Aristophon, 65
Aristotle, 121, 221–222

arkteia, 170–171, 173
arming scenes, 24, 26
Arrhephoroi, Arrhephoria, 170, 173
Artemis Agrotera, 106, 183, 184
  See also Temple on the Ilissos
Artemis Brauronia, sanctuary of, 169, 170–171
Artemisia, 96
Aspasia, 224
Athena, 30, 31, 32, 33, 38, 43–44, 69, 93, 187–189, 222, 226
  birth of, 141, 189
  contest with Poseidon, 169
  as embodiment of *tekhne,* 113, 170
  on Nike temple east frieze, 187–189
  statue of, in Temple of Ares, 119–120, 121
  statue of, in Temple of Hephaistos, 114, 124
Athena Areia, 188
  at Acharnai, 120, 123
  at Plataia, 82, 113, 267
Athena Chalkioikos, 114–115
Athena Ergane, 170
Athena Giustiniani, 119, 125–128
Athena Hygieia, 124, 188
Athena Nike. *See* Temple of Athena Nike
Athena of Pallene (Athena Pallenis), 121–123, 127
Athena Parthenos
  statue of, 31, 43, 44, 65, 112, 113–114, 140, 141, 142, 150, 170, 189, 223, 226, 227, 228, 235
Athena Polias
  altar of, 169
  olive wood statue (*xoanon*) of, 112, 114, 169, 171
  See also Temple of Athena Polias
Athena Promachos, 114
Athens, passim
  funerary customs at, 13–14, 15–16
  as Neoclassical ideal, 239
  under Roman rule, 201–214
Augustus, 119, 125, 128, 220–221, 225, 226

bail oinochoai, 13–21
Bakchylides, 98
Blond Boy, 137
Boardman, J., 267
Boreas and Oreithyia, 171, 183
Brauron, 171, 183
Bryaxis, 197
Brygos Painter, 41

Castriota, D., 267–268
cavalry, 24, 30, 147, 148, 149, 158–159
  See also horsemen
Centauromachy, 137, 138, 141
Chalkeia festival, 169–170
chryselephantine technique, 111, 112, 113–114, 115
Cicero, 13, 55, 235
Codrus Painter, 57
cult images, 111–115
  as modern construct, 111–112

Deconstruction, 261–262
Delian League, 90, 91, 96, 101, 268
Delphi
  Argive dedication at, 67, 78, 80
  Athena Pronaia sanctuary, 121
  Knidian Lesche at, 63–64, 65, 67–68, 69, 76–77, 81–85, 97, 107, 181, 184, 186, 267–268
  Marathon monument at, 69, 127
  Siphnian Treasury at, 69
  Temple of Apollo, 142
Demosion Sema, 13
Demosthenes (general), 5, 81
Demosthenes (orator), 69, 208
  Philippics by, 171
  statue of, 119
departure scenes, 23–35
Dinos Painter, 28, 29, 30, 32, 33
Dio Chrysostom, 205–206, 212, 222
Dionysos
  chryselephantine statue of, by Alkamenes, 113
  at Delphi, 112
  on Nike temple frieze, 187
  in Parthenon's east pediment, 140
dokimasia, 150
Dresden-Bologna Athena ("Lemnia"), 127–128

Eleusinian Mysteries, 180, 182, 183–184, 213
Elgin marbles, 241, 243
Elpis (Hope), 37–44
Enyo, 119–120
ephebeia, 31–32, 33
ephebes, 24, 30–33, 149, 202, 203, 206, 207
Ephoros, 219
Epimetheus, 38, 40
epitaphios logos. See Funeral Oration
Erechtheion, 124, 169, 172, 241
Erechtheus, 165, 169, 186
Eretria Painter, 28
Erichthonios, 28, 43–44, 127, 165, 170, 188, 189
ethos, 85, 93, 124, 268
Eukleia, 56
Euripides, 52, 167
  Erechtheus, 43
  Helen, 54–55, 56
  Herakleidai, 121, 123, 125
  Iphigeneia at Aulis, 57

Medea, 173
Orestes, 59
Trojan Women, 54
Eurymedon, 81, 82, 84, 99–101
Euthydikos kore, 137–138
Euthymides, 26
Eutychides, 195
Exekias, 267

Favorinus, 207, 208
Foundry Painter, 38
Freud, S., 249, 250
funeral oration (*epitaphios logos*), 13, 91
See also Perikles

Gigantomachy, 31, 66, 141, 149, 170
Gitiadas, 115
Gorgias, 54, 56, 60, 259
Graces, 187, 189
Greek Revival, 240, 241
gymnasion, 202, 206

Hadrian, 89, 201, 202, 212–213, 218, 223
portraits of, 212–213
Harmodios, 137, 139
Hector Painter, 26, 29, 33
Heimarmene Painter, 50–52, 53
Helen, 47–60
painting of, by Zeuxis, 55, 60
Heliodoros (*kosmetes*)
herm portrait of, 203–207, 208
Henderson, J., 261–262
Hephaisteion. *See* Temple of Hephaistos
Hephaistos, 38–40, 43–44, 121, 170, 187, 188
on Nike temple east frieze, 189
Hera, 56
chryselephantine statue of, at Argos, 111
on Nike temple frieze, 188
pear wood statue of, at Argos, 111
statue of, at Olympia, 112
Heraion of Argos, 111
Herakles, 40–41, 188
Hermes, 207
on Nike temple frieze, 188
Propylaios, 188
Hermippos, 2
herms, 202, 203, 206–207
See also Heliodoros; *kosmetai*
Herodes Atticus, portraits of, 202, 210–211, 213
Herodotos, 7–8, 41, 56, 66, 78, 89, 91, 93, 96, 106, 121, 183, 184, 226, 227
heroic nudity, 29, 107

Hesiod, 42, 44, 262
Catalogue of Women, 56
Theogony, 38, 41, 43
Works and Days, 37, 38–39, 40, 42, 43, 165
hippeis. See horsemen
Homer, 48, 67, 262
Iliad, 40, 41, 43, 47, 48, 49, 51, 53, 56, 113
Odyssey, 49, 83, 165, 181, 182
Hope-Farnese Athena, 124
hoplites, 24–30, 31, 32, 33, 147, 148, 149, 186
hoplitodromos, 31
horsemen
on Parthenon frieze, 147–159
Hygieia, 188, 189

Iktinos, 136, 138, 142
Ilioupersis. *See* Parthenon, metopes of; Stoa Poikile; Temple on the Ilissos
Ilissos Temple. *See* Temple on the Ilissos
Ion, 225, 226, 228
Ionic order, 105, 108, 135, 138, 177

Kallikrates, 136, 142, 177
Kimon, 7, 66, 67, 75, 78, 81, 82, 83, 84, 85, 90, 91, 96, 99, 100, 101, 225, 226, 267, 268, 269
building program of, 74, 79, 81
Kleon, 80
Kleophon Painter, 32–33
Kleophrades Painter, 84–85
Knidian Lesche. *See* Delphi; Polygnotos
Konstantinou, D., 245–246
kosmetai, 201–214
Kratinos
Nemesis by, 54
Kritios and Nesiotes, 137
Kritios Boy, 265
Kypria, 50

Lampon, 226
Leochares, 196
LeQuire, A., 113
Libon of Elis, 136, 140
Lissarrague, F., 260–261, 265–266
Lokros of Paros, 119–121, 123, 125
long walls, 7, 8
Lykaon Painter, 29, 31
Lysias, 94, 96
Lysippos, 195, 256

Makron, 48, 49, 50, 57, 60
Marathon. *See* Stoa Poikile
Margaritis, Ph., 245–246

Meidias Painter, 56–60
Meidias Painter Workshop, 55–56
Melissos, 227
Menander
  Dyskolos, 180
Menelaos, 48–49, 53
Metrodoros of Lampsakos, 113, 210
Mikon, 63, 64, 66, 69, 70, 74, 76, 77, 81, 93–94, 96, 99, 101, 137
  See also Stoa Poikile; Theseion
Myron, 71, 114
  Athena by, 126, 127

Naukydes
  Diskobolos by, 123–124
  statue of Hebe by, 111
Nekyia. *See* Polygnotos
Nemesis, 51, 53–54, 113, 188
  statue of, by Agorakritos, 53, 113, 119, 125, 126, 127, 189
  Temple of, at Rhamnous, 53–54, 68, 124, 125
Nike, 30–31, 33, 141, 142, 188, 238
Niobid Painter, 24, 27–28, 32, 64, 69–70, 107, 127

Odysseus
Oinoe. *See* Stoa Poikile
Older Parthenon, 135, 138
Olympia
  Philippeion, 115
  See also Temple of Zeus
Onasos (*kosmetes*)
  portrait of, 209–211, 213
Osborne, R., 265–267
Ovid, 165, 166
Owl Pillar Group, 38

paideia, 201
Painter of Bologna 279, 94
Painter of the Woolly Satyrs, 137
Paionios, 136, 142
Pallene, 119, 121, 128
Pamphilos, 78–79
Panainos, 66, 77, 81, 101, 141
Panathenaia festival, 147–149, 150, 159, 169–171
Panathenaic *peplos,* 148–149, 169–170
Pandion, 28–29, 165, 167–168, 169, 172
Pandora, 37–44, 141, 189
Pandrosos, 170
Panhellion, 212
Paris, 47–60
Parrhasios, 93
Parthenon, 44, 89, 90, 114, 124, 135–136, 138–142, 148, 154, 168, 169, 170, 190, 221, 222, 228, 241, 242, 267
  akroteria of, 142
  frieze of, 68, 69, 104, 105, 106, 127, 128, 141, 147–159, 166, 169, 172, 178, 268
  metopes of, 31, 69, 122, 138–139, 141, 169, 170, 172, 266
  optical refinements of, 158
  pediments, 108, 128, 139–140, 141, 169, 172, 189
  peplos scene, on frieze, 148–149
  plan of, 135–136, 138
  reflecting pool in, 142
  relation of, to Older Parthenon, 135, 138
  See also Athena Parthenos
Pausanias, 53, 56, 63–64, 66, 67, 68–69, 74–81, 83–84, 90–92, 96–97, 101, 107, 111, 112, 113, 114–115, 119–121, 125, 136, 140, 141, 142, 163, 165, 166–168, 169, 170, 171, 181, 184–185, 186, 240
Pausias, 67
Peisianax, 81, 90
Peisistratos, 121, 218, 223, 226, 267
Peleus Painter, 30, 31
Peloponnesian War, 1–9, 30, 48, 54, 80, 81, 91, 107, 108, 121, 172–173, 184, 190, 258–259, 272
Pergamon, 112
Perikles, passim
  building program of, 74, 108, 124, 136, 223–224, 226, 228
  cavalry reform of, 148, 149–150, 158–159
  Funeral Oration of, 13, 26, 29, 30, 33, 148, 150, 172
  as new Peisistratos, 218, 223, 226
  parodied as Zeus, 54
  in Plutarch, 217–229
  portraits of, 228
  as *strategos* (general), 1–9
  as subject of Second Sophistic, 208
peripoloi, 24, 30
Persians, Persian Wars, 3, 64, 68, 71, 78, 84, 90, 91, 93, 94, 114, 121, 141, 171, 183, 184, 186, 188, 238, 267, 269
  feminization of, 94–96, 99–101
  See also Stoa Poikile, *Battle of Marathon*
Pheidias, 66, 77, 101, 113, 125, 136, 139, 140, 141, 142, 150, 178, 195, 196, 221–224, 225, 227, 229, 258, 264, 265
  Aphrodite Ourania by, in Athens, 113
  Aphrodite Ourania, by, at Elis, 113
  Athena by, at Elis, 113
  Athena by, at Pallene, 113
  Athena Areia by, at Plataia, 82, 113
  Athena Lemnia by, 127–128
  Athena Parthenos by, 31, 43, 44, 65, 112, 113–114, 140, 141, 142, 150, 189, 223, 226, 228, 235
  Bronze Athena (Promachos) by, 114
  Marathon group at Delphi by, 69, 127
  and Parthenon frieze, 150
  self-portrait of, 226, 228, 235
  Zeus at Olympia by, 112, 113, 136, 140–142, 178, 189, 195, 196, 222–223

Philemon, 222
Philip of Makedon, 115
Philokles, 172
Philomela, 165, 169–170, 171
Phormio, 172
Pinakotheke (Propylaia), 52, 67
plague, 5, 8–9
Plataia, 91–92, 96, 184, 186, 268
  Oath of, 238
  sanctuary of Athena, 82, 267
Plato, 202, 217, 219, 220, 222, 228
Pliny, 65, 66, 67, 77, 92, 101, 115, 123, 141
Plutarch
  Life of Alkibiades, 222
  Life of Kimon by, 67, 97
  Life of Perikles by, 1, 3–4, 9, 124, 217–229, 235
  Life of Theseus by, 93, 121
Polemon, 66, 68, 69, 207–208, 213
Pollitt, J. J., 1, 13, 23, 89, 93, 98, 111, 113, 115, 119, 148, 152, 163, 169, 201, 217, 235
  career of, xv–xvi
  influence of, 201, 255–272
Polygnotos (panel or mural painter), 52, 63–64, 65, 66–68, 69, 73, 74, 77, 81–85, 97, 99, 101
  Ilioupersis by (at Delphi), 64, 67, 76–77, 81, 82–83, 84, 97, 98, 107–108, 268
  Ilioupersis by (in Stoa Poikile), 66–67, 76, 81, 82–83, 92, 97–99, 184
  Nekyia by (Delphi), 65, 82, 83–84, 107, 181–182, 184, 186
  Odysseus and the Suitors by (at Plataia), 82
  as painter of *ethos,* 85, 98
  painting at Thespiae by, 67
  Warrior by, 66
Polygnotos (vase-painter), 30, 38
Polykleitos, 123, 124, 222, 265
  statue of Hera by, 111
portraiture, 67
  of *kosmetai,* 201–214
  of Perikles, 228
  of Roman emperors, 202, 203–205, 209, 212–213
  See also self-portraiture
Poseidon
  contest of, with Athena, 169
  on Nike temple frieze, 188
  statue of, near Naupaktos, 114–115
Poststructuralism, 261–262, 270
Praxiteles, 55, 120
Prokne and Itys. *See* Alkamenes
Prometheus, 40, 43
Propylaia, 52, 124, 168, 188, 226, 238, 240, 241, 242, 243, 244
Protagoras, 227
Pseudo-Demosthenes, 79
Pyrrhos, 124

Quintilian, 141

Rhamnous, 53
  See also Temple of Nemesis
Robertson, J., 244, 247
Rumine, G. de, 246

Salamis, 96
Sappho Painter, 16, 18
Sarapis, 197, 198
Sebah, P., 248
Second Sophistic, 201, 207, 208, 209, 210, 212, 213
Seleukia Pieria, 195–198
self-portraiture
  in the Renaissance, 233–235
Shanks, M., 263–264
Simonides, 81
Sokrates, 93, 220
Sophokles
  Oedipus at Colonus by, 147
  Oinomaos by, 137
  portraits of, 77, 210
  Tereus by, 165, 167–168, 171, 172
  Trachiniai, 228
Sphakteria, 80, 91, 92
Spivey, N., 264–265
Stesichoros, 49, 54, 56, 59
Stillman, W. J., 247
Stoa Poikile, 65–70, 73–85, 89–101, 135, 267
  Amazonomachy in, 66, 67, 73, 74, 76, 77, 78, 80, 90–91, 92, 93–94, 96–97, 98, 99, 101
  Battle of Marathon in, 65, 66, 67–70, 73, 74–75, 76, 77, 78, 79, 80, 90, 91, 92–93, 96, 99–101, 185–186
  Battle of Oinoe in, 66, 67, 68–69, 74–75, 76, 77, 78–81, 90, 91–92, 186
  Ilioupersis in, 66–67, 73, 74, 76, 77, 78, 79, 80, 82, 90, 91, 92, 97–99, 101
  Sophokles portrait in, 77
  Spartan shields in, 77, 80, 91, 92
  Suppliant Herakleidai in, 77, 78–79
Stoicism, 89
Strabo, 112, 113, 140
strategos, -oi, 1, 7, 202
Structuralism, 260–262, 269, 271
Stuart, J., and N. Revett, 103, 104, 178, 184, 240
Suessula Painter, 66
Suppliant Herakleidai (painting). *See* Stoa Poikile

Temple of Apollo (Bassai), 266
Temple of Apollo (Delphi), 112
Temple of Ares (Agora), 119–121, 124, 125, 128
Temple of Athena Areia (Plataia), 267
Temple of Athena at Paestum, 135

Temple of Athena at Pallene, 121, 125
  See also Temple of Ares
Temple of Athena Chalkioikos (Sparta), 114–115
Temple of Athena Nike, 90, 113, 124, 177, 184–190, 238–250
  altar of, 238
  cult statue, 113, 238
  date of, 178
  frieze of, 81, 104, 106, 177, 184–190
  in nineteenth-century photography, 244–250
  parapet of, 239, 248
  post-Classical history of, 238–239
  restoration of, in nineteenth century, 242–243
Temple of Athena Polias (*Archaios Neos*), 113, 135, 169
Temple of Hephaistos (Hephaisteion, or Theseion), 43–44, 53, 69, 74, 105, 106, 114, 124–125
  frieze of, 121–123, 125, 127, 128
  metopes, 125
  pediments, 125
  statues in, 114, 115, 124
Temple of Hera (Heraion) at Argos, 111
Temple of Hera at Olympia, 112
Temple of Nemesis at Rhamnous, 53–54, 68, 124, 125
Temple of Olympian Zeus, Athens, 213
Temple of Poseidon, Sounion, 112, 124, 125
Temple of Zeus, Nemea, 112
Temple of Zeus, Olympia, 64, 76, 136–142
  akroteria, 136, 142
  metopes, 64, 128, 138, 140, 141
  pediments, 76, 136–142, 266
  reflecting pool in, 140, 142
  remodeling of, 140
  See also Zeus, chryselephantine statue of
Temple of Zeus and Athena of the Palladion, 182
Temple on the Ilissos, 177–184, 189–190
  date of, 103, 104–105, 108, 178
  frieze of, 103–109, 177–184, 189–190
Theon of Smyrna, portrait of, 202, 210, 211, 213
Theophrastos, 228
Thermon, 166
Theseion (Early Classical sanctuary), 70, 74, 76, 81, 83, 93, 137, 267
Theseion (High Classical temple). *See* Temple of Hephaistos
Thorikos, 54
Thukydides (historian), 2–3, 5–6, 8, 9, 13, 26, 29, 149, 171, 172, 217, 219, 225, 226, 229
Thukydides, son of Melesias, 225, 226
Tolmides, 3
Torre Nuova sarcophagus, 104, 180–182
Trajan, 202
Troy, Trojans. *See* Polygnotos; Stoa Poikile, *Ilioupersis* in; Temple on the Ilissos
Tyche of Antioch, 195
Tyrannicides, 137

Valerius Maximus, 218, 223
Vasari, 233–234
Velletri Athena, 124, 126, 127
Voltaire, 221

Webster, T. B. L., 257
White-ground lekythoi, 13, 15, 19, 24, 32
Whitley, J., 262–263, 264
Winckelmann, J., 246, 248, 256

Xanthippos, 227
Xenophon, 150, 156, 158
  Memorabilia, 93
Xenotimos Painter, 58

Zeno, 225
Zeus, 39–40, 44, 53, 54, 207
  chryselephantine statue of, at Olympia, 112, 113, 136, 140–142, 178, 189, 195, 196, 222–223
  chryselephantine statue of (Seleukid), 196, 197
  Ithomatas, 114
  Kasios, from Seleukia Pieria, 195–198
  on Nike temple frieze, 188
  in Parthenon east pediment, 139–140, 189
  standing statue of, in Hera temple (Olympia), 112
Zeuxis, 55, 60